PEARSON CUSTOM
BUSINESS RESOURCES

Cost Accounting, 15/e
Horngren   Datar   Rajan
Custom Edition for ACCT 520
Metropolitan State University

PEARSON

ISBN 10: 1-269-68299-7
ISBN 13: 978-1-269-68299-2

PEARSON

Table of Contents

Flexible Budgets, Direct-Cost Variances, and Management Control

From Chapter 7 of *Cost Accounting: A Managerial Emphasis*, Fifteenth Edition. Charles T. Horngren, Srikant M. Datar, Madhav V. Rajan. Copyright © 2015 by Pearson Education, Inc. All rights reserved.

Flexible Budgets, Direct-Cost Variances, and Management Control

Learning Objectives

1 Understand static budgets and static-budget variances

2 Examine the concept of a flexible budget and learn how to develop it

3 Calculate flexible-budget variances and sales-volume variances

4 Explain why standard costs are often used in variance analysis

5 Compute price variances and efficiency variances for direct-cost categories

6 Understand how managers use variances

7 Describe benchmarking and explain its role in cost management

Every organization, regardless of its profitability or growth, has to step back and take a hard look at its spending decisions.

And when customers are affected by a recession, the need for managers to use budgeting and variance analysis tools for cost control becomes especially critical. By studying variances, managers can focus on where specific performances have fallen short and use the information they learn to make corrective adjustments and achieve significant savings for their companies. The drive to achieve cost reductions might seem at odds with the growing push for organizations to pursue environmentally sound business practices. To the contrary, managers looking to be more efficient with their plants and operations have found that cornerstones of the sustainability movement, such as reducing waste and power usage, offer fresh ways to help them manage risk and control costs, as the following article shows.

Going for the (Other) Green: Reducing Standard Costs[1]

While Whole Foods and IKEA have long been associated with eco-friendliness, sustainable practices have been spreading far beyond these early adopters to a broad swath of businesses. In recent years, managers in some unlikely industries have discovered that the financial benefits of sustainability can manifest themselves in numerous ways. One surprising way involves companies going green to reduce their standard costs.

At APC Construction, a small road-builder in Colorado, the company increased the amount of recycled asphalt it uses in its production process—purely out of necessity. When the cost of standard asphalt cement skyrocketed from $180 per ton in 2003 to $600 per ton in 2008, the company needed to rein in its standard costs for cement. As a result, the company began increasing the amount of recycled ingredients in its product. "With a 30% recycled product, you're looking at a savings of almost $8 per ton," says Bob Stewart, the company's finance chief. "You're reducing the amount of energy you use to crush the rock and you're preserving natural resources."

Urschel Laboratories, a maker of capital equipment for the food processing and chemical industries, simultaneously reduced its freight costs and carbon footprint. With

---

[1] *Source:* Kate O'Sullivan, "Going for the Green" Sept. 01, 2011, CFO Magazine.

oil prices rising, some of Urschel's carriers began adding fuel surcharges to ship the company's machinery. Since much of what the company sells is heavy equipment, Urschel found that its customers often had enough lead time to wait 4 to 6 weeks for their orders to arrive by sea, a practice that costs the company half of what air freight—its former standard—costs. This lowered the company's standard costs for shipping while reducing the amount of fuel oil required to ship its equipment to customers around the world.

Understanding the behavior of costs, planning for them, performing variance analysis, and acting appropriately on the results are critical functions for managers. For retailers such as McDonald's and Dunkin' Donuts, an intricate understanding of direct costs is essential in order to make each high-quality food item and beverage at the lowest possible cost. Similarly, organizations ranging from General Electric and Bank of America to sports teams such as the Sacramento Kings have to manage costs and analyze variances for long-term sustainability.

Budgets help managers with their planning function. We now explain how budgets, specifically flexible budgets, are used to compute variances, which assist managers in their control function. Flexible budgets and variances enable managers to compare a firm's actual results with its planned performance, understand why the two differ, and learn what improvements can be made. Variance analysis supports the critical final function in the five-step decision-making process by enabling managers to *evaluate performance and learn* after decisions are implemented. In this chapter, we explain how.

Static Budgets and Variances

A **variance** is the difference between actual results and expected performance. The expected performance is also called **budgeted performance**, which is a point of reference for making comparisons.

The Use of Variances

Variances bring together the planning and control functions of management and facilitate management by exception. **Management by exception** is a practice whereby managers focus more closely on areas that are not operating as expected and less closely on areas that are. Consider the scrap and rework costs at a Maytag appliances plant. If the plant's actual costs are much higher than originally budgeted, the variances will prompt managers to find out why and correct the problem so future operations result in less scrap and rework. Sometimes a large positive variance may occur, such as a significant decrease in the manufacturing costs of a product. Managers will try to understand the reasons for the decrease (better operator training or changes in manufacturing methods, for example) so these practices can be continued and implemented by other divisions within the organization.

Variances are also used for evaluating performance and to motivate managers. Production-line managers at Maytag may have quarterly efficiency incentives linked to achieving a budgeted amount of operating costs.

Sometimes variances suggest that the company should consider a change in strategy. For example, large negative variances caused by excessive defect rates for a new product may suggest a flawed product design. Managers may then want to investigate the product design and potentially change the mix of products being offered. Variances also help managers make more informed predictions about the future and thereby improve the quality of the five-step decision-making process.

The benefits of variance analysis are not restricted to companies. In today's difficult economic environment, public officials have realized that the ability to make timely tactical changes based on variance information can result in their having to make fewer draconian adjustments later. For example, the city of Scottsdale, Arizona, monitors its tax and fee performance against expenditures monthly. Why? One of the city's goals is to keep its water usage rates stable. By monitoring the extent to which the city's water revenues are matching its current expenses, Scottsdale can avoid sudden spikes in the rate it charges residents for water as well as finance water-related infrastructure projects.[2]

How important of a decision-making tool is variance analysis? Very. A recent survey by the United Kingdom's Chartered Institute of Management Accountants found that it was easily the most popular costing tool used by organizations of all sizes.

Static Budgets and Static-Budget Variances

We will take a closer look at variances by examining one company's accounting system. As you study the exhibits in this chapter, note that "level" followed by a number denotes the amount of detail shown by a variance analysis. Level 1 reports the least detail; level 2 offers more information; and so on.

Consider Webb Company, a firm that manufactures and sells jackets. The jackets require tailoring and many other hand operations. Webb sells exclusively to distributors, who in turn sell to independent clothing stores and retail chains. For simplicity, we assume the following:

1. Webb's only costs are in the manufacturing function; Webb incurs no costs in other value-chain functions, such as marketing and distribution.
2. All units manufactured in April 2014 are sold in April 2014.
3. There is no direct materials inventory at either the beginning or the end of the period. No work-in-process or finished goods inventories exist at either the beginning or the end of the period.

Webb has three variable-cost categories. The budgeted variable cost per jacket for each category is as follows:

Cost Category	Variable Cost per Jacket
Direct materials costs	$60
Direct manufacturing labor costs	16
Variable manufacturing overhead costs	12
Total variable costs	$88

The *number of units manufactured* is the cost driver for direct materials, direct manufacturing labor, and variable manufacturing overhead. The relevant range for the cost driver is from 0 to 12,000 jackets. Budgeted and actual data for April 2014 are:

Budgeted fixed costs for production between 0 and 12,000 jackets	$276,000
Budgeted selling price	$ 120 per jacket
Budgeted production and sales	12,000 jackets
Actual production and sales	10,000 jackets

---

[2] For an excellent discussion and other related examples from governmental settings, see Kavanagh S., and C. Swanson. 2009. Tactical financial management: Cash flow and budgetary variance analysis. *Government Finance Review*, October 1.

Level 1 Analysis

	Actual Results (1)	Static-Budget Variances (2) = (1) – (3)	Static Budget (3)
Units sold	10,000	2,000 U	12,000
Revenues	$1,250,000	$190,000 U	$1,440,000
Variable costs			
Direct materials	621,600	98,400 F	720,000
Direct manufacturing labor	198,000	6,000 U	192,000
Variable manufacturing overhead	130,500	13,500 F	144,000
Total variable costs	950,100	105,900 F	1,056,000
Contribution margin	299,900	84,100 U	384,000
Fixed costs	285,000	9,000 U	276,000
Operating income	$ 14,900	$ 93,100 U	$ 108,000
		$ 93,100 U	
		Static-budget variance	

[a]F = favorable effect on operating income; U = unfavorable effect on operating income.

The **static budget**, or master budget, is based on the level of output planned at the start of the budget period. The master budget is called a static budget because the budget for the period is developed around a single (static) planned output level. Exhibit 1, column 3, presents the static budget for Webb Company for April 2014 that was prepared at the end of 2013. For each line item in the income statement, Exhibit 1, column 1, displays data for the actual April results. For example, actual revenues are $1,250,000, and the actual selling price is $1,250,000 ÷ 10,000 jackets = $125 per jacket—compared with the budgeted selling price of $120 per jacket. Similarly, actual direct materials costs are $621,600, and the direct material cost per jacket is $621,600 ÷ 10,000 = $62.16 per jacket—compared with the budgeted direct material cost per jacket of $60. We describe potential reasons and explanations for these differences as we discuss different variances throughout the chapter.

The **static-budget variance** (see Exhibit 1, column 2) is the difference between the actual result and the corresponding budgeted amount in the static budget.

A **favorable variance**—denoted F in this text—has the effect, when considered in isolation, of increasing operating income relative to the budgeted amount. For revenue items, F means actual revenues exceed budgeted revenues. For cost items, F means actual costs are less than budgeted costs. An **unfavorable variance**—denoted U in this text—has the effect, when viewed in isolation, of decreasing operating income relative to the budgeted amount. Unfavorable variances are also called *adverse variances* in some countries, such as the United Kingdom.

The unfavorable static-budget variance for operating income of $93,100 in Exhibit 1 is calculated by subtracting static-budget operating income of $108,000 from actual operating income of $14,900:

$$\text{Static-budget variance for operating income} = \text{Actual result} - \text{Static-budget amount}$$

$$= \$14,900 - \$108,000$$

$$= \$93,100 \text{ U}.$$

The analysis in Exhibit 1 provides managers with additional information on the static-budget variance for operating income of $93,100 U. The more detailed breakdown indicates how the line items that comprise operating income—revenues, individual variable costs, and fixed costs—add up to the static-budget variance of $93,100.

Decision Point

What are static budgets and static-budget variances?

Recall that Webb produced and sold only 10,000 jackets, although managers anticipated an output of 12,000 jackets in the static budget. *Managers want to know how much of the static-budget variance is due to Webb inaccurately forecasting what it expected to produce and sell and how much is due to how it actually performed manufacturing and selling 10,000 jackets.* Managers, therefore, create a flexible budget, which enables a more in-depth understanding of deviations from the static budget.

Flexible Budgets

Learning Objective 2

Examine the concept of a flexible budget

...the budget that is adjusted (flexed) to recognize the actual output level

and learn how to develop it

...proportionately increase variable costs; keep fixed costs the same

A **flexible budget** calculates budgeted revenues and budgeted costs based on *the actual output in the budget period.* The flexible budget is prepared at the end of the period (April 2014 for Webb), after managers know the actual output of 10,000 jackets. The flexible budget is the *hypothetical* budget that Webb would have prepared at the start of the budget period if it had correctly forecast the actual output of 10,000 jackets. In other words, the flexible budget is not the plan Webb initially had in mind for April 2014 (remember Webb planned for an output of 12,000 jackets). Rather, it is the budget Webb *would have* put together for April if it knew in advance that the output for the month would be 10,000 jackets. In preparing the flexible budget, note that:

- The budgeted selling price is the same $120 per jacket used in the static budget.
- The budgeted unit variable cost is the same $88 per jacket used in the static budget.
- The budgeted *total* fixed costs are the same static-budget amount of $276,000. Why? Because the 10,000 jackets produced falls within the relevant range of 0 to 12,000 jackets. Therefore, Webb would have budgeted the same amount of fixed costs, $276,000, whether it anticipated making 10,000 or 12,000 jackets.

The *only* difference between the static budget and the flexible budget is that the static budget is prepared for the planned output of 12,000 jackets, whereas the flexible budget is prepared retroactively based on the actual output of 10,000 jackets. In other words, the static budget is being "flexed," or adjusted, from 12,000 jackets to 10,000 jackets.[3] The flexible budget for 10,000 jackets assumes all costs are either completely variable or completely fixed with respect to the number of jackets produced.

Webb develops its flexible budget in three steps.

Step 1: Identify the Actual Quantity of Output. In April 2014, Webb produced and sold 10,000 jackets.

Step 2: Calculate the Flexible Budget for Revenues Based on the Budgeted Selling Price and Actual Quantity of Output.

$$\text{Flexible-budget revenues} = \$120 \text{ per jacket} \times 10,000 \text{ jackets}$$
$$= \$1,200,000$$

Step 3: Calculate the Flexible Budget for Costs Based on the Budgeted Variable Cost per Output Unit, Actual Quantity of Output, and Budgeted Fixed Costs.

Flexible-budget variable costs	
Direct materials, $60 per jacket × 10,000 jackets	$ 600,000
Direct manufacturing labor, $16 per jacket × 10,000 jackets	160,000
Variable manufacturing overhead, $12 per jacket × 10,000 jackets	120,000
Total flexible-budget variable costs	880,000
Flexible-budget fixed costs	276,000
Flexible-budget total costs	$1,156,000

---

[3] Suppose Webb, when preparing its annual budget for 2014 at the end of 2013, had perfectly anticipated that its output in April 2014 would equal 10,000 jackets. Then the flexible budget for April 2014 would be identical to the static budget.

| Exhibit 2 | Level 2 Flexible-Budget-Based Variance Analysis for Webb Company for April 2014[a] |

Level 2 Analysis

	Actual Results (1)	Flexible-Budget Variances (2) = (1) − (3)	Flexible Budget (3)	Sales-Volume Variances (4) = (3) − (5)	Static Budget (5)
Units sold	10,000	0	10,000	2,000 U	12,000
Revenues	$1,250,000	$50,000 F	$1,200,000	$240,000 U	$1,440,000
Variable costs					
Direct materials	621,600	21,600 U	600,000	120,000 F	720,000
Direct manufacturing labor	198,000	38,000 U	160,000	32,000 F	192,000
Variable manufacturing overhead	130,500	10,500 U	120,000	24,000 F	144,000
Total variable costs	950,100	70,100 U	880,000	176,000 F	1,056,000
Contribution margin	299,900	20,100 U	320,000	64,000 U	384,000
Fixed manufacturing costs	285,000	9,000 U	276,000	0	276,000
Operating income	$ 14,900	$29,100 U	$ 44,000	$ 64,000 U	$ 108,000

Level 2 $29,100 U $ 64,000 U

Flexible-budget variance   Sales-volume variance

Level 1 $93,100 U

Static-budget variance

[a]F = favorable effect on operating income; U = unfavorable effect on operating income.

These three steps enable Webb to prepare a flexible budget, as shown in Exhibit 2, column 3. The flexible budget allows for a more detailed analysis of the $93,100 unfavorable static-budget variance for operating income.

Flexible-Budget Variances and Sales-Volume Variances

Exhibit 2 shows the flexible-budget-based variance analysis for Webb, which subdivides the $93,100 unfavorable static-budget variance for operating income into two parts: a flexible-budget variance of $29,100 U and a sales-volume variance of $64,000 U. The **sales-volume variance** is the difference between a flexible-budget amount and the corresponding static-budget amount. The **flexible-budget variance** is the difference between an actual result and the corresponding flexible-budget amount.

Sales-Volume Variances

Keep in mind that the flexible-budget amounts in column 3 of Exhibit 2 and the static-budget amounts in column 5 are both computed using budgeted selling prices, budgeted variable cost per jacket, and budgeted fixed costs. The difference between the static-budget and the flexible-budget amounts is called the sales-volume variance because it arises *solely* from the difference between the 10,000 actual quantity (or volume) of jackets sold and the 12,000 quantity of jackets expected to be sold in the static budget.

$$\text{Sales-volume variance for operating income} = \text{Flexible-budget amount} - \text{Static-budget amount}$$

$$= \$44,000 - \$108,000$$

$$= \$64,000 \text{ U}$$

Decision Point

How can managers develop a flexible budget and why is it useful to do so?

Learning Objective 3

Calculate flexible-budget variances

...each flexible-budget variance is the difference between an actual result and a flexible-budget amount

and sales-volume variances

...each sales-volume variance is the difference between a flexible-budget amount and a static-budget amount

The sales-volume variance in operating income for Webb measures the change in the budgeted contribution margin because Webb sold only 10,000 jackets rather than the budgeted 12,000.

$$\begin{aligned}
\begin{pmatrix} \text{Sales-volume} \\ \text{variance for} \\ \text{operating income} \end{pmatrix} &= \begin{pmatrix} \text{Budgeted contribution} \\ \text{margin per unit} \end{pmatrix} \times \begin{pmatrix} \text{Actual units} \\ \text{sold} \end{pmatrix} - \begin{pmatrix} \text{Static-budget} \\ \text{units sold} \end{pmatrix} \\
&= \begin{pmatrix} \text{Budgeted selling} \\ \text{price} \end{pmatrix} - \begin{pmatrix} \text{Budgeted variable} \\ \text{cost per unit} \end{pmatrix} \times \begin{pmatrix} \text{Actual units} \\ \text{sold} \end{pmatrix} - \begin{pmatrix} \text{Static-budget} \\ \text{units sold} \end{pmatrix} \\
&= (\$120 \text{ per jacket} - \$88 \text{ per jacket}) \times (10,000 \text{ jackets} - 12,000 \text{ jackets}) \\
&= \$32 \text{ per jacket} \times (-2,000 \text{ jackets}) \\
&= \$64,000 \text{ U}
\end{aligned}$$

Exhibit 2, column 4, shows the components of this overall variance by identifying the sales-volume variance for each of the line items in the income statement. The unfavorable sales-volume variance in operating income arises because of one or more of the following reasons:

1. Failure of Webb's managers to execute the sales plans
2. Weaker than anticipated overall demand for jackets
3. Competitors taking away market share from Webb
4. Unexpected changes in customer tastes and preferences away from Webb's designs
5. Quality problems leading to customer dissatisfaction with Webb's jackets

How Webb responds to the unfavorable sales-volume variance will depend on what its managers believe caused the variance. For example, if Webb's managers believe the unfavorable sales-volume variance was caused by market-related reasons (reasons 1, 2, 3, or 4), the sales manager would be in the best position to explain what happened and suggest corrective actions that may be needed, such as sales promotions, market studies, or changes to advertising plans. If, however, managers believe the unfavorable sales-volume variance was caused by unanticipated quality problems (reason 5), the production manager would be in the best position to analyze the causes and suggest strategies for improvement, such as changes in the manufacturing process or investments in new machines.

The static-budget variances compared actual revenues and costs for 10,000 jackets against budgeted revenues and costs for 12,000 jackets. A portion of this difference, the sales-volume variance, reflects the effects of selling fewer units or inaccurate forecasting of sales. By removing this component from the static-budget variance, managers can compare their firm's revenues earned and costs incurred for April 2014 against the flexible budget—the revenues and costs Webb would have budgeted for the 10,000 jackets actually produced and sold. *Flexible-budget variances are a better measure of sales price and cost performance than static-budget variances because they compare actual revenues to budgeted revenues and actual costs to budgeted costs for the same 10,000 jackets of output.* Concepts in Action: Flexible Budgets at Corning shows the importance of flexible budgets for conducting variance analysis and in enabling a company to manage its business in an uncertain environment.

Flexible-Budget Variances

The first three columns of Exhibit 2 compare Webb's actual results with its flexible-budget amounts. The flexible-budget variances for each line item in the income statement are shown in column 2:

$$\frac{\text{Flexible-budget}}{\text{variance}} = \frac{\text{Actual}}{\text{result}} - \frac{\text{Flexible-budget}}{\text{amount}}$$

The operating income line in Exhibit 2 shows the flexible-budget variance is $29,100 U ($14,900 – $44,000). The $29,100 U arises because the actual selling price, actual variable

Concepts in Action ▶ Flexible Budgets at Corning

Historically, the rule of business budgeting was simple: Make a budget and stick to it. In today's fast-changing environment, however, many companies are pairing their annual "static" budget with a flexible budget that adjusts for changes in the volume of activity. Corning, the 160-year-old maker of specialty glass and ceramics, uses a flexible budget to quickly accommodate the impact of significant changes that affect its business.

Each year, Corning pulls together its annual budget. While managers still work to make sure that budget is achieved, it cannot predict the actions of Corning's customers and competitors with 100% accuracy. For instance, Apple uses the company's scratch-resistant Gorilla Glass on its iPhone screens. If Apple decides to expedite the production of its newest iPhone model, Corning may have to unexpectedly ramp up its Gorilla Glass manufacturing, which has both unexpected costs and revenues. At Corning, management accountants and finance executives produce rolling forecasts each month to address what the company thinks will happen for the rest of the quarter. According to Tony Tripeny, Corning's senior vice president and corporate controller, "Based on this analysis, we will go to the business units and say, 'What are you going to do differently? What actions are you going to take, and how is that different from what we had assumed with the budget?'"

By using a flexible budget, Corning managers can analyze uncertainty, improve performance evaluation, and conduct useful variance analysis that helps the company stay on track. So, why does Corning develop a detailed budget at all? It has specific benefits, explains Tripeny. As an example, he cites the relationship of a budget to Corning's resolve to be the lowest-cost producer in its markets. "During the budget process, we set up specific objectives, like targets for manufacturing costs," he says. "Even though the business might change during the year, it normally doesn't change enough to alter the manufacturing-performance targets. From a control standpoint, a budget still has value, but it shouldn't guide how you manage the business, which is about perceiving what's ahead and acting on it quicker than the competition."

Sources: Pogue, David. 2010. Gorilla Glass, the smartphone's unsung hero. Pogue's Posts (blog), *New York Times*, December 9. http://pogue.blogs.nytimes.com; Banham, Russ. 2011. Let it roll. *CFO Magazine*, May.

cost per unit, and actual fixed costs differ from their budgeted amounts. The actual results and budgeted amounts for the selling price and variable cost per unit are as follows:

	Actual Result	Budgeted Amount
Selling price	$125.00 ($1,250,000 ÷ 10,000 jackets)	$120.00 ($1,200,000 ÷ 10,000 jackets)
Variable cost per jacket	$ 95.01 ($ 950,100 ÷ 10,000 jackets)	$ 88.00 ($ 880,000 ÷ 10,000 jackets)

The flexible-budget variance for revenues is called the **selling-price variance** because it arises solely from the difference between the actual selling price and the budgeted selling price:

$$
\begin{aligned}
\text{Selling-price variance} &= \left(\begin{array}{c} \text{Actual} \\ \text{selling price} \end{array} - \begin{array}{c} \text{Budgeted} \\ \text{selling price} \end{array} \right) \times \begin{array}{c} \text{Actual} \\ \text{units sold} \end{array} \\
&= (\$125\,\text{per jacket} - \$120\,\text{per jacket}) \times 10{,}000\,\text{jackets} \\
&= \$50{,}000\,\text{F}
\end{aligned}
$$

Webb has a favorable selling-price variance because the $125 actual selling price exceeds the $120 budgeted amount, which increases operating income. Marketing managers are generally in the best position to understand and explain the reason for a selling price difference. For example, was the difference due to better quality? Or was it due to an overall increase in market prices? Webb's managers concluded it was due to a general increase in prices.

The flexible-budget variance for total variable costs is unfavorable ($70,100 U) for the actual output of 10,000 jackets. It's unfavorable because of one or both of the following:

- Webb used greater quantities of inputs (such as direct manufacturing labor-hours) compared to the budgeted quantities of inputs.
- Webb incurred higher prices per unit for the inputs (such as the wage rate per direct manufacturing labor-hour) compared to the budgeted prices per unit of the inputs.

Higher input quantities and/or higher input prices relative to the budgeted amounts could be the result of Webb deciding to produce a better product than what was planned or the result of inefficiencies related to Webb's manufacturing and purchasing operations or both. *You should always think of variance analysis as providing suggestions for further investigation rather than as establishing conclusive evidence of good or bad performance.*

The actual fixed costs of $285,000 are $9,000 more than the budgeted amount of $276,000. This unfavorable flexible-budget variance reflects unexpected increases in the cost of fixed indirect resources, such as the factory's rent or supervisors' salaries.

In the rest of this chapter, we will focus on variable direct-cost input variances.

Decision Point

How are flexible-budget and sales-volume variances calculated?

Learning Objective 4

Explain why standard costs are often used in variance analysis

...standard costs exclude past inefficiencies and take into account expected future changes

Standard Costs for Variance Analysis

To gain further insight, a company will subdivide the flexible-budget variance for its direct-cost inputs into two more-detailed variances:

1. A price variance that reflects the difference between an actual input price and a budgeted input price
2. An efficiency variance that reflects the difference between an actual input quantity and a budgeted input quantity

We will call these level 3 variances. Managers generally have more control over efficiency variances than price variances because the quantity of inputs used is primarily affected by factors inside the company (such as the efficiency with which operations are performed), whereas changes in the price of materials or in wage rates may be largely dictated by market forces outside the company.

Obtaining Budgeted Input Prices and Budgeted Input Quantities

To calculate price and efficiency variances, Webb needs to obtain budgeted input prices and budgeted input quantities. Webb's three main sources for this information are: (1) past data, (2) data from similar companies, and (3) standards. Each source has its advantages and disadvantages.

1. **Actual input data from past periods.** Most companies have past data on actual input prices and actual input quantities. These historical data could be analyzed for trends or patterns to obtain estimates of budgeted prices and quantities.

   Advantages: Past data represent quantities and prices that are real rather than hypothetical, so they can be very useful benchmarks for measuring improvements in performance. Moreover, past data are typically easy to collect at a low cost.

   Disadvantages: A firm's inefficiencies, such as the wastage of direct materials, are incorporated in past data. Consequently, the data do not represent the performance the firm could have ideally attained, only the performance it achieved in the past. Past data also do not incorporate any changes expected for the budget period, such as improvements resulting from new investments in technology.

2. **Data from other companies that have similar processes.** Another source of information is data from peer companies or companies that have similar processes, which can serve as a benchmark. For example, Baptist Healthcare System in Louisville, Kentucky, benchmarks its labor performance data against those of similar top-ranked hospitals.

   Advantages: Data from other companies can provide a firm useful information about how it's performing relative to its competitors.

   Disadvantages: Input-price and input-quantity data from other companies are often not available or may not be comparable to a particular company's situation. Consider American Apparel, which makes more than 1 million articles of clothing a week. At its sole factory, in Los Angeles, workers receive hourly wages, piece rates, and medical benefits well in excess of those paid by its competitors, virtually all of whom are offshore and have significantly lower production costs. (We will discuss benchmarking in more detail later in the chapter.)

3. **Standards developed by the firm itself.** A **standard** is a carefully determined price, cost, or quantity that is used as a benchmark for judging performance. Standards are usually expressed on a per-unit basis. Consider how Webb determines its direct manufacturing labor standards. Webb conducts engineering studies to obtain a detailed breakdown of the steps required to make a jacket. Each step is assigned a standard time based on work performed by a *skilled* worker using equipment operating in an *efficient* manner. Similarly, Webb determines the standard quantity of square yards of cloth based on what is required by a skilled operator to make a jacket.

   Advantages: Standard times (1) aim to exclude past inefficiencies and (2) take into account changes expected to occur in the budget period. An example of the latter would be a decision by Webb's managers to lease new, faster, and more accurate sewing machines. Webb would incorporate the resulting higher level of efficiency into the new standards it sets.

   Disdvantages: Because they are not based on realized benchmarks, the standards might not be achievable, and workers could get discouraged trying to meet them.

The term *standard* refers to many different things:

- A **standard input** is a carefully determined quantity of input, such as square yards of cloth or direct manufacturing labor-hours, required for one unit of output, such as a jacket.
- A **standard price** is a carefully determined price a company expects to pay for a unit of input. In the Webb example, the standard wage rate the firm expects to pay its operators is an example of a standard price of a direct manufacturing labor-hour.
- A **standard cost** is a carefully determined cost of a unit of output, such as the standard direct manufacturing labor cost of a jacket at Webb.

$$\text{Standard cost per output unit for each variable direct-cost input} = \text{Standard input allowed for one output unit} \times \text{Standard price per input unit}$$

Standard direct material cost per jacket: 2 square yards of cloth input allowed per output unit (jacket) manufactured, at $30 standard price per square yard

Standard direct material cost per jacket $= 2$ square yards $\times$ $30 per square yard $=$ $60

Standard direct manufacturing labor cost per jacket: 0.8 manufacturing labor-hour of input allowed per output unit manufactured, at $20 standard price per hour

Standard direct manufacturing labor cost per jacket $= 0.8$ labor-hour $\times$ $20 per labor-hour $=$ $16

How are the words *budget* and *standard* related? Budget is the broader term. To clarify, budgeted input prices, input quantities, and costs need *not* be based on standards. As we saw previously, they could be based on past data or competitive benchmarks. However, when standards *are* used to obtain budgeted input quantities and prices, the terms *standard* and *budget* are used interchangeably. The standard cost of each input required for one unit of output is determined by the standard quantity of the input required for one unit of output and the standard price per input unit. Notice how the standard-cost computations shown previously for direct materials and direct manufacturing labor result in the budgeted direct material cost per jacket of $60 and the budgeted direct manufacturing labor cost of $16 referred to earlier.

In its standard costing system, Webb uses standards that are attainable by operating efficiently but that allow for normal disruptions. A normal disruption could include, for example, a short delay in the receipt of materials needed to produce the jackets or a production delay because a piece of equipment needed a minor repair. An alternative is to set more-challenging standards that are more difficult to attain. Setting challenging standards can increase the motivation of employees and a firm's performance. However, as we have indicated, if workers believe the standards are unachievable, they can become frustrated and the firm's performance could suffer.

Decision Point

What is a standard cost and what are its purposes?

Learning Objective 5

Compute price variances

...each price variance is the difference between an actual input price and a budgeted input price

and efficiency variances

...each efficiency variance is the difference between an actual input quantity and a budgeted input quantity for actual output

for direct-cost categories

Price Variances and Efficiency Variances for Direct-Cost Inputs

Consider Webb's two direct-cost categories. The actual cost for each of these categories for the 10,000 jackets manufactured and sold in April 2014 is as follows:

Direct Materials Purchased and Used[4]

1. Square yards of cloth input purchased and used	22,200
2. Actual price incurred per square yard	$ 28
3. Direct material costs (22,200 × $28) [shown in Exhibit 2, column 1]	$621,600

Direct manufacturing Labor used

1. Direct manufacturing labor-hours used	9,000
2. Actual price incurred per direct manufacturing labor-hour	$ 22
3. Direct manufacturing labor costs (9,000 × $22) [shown in Exhibit 2, column 1]	$198,000

Let's use the Webb Company data to illustrate the price variance and the efficiency variance for direct-cost inputs.

A **price variance** is the difference between actual price and budgeted price, multiplied by the actual input quantity, such as direct materials purchased. A price variance is sometimes called a **rate variance**, especially when it's used to describe the price variance for direct manufacturing labor. An **efficiency variance** is the difference between the actual input quantity used (such as square yards of cloth) and the budgeted input quantity allowed for actual output, multiplied by budgeted price. An efficiency variance is sometimes called a **usage variance**. Let's explore price and efficiency variances in greater detail so we can see how managers use them.

Price Variances

The formula for computing the price variance is as follows:

$$\frac{\text{Price}}{\text{variance}} = \left(\begin{array}{c} \text{Actual price} \\ \text{of input} \end{array} - \begin{array}{c} \text{Budgeted price} \\ \text{of input} \end{array} \right) \times \begin{array}{c} \text{Actual quantity} \\ \text{of input} \end{array}$$

The price variances for Webb's two direct-cost categories are as follows:

Direct-Cost Category	(Actual price of input − Budgeted price of input) ×	Actual quantity of input	=	Price Variance
Direct materials	($28 per sq. yard) − $30 per sq. yard) × 22,200 square yards		=	$44,400 F
Direct manufacturing labor	($22 per hour − $20 per hour) × 9,000 hours		=	$18,000 U

---

[4] The Problem for Self-Study relaxes the assumption that the quantity of direct materials used equals the quantity of direct materials purchased.

The direct materials price variance is favorable because the actual price of cloth is less than the budgeted price, resulting in an increase in operating income. The direct manufacturing labor price variance is unfavorable because the actual wage rate paid to labor is more than the budgeted rate, resulting in a decrease in operating income.

Managers should always consider a broad range of possible causes for a price variance. For example, Webb's favorable direct materials price variance could be due to one or more of the following:

- Webb's purchasing manager negotiated the direct materials prices more skillfully than was planned for in the budget.
- The purchasing manager switched to a lower-price supplier.
- The purchasing manager ordered larger quantities than the quantities budgeted, thereby obtaining quantity discounts.
- Direct materials prices decreased unexpectedly due to an oversupply of materials in the industry.
- The budgeted purchase prices of direct materials were set too high because managers did not carefully analyze market conditions.
- The purchasing manager negotiated favorable prices because he was willing to accept unfavorable terms on factors other than prices (such as agree to lower-quality material).

How Webb's managers respond to the direct materials price variance depends on what they believe caused it. For example, if they believe the purchasing manager received quantity discounts by ordering a larger amount of materials than budgeted, Webb could investigate whether the larger quantities resulted in higher storage costs for the firm. If the increase in storage and inventory holding costs exceeds the quantity discounts, purchasing in larger quantities is not beneficial. Some companies have reduced their materials storage areas to prevent their purchasing managers from ordering in larger quantities.

Efficiency Variance

For any actual level of output, the efficiency variance is the difference between the actual quantity of input used and the budgeted quantity of input allowed for that output level, multiplied by the budgeted input price:

$$\text{Efficiency variance} = \left(\begin{array}{c} \text{Actual} \\ \text{quantity of} \\ \text{input used} \end{array} - \begin{array}{c} \text{Budgeted quantity} \\ \text{of input allowed} \\ \text{for actual output} \end{array} \right) \times \begin{array}{c} \text{Budgeted price} \\ \text{of input} \end{array}$$

The idea here is that, given a certain output level, a company is inefficient if it uses a larger quantity of input than budgeted. Conversely, a company is efficient if it uses a smaller input quantity than was budgeted for that output level.

The efficiency variances for each of Webb's direct-cost categories are as follows:

Direct-Cost Category	$\left(\begin{array}{c} \text{Actual} \\ \text{quantity of} \\ \text{input used} \end{array} - \begin{array}{c} \text{Budgeted quantity} \\ \text{of input allowed} \\ \text{for actual output} \end{array} \right)$	$\times$ Budgeted price of input	= Efficiency variance
Direct materials	[22,200 sq. yds. − (10,000 units × 2 sq. yds./unit)]	× $30 per sq. yard	
	= (22,200 sq. yds. − 20,000 sq. yds.)	× $30 per sq. yard	= $66,000 U
Direct manufacturing labor	[9,000 hours − (10,000 units × 0.8 hour/unit)]	× $20 per hour	
	= (9,000 hours − 8,000 hours)	× $20 per hour	= 20,000 U

The two manufacturing efficiency variances—the direct materials efficiency variance and the direct manufacturing labor efficiency variance—are each unfavorable. Why? Because given the firm's actual output, more of these inputs were used than were budgeted for. This lowered Webb's operating income.

As with price variances, there is a broad range of possible causes for these efficiency variances. For example, Webb's unfavorable efficiency variance for direct manufacturing labor could be because of one or more of the following:

- Webb's workers took longer to make each jacket because they worked more slowly or made poor-quality jackets that required reworking.
- Webb's personnel manager hired underskilled workers.
- Webb's production scheduler inefficiently scheduled work, resulting in more manufacturing labor time than budgeted being used per jacket.
- Webb's maintenance department did not properly maintain machines, resulting in more manufacturing labor time than budgeted being used per jacket.
- Webb's budgeted time standards were too tight because the skill levels of employees and the environment in which they operated weren't accurately evaluated.

Suppose Webb's managers determine that the unfavorable variance is due to poor machine maintenance. Webb could then establish a team consisting of plant engineers and machine operators to develop a maintenance schedule to reduce future breakdowns and prevent adverse effects on labor time and product quality.[5]

Exhibit 3 provides an alternative way to calculate price and efficiency variances. It shows how the price variance and the efficiency variance subdivide the flexible-budget variance. Consider direct materials. The direct materials flexible-budget variance of $21,600 U is the difference between the actual costs incurred (actual input quantity × actual price) of $621,600 shown in column 1 and the flexible budget (budgeted input quantity allowed

| Exhibit 3 | Columnar Presentation of Variance Analysis: Direct Costs for Webb Company for April 2014[a] |

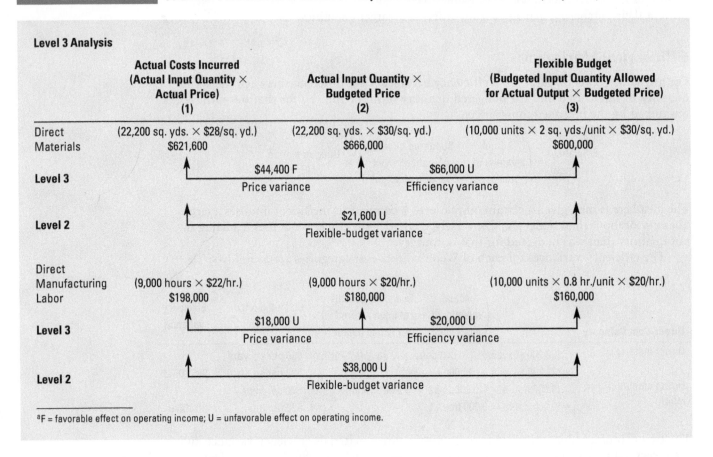

Level 3 Analysis

	Actual Costs Incurred (Actual Input Quantity × Actual Price) (1)	Actual Input Quantity × Budgeted Price (2)	Flexible Budget (Budgeted Input Quantity Allowed for Actual Output × Budgeted Price) (3)
Direct Materials	(22,200 sq. yds. × $28/sq. yd.) $621,600	(22,200 sq. yds. × $30/sq. yd.) $666,000	(10,000 units × 2 sq. yds./unit × $30/sq. yd.) $600,000
Level 3		$44,400 F Price variance	$66,000 U Efficiency variance
Level 2		$21,600 U Flexible-budget variance	
Direct Manufacturing Labor	(9,000 hours × $22/hr.) $198,000	(9,000 hours × $20/hr.) $180,000	(10,000 units × 0.8 hr./unit × $20/hr.) $160,000
Level 3		$18,000 U Price variance	$20,000 U Efficiency variance
Level 2		$38,000 U Flexible-budget variance	

[a]F = favorable effect on operating income; U = unfavorable effect on operating income.

---

[5] When there are multiple inputs, such as different types of materials, that can be substituted for one another, the efficiency variance can be further decomposed into mix and yield variances. The appendix to this chapter describes how these variances are calculated.

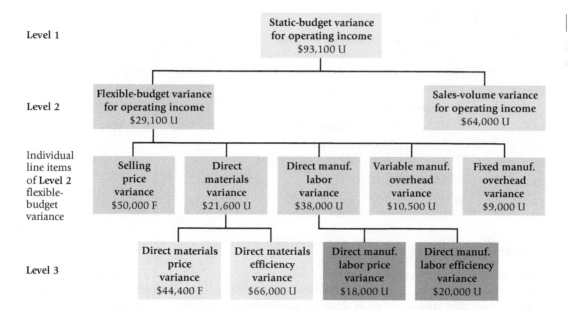

Exhibit 4

Summary of Level 1, 2, and 3 Variance Analyses

for actual output × budgeted price) of $600,000 shown in column 3. Column 2 (actual input quantity × budgeted price) is inserted between column 1 and column 3. The difference between columns 1 and 2 is the price variance of $44,400 F. This price variance occurs because the same actual input quantity (22,200 sq. yds.) is multiplied by the *actual price* ($28) in column 1 and the *budgeted price* ($30) in column 2. The difference between columns 2 and 3 is the efficiency variance of $66,000 U because the same budgeted price ($30) is multiplied by the *actual input quantity* (22,200 sq. yds) in column 2 and the *budgeted input quantity allowed for actual output* (20,000 sq. yds.) in column 3. The sum of the direct materials price variance, $44,400 F, and the direct materials efficiency variance, $66,000 U, equals the direct materials flexible budget variance, $21,600 U.

Exhibit 4 provides a summary of the different variances. Note how the variances at each higher level provide disaggregated and more detailed information for evaluating performance.

We now present Webb's journal entries under its standard costing system.

Journal Entries Using Standard Costs

Our focus is on direct materials and direct manufacturing labor. All the numbers included in the following journal entries are found in Exhibit 3.

Note: In each of the following entries, unfavorable variances are always debits (they decrease operating income), and favorable variances are always credits (they increase operating income).

Journal Entry 1A

Isolate the direct materials price variance at the time the materials were purchased. This is done by increasing (debiting) the Direct Materials Control account by the standard price Webb established for purchasing the materials. This is the earliest time possible to isolate this variance.

1a.	Direct Materials Control		
	(22,200 square yards × $30 per square yard)	666,000	
	Direct Materials Price Variance		
	(22,200 square yards × $2 per square yard)		44,400
	Accounts Payable Control		
	(22,200 square yards × $28 per square yard)		621,600
	This records the direct materials purchased.		

Journal Entry 1B

Isolate the direct materials efficiency variance at the time the direct materials are used by increasing (debiting) the Work-in-Process Control account. Use the standard quantities allowed for the actual output units manufactured times their standard purchase prices.

1b.	Work-in-Process Control		
	(10,000 jackets × 2 yards per jacket × $30 per square yard)	600,000	
	Direct Materials Efficiency Variance		
	(2,200 square yards × $30 per square yard)	66,000	
	Direct Materials Control		
	(22,200 square yards × $30 per square yard)		666,000
	This records the direct materials used.		

Journal Entry 2

Isolate the direct manufacturing labor price variance and efficiency variance at the time the labor is used by increasing (debiting) the Work-in-Process Control by the standard hours and standard wage rates allowed for the actual units manufactured. Note that the Wages Payable Control account measures the actual amounts payable to workers based on the actual hours they worked and their actual wage rate.

2.	Work-in-Process Control		
	(10,000 jackets × 0.80 hour per jacket × $20 per hour)	160,000	
	Direct Manufacturing Labor Price Variance		
	(9,000 hours × $2 per hour)	18,000	
	Direct Manufacturing Labor Efficiency Variance		
	(1,000 hours × $20 per hour)	20,000	
	Wages Payable Control		
	(9,000 hours × $22 per hour)		198,000
	This records the liability for Webb's direct manufacturing labor costs.		

You have learned how standard costing and variance analysis help managers focus on areas not operating as expected. The journal entries here point to another advantage of standard costing systems: standard costs simplify product costing. As each unit is manufactured, costs are assigned to it using the standard cost of direct materials, the standard cost of direct manufacturing labor, and the standard manufacturing overhead cost.

From the perspective of control, all variances should be isolated at the earliest possible time. For example, by isolating the direct materials price variance at the time materials are purchased, managers can take corrective actions—such as trying to obtain cost reductions from the firm's current suppliers or obtaining price quotes from other potential suppliers—immediately when a large unfavorable variance is known rather than waiting until after the materials are used in production.

If the variance accounts are immaterial in amount at the end of the fiscal year, they are written off to the cost of goods sold. For simplicity, we assume that the balances in the different direct cost variance accounts as of April 2014 are also the balances at the end of 2014 and are immaterial in total. Webb would record the following journal entry to write off the direct cost variance accounts to the Cost of Goods Sold account.

Cost of Goods Sold	59,600	
Direct Materials Price Variance	44,400	
Direct Materials Efficiency Variance		66,000
Direct Manufacturing Labor Price Variance		18,000
Direct Manufacturing Labor Efficiency Variance		20,000

Alternatively, assuming Webb has inventories at the end of the fiscal year and the variances are material in their amounts, the variance accounts will be prorated among the cost of goods sold and various inventory accounts. For example, the Direct Materials Price Variance will be prorated among Materials Control, Work-in-Process Control, Finished Goods Control, and Cost of Goods Sold on the basis of the standard costs of direct materials in each account's ending balance. Direct Materials Efficiency Variance is prorated among Work-in-Process Control, Finished Goods Control, and Cost of Goods Sold on the basis of the direct material costs in each account's ending balance (after proration of the direct materials price variance).

Many accountants, industrial engineers, and managers argue that to the extent variances measure inefficiency during the year, they should be written off against income for that period instead of being prorated among inventories and the cost of goods sold. These people believe it's better to apply a combination of the write-off and proration methods for each individual variance. That way, unlike full proration, the firm doesn't end up carrying the costs of inefficiency as part of its inventoriable costs. Consider the efficiency variance: The portion of the variance due to avoidable inefficiencies should be written off to cost of goods sold. In contrast, the portion that is unavoidable should be prorated. Likewise, if a portion of the direct materials price variance is unavoidable because it is entirely caused by general market conditions, it too should be prorated.

Implementing Standard Costing

Standard costing provides valuable information that is used for the management and control of materials, labor, and other activities related to production.

Standard Costing and Information Technology

Both large and small firms are increasingly using computerized standard costing systems. For example, companies such as Sandoz, a maker of generic drugs, and Dell store standard prices and standard quantities in their computer systems. A bar code scanner records the receipt of materials, immediately costing each material using its stored standard price. The receipt of materials is then matched with the firm's purchase orders and recorded in accounts payable, and the direct material price variance is isolated.

The direct materials efficiency variance is calculated as output is completed by comparing the standard quantity of direct materials that should have been used with the computerized request for direct materials submitted by an operator on the production floor. Labor variances are calculated as employees log into production-floor terminals and punch in their employee numbers, start and end times, and the quantity of product they helped produce. Managers use this instantaneous feedback from variances to immediately detect and correct any cost-related problem.

Wide Applicability of Standard Costing

Manufacturing firms as well as firms in the service sector find standard costing to be a useful tool. Companies implementing total quality management programs use standard costing to control materials costs. Service-sector companies such as McDonald's are labor intensive and use standard costs to control labor costs. Companies that have implemented computer-integrated manufacturing (CIM), such as Toyota, use flexible budgeting and standard costing to manage activities such as materials handling and setups. The growing use of Enterprise Resource Planning (ERP) systems has made it easy for firms to keep track of the standard, average, and actual costs of items in inventory and to make real-time assessments of variances. Managers use variance information to identify areas of the firm's manufacturing or purchasing process that most need attention.

Decision Point

Why should a company calculate price and efficiency variances?

Concepts in Action ▶ Starbucks Reduces Direct-Cost Variances to Brew a Turnaround

Along with coffee, Starbucks brewed profitable growth for many years. But when consumers tightened their purse strings amid the recent recession, the company was in serious trouble. With customers cutting back and lower-priced competition—from Dunkin' Donuts and McDonald's among others—increasing, Starbucks' profit margins were under attack.

For Starbucks, profitability depends on making each beverage at the lowest possible cost. In each Starbucks store, the two key direct costs are materials and labor. Materials costs at Starbucks include coffee beans, milk, flavoring syrups, pastries, paper cups, and lids. To reduce budgeted costs for materials, Starbucks sought to avoid waste and spoilage by no longer brewing decaffeinated and darker coffee blends in the afternoon and evening, when store traffic is slower. With milk prices rising, the company switched to 2% milk, which is healthier and costs less, and redoubled efforts to reduce milk-related spoilage. To reduce labor costs, stores employed fewer baristas. In other stores, Starbucks adopted many "lean" production techniques to make its drink-making processes more efficient. While some changes seem small—keeping bins of coffee beans on top of the counter so baristas don't have to bend over and moving bottles of flavored syrups closer to where drinks are made—some stores experienced a 10% increase in transactions using the same number of workers or fewer.

Starbucks' focus on reducing direct-cost variances paid off. The company has reduced its store operating expenses from 36.1% of total net revenue in 2008 to 29.5% in 2012. Continued focus on direct-cost variances will remain critical to the company's future success in any economic climate.

Sources: Adamy, Janet. 2009. Starbucks brews up new cost cuts by putting lid on afternoon decaf. *Wall Street Journal*, January 28; Harris, Craig. 2007. Starbucks slips; lattes rise. *Seattle Post Intelligencer*, July 23; Jargon, Julie. 2010. Starbucks growth revives, perked by Via. *Wall Street Journal*, January 21; Jargon, Julie. 2009. Latest Starbucks buzzword: 'Lean' Japanese techniques. *Wall Street Journal*, August 4; Kesmodel, David. 2009. Starbucks sees demand stirring again. *Wall Street Journal*, November 6; Starbucks Corporation, 2012 Annual Report (Seattle: Starbucks Corporation, 2013); and Starbucks Corporation, 2008 Annual Report (Seattle: Starbucks Corporation, 2009).

Learning Objective 6

Understand how managers use variances

...managers use variances to improve future performance

Management's Use of Variances

Managers and management accountants use variances to evaluate performance after decisions are implemented, to trigger organization learning, and to make continuous improvements. Variances serve as an early warning system to alert managers to existing problems or to prospective opportunities. When done well, variance analysis enables managers to evaluate the effectiveness of the actions and performance of personnel in the current period, as well as to fine-tune strategies for achieving improved performance in the future. Concepts in Action: Starbucks Reduces Direct-Cost Variances to Brew a Turnaround shows the huge payoff the coffee retailing giant has reaped from paying careful attention to variance analysis wth respect to its direct costs.

Multiple Causes of Variances

To interpret variances correctly and make appropriate decisions based on them, managers need to recognize that variances can have multiple causes. Managers must not interpret variances in isolation of each other. The causes of variances in one part of the value chain can be the result of decisions made in another part of the value chain. Consider an unfavorable direct materials efficiency variance on Webb's production line. Possible operational causes of this variance across the value chain of the company are:

1. Poor design of products or processes
2. Poor work on the production line because of underskilled workers or faulty machines
3. Inappropriate assignment of labor or machines to specific jobs
4. Congestion due to scheduling a large number of rush orders placed by Webb's sales representatives
5. Webb's cloth suppliers not manufacturing materials of uniformly high quality

Item 5 offers an even broader reason for the cause of the unfavorable direct materials efficiency variance by considering inefficiencies in the supply chain of companies—in this case, by the cloth suppliers for Webb's jackets. Whenever possible, managers must attempt to understand the root causes of the variances.

When to Investigate Variances

Because a standard is not a single measure but rather a range of acceptable input quantities, costs, output quantities, or prices, managers should expect small variances to arise. A variance within an acceptable range is considered to be an "in-control occurrence" and calls for no investigation or action by managers. So when do managers need to investigate variances?

Frequently, managers investigate variances based on subjective judgments or rules of thumb. For critical items, such as product defects, even a small variance can prompt an investigation. For other items, such as direct material costs, labor costs, and repair costs, companies generally have rules such as "investigate all variances exceeding $5,000 or 20% of the budgeted cost, whichever is lower." The idea is that a 4% variance in direct material costs of $1 million—a $40,000 variance—deserves more attention than a 15% variance in repair costs of $10,000—a $1,500 variance. In other words, variance analysis is subject to the same cost–benefit test as all other phases of a management control system.

Using Variances for Performance Measurement

Managers often use variance analysis when evaluating the performance of their employees or business units. Two attributes of performance are commonly evaluated:

1. **Effectiveness:** the degree to which a predetermined objective or target is met, such as the sales, market share, and customer satisfaction ratings of Starbucks' VIA® Ready Brew line of instant coffees.
2. **Efficiency:** the relative amount of inputs used to achieve a given output level. For example, the smaller the quantity of Arabica beans used to make a given number of VIA packets or the greater the number of VIA packets made from a given quantity of beans, the greater the efficiency.

As we discussed earlier, it is important to understand the causes of a variance before using it for performance evaluation. Suppose a purchasing manager for Starbucks has just negotiated a deal that results in a favorable price variance for direct materials. The deal could have achieved a favorable variance for any or all of the following reasons:

1. The purchasing manager bargained effectively with suppliers.
2. The purchasing manager secured a discount for buying in bulk with fewer purchase orders. (However, buying larger quantities than necessary for the short run resulted in excessive inventory.)
3. The purchasing manager accepted a bid from the lowest-priced supplier without fully checking the supplier's quality-monitoring procedures.

If the purchasing manager's performance is evaluated solely on price variances, then the evaluation will be positive. Reason 1 would support this conclusion: The purchasing manager bargained effectively. Reasons 2 and 3, buying in bulk or buying without checking the supplier's quality-monitoring procedures, will lead to short-run gains. But should these lead to a positive evaluation for the purchasing manager? Not necessarily. These short-run gains could be offset by higher inventory storage costs or higher inspection costs and defect rates. Starbucks may ultimately lose more money because of reasons 2 and 3 than it gains from the favorable price variance.

Bottom line: Managers should not automatically interpret a favorable variance as "good news" or assume it means their subordinates performed well.

Firms benefit from variance analysis because it highlights individual aspects of performance. However, if any single performance measure (for example, achieving a certain labor efficiency variance or a certain consumer rating) is overemphasized, managers will tend to make decisions that will cause the particular performance measure to look good. These actions may conflict with the company's overall goals, inhibiting the goals from being achieved. This faulty perspective on performance usually arises when top management designs a performance evaluation and reward system that does not emphasize total company objectives.

Organization Learning

The goal of variance analysis is for managers to understand why variances arise, to learn, and to improve their firm's future performance. For instance, to reduce the unfavorable direct materials efficiency variance, Webb's managers may attempt to improve the design of its jackets, the commitment of its workers to do the job right the first time, and the quality of the materials. Sometimes an unfavorable direct materials efficiency variance may signal a need to change the strategy related to a product, perhaps because it cannot be made at a low enough cost. Variance analysis should not be used to "play the blame game" (find someone to blame for every unfavorable variance) but to help managers learn about what happened and how to perform better in the future.

Companies need to strike a delicate balance between using variances to evaluate the performance of managers and employees and improve learning within the organization. If the performance evaluation aspect is overemphasized, managers will focus on setting and meeting targets that are easy to attain rather than targets that are challenging, require creativity and resourcefulness, and result in continuous improvement. For example, Webb's manufacturing manager will prefer an easy standard that allows workers ample time to manufacture a jacket. But that will provide the manufacturing department little incentive to improve processes and identify methods to reduce production times and costs. Alternatively, the manufacturing manager might urge workers to produce jackets within the time allowed, even if this leads to poorer quality jackets being produced, which would later hurt revenues. If variance analysis is seen as a way to promote learning within the organization, negative effects such as these can be minimized.

Continuous Improvement

Managers can also use variance analysis to create a virtuous cycle of continuous improvement. How? By repeatedly identifying the causes of variances, taking corrective actions, and evaluating the results. Improvement opportunities are often easier to identify when the company first produces a product. Once managers identify easy improvements, much more ingenuity may be required to identify successive ones. Some companies use kaizen budgeting to specifically target reductions in budgeted costs over successive periods. The advantage of kaizen budgeting is that it makes continuous improvement goals explicit.

Financial and Nonfinancial Performance Measures

Almost all companies use a combination of financial and nonfinancial performance measures for planning and control rather than relying exclusively on either type of measure. To control a production process, supervisors cannot wait for an accounting report with variances reported in dollars. Instead, timely nonfinancial performance measures are frequently used for control purposes. For example, Nissan and many other manufacturers display real-time defect rates and production levels on large LED screens throughout their plants for workers and managers to see.

In Webb's cutting room, cloth is laid out and cut into pieces, which are then matched and assembled. Managers exercise control in the cutting room by observing workers and by focusing on *nonfinancial measures*, such as number of square yards of cloth used to produce 1,000 jackets or the percentage of jackets started and completed without requiring any rework. Webb's production workers find these nonfinancial measures easy to understand. Webb's managers also use *financial measures* to evaluate the overall cost efficiency with which operations are being run and to help guide decisions about, say, changing the mix of inputs used in manufacturing jackets. Financial measures are critical in a company because they indicate the economic impact of diverse physical activities. This knowledge allows managers to make trade-offs, such as increasing the costs of one physical activity (say, cutting) to reduce the costs of another physical measure (say, defects).

Decision Point

How do managers use variances?

Benchmarking and Variance Analysis

Webb Company based its budgeted amounts on analysis of its own operations. We now turn to the situation in which companies develop standards based on the operations of other companies. **Benchmarking** is the continuous process of comparing your firm's performance levels against the best levels of performance in competing companies or in companies having similar processes. When benchmarks are used as standards, managers and management accountants know that the company will be competitive in the marketplace if it can meet or beat those standards.

Companies develop benchmarks and calculate variances on items that are the most important to their businesses. A common unit of measurement used to compare the efficiency of airlines is cost per available seat mile. Available seat mile (ASM) is a measure of airline size and equals the total seats in a plane multiplied by the distance the plane traveled. Consider the cost per available seat mile for United. Assume United uses data from each of six competing U.S. airlines in its benchmark cost comparisons. Summary data are in Exhibit 5. The benchmark companies are in alphabetical order in column A. Also reported in Exhibit 5 are operating cost per ASM, operating revenue per ASM, operating income per ASM, fuel cost per ASM, labor cost per ASM, and total available seat miles for each airline. The slow recovery of the travel industry from the recession induced by the financial crisis is evident in the fact that only five of the seven airlines have positive levels of operating income.

How well did United manage its costs? The answer depends on which specific benchmark is being used for comparison. United's actual operating cost of 14.19 cents per ASM is above the average operating cost of 12.91 cents per ASM of the six other airlines. Moreover, United's operating cost per ASM is 24.2% higher than JetBlue Airways, the lowest-cost competitor at 11.42 cents per ASM [(14.19 − 11.42) ÷ 11.42 = 0.242]. So why is United's operating cost per ASM so high? Columns E and F suggest that both fuel cost and labor cost are possible reasons. These benchmarking data alert management at United that it needs to become more efficient in its use of both material and labor inputs to become more cost competitive.

It can be difficult for firms to find appropriate benchmarks such as those in Exhibit 5. Many companies purchase benchmark data from consulting firms. Another problem is ensuring the benchmark numbers are comparable. In other words, there needs to be an "apples to apples" comparison. Differences can exist across companies in their strategies, inventory costing methods, depreciation methods, and so on. For example, JetBlue serves fewer cities and flies mostly long-haul routes compared with United, which serves almost all major U.S. cities and several international cities and flies both long-haul and short-haul routes. Southwest Airlines differs from United because it specializes in short-haul direct flights and offers fewer services on board its planes. Because United's strategy is different from the strategies of JetBlue and Southwest, one might expect its cost per ASM to be different, too. United's strategy is more comparable to the strategies of American, Delta, and U.S. Airways. Note that its costs per ASM are relatively more competitive with these airlines. But United

Learning Objective 7

Describe benchmarking and explain its role in cost management

...benchmarking compares actual performance against the best levels of performance

Exhibit 5	Available Seat Mile (ASM) Benchmark Comparison of United Airlines with Six Other Airlines

	Home	Insert	Page Layout	Formulas	Data	Review	View	

	A	B	C	D	E	F	G
1		Operating Cost	Operating Revenue	Operating Income	Fuel Cost	Labor Cost	Total ASMs
2		(Cents per ASM)	(Cents per ASM)	(Cents per ASM)	(Cents per ASM)	(Cents per ASM)	(Millions)
3	Airline	(1)	(2)	(3) = (2) – (1)	(4)	(5)	(6)
4							
5	United Airlines	14.19	13.10	- 1.09	4.90	4.24	216,299
6	Airlines used as benchmarks:						
7	Alaska Airlines	11.90	13.09	1.19	4.10	3.53	28,185
8	American Airlines	14.26	13.47	-0.79	4.90	4.28	152,627
9	Delta Airlines	13.80	14.48	0.68	5.00	3.86	200,880
10	JetBlue Airways	11.42	11.96	0.54	4.40	2.76	40,095
11	Southwest Airlines	12.83	13.29	0.46	4.60	3.90	128,272
12	U.S. Airways	13.25	13.49	0.24	4.60	3.54	74,204
13	Average of airlines						
14	used as benchmarks	12.91	13.30	0.39	4.60	3.65	104,044
15							
16	Source: 2012 data from the MIT Global Airline Industry Program						

Decision Point

What is benchmarking and why is it useful?

competes head to head with JetBlue and Southwest in several cities and markets, so it still needs to benchmark against these carriers as well.

United's management accountants can use benchmarking data to address several questions. How do factors such as plane size and type or the duration of flights affect the cost per ASM? Do airlines differ in their fixed cost/variable cost structures? To what extent can United's performance be improved by rerouting flights, using different types of aircraft on different routes, or changing the frequency or timing of specific flights? What explains revenue differences per ASM across airlines? Is it differences in the service quality passengers perceive or differences in an airline's competitive power at specific airports? Management accountants are more valuable to managers when they use benchmarking data to provide insight into *why* costs or revenues differ across companies or within plants of the same company, as distinguished from simply reporting the magnitude of the differences.

Problem for Self-Study

O'Shea Company manufactures ceramic vases. It uses its standard costing system when developing its flexible-budget amounts. In September 2014, 2,000 finished units were produced. The following information relates to its two direct manufacturing cost categories: direct materials and direct manufacturing labor.

Direct materials used were 4,400 kilograms (kg). The standard direct materials input allowed for one output unit is 2 kilograms at $15 per kilogram. O'Shea purchased 5,000 kilograms of materials at $16.50 per kilogram, a total of $82,500. (This Problem for Self-Study illustrates how to calculate direct materials variances when the quantity of materials *purchased* in a period differs from the quantity of materials *used* in that period.)

Actual direct manufacturing labor-hours were 3,250, at a total cost of $66,300. Standard manufacturing labor time allowed is 1.5 hours per output unit, and the standard direct manufacturing labor cost is $20 per hour.

1. Calculate the direct materials price variance and efficiency variance and the direct manufacturing labor price variance and efficiency variance. Base the direct materials price variance on a flexible budget for *actual quantity purchased*, but base the direct materials efficiency variance on a flexible budget for *actual quantity used*.
2. Prepare journal entries for a standard costing system that isolates variances at the earliest possible time.

Solution

1. Exhibit 6 shows how the columnar presentation of variances introduced in Exhibit 3 can be adjusted for the difference in timing between purchase and use of materials. Note, in particular, the two sets of computations in column 2 for direct materials—the $75,000 for direct materials purchased and the $66,000 for direct materials used. The direct materials price variance is calculated on purchases so that managers responsible for the purchase can immediately identify and isolate reasons for the variance and initiate any desired corrective action. The efficiency variance is the responsibility of the production manager, so this variance is identified only at the time materials are used.

2.

Materials Control (5,000 kg × $15 per kg)	75,000	
Direct Materials Price Variance (5,000 kg × $1.50 per kg)	7,500	
Accounts Payable Control (5,000 kg × $16.50 per kg)		82,500
Work-in-Process Control (2,000 units × 2 kg per unit × $15 per kg)	60,000	
Direct Materials Efficiency Variance (400 kg × $15 per kg)	6,000	
Materials Control (4,400 kg × $15 per kg)		66,000
Work-in-Process Control (2,000 units × 1.5 hours per unit × $20 per hour)	60,000	
Direct Manufacturing Labor Price Variance (3,250 hours × $0.40 per hour)	1,300	
Direct Manufacturing Labor Efficiency Variance (250 hours × $20 per hour)	5,000	
Wages Payable Control (3,250 hours × $20.40 per hour)		66,300

Note: All the variances are debits because they are unfavorable and therefore reduce operating income.

Exhibit 6   Columnar Presentation of Variance Analysis for O'Shea Company: Direct Materials and Direct Manufacturing Labor for September 2014

Level 3 Analysis

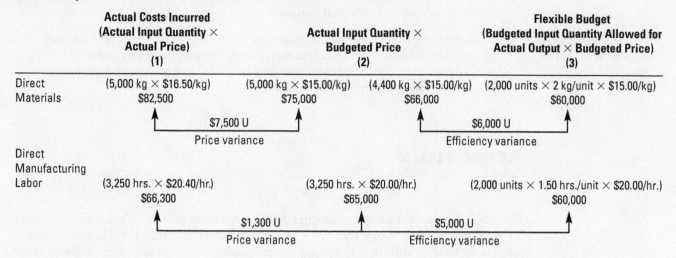

[a]F = favorable effect on operating income; U = unfavorable effect on operating income.

▶ Decision Points

The following question-and-answer format summarizes the chapter's learning objectives. Each decision presents a key question related to a learning objective. The guidelines are the answer to that question.

Decision	Guidelines
1. What are static budgets and static-budget variances?	A static budget is based on the level of output planned at the start of the budget period. The static-budget variance is the difference between the actual result and the corresponding budgeted amount in the static budget.
2. How can managers develop a flexible budget, and why is it useful to do so?	A flexible budget is adjusted (flexed) to recognize the actual output level of the budget period. Managers use a three-step procedure to develop a flexible budget. When all costs are either variable or fixed with respect to output, these three steps require only information about the budgeted selling price, budgeted variable cost per output unit, budgeted fixed costs, and actual quantity of output units. Flexible budgets help managers gain more insight into the causes of variances than is available from static budgets.
3. How are flexible-budget and sales-volume variances calculated?	The static-budget variance can be subdivided into a flexible-budget variance (the difference between the actual result and the corresponding flexible-budget amount) and a sales-volume variance (the difference between the flexible-budget amount and the corresponding static-budget amount).
4. What is a standard cost and what are its purposes?	A standard cost is a carefully determined cost used as a benchmark for judging performance. The purposes of a standard cost are to exclude past inefficiencies and to take into account changes expected to occur in the budget period.
5. Why should a company calculate price and efficiency variables?	The computation of price and efficiency variances helps managers gain insight into two different—but not independent—aspects of performance. The price variance focuses on the difference between the actual input price and the budgeted input price. The efficiency variance focuses on the difference between the actual quantity of input and the budgeted quantity of input allowed for actual output.
6. How do managers use variances?	Managers use variances for control, decision-making, performance evaluation, organization learning, and continuous improvement. When using variances for these purposes, managers should consider several variances together rather than focusing only on an individual variance.
7. What is benchmarking and why is it useful?	Benchmarking is the continuous process of comparing your firm's performance against the best levels of performance in competing companies or companies with similar processes. Benchmarking measures how well a company and its managers are doing in comparison to other organizations.

Appendix

Mix and Yield Variances for Substitutable Inputs

The Webb Company example illustrates how to calculate price and efficiency variances for production inputs when there is a single form of each input. For example, there is a single material (cloth) that is needed for production and a single type of direct labor employed by Webb. But what if managers have leeway in combining and substituting inputs? For example, Del Monte can combine material inputs (such as pineapples, cherries, and grapes) in varying proportions for its cans of fruit cocktail. Within limits, these individual fruits are *substitutable inputs* in making the fruit cocktail.

We illustrate how the efficiency variance discussed in this chapter can be subdivided into variances that highlight the financial impact of input mix and input yield when inputs are substitutable. Consider Delpino Corporation, which makes tomato ketchup. Our example focuses on direct material inputs and substitution among three of these inputs. The same approach can also be used to examine substitutable direct manufacturing labor inputs.

To produce ketchup of a specified consistency, color, and taste, Delpino mixes three types of tomatoes grown in different regions: Latin American tomatoes (Latoms), California tomatoes (Caltoms), and Florida tomatoes (Flotoms). Delpino's production standards require 1.60 tons of tomatoes to produce 1 ton of ketchup; 50% of the tomatoes are budgeted to be Latoms, 30% Caltoms, and 20% Flotoms. The direct material inputs budgeted to produce 1 ton of ketchup are as follows:

0.80 (50% of 1.6) ton of Latoms at $70 per ton	$ 56.00
0.48 (30% of 1.6) ton of Caltoms at $80 per ton	38.40
0.32 (20% of 1.6) ton of Flotoms at $90 per ton	28.80
Total budgeted cost of 1.6 tons of tomatoes	$123.20

Budgeted average cost per ton of tomatoes is $123.20 ÷ 1.60 tons = $77 per ton.

Because Delpino uses fresh tomatoes to make ketchup, no inventories of tomatoes are kept. Purchases are made as needed, so all price variances relate to tomatoes purchased and used. Actual results for June 2014 show that a total of 6,500 tons of tomatoes were used to produce 4,000 tons of ketchup:

3,250	tons of Latoms at actual cost of $70 per ton	$227,500
2,275	tons of Caltoms at actual cost of $82 per ton	186,550
975	tons of Flotoms at actual cost of $96 per ton	93,600
6,500	tons of tomatoes	507,650
	Budgeted cost of 4,000 tons of ketchup at $123.20 per ton	492,800
	Flexible-budget variance for direct materials	$ 14,850 U

Given the standard ratio of 1.60 tons of tomatoes to 1 ton of ketchup, 6,400 tons of tomatoes should be used to produce 4,000 tons of ketchup. At standard mix, quantities of each type of tomato required are as follows:

Latoms:	0.50 × 6,400 = 3,200 tons
Caltoms:	0.30 × 6,400 = 1,920 tons
Flotoms:	0.20 × 6,400 = 1,280 tons

Direct Materials Price and Efficiency Variances

Exhibit 7 presents in columnar format the analysis of the flexible-budget variance for direct materials discussed in the body of the chapter. The materials price and efficiency variances are calculated separately for each input material and then added together. The variance analysis prompts Delpino to investigate the unfavorable price and efficiency variances. Why did it pay more for tomatoes and use greater quantities than it had budgeted? Were actual market prices of tomatoes higher, in general, or could the purchasing department have negotiated lower prices? Did the inefficiencies result from inferior tomatoes or from problems in processing?

Direct Materials Mix and Direct Materials Yield Variances

Managers sometimes have discretion to substitute one material for another. The manager of Delpino's ketchup plant has some leeway in combining Latoms, Caltoms, and Flotoms without affecting the ketchup's quality. We will assume that to maintain quality, mix percentages of each type of tomato can only vary up to 5% from standard mix. For example, the percentage of Caltoms in the mix can vary between 25% and 35% (30% ± 5%).

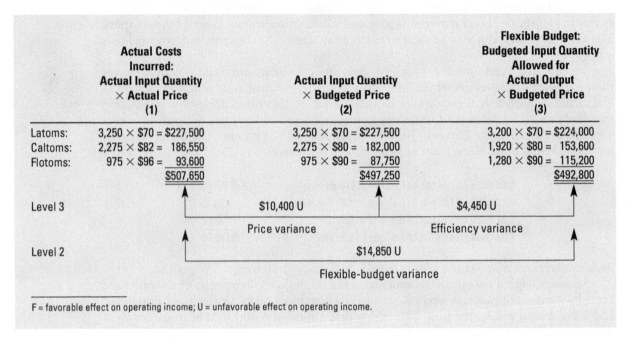

| | **Exhibit 7** | Direct Materials Price and Efficiency Variances for the Delpino Corporation for June 2014 |

	Actual Costs Incurred: Actual Input Quantity × Actual Price (1)	Actual Input Quantity × Budgeted Price (2)	Flexible Budget: Budgeted Input Quantity Allowed for Actual Output × Budgeted Price (3)
Latoms:	3,250 × $70 = $227,500	3,250 × $70 = $227,500	3,200 × $70 = $224,000
Caltoms:	2,275 × $82 = 186,550	2,275 × $80 = 182,000	1,920 × $80 = 153,600
Flotoms:	975 × $96 = 93,600	975 × $90 = 87,750	1,280 × $90 = 115,200
	$507,650	$497,250	$492,800

Level 3   ↑——— $10,400 U ———↑   ↑——— $4,450 U ———↑

               Price variance   Efficiency variance

Level 2   ↑——————————— $14,850 U ———————————↑

                    Flexible-budget variance

F = favorable effect on operating income; U = unfavorable effect on operating income.

When inputs are substitutable, direct materials efficiency improvement relative to budgeted costs can come from two sources: (1) using a cheaper mix to produce a given quantity of output, measured by the direct materials mix variance, and (2) using less input to achieve a given quantity of output, measured by the direct materials yield variance.

Holding actual total quantity of all direct materials inputs used constant, the total **direct materials mix variance** is the difference between (1) budgeted cost for actual mix of actual total quantity of direct materials used and (2) budgeted cost of budgeted mix of actual total quantity of direct materials used. Holding budgeted input mix constant, the **direct materials yield variance** is the difference between (1) budgeted cost of direct materials based on actual total quantity of direct materials used and (2) flexible-budget cost of direct materials based on budgeted total quantity of direct materials allowed for actual output produced. Exhibit 8 presents the direct materials mix and yield variances for the Delpino Corporation.

Direct Materials Mix Variance

The total direct materials mix variance is the sum of the direct materials mix variances for each input:

$$
\begin{pmatrix} \text{Direct} \\ \text{materials} \\ \text{mix variance} \\ \text{for each input} \end{pmatrix} = \begin{pmatrix} \text{Actual total} \\ \text{quantity of all} \\ \text{direct materials} \\ \text{inputs used} \end{pmatrix} \times \begin{pmatrix} \text{Actual} \\ \text{direct materials} \\ \text{input mix} \\ \text{percentage} \end{pmatrix} - \begin{pmatrix} \text{Budgeted} \\ \text{direct materials} \\ \text{input mix} \\ \text{percentage} \end{pmatrix} \times \begin{pmatrix} \text{Budegeted} \\ \text{price of} \\ \text{direct materials} \\ \text{input} \end{pmatrix}
$$

The direct materials mix variances are as follows:

Latoms:	6,500 tons × (0.50 − 0.50) × $70 per ton = 6,500 × 0.00 × $70	= $ 0
Caltoms:	6,500 tons × (0.35 − 0.30) × $80 per ton = 6,500 × 0.05 × $80	= 26,000 U
Flotoms:	6,500 tons × (0.15 − 0.20) × $90 per ton = 6,500 × −0.05 × $90	= 29,250 F
Total direct materials mix variance		$ 3,250 F

| Exhibit 8 | Total Direct Materials Yield and Mix Variances for the Delpino Corporation for June 2014 |

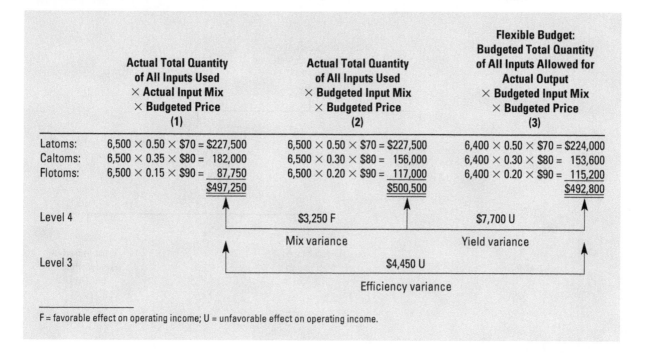

The total direct materials mix variance is favorable because relative to the budgeted mix, Delpino substitutes 5% of the cheaper Caltoms for 5% of the more-expensive Flotoms.

Direct Materials Yield Variance

The direct materials yield variance is the sum of the direct materials yield variances for each input:

$$
\begin{pmatrix} \text{Direct} \\ \text{materials} \\ \text{yield variance} \\ \text{for each input} \end{pmatrix} = \begin{pmatrix} \text{Actual total} & & \text{Budgeted total} \\ \text{quantity of} & & \text{quantity of all} \\ \text{all direct} & - & \text{direct materials} \\ \text{materials} & & \text{input allowed} \\ \text{inputs used} & & \text{for actual output} \end{pmatrix} \times \begin{pmatrix} \text{Budgeted} \\ \text{direct materials} \\ \text{input mix} \\ \text{percentage} \end{pmatrix} \times \begin{pmatrix} \text{Budegeted} \\ \text{price of} \\ \text{direct materials} \\ \text{input} \end{pmatrix}
$$

The direct materials yield variances are as follows:

Latoms:	(6,500 − 6,400) tons × 0.50 × $70 per ton = 100 × 0.50 × $70 = $3,500 U
Caltoms:	(6,500 − 6,400) tons × 0.30 × $80 per ton = 100 × 0.30 × $80 = 2,400 U
Flotoms:	(6,500 − 6,400) tons × 0.20 × $90 per ton = 100 × 0.20 × $90 = 1,800 U
Total direct materials yield variance	$7,700 U

The total direct materials yield variance is unfavorable because Delpino used 6,500 tons of tomatoes rather than the 6,400 tons that it should have used to produce 4,000 tons of ketchup. Holding the budgeted mix and budgeted prices of tomatoes constant, the budgeted cost per ton of tomatoes in the budgeted mix is $77 per ton. The unfavorable yield variance represents the budgeted cost of using 100 more tons of tomatoes, (6,500 − 6,400) tons × $77 per ton = $7,700 U. Delpino would want to investigate reasons for this unfavorable yield variance. For example, did the substitution of the cheaper Caltoms for Flotoms that resulted in the favorable mix variance also cause the unfavorable yield variance?

27

The direct materials variances computed in Exhibits 7 and 8 can be summarized as follows:

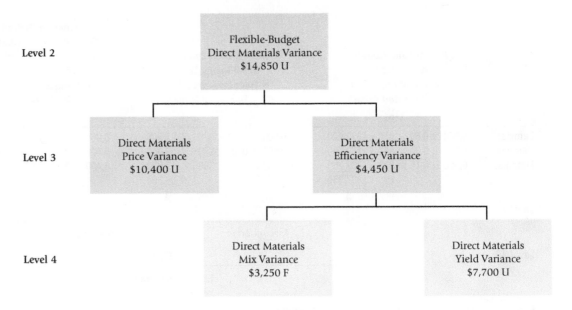

	Flexible-Budget Direct Materials Variance $14,850 U
Level 2	

| Level 3 | Direct Materials Price Variance $10,400 U | Direct Materials Efficiency Variance $4,450 U |

| Level 4 | Direct Materials Mix Variance $3,250 F | Direct Materials Yield Variance $7,700 U |

Terms to Learn

This chapter contains definitions of the following important terms:

benchmarking	flexible budget	standard cost
budgeted performance	flexible-budget variance	standard input
direct materials mix variance	management by exception	standard price
direct materials yield variance	price variance	static budget
effectiveness	rate variance	static-budget variance
efficiency	sales-volume variance	unfavorable variance
efficiency variance	selling-price variance	usage variance
favorable variance	standard	variance

Assignment Material

Questions

1 What is the relationship between management by exception and variance analysis?
2 What are two possible sources of information a company might use to compute the budgeted amount in variance analysis?
3 Distinguish between a favorable variance and an unfavorable variance.
4 What is the key difference between a static budget and a flexible budget?
5 Why might managers find a flexible-budget analysis more informative than a static-budget analysis?
6 Describe the steps in developing a flexible budget.
7 List four reasons for using standard costs.
8 How might a manager gain insight into the causes of a flexible-budget variance for direct materials?
9 List three causes of a favorable direct materials price variance.
10 Describe three reasons for an unfavorable direct manufacturing labor efficiency variance.
11 How does variance analysis help in continuous improvement?
12 Why might an analyst examining variances in the production area look beyond that business function for explanations of those variances?

13 Comment on the following statement made by a plant manager: "Meetings with my plant accountant are frustrating. All he wants to do is pin the blame on someone for the many variances he reports."

14 How can the sales-volume variance be decomposed further to obtain useful information?

15 "Benchmarking against other companies enables a company to identify the lowest-cost producer. This amount should become the performance measure for next year." Do you agree?

Exercises

MyAccountingLab

16 Flexible budget. Brabham Enterprises manufactures tires for the Formula I motor racing circuit. For August 2014, it budgeted to manufacture and sell 3,000 tires at a variable cost of $74 per tire and total fixed costs of $54,000. The budgeted selling price was $110 per tire. Actual results in August 2014 were 2,800 tires manufactured and sold at a selling price of $112 per tire. The actual total variable costs were $229,600, and the actual total fixed costs were $50,000.

Required

1. Prepare a performance report (akin to Exhibit 2) that uses a flexible budget and a static budget.
2. Comment on the results in requirement 1.

17 Flexible budget. Connor Company's budgeted prices for direct materials, direct manufacturing labor, and direct marketing (distribution) labor per attaché case are $40, $8, and $12, respectively. The president is pleased with the following performance report:

	Actual Costs	Static Budget	Variance
Direct materials	$364,000	$400,000	$36,000 F
Direct manufacturing labor	78,000	80,000	2,000 F
Direct marketing (distribution) labor	110,000	120,000	10,000 F

Actual output was 8,800 attaché cases. Assume all three direct-cost items shown are variable costs.

Required

Is the president's pleasure justified? Prepare a revised performance report that uses a flexible budget and a static budget.

18 Flexible-budget preparation and analysis. Bank Management Printers, Inc., produces luxury checkbooks with three checks and stubs per page. Each checkbook is designed for an individual customer and is ordered through the customer's bank. The company's operating budget for September 2014 included these data:

Number of checkbooks	15,000
Selling price per book	$ 20
Variable cost per book	$ 8
Fixed costs for the month	$145,000

The actual results for September 2014 were as follows:

Number of checkbooks produced and sold	12,000
Average selling price per book	$ 21
Variable cost per book	$ 7
Fixed costs for the month	$150,000

The executive vice president of the company observed that the operating income for September was much lower than anticipated, despite a higher-than-budgeted selling price and a lower-than-budgeted variable cost per unit. As the company's management accountant, you have been asked to provide explanations for the disappointing September results.

Bank Management develops its flexible budget on the basis of budgeted per-output-unit revenue and per-output-unit variable costs without detailed analysis of budgeted inputs.

Required

1. Prepare a static-budget-based variance analysis of the September performance.
2. Prepare a flexible-budget-based variance analysis of the September performance.
3. Why might Bank Management find the flexible-budget-based variance analysis more informative than the static-budget-based variance analysis? Explain your answer.

19 Flexible budget, working backward. The Clarkson Company produces engine parts for car manufacturers. A new accountant intern at Clarkson has accidentally deleted the calculations on the company's variance analysis calculations for the year ended December 31, 2014. The following table is what remains of the data.

	A	B	C	D	E	F
1	Performance Report, Year Ended December 31, 2014					
2						
3		Actual Results	Flexible-Budget Variances	Flexible Budget	Sales-Volume Variances	Static Budget
4	Units sold	130,000				120,000
5	Revenues (sales)	$715,000				$420,000
6	Variable costs	515,000				240,000
7	Contribution margin	200,000				180,000
8	Fixed costs	140,000				120,000
9	Operating income	$ 60,000				$ 60,000

Required

1. Calculate all the required variances. (If your work is accurate, you will find that the total static-budget variance is $0.)
2. What are the actual and budgeted selling prices? What are the actual and budgeted variable costs per unit?
3. Review the variances you have calculated and discuss possible causes and potential problems. What is the important lesson learned here?

20 Flexible-budget and sales volume variances. Luster, Inc., produces the basic fillings used in many popular frozen desserts and treats—vanilla and chocolate ice creams, puddings, meringues, and fudge. Luster uses standard costing and carries over no inventory from one month to the next. The ice-cream product group's results for June 2014 were as follows:

	A	B	C
1	Performance Report, June 2014		
2		Actual Results	Static Budget
3	Units (pounds)	350,000	335,000
4	Revenues	$2,012,500	$1,976,500
5	Variable manufacturing costs	1,137,500	1,038,500
6	Contribution margin	$875,000	$938,000

Sam Adler, the business manager for ice-cream products, is pleased that more pounds of ice cream were sold than budgeted and that revenues were up. Unfortunately, variable manufacturing costs went up, too. The bottom line is that contribution margin declined by $63,000, which is less than 3% of the budgeted revenues of $1,976,500. Overall, Adler feels that the business is running fine.

Required

1. Calculate the static-budget variance in units, revenues, variable manufacturing costs, and contribution margin. What percentage is each static-budget variance relative to its static-budget amount?
2. Break down each static-budget variance into a flexible-budget variance and a sales-volume variance.
3. Calculate the selling-price variance.
4. Assume the role of management accountant at Luster. How would you present the results to Sam Adler? Should he be more concerned? If so, why?

21 Price and efficiency variances. Peterson Foods manufactures pumpkin scones. For January 2014, it budgeted to purchase and use 15,000 pounds of pumpkin at $0.89 a pound. Actual purchases and usage for January 2014 were 16,000 pounds at $0.82 a pound. Peterson budgeted for 60,000 pumpkin scones. Actual output was 60,800 pumpkin scones.

1. Compute the flexible-budget variance.
2. Compute the price and efficiency variances.
3. Comment on the results for requirements 1 and 2 and provide a possible explanation for them.

22 **Materials and manufacturing labor variances.** Consider the following data collected for Great Homes, Inc.:

	Direct Materials	Direct Manufacturing Labor
Cost incurred: Actual inputs × actual prices	$200,000	$90,000
Actual inputs × standard prices	214,000	86,000
Standard inputs allowed for actual output × standard prices	225,000	80,000

Compute the price, efficiency, and flexible-budget variances for direct materials and direct manufacturing labor.

23 **Direct materials and direct manufacturing labor variances.** SallyMay, Inc., designs and manufactures T-shirts. It sells its T-shirts to brand-name clothes retailers in lots of one dozen. SallyMay's May 2013 static budget and actual results for direct inputs are as follows:

Static Budget

Number of T-shirt lots (1 lot = 1 dozen)	400

Per Lot of T-shirts:

Direct materials	14 meters at $1.70 per meter = $23.80
Direct manufacturing labor	1.6 hours at $8.10 per hour = $12.96

Actual Results

Number of T-shirt lots sold	450

Total Direct Inputs:

Direct materials	6,840 meters at $1.95 per meter = $13,338
Direct manufacturing labor	675 hours at $8.20 per hour = $5,535

SallyMay has a policy of analyzing all input variances when they add up to more than 10% of the total cost of materials and labor in the flexible budget, and this is true in May 2013. The production manager discusses the sources of the variances: "A new type of material was purchased in May. This led to faster cutting and sewing, but the workers used more material than usual as they learned to work with it. For now, the standards are fine."

1. Calculate the direct materials and direct manufacturing labor price and efficiency variances in May 2013. What is the total flexible-budget variance for both inputs (direct materials and direct manufacturing labor) combined? What percentage is this variance of the total cost of direct materials and direct manufacturing labor in the flexible budget?
2. Sally King, the CEO, is concerned about the input variances. But she likes the quality and feel of the new material and agrees to use it for one more year. In May 2014, SallyMay again produces 450 lots of T-shirts. Relative to May 2013, 2% less direct material is used, direct material price is down 5%, and 2% less direct manufacturing labor is used. Labor price has remained the same as in May 2013. Calculate the direct materials and direct manufacturing labor price and efficiency variances in May 2014. What is the total flexible-budget variance for both inputs (direct materials and direct manufacturing labor) combined? What percentage is this variance of the total cost of direct materials and direct manufacturing labor in the flexible budget?
3. Comment on the May 2014 results. Would you continue the "experiment" of using the new material?

24 **Price and efficiency variances, journal entries.** The Schuyler Corporation manufactures lamps. It has set up the following standards per finished unit for direct materials and direct manufacturing labor:

Direct materials: 10 lb. at $4.50 per lb.	$45.00
Direct manufacturing labor: 0.5 hour at $30 per hour	15.00

The number of finished units budgeted for January 2014 was 10,000; 9,850 units were actually produced.

Actual results in January 2014 were as follows:

> Direct materials: 98,055 lb. used
> Direct manufacturing labor: 4,900 hours $154,350

Assume that there was no beginning inventory of either direct materials or finished units.

During the month, materials purchased amounted to 100,000 lb., at a total cost of $465,000. Input price variances are isolated upon purchase. Input-efficiency variances are isolated at the time of usage.

Required

1. Compute the January 2014 price and efficiency variances of direct materials and direct manufacturing labor.
2. Prepare journal entries to record the variances in requirement 1.
3. Comment on the January 2014 price and efficiency variances of Schuyler Corporation.
4. Why might Schuyler calculate direct materials price variances and direct materials efficiency variances with reference to different points in time?

25 Materials and manufacturing labor variances, standard costs. Dunn, Inc., is a privately held furniture manufacturer. For August 2014, Dunn had the following standards for one of its products, a wicker chair:

	Standards per Chair
Direct materials	2 square yards of input at $5 per square yard
Direct manufacturing labor	0.5 hour of input at $10 per hour

The following data were compiled regarding *actual performance*: actual output units (chairs) produced, 2,000; square yards of input purchased and used, 3,700; price per square yard, $5.10; direct manufacturing labor costs, $8,820; actual hours of input, 900; labor price per hour, $9.80.

1. Show computations of price and efficiency variances for direct materials and direct manufacturing labor. Give a plausible explanation of why each variance occurred.
2. Suppose 6,000 square yards of materials were purchased (at $5.10 per square yard), even though only 3,700 square yards were used. Suppose further that variances are identified at their most timely control point; accordingly, direct materials price variances are isolated and traced at the time of purchase to the purchasing department rather than to the production department. Compute the price and efficiency variances under this approach.

26 Journal entries and T-accounts (continuation of 25). Prepare journal entries and post them to T-accounts for all transactions in Exercise 25, including requirement 2. Summarize how these journal entries differ from normal-costing entries.

27 Price and efficiency variances, benchmarking. Topiary Co. produces molded plastic garden pots and other plastic containers. In June 2014, Topiary produces 1,000 lots (each lot is 12 dozen pots) of its most popular line of pots, the 14-inch "Grecian urns," at each of its two plants, which are located in Mineola and Bayside. The production manager, Janice Roberts, asks her assistant, Alastair Ramy, to find out the precise per-unit budgeted variable costs at the two plants and the variable costs of a competitor, Land Art, who offers similar-quality pots at cheaper prices. Ramy pulls together the following information for each lot:

Per lot	Mineola Plant	Bayside Plant	Land Art
Direct materials	13.50 lbs. @ $9.20 per lb.	14.00 lbs. @ $9.00 per lb.	13.00 lbs. @ $8.80 per lb.
Direct labor	3 hrs. @ $10.15 per hr.	2.7 hrs. @ $10.20 per hr.	2.5 hrs. @ $10.00 per hr.
Variable overhead	$12 per lot	$11 per lot	$11 per lot

Required

1. What is the budgeted variable cost per lot at the Mineola Plant, the Bayside Plant, and at Land Art?
2. Using the Land Art data as the standard, calculate the direct materials and direct labor price and efficiency variances for the Mineola and Bayside plants.
3. What advantage does Topiary get by using Land Art's benchmark data as standards in calculating its variances? Identify two issues that Roberts should keep in mind in using the Land Art data as the standards.

28 Static and flexible budgets, service sector. Student Finance (StuFi) is a startup that aims to use the power of social communities to transform the student loan market. It connects participants through a dedicated lending pool, enabling current students to borrow from a school's alumni community. StuFi's revenue model is to take an upfront fee of 40 basis points (0.40%) *each* from the alumni investor and the student borrower for every loan originated on its platform.

StuFi hopes to go public in the near future and is keen to ensure that its financial results are in line with that ambition. StuFi's budgeted and actual results for the third quarter of 2014 are presented below.

	A	B	C	D	E
		Home Insert Page Layout Formulas Data Review View			
1		Static Budget		Actual Results	
2	New loans originated	8,200		10,250	
3	Average amount of loan	$145,000		$162,000	
4	Variable costs per loan:				
5	Professional labor	$360	(8 hrs at $45 per hour)	$475	(9.5 hrs at $50 per hour)
6	Credit verification	$100		$100	
7	Federal documentation fees	$120		$125	
8	Courier services	$50		$54	
9	Administrative costs (fixed)	$800,000		$945,000	
10	Technology costs (fixed)	$1,300,000		$1,415,000	

Required

1. Prepare StuFi's static budget of operating income for the third quarter of 2014.
2. Prepare an analysis of variances for the third quarter of 2014 along the lines of Exhibit 2; identify the sales volume and flexible budget variances for operating income.
3. Compute the professional labor price and efficiency variances for the third quarter of 2014.
4. What factors would you consider in evaluating the effectiveness of professional labor in the third quarter of 2014.

Problems

MyAccountingLab

29 Flexible budget, direct materials, and direct manufacturing labor variances. Milan Statuary manufactures bust statues of famous historical figures. All statues are the same size. Each unit requires the same amount of resources. The following information is from the static budget for 2014:

Expected production and sales	6,100 units
Expected selling price per unit	$ 700
Total fixed costs	$1,350,000

Standard quantities, standard prices, and standard unit costs follow for direct materials and direct manufacturing labor:

	Standard Quantity	Standard Price	Standard Unit Cost
Direct materials	16 pounds	$14 per pound	$224
Direct manufacturing labor	3.8 hours	$ 30 per hour	$114

During 2014, actual number of units produced and sold was 5,100, at an average selling price of $730. Actual cost of direct materials used was $1,149,400, based on 70,000 pounds purchased at $16.42 per pound. Direct manufacturing labor-hours actually used were 17,000, at the rate of $33.70 per hour. As a result, actual direct manufacturing labor costs were $572,900. Actual fixed costs were $1,200,000. There were no beginning or ending inventories.

1. Calculate the sales-volume variance and flexible-budget variance for operating income.
2. Compute price and efficiency variances for direct materials and direct manufacturing labor.

Required

30 Variance analysis, nonmanufacturing setting. Marcus McQueen has run In-A-Flash Car Detailing for the past 10 years. His static budget and actual results for June 2014 are provided next. Marcus has one employee who has been with him for all 10 years that he has been in business. In addition, at any given time he also employs two other less experienced workers. It usually takes each employee 2 hours to detail a vehicle, regardless of his or her experience. Marcus pays his experienced employee $30 per vehicle and the other two employees $15 per vehicle. There were no wage increases in June.

In-A-Flash Car Detailing
Actual and Budgeted Income Statements
For the Month Ended June 30, 2014

	Budget	Actual
Cars detailed	280	320
Revenue	$53,200	$72,000
Variable costs		
Costs of supplies	1,260	1,360
Labor	6,720	8,400
Total variable costs	7,980	9,760
Contribution margin	45,220	62,240
Fixed costs	9,800	9,800
Operating income	$35,420	$52,440

Required

1. How many cars, on average, did Marcus budget for each employee? How many cars did each employee actually detail?
2. Prepare a flexible budget for June 2014.
3. Compute the sales price variance and the labor efficiency variance for each labor type.
4. What information, in addition to that provided in the income statements, would you want Marcus to gather, if you wanted to improve operational efficiency?

31 Comprehensive variance analysis, responsibility issues. (CMA, adapted) Ultra, Inc., manufactures a full line of well-known sunglasses frames and lenses. Ultra uses a standard costing system to set attainable standards for direct materials, labor, and overhead costs. Ultra reviews and revises standards annually as necessary. Department managers, whose evaluations and bonuses are affected by their department's performance, are held responsible to explain variances in their department performance reports.

Recently, the manufacturing variances in the Delta prestige line of sunglasses have caused some concern. For no apparent reason, unfavorable materials and labor variances have occurred. At the monthly staff meeting, John Puckett, manager of the Image line, will be expected to explain his variances and suggest ways of improving performance. Barton will be asked to explain the following performance report for 2014:

	Actual Results	Static-Budget Amounts
Units sold	7,300	7,800
Revenues	$576,700	$608,400
Variable manufacturing costs	346,604	273,000
Fixed manufacturing costs	111,000	114,000
Gross margin	119,096	221,400

Barton collected the following information:
    Three items comprised the standard variable manufacturing costs in 2014:

- Direct materials: Frames. Static budget cost of $35,880. The standard input for 2014 is 2.00 ounces per unit.

- Direct materials: Lenses. Static budget costs of $96,720. The standard input for 2014 is 4.00 ounces per unit.

- Direct manufacturing labor: Static budget costs of $140,400. The standard input for 2014 is 1 hour per unit.

Assume there are no variable manufacturing overhead costs.
    The actual variable manufacturing costs in 2014 were as follows:

- Direct materials: Frames. Actual costs of $70,080. Actual ounces used were 4.00 ounces per unit.
- Direct materials: Lenses. Actual costs of $131,400. Actual ounces used were 6.00 ounces per unit.
- Direct manufacturing labor: Actual costs of $145,124. The actual labor rate was $14.20 per hour.

Required

1. Prepare a report that includes the following:
   a. Selling-price variance
   b. Sales-volume variance and flexible-budget variance for operating income in the format of the analysis in Exhibit 2

   c. Price and efficiency variances for the following:
- Direct materials: frames
- Direct materials: lenses
- Direct manufacturing labor

2. Give three possible explanations for each of the three price and efficiency variances at Ultra in requirement 1c.

32 Possible causes for price and efficiency variances. You are a student preparing for a job interview with a *Fortune* 100 consumer products manufacturer. You are applying for a job in the finance department. This company is known for its rigorous case-based interview process. One of the students who successfully obtained a job with them upon graduation last year advised you to "know your variances cold!" When you inquired further, she told you that she had been asked to pretend that she was investigating wage and materials variances. Per her advice, you have been studying the causes and consequences of variances. You are excited when you walk in and find that the first case deals with variance analysis. You are given the following data for May for a detergent bottling plant located in Mexico:

Actual

Bottles filled	360,000
Direct materials used in production	6,300,000 oz.
Actual direct material cost	2,205,000 pesos
Actual direct manufacturing labor-hours	24,500 hours
Actual direct labor cost	739,165 pesos

Standards

Purchase price of direct materials	0.34 pesos/oz
Bottle size	15 oz.
Wage rate	29.30 pesos/hour
Bottles per minute	0.50

Please respond to the following questions as if you were in an interview situation:

Required

1. Calculate the materials efficiency and price variance and the wage and labor efficiency variances for the month of May.
2. You are given the following context: "Union organizers are targeting our detergent bottling plant in Puebla, Mexico, for a union." Can you provide a better explanation for the variances that you have calculated on the basis of this information?

33 Material cost variances, use of variances for performance evaluation. Katharine Johnson is the owner of Best Bikes, a company that produces high-quality cross-country bicycles. Best Bikes participates in a supply chain that consists of suppliers, manufacturers, distributors, and elite bicycle shops. For several years Best Bikes has purchased titanium from suppliers in the supply chain. Best Bikes uses titanium for the bicycle frames because it is stronger and lighter than other metals and therefore increases the quality of the bicycle. Earlier this year, Best Bikes hired Michael Bentfield, a recent graduate from State University, as purchasing manager. Michael believed that he could reduce costs if he purchased titanium from an online marketplace at a lower price.

Best Bikes established the following standards based upon the company's experience with previous suppliers. The standards are as follows:

Cost of titanium	$18 per pound
Titanium used per bicycle	8 lbs.

Actual results for the first month using the online supplier of titanium are as follows:

Bicycles produced	400
Titanium purchased	5,200 lb. for $88,400
Titanium used in production	4,700 lb.

Required

1. Compute the direct materials price and efficiency variances.
2. What factors can explain the variances identified in requirement 1? Could any other variances be affected?
3. Was switching suppliers a good idea for Best Bikes? Explain why or why not.

4. Should Michael Bentfield's performance evaluation be based solely on price variances? Should the production manager's evaluation be based solely on efficiency variances? Why is it important for Katharine Johnson to understand the causes of a variance before she evaluates performance?
5. Other than performance evaluation, what reasons are there for calculating variances?
6. What future problems could result from Best Bikes' decision to buy a lower quality of titanium from the online marketplace?

34 Direct manufacturing labor and direct materials variances, missing data. (CMA, heavily adapted) Young Bay Surfboards manufactures fiberglass surfboards. The standard cost of direct materials and direct manufacturing labor is $223 per board. This includes 40 pounds of direct materials, at the budgeted price of $2 per pound, and 10 hours of direct manufacturing labor, at the budgeted rate of $14.30 per hour. Following are additional data for the month of July:

Units completed	5,500 units
Direct material purchases	160,000 pounds
Cost of direct material purchases	$432,000
Actual direct manufacturing labor-hours	41,000 hours
Actual direct labor cost	$594,500
Direct materials efficiency variance	$ 1,700 F

There were no beginning inventories.

Required

1. Compute direct manufacturing labor variances for July.
2. Compute the actual pounds of direct materials used in production in July.
3. Calculate the actual price per pound of direct materials purchased.
4. Calculate the direct materials price variance.

35 Direct materials efficiency, mix, and yield variances. Nature's Best Nuts produces specialty nut products for the gourmet and natural foods market. Its most popular product is Zesty Zingers, a mixture of roasted nuts that are seasoned with a secret spice mixture and sold in 1-pound tins. The direct materials used in Zesty Zingers are almonds, cashews, pistachios, and seasoning. For each batch of 100 tins, the budgeted quantities and budgeted prices of direct materials are as follows:

	Quantity for One Batch	Price of Input
Almonds	180 cups	$1 per cup
Cashews	300 cups	$2 per cup
Pistachios	90 cups	$3 per cup
Seasoning	30 cups	$6 per cup

Changing the standard mix of direct material quantities slightly does not significantly affect the overall end product, particularly for the nuts. In addition, not all nuts added to production end up in the finished product, as some are rejected during inspection.

In the current period, Nature's Best made 2,500 tins of Zesty Zingers in 25 batches with the following actual quantity, cost, and mix of inputs:

	Actual Quantity	Actual Cost	Actual Mix
Almonds	5,280 cups	$ 5,280	33%
Cashews	7,520 cups	15,040	47%
Pistachios	2,720 cups	8,160	17%
Seasoning	480 cups	2,880	3%
Total actual	16,000 cups	$31,360	100%

Required

1. What is the budgeted cost of direct materials for the 2,500 tins?
2. Calculate the total direct materials efficiency variance.
3. Why is the total direct materials price variance zero?
4. Calculate the total direct materials mix and yield variances. What are these variances telling you about the 2,500 tins produced this period? Are the variances large enough to investigate?

36 Direct materials and manufacturing labor variances, solving unknowns. (CPA, adapted) On May 1, 2014, Lowell Company began the manufacture of a new paging machine known as Dandy. The company installed a standard costing system to account for manufacturing costs. The standard costs for a unit of Dandy follow:

Direct materials (2 lb. at $3 per lb.)	$6.00
Direct manufacturing labor (1/2 hour at $16 per hour)	8.00
Manufacturing overhead (80% of direct manufacturing labor costs)	6.40
	$20.40

The following data were obtained from Lowell's records for the month of May:

	Debit	Credit
Revenues		$150,000
Accounts payable control (for May's purchases of direct materials)		36,300
Direct materials price variance	$4,500	
Direct materials efficiency variance	2,900	
Direct manufacturing labor price variance	1,700	
Direct manufacturing labor efficiency variance		2,000

Actual production in May was 4,700 units of Dandy, and actual sales in May were 3,000 units.

The amount shown for direct materials price variance applies to materials purchased during May. There was no beginning inventory of materials on May 1, 2014.

Compute each of the following items for Lowell for the month of May. Show your computations.

Required

1. Standard direct manufacturing labor-hours allowed for actual output produced
2. Actual direct manufacturing labor-hours worked
3. Actual direct manufacturing labor wage rate
4. Standard quantity of direct materials allowed (in pounds)
5. Actual quantity of direct materials used (in pounds)
6. Actual quantity of direct materials purchased (in pounds)
7. Actual direct materials price per pound

37 Direct materials and manufacturing labor variances, journal entries. Zanella's Smart Shawls, Inc., is a small business that Zanella developed while in college. She began hand-knitting shawls for her dorm friends to wear while studying. As demand grew, she hired some workers and began to manage the operation. Zanella's shawls require wool and labor. She experiments with the type of wool that she uses, and she has great variety in the shawls she produces. Zanella has bimodal turnover in her labor. She has some employees who have been with her for a very long time and others who are new and inexperienced.

Zanella uses standard costing for her shawls. She expects that a typical shawl should take 3 hours to produce, and the standard wage rate is $9.00 per hour. An average shawl uses 13 skeins of wool. Zanella shops around for good deals and expects to pay $3.40 per skein.

Zanella uses a just-in-time inventory system, as she has clients tell her what type and color of wool they would like her to use.

For the month of April, Zanella's workers produced 200 shawls using 580 hours and 3,500 skeins of wool. Zanella bought wool for $9,000 (and used the entire quantity) and incurred labor costs of $5,520.

Required

1. Calculate the price and efficiency variances for the wool and the price and efficiency variances for direct manufacturing labor.
2. Record the journal entries for the variances incurred.
3. Discuss logical explanations for the combination of variances that Zanella experienced.

38 Use of materials and manufacturing labor variances for benchmarking. You are a new junior accountant at In Focus Corporation, maker of lenses for eyeglasses. Your company sells generic-quality lenses for a moderate price. Your boss, the controller, has given you the latest month's report for the lens trade association. This report includes information related to operations for your firm and three of your competitors within the trade association. The report also includes information related to the industry benchmark for each line item in the report. You do not know which firm is which, except that you know you are Firm A.

Unit Variable Costs
Member Firms
For the Month Ended September 30, 2014

	Firm A	Firm B	Firm C	Firm D	Industry Benchmark	
Materials input	2.15	2.00	2.20	2.60	2.15	oz. of glass
Materials price	$ 5.00	$ 5.25	$ 5.10	$ 4.50	$ 5.10	per oz.
Labor-hours used	0.75	1.00	0.65	0.70	0.70	hours
Wage rate	$14.50	$14.00	$14.25	$15.25	$12.50	per DLH
Variable overhead rate	$ 9.25	$14.00	$ 7.75	$11.75	$12.25	per DLH

Required

1. Calculate the total variable cost per unit for each firm in the trade association. Compute the percent of total for the material, labor, and variable overhead components.
2. Using the trade association's industry benchmark, calculate direct materials and direct manufacturing labor price and efficiency variances for the four firms. Calculate the percent over standard for each firm and each variance.
3. Write a brief memo to your boss outlining the advantages and disadvantages of belonging to this trade association for benchmarking purposes. Include a few ideas to improve productivity that you want your boss to take to the department heads' meeting.

39 Direct labor variances: price, efficiency, mix, and yield. Trevor Joseph employs two workers in his guitar-making business. The first worker, George, has been making guitars for 20 years and is paid $30 per hour. The second worker, Earl, is less experienced and is paid $20 per hour. One guitar requires, on average, 10 hours of labor. The budgeted direct labor quantities and prices for one guitar are as follows:

	Quantity	Price per Hour of Labor	Cost for One Guitar
George	6 hours	$30 per hour	$180
Earl	4 hours	$20 per hour	80

That is, each guitar is budgeted to require 10 hours of direct labor, composed of 60% of George's labor and 40% of Earl's, although sometimes Earl works more hours on a particular guitar and George less, or vice versa, with no obvious change in the quality or function of the guitar.

During the month of August, Joseph manufactures 25 guitars. Actual direct labor costs are as follows:

George (145 hours)	$4,350
Earl (108 hours)	2,160
Total actual direct labor cost	$6,510

Required

1. What is the budgeted cost of direct labor for 25 guitars?
2. Calculate the total direct labor price and efficiency variances.
3. For the 25 guitars, what is the total actual amount of direct labor used? What is the actual direct labor input mix percentage? What is the budgeted amount of George's and Earl's labor that should have been used for the 25 guitars?
4. Calculate the total direct labor mix and yield variances. How do these numbers relate to the total direct labor efficiency variance? What do these variances tell you?

40 Direct-cost and selling price variances. MicroDisk is the market leader in the Secure Digital (SD) card industry and sells memory cards for use in portable devices such as mobile phones, tablets, and digital cameras. Its most popular card is the Mini SD, which it sells to OEMs as well as through outlets such as Target and Walmart for an average selling price of $8. MicroDisk has a standard monthly production level of

420,000 Mini SDs in its Taiwan facility. The standard input quantities and prices for direct-cost inputs are as follows:

	Quantity per		Standard	
Cost Item	Mini SD card		Unit Costs	
Direct materials				
Specialty polymer	17	mm	$0.05	/mm
Connector pins	10	units	0.10	/unit
Wi-Fi transreceiver	1	unit	0.50	/unit
Direct manufacturing labor				
Setup	1	min.	24.00	/hr.
Fabrication	2	min.	30.00	/hr.

Phoebe King, the CEO, is disappointed with the results for June 2014, especially in comparison to her expectations based on the standard cost data.

Performance Report, June 2014			
	Actual	Budget	Variance
Output units	462,000	420,000	42,000 F
Revenues	$3,626,700	$3,360,000	$266,700 F
Direct materials	1,200,000	987,000	213,000 U
Direct manufacturing labor	628,400	588,000	40,400 U

King observes that despite the significant increase in the output of Mini SDs in June, the product's contribution to the company's profitability has been lower than expected. She gathers the following information to help analyze the situation:

Input Usage Report, June 2014			
Cost Item	Quantity		Actual Cost
Direct materials			
Specialty polymer	8,300,000	mm	$415,000
Connector pins	5,000,000	units	550,000
Wi-Fi transreceiver	470,000	units	235,000
Direct manufacturing labor			
Setup	455,000	min.	182,000
Fabrication	864,000	min.	446,400

Calculate the following variances. Comment on the variances and provide potential reasons why they might have arisen, with particular attention to the variances that may be related to one another:

1. Selling-price variance
2. Direct materials price variance, for each category of materials
3. Direct materials efficiency variance, for each category of materials

Required

4. Direct manufacturing labor price variance, for setup and fabrication
5. Direct manufacturing labor efficiency variance, for setup and fabrication.

41 Comprehensive variance analysis review. Vivus Bioscience produces a generic statin pill that is used to treat patients with high cholesterol. The pills are sold in blister packs of 10. Vivus employs a team of sales representatives who are paid varying amounts of commission.

Given the narrow margins in the generic drugs industry, Vivus relies on tight standards and cost controls to manage its operations. Vivus has the following budgeted standards for the month of April 2014:

Average selling price per pack	$ 7.20
Total direct materials cost per pack	$ 1.80
Direct manufacturing labor cost per hour	$ 14.40
Average labor productivity rate (packs per hour)	280
Sales commission cost per unit	$ 0.36
Fixed administrative and manufacturing overhead	$960,000

Vivus budgeted sales of 1,400,000 packs for April. At the end of the month, the controller revealed that actual results for April had deviated from the budget in several ways:

- Unit sales and production were 90% of plan.
- Actual average selling price increased to $7.30.
- Productivity dropped to 250 packs per hour.
- Actual direct manufacturing labor cost was $14.60 per hour.
- Actual total direct material cost per unit increased to $1.90.
- Actual sales commissions were $0.30 per unit.
- Fixed overhead costs were $12,000 above budget.

Calculate the following amounts for Vivus for April 2014:

Required

1. Static-budget and actual operating income
2. Static-budget variance for operating income
3. Flexible-budget operating income
4. Flexible-budget variance for operating income
5. Sales-volume variance for operating income
6. Price and efficiency variances for direct manufacturing labor
7. Flexible-budget variance for direct manufacturing labor

42 Price and efficiency variances, benchmarking and ethics. Sunto Scientific manufactures GPS devices for a chain of retail stores. Its most popular model, the Magellan XS, is assembled in a dedicated facility in Savannah, Georgia. Sunto is keenly aware of the competitive threat from smartphones that use Google Maps and has put in a standard cost system to manage production of the Magellan XS. It has also implemented a just-in-time system so the Savannah facility operates with no inventory of any kind.

Producing the Magellan XS involves combining a navigation system (imported from Sunto's plant in Dresden at a fixed price), an LCD screen made of polarized glass, and a casing developed from specialty plastic. The budgeted and actual amounts for Magellan XS for July 2014 were as follows:

	Budgeted Amounts	Actual Amounts
Magellan XS units produced	4,000	4,400
Navigation system cost	$81,600	$89,000
Navigation systems	4,080	4,450
Polarized glass cost	$40,000	$40,300
Sheets of polarized glass used	800	816
Plastic casing cost	$12,000	$12,500
Ounces of specialty plastic used	4,000	4,250
Direct manufacturing labor costs	$36,000	$37,200
Direct manufacturing labor-hours	2,000	2,040

The controller of the Savannah plant, Jim Williams, is disappointed with the standard costing system in place. The standards were developed on the basis of a study done by an outside consultant at the start of the year. Williams points out that he has rarely seen a significant unfavorable variance under this system. He observes that even at the present level of output, workers seem to have a substantial amount of idle time. Moreover, he is concerned that the production supervisor, John Kelso, is aware of the issue but is unwilling to tighten the standards because the current lenient benchmarks make his performance look good.

Required

1. Compute the price and efficiency variances for the three categories of direct materials and for direct manufacturing labor in July 2014.
2. Describe the types of actions the employees at the Savannah plant may have taken to reduce the accuracy of the standards set by the outside consultant. Why would employees take those actions? Is this behavior ethical?
3. If Williams does nothing about the standard costs, will his behavior violate any of the standards of ethical conduct for practitioners described in the IMA Statement of Ethical Professional Practice?
4. What actions should Williams take?
5. Williams can obtain benchmarking information about the estimated costs of Sunto's competitors such as Garmin and TomTom from the Competitive Intelligence Institute (CII). Discuss the pros and cons of using the CII information to compute the variances in requirement 1.

Glossary

Benchmarking. The continuous process of comparing the levels of performance in producing products and services and executing activities against the best levels of performance in competing companies or in companies having similar processes.

Budgeted performance. Expected performance or a point of reference to compare actual results.

Direct materials mix variance. The difference between (1) budgeted cost for actual mix of the actual total quantity of direct materials used and (2) budgeted cost of budgeted mix of the actual total quantity of direct materials used.

Direct materials yield variance. The difference between (1) budgeted cost of direct materials based on the actual total quantity of direct materials used and (2) flexible-budget cost of direct materials based on the budgeted total quantity of direct materials allowed for the actual output produced.

Effectiveness. The degree to which a predetermined objective or target is met.

Efficiency. The relative amount of inputs used to achieve a given output level.

Efficiency variance. The difference between actual input quantity used and budgeted input quantity allowed for actual output, multiplied by budgeted price. Also called *usage variance*.

Favorable variance. Variance that has the effect of increasing operating income relative to the budgeted amount. Denoted F.

Flexible budget. Budget developed using budgeted revenues and budgeted costs based on the actual output in the budget period.

Flexible-budget variance. The difference between an actual result and the corresponding flexible-budget amount based on the actual output level in the budget period.

Management by exception. Practice of focusing management attention on areas not operating as expected and giving less attention to areas operating as expected.

Price variance. The difference between actual price and budgeted price multiplied by actual quantity of input. Also called *rate variance*.

Rate variance. See *price variance*.

Sales-volume variance. The difference between a flexible-budget amount and the corresponding static-budget amount.

Selling-price variance. The difference between the actual selling price and the budgeted selling price multiplied by the actual units sold.

Standard. A carefully determined price, cost, or quantity that is used as a benchmark for judging performance. It is usually expressed on a per unit basis.

Standard cost. A carefully determined cost of a unit of output.

Standard input.   A carefully determined quantity of input required for one unit of output.

Standard price.   A carefully determined price that a company expects to pay for a unit of input.

Static budget.   Budget based on the level of output planned at the start of the budget period.

Static-budget variance.   Difference between an actual result and the corresponding budgeted amount in the static budget.

Unfavorable variance.   Variance that has the effect of decreasing operating income relative to the budgeted amount. Denoted U.

Usage variance.   See *efficiency variance*.

Variance.   The difference between actual result and expected performance.

Photo Credits

Credits are listed in order of appearance.

Photo 1: Alexandru Magurean/Getty Images
Photo 2: Rachel Youdelman/Pearson Education, Inc
Photo 3: Soultana Koleska/Alamy

Flexible Budgets, Overhead Cost Variances, and Management Control

From Chapter 8 of *Cost Accounting: A Managerial Emphasis,* Fifteenth Edition. Charles T. Horngren, Srikant M. Datar, Madhav V. Rajan. Copyright © 2015 by Pearson Education, Inc. All rights reserved.

Flexible Budgets, Overhead Cost Variances, and Management Control

Learning Objectives

1. Explain the similarities and differences in planning variable overhead costs and fixed overhead costs

2. Develop budgeted variable overhead cost rates and budgeted fixed overhead cost rates

3. Compute the variable overhead flexible-budget variance, the variable overhead efficiency variance, and the variable overhead spending variance

4. Compute the fixed overhead flexible-budget variance, the fixed overhead spending variance, and the fixed overhead production-volume variance

5. Show how the 4-variance analysis approach reconciles the actual overhead incurred with the overhead amounts allocated during the period

6. Explain the relationship between the sales-volume variance and the production-volume variance

7. Calculate variances in activity-based costing

8. Examine the use of overhead variances in nonmanufacturing settings

What do this week's weather forecast and an organization's performance have in common?

Much of the time, reality doesn't match what people expect. Rain that results in a little league game being canceled may suddenly give way to sunshine. Business owners expecting to "whistle their way to the bank" may change their tune after tallying their monthly bills and discovering that skyrocketing operational costs have significantly reduced their profits. Differences, or variances, are all around us.

Analyzing variances is a valuable activity for firms because the process highlights the areas where performance most lags expectations. By using this information to make corrective adjustments, companies can achieve significant savings. Furthermore, the process of setting up standards requires firms to have a thorough understanding of their fixed and variable overhead costs, which brings its own benefits, as the following article shows.

Planning Fixed and Variable Overhead Costs at Tesla Motors[1]

Managers frequently review the differences, or variances, in overhead costs and make changes in the operations of a business. Sometimes staffing levels are increased or decreased, while at other times managers identify ways to use fewer resources like, say, office supplies and travel for business meetings that don't add value to the products and services that customers buy.

Tesla Motors is a Silicon Valley–based electric car manufacturer. To develop its renowned Model S all-electric plug-in sedan—*Consumer Reports* recently called it the best car it ever tested—Tesla Motors required an in-depth understanding of its fixed and variable overhead costs for planning and control purposes.

Automobile manufacturing is an industry with significant fixed overhead costs. As a new company, Tesla Motors made the strategic decision to make up-front fixed

[1] *Sources:* Ohnsman, Alan. 2012. Tesla Motors cuts factory cost to try to generate profit. *Bloomberg*, http://www.bloomberg.com/news/2012-04-12/tesla-motors-cuts-factory-cost-to-try-to-generate-profit.html, April 12; Tesla Motors, Inc. 2013. March 31, 2013 Form 10-Q (filed May 10); Valdes-Dapena, Peter. 2013. Tesla: Consumer Reports' best car ever tested. *CNNMoney.com*, http://money.cnn.com/2013/05/09/autos/tesla-models-consumer-reports/index.html, May 9; White, Joseph. 2013. Tesla has a fresh $1 billion—and lots of ways to spend it. *Corporate Intelligence (blog), The Wall Street Journal*, http://blogs.wsj.com/corporate-intelligence/, May 17.

investments designed to benefit the company for many years. These resulted in various fixed overhead costs including depreciation and taxes on its new state-of-the-art factory, assembly line supervisors, insurance, and salaries for the engineers that design the battery packs and electric motors that power its specially designed vehicles. Variable costs for Tesla Motors include utilities, office supplies, advertising, and promotion costs among many others.

Understanding its fixed and variable overhead costs allows Tesla Motors' management accountants to develop the company's budgeted fixed and variable overhead cost rates for each Model S produced. Also, using flexible budgeting, the company can make strategic changes based on activity. For instance, when Tesla Motors began expanding sales beyond North America in early 2013, the company added new sales and marketing staff to support the growth of the business, which then resulted in a new variable overhead cost rate.

Companies such as DuPont, International Paper, and U.S. Steel, which invest heavily in capital equipment, and Amazon.com and Yahoo!, which invest large amounts in software, have high overhead costs. As the Tesla example suggests, understanding the behavior of overhead costs, planning for them, analyzing the variances related to them, and acting appropriately on the results are critical for a company.

Managers use flexible budgets and variance analysis to help plan and control the direct-cost categories of direct materials and direct manufacturing labor. In this chapter, you will learn how managers plan for and control the indirect-cost categories of variable manufacturing overhead and fixed manufacturing overhead. This chapter also explains why managers should be careful when interpreting variances based on overhead-cost concepts developed primarily for financial reporting purposes.

Planning of Variable and Fixed Overhead Costs

We'll use the Webb Company example to illustrate the planning and control of variable and fixed overhead costs. Webb manufactures jackets it sells to distributors, who in turn sell them to independent clothing stores and retail chains. Because we assume Webb's only costs are manufacturing costs, for simplicity we use the term "overhead costs" instead of "manufacturing overhead costs" in this chapter. Webb's variable overhead costs include energy, machine maintenance, engineering support, and indirect materials. Webb's fixed overhead costs include plant leasing costs, depreciation on plant equipment, and the salaries of the plant managers.

Planning Variable Overhead Costs

To effectively plan variable overhead costs for a product or service, managers must focus on the activities that create a superior product or service for their customers and eliminate activities that do not add value. For example, customers expect Webb's jackets to last, so

Learning Objective 1

Explain the similarities and differences in planning variable overhead costs and fixed overhead costs

…for both, plan only essential activities and be efficient; fixed overhead costs are usually determined well before the budget period begins

Webb's managers consider sewing to be an essential activity. Therefore, maintenance activities for sewing machines, which are included in Webb's variable overhead costs, are also essential activities for which management must plan. Such maintenance should be done in a cost-effective way, such as by scheduling periodic equipment maintenance rather than waiting for sewing machines to break down. For many companies today, it is critical to plan for ways to reduce the consumption of energy, a rapidly growing component of variable overhead costs. Webb installs smart meters in order to monitor energy use in real time and steer production operations away from peak consumption periods.

Planning Fixed Overhead Costs

Planning fixed overhead costs is similar to planning variable overhead costs—undertake only essential activities and then plan to be efficient in that undertaking. But there is an additional strategic issue when it comes to planning fixed overhead costs: choosing the appropriate level of capacity or investment that will benefit the company in the long run. Consider Webb's leasing of sewing machines, each of which has a fixed cost per year. Leasing too many machines will result in overcapacity and unnecessary fixed leasing costs. Leasing too few machines will result in an inability to meet demand, lost sales of jackets, and unhappy customers. Consider AT&T, which did not initially foresee the iPhone's appeal or the proliferation of "apps" and consequently did not upgrade its network sufficiently to handle the resulting data traffic. AT&T subsequently had to impose limits on how customers could use the iPhone (such as by curtailing tethering and the streaming of Webcasts). This explains why following the iPhone's release, at one point AT&T had the lowest customer satisfaction ratings among all major carriers.

The planning of fixed overhead costs differs from the planning of variable overhead costs in another regard as well: timing. At the start of a budget period, management will have made most of the decisions determining the level of fixed overhead costs to be incurred. But it's the day-to-day, ongoing operating decisions that mainly determine the level of variable overhead costs incurred in that period. For example, the variable overhead costs of hospitals, which include the costs of disposable supplies, doses of medication, suture packets, and medical waste disposal, are a function of the number and nature of procedures carried out, as well as the practice patterns of the physicians. However, most of the costs of providing hospital service are fixed overhead costs—those related to buildings, equipment, and salaried labor. These costs are unrelated to a hospital's volume of activity.[2]

Decision Point

How do managers plan variable overhead costs and fixed overhead costs?

Learning Objective 2

Develop budgeted variable overhead cost rates

...budgeted variable costs divided by quantity of cost-allocation base

and budgeted fixed overhead cost rates

...budgeted fixed costs divided by quantity of cost-allocation base

Standard Costing at Webb Company

Webb uses standard costing. This chapter explains how the standards for Webb's manufacturing overhead costs are developed. **Standard costing** is a costing system that (1) traces direct costs to output produced by multiplying the standard prices or rates by the standard quantities of inputs allowed for actual outputs produced and (2) allocates overhead costs on the basis of the standard overhead-cost rates times the standard quantities of the allocation bases allowed for the actual outputs produced.

The standard cost of Webb's jackets can be computed at the start of the budget period. This feature of standard costing simplifies record keeping because no record is needed of the actual overhead costs or of the actual quantities of the cost-allocation bases used for making the jackets. What managers *do* need are the standard overhead cost rates for Webb's variable and fixed overhead. Management accountants calculate these cost rates based on the planned amounts of variable and fixed overhead and the standard

---

[2] Free-standing surgery centers have thrived because they have lower fixed overhead costs compared to traditional hospitals. For an enlightening summary of costing issues in health care, see A. Macario. 2010. "What does one minute of operating room time cost?" *Journal of Clinical Anesthesia*, June.

quantities of the allocation bases. We describe these computations next. Note that once managers set these standards, the costs of using standard costing are low relative to the costs of using actual costing or normal costing.

Developing Budgeted Variable Overhead Rates

Budgeted variable overhead cost-allocation rates can be developed in four steps. Throughout the chapter, we use the broader term *budgeted rate* rather than *standard rate*. When standard costing is used, the budgeted rates are standard rates.

Step 1: Choose the Period to Be Used for the Budget. Webb uses a 12-month budget period. There are two reasons for using annual overhead rates rather than, say, monthly rates. The first relates to the numerator, such as reducing the influence of seasonality on the firm's cost structure. The second relates to the denominator, such as reducing the effect of varying output and number of days in a month. In addition, setting overhead rates once a year rather than 12 times a year saves managers time.

Step 2: Select the Cost-Allocation Bases to Use in Allocating the Variable Overhead Costs to the Output Produced. Webb's operating managers select machine-hours as the cost-allocation base because they believe that machine-hours is the only cost driver of variable overhead. Based on an engineering study, Webb estimates it will take 0.40 of a machine-hour per actual output unit. For its budgeted output of 144,000 jackets in 2014, Webb budgets 57,600 (0.40 × 144,000) machine-hours.

Step 3: Identify the Variable Overhead Costs Associated with Each Cost-Allocation Base. Webb groups all of its variable overhead costs, including the costs of energy, machine maintenance, engineering support, indirect materials, and indirect manufacturing labor, in a single cost pool. Webb's total budgeted variable overhead costs for 2014 are $1,728,000.

Step 4: Compute the Rate per Unit of Each Cost-Allocation Base Used to Allocate the Variable Overhead Costs to the Output Produced. Dividing the amount in Step 3 ($1,728,000) by the amount in Step 2 (57,600 machine-hours), Webb estimates a rate of $30 per standard machine-hour for allocating its variable overhead costs.

When standard costing is used, the variable overhead rate per unit of the cost-allocation base ($30 per machine-hour for Webb) is generally expressed as a standard rate per output unit. Webb calculates the budgeted variable overhead cost rate per output unit as follows:

$$\begin{matrix} \text{Budgeted variable} & & \text{Budgeted input} & & \text{Budgeted variable} \\ \text{overhead cost rate} & = & \text{allowed per} & \times & \text{overhead cost rate} \\ \text{per output unit} & & \text{output unit} & & \text{per input unit} \end{matrix}$$

$$= 0.40 \text{ hour per jacket} \times \$30 \text{ per hour}$$

$$= \$12 \text{ per jacket}$$

The $12-per-jacket rate is the budgeted variable overhead cost rate in Webb's static budget for 2014 as well as in the monthly performance reports the firm prepares during 2014.

The $12-per-jacket rate represents the amount by which managers expect Webb's variable overhead costs to change when the amount of output changes. As the number of jackets manufactured increases, the variable overhead costs allocated to output (for inventory costing) increase at the rate of $12 per jacket. The $12 per jacket represents the firm's total variable overhead costs per unit of output, including the costs of energy, repairs, indirect labor, and so on. Managers help control variable overhead costs by setting a budget for each of these line items and then investigating the possible causes of any significant variances.

Developing Budgeted Fixed Overhead Rates

Fixed overhead costs are, by definition, a lump sum of costs that remains unchanged for a given period, despite wide changes in a firm's level of activity or output. Fixed costs are included in flexible budgets, but they remain the same within the relevant range of activity regardless of the output level chosen to "flex" the variable costs and revenues. Webb's monthly fixed overhead costs of $276,000 are the same in the static budget as they are in the flexible budget. Do not assume, however, that these costs can never be changed. Managers can reduce them by selling equipment or laying off employees, for example. But the costs are fixed in the sense that, unlike variable costs such as direct material costs, fixed costs do not *automatically* increase or decrease with the level of activity within the relevant range.

The process of developing the budgeted fixed overhead rate is the same as the one for calculating the budgeted variable overhead rate. The steps are as follows:

Step 1: Choose the Period to Use for the Budget. As with variable overhead costs, the budget period for fixed overhead costs is typically one year, to help smooth out seasonal effects.

Step 2: Select the Cost-Allocation Bases to Use in Allocating the Fixed Overhead Costs to the Output Produced. Webb uses machine-hours as the only cost-allocation base for the firm's fixed overhead costs. Why? Because Webb's managers believe that, in the long run, the company's fixed overhead costs will increase or decrease to the levels needed to support the amount of machine-hours. Therefore, in the long run, the amount of machine-hours used is the only cost driver of fixed overhead costs. The number of machine-hours is the denominator in the budgeted fixed overhead rate computation and is called the **denominator level.** For simplicity, we assume Webb expects to operate at capacity in fiscal year 2014, with a budgeted usage of 57,600 machine-hours for a budgeted output of 144,000 jackets.[3]

Step 3: Identify the Fixed Overhead Costs Associated with Each Cost-Allocation Base. Because Webb identifies a single cost-allocation base—machine-hours—to allocate fixed overhead costs, it groups all such costs into a single cost pool. Costs in this pool include depreciation on plant and equipment, plant and equipment leasing costs, and the plant manager's salary. Webb's fixed overhead budget for 2014 is $3,312,000.

Step 4: Compute the Rate per Unit of Each Cost-Allocation Base Used to Allocate Fixed Overhead Costs to the Output Produced. By dividing the $3,312,000 from Step 3 by the 57,600 machine-hours from Step 2, Webb estimates a fixed overhead cost rate of $57.50 per machine-hour:

$$\begin{array}{c} \text{Budgeted fixed} \\ \text{overhead cost per} \\ \text{unit of cost-allocation} \\ \text{base} \end{array} = \frac{\begin{array}{c}\text{Budgeted total costs} \\ \text{in fixed overhead cost pool}\end{array}}{\begin{array}{c}\text{Budgeted total quantity of} \\ \text{cost-allocation base}\end{array}} = \frac{\$3{,}312{,}000}{57{,}600} = \$57.50 \text{ per machine-hour}$$

Under standard costing, the $57.50 fixed overhead cost per machine-hour is usually expressed as a standard cost per output unit. Recall that Webb's engineering study estimates that it will take 0.40 machine-hour per output unit. Webb can now calculate the budgeted fixed overhead cost per output unit as follows:

$$\begin{array}{c} \text{Budgeted fixed} \\ \text{overhead cost per} \\ \text{output unit} \end{array} = \begin{array}{c} \text{Budgeted quantity} \\ \text{of cost-allocation} \\ \text{base allowed per} \\ \text{output unit} \end{array} \times \begin{array}{c} \text{Budgeted fixed} \\ \text{overhead cost} \\ \text{per unit of} \\ \text{cost-allocation base} \end{array}$$

$$= 0.40 \text{ of a machine-hour per jacket} \times \$57.50 \text{ per machine-hour}$$

$$= \$23.00 \text{ per jacket}$$

When preparing monthly budgets for 2014, Webb divides the $3,312,000 annual total fixed costs into 12 equal monthly amounts of $276,000.

---

[3] Because Webb plans its capacity over multiple periods, anticipated demand in 2014 could be such that budgeted output for 2014 is less than Webb's capacity. Companies vary in the denominator levels they choose. Some choose budgeted output and others choose capacity. In either case, the approach and analysis presented in this chapter is unchanged.

Variable Overhead Cost Variances

Learning
Objective **3**

We now illustrate how the budgeted variable overhead rate is used to compute Webb's variable overhead cost variances. The following data are for April 2014, when Webb produced and sold 10,000 jackets:

	Actual Result	Flexible-Budget Amount
1. Output units (jackets)	10,000	10,000
2. Machine-hours per output unit	0.45	0.40
3. Machine-hours (1 × 2)	4,500	4,000
4. Variable overhead costs	$130,500	$120,000
5. Variable overhead costs per machine-hour (4 ÷ 3)	$ 29.00	$ 30.00
6. Variable overhead costs per output unit (4 ÷ 1)	$ 13.05	$ 12.00

Compute the variable overhead flexible-budget variance,

...difference between actual variable overhead costs and flexible-budget variable overhead amounts

the variable overhead efficiency variance,

...difference between actual quantity of cost-allocation base and budgeted quantity of cost-allocation base

and the variable overhead spending variance

...difference between actual variable overhead cost rate and budgeted variable overhead cost rate

The flexible budget enables Webb to highlight the differences between actual costs and actual quantities versus budgeted costs and budgeted quantities for the actual output level of 10,000 jackets.

Flexible-Budget Analysis

The **variable overhead flexible-budget variance** measures the difference between actual variable overhead costs incurred and flexible-budget variable overhead amounts.

$$\frac{\text{Variable overhead}}{\text{flexible-budget variance}} = \frac{\text{Actual costs}}{\text{incurred}} - \frac{\text{Flexible-budget}}{\text{amount}}$$

$$= \$130,500 - \$120,000$$

$$= \$10,500 \text{ U}$$

This $10,500 unfavorable flexible-budget variance means Webb's actual variable overhead exceeded the flexible-budget amount by $10,500 for the 10,000 jackets actually produced and sold. Webb's managers would want to know why. Did Webb use more machine-hours than planned to produce the 10,000 jackets? If so, was it because workers were less skilled than expected in using machines? Or did Webb spend more on variable overhead costs, such as maintenance?

Webb's managers can get further insight into the reason for the $10,500 unfavorable variance by subdividing it into the efficiency variance and spending variance.

Variable Overhead Efficiency Variance

The **variable overhead efficiency variance** is the difference between actual quantity of the cost-allocation base used and budgeted quantity of the cost-allocation base that should have been used to produce the actual output, multiplied by the budgeted variable overhead cost per unit of the cost-allocation base.

$$\frac{\text{Variable overhead efficiency variance}}{} = \left(\begin{array}{c} \text{Actual quantity of} \\ \text{variable overhead} \\ \text{cost-allocation base} \\ \text{used for actual} \\ \text{output} \end{array} - \begin{array}{c} \text{Budgeted quantity of} \\ \text{variable overhead} \\ \text{cost-allocation base} \\ \text{allowed for} \\ \text{actual output} \end{array} \right) \times \begin{array}{c} \text{Budgeted variable} \\ \text{overhead cost per unit} \\ \text{of cost-allocation base} \end{array}$$

$$= (4,500 \text{ hours} - 0.40 \text{ hr./unit} \times 10,000 \text{ units}) \times \$30 \text{ per hour}$$

$$= (4,500 \text{ hours} - 4,000 \text{ hours}) \times \$30 \text{ per hour}$$

$$= \$15,000 \text{ U}$$

Columns 2 and 3 of Exhibit 1 depict the variable overhead efficiency variance. Note the variance arises solely because of the difference between the actual quantity (4,500 hours)

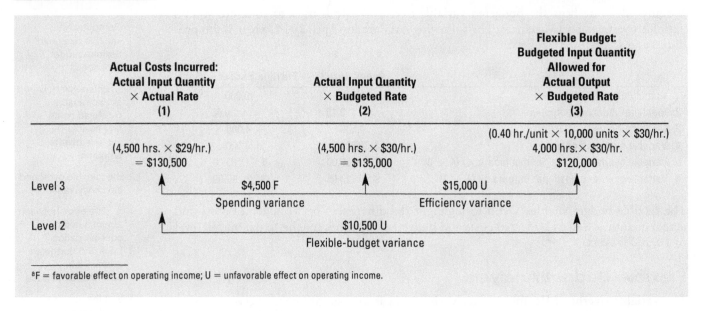

Exhibit 1 Columnar Presentation of Variable Overhead Variance Analysis: Webb Company for April 2014[a]

	Actual Costs Incurred: Actual Input Quantity × Actual Rate (1)		Actual Input Quantity × Budgeted Rate (2)		Flexible Budget: Budgeted Input Quantity Allowed for Actual Output × Budgeted Rate (3)
					(0.40 hr./unit × 10,000 units × $30/hr.) 4,000 hrs.× $30/hr.
	(4,500 hrs. × $29/hr.) = $130,500		(4,500 hrs. × $30/hr.) = $135,000		$120,000
Level 3		$4,500 F Spending variance		$15,000 U Efficiency variance	
Level 2			$10,500 U Flexible-budget variance		

[a]F = favorable effect on operating income; U = unfavorable effect on operating income.

and budgeted quantity (4,000 hours) of the cost-allocation base. The variable overhead efficiency variance is computed the same way the efficiency variance for direct-cost items is. However, the interpretation of the variance is somewhat different. The efficiency variances for direct-cost items are based on the differences between the actual inputs used and the budgeted inputs allowed for the actual output produced. For example, a forensic laboratory (the kind popularized by television shows such as *CSI* and *Dexter*) would calculate a direct labor efficiency variance based on whether the lab used more or fewer hours than the standard hours allowed for the actual number of DNA tests. In contrast, the efficiency variance for variable overhead is based on the efficiency with which *the cost-allocation base* is used. Webb's unfavorable variable overhead efficiency variance of $15,000 means that the actual machine-hours (the cost-allocation base) of 4,500 hours was higher than the budgeted machine-hours of 4,000 hours allowed to manufacture 10,000 jackets and this, to the extent machine-hours are a cost driver for variable overhead, pushed up the potential spending on variable overhead.

The following table shows possible causes for Webb's actual machine-hours exceeding the budgeted machine-hours and Webb's potential responses to each of these causes.

Possible Causes for Exceeding Budget	Potential Management Responses
1. Workers were less efficient than expected in using machines.	1. Encourage the human resources department to implement better employee-hiring practices and training procedures.
2. The production scheduler inefficiently scheduled jobs, resulting in more machine-hours used than budgeted.	2. Improve plant operations by installing production-scheduling software.
3. Machines were not maintained in good operating condition.	3. Ensure preventive maintenance is done on all machines.
4. Webb's sales staff promised a distributor a rush delivery, which resulted in more machine-hours used than budgeted.	4. Coordinate production schedules with sales staff and distributors and share information with them.
5. Budgeted machine time standards were set too tight.	5. Commit more resources to develop appropriate standards.

Note how, depending on the cause(s) of the $15,000 U variance, corrective actions may need to be taken not just in manufacturing but also in other business functions of the value chain, such as sales and distribution.

Webb's managers discovered that one reason for the unfavorable variance was that workers were underskilled. As a result, Webb is improving its hiring and training practices. Insufficient maintenance performed in the 2 months prior to April 2014 was another reason. A former plant manager had delayed the maintenance in an attempt to meet Webb's monthly cost targets. Managers should not focus on meeting short-run cost targets if they are likely to result in harmful long-run consequences. For example, if Webb's employees were to hurt themselves while operating poorly maintained machinery, the consequences would not only be harmful, they could be deadly. Webb is now strengthening its internal maintenance procedures so that failure to do monthly maintenance as needed will raise a "red flag" that must be immediately explained to management. Webb is also taking a hard look at its evaluation practices to determine if they inadvertently pressure managers to fixate on short-term targets to the long-run detriment of the firm.

Variable Overhead Spending Variance

The **variable overhead spending variance** is the difference between the actual variable overhead cost per unit of the cost-allocation base and the budgeted variable overhead cost per unit of the cost-allocation base, multiplied by the actual quantity of variable overhead cost-allocation base used.

$$\begin{pmatrix} \text{Variable} \\ \text{overhead} \\ \text{spending} \\ \text{variance} \end{pmatrix} = \begin{pmatrix} \text{Actual variable} & & \text{Budgeted variable} \\ \text{overhead cost per unit} & - & \text{overhead cost per unit} \\ \text{of cost-allocation base} & & \text{of cost-allocation base} \end{pmatrix} \times \begin{pmatrix} \text{Actual quantity of} \\ \text{variable overhead} \\ \text{cost-allocation base} \\ \text{used} \end{pmatrix}$$

$$= (\$29 \text{ per machine-hour} - \$30 \text{ per machine-hour}) \times 4,500 \text{ machine-hours}$$

$$= (-\$1 \text{ per machine-hour}) \times 4,500 \text{ machine-hours}$$

$$= \$4,500 \text{ F}$$

Webb operated in April 2014 with a lower-than-budgeted variable overhead cost per machine-hour, so there is a favorable variable overhead spending variance. Columns 1 and 2 in Exhibit 1 depict this variance.

To understand why the favorable variable overhead spending variance occurred, Webb's managers need to recognize why *actual* variable overhead cost per unit of the cost-allocation base ($29 per machine-hour) is *lower* than the *budgeted* variable overhead cost per unit of the cost-allocation base ($30 per machine-hour).

Overall, Webb used 4,500 machine-hours, which is 12.5% greater than the flexible-budget amount of 4,000 machine-hours. However, actual variable overhead costs of $130,500 are only 8.75% greater than the flexible-budget amount of $120,000. Thus, relative to the flexible budget, the percentage increase in actual variable overhead costs is *less* than the percentage increase in machine-hours. Consequently, the actual variable overhead cost per machine-hour is lower than the budgeted amount, resulting in a favorable variable overhead spending variance.

Recall that variable overhead costs include costs of energy, machine maintenance, indirect materials, and indirect labor. Two possible reasons why the percentage increase in actual variable overhead costs is less than the percentage increase in machine-hours are as follows:

1. The actual prices of the individual inputs included in variable overhead costs, such as the price of energy, indirect materials, or indirect labor, are lower than budgeted prices of these inputs. For example, the actual price of electricity may only be $0.09 per kilowatt-hour, compared with a price of $0.10 per kilowatt-hour in the flexible budget.

2. Relative to the flexible budget, the percentage increase in the actual use of individual items in the variable overhead-cost pool is less than the percentage increase in machine-hours. Compared with the flexible-budget amount of 30,000 kilowatt-hours, suppose the actual energy use was 32,400 kilowatt-hours, or 8% higher. The fact that this is a smaller percentage increase than the 12.5% increase in machine-hours (4,500 actual

machine-hours versus a flexible budget of 4,000 machine-hours) will lead to a favorable variable overhead spending variance, which can be partially or completely traced to the efficient use of energy and other variable overhead items.

As part of the last stage of the five-step decision-making process, Webb's managers will need to examine the signals provided by the variable overhead variances to *evaluate the firm's performance and learn*. By understanding the reasons for these variances, Webb can take appropriate actions and make more precise predictions in order to achieve improved results in future periods.

For example, Webb's managers must examine why the actual prices of variable overhead cost items are different from the budgeted prices. The differences could be the result of skillful negotiation on the part of the purchasing manager, oversupply in the market, or lower quality of inputs such as indirect materials. Webb's response depends on what is believed to be the cause of the variance. If the concerns are about quality, for instance, Webb may want to put in place new quality management systems.

Similarly, Webb's managers should understand the possible causes for the efficiency with which variable overhead resources are used. These causes include the skill levels of workers, maintenance of machines, and the efficiency of the manufacturing process. Webb's managers discovered that Webb used fewer indirect labor resources per machine-hour because of manufacturing process improvements. As a result, the firm began organizing cross-functional teams to see if more process improvements could be achieved.

We emphasize that a manager should not always view a favorable variable overhead spending variance as desirable. For example, the variable overhead spending variance would be favorable if Webb's managers purchased lower-priced, poor-quality indirect materials, hired less-talented supervisors, or performed less machine maintenance. These decisions, however, are likely to hurt product quality and harm the long-run prospects of the business.

To clarify the concepts of variable overhead efficiency variance and variable overhead spending variance, consider the following example. Suppose that (a) energy is the only item of variable overhead cost and machine-hours is the cost-allocation base; (b) actual machine-hours used equals the number of machine-hours under the flexible budget; and (c) the actual price of energy equals the budgeted price. From (a) and (b), it follows that there is no efficiency variance—the company has been efficient with respect to the number of machine-hours (the cost-allocation base) used to produce the actual output. However, and despite (c), there could still be a spending variance. Why? Because even though the company used the correct number of machine-hours, the energy consumed *per machine-hour* could be higher than budgeted (for example, because the machines have not been maintained correctly). The cost of this higher energy usage would be reflected in an unfavorable spending variance.

Journal Entries for Variable Overhead Costs and Variances

We now prepare journal entries for the Variable Overhead Control account and the contra account Variable Overhead Allocated.

Entries for variable overhead for April 2014 (data from Exhibit 1) are as follows:

1. Variable Overhead Control   130,500
     Accounts Payable and various other accounts   130,500
   To record actual variable overhead costs incurred.
2. Work-in-Process Control   120,000
     Variable Overhead Allocated   120,000
   To record variable overhead cost allocated
     (0.40 machine-hour/unit × 10,000 units × $30/machine-hour). (The costs accumulated in Work-in-Process Control are transferred to Finished Goods Control when production is completed and to Cost of Goods Sold when the products are sold.)

3. Variable Overhead Allocated   120,000

   Variable Overhead Efficiency Variance   15,000

    Variable Overhead Control   130,500

    Variable Overhead Spending Variance   4,500

   This records the variances for the accounting period.

These variances are the underallocated or overallocated variable overhead costs. At the end of the fiscal year, the variance accounts are written off to cost of goods sold if immaterial in amount. If the variances are material in amount, they are prorated among the Work-in-Process Control, Finished Goods Control, and Cost of Goods Sold accounts on the basis of the variable overhead allocated to these accounts. Only unavoidable costs are prorated. Any part of the variances attributable to avoidable inefficiency is written off in the period. Assume that the balances in the variable overhead variance accounts as of April 2014 are also the balances at the end of the 2014 fiscal year and are immaterial in amount. The following journal entry records the write-off of the variance accounts to the cost of goods sold:

Cost of Goods Sold   10,500

Variable Overhead Spending Variance   4,500

  Variable Overhead Efficiency Variance   15,000

Next we demonstrate how to calculate fixed overhead cost variances.

Decision Point

What variances can be calculated for variable overhead costs?

Fixed Overhead Cost Variances

Learning Objective 4

Compute the fixed overhead flexible-budget variance,

...difference between actual fixed overhead costs and flexible-budget fixed overhead amounts

the fixed overhead spending variance,

...same as the preceding explanation

and the fixed overhead production-volume variance

...difference between budgeted fixed overhead and fixed overhead allocated on the basis of actual output produced

The flexible-budget amount for a fixed-cost item is also the amount included in the static budget prepared at the start of the period. No adjustment is required for differences between actual output and budgeted output for fixed costs because fixed costs are unaffected by changes in the output level within the relevant range. At the start of 2014, Webb budgeted its fixed overhead costs to be $276,000 per month. The actual amount for April 2014 turned out to be $285,000. The **fixed overhead flexible-budget variance** is the difference between actual fixed overhead costs and fixed overhead costs in the flexible budget:

$$\text{Fixed overhead flexible-budget variance} = \text{Actual costs incurred} - \text{Flexible-budget amount}$$

$$= \$285{,}000 - \$276{,}000$$

$$= \$9{,}000 \text{ U}$$

The variance is unfavorable because the $285,000 actual fixed overhead costs exceed the $276,000 budgeted for April 2014, which decreases that month's operating income by $9,000.

  The variable overhead flexible-budget variance described earlier in this chapter was subdivided into a spending variance and an efficiency variance. There is no efficiency variance for fixed overhead costs. That's because a given lump sum of fixed overhead costs will be unaffected by how efficiently machine-hours are used to produce output in a given budget period. As we will see later on, this does not mean that a company cannot be efficient or inefficient in its use of fixed-overhead-cost resources. As Exhibit 2 shows, because there is no efficiency variance, the **fixed overhead spending variance** is the same amount as the fixed overhead flexible-budget variance:

$$\text{Fixed overhead spending variance} = \text{Actual costs incurred} - \text{Flexible-budget amount}$$

$$= \$285{,}000 - \$276{,}000$$

$$= \$9{,}000 \text{ U}$$

Reasons for the unfavorable spending variance could be higher plant-leasing costs, higher depreciation on plant and equipment, or higher administrative costs, such as a higher-than-budgeted

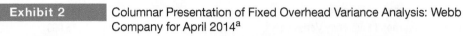

| Exhibit 2 | Columnar Presentation of Fixed Overhead Variance Analysis: Webb Company for April 2014[a] |

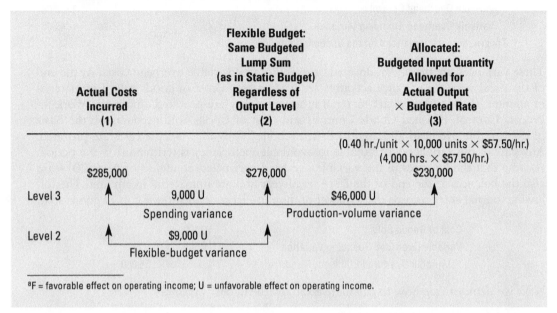

[a]F = favorable effect on operating income; U = unfavorable effect on operating income.

salary paid to the plant manager. Webb investigated this variance and found that there was a $9,000 per month unexpected increase in its equipment-leasing costs. However, managers concluded that the new lease rates were competitive with lease rates available elsewhere. If this were not the case, Webb would look to lease equipment from other suppliers.

Production-Volume Variance

The **production-volume variance** arises only for fixed costs. It is the difference between the budgeted fixed overhead and the fixed overhead allocated on the basis of actual output produced. Recall that at the start of the year, Webb calculated a budgeted fixed overhead rate of $57.50 per machine-hour based on monthly budgeted fixed overhead costs of $276,000. Under standard costing, Webb's fixed overhead costs are allocated to the actual output produced during each period at the rate of $57.50 per standard machine-hour, which is equivalent to a rate of $23 per jacket (0.40 machine-hour per jacket × $57.50 per machine-hour). If Webb produces 1,000 jackets, $23,000 ($23 per jacket × 1,000 jackets) out of April's budgeted fixed overhead costs of $276,000 will be allocated to the jackets. If Webb produces 10,000 jackets, $230,000 ($23 per jacket × 10,000 jackets) will be allocated. Only if Webb produces 12,000 jackets (that is, operates, as budgeted, at capacity) will all $276,000 ($23 per jacket × 12,000 jackets) of the budgeted fixed overhead costs be allocated to the jacket output. The key point here is that even though Webb budgeted its fixed overhead costs to be $276,000, it does not necessarily allocate all these costs to output. The reason is that Webb budgets $276,000 of fixed costs to support its planned production of 12,000 jackets. If Webb produces fewer than 12,000 jackets, it only allocates the budgeted cost of capacity actually needed and used to produce the jackets.

The production-volume variance, also referred to as the **denominator-level variance**, is the difference between the budgeted and allocated fixed overhead amounts. Note that the allocated overhead can be expressed in terms of allocation-base units (machine-hours for Webb) or in terms of the budgeted fixed cost per unit:

$$\frac{\text{Production}}{\text{volume variance}} = \frac{\text{Budgeted}}{\text{fixed overhead}} - \frac{\text{Fixed overhead allocated}}{\text{for actual output units produced}}$$

$$= \$276,000 - (0.40 \text{ hour per jacket} \times \$57.50 \text{ per hour} \times 10,000 \text{ jackets})$$

$$= \$276,000 - (\$23 \text{ per jacket} \times 10,000 \text{ jackets})$$

$$= \$276,000 - \$230,000$$

$$= \$46,000 \text{ U}$$

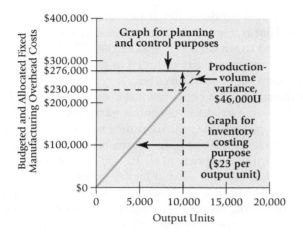

Exhibit 3

Behavior of Fixed
Manufacturing
Overhead Costs:
Budgeted for Planning
and Control Purposes
and Allocated for
Inventory Costing
Purposes for Webb
Company for April 2014

As shown in Exhibit 2, the budgeted fixed overhead ($276,000) will be the lump sum shown in the static budget and also in any flexible budget within the relevant range. The fixed overhead allocated ($230,000) is the amount of fixed overhead costs allocated; it is calculated by multiplying the number of output units produced during the budget period (10,000 units) by the budgeted cost per output unit ($23). The $46,000 U production-volume variance can also be thought of as $23 per jacket × 2,000 jackets that were *not* produced. We will explore possible causes for the unfavorable production-volume variance and its management implications in the following section.

Exhibit 3 shows Webb's production-volume variance. For planning and control purposes, Webb's fixed (manufacturing) overhead costs do not change in the 0- to 12,000-unit relevant range. Contrast this behavior of fixed costs with how these costs are depicted for the purpose of inventory costing in Exhibit 3. Under Generally Accepted Accounting Principles (GAAP), fixed (manufacturing) overhead costs are allocated as an inventoriable cost to the output units produced. Every output unit that Webb manufactures will increase the fixed overhead allocated to products by $23. That is, for purposes of allocating fixed overhead costs to jackets, these costs are viewed *as if* they had a variable-cost behavior pattern. As the graph in Exhibit 3 shows, the difference between the $276,000 in fixed overhead costs budgeted and the $230,000 of costs allocated is the $46,000 unfavorable production-volume variance.

Managers should always be careful to distinguish the true behavior of fixed costs from the manner in which fixed costs are assigned to products. In particular, although fixed costs are unitized and allocated for inventory costing purposes, managers should be wary of using the same unitized fixed overhead costs for planning and control purposes. When forecasting fixed costs, managers should concentrate on total lump-sum costs instead of unitized costs. Similarly, when managers are looking to assign costs for control purposes or identify the best way to use capacity resources fixed in the short run, the use of unitized fixed costs often leads to incorrect decisions.

Interpreting the Production-Volume Variance

Lump-sum fixed costs represent the costs of acquiring capacity. These costs do not decrease automatically if the capacity needed turns out to be less than the capacity acquired. Sometimes costs are fixed for a specific time period for contractual reasons, such as an annual lease contract for a plant. At other times, costs are fixed because capacity has to be acquired or disposed of in fixed increments, or lumps. For example, suppose that acquiring a sewing machine gives Webb the ability to produce 1,000 jackets. If it is not possible to buy or lease a fraction of a machine, Webb can add capacity only in increments of 1,000 jackets. That is, Webb may choose capacity levels of 10,000, 11,000, or 12,000 jackets, but nothing in between.

Webb's management would want to analyze the $46,000 unfavorable production-volume variance. Why did this overcapacity occur? Why were 10,000 jackets produced instead of 12,000? Is demand weak? Should Webb reevaluate its product and marketing strategies? Is there a quality problem? Or did Webb make a strategic mistake by acquiring too much capacity? The causes of the $46,000 unfavorable production-volume variance will determine the actions Webb's managers take in response to the variance.

In contrast, a favorable production-volume variance indicates an overallocation of fixed overhead costs. That is, the overhead costs allocated to the actual output produced exceed the budgeted fixed overhead costs of $276,000. The favorable production-volume variance is composed of the fixed costs recorded in excess of $276,000.

Be careful when drawing conclusions about a company's capacity planning whether the production-volume variance is either favorable or unfavorable. To correctly interpret Webb's $46,000 unfavorable production-volume variance, its managers should consider why it sold only 10,000 jackets in April. Suppose a new competitor gained market share by pricing its jackets lower than Webb's. To sell the budgeted 12,000 jackets, Webb might have had to reduce its own selling price on all 12,000 jackets. Suppose it decided that selling 10,000 jackets at a higher price yielded higher operating income than selling 12,000 jackets at a lower price. The production-volume variance does not take into account such information. The failure of the production-volume variance to consider such information is why Webb should not interpret the $46,000 U amount as the total economic cost of selling 2,000 jackets fewer than the 12,000 jackets budgeted. If, however, Webb's managers anticipate they will not need capacity beyond 10,000 jackets, they may reduce the excess capacity, say, by canceling the lease on some of the machines.

Companies plan their plant capacity strategically on the basis of market information about how much capacity will be needed over some future time horizon. For 2014, Webb's budgeted quantity of output is equal to the maximum capacity of the plant for that budget period. Actual demand (and quantity produced) turned out to be below the budgeted quantity of output, so Webb reports an unfavorable production-volume variance for April 2014. However, it would be incorrect to conclude that Webb's management made a poor planning decision regarding its plant capacity. The demand for Webb's jackets might be highly uncertain. Given this uncertainty and the cost of not having sufficient capacity to meet sudden demand surges (including lost contribution margins as well as reduced repeat business), Webb's management may have made a wise capacity choice for 2014.

So what should Webb's managers ultimately do about the unfavorable variance in April? Should they try to reduce capacity, increase sales, or do nothing? Based on their analysis of the situation, Webb's managers decided to reduce some capacity but continued to maintain some excess capacity to accommodate unexpected surges in demand. Concepts in Action: Variance Analysis and Standard Costing Help Sandoz Manage Its Overhead Costs highlights another example of managers using variances to help guide their decisions.

Next we describe the journal entries Webb would make to record fixed overhead costs using standard costing.

Journal Entries for Fixed Overhead Costs and Variances

We illustrate journal entries for fixed overhead costs for April 2014 using the Fixed Overhead Control account and the contra account Fixed Overhead Allocated (data from Exhibit 2).

1. Fixed Overhead Control   285,000

    Salaries Payable, Accumulated Depreciation, and various other accounts   285,000

    To record actual fixed overhead costs incurred.

2. Work-in-Process Control   230,000

    Fixed Overhead Allocated   230,000

    To record fixed overhead costs allocated.

    (0.40 machine-hour/unit $\times$ 10,000 units $\times$ $57.50/machine-hour). (The costs accumulated in Work-in-Process Control are transferred to Finished Goods Control when production is completed and to the Cost of Goods Sold when the products are sold.)

3. Fixed Overhead Allocated   230,000

    Fixed Overhead Spending Variance   9,000

    Fixed Overhead Production-Volume Variance   46,000

    Fixed Overhead Control   285,000

    To record variances for the accounting period.

Concepts in Action

Variance Analysis and Standard Costing Help Sandoz Manage Its Overhead Costs

Sandoz US, the $8.7 billion subsidiary of Swiss-based Novartis AG, is one of the world's largest generic drug manufacturers. Market pricing pressure means that Sandoz operates on razor-thin margins. As a result, Sandoz must tackle the challenge of accounting for overhead costs. Sandoz uses standard costing and variance analysis to manage its overhead costs.

Each year, Sandoz prepares an overhead budget based on a detailed production plan, planned overhead spending, and other factors. Sandoz then uses activity-based costing to assign budgeted overhead costs to different work centers (for example, mixing, blending, tableting, testing, and packaging). Finally, overhead costs are assigned to products based on the activity levels required by each product at each work center. The resulting standard product cost is used in product profitability analysis and as a basis for making pricing decisions. The two main focal points in Sandoz's performance analyses are overhead absorption analysis and manufacturing overhead variance analysis.

Each month, Sandoz uses absorption analysis to compare its actual production and actual costs to the standard costs of its processed inventory. The monthly analysis evaluates two key trends:

1. Are costs in line with the budget? If not, the reasons are examined and the accountable managers are notified.

2. Are production volume and product mix conforming to plan? If not, Sandoz reviews and adjusts the capacities of its machines, and the absorption trend is deemed to be permanent.

Manufacturing overhead variances are examined at the work center level. These variances help determine when equipment is not running as expected so it can be repaired or replaced. Variances also help in identifying inefficiencies in processing and setup and cleaning times, which leads to more efficient ways to use equipment. Sometimes, the manufacturing overhead variance analysis leads to the review and improvement of the standards themselves—a critical element in planning the level of plant capacity. Managers also review the company's current and future capacity on a monthly basis to identify constraints and future capital needs.

Sources: Novartis AG. 2013. December 31, 2012 Form 20-F (filed January 23, 2013), accessed May 2013; and conversations with and documents prepared by Eric Evans and Erich Erchr (of Sandoz US), 2004.

Overall, $285,000 of fixed overhead costs were incurred during April, but only $230,000 were allocated to jackets. The difference of $55,000 is the underallocated fixed overhead costs. The third entry illustrates how the fixed overhead spending variance of $9,000 and the fixed overhead production-volume variance of $46,000 together record this amount in a standard costing system.

At the end of the fiscal year, the fixed overhead spending variance is written off to the cost of goods sold if it is immaterial in amount or prorated among Work-in-Process Control, Finished Goods Control, and Cost of Goods Sold on the basis of the fixed overhead allocated to these accounts. Some companies combine the write-off and proration methods—that is, they write off the portion of the variance that is due to inefficiency and could have been avoided and prorate the portion of the variance that is unavoidable. Assume that the balance in the Fixed

Overhead Spending Variance account as of April 2014 is also the balance at the end of 2014 and is immaterial in amount. The following journal entry records the write-off to Cost of Goods Sold.

Cost of Goods Sold	9,000	
Fixed Overhead Spending Variance		9,000

We now consider the production-volume variance. Assume that the balance in the Fixed Overhead Production-Volume Variance account as of April 2014 is also the balance at the end of 2014. Also assume that some of the jackets manufactured during 2014 are in work-in-process and finished goods inventory at the end of the year. Many management accountants make a strong argument for writing off to Cost of Goods Sold and not prorating an unfavorable production-volume variance. Proponents of this argument contend that the unfavorable production-volume variance of $46,000 measures the cost of resources expended for 2,000 jackets that were not produced ($23 per jacket × 2,000 jackets = $46,000). Prorating these costs would inappropriately allocate the fixed overhead costs incurred for the 2,000 jackets not produced to the jackets that were produced. The jackets produced already bear their representative share of fixed overhead costs of $23 per jacket. Therefore, this argument favors charging the unfavorable production-volume variance against the year's revenues so that fixed costs of unused capacity are not carried in work-in-process inventory and finished goods inventory.

There is, however, an alternative view. This view regards the denominator level as a "soft" rather than a "hard" measure of the fixed resources required and needed to produce each jacket. Suppose that either because of the design of the jacket or the functioning of the machines, it took more machine-hours than previously thought to manufacture each jacket. Consequently, Webb could make only 10,000 jackets rather than the planned 12,000 in April. In this case, the $276,000 of budgeted fixed overhead costs support the production of the 10,000 jackets manufactured. Under this reasoning, prorating the fixed overhead production-volume variance would appropriately spread the fixed overhead costs among the Work-in-Process Control, Finished Goods Control, and Cost of Goods Sold accounts.

What about a favorable production-volume variance? Suppose Webb manufactured 13,800 jackets in April 2014.

$$\text{Production-volume variance} = \begin{matrix} \text{Budgeted} \\ \text{fixed} \\ \text{overhead} \end{matrix} - \begin{matrix} \text{Fixed overhead allocated using} \\ \text{budgeted cost per output unit overhead} \\ \text{allowed for actual output produced} \end{matrix}$$

$$= \$276,000 - (\$23 \text{ per jacket} \times 13,800 \text{ jackets})$$

$$= \$276,000 - \$317,400 = \$41,400 \text{ F}$$

Because actual production exceeded the planned capacity level, clearly the fixed overhead costs of $276,000 supported the production of all 13,800 jackets and should therefore be allocated to them. Prorating the favorable production-volume variance achieves this outcome and reduces the amounts in the Work-in-Process Control, Finished Goods Control, and Cost of Goods Sold accounts. Proration is also the more conservative approach in the sense that it results in a lower operating income than if the entire favorable production-volume variance were credited to Cost of Goods Sold.

Another point relevant to this discussion is that if variances are always written off to Cost of Goods Sold, a company could set its standards to either increase (for financial reporting purposes) or decrease (for tax purposes) its operating income. In other words, always writing off variances invites gaming behavior. For example, Webb could generate a favorable production-volume variance by setting the denominator level used to allocate the firm's fixed overhead costs low and thereby increase its operating income. Or the firm could do just the opposite if it wanted to decrease its operating income to lower its taxes. The proration method has the effect of approximating the allocation of fixed costs based on actual costs and actual output, so it is not susceptible to this type of manipulation.

There is no clear-cut or preferred approach for closing out the production-volume variance. The appropriate accounting procedure is a matter of judgment and depends on the circumstances of each case. Variations of the proration method may be desirable. For example, a company may choose to write off a portion of the production-volume variance and prorate the rest. The goal is to write off that part of the production-volume variance that represents the cost of capacity not used to support the production of output during the period. The rest of the production-volume variance is prorated to Work-in-Process Control, Finished Goods Control, and Cost of Goods Sold.

If Webb were to write off the production-volume variance to Cost of Goods Sold, it would make the following journal entry.

Cost of Goods Sold	46,000	
Fixed Overhead Production-Volume Variance		46,000

Decision Point

What variances can be calculated for fixed overhead costs?

Integrated Analysis of Overhead Cost Variances

As our discussion indicates, the variance calculations for variable overhead and fixed overhead differ:

- Variable overhead has no production-volume variance.
- Fixed overhead has no efficiency variance.

Exhibit 4 presents an integrated summary of the variable overhead variances and the fixed overhead variances computed using standard costs for April 2014. Panel A shows the variances for variable overhead, whereas Panel B contains the fixed overhead variances. As you study Exhibit 4, note how the columns in Panels A and B are aligned to measure the different variances. In both Panels A and B,

- the difference between columns 1 and 2 measures the spending variance.
- the difference between columns 2 and 3 measures the efficiency variance (if applicable).
- the difference between columns 3 and 4 measures the production-volume variance (if applicable).

Panel A contains an efficiency variance; Panel B has no efficiency variance for fixed overhead. As we discussed, a lump-sum amount of fixed costs will be unaffected by the degree of operating efficiency in a given budget period.

Panel A does not have a production-volume variance because the amount of variable overhead allocated is always the same as the flexible-budget amount. Variable costs never have any unused capacity. When production and sales decline from 12,000 jackets to 10,000 jackets, budgeted variable overhead costs proportionately decline. Fixed costs are different. Panel B has a production-volume variance (see Exhibit 3) because Webb did not use some of the fixed overhead capacity it had acquired when it planned to produce 12,000 jackets.

Learning Objective 5

Show how the 4-variance analysis approach reconciles the actual overhead incurred with the overhead amounts allocated during the period

...the 4-variance analysis approach identifies spending and efficiency variances for variable overhead costs and spending and production-volume variances for fixed overhead costs

4-Variance Analysis

When all of the overhead variances are presented together as in Exhibit 4, we refer to it as a 4-variance analysis:

4-Variance Analysis

	Spending Variance	Efficiency Variance	Production-Volume Variance
Variable overhead	$4,500 F	$15,000 U	Never a variance
Fixed overhead	$9,000 U	Never a variance	$46,000 U

Note that the 4-variance analysis provides the same level of information as the variance analysis carried out earlier for variable overhead and fixed overhead separately

| Exhibit 4 | Columnar Presentation of Integrated Variance Analysis: Webb Company for April 2014[a] |

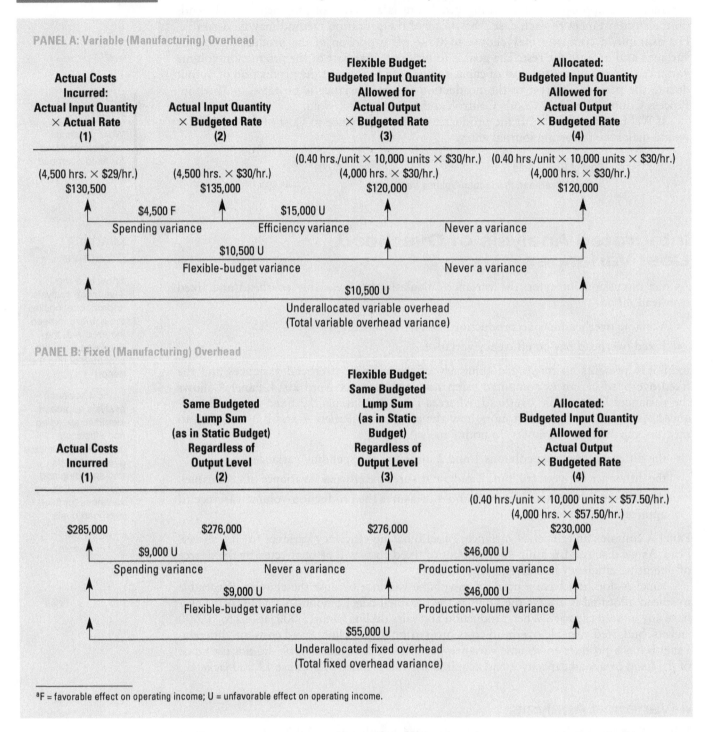

PANEL A: Variable (Manufacturing) Overhead

| Actual Costs Incurred: Actual Input Quantity × Actual Rate (1) | Actual Input Quantity × Budgeted Rate (2) | Flexible Budget: Budgeted Input Quantity Allowed for Actual Output × Budgeted Rate (3) | Allocated: Budgeted Input Quantity Allowed for Actual Output × Budgeted Rate (4) |

(4,500 hrs. × $29/hr.) $130,500

(4,500 hrs. × $30/hr.) $135,000

(0.40 hrs./unit × 10,000 units × $30/hr.) (4,000 hrs. × $30/hr.) $120,000

(0.40 hrs./unit × 10,000 units × $30/hr.) (4,000 hrs. × $30/hr.) $120,000

$4,500 F — Spending variance

$15,000 U — Efficiency variance

Never a variance

$10,500 U — Flexible-budget variance

Never a variance

$10,500 U
Underallocated variable overhead
(Total variable overhead variance)

PANEL B: Fixed (Manufacturing) Overhead

| Actual Costs Incurred (1) | Same Budgeted Lump Sum (as in Static Budget) Regardless of Output Level (2) | Flexible Budget: Same Budgeted Lump Sum (as in Static Budget) Regardless of Output Level (3) | Allocated: Budgeted Input Quantity Allowed for Actual Output × Budgeted Rate (4) |

(0.40 hrs./unit × 10,000 units × $57.50/hr.) (4,000 hrs. × $57.50/hr.) $230,000

$285,000

$276,000

$276,000

$9,000 U — Spending variance

Never a variance

$46,000 U — Production-volume variance

$9,000 U — Flexible-budget variance

$46,000 U — Production-volume variance

$55,000 U
Underallocated fixed overhead
(Total fixed overhead variance)

[a]F = favorable effect on operating income; U = unfavorable effect on operating income.

(in Exhibits 1 and 2, respectively), but it does so in a unified presentation that also indicates those variances that are never present.

As with other variances, the variances in Webb's 4-variance analysis are not necessarily independent of each other. For example, Webb may purchase lower-quality machine fluids (leading to a favorable variable overhead spending variance), which results in the machines taking longer to operate than budgeted (causing an unfavorable variable overhead efficiency variance), and producing less than budgeted output (causing an unfavorable production-volume variance).

Combined Variance Analysis

To keep track of all that is happening within their areas of responsibility, managers in large, complex businesses, such as General Electric and Disney, use detailed 4-variance analysis. Doing so helps them identify and focus attention on the areas not operating as expected. Managers of small businesses understand their operations better based on personal observations and nonfinancial measures. They find less value in doing the additional measurements required for 4-variance analyses. For example, to simplify their costing systems, small companies may not distinguish variable overhead incurred from fixed overhead incurred because making this distinction is often not clear-cut. Many costs such as supervision, quality control, and materials handling have both variable- and fixed-cost components that may not be easy to separate. Managers may therefore use a less detailed analysis that *combines* the variable overhead and fixed overhead into a single total overhead cost.

When a single total overhead cost category is used, it can still be analyzed in depth. The variances are now the sums of the variable overhead and fixed overhead variances for that level, as computed in Exhibit 4. The combined variance analysis looks as follows:

Combined 3-Variance Analysis

	Spending Variance	Efficiency Variance	Production-Volume Variance
Total overhead	$4,500 U	$15,000 U	$46,000 U

The accounting for 3-variance analysis is simpler than for 4-variance analysis, but some information is lost because the variable and fixed overhead spending variances are combined into a single total overhead spending variance.

Finally, the overall **total-overhead variance** is given by the sum of the preceding variances. In the Webb example, this equals $65,500 U. Note that this amount, which aggregates the flexible-budget and production-volume variances, equals the total amount of underallocated (or underapplied) overhead costs. Using figures from Exhibit 4, the $65,500 U total-overhead variance is the difference between (a) the total actual overhead incurred ($130,500 + $285,000 = $415,500) and (b) the overhead allocated ($120,000 + $230,000 = $350,000) to the actual output produced. If the total-overhead variance were favorable, it would have corresponded instead to the amount of overapplied overhead costs.

Production-Volume Variance and Sales-Volume Variance

As we complete our study of variance analysis for Webb Company, it is helpful to step back to see the "big picture" and to link the accounting and performance evaluation functions of standard costing. A static-budget variance of $93,100 U can be identified as the difference between the static budget operating income of $108,000 and the actual operating income of $14,900. That static-budget variance of $93,100 U can be subdivided into a flexible-budget variance of $29,100 U and a sales-volume variance of $64,000 U. More detailed variances subdivide, whenever possible, individual flexible-budget variances for the selling price, direct materials, direct manufacturing labor, and variable overhead. For the fixed overhead, we noted that the flexible-budget variance is the same as the spending variance. Where does the production-volume variance belong then? As you shall see, the production-volume variance is a component of the sales-volume variance. Under our assumption of actual production and sales of 10,000 jackets, Webb's

Decision Point

What is the most detailed way for a company to reconcile actual overhead incurred with the amount allocated during a period?

Learning Objective 6

Explain the relationship between the sales-volume variance and the production-volume variance

...the production-volume and operating-income volume variances together comprise the sales-volume variance

costing system debits to Work-in-Process Control the standard costs of the 10,000 jackets produced. These amounts are then transferred to Finished Goods and finally to Cost of Goods Sold:

Direct materials	
($60 per jacket × 10,000 jackets)	$ 600,000
Direct manufacturing labor	
($16 per jacket × 10,000 jackets)	160,000
Variable overhead	
($12 per jacket × 10,000 jackets)	120,000
Fixed overhead	
($23 per jacket × 10,000 jackets)	230,000
Cost of goods sold at standard cost	
($111 per jacket × 10,000 jackets)	$1,110,000

Webb's costing system also records the revenues from the 10,000 jackets sold at the budgeted selling price of $120 per jacket. The net effect of these entries on Webb's budgeted operating income is as follows:

Revenues at budgeted selling price	
($120 per jacket × 10,000 jackets)	$1,200,000
Cost of goods sold at standard cost	
($111 per jacket × 10,000 jackets)	1,110,000
Operating income based on budgeted profit per jacket	
($9 per jacket × 10,000 jackets)	$ 90,000

A crucial point to keep in mind is that under standard costing, fixed overhead costs are treated as if they are a variable cost. That is, in determining the budgeted operating income of $90,000, only $230,000 ($23 per jacket × 10,000 jackets) of the fixed overhead costs are considered, whereas the budgeted fixed overhead costs are $276,000. Webb's accountants then record the $46,000 unfavorable production-volume variance (the difference between the budgeted fixed overhead costs, $276,000, and allocated fixed overhead costs, $230,000), as well as the various flexible-budget variances (including the fixed overhead spending variance) that total $29,100 unfavorable. This results in actual operating income of $14,900 as follows:

Operating income based on budgeted profit per jacket	
($9 per jacket × 10,000 jackets)	$ 90,000
Unfavorable production-volume variance	(46,000)
Flexible-budget operating income	44,000
Unfavorable flexible-budget variance for operating income	(29,100)
Actual operating income	$ 14,900

In contrast, the static-budget operating income of $108,000 is not entered in Webb's costing system because standard costing records budgeted revenues, standard costs, and variances only for the 10,000 jackets actually produced and sold, not for the 12,000 jackets that were *planned* to be produced and sold. As a result, the sales-volume variance of $64,000 U, which is the difference between the static-budget operating income of $108,000 and the flexible-budget operating income of $44,000, is never actually recorded under standard costing. Nevertheless, the sales-volume variance is useful because it helps managers understand the lost contribution margin from selling 2,000 fewer jackets (the sales-volume variance assumes fixed costs remain at the budgeted level of $276,000).

The sales-volume variance has two components. They are as follows:

1. A difference between the static-budget operating income of $108,000 for 12,000 jackets and the budgeted operating income of $90,000 for 10,000 jackets. This is the

operating-income volume variance of $18,000 U ($108,000 − $90,000). It reflects the fact that Webb produced and sold 2,000 fewer units than budgeted.

2. A difference between the budgeted operating income of $90,000 and the flexible budget operating income of $44,000 for the 10,000 actual units. This difference arises because Webb's costing system treats fixed costs as if they behave in a variable manner and assumes fixed costs equal the allocated amount of $230,000, rather than the budgeted fixed costs of $276,000. Of course, this difference is precisely the production-volume variance of $46,000 U.

In summary, we have the following:

	Operating-income volume variance	$18,000 U
(+)	Production-volume variance	46,000 U
Equals	Sales-volume variance	$64,000 U

We can now provide a summary (see Exhibit 5) that formally disaggregates the static-budget variance of $93,100 U into its components.

We next describe the use of variance analysis in activity-based costing systems.

Variance Analysis and Activity-Based Costing

Activity-based costing (ABC) systems focus on individual activities as the fundamental cost objects. ABC systems classify the costs of various activities into a cost hierarchy—output unit-level costs, batch-level costs, product-sustaining costs, and facility-sustaining costs. In this section, we show how a company that has an ABC system and batch-level costs can benefit from variance analysis. Batch-level costs are the costs of activities related to a group of units of products or services rather than to each individual

Exhibit 5	Summary of Levels 1, 2, and 3 Variance Analysis: Webb Company for April 2014

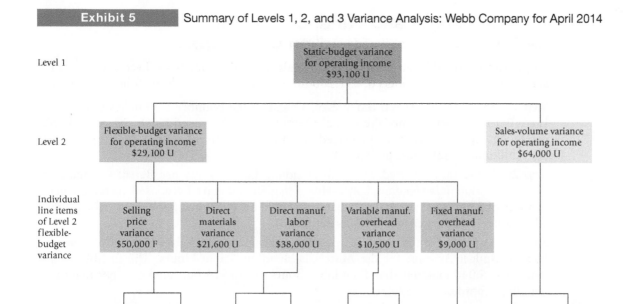

63

unit of product or service. We illustrate variance analysis for variable batch-level direct costs and fixed batch-level setup overhead costs.[4]

Consider Lyco Brass Works, which manufactures many different types of faucets and brass fittings. Because of the wide range of products it produces, Lyco uses an activity-based costing system. In contrast, Webb uses a simple costing system because it makes only one type of jacket. One of Lyco's products is Elegance, a decorative brass faucet for home spas. Lyco produces Elegance in batches.

For each product Lyco makes, it uses dedicated materials-handling labor to bring materials to the production floor, transport items in process from one work center to the next, and take the finished goods to the shipping area. Therefore, materials-handling labor costs for Elegance are direct costs of Elegance. Because the materials for a batch are moved together, materials-handling labor costs vary with number of batches rather than with number of units in a batch. Materials-handling labor costs are variable direct batch-level costs.

To manufacture a batch of Elegance, Lyco must set up the machines and molds. Employees must be highly skilled to set up the machines and molds. Hence, a separate setup department is responsible for setting up the machines and molds for different batches of products. Setup costs are overhead costs. For simplicity, assume that setup costs are fixed with respect to the number of setup-hours. The costs consist of salaries paid to engineers and supervisors and the costs of leasing setup equipment.

Information regarding Elegance for 2014 follows:

	Actual Result	Static-Budget Amount
1. Units of Elegance produced and sold	151,200	180,000
2. Batch size (units per batch)	140	150
3. Number of batches (Line 1 ÷ Line 2)	1,080	1,200
4. Materials-handling labor-hours per batch	5.25	5
5. Total materials-handling labor-hours (Line 3 × Line 4)	5,670	6,000
6. Cost per materials-handling labor-hour	$ 14.50	$ 14
7. Total materials-handling labor costs (Line 5 × Line 6)	$ 82,215	$ 84,000
8. Setup-hours per batch	6.25	6
9. Total setup-hours (Line 3 × Line 8)	6,750	7,200
10. Total fixed setup overhead costs	$220,000	$216,000

Flexible Budget and Variance Analysis for Direct Materials-Handling Labor Costs

To prepare the flexible budget for the materials-handling labor costs, Lyco starts with the actual units of output produced, 151,200 units, and proceeds with the following steps.

Step 1: Using the Budgeted Batch Size, Calculate the Number of Batches that Should Have Been Used to Produce the Actual Output. At the budgeted batch size of 150 units per batch, Lyco should have produced the 151,200 units of output in 1,008 batches (151,200 units ÷ 150 units per batch).

Step 2: Using the Budgeted Materials-Handling Labor-Hours per Batch, Calculate the Number of Materials-Handling Labor-Hours that Should Have Been Used. At the budgeted quantity of 5 hours per batch, 1,008 batches should have required 5,040 materials-handling labor-hours (1,008 batches × 5 hours per batch).

Step 3: Using the Budgeted Cost per Materials-Handling Labor-Hour, Calculate the Flexible-Budget Amount for the Materials-Handling Labor-Hours. The flexible-budget amount is 5,040 materials-handling labor-hours × the $14 budgeted cost per materials-handling labor-hour = $70,560.

Note how the flexible-budget calculations for the materials-handling labor costs focus on batch-level quantities (materials-handling labor-hours per batch rather than per unit). The flexible-budget quantity computations focus at the appropriate level of the cost hierarchy.

---

[4] The techniques we demonstrate can be applied to analyze variable batch-level overhead costs as well.

For example, because materials handling is a batch-level cost, the flexible-budget quantity calculations are made at the batch level—the quantity of materials-handling labor-hours that Lyco should have used based on the number of batches it should have used to produce the actual quantity of 151,200 units. If a cost had been a product-sustaining cost—such as product design cost—the flexible-budget quantity computations would focus at the product-sustaining level, for example, by evaluating the actual complexity of the product's design relative to the budget.

The flexible-budget variance for the materials-handling labor costs can now be calculated as follows:

$$\frac{\text{Flexible-budget}}{\text{variance}} = \text{Actual costs} - \text{Flexible-budget costs}$$
$$= (5,670 \text{ hours} \times \$14.50 \text{ per hour}) - (5,040 \text{ hours} \times \$14 \text{ per hour})$$
$$= \$82,215 - \$70,560$$
$$= \$11,655 \text{ U}$$

The unfavorable variance indicates that materials-handling labor costs were $11,655 higher than the flexible-budget target. We can get some insight into the possible reasons for this unfavorable outcome by examining the price and efficiency components of the flexible-budget variance. Exhibit 6 presents the variances in columnar form.

$$\frac{\text{Price}}{\text{variance}} = \left(\frac{\text{Actual price}}{\text{of input}} - \frac{\text{Budgeted price}}{\text{of input}}\right) \times \frac{\text{Actual quantity}}{\text{of input}}$$
$$= (\$14.50 \text{ per hour} - \$14 \text{ per hour}) \times 5,670 \text{ hours}$$
$$= \$0.50 \text{ per hour} \times 5,670 \text{ hours}$$
$$= \$2,835 \text{ U}$$

The unfavorable price variance for materials-handling labor indicates that the $14.50 actual cost per materials-handling labor-hour exceeds the $14.00 budgeted cost per materials-handling labor-hour. This variance could be the result of Lyco's human resources manager negotiating wage rates less skillfully or of wage rates increasing unexpectedly due to a scarcity of labor.

$$\frac{\text{Efficiency}}{\text{variance}} = \left(\begin{array}{c}\text{Actual} \\ \text{quantity of} \\ \text{input used}\end{array} - \begin{array}{c}\text{Budgeted quantity} \\ \text{of input allowed} \\ \text{for actual output}\end{array}\right) \times \frac{\text{Budgeted price}}{\text{of input}}$$
$$= (5,670 \text{ hours} - 5,040 \text{ hours}) \times \$14 \text{ per hour}$$
$$= 630 \text{ hours} \times \$14 \text{ per hour}$$
$$= \$8,820 \text{ U}$$

Exhibit 6	Columnar Presentation of Variance Analysis for Direct Materials-Handling Labor Costs: Lyco Brass Works for 2014[a]

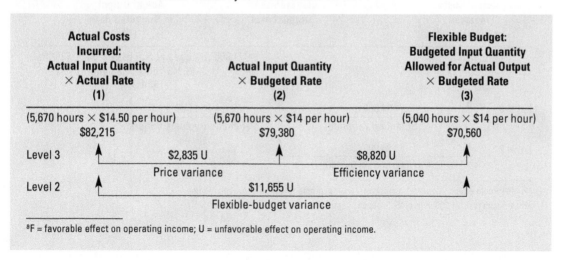

Actual Costs Incurred: Actual Input Quantity × Actual Rate (1)		Actual Input Quantity × Budgeted Rate (2)		Flexible Budget: Budgeted Input Quantity Allowed for Actual Output × Budgeted Rate (3)
(5,670 hours × $14.50 per hour) $82,215		(5,670 hours × $14 per hour) $79,380		(5,040 hours × $14 per hour) $70,560
Level 3	$2,835 U		$8,820 U	
	Price variance		Efficiency variance	
Level 2		$11,655 U		
		Flexible-budget variance		

[a]F = favorable effect on operating income; U = unfavorable effect on operating income.

The unfavorable efficiency variance indicates that the 5,670 actual materials-handling labor-hours exceeded the 5,040 budgeted materials-handling labor-hours for the actual output. Possible reasons for the unfavorable efficiency variance are as follows:

- Smaller actual batch sizes of 140 units, instead of the budgeted batch sizes of 150 units, resulted in Lyco producing the 151,200 units in 1,080 batches instead of 1,008 (151,200 ÷ 150) batches
- The actual materials-handling labor-hours per batch (5.25 hours) were higher than the budgeted materials-handling labor-hours per batch (5 hours)

Reasons for smaller-than-budgeted batch sizes could include quality problems when batch sizes exceed 140 faucets and high costs of carrying inventory.

Possible reasons for the larger actual materials-handling labor-hours per batch are as follows:

- Inefficient layout of the Elegance production line
- Materials-handling labor having to wait at work centers before picking up or delivering materials
- Unmotivated, inexperienced, and underskilled employees
- Very tight standards for materials-handling time

Identifying the reasons for the efficiency variance helps Lyco's managers develop a plan for improving its materials-handling labor efficiency and take corrective action that will be incorporated into future budgets.

We now consider fixed setup overhead costs.

Flexible Budget and Variance Analysis for Fixed Setup Overhead Costs

Exhibit 7 presents the variances for fixed setup overhead costs in columnar form.

Exhibit 7 Columnar Presentation of Fixed Setup Overhead Variance Analysis: Lyco Brass Works for 2014[a]

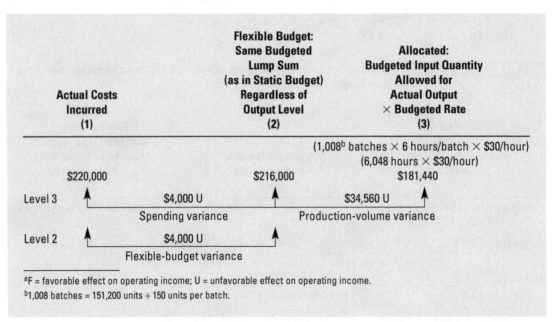

[a]F = favorable effect on operating income; U = unfavorable effect on operating income.
[b]1,008 batches = 151,200 units ÷ 150 units per batch.

Lyco's fixed setup overhead flexible-budget variance is calculated as follows:

$$
\begin{array}{c}
\text{Fixed-setup} \\
\text{overhead} \\
\text{flexible-budget} \\
\text{variance}
\end{array}
=
\begin{array}{c}
\text{Actual costs} \\
\text{incurred}
\end{array}
-
\begin{array}{c}
\text{Flexible-budget} \\
\text{costs}
\end{array}
$$

$$= \$220{,}000 - \$216{,}000$$

$$= \$4{,}000 \text{ U}$$

Note that the flexible-budget amount for the fixed setup overhead costs equals the static-budget amount of $216,000. That's because there is no "flexing" of fixed costs. Moreover, because the fixed overhead costs have no efficiency variance, the fixed setup overhead spending variance is the same as the fixed overhead flexible-budget variance. The spending variance could be unfavorable because of higher leasing costs of new setup equipment or higher salaries paid to engineers and supervisors. Lyco may have incurred these costs to alleviate some of the difficulties it was having in setting up machines.

To calculate the production-volume variance, Lyco first computes the budgeted cost-allocation rate for the fixed setup overhead costs using the same four-step approach.

Step 1: Choose the Period to Use for the Budget. Lyco uses a period of 12 months (the year 2014).

Step 2: Select the Cost-Allocation Base to Use in Allocating the Fixed Overhead Costs to the Output Produced. Lyco uses budgeted setup-hours as the cost-allocation base for fixed setup overhead costs. Budgeted setup-hours in the static budget for 2014 are 7,200 hours.

Step 3: Identify the Fixed Overhead Costs Associated with the Cost-Allocation Base. Lyco's fixed setup overhead cost budget for 2014 is $216,000.

Step 4: Compute the Rate per Unit of the Cost-Allocation Base Used to Allocate the Fixed Overhead Costs to the Output Produced. Dividing the $216,000 from Step 3 by the 7,200 setup-hours from Step 2, Lyco estimates a fixed setup overhead cost rate of $30 per setup-hour:

$$
\begin{array}{c}
\text{Budgeted fixed} \\
\text{setup overhead} \\
\text{cost per unit of} \\
\text{cost-allocation base}
\end{array}
=
\begin{array}{c}
\text{Budgeted total costs} \\
\text{in fixed overhead cost pool} \\
\hline
\text{Budgeted total quantity of} \\
\text{cost-allocation base}
\end{array}
=
\frac{\$216{,}000}{7{,}200 \text{ setup hours}}
$$

$$= \$30 \text{ per setup-hour}$$

$$
\begin{array}{c}
\text{Production-volume} \\
\text{variance for} \\
\text{fixed setup} \\
\text{overhead costs}
\end{array}
=
\begin{array}{c}
\text{Budgeted} \\
\text{fixed setup} \\
\text{overhead} \\
\text{costs}
\end{array}
-
\begin{array}{c}
\text{Fixed setup overhead} \\
\text{allocation using budgeted} \\
\text{input allowed for actual} \\
\text{output units produced}
\end{array}
$$

$$= \$216{,}000 - (1{,}008 \text{ batches} \times 6 \text{ hours/batch}) \times \$30/\text{hour}$$

$$= \$216{,}000 - (6{,}048 \text{ hours} \times \$30/\text{hour})$$

$$= \$216{,}000 - \$181{,}440$$

$$= \$34{,}560 \text{ U}$$

During 2014, Lyco planned to produce 180,000 units of Elegance but actually produced 151,200 units. The unfavorable production-volume variance measures the amount of extra fixed setup costs Lyco incurred for setup capacity it did not use. One interpretation is that the unfavorable $34,560 production-volume variance represents an inefficient use of the company's setup capacity. However, Lyco may have earned higher operating income by selling 151,200 units at a higher price than 180,000 units at a lower price. As a result, Lyco's managers should interpret the production-volume variance cautiously because it does not consider the effect of output on selling prices and operating income.

◀ **Decision Point**

How can variance analysis be used in an activity-based costing system?

Overhead Variances in Nonmanufacturing Settings

Our Webb Company example examined variable and fixed manufacturing overhead costs. Managers can also use variance analysis to examine the overhead costs of the nonmanufacturing areas of the company and to make decisions about (1) pricing, (2) managing costs, and (3) the mix of products to make. For example, when product distribution costs are high, as they are in the automobile, consumer durables, cement, and steel industries, standard costing can provide managers with reliable and timely information on variable distribution overhead spending variances and efficiency variances.

What about service-sector companies such as airlines, hospitals, hotels, and railroads? How can they benefit from variance analyses? The output measures these companies commonly use are passenger-miles flown, patient days provided, room-days occupied, and ton-miles of freight hauled, respectively. Few costs can be traced to these outputs in a cost-effective way. Most of the costs are fixed overhead costs, such as the costs of equipment, buildings, and staff. Using capacity effectively is the key to profitability, and fixed overhead variances can help managers in this task. Retail businesses, such as Kmart, also have high capacity-related fixed costs (lease and occupancy costs). In the case of Kmart, sales declines resulted in unused capacity and unfavorable fixed-cost variances. Kmart reduced its fixed costs by closing some of its stores, but it also had to file for Chapter 11 bankruptcy.

Consider the following data for United Airlines for selected years from the past decade. Available seat miles (ASMs) are the actual seats in an airplane multiplied by the distance the plane traveled.

Year	Total ASMs (Millions) (1)	Operating Revenue per ASM (2)	Operating Cost per ASM (3)	Operating Income per ASM (4) = (2) − (3)
2000	175,493	10.2 cents	10.0 cents	0.2 cents
2003	136,566	8.6 cents	9.8 cents	−1.2 cents
2006	143,085	10.6 cents	10.8 cents	−0.2 cents
2008	135,859	11.9 cents	13.6 cents	−1.4 cents
2011	118,973	13.1 cents	13.5 cents	−0.4 cents

When air travel declined after terrorists hijacked a number of commercial jets on September 11, 2001, United's revenues fell. However most of the company's fixed costs—for its airport facilities, equipment, personnel, and so on—did not. United had a large unfavorable production-volume variance because its capacity was underutilized. As column 1 of the table indicates, United responded by reducing its capacity substantially over the next few years. Available seat miles (ASMs) declined from 175,493 million in 2000 to 136,566 million in 2003. Yet United was unable to fill even the planes it had retained, so its revenue per ASM declined (column 2) and its cost per ASM stayed roughly the same (column 3). United filed for Chapter 11 bankruptcy in December 2002 and began seeking government guarantees to obtain the loans it needed. Subsequently, strong demand for airline travel, as well as productivity improvements resulting from the more efficient use of resources and networks, led to increased traffic and higher average ticket prices. By maintaining a disciplined approach to capacity and tight control over growth, United saw over a 20% increase in its revenue per ASM between 2003 and 2006. The improvement in performance allowed United to come out of bankruptcy on February 1, 2006. In the past few years, however, the global recession and soaring jet fuel prices have had a significant negative impact on United's performance, as reflected in the continued negative operating incomes and the further decline in capacity. In May 2010, a merger agreement was reached between United and Continental Airlines, and Continental was dissolved in 2012.

Financial and Nonfinancial Performance Measures

The overhead variances discussed in this chapter are examples of financial performance measures. As the preceding examples illustrate, nonfinancial measures such as those related to capacity utilization and physical measures of input usage also provide useful information. The nonfinancial measures that managers of Webb would likely find helpful in planning and controlling its overhead costs include the following:

1. Quantity of actual indirect materials used per machine-hour, relative to the quantity of budgeted indirect materials used per machine-hour

2. Actual energy used per machine-hour, relative to the budgeted energy used per machine-hour

3. Actual machine-hours per jacket, relative to the budgeted machine-hours per jacket

These performance measures, like the financial variances discussed in this chapter, alert managers to problems and probably would be reported daily or hourly on the production floor. The overhead variances we discussed in this chapter capture the financial effects of items such as the three factors listed, which in many cases first appear as nonfinancial performance measures. An especially interesting example along these lines comes from Japan: Some Japanese companies have begun reining in their CO_2 emissions in part by doing a budgeted-to-actual variance analysis of the emissions. The goal is to make employees aware of the emissions and reduce them in advance of greenhouse-gas reduction plans being drawn up by the Japanese government.

Finally, both financial and nonfinancial performance measures are used to evaluate the performance of managers. Exclusive reliance on either is always too simplistic because each gives a different perspective on performance. Nonfinancial measures (such as those described previously) provide feedback on individual aspects of a manager's performance, whereas financial measures evaluate the overall effect of and the tradeoffs among different nonfinancial performance measures.

◀ **Decision Point**

How are overhead variances useful in nonmanufacturing settings?

Problem for Self-Study

Nina Garcia is the newly appointed president of Laser Products. She is examining the May 2014 results for the Aerospace Products Division. This division manufactures wing parts for satellites. Garcia's current concern is with manufacturing overhead costs at the Aerospace Products Division. Both variable and fixed overhead costs are allocated to the wing parts on the basis of laser-cutting-hours. The following budget information is available:

Budgeted variable overhead rate	$200 per hour
Budgeted fixed overhead rate	$240 per hour
Budgeted laser-cutting time per wing part	1.5 hours
Budgeted production and sales for May 2014	5,000 wing parts
Budgeted fixed overhead costs for May 2014	$1,800,000

Actual results for May 2014 are as follows:

Wing parts produced and sold	4,800 units
Laser-cutting-hours used	8,400 hours
Variable overhead costs	$1,478,400
Fixed overhead costs	$1,832,200

1. Compute the spending variance and the efficiency variance for variable overhead.
2. Compute the spending variance and the production-volume variance for fixed overhead.
3. Give two explanations for each of the variances calculated in requirements 1 and 2.

Required

Solution

1 and 2. See Exhibit 8.

3. a. Variable overhead spending variance, $201,600 F. One possible reason for this variance is that the actual prices of individual items included in variable overhead (such as cutting fluids) are lower than budgeted prices. A second possible reason is that the percentage increase in the actual quantity usage of individual items in the variable overhead cost pool is less than the percentage increase in laser-cutting-hours compared to the flexible budget.

   b. Variable overhead efficiency variance, $240,000 U. One possible reason for this variance is inadequate maintenance of laser machines, causing them to take more

Exhibit 8	Columnar Presentation of Integrated Variance Analysis: Laser Products for May 2014[a]

PANEL A: Variable (Manufacturing) Overhead

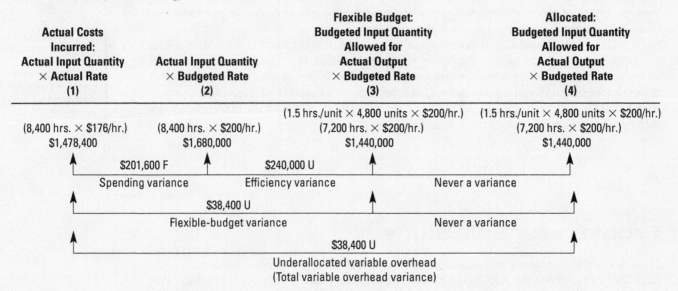

PANEL B: Fixed (Manufacturing) Overhead

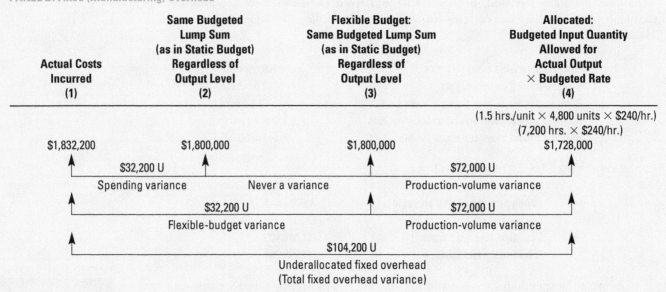

[a]F = favorable effect on operating income; U = unfavorable effect on operating income.

Source: Republished with permission of Strategic Finance by Paul Sherman. Copyright 2003 by Institute of Management Accountants. Permission conveyed through Copyright Clearance Center, Inc.

laser-cutting time per wing part. A second possible reason is use of undermotivated, inexperienced, or underskilled workers operating the laser-cutting machines, resulting in more laser-cutting time per wing part.

c. Fixed overhead spending variance, $32,200 U. One possible reason for this variance is that the actual prices of individual items in the fixed-cost pool unexpectedly increased from the prices budgeted (such as an unexpected increase in the cost of leasing each machine). A second possible reason is that the Aerospace Products Division had to lease more machines or hire more supervisors than had been budgeted.

d. Production-volume variance, $72,000 U. Actual production of wing parts is 4,800 units, compared with 5,000 units budgeted. One possible reason for this variance is demand factors, such as a decline in an aerospace program that led to a decline in demand for aircraft parts. A second possible reason is supply factors, such as a production stoppage due to labor problems or machine breakdowns.

▶ Decision Points

The following question-and-answer format summarizes the chapter's learning objectives. Each decision presents a key question related to a learning objective. The guidelines are the answer to that question.

Decision	Guidelines
1. How do managers plan variable overhead costs and fixed overhead costs?	Planning of both variable and fixed overhead costs involves undertaking only activities that add value and then being efficient in that undertaking. The key difference is that for variable-cost planning, ongoing decisions during the budget period play a much larger role; for fixed-cost planning, most key decisions are made before the start of the period.
2. How are budgeted variable overhead and fixed overhead cost rates calculated?	The budgeted variable (fixed) overhead cost rate is calculated by dividing the budgeted variable (fixed) overhead costs by the denominator level of the cost-allocation base.
3. What variances can be calculated for variable overhead costs?	When the flexible budget for variable overhead is developed, an overhead efficiency variance and an overhead spending variance can be computed. The variable overhead efficiency variance focuses on the difference between the actual quantity of the cost-allocation base used relative to the budgeted quantity of the cost-allocation base. The variable overhead spending variance focuses on the difference between the actual variable overhead cost per unit of the cost-allocation base relative to the budgeted variable overhead cost per unit of the cost-allocation base.
4. What variances can be calculated for fixed overhead costs?	For fixed overhead, the static and flexible budgets coincide. The difference between the budgeted and actual amount of fixed overhead is the flexible-budget variance, also referred to as the spending variance. The production-volume variance measures the difference between the budgeted fixed overhead and the fixed overhead allocated on the basis of actual output produced.
5. What is the most detailed way for a company to reconcile actual overhead incurred with the amount allocated during a period?	A 4-variance analysis presents spending and efficiency variances for variable overhead costs and spending and production-volume variances for fixed overhead costs. By analyzing these four variances together, managers can reconcile the actual overhead costs with the amount of overhead allocated to the output produced during a period.
6. What is the relationship between the sales-volume variance and the production-volume variance?	The production-volume variance is a component of the sales-volume variance. The production-volume and operating-income volume variances together comprise the sales-volume variance.

Decision	Guidelines
7. How can variance analysis be used in an activity-based costing system?	Flexible budgets in ABC systems give insight into why actual activity costs differ from budgeted activity costs. Using output and input measures for an activity, a comprehensive variance analysis can be conducted.
8. How are overhead variances useful in nonmanufacturing settings?	Managers can analyze variances for all variable overhead costs, including those outside the manufacturing function. The analysis can be used to make pricing and product mix decisions and to manage costs. Fixed overhead variances are especially important in service settings, where using capacity effectively is the key to profitability. In all cases, the information provided by variances can be supplemented by the use of suitable nonfinancial metrics.

Terms to Learn

The chapter contains definitions of the following important terms:

denominator level

denominator-level variance

fixed overhead flexible-budget variance

fixed overhead spending variance

operating-income volume variance

production-volume variance

standard costing

total-overhead variance

variable overhead efficiency variance

variable overhead flexible-budget variance

variable overhead spending variance

Assignment Material

MyAccountingLab

Questions

1 How do managers plan for variable overhead costs?
2 How does the planning of fixed overhead costs differ from the planning of variable overhead costs?
3 How does standard costing differ from actual costing?
4 What are the steps in developing a budgeted variable overhead cost-allocation rate?
5 What are the factors that affect the spending variance for variable manufacturing overhead?
6 Assume variable manufacturing overhead is allocated using machine-hours. Give three possible reasons for a favorable variable overhead efficiency variance.
7 Describe the difference between a direct materials efficiency variance and a variable manufacturing overhead efficiency variance.
8 What are the steps in developing a budgeted fixed overhead rate?
9 Why is the flexible-budget variance the same amount as the spending variance for fixed manufacturing overhead?
10 Explain how the analysis of fixed manufacturing overhead costs differs for (a) planning and control and (b) inventory costing for financial reporting.
11 Provide one caveat that will affect whether a production-volume variance is a good measure of the economic cost of unused capacity.
12 "The production-volume variance should always be written off to Cost of Goods Sold." Do you agree? Explain.
13 What are the variances in a 4-variance analysis?
14 "Overhead variances should be viewed as interdependent rather than independent." Give an example.
15 Describe how flexible-budget variance analysis can be used in the control of costs of activity areas.

MyAccountingLab

Exercises

16 **Variable manufacturing overhead, variance analysis.** Esquire Clothing is a manufacturer of designer suits. The cost of each suit is the sum of three variable costs (direct material costs, direct

manufacturing labor costs, and manufacturing overhead costs) and one fixed-cost category (manufacturing overhead costs). Variable manufacturing overhead cost is allocated to each suit on the basis of budgeted direct manufacturing labor-hours per suit. For June 2014, each suit is budgeted to take 4 labor-hours. Budgeted variable manufacturing overhead cost per labor-hour is $12. The budgeted number of suits to be manufactured in June 2014 is 1,040.

Actual variable manufacturing costs in June 2014 were $52,164 for 1,080 suits started and completed. There were no beginning or ending inventories of suits. Actual direct manufacturing labor-hours for June were 4,536.

1. Compute the flexible-budget variance, the spending variance, and the efficiency variance for variable manufacturing overhead.
2. Comment on the results.

Required

17 Fixed manufacturing overhead, variance analysis (continuation of 16). Esquire Clothing allocates fixed manufacturing overhead to each suit using budgeted direct manufacturing labor-hours per suit. Data pertaining to fixed manufacturing overhead costs for June 2014 are budgeted, $62,400, and actual, $63,916.

1. Compute the spending variance for fixed manufacturing overhead. Comment on the results.
2. Compute the production-volume variance for June 2014. What inferences can Esquire Clothing draw from this variance?

Required

18 Variable manufacturing overhead variance analysis. The French Bread Company bakes baguettes for distribution to upscale grocery stores. The company has two direct-cost categories: direct materials and direct manufacturing labor. Variable manufacturing overhead is allocated to products on the basis of standard direct manufacturing labor-hours. Following is some budget data for the French Bread Company:

Direct manufacturing labor use	0.02 hours per baguette
Variable manufacturing overhead	$10.00 per direct manufacturing labor-hour

The French Bread Company provides the following additional data for the year ended December 31, 2014:

Planned (budgeted) output	3,200,000 baguettes
Actual production	2,800,000 baguettes
Direct manufacturing labor	50,400 hours
Actual variable manufacturing overhead	$680,400

1. What is the denominator level used for allocating variable manufacturing overhead? (That is, for how many direct manufacturing labor-hours is French Bread budgeting?)
2. Prepare a variance analysis of variable manufacturing overhead. Use Exhibit 4 for reference.
3. Discuss the variances you have calculated and give possible explanations for them.

Required

19 Fixed manufacturing overhead variance analysis (continuation of 18). The French Bread Company also allocates fixed manufacturing overhead to products on the basis of standard direct manufacturing labor-hours. For 2014, fixed manufacturing overhead was budgeted at $4.00 per direct manufacturing labor-hour. Actual fixed manufacturing overhead incurred during the year was $272,000.

1. Prepare a variance analysis of fixed manufacturing overhead cost. Use Exhibit 4 as a guide.
2. Is fixed overhead underallocated or overallocated? By what amount?
3. Comment on your results. Discuss the variances and explain what may be driving them.

Required

20 Manufacturing overhead, variance analysis. The Principles Corporation is a manufacturer of centrifuges. Fixed and variable manufacturing overheads are allocated to each centrifuge using budgeted assembly-hours. Budgeted assembly time is 2 hours per unit. The following table shows the budgeted amounts and actual results related to overhead for June 2014.

	Home	Insert	Page Layout	Formulas	Data	Review	View	
	A	B	C	D	E		F	G
1			The Principles Corporation (June 2014)				Actual Results	Static Budget
2	Number of centrifuges assembled and sold						225	110
3	Hours of assembly time						360	
4	Variable manufacturing overhead cost per hour of assembly time							$32.00
5	Variable manufacturing overhead costs						$11,933	
6	Fixed manufacturing overhead costs						$12,180	$10,780

Flexible Budgets, Overhead Cost Variances, and Management Control

1. Prepare an analysis of all variable manufacturing overhead and fixed manufacturing overhead variances using the columnar approach in Exhibit 4.
2. Prepare journal entries for Principles' June 2014 variable and fixed manufacturing overhead costs and variances; write off these variances to cost of goods sold for the quarter ending June 30, 2014.
3. How does the planning and control of variable manufacturing overhead costs differ from the planning and control of fixed manufacturing overhead costs?

21 4-variance analysis, fill in the blanks. Rozema, Inc., produces chemicals for large biotech companies. It has the following data for manufacturing overhead costs during August 2015:

	Variable	Fixed
Actual costs incurred	$31,000	$18,000
Costs allocated to products	33,000	14,600
Flexible budget	——	13,400
Actual input × budgeted rate	30,800	——

Use F for favorable and U for unfavorable:

	Variable	Fixed
(1) Spending variance	$____	$____
(2) Efficiency variance	____	____
(3) Production-volume variance	____	____
(4) Flexible-budget variance	____	____
(5) Underallocated (overallocated) manufacturing overhead	____	____

22 Straightforward 4-variance overhead analysis. The Lopez Company uses standard costing in its manufacturing plant for auto parts. The standard cost of a particular auto part, based on a denominator level of 4,000 output units per year, included 6 machine-hours of variable manufacturing overhead at $8 per hour and 6 machine-hours of fixed manufacturing overhead at $15 per hour. Actual output produced was 4,400 units. Variable manufacturing overhead incurred was $245,000. Fixed manufacturing overhead incurred was $373,000. Actual machine-hours were 28,400.

1. Prepare an analysis of all variable manufacturing overhead and fixed manufacturing overhead variances, using the 4-variance analysis in Exhibit 4.
2. Prepare journal entries using the 4-variance analysis.
3. Describe how individual fixed manufacturing overhead items are controlled from day to day.
4. Discuss possible causes of the fixed manufacturing overhead variances.

23 Straightforward coverage of manufacturing overhead, standard-costing system. The Singapore division of a Canadian telecommunications company uses standard costing for its machine-paced production of telephone equipment. Data regarding production during June are as follows:

Variable manufacturing overhead costs incurred	$618,840
Variable manufacturing overhead cost rate	$8 per standard machine-hour
Fixed manufacturing overhead costs incurred	$145,790
Fixed manufacturing overhead costs budgeted	$144,000
Denominator level in machine-hours	72,000
Standard machine-hour allowed per unit of output	1.2
Units of output	65,500
Actual machine-hours used	76,400
Ending work-in-process inventory	0

1. Prepare an analysis of all manufacturing overhead variances. Use the 4-variance analysis framework illustrated in Exhibit 4.
2. Prepare journal entries for manufacturing overhead costs and their variances.
3. Describe how individual variable manufacturing overhead items are controlled from day to day.
4. Discuss possible causes of the variable manufacturing overhead variances.

24 Overhead variances, service sector. Easy Meals Now (EMN) operates a meal home-delivery service. It has agreements with 20 restaurants to pick up and deliver meals to customers who phone or fax orders to EMN. EMN allocates variable and fixed overhead costs on the basis of delivery time. EMN's owner, Steve Roberts, obtains the following information for May 2014 overhead costs:

	Home Insert Page Layout Formulas Data Review		
	A	B	C
1	**Easy Meals Now (May 2014)**	**Actual Results**	**Static Budget**
2	Output units (number of deliveries)	8,600	12,000
3	Hours per delivery		0.70
4	Hours of delivery time	5,660	
5	Variable overhead cost per hour of delivery time		$1.75
6	Variable overhead costs	$11,320	
7	Fixed overhead costs	$39,600	$33,600

Required

1. Compute spending and efficiency variances for EMN's variable overhead in May 2014.
2. Compute the spending variance and production-volume variance for EMN's fixed overhead in May 2014.
3. Comment on EMN's overhead variances and suggest how Steve Roberts might manage EMN's variable overhead differently from its fixed overhead costs.

25 Total overhead, 3-variance analysis. Ames Air Force Base has a bay that specializes in maintenance for aircraft engines. It uses standard costing and flexible budgets to account for this activity. For 2014, budgeted variable overhead at a level of 8,000 standard monthly direct labor-hours was $64,000; budgeted total overhead at 10,000 standard monthly direct labor-hours was $197,600. The standard cost allocated to repair output included a total overhead rate of 120% of standard direct labor costs.

For February, Ames incurred total overhead of $249,000 and direct labor costs of $202,440. The direct labor price variance was $9,640 unfavorable. The direct labor flexible-budget variance was $14,440 unfavorable. The standard labor price was $16 per hour. The production-volume variance was $14,000 favorable.

Required

1. Compute the direct labor efficiency variance.
2. Compute the denominator level and the spending and efficiency variances for total overhead.
3. Describe how individual variable overhead items are controlled from day to day. Also, describe how individual fixed overhead items are controlled.

26 Production-volume variance analysis and sales volume variance. Marissa Designs, Inc., makes jewelry in the shape of geometric patterns. Each piece is handmade and takes an average of 1.5 hours to produce because of the intricate design and scrollwork. Marissa uses direct labor-hours to allocate the overhead cost to production. Fixed overhead costs, including rent, depreciation, supervisory salaries, and other production expenses, are budgeted at $10,800 per month. These costs are incurred for a facility large enough to produce 1,200 pieces of jewelry a month.

During the month of February, Marissa produced 720 pieces of jewelry and actual fixed costs were $11,400.

Required

1. Calculate the fixed overhead spending variance and indicate whether it is favorable (F) or unfavorable (U).
2. If Marissa uses direct labor-hours available at capacity to calculate the budgeted fixed overhead rate, what is the production-volume variance? Indicate whether it is favorable (F) or unfavorable (U).
3. An unfavorable production-volume variance could be interpreted as the economic cost of unused capacity. Why would Marissa be willing to incur this cost?
4. Marissa's budgeted variable cost per unit is $25, and it expects to sell its jewelry for $55 apiece. Compute the sales-volume variance and reconcile it with the production-volume variance calculated in requirement 2. What does each concept measure?

27 Overhead variances, service setting. Munich Partners provides a diverse array of back office services to its clients in the financial services industry, ranging from record keeping and compliance to order processing and trade settlement. Munich has grown increasingly reliant on technology to acquire, retain, and serve its clients. Worried that its spending on information technology is getting out of control, Munich has recently embraced variance analysis as a tool for cost management.

After some study, Munich determines that its variable and fixed technology overhead costs are both driven by the processing time involved in meeting client requests. This is typically measured in CPU units of usage of a high-performance computing cluster. Munich's primary measure of output is the number of client interactions its partners have in a given period.

The following information pertains to the first quarter of 2014 (dollars in thousands):

Budgeted Output Units	14,000 client interactions
Budgeted Fixed Technology Overhead	$ 11,200
Budgeted Variable Technology Overhead	$ 1.50 per CPU unit
Budgeted CPU units	0.2 units per client interaction
Fixed Technology Overhead incurred	$ 12,200
CPU Units used	4,000
Variable Technology Overhead incurred	$ 5,500
Actual Output Units	15,000 client interactions

1. Calculate the variable overhead spending and efficiency variances, and indicate whether each is favorable (F) or unfavorable (U).
2. Calculate the fixed overhead spending and production volume variances, and indicate whether each is favorable (F) or unfavorable (U).
3. Comment on Munich Partners' overhead variances. In your view, is the firm right to be worried about its control over technology spending?

28 Identifying favorable and unfavorable variances. Purdue, Inc., manufactures tires for large auto companies. It uses standard costing and allocates variable and fixed manufacturing overhead based on machine-hours. For each independent scenario given, indicate whether each of the manufacturing variances will be favorable or unfavorable or, in case of insufficient information, indicate "CBD" (cannot be determined).

Scenario	Variable Overhead Spending Variance	Variable Overhead Efficiency Variance	Fixed Overhead Spending Variance	Fixed Overhead Production-Volume Variance
Production output is 6% less than budgeted, and actual fixed manufacturing overhead costs are 5% more than budgeted				
Production output is 13% less than budgeted; actual machine-hours are 7% more than budgeted				
Production output is 10% more than budgeted				
Actual machine-hours are 20% less than flexible-budget machine-hours				
Relative to the flexible budget, actual machine-hours are 15% less, and actual variable manufacturing overhead costs are 20% greater				

29 Flexible-budget variances. Michael Roberts is a cost accountant and business analyst for Darby Design Company (DDC), which manufactures expensive brass doorknobs. DDC uses two direct cost categories: direct materials and direct manufacturing labor. Roberts feels that manufacturing overhead is most closely related to material usage. Therefore, DDC allocates manufacturing overhead to production based upon pounds of materials used.

At the beginning of 2014, DDC budgeted annual production of 410,000 doorknobs and adopted the following standards for each doorknob:

	Input	Cost/Doorknob
Direct materials (brass)	0.3 lb. @ $9/lb.	$ 2.70
Direct manufacturing labor	1.2 hours @ $16/hour	19.20
Manufacturing overhead:		
Variable	$4/lb. × 0.3 lb.	1.20
Fixed	$14/lb. × 0.3 lb.	4.20
Standard cost per doorknob		$27.30

Actual results for April 2014 were as follows:

Production	32,000 doorknobs
Direct materials purchased	12,900 lb. at $10/lb.
Direct materials used	9,000 lbs.
Direct manufacturing labor	29,600 hours for $621,600
Variable manufacturing overhead	$ 64,900
Fixed manufacturing overhead	$160,000

Required

1. For the month of April, compute the following variances, indicating whether each is favorable (F) or unfavorable (U):
   a. Direct materials price variance (based on purchases)
   b. Direct materials efficiency variance
   c. Direct manufacturing labor price variance
   d. Direct manufacturing labor efficiency variance
   e. Variable manufacturing overhead spending variance
   f. Variable manufacturing overhead efficiency variance
   g. Production-volume variance
   h. Fixed manufacturing overhead spending variance

2. Can Roberts use any of the variances to help explain any of the other variances? Give examples.

Problems

MyAccountingLab

30 Comprehensive variance analysis. Chef Whiz manufactures premium food processors. The following are some manufacturing overhead data for Chef Whiz for the year ended December 31, 2014:

Manufacturing Overhead	Actual Results	Flexible Budget	Allocated Amount
Variable	$51,480	$79,950	$79,950
Fixed	350,210	343,980	380,250

Budgeted number of output units: 588
Planned allocation rate: 3 machine-hours per unit
Actual number of machine-hours used: 1,170
Static-budget variable manufacturing overhead costs: $72,324

Compute the following quantities (you should be able to do so in the prescribed order):

Required

1. Budgeted number of machine-hours planned
2. Budgeted fixed manufacturing overhead costs per machine-hour
3. Budgeted variable manufacturing overhead costs per machine-hour
4. Budgeted number of machine-hours allowed for actual output produced
5. Actual number of output units
6. Actual number of machine-hours used per output unit

31 Journal entries (continuation of 30).

1. Prepare journal entries for variable and fixed manufacturing overhead (you will need to calculate the various variances to accomplish this).
2. Overhead variances are written off to the Cost of Goods Sold (COGS) account at the end of the fiscal year. Show how COGS is adjusted through journal entries.

Required

32 Graphs and overhead variances. Best Around, Inc., is a manufacturer of vacuums and uses standard costing. Manufacturing overhead (both variable and fixed) is allocated to products on the basis of budgeted machine-hours. In 2014, budgeted fixed manufacturing overhead cost was $17,000,000. Budgeted variable manufacturing overhead was $10 per machine-hour. The denominator level was 1,000,000 machine-hours.

Required

1. Prepare a graph for fixed manufacturing overhead. The graph should display how Best Around, Inc.'s fixed manufacturing overhead costs will be depicted for the purposes of (a) planning and control and (b) inventory costing.

2. Suppose that 1,125,000 machine-hours were allowed for actual output produced in 2014, but 1,200,000 actual machine-hours were used. Actual manufacturing overhead was $12,075,000, variable, and $17,100,000, fixed. Compute (a) the variable manufacturing overhead spending and efficiency variances and (b) the fixed manufacturing overhead spending and production-volume variances. Use the columnar presentation illustrated in Exhibit 4.

3. What is the amount of the under- or overallocated variable manufacturing overhead and the under- or overallocated fixed manufacturing overhead? Why are the flexible-budget variance and the under- or overallocated overhead amount always the same for variable manufacturing overhead but rarely the same for fixed manufacturing overhead?

4. Suppose the denominator level was 1,700,000 rather than 1,000,000 machine-hours. What variances in requirement 2 would be affected? Recompute them.

33 Overhead variance, missing information. Consider the following two situations—cases A and B—independently. Data refer to operations for April 2014. For each situation, assume standard costing. Also assume the use of a flexible budget for control of variable and fixed manufacturing overhead based oı machine-hours.

		Cases	
		A	B
(1)	Fixed manufacturing overhead incurred	$ 84,920	$23,180
(2)	Variable manufacturing overhead incurred	$120,400	—
(3)	Denominator level in machine-hours	—	1,000
(4)	Standard machine-hours allowed for actual output achieved	6,200	—
(5)	Fixed manufacturing overhead (per standard machine-hour)	—	—
Flexible-Budget Data:			
(6)	Variable manufacturing overhead (per standard machine-hour)	—	$ 42.00
(7)	Budgeted fixed manufacturing overhead	$ 88,200	$20,000
(8)	Budgeted variable manufacturing overhead[a]	—	—
(9)	Total budgeted manufacturing overhead[a]	—	—
Additional Data:			
(10)	Standard variable manufacturing overhead allocated	$124,000	—
(11)	Standard fixed manufacturing overhead allocated	$ 86,800	—
(12)	Production-volume variance	—	$ 4,000 F
(13)	Variable manufacturing overhead spending variance	$ 5,000 F	$ 2,282 F
(14)	Variable manufacturing overhead efficiency variance	—	$ 2,478 F
(15)	Fixed manufacturing overhead spending variance	—	—
(16)	Actual machine-hours used	—	—

[a]For standard machine-hours allowed for actual output produced.

Required

Fill in the blanks under each case. [*Hint:* Prepare a worksheet similar to that in Exhibit 4. Fill in the knowns and then solve for the unknowns.]

34 Flexible budgets, 4-variance analysis. (CMA, adapted) Wilson Products uses standard costing. It allocates manufacturing overhead (both variable and fixed) to products on the basis of standard direct manufacturing labor-hours (DLH). Wilson Products develops its manufacturing overhead rate from the current annual budget. The manufacturing overhead budget for 2014 is based on budgeted output of 672,000 units, requiring 3,360,000 DLH. The company is able to schedule production uniformly throughout the year.

A total of 72,000 output units requiring 321,000 DLH was produced during May 2014. Manufacturing overhead (MOH) costs incurred for May amounted to $355,800. The actual costs, compared with the annual budget and 1/12 of the annual budget, are as follows:

Annual Manufacturing Overhead Budget 2014

	Total Amount	Per Output Unit	Per DLH Input Unit	Monthly MOH Budget May 2014	Actual MOH Costs for May 2014
Variable MOH					
Indirect manufacturing labor	$1,008,000	$1.50	$0.30	$ 84,000	$ 84,000
Supplies	672,000	1.00	0.20	56,000	117,000
Fixed MOH					
Supervision	571,200	0.85	0.17	47,600	41,000
Utilities	369,600	0.55	0.11	30,800	55,000
Depreciation	705,600	1.05	0.21	58,800	88,800
Total	$3,326,400	$4.95	$0.99	$277,200	$355,800

Calculate the following amounts for Wilson Products for May 2014:

Required

1. Total manufacturing overhead costs allocated
2. Variable manufacturing overhead spending variance
3. Fixed manufacturing overhead spending variance
4. Variable manufacturing overhead efficiency variance
5. Production-volume variance

Be sure to identify each variance as favorable (F) or unfavorable (U).

35 Activity-based costing, batch-level variance analysis. Audrina's Fleet Feet, Inc., produces dance shoes for stores all over the world. While the pairs of shoes are boxed individually, they are crated and shipped in batches. The shipping department records both variable direct batch-level costs and fixed batch-level overhead costs. The following information pertains to shipping department costs for 2014.

	Static-Budget Amounts	Actual Results
Pairs of shoes shipped	225,000	180,000
Average number of pairs of shoes per crate	15	10
Packing hours per crate	0.9 hours	1.1 hour
Variable direct cost per hour	$18	$16
Fixed overhead cost	$54,000	$56,500

Required

1. What is the static budget number of crates for 2014?
2. What is the flexible budget number of crates for 2014?
3. What is the actual number of crates shipped in 2014?
4. Assuming fixed overhead is allocated using crate-packing hours, what is the predetermined fixed overhead allocation rate?
5. For variable direct batch-level costs, compute the price and efficiency variances.
6. For fixed overhead costs, compute the spending and the production-volume variances.

36 Overhead variances and sales volume variance. Birken Company manufactures shopping bags made of recycled plastic that it plans to sell for $5 each. Birken budgets production and sales of 800,000 bags for 2014, with a standard of 400,000 machine-hours for the whole year. Budgeted fixed overhead costs are $500,000, and variable overhead cost is $1.60 per machine-hour.

Because of increased demand, Birken actually produced and sold 900,000 bags in 2014, using a total of 440,000 machine-hours. Actual variable overhead costs are $699,600 and actual fixed overhead is $501,900. Actual selling price is $6 per bag.

Direct materials and direct labor actual costs were the same as standard costs, which were $1.20 per unit and $1.80 per unit, respectively.

Required

1. Calculate the variable overhead and fixed overhead variances (spending, efficiency, spending, and volume).
2. Create a chart showing Flexible Budget Variances and Sales Volume Variances for revenues, costs, contribution margin, and operating income.
3. Calculate the operating income based on budgeted profit per shopping bag.

4. Reconcile the budgeted operating income from requirement 3 to the actual operating income from your chart in requirement 2.
5. Calculate the operating income volume variance and show how the sales volume variance is composed of the production volume variance and the operating income volume variance.

37 Activity-based costing, batch-level variance analysis. Rae Steven Publishing Company specializes in printing specialty textbooks for a small but profitable college market. Due to the high setup costs for each batch printed, Rae Steven holds the book requests until demand for a book is approximately 520. At that point Rae Steven will schedule the setup and production of the book. For rush orders, Rae Steven will produce smaller batches for an additional charge of $987 per setup.

Budgeted and actual costs for the printing process for 2014 were as follows:

	Static-Budget Amounts	Actual Results
Number of books produced	197,600	225,680
Average number of books per setup	520	496
Hours to set up printers	7 hours	7.5 hours
Direct variable cost per setup-hour	$130	$70
Total fixed setup overhead costs	$53,200	$68,000

Required

1. What is the static budget number of setups for 2014?
2. What is the flexible budget number of setups for 2014?
3. What is the actual number of setups in 2014?
4. Assuming fixed setup overhead costs are allocated using setup-hours, what is the predetermined fixed setup overhead allocation rate?
5. Does Rae Steven's charge of $987 cover the budgeted direct variable cost of an order? The budgeted total cost?
6. For direct variable setup costs, compute the price and efficiency variances.
7. For fixed setup overhead costs, compute the spending and the production-volume variances.
8. What qualitative factors should Rae Steven consider before accepting or rejecting a special order?

38 Comprehensive review, working backward from given variances. The Gallo Company uses a flexible budget and standard costs to aid planning and control of its machining manufacturing operations. Its costing system for manufacturing has two direct-cost categories (direct materials and direct manufacturing labor—both variable) and two overhead-cost categories (variable manufacturing overhead and fixed manufacturing overhead, both allocated using direct manufacturing labor-hours).

At the 50,000 budgeted direct manufacturing labor-hour level for August, budgeted direct manufacturing labor is $1,250,000, budgeted variable manufacturing overhead is $500,000, and budgeted fixed manufacturing overhead is $1,000,000.

The following actual results are for August:

Direct materials price variance (based on purchases)	$179,300 F
Direct materials efficiency variance	75,900 U
Direct manufacturing labor costs incurred	535,500
Variable manufacturing overhead flexible-budget variance	10,400 U
Variable manufacturing overhead efficiency variance	18,100 U
Fixed manufacturing overhead incurred	957,550

The standard cost per pound of direct materials is $11.50. The standard allowance is 6 pounds of direct materials for each unit of product. During August, 20,000 units of product were produced. There was no beginning inventory of direct materials. There was no beginning or ending work in process. In August, the direct materials price variance was $1.10 per pound.

In July, labor unrest caused a major slowdown in the pace of production, resulting in an unfavorable direct manufacturing labor efficiency variance of $40,000. There was no direct manufacturing labor price variance. Labor unrest persisted into August. Some workers quit. Their replacements had to be hired at higher wage rates, which had to be extended to all workers. The actual average wage rate in August exceeded the standard average wage rate by $0.50 per hour.

1. Compute the following for August:
   a. Total pounds of direct materials purchased
   b. Total number of pounds of excess direct materials used
   c. Variable manufacturing overhead spending variance
   d. Total number of actual direct manufacturing labor-hours used
   e. Total number of standard direct manufacturing labor-hours allowed for the units produced
   f. Production-volume variance

2. Describe how Gallo's control of variable manufacturing overhead items differs from its control of fixed manufacturing overhead items.

39 Review, 3-variance analysis. (CPA, adapted) The Brown Manufacturing Company's costing system has two direct-cost categories: direct materials and direct manufacturing labor. Manufacturing overhead (both variable and fixed) is allocated to products on the basis of standard direct manufacturing labor-hours (DLH). At the beginning of 2014, Beal adopted the following standards for its manufacturing costs:

	Input	Cost per Output Unit
Direct materials	5 lb. at $4 per lb.	$ 20.00
Direct manufacturing labor	4 hrs. at $16 per hr.	64.00
Manufacturing overhead:		
Variable	$8 per DLH	32.00
Fixed	$9 per DLH	36.00
Standard manufacturing cost per output unit		$152.00

The denominator level for total manufacturing overhead per month in 2014 is 37,000 direct manufacturing labor-hours. Beal's flexible budget for January 2014 was based on this denominator level. The records for January indicated the following:

Direct materials purchased	40,300 lb. at $3.80 per lb.
Direct materials used	37,300 lb.
Direct manufacturing labor	31,400 hrs. at $16.25 per hr.
Total actual manufacturing overhead (variable and fixed)	$650,000
Actual production	7,600 output units

1. Prepare a schedule of total standard manufacturing costs for the 7,600 output units in January 2014.
2. For the month of January 2014, compute the following variances, indicating whether each is favorable (F) or unfavorable (U):
   a. Direct materials price variance, based on purchases
   b. Direct materials efficiency variance
   c. Direct manufacturing labor price variance
   d. Direct manufacturing labor efficiency variance
   e. Total manufacturing overhead spending variance
   f. Variable manufacturing overhead efficiency variance
   g. Production-volume variance

40 Non-financial variances. Max Canine Products produces high-quality dog food distributed only through veterinary offices. To ensure that the food is of the highest quality and has taste appeal, Max Canine has a rigorous inspection process. For quality control purposes, Max Canine has a standard based on the pounds of food inspected per hour and the number of pounds that pass or fail the inspection.

Max Canine expects that for every 13,000 pounds of food produced, 1,300 pounds of food will be inspected. Inspection of 1,300 pounds of dog food should take 1 hour. Max Canine also expects that 5% of the food inspected will fail the inspection. During the month of May, Supreme produced 2,990,000 pounds of food and inspected 292,500 pounds of food in 200 hours. Of the 292,500 pounds of food inspected, 15,625 pounds of food failed to pass the inspection.

1. Compute two variances that help determine whether the time spent on inspections was more or less than expected. (Follow a format similar to the one used for the variable overhead spending and efficiency variances, but without prices.)
2. Compute two variances that can be used to evaluate the percentage of the food that fails the inspection.

41 Overhead variances, service sector. Cavio is a cloud service provider that offers computing resources to handle enterprise-wide applications. For March 2014, Cavio estimates that it will provide 18,000 RAM hours of services to clients. The budgeted variable overhead rate is $6 per RAM hour.

At the end of March, there is a $500 favorable spending variance for variable overhead and a $1,575 unfavorable spending variance for fixed overhead. For the services actually provided during the month, 14,850 RAM hours are budgeted and 15,000 RAM hours are actually used. Total actual overhead costs are $119,875.

Required

1. Compute efficiency and flexible-budget variances for Cavio's variable overhead in March 2014. Will variable overhead be over- or underallocated? By how much?
2. Compute production-volume and flexible-budget variances for Cavio's fixed overhead in March 2014. Will fixed overhead be over- or underallocated? By how much?

42 Direct-cost and overhead variances, income statement. The Kordell Company started business on January 1, 2013, in Raleigh. The company adopted a standard absorption costing system for its one product—a football for use in collegiate intramural sports. Because of the extensive handcrafting needed to do quality assurance on the final product, Kordell chose direct labor as the application base for overhead and decided to use the proration method to account for variances at year-end.

Kordell expected to make and sell 80,000 footballs the first year; each football was budgeted to use 1 pound of leather and require 15 minutes of direct labor work. The company expected to pay $1 for each pound of leather and compensate workers at an hourly wage of $16. Kordell has no variable overhead costs, but expected to spend $200,000 on fixed manufacturing overhead in 2013.

In 2013, Kordell actually made 100,000 footballs and sold 80,000 of them for a total revenue of $1 million. The expenses incurred were as follows:

Fixed manufacturing costs	$300,000
Leather costs (110,000 pounds bought and used)	$121,000
Direct labor costs (30,000 hours)	$465,000

Required

1. Compute the following variances for 2013, and indicate whether each is favorable (F) or unfavorable (U):
   a. Direct materials efficiency variance
   b. Direct materials price variance
   c. Direct labor efficiency variance
   d. Direct labor price variance
   e. Total manufacturing overhead spending variance
   f. Fixed overhead flexible budget variance
   g. Fixed overhead production-volume variance
2. Compute Kordell Company's gross margin for its first year of operation.

43 Overhead variances, ethics. Hartmann Company uses standard costing. The company has two manufacturing plants, one in Georgia and the other in Alabama. For the Georgia plant, Hartmann has budgeted annual output of 2,000,000 units. Standard labor-hours per unit are 0.50, and the variable overhead rate for the Georgia plant is $3.30 per direct labor-hour. Fixed overhead for the Georgia plant is budgeted at $2,400,000 for the year.

For the Alabama plant, Hartmann has budgeted annual output of 2,100,000 units with standard labor-hours also 0.50 per unit. However, the variable overhead rate for the Alabama plant is $3.10 per hour, and the budgeted fixed overhead for the year is only $2,205,000.

Firm management has always used variance analysis as a performance measure for the two plants and has compared the results of the two plants.

Tom Saban has just been hired as a new controller for Hartmann. Tom is good friends with the Alabama plant manager and wants him to get a favorable review. Tom suggests allocating the firm's budgeted common fixed costs of $3,150,000 to the two plants, but on the basis of one-third to the Alabama plant and two-thirds to the Georgia plant. His explanation for this allocation base is that Georgia is a more expensive state than Alabama.

At the end of the year, the Georgia plant reported the following actual results: output of 1,950,000 using 1,020,000 labor-hours in total, at a cost of $3,264,000 in variable overhead and $2,440,000 in fixed overhead.

Actual results for the Alabama plant are an output of 2,175,000 units using 1,225,000 labor-hours with a variable cost of $3,920,000 and fixed overhead cost of $2,300,000. The actual common fixed costs for the year were $3,075,000.

1. Compute the budgeted fixed cost per labor-hour for the fixed overhead separately for each plant:
   a. Excluding allocated common fixed costs
   b. Including allocated common fixed costs
2. Compute the variable overhead spending variance and the variable overhead efficiency variance separately for each plant.
3. Compute the fixed overhead spending and volume variances for each plant:
   a. Excluding allocated common fixed costs
   b. Including allocated common fixed costs
4. Did Tom Saban's attempt to make the Alabama plant look better than the Georgia plant by allocating common fixed costs work? Why or why not?
5. Should common fixed costs be allocated in general when variances are used as performance measures? Why or why not?
6. What do you think of Tom Saban's behavior overall?

Glossary

Denominator level.   The denominator in the budgeted fixed overhead rate computation.

Denominator-level variance.   See *production-volume variance*.

Fixed overhead flexible-budget variance.   The difference between actual fixed overhead costs and fixed overhead costs in the flexible budget.

Fixed overhead spending variance.   Same as the fixed overhead flexible-budget variance. The difference between actual fixed overhead costs and fixed overhead costs in the flexible budget.

Operating-income volume variance.   The difference between static-budget operating income and the operating income based on budgeted profit per unit and actual units of output.

Production-volume variance.   The difference between budgeted fixed overhead and fixed overhead allocated on the basis of actual output produced. Also called *denominator-level variance*.

Standard costing.   Costing system that traces direct costs to output produced by multiplying the standard prices or rates by the standard quantities of inputs allowed for actual outputs produced and allocates overhead costs on the basis of the standard overhead-cost rates times the standard quantities of the allocation bases allowed for the actual outputs produced.

Total-overhead variance.   The sum of the flexible-budget variance and the production-volume variance.

Variable overhead efficiency variance.   The difference between the actual quantity of variable overhead cost-allocation base used and budgeted quantity of variable overhead cost-allocation base that should have been used to produce actual output, multiplied by budgeted variable overhead cost per unit of cost-allocation base.

Variable overhead flexible-budget variance.   The difference between actual variable overhead costs incurred and flexible-budget variable overhead amounts.

Variable overhead spending variance.   The difference between actual variable overhead cost per unit and budgeted variable overhead cost per unit of the cost-allocation base, multiplied by actual quantity of variable overhead cost-allocation base used for actual output.

Photo Credits

Credits are listed in order of appearance.

Photo 1: MShieldsPhotos/Alamy
Photo 2: Liaison/Getty Images

Inventory Costing
and Capacity
Analysis

From Chapter 9 of *Cost Accounting: A Managerial Emphasis,* Fifteenth Edition. Charles T. Horngren, Srikant M. Datar, Madhav V. Rajan. Copyright © 2015 by Pearson Education, Inc. All rights reserved.

Inventory Costing and Capacity Analysis

Learning Objectives

1 Identify what distinguishes variable costing from absorption costing.

2 Compute income under variable costing and absorption costing, and explain the difference in income.

3 Understand how absorption costing can provide undesirable incentives for managers to build up inventory.

4 Differentiate throughput costing from variable costing and absorption costing.

5 Describe the various capacity concepts that firms can use in absorption costing.

6 Examine the key factors managers use to choose a capacity level to compute the budgeted fixed manufacturing cost rate.

7 Understand other issues that play an important role in capacity planning and control.

Few numbers capture the attention of managers and shareholders more than operating profits.

In industries that require significant upfront investments in capacity, two key decisions have a substantial impact on corporate profits: (1) How much money a firm spends on fixed investments and (2) the extent to which the firm eventually utilizes capacity to meet customer demand. Unfortunately, the compensation and reward systems of a firm, as well as the choice of inventory-costing methods, may induce managers to make decisions that benefit short-term earnings at the expense of a firm's long-term health. It may take a substantial external shock, like a sharp economic slowdown, to motivate managers to make the right capacity and inventory choices, as the following article illustrates.

Lean Manufacturing Helps Companies Reduce Inventory and Survive the Recession[1]

Can changing the way a mattress is pieced together help a company stay in business and remain profitable during a recession? For Sealy, the world's largest mattress manufacturer, the answer was a resounding "yes!"

Sealy used to manufacture as many mattresses as its resources allowed, regardless of customer orders. While factories operated at peak capacity, inventory often piled up, which cost the company millions of dollars each year. During the recent recession, Sealy was among thousands of manufacturers that remained profitable by changing its production plans to become more cost-efficient. Sealy adopted a policy of lean manufacturing, that is, producing only completed units and initiating production only in response to actual customer orders.

While Sealy launched its lean strategy in 2004, it intensified that strategy during the recession. The firm reconfigured old manufacturing processes to be more efficient. As a result:

- Each bed is now completed in 4 hours, down from 21.
- Median delivery times from Sealy to its retailers were cut to 60 hours, down from 72.

---

[1] *Sources:* Davidson, Paul. 2009. Lean manufacturing helps companies survive recession. *USA Today*, November 2; Sealy Corporation. 2011 Annual Report. Trinity, NC: Sealy Corporation, 2012; Sealy Corporation. 2009 Annual Report. Trinity, NC: Sealy Corporation, 2010; Hsu, Tiffany. 2012. Mattress mates: Tempur-Pedic buys Sealy for $1.3 billion. *The Los Angeles Times*, September 27.

- Raw-material inventories were cut by 50%.
- The company now adheres to a precise production schedule based on orders from retailers. While factories no longer run at full capacity, no mattress is made now until a customer orders it.

Sealy's manufacturing and inventory strategy was key to its survival during the recession and beyond. From 2008 to 2011, Sealy's lean manufacturing successfully reduced its inventory costs by 12%, or $7.6 million. This reduction enhanced the company's operations and made it an attractive acquisition target. In 2012, rival Tempur-Pedic purchased Sealy for $1.3 billion to create one of the largest companies in the competitive bedding industry.

Managers in industries with high fixed costs, like manufacturing, must manage capacity levels and make decisions about how to use available capacity. Managers must also decide on a production and inventory policy (as Sealy did). These decisions and the accounting choices managers make affect the operating incomes of manufacturing companies. This chapter focuses on two types of cost accounting choices:

1. *The inventory-costing choice* determines which manufacturing costs are treated as inventoriable costs. *Inventoriable costs* are all costs of a product that are regarded as assets when they are incurred and expensed as cost of goods sold when the product is sold. There are three types of inventory costing methods: absorption costing, variable costing, and throughput costing.

2. *The denominator-level capacity choice* focuses on the cost allocation base used to set budgeted fixed manufacturing cost rates. There are four possible choices of capacity levels: theoretical capacity, practical capacity, normal capacity utilization, and master-budget capacity utilization.

Variable and Absorption Costing

The two most common methods of costing inventories in manufacturing companies are *variable costing* and *absorption costing*. We describe each in this section and then discuss them in detail, using a hypothetical telescope-manufacturing company as an example.

Variable Costing

Variable costing is a method of inventory costing in which all variable manufacturing costs (direct and indirect) are included as inventoriable costs. All fixed manufacturing costs are excluded from inventoriable costs and are instead treated as costs of the period in which they are incurred. Note that *variable costing* is an imprecise term to describe this inventory-costing method because only variable manufacturing costs are inventoried; variable nonmanufacturing costs are still treated as period costs and are expensed. Another common term used to describe this method is **direct costing**. This term is also imprecise because variable costing considers variable manufacturing overhead (an indirect cost) as inventoriable, while excluding direct marketing costs, for example.

Absorption Costing

Absorption costing is a method of inventory costing in which all variable manufacturing costs and all fixed manufacturing costs are included as inventoriable costs. That is, inventory "absorbs" all manufacturing costs.

Under both variable costing and absorption costing, all variable manufacturing costs are inventoriable costs and all nonmanufacturing costs in the value chain (such as research and development and marketing), whether variable or fixed, are period costs and are recorded as expenses when incurred.

Comparing Variable and Absorption Costing

The easiest way to understand the difference between variable costing and absorption costing is with an example. In this chapter, we will study Stassen Company, an optical consumer-products manufacturer, and focus on its product line of high-end telescopes for aspiring astronomers.

Stassen uses standard costing:

- Direct costs are traced to products using standard prices and standard inputs allowed for actual outputs produced.

- Indirect (overhead) manufacturing costs are allocated using standard indirect rates times standard inputs allowed for actual outputs produced.

Stassen's management wants to prepare an income statement for 2014 (the fiscal year just ended) to evaluate the performance of the telescope product line. The operating information for the year is as follows:

	Home	Insert	Page Layout	Formulas	Data
		A			B
1					**Units**
2	Beginning inventory				0
3	Production				8,000
4	Sales				6,000
5	Ending inventory				2,000

Actual price and cost data for 2014 are as follows:

	Home	Insert	Page Layout	Formulas	Data	Review
		A				B
10	Selling price					$ 1,000
11	Variable manufacturing cost per unit					
12	Direct material cost per unit					$ 110
13	Direct manufacturing labor cost per unit					40
14	Manufacturing overhead cost per unit					50
15	Total variable manufacturing cost per unit					$ 200
16	Variable marketing cost per unit sold					$ 185
17	Fixed manufacturing costs (all indirect)					$1,080,000
18	Fixed marketing costs (all indirect)					$1,380,000

For simplicity and to focus on the main ideas, we assume the following about Stassen:

- Stassen incurs manufacturing and marketing costs only. The cost driver for all variable manufacturing costs is units produced; the cost driver for variable marketing costs is units sold. There are no batch-level costs and no product-sustaining costs.

- There are no price variances, efficiency variances, or spending variances. Therefore, the *budgeted* (standard) price and cost data for 2014 are the same as the *actual* price and cost data.

- Work-in-process inventory is zero.

- Stassen budgeted production of 8,000 units for 2014. This was used to calculate the budgeted fixed manufacturing cost per unit of $135 ($1,080,000/8,000 units).[2]

- Stassen budgeted sales of 6,000 units for 2014, which is the same as the actual sales for 2014.

- The actual production for 2014 is 8,000 units. As a result, there is no production-volume variance for manufacturing costs in 2014. A later example, based on data for 2015, does include production-volume variances. However, even in that case, the income statement contains no variances other than the production-volume variance.

- Variances are written off to cost of goods sold in the period (year) in which they occur.

Based on the preceding information, Stassen's inventoriable costs per unit produced in 2014 under the two inventory costing methods are as follows:

	Variable Costing		Absorption Costing	
Variable manufacturing cost per unit produced:				
Direct materials	$110		$110	
Direct manufacturing labor	40		40	
Manufacturing overhead	50	$200	50	$200
Fixed manufacturing cost per unit produced		—		135
Total inventoriable cost per unit produced		$200		$335

> *To summarize, the main difference between variable costing and absorption costing is the accounting for fixed manufacturing costs:*

- Under variable costing, fixed manufacturing costs are not inventoried; they are treated as an expense of the period.

- Under absorption costing, fixed manufacturing costs are inventoriable costs. In our example, the standard fixed manufacturing cost is $135 per unit ($1,080,000 ÷ 8,000 units) produced.

Decision Point

How does variable costing differ from absorption costing?

Variable vs. Absorption Costing: Operating Income and Income Statements

Learning Objective 2

Compute income under absorption costing

...using the gross-margin format

and variable costing,

...using the contribution-margin format

and explain the difference in income

...affected by the unit level of production and sales under absorption costing, but only the unit level of sales under variable costing

When comparing variable and absorption costing, we must also take into account whether we are looking at short- or long-term numbers. How does the data for a one-year period differ from that of a two-year period under variable and absorption costing?

Comparing Income Statements for One Year

What will Stassen's operating income be if it uses variable costing or absorption costing? The differences between these methods are apparent in Exhibit 1. Panel A shows the variable costing income statement and Panel B the absorption-costing income statement for Stassen's telescope product line for 2014. The variable-costing income statement uses the contribution-margin format. The absorption-costing income statement uses the gross-margin format. Why these different formats? The distinction between variable costs and fixed costs is central to

---

[2] Throughout this section, we use budgeted output as the basis for calculating the fixed manufacturing cost per unit for ease of exposition. In the latter half of this chapter, we consider the relative merits of alternative denominator-level choices for calculating this unit cost.

Exhibit 1 Comparison of Variable Costing and Absorption Costing for Stassen Company: Telescope Product-Line Income Statements for 2014

	A	B	C	D	E	F	G
	Home Insert Page Layout Formulas Data Review View						
1	Panel A: VARIABLE COSTING				Panel B: ABSORPTION COSTING		
2	Revenues: $1,000 × 6,000 units		$6,000,000		Revenues: $1,000 × 6,000 units		$6,000,000
3	Variable cost of goods sold:				Cost of goods sold:		
4	Beginning inventory	$ 0			Beginning inventory	$ 0	
5	Variable manufacturing costs: $200 × 8,000 units	1,600,000			Variable manufacturing costs: $200 × 8,000 units	1,600,000	
6					Allocated fixed manufacturing costs: $135 × 8,000 units	1,080,000	
7	Cost of goods available for sale	1,600,000			Cost of goods available for sale	2,680,000	
8	Deduct ending inventory: $200 × 2,000 units	(400,000)			Deduct ending inventory: $335 × 2,000 units	(670,000)	
9	Variable cost of goods sold		1,200,000		Cost of goods sold		2,010,000
10	Variable marketing costs: $185 × 6,000 units sold		1,110,000				
11	Contribution margin		3,690,000		Gross Margin		3,990,000
12	Fixed manufacturing costs		1,080,000		Variable marketing costs: $185 × 6,000 units sold		1,110,000
13	Fixed marketing costs		1,380,000		Fixed marketing costs		1,380,000
14	Operating income		$1,230,000		Operating Income		$1,500,000
15							
16	Manufacturing costs expensed in Panel A:				Manufacturing costs expensed in Panel B:		
17	Variable cost of goods sold		$1,200,000				
18	Fixed manufacturing costs		1,080,000				
19	Total		$2,280,000		Cost of goods sold		$2,010,000

variable costing, and it is highlighted by the contribution-margin format. Similarly, the distinction between manufacturing and nonmanufacturing costs is central to absorption costing, and it is highlighted by the gross-margin format.

Absorption-costing income statements do not need to differentiate between variable and fixed costs. However, we will make this distinction between variable and fixed costs in the Stassen example to show how individual line items are classified differently under variable costing and absorption costing. In Exhibit 1, Panel B, note that inventoriable cost is $335 per unit under absorption costing: allocated fixed manufacturing costs of $135 per unit plus variable manufacturing costs of $200 per unit.

Notice how the fixed manufacturing costs of $1,080,000 are accounted for under variable costing and absorption costing in Exhibit 1. The income statement under variable costing deducts the $1,080,000 lump sum as an expense for 2014. In contrast, under absorption costing, the $1,080,000 ($135 per unit × 8,000 units) is initially treated as an inventoriable cost in 2014. Of this $1,080,000, $810,000 ($135 per unit × 6,000 units sold) subsequently becomes a part of cost of goods sold in 2014, and $270,000 ($135 per unit × 2,000 units) remains an asset—part of ending finished goods inventory on December 31, 2014.

Operating income is $270,000 higher under absorption costing compared with variable costing because only $810,000 of fixed manufacturing costs are expensed under absorption costing, whereas all $1,080,000 of fixed manufacturing costs are expensed under variable costing. Note that the variable manufacturing cost of $200 per unit is accounted for the same way in both income statements in Exhibit 1.

These points can be summarized as follows:

	Variable Costing	Absorption Costing
Variable manufacturing costs: $200 per telescope produced	Inventoriable	Inventoriable
Fixed manufacturing costs: $1,080,000 per year	Deducted as an expense of the period	Inventoriable at $135 per telescope produced using budgeted denominator level of 8,000 units produced per year ($1,080,000 ÷ 8,000 units = $135 per unit)

The basis of the difference between variable costing and absorption costing is how fixed manufacturing costs are accounted for. If inventory levels change, operating income will differ between the two methods because of the difference in accounting for fixed manufacturing costs. To see this difference, let's compare telescope sales of 6,000, 7,000, and 8,000 units by Stassen in 2014, when 8,000 units were produced. Of the $1,080,000 total fixed manufacturing costs, the amount expensed in the 2014 income statement under each of these scenarios would be as follows:

	Home	Insert	Page Layout	Formulas	Data	Review	View		
	A	B	C	D	E		G	H
1			Variable Costing				Absorption Costing	
2							Fixed Manufacturing Costs	
3	Units	Ending	Fixed Manufacturing Costs				Included in Inventory	Amount Expensed
4	Sold	Inventory	Included in Inventory	Amount Expensed			=$135 × Ending Inv.	=$135 × Units Sold
5	6,000	2,000	$0	$1,080,000			$270,000	$ 810,000
6	7,000	1,000	$0	$1,080,000			$135,000	$ 945,000
7	8,000	0	$0	$1,080,000			$ 0	$1,080,000

In the last scenario, where 8,000 units are produced and sold, both variable and absorption costing report the same net income because inventory levels are unchanged. This chapter's appendix describes how the choice of variable costing or absorption costing affects the breakeven quantity of sales when inventory levels are allowed to vary.

Comparing Income Statements for Multiple Years

To get a more comprehensive view of the effects of variable costing and absorption costing, Stassen's management accountants prepare income statements for two years of operations, starting with 2014. The data are given in units in the following table:

	Home	Insert	Page Layout	Formulas
	E	F	G	
1		2014	2015	
2	Budgeted production	8,000	8,000	
3	Beginning inventory	0	2,000	
4	Actual production	8,000	5,000	
5	Sales	6,000	6,500	
6	Ending inventory	2,000	500	

All other 2014 data given earlier for Stassen also apply for 2015.

In 2015, Stassen has a production-volume variance because actual telescope production differs from the budgeted level of production of 8,000 units per year used to calculate the budgeted fixed manufacturing cost per unit. The actual quantity sold for 2015 is 6,500 units, which is the same as the sales quantity budgeted for that year.

Exhibit 2 presents the income statement under variable costing in Panel A and the income statement under absorption costing in Panel B for 2014 and 2015. As you study Exhibit 2, note that the 2014 columns in both Panels A and B show the same figures as Exhibit 1. The 2015 column is similar to 2014 *except for the production-volume variance line item under absorption costing in Panel B*. Keep in mind the following points about absorption costing as you study Panel B of Exhibit 2:

1. The $135 fixed manufacturing cost rate is based on the budgeted denominator capacity level of 8,000 units in 2014 and 2015 ($1,080,000 ÷ 8,000 units = $135 per unit). Whenever production (the quantity produced, not the quantity sold) deviates from the denominator level, there will be a production-volume variance. The amount of Stassen's production-volume variance is determined by multiplying $135 per unit by the difference between the actual level of production and the denominator level.

Exhibit 2   Comparison of Variable Costing and Absorption Costing for Stassen Company: Telescope Product-Line Income Statements for 2014 and 2015

	Home	Insert	Page Layout	Formulas	Data	Review	View			
		A				B	C	D	E	
1	Panel A: VARIABLE COSTING									
2							2014		2015	
3	Revenues: $1,000 × 6,000; 6,500 units						$6,000,000		$6,500,000	
4	Variable cost of goods sold:									
5	Beginning inventory: $200 × 0; 2,000 units					$ 0		$ 400,000		
6	Variable manufacturing costs: $200 × 8,000; 5,000 units					1,600,000		1,000,000		
7	Cost of goods available for sale					1,600,000		1,400,000		
8	Deduct ending inventory: $200 × 2,000; 500 units					(400,000)		(100,000)		
9	Variable cost of goods sold						1,200,000		1,300,000	
10	Variable marketing costs: $185 × 6,000; 6,500 units						1,110,000		1,202,500	
11	Contribution margin						3,690,000		3,997,500	
12	Fixed manufacturing costs						1,080,000		1,080,000	
13	Fixed marketing costs						1,380,000		1,380,000	
14	Operating income						$1,230,000		$1,537,500	
15										
16	Panel B: ABSORPTION COSTING									
17							2014		2015	
18	Revenues: $1,000 × 6,000; 6,500 units						$6,000,000		$6,500,000	
19	Cost of goods sold:									
20	Beginning inventory: $335 × 0; 2,000 units					0		670,000		
21	Variable manufacturing costs: $200 × 8,000; 5,000 units					1,600,000		1,000,000		
22	Allocated fixed manufacturing costs: $135 × 8,000; 5,000 units					1,080,000		675,000		
23	Cost of goods available for sale					2,680,000		2,345,000		
24	Deduct ending inventory: $335 × 2,000; 500 units					(670,000)		(167,500)		
25	Adjustment for production-volume variance[a]					$ 0		$ 405,000	U	
26	Cost of goods sold						2,010,000		2,582,500	
27	Gross Margin						3,990,000		3,917,500	
28	Variable marketing costs: $185 × 6,000; 6,500 units						1,110,000		1,202,500	
29	Fixed marketing costs						1,380,000		1,380,000	
30	Operating Income						$1,500,000		$1,335,000	
31										
32	[a]Production-volume variance = Budgeted fixed manufacturing costs – Fixed manufacturing overhead allocated using budgeted cost per output unit allowed for actual output produced (Panel B, line 22)									
33	2014: $1,080,000 – ($135 × 8,000) = $1,080,000 – $1,080,000 = $0									
34	2015: $1,080,000 – ($135 × 5,000) = $1,080,000 – $675,000 = $405,000 U									
35										
36	Production-volume variance can also be calculated as follows:									
37	Fixed manufacturing cost per unit × (Denominator level – Actual output units produced)									
38	2014: $135 × (8,000 – 8,000) units = $135 × 0 = $0									
39	2015: $135 × (8,000 – 5,000) units = $135 × 3,000 = $405,000 U									

Recall how standard costing works under absorption costing. Each time a unit is manufactured, $135 of fixed manufacturing costs is included in the cost of goods manufactured and available for sale. In 2015, when 5,000 units are manufactured, $675,000 ($135 per unit × 5,000 units) of fixed manufacturing costs is included in the cost of goods available for sale (see Exhibit 2, Panel B, line 22). Total fixed manufacturing costs for 2015 are $1,080,000. The production-volume variance of $405,000 U equals the difference between $1,080,000 and $675,000. In Panel B, note how, for each year, the fixed manufacturing costs included in the cost of goods available for sale plus the production-volume variance always equals $1,080,000.

2. As a result of the production-volume variance, note that the absorption costing income is lower in 2015 than in 2014 even though Stassen sold 500 more units. We explore the impact of production levels on income under absorption costing in greater detail later in this chapter.

3. The production-volume variance, which relates only to fixed manufacturing overhead, exists under absorption costing but not under variable costing. Under variable costing, fixed manufacturing costs of $1,080,000 are always treated as an expense of the period, regardless of the level of production (and sales).

Here's a summary (using information from Exhibit 2) of the operating-income differences for Stassen Company during 2014 and 2015:

	2014	2015
1. Absorption-costing operating income	$1,500,000	$1,335,000
2. Variable-costing operating income	$1,230,000	$1,537,500
3. Difference: (1) – (2)	$ 270,000	$ (202,500)

The sizeable differences in the preceding table illustrate why managers whose performance is measured by reported income are concerned about the choice between variable costing and absorption costing.

Why do variable costing and absorption costing report different operating income numbers? In general, if inventory increases during an accounting period, less operating income will be reported under variable costing than absorption costing. Conversely, if inventory decreases, more operating income will be reported under variable costing than absorption costing. The difference in reported operating income is due solely to (a) moving fixed manufacturing costs into inventories as inventories increase and (b) moving fixed manufacturing costs out of inventories as inventories decrease under absorption costing.

The difference between operating income under absorption costing and variable costing can be computed by formula 1, which focuses on fixed manufacturing costs in beginning inventory and ending inventory:

	A	B	C	D	E	F	G	H
1	Formula 1							
2						Fixed manufacturing		Fixed manufacturing
3		Absorption-costing	–	Variable-costing	=	costs in ending inventory	–	costs in beginning inventory
4		operating income		operation income		under absorption costing		under absorption costing
5	2014	$1,500,000	–	$1,230,000	=	($135 × 2,000 units)	–	($135 × 0 units)
6		$270,000			=	$270,000		
7								
8	2015	$1,335,000	–	$1,537,500	=	($135 × 500 units)	–	($135 × 2,000 units)
9		($202,500)			=	($202,500)		

Fixed manufacturing costs in ending inventory are deferred to a future period under absorption costing. For example, $270,000 of fixed manufacturing overhead is deferred to 2015 at December 31, 2014. Under variable costing, all $1,080,000 of fixed manufacturing costs are treated as an expense of 2014.

Recall that

$$\frac{\text{Beginning}}{\text{inventory}} + \frac{\text{Cost of goods}}{\text{manufactured}} = \frac{\text{Cost of goods}}{\text{sold}} + \frac{\text{Ending}}{\text{Inventory}}$$

Therefore, instead of focusing on fixed manufacturing costs in ending and beginning inventory (as in formula 1), we could alternatively look at fixed manufacturing costs in units produced and units sold. The latter approach (see formula 2) highlights how fixed manufacturing costs move between units produced and units sold during the fiscal year.

	A	B	C	D	E	F	G	H
12	**Formula 2**							
13						**Fixed manufacturing costs**		**Fixed manufacturing costs**
14		**Absorption-costing**	–	**Variable-costing**	=	**inventoried in units produced**	–	**in cost of goods sold**
15		**operating income**		**operation income**		**under absorption costing**		**under absorption costing**
16	**2014**	$1,500,000	–	$1,230,000	=	($135 × 8,000 units)	–	($135 × 6,000 units)
17		$270,000			=	$270,000		
18								
19	**2015**	$1,335,000	–	$1,537,500	=	($135 × 5,000 units)	–	($135 × 6,500 units)
20		($202,500)			=	($202,500)		

Managers face increasing pressure to reduce inventory levels. Some companies are achieving steep reductions in inventory levels using policies such as just-in-time production—a production system under which products are manufactured only when needed. Formula 1 illustrates that, as Stassen reduces its inventory levels, operating income differences between absorption costing and variable costing become immaterial. Consider, for example, the formula for 2014. If instead of 2,000 units in ending inventory, Stassen had only 2 units in ending inventory, the difference between absorption-costing operating income and variable-costing operating income would drop from $270,000 to just $270.

Variable Costing and the Effect of Sales and Production on Operating Income

Given a constant contribution margin per unit and constant fixed costs, the period-to-period change in operating income under variable costing is *driven solely by changes in the quantity of units actually sold.* Consider the variable-costing operating income of Stassen in 2015 versus 2014. Recall the following:

$$\frac{\text{Contribution}}{\text{margin per unit}} = \text{Selling price} - \frac{\text{Variable manufacturing}}{\text{cost per unit}} - \frac{\text{Variable marketing}}{\text{cost per unit}}$$

$$= \$1,000 \text{ per unit} - \$200 \text{ per unit} - \$185 \text{ per unit}$$

$$= \$615 \text{ per unit}$$

$$\frac{\text{Change in}}{\text{variable-costing}} = \frac{\text{Contribution}}{\text{margin}} \times \frac{\text{Change in quantity}}{\text{of units sold}}$$
$$\text{operating income} \quad \text{per unit}$$

$$\text{2015 vs. 2014: } \$1,537,500 - \$1,230,000 = \$615 \text{ per unit} \times (6,500 \text{ unit} - 6,000 \text{ units})$$

$$\$307,500 = \$307,500$$

Decision Point

How does income differ under variable and absorption costing?

Under variable costing, Stassen managers cannot increase operating income by "producing for inventory." Why not? Because, as you can see from the preceding computations, when using variable costing, only the quantity of units sold drives operating income. We'll explain later in this chapter that absorption costing enables managers to increase operating income by increasing the unit level of sales, as well as by producing more units. Before you proceed to the next section, make sure that you examine Exhibit 3 for a detailed comparison of the differences between variable costing and absorption costing.

Exhibit 3	Comparative Income Effects of Variable Costing and Absorption Costing

Question	Variable Costing	Absorption Costing	Comment
Are fixed manufacturing costs inventoried?	No	Yes	Basic theoretical question of when these costs should be expensed
Is there a production-volume variance?	No	Yes	Choice of denominator level affects measurement of operating income under absorption costing only
Are classifications between variable and fixed costs routinely made?	Yes	Infrequently	Absorption costing can be easily modified to obtain subclassifications for variable and fixed costs, if desired (for example, see Exhibit 1, Panel B)
How do changes in unit inventory levels affect operating income?[a]			Differences are attributable to the timing of when fixed manufacturing costs are expensed
Production = sales	Equal	Equal	
Production > sales	Lower[b]	Higher[c]	
Production < sales	Higher	Lower	
What are the effects on cost-volume-profit relationship (for a given level of fixed costs and a given contribution margin per unit)?	Driven by unit level of sales	Driven by (a) unit level of sales, (b) unit level of production, and (c) chosen denominator level	Management control benefit: Effects of changes in production level on operating income are easier to understand under variable costing

[a]Assuming that all manufacturing variances are written off as period costs, that no change occurs in work-in-process inventory, and no change occurs in the budgeted fixed manufacturing cost rate between accounting periods.

[b]That is, lower operating income than under absorption costing.

[c]That is, higher operating income than under variable costing.

Absorption Costing and Performance Measurement

Learning Objective 3

Understand how absorption costing can provide undesirable incentives for managers to build up inventory

...producing more units for inventory absorbs fixed manufacturing costs and increases operating income

Absorption costing is the required inventory method for external financial reporting in most countries (we provide potential reasons for this rule later in the chapter). Many companies use absorption costing for internal accounting as well because:

- It is cost-effective and less confusing for managers to use one common method of inventory costing for both external and internal reporting and performance evaluation.

- It can help prevent managers from taking actions that make their performance measure look good but that hurt the income they report to shareholders.

- It measures the cost of all manufacturing resources, whether variable or fixed, necessary to produce inventory. Many companies use inventory costing information for long-run decisions, such as pricing and choosing a product mix. For these long-run decisions, inventory costs should include both variable *and* fixed costs.

An important attribute of absorption costing is that it enables a manager to increase margins and operating income by producing more ending inventory. Producing for inventory is justified when a firm's managers anticipate rapid growth in demand and want to produce and store additional units to deal with possible production shortages in the next year. For example, with the recent improvement in the national economy, manufacturers of energy-efficient doors and windows are stepping up production in order to take advantage of an anticipated rebound in the housing market. But, under absorption costing, Stassen's managers may be tempted to produce inventory even when they *do not* anticipate customer demand to grow. The reason is that this production leads to higher operating income, which can benefit managers in two ways: directly, because higher incomes typically result in a higher bonus for the manager, and indirectly, because greater income levels have a positive effect on stock price, which increases managers' stock-based compensation. But higher income results in the company paying higher taxes. Shareholders and supporters of good corporate governance would also argue that it is unethical for managers to take actions that are intended solely to increase their compensation rather than to improve the company. Producing for inventory is a risky strategy, especially in industries with volatile demand or high risk of product obsolescence because of the pace at which innovation is occuring. For example, the new BlackBerry Z10 smartphone has seen declining sell-through rates and higher levels of inventory and is being sold at deeply discounted prices in the United Kingdom. Concepts in Action: Absorption Costing and the Bankruptcy of U.S. Automakers illustrates the dramatic negative impact of producing for inventory in the auto industry.

To reduce the undesirable incentives to build up inventories that absorption costing can create, a number of companies use variable costing for internal reporting. Variable costing focuses attention on distinguishing variable manufacturing costs from fixed manufacturing costs. This distinction is important for short-run decision making.

Companies that use both methods for internal reporting—variable costing for short-run decisions and performance evaluation and absorption costing for long-run decisions—benefit from the different advantages of both. Surveys sponsored by Chartered Institute of Management Accountants (United Kingdom), the world's largest professional body of management accountants, have shown that while most organizations employ absorption costing systems, more than 75% indicate the use of variable costing information as either the most important or second most important measure for decision-making purposes.

In the next section, we explore in more detail the challenges that arise from absorption costing.

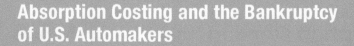

Concepts in Action ▶ Absorption Costing and the Bankruptcy of U.S. Automakers

In the years leading up to the 2008 recession, General Motors, Ford, and Chrysler were producing new vehicles in excess of market demand. This led to large inventories on car dealers' lots across the United States. At the same time, profits were rising and executives at these three companies were achieving their short-term incentive targets. How is this possible? Absorption costing may hold the answer.

In 2009, General Motors and Chrysler filed for bankruptcy and appealed for government aid. Yet these automakers had abundant excess capacity. They also had enormous fixed costs, from factories and machinery to workers whose contracts protected them from layoffs when demand was low. To "absorb" these costs, the automakers produced more cars while using absorption costing. The more vehicles they made, the lower the cost per vehicle, and the higher the profits on their income statements. In effect, the automakers shifted costs from their income statements to their balance sheets.

Ultimately, this practice hurt the automakers by driving up advertising and inventory costs. "When the dealers couldn't sell the cars, they would sit on the lots," says Dr. Karen Sedatole, a Michigan State professor who recently co-authored a study on the topic. "They'd have to go in and replace the tires, and there were costs associated with that." The companies also had to pay to advertise their cars, often at discounted prices using rebates, employee pricing, and 0% financing promotions. General Motors and Chrysler ran out of cash for operations and making loans available for car buyers. In January 2009, the U.S. government used $24.9 billion in bailout funds to rescue General Motors and Chrysler.

Sources: Based on Marielle Segarra, "Lots of Trouble," *CFO Magazine* (March 2012); and Bruggen, A., R. Krishnan, and K. L. Sedatole. 2011. Drivers and Consequences of Short-Term Production Decisions: Evidence from the Auto Industry. *Contemporary Accounting Research* 28 (1):83–123.

Undesirable Buildup of Inventories

If a manager's bonus is based on reported absorption-costing operating income, that manager may be motivated to build up an undesirable level of inventories. Assume that Stassen's managers have such a bonus plan. Exhibit 4 shows how Stassen's absorption costing operating income for 2015 changes as the production level changes. This exhibit assumes that the production-volume variance is written off to cost of goods sold at the end of each year. Beginning inventory of 2,000 units and sales of 6,500 units for 2015 are unchanged from the case shown in Exhibit 2. *As you review* Exhibit 4, *keep in mind that the computations are basically the same as those in* Exhibit 2.

Exhibit 4 shows that production of 4,500 units meets the 2015 sales budget of 6,500 units (2,000 units from beginning inventory +4,500 units produced). Operating income at this production level is $1,267,500. By producing more than 4,500 units, commonly referred to as *producing for inventory*, Stassen increases absorption-costing operating income. Each additional unit in 2015 ending inventory will increase operating income by $135. For example, if 9,000 units are produced (column H in Exhibit 4), ending inventory will be 4,500 units and operating income increases to $1,875,000. This amount is $607,500 more than the operating income with zero ending inventory ($1,875,000 – $1,267,500, or 4,500 units × $135 per unit = $607,500). By producing 4,500 units for inventory, the company using absorption costing includes $607,500 of fixed manufacturing costs in finished goods inventory, so those costs are not expensed in 2015.

The scenarios outlined in Exhibit 4 raise three other important points. First, column D is the base-case setting and just restates the 2015 absorption costing results from Panel B of Exhibit 2. Second, column F highlights that when inventory levels are unchanged, that is, production equals sales, the absorption costing income equals the income under variable costing (see Panel A of Exhibit 2 for comparison). Third, the example in Exhibit 4 focuses on one year, 2015. A Stassen manager who built up an inventory of 4,500 telescopes at the end of 2015 would have to further increase ending inventories in 2016 to increase that year's operating income by producing for inventory. There are limits to how much inventory levels can be increased over time because of physical constraints

Exhibit 4	Effect on Absorption-Costing Operating Income of Different Production Levels for Stassen Company: Telescope Product-Line Income Statement for 2015 at Sales of 6,500 Units

	Home	Insert	Page Layout	Formulas	Data	Review	View				
	A				B	C	D	E	F	G	H	I
1	Unit Data											
2	Beginning inventory				2,000		2,000		2,000		2,000	
3	Production				4,500		5,000		6,500		9,000	
4	Goods available for sale				6,500		7,000		8,500		11,000	
5	Sales				6,500		6,500		6,500		6,500	
6	Ending inventory				0		500		2,000		4,500	
7												
8	Income Statement											
9	Revenues				$6,500,000		$6,500,000		$6,500,000		$6,500,000	
10	Cost of goods sold:											
11	Beginning inventory: $335 × 2,000				670,000		670,000		670,000		670,000	
12	Variable manufacturing costs: $200 × production				900,000		1,000,000		1,300,000		1,800,000	
13	Allocated fixed manufacturing costs: $135 × production				607,500		675,000		877,500		1,215,000	
14	Cost of goods available for sale				2,177,500		2,345,000		2,847,500		3,685,000	
15	Deduct ending inventory: $335 × ending inventory				0		(167,500)		(670,000)		(1,507,500)	
16	Adjustment for production-volume variance[a]				472,500	U	405,000	U	202,500	U	(135,000)	F
17	Cost of goods sold				2,650,000		2,582,500		2,380,000		2,042,500	
18	Gross Margin				3,850,000		3,917,500		4,120,000		4,457,500	
19	Marketing costs: $1,380,000 + ($185 per unit × 6,500 units sold)				2,582,500		2,582,500		2,582,500		2,582,500	
20	Operating Income				$1,267,500		$1,335,000		$1,537,500		$1,875,000	
21												
22	[a]Production-volume variance = Budgeted fixed manufacturing costs − Allocated fixed manufacturing costs (Income Statement, line 13)											
23	At production of 4,500 units: $1,080,000 − $607,500 = $472,500 U											
24	At production of 5,000 units: $1,080,000 − $675,000 = $405,000 U											
25	At production of 6,500 units: $1,080,000 − $877,500 = $202,500 U											
26	At production of 9,000 units: $1,080,000 − $1,215,000 = ($135,000) F											

on storage space and management controls. Such limits reduce the likelihood of incurring some of absorption costing's undesirable effects. Nevertheless, managers do have the ability and incentive to move costs in and out of inventory in order to manage operating income under absorption costing.

Top management can implement checks and balances that limit managers from producing for inventory under absorption costing. However, the practice cannot be completely prevented. There are many subtle ways a manager can produce for inventory that may not be easy to detect. For example, consider the following scenarios:

- A plant manager may switch to manufacturing products that absorb the highest amount of fixed manufacturing costs, regardless of the customer demand for these products (called "cherry picking" the production line). Delaying the production of items that absorb the least or lower fixed manufacturing costs could lead to failure to meet promised customer delivery dates (which, over time, can result in unhappy customers).

- A plant manager may accept a particular order to increase production, even though another plant in the same company is better suited to handle that order.

- To increase production, a manager may defer maintenance of equipment beyond the current period. Although operating income in this period may increase as a result, future operating income could decrease by a larger amount if repair costs increase and equipment becomes less efficient.

Proposals for Revising Performance Evaluation

Top management, with help from the controller and management accountants, can take several steps to reduce the undesirable effects of absorption costing.

- Focus on careful budgeting and inventory planning to reduce management's freedom to build up excess inventory. For example, the budgeted monthly balance sheets have estimates of the dollar amount of inventories. If actual inventories exceed these dollar amounts, top management can investigate the inventory buildups.

- Incorporate a carrying charge for inventory in the internal accounting system. For example, the company could assess an inventory carrying charge of 1% per month on the investment tied up in inventory and for spoilage and obsolescence when it evaluates a manager's performance. An increasing number of companies are beginning to adopt this inventory carrying charge.

- Change the period used to evaluate performance. Critics of absorption costing give examples in which managers take actions that maximize quarterly or annual income at the potential expense of long-run income. When their performance is evaluated over a three- to five-year period, managers will be less tempted to produce for inventory.

- Include nonfinancial as well as financial variables in the measures used to evaluate performance. Examples of nonfinancial measures that can be used to monitor the performance of Stassen's managers in 2015 (see column H of Exhibit 4) are as follows:

$$(a) \quad \frac{\text{Ending inventory in units in 2015}}{\text{Beginning inventory in units in 2015}} = \frac{4,500}{2,000} = 2.25$$

$$(b) \quad \frac{\text{Units produced in 2015}}{\text{Units sold in 2015}} = \frac{9,000}{6,500} = 1.38$$

Decision Point

Why might managers build up finished goods inventory if they use absorption costing?

Top management would want to see production equal to sales and relatively stable levels of inventory. Companies that manufacture or sell several products could report these two measures for each of the products they manufacture and sell.

Besides the formal performance measurement systems, companies develop codes of conduct to discourage behavior that benefits managers but not the company and build values and cultures that focus on behaving ethically.

Comparing Inventory Costing Methods

Before we begin our discussion of capacity, we will look at *throughput costing*, a variation of variable costing, and compare the various costing methods.

Throughput Costing

Some managers believe that even variable costing promotes an excessive amount of costs being inventoried. They argue that only direct materials, such as the lenses, casing, scope, and mount in the case of Stassen's telescopes, are "truly variable" in output. **Throughput costing**, which is also called **super-variable costing**, is an extreme form of variable costing in which only direct material costs are included as inventoriable costs. All other costs are costs of the period in which they are incurred. In particular, variable direct manufacturing labor costs and variable manufacturing overhead costs are regarded as period costs and are deducted as expenses of the period.

Exhibit 5 is the throughput-costing income statement for Stassen Company for 2014 and 2015. *Throughput margin* equals revenues minus all direct material cost of the goods sold. Compare the operating income amounts reported in Exhibit 5 with those for absorption costing and variable costing:

	2014	2015
Absorption-costing operating income	$1,500,000	$1,335,000
Variable-costing operating income	$1,230,000	$1,537,500
Throughput-costing operating income	$1,050,000	$1,672,500

Only the $110 direct material cost per unit is inventoriable under throughput costing, compared with $335 per unit for absorption costing and $200 per unit for variable costing. When the production quantity exceeds sales, as in 2014, throughput costing results in the largest amount of expenses in the current period's income statement. Advocates of throughput costing say it provides managers less incentive to produce for inventory than either variable costing or, especially, absorption costing. Throughput costing is a more

	A	B	C
		2014	2015
2	Revenues: $1,000 × 6,000; 6,500 units	$6,000,000	$6,500,000
3	Direct material cost of goods sold		
4	Beginning inventory: $110 × 0; 2,000 units	0	220,000
5	Direct materials: $110 × 8,000; 5,000 units	880,000	550,000
6	Cost of goods available for sale	880,000	770,000
7	Deduct ending inventory: $110 × 2,000; 500 units	(220,000)	(55,000)
8	Direct material cost of goods sold	660,000	715,000
9	Throughput margin[a]	5,340,000	5,785,000
10	Manufacturing costs (other than direct materials)[b]	1,800,000	1,530,000
11	Marketing costs[c]	2,490,000	2,582,500
12	Operating income	$1,050,000	$1,672,500
13			
14	[a]Throughput margin equals revenues minus all direct material cost of goods sold		
15	[b]Fixed manuf. costs + [(variable manuf. labor cost per unit + variable manuf. overhead cost per unit) × units produced]; $1,080,000 + [($40 + $50) × 8,000; 5,000 units]		
16	[c]Fixed marketing costs + (variable marketing cost per unit × units sold);		
17	$1,380,000 + ($185 × 6,000; 6,500 units)		

recent phenomenon in comparison with variable costing and absorption costing and has avid supporters, but so far it has not been widely adopted.[3]

A Comparison of Alternative Inventory-Costing Methods

Variable costing and absorption costing may be combined with actual, normal, or standard costing. Exhibit 6 compares product costing under these six alternative inventory-costing systems.

Variable costing has been controversial among accountants because of how it affects *external reporting*, not because of disagreement about the need to delineate between variable and fixed costs for internal planning and control. Accountants who favor variable costing for external reporting maintain that the fixed portion of manufacturing costs is more closely related to the capacity to produce than to the actual production of specific units. Fixed costs should therefore be expensed, not inventoried.

Accountants who support absorption costing for *external reporting* maintain that inventories should carry a fixed-manufacturing-cost component because both variable manufacturing costs and fixed manufacturing costs are necessary to produce goods. Therefore, both types of costs should be inventoried in order to match all manufacturing costs to revenues, regardless of their different behavior patterns. For external reporting to shareholders, companies around the globe tend to follow the generally accepted accounting principle that all manufacturing costs are inventoriable. This also eases the burden on firms and auditors to attempt to disentangle fixed and variable costs of production, a distinction that is not always clear-cut in practice.

Similarly, for tax reporting in the United States, managers must take direct production costs, as well as fixed and variable indirect production costs, into account in the computation of inventoriable costs in accordance with the "full absorption" method of inventory costing. Indirect production costs include items such as rent, utilities, maintenance, repair

---

Exhibit 6 Comparison of Alternative Inventory-Costing Systems

		Actual Costing	**Normal Costing**	**Standard Costing**
Absorption Costing	Variable Costing	**Variable Direct Manufacturing Cost**	Actual prices × Actual quantity of inputs used	Actual prices × Actual quantity of inputs used	Standard prices × Standard quantity of inputs allowed for actual output achieved
		Variable Manufacturing Overhead Costs	Actual variable overhead rates × Actual quantity of cost-allocation bases used	Budgeted variable overhead rates × Actual quantity of cost-allocation bases used	Standard variable overhead rates × Standard quantity of cost-allocation bases allowed for actual output achieved
		Fixed Direct Manufacturing Costs	Actual prices × Actual quantity of inputs used	Actual prices × Actual quantity of inputs used	Standard prices × Standard quantity of inputs allowed for actual output achieved
		Fixed Manufacturing Overhead Costs	Actual fixed overhead rates × Actual quantity of cost-allocation bases used	Budgeted fixed overhead rates × Actual quantity of cost-allocation bases used	Standard fixed overhead rates × Standard quantity of cost-allocation bases allowed for actual output achieved

---

[3] See E. Goldratt, *The Theory of Constraints* (New York: North River Press, 1990); E. Noreen, D. Smith, and J. Mackey, *The Theory of Constraints and Its Implications for Management Accounting* (New York: North River Press, 1995).

expenses, indirect materials, and indirect labor. For other indirect cost categories (including depreciation, insurance, taxes, officers' salaries, factory administrative expenses, and strike-related costs), the portion of the cost that is "incident to and necessary for production or manufacturing operations or processes" is inventoriable for tax purposes *only* if it is treated as inventoriable for the purposes of financial reporting. Accordingly, managers must often allocate costs between those portions related to manufacturing activities and those not related to manufacturing.[4]

Decision Point

How does throughput costing differ from variable costing and absorption costing?

Denominator-Level Capacity Concepts and Fixed-Cost Capacity Analysis

We have seen that the difference between variable and absorption costing methods arises solely from the treatment of fixed manufacturing costs. Spending on fixed manufacturing costs enables firms to obtain the scale or capacity needed to satisfy the expected market demand from customers. Determining the "right" amount of spending, or the appropriate level of capacity, is one of the most strategic and most difficult decisions managers face. Having too much capacity to produce relative to that needed to meet market demand means firms will incur some costs of unused capacity. Having too little capacity to produce means that demand from some customers may be unfilled. These customers may go to other sources of supply and never return. Both managers and accountants must understand these issues that arise with capacity costs.

We start this section by analyzing a key question in absorption costing: Given a firm's level of spending on fixed manufacturing costs, what capacity level should managers and accountants use to compute the fixed manufacturing cost per unit produced? We then study the broader question of how a firm should decide on its level of capacity investment.

Absorption Costing and Alternative Denominator-Level Capacity Concepts

Normal costing and standard costing report costs in an ongoing timely manner throughout a fiscal year. The choice of the capacity level used to allocate budgeted fixed manufacturing costs to products can greatly affect the operating income reported under normal costing or standard costing and the product-cost information available to managers.

Consider the Stassen Company example again. Recall that the annual fixed manufacturing costs of the production facility are $1,080,000. Stassen currently uses absorption costing with standard costs for external reporting purposes, and it calculates its budgeted fixed manufacturing rate on a per unit basis. We will now examine four different capacity levels used as the denominator to compute the budgeted fixed manufacturing cost rate: theoretical capacity, practical capacity, normal capacity utilization, and master-budget capacity utilization.

Theoretical Capacity and Practical Capacity

In business and accounting, capacity ordinarily means a "constraint," an "upper limit." **Theoretical capacity** is the level of capacity based on producing at full efficiency all the time. Stassen can produce 25 units per shift when the production lines are operating at maximum speed. If we assume 360 days per year, the theoretical annual capacity for 2 shifts per day is as follows:

$$25 \text{ units per shift} \times 2 \text{ shifts per day} \times 360 \text{ days} = 18,000 \text{ units}$$

---

[4] Details regarding tax rules can be found in Section 1.471-11 of the U.S. Internal Revenue Code: Inventories of Manufacturers (see http://ecfr.gpoaccess.gov). Costs not related to production, such as marketing, distribution, or research expenses, are treated as period expenses for financial reporting. Under U.S. tax rules, a firm can still consider these costs as inventoriable for tax purposes provided that it does so consistently.

Theoretical capacity is theoretical in the sense that it does not allow for any slowdowns due to plant maintenance, shutdown periods, or interruptions because of downtime on the assembly lines. Theoretical capacity levels are unattainable in the real world, but they represent the ideal goal of capacity utilization a company can aspire to.

Practical capacity is the level of capacity that reduces theoretical capacity by considering unavoidable operating interruptions, such as scheduled maintenance time and shutdowns for holidays. Assume that practical capacity is the practical production rate of 20 units per shift (as opposed to 25 units per shift under theoretical capacity) for 2 shifts per day for 300 days a year (as opposed to 360 days a year under theoretical capacity). The practical annual capacity is as follows:

$$20 \text{ units per shift} \times 2 \text{ shifts per day} \times 300 \text{ days} = 12,000 \text{ units}$$

Engineering and human resource factors are both important when estimating theoretical or practical capacity. Engineers at the Stassen facility can provide input on the technical capabilities of machines for cutting and polishing lenses. Human resources can evaluate employee safety factors, such as increased injury risk when the line operates at faster speeds.

Normal Capacity Utilization and Master-Budget Capacity Utilization

Both theoretical capacity and practical capacity measure capacity levels in terms of what a plant can *supply*—available capacity. In contrast, normal capacity utilization and master-budget capacity utilization measure capacity levels in terms of *demand* for the output of the plant, that is, the amount of available capacity the plant expects to use based on the demand for its products. In many cases, budgeted demand is well below production capacity available.

Normal capacity utilization is the level of capacity utilization that satisfies average customer demand over a period (say, two to three years) that includes seasonal, cyclical, and trend factors. **Master-budget capacity utilization** is the level of capacity utilization that managers expect for the current budget period, which is typically one year. These two capacity-utilization levels can differ quite significantly in industries that face cyclical demand patterns. For example:

- The automobile industry may have a period of high demand due to low interest rates or a period of low demand due to a recession.
- The semiconductor industry may have a period of high demand if companies update employee computers or a period of low demand if companies downsize.

Consider Stassen's master budget for 2014, based on production of 8,000 telescopes per year. Despite using this master-budget capacity-utilization level of 8,000 telescopes for 2014, top management believes that over the next three years the normal (average) annual production level will be 10,000 telescopes. It views 2014's budgeted production level of 8,000 telescopes to be "abnormally" low because a major competitor has been sharply reducing its selling price and spending a lot of money on advertising. Stassen expects that the competitor's lower price and advertising blitz will not be a long-run phenomenon and that, by 2015 and beyond, Stassen's production and sales will be higher.

Effect on Budgeted Fixed Manufacturing Cost Rate

We now illustrate how each of these four denominator levels affects the budgeted fixed manufacturing cost rate. Stassen has budgeted (standard) fixed manufacturing overhead costs of $1,080,000 for 2014. This lump-sum is incurred to provide the capacity to produce telescopes. The amount includes, among other costs, leasing costs for the facility and the compensation of the facility managers. The budgeted fixed manufacturing cost rates for 2014 for each of the four capacity-level concepts are as follows:

	Home	Insert	Page Layout	Formulas	Data	Review	View	
	A		B	C	D			
1			Budgeted Fixed	Budget	Budgeted Fixed			
2	Denominator-Level		Manufacturing	Capacity Level	Manufacturing			
3	Capacity Concept		Costs per Year	(in units)	Cost per Unit			
4	(1)		(2)	(3)	(4) = (2)/(3)			
5	Theoretical capacity		$1,080,000	18,000	$ 60			
6	Practical capacity		$1,080,000	12,000	$ 90			
7	Normal capacity utilization		$1,080,000	10,000	$108			
8	Master-budget capacity utilization		$1,080,000	8,000	$135			

The significant difference in cost rates (from $60 to $135) arises because of large differences in budgeted capacity levels under the different capacity concepts.

Budgeted (standard) variable manufacturing cost is $200 per unit. The total budgeted (standard) manufacturing cost per unit for alternative capacity-level concepts is as follows:

	Home	Insert	Page Layout	Formulas	Data	Review	View	
	A		B	C	D			
1			Budgeted Variable	Budgeted Fixed	Budgeted Total			
2	Denominator-Level		Manufacturing	Manufacturing	Manufacturing			
3	Capacity Concept		Cost per Unit	Cost per Unit	Cost per Unit			
4	(1)		(2)	(3)	(4) = (2) + (3)			
5	Theoretical capacity		$200	$ 60	$260			
6	Practical capacity		$200	$ 90	$290			
7	Normal capacity utilization		$200	$108	$308			
8	Master-budget capacity utilization		$200	$135	$335			

Because different denominator-level capacity concepts yield different budgeted fixed manufacturing costs per unit, Stassen must decide which capacity level to use. Stassen is not required to use the same capacity-level concept, say, for management planning and control, external reporting to shareholders, and income tax purposes.

Choosing a Capacity Level

As we just saw, at the start of each fiscal year, managers determine different denominator levels for the different capacity concepts and calculate different budgeted fixed manufacturing costs per unit. We now discuss different denominator-level choices for different purposes, including (a) product costing and capacity management, (b) pricing, (c) performance evaluation, (d) external reporting, and (e) tax requirements.

Product Costing and Capacity Management

Data from normal costing or standard costing are often used in pricing or product-mix decisions. As the Stassen example illustrates, use of theoretical capacity results in an unrealistically small fixed manufacturing cost per unit because it is based on an idealistic and unattainable level of capacity. Theoretical capacity is rarely used to calculate budgeted fixed manufacturing cost per unit because it departs significantly from the real capacity available to a company.

Decision Point

What are the various capacity levels a company can use to compute the budgeted fixed manufacturing cost rate?

Learning Objective 6

Examine the key factors in choosing a capacity level to compute the budgeted fixed manufacturing cost rate

...managers must consider the effect a capacity level has on product costing, pricing decisions, performance evaluation, and financial and tax statements

Many companies favor practical capacity as the denominator to calculate budgeted fixed manufacturing cost per unit. Practical capacity in the Stassen example represents the maximum number of units (12,000) that Stassen can reasonably expect to produce per year for the $1,080,000 it will spend annually on capacity. If Stassen had consistently planned to produce fewer units, say 6,000 telescopes each year, it would have built a smaller plant and incurred lower costs.

Stassen budgets $90 in fixed manufacturing cost per unit based on the $1,080,000 it costs to acquire the capacity to produce 12,000 units. This level of plant capacity is an important strategic decision that managers make well before Stassen uses the capacity and even before Stassen knows how much of the capacity it will actually use. That is, budgeted fixed manufacturing cost of $90 per unit measures the *cost per unit of supplying the capacity*.

Demand for Stassen's telescopes in 2014 is expected to be 8,000 units, which is 4,000 units lower than the practical capacity of 12,000 units. However, it costs Stassen $1,080,000 per year to acquire the capacity to make 12,000 units, so the cost of *supplying* the capacity needed to make 12,000 units is still $90 per unit. The capacity and its cost are fixed *in the short run*; unlike variable costs, the capacity supplied does not automatically reduce to match the capacity needed in 2014. As a result, not all of the capacity supplied at $90 per unit will be needed or used in 2014. Using practical capacity as the denominator level, managers can subdivide the cost of resources supplied into used and unused components. At the supply cost of $90 per unit, the manufacturing resources that Stassen will use equal $720,000 ($90 per unit × 8,000 units). Manufacturing resources that Stassen will not use are $360,000 [$90 per unit × (12,000 − 8,000) units].

Using practical capacity as the denominator level sets the cost of capacity at the cost of supplying the capacity, regardless of the demand for the capacity. Highlighting the cost of capacity acquired but not used directs managers' attention toward managing unused capacity, perhaps by designing new products to fill unused capacity, by leasing unused capacity to others, or by eliminating unused capacity. In contrast, using either of the capacity levels based on the demand for Stassen's telescopes—master-budget capacity utilization or normal capacity utilization—hides the amount of unused capacity. If Stassen had used master-budget capacity utilization as the capacity level, it would have calculated budgeted fixed manufacturing cost per unit as $135 ($1,080,000 ÷ 8,000 units). This calculation does not use data about practical capacity, so it does not separately identify the cost of unused capacity. Note, however, that the cost of $135 per unit includes a charge for unused capacity: It is composed of the $90 fixed manufacturing resource that would be used to produce each unit at practical capacity plus the cost of unused capacity allocated to each unit, $45 per unit ($360,000 ÷ 8,000 units).

From the perspective of long-run product costing, which cost of capacity should Stassen use for pricing purposes or for benchmarking its product cost structure against competitors: $90 per unit based on practical capacity or $135 per unit based on master-budget capacity utilization? Probably the $90 per unit based on practical capacity. Why? Because $90 per unit represents the budgeted cost per unit of only the capacity used to produce the product, and it explicitly excludes the cost of any unused capacity. Stassen's customers will be willing to pay a price that covers the cost of the capacity actually used but will not want to pay for unused capacity that provides no other benefits to them. Customers expect Stassen to manage its unused capacity or to bear the cost of unused capacity, not pass it along to them. Moreover, if Stassen's competitors manage unused capacity more effectively, the cost of capacity in the competitors' cost structures (which guides competitors' pricing decisions) is likely to approach $90. In the next section, we show how using normal capacity utilization or master-budget capacity utilization can result in managers setting selling prices that are not competitive.

Pricing Decisions and the Downward Demand Spiral

The **downward demand spiral** for a company is the continuing reduction in the demand for its products that occurs when competitor prices are not met; as demand drops further, higher and higher unit costs result in greater reluctance to meet competitors' prices.

The easiest way to understand the downward demand spiral is with an example. Assume Stassen uses master-budget capacity utilization of 8,000 units for product costing in 2014. The resulting manufacturing cost is $335 per unit ($200 variable manufacturing cost per unit + $135 fixed manufacturing cost per unit). Assume that in December 2013, a competitor offers to supply a major customer of Stassen (a customer who was expected to purchase 2,000 units in 2014) telescopes at $300 per unit. The Stassen manager doesn't want to show a loss on the account and wants to recoup all costs in the long run, so the manager declines to match the competitor's price. The account is lost. The loss means budgeted fixed manufacturing costs of $1,080,000 will be spread over the remaining master-budget volume of 6,000 units at a rate of $180 per unit ($1,080,000 ÷ 6,000 units).

Suppose yet another Stassen customer, who also accounts for 2,000 units of budgeted volume, receives a bid from a competitor at a price of $350 per unit. The Stassen manager compares this bid with his revised unit cost of $380 ($200 + $180) and declines to match the competition, and the account is lost. Planned output would shrink further to 4,000 units. Budgeted fixed manufacturing cost per unit for the remaining 4,000 telescopes would now be $270 ($1,080,000 ÷ 4,000 units). The following table shows the effect of spreading fixed manufacturing costs over a shrinking amount of master-budget capacity utilization:

	Home	Insert	Page Layout	Formulas	Data	Review	View	
	A		B		C		D	
1	Master-Budget				Budgeted Fixed			
2	Capacity Utilization		Budgeted Variable		Manufacturing		Budgeted Total	
3	Denominator Level		Manufacturing Cost		Cost per Unit		Manufacturing	
4	(Units)		per Unit		[$1,080,000 ÷ (1)]		Cost per Unit	
5	(1)		(2)		(3)		(4) = (2) + (3)	
6	8,000		$200		$135		$335	
7	6,000		$200		$180		$380	
8	4,000		$200		$270		$470	
9	3,000		$200		$360		$560	

Practical capacity, by contrast, is a stable measure. The use of practical capacity as the denominator to calculate budgeted fixed manufacturing cost per unit avoids the recalculation of unit costs when expected demand levels change because the fixed cost rate is calculated based on *capacity available* rather than *capacity used to meet demand*. Managers who use reported unit costs in a mechanical way to set prices are less likely to promote a downward demand spiral when they use practical capacity than when they use normal capacity utilization or master-budget capacity utilization.

Using practical capacity as the denominator level also gives the manager a more accurate idea of the resources needed and used to produce a unit by excluding the cost of unused capacity. As discussed earlier, the cost of manufacturing resources supplied to produce a telescope is $290 ($200 variable manufacturing cost per unit plus $90 fixed manufacturing cost per unit). This cost is lower than the prices Stassen's competitors offer and would have correctly led the manager to match the prices and retain the accounts (assuming for purposes of this discussion that Stassen has no other costs). If, however, the prices competitors offered were lower than $290 per unit, the Stassen manager would not recover the cost of resources used to supply telescopes. This would signal to the manager that Stassen was noncompetitive even if it had no unused capacity. The only way for Stassen to be profitable and retain customers in the long run would be to reduce its manufacturing cost per unit.[5]

Performance Evaluation

Consider how the choice among normal capacity utilization, master-budget capacity utilization, and practical capacity affects how a company evaluates its marketing manager. Normal capacity utilization is often used as a basis for long-run plans. Normal

---

[5] The downward demand spiral is currently at work in the traditional landline phone industry. As more telephone customers shift services to wireless or Internet-based options, Verizon and AT&T, the two largest telephone service providers in the United States, are reducing their focus on providing copper-wire telephone service to homes and business. As AT&T told the U.S. Federal Communications Commission, "The business model for legacy phone services is in a death spiral."

capacity utilization depends on the time span selected and the forecasts made for each year. *However, normal capacity utilization is an average that provides no meaningful feedback to the marketing manager for a particular year.* Using normal capacity utilization to judge current performance of a marketing manager is an example of a company misusing a long-run measure for a short-run purpose. The company should use master-budget capacity utilization, rather than normal capacity utilization or practical capacity, to evaluate a marketing manager's performance in the current year because the master budget is the principal short-run planning and control tool. Managers feel more obligated to reach the levels specified in the master budget, which the company should have carefully set in relation to the maximum opportunities for sales in the current year.

When large differences exist between practical capacity and master-budget capacity utilization, several companies (such as Texas Instruments, Polysar, and Sandoz) classify the difference as *planned unused capacity*. One reason for this approach is performance evaluation. Consider our Stassen telescope example. The managers in charge of capacity planning usually do not make pricing decisions. Top management decided to build a production facility with 12,000 units of practical capacity, focusing on demand over the next five years. But Stassen's marketing managers, who are mid-level managers, make the pricing decisions. These marketing managers believe they should be held accountable only for the manufacturing overhead costs related to their potential customer base in 2014. The master-budget capacity utilization suggests a customer base in 2014 of 8,000 units (2/3 of the 12,000 practical capacity). Using responsibility accounting principles, only 2/3 of the budgeted total fixed manufacturing costs ($1,080,000 \times 2/3 = \$720,000$) would be attributed to the fixed capacity costs of meeting 2014 demand. The remaining 1/3 of the numerator ($1,080,000 \times 1/3 = \$360,000$) would be separately shown as the capacity cost of meeting increases in long-run demand expected to occur beyond 2014.[6]

External Reporting

The magnitude of the favorable/unfavorable production-volume variance under absorption costing is affected by the choice of the denominator level used to calculate the budgeted fixed manufacturing cost per unit. Assume the following actual operating information for Stassen in 2014:

	A	B	C
	Home Insert Page Layout Formulas Data		
	A	B	C
1	Beginning inventory	0	
2	Production	8,000	units
3	Sales	6,000	units
4	Ending inventory	2,000	units
5	Selling price	$ 1,000	per unit
6	Variable manufacturing cost	$ 200	per unit
7	Fixed manufacturing costs	$ 1,080,000	
8	Variable marketing cost	$ 185	per unit sold
9	Fixed marketing costs	$ 1,380,000	

Note that this is the same data used to calculate the income under variable and absorption costing for Stassen in Exhibit 1. As before, we assume that there are no price, spending, or efficiency variances in manufacturing costs.

---

[6] For further discussion, see T. Klammer, *Capacity Measurement and Improvement* (Chicago: Irwin, 1996). This research was facilitated by CAM-I, an organization promoting innovative cost management practices. CAM-I's research on capacity costs explores how companies can identify types of capacity costs that can be reduced (or eliminated) without affecting the required output to meet customer demand. An example is improving processes to successfully eliminate the costs of capacity held in anticipation of handling difficulties due to imperfect coordination with suppliers and customers.

The equation used to calculate the production-volume variance is:

$$\text{Production-volume variance} = \left(\begin{array}{c}\text{Budgeted} \\ \text{fixed} \\ \text{manufacturing} \\ \text{overhead}\end{array}\right) - \left(\begin{array}{c}\text{Fixed manufacturing overhead allocated using} \\ \text{budgeted cost per output unit} \\ \text{allowed for actual output produced}\end{array}\right)$$

The four different capacity-level concepts result in four different budgeted fixed manufacturing overhead cost rates per unit. The different rates will result in different amounts of fixed manufacturing overhead costs allocated to the 8,000 units actually produced and different amounts of production-volume variance. Using the budgeted fixed manufacturing costs of $1,080,000 (equal to actual fixed manufacturing costs) and the rates calculated for different denominator levels, the production-volume variance computations are as follows:

Production-volume variance (theoretical capacity)
= $1,080,000 − (8,000 units × $60 per unit)
= $1,080,000 − 480,000
= $600,000 U

Production-volume variance (practical capacity)
= $1,080,000 − (8,000 units × $90 per unit)
= $1,080,000 − 720,000
= $360,000 U

Production-volume variance (normal capacity utilization) = $1,080,00 − (8,000 units × $108 per unit)
= $1,080,000 − 864,000
= $216,000 U

Production-volume variance (master-budget capacity utilization)
= $1,080,000 − (8,000 units × $135 per unit)
= $1,080,000 − 1,080,000
= $0

How Stassen disposes of its production-volume variance at the end of the fiscal year will determine the effect this variance has on the company's operating income. We now discuss the three alternative approaches Stassen can use to dispose of the production-volume variance.

1. **Adjusted allocation-rate approach.** This approach restates all amounts in the general and subsidiary ledgers by using actual rather than budgeted cost rates. Given that actual fixed manufacturing costs are $1,080,000 and actual production is 8,000 units, the recalculated fixed manufacturing cost is $135 per unit ($1,080,000 ÷ 8,000 actual units). Under the adjusted allocation-rate approach, the choice of the capacity level used to calculate the budgeted fixed manufacturing cost per unit has no impact on year-end financial statements. In effect, actual costing is adopted at the end of the fiscal year.

2. **Proration approach.** The underallocated or overallocated overhead is spread among ending balances in Work-in-Process Control, Finished Goods Control, and Cost of Goods Sold. The proration restates the ending balances in these accounts to what they would have been if actual cost rates had been used rather than budgeted cost rates. The proration approach also results in the choice of the capacity level used to calculate the budgeted fixed manufacturing cost per unit having no effect on year-end financial statements.

3. **Write-off variances to cost of goods sold approach.** Exhibit 7 shows how use of this approach affects Stassen's operating income for 2014. Recall that the ending inventory on December 31, 2014, is 2,000 units. Using master-budget capacity utilization as the denominator level results in assigning the highest amount of fixed manufacturing cost per unit to the 2,000 units in ending inventory (see the line item "deduct ending inventory" in Exhibit 7). Accordingly, operating income is highest using master-budget capacity utilization. The differences in operating income for the four denominator-level

concepts in Exhibit 7 are due to these different amounts of fixed manufacturing overhead being inventoried at the end of 2014:

Fixed Manufacturing Overhead in December 31, 2014, Inventory

Theoretical capacity	2,000 units × $60 per unit = $120,000
Practical capacity	2,000 units × $90 per unit = $180,000
Normal capacity utilization	2,000 units × $108 per unit = $216,000
Master-budget capacity utilization	2,000 units × $135 per unit = $270,000

In Exhibit 7, for example, the $54,000 difference ($1,500,000 − $1,446,000) in operating income between master-budget capacity utilization and normal capacity utilization is due to the difference in fixed manufacturing overhead inventoried ($270,000 − $216,000).

To summarize, the common factor behind the increasing operating-income numbers in Exhibit 4 and Exhibit 7 is the increasing amount of fixed manufacturing costs incurred that is included in ending inventory. The amount of fixed manufacturing costs inventoried depends on two factors: the number of units in ending inventory and the rate at which fixed manufacturing costs are allocated to each unit. Exhibit 4 shows the effect on operating income of increasing the number of units in ending inventory (by increasing production). Exhibit 7 shows the effect on operating income of increasing the

Exhibit 7 Income-Statement Effects of Using Alternative Capacity-Level Concepts: Stassen Company for 2014

	A	B	C	D	E	F	G	H	I
1		Theoretical Capacity		Practical Capacity		Normal Capacity Utilization		Master-Budget Capacity Utilization	
2	Denominator level in units	18,000		12,000		10,000		8,000	
3	Revenues[a]	$6,000,000		$6,000,000		$6,000,000		$6,000,000	
4	Cost of goods sold								
5	Beginning inventory	0		0		0		0	
6	Variable manufacturing costs[b]	1,600,000		1,600,000		1,600,000		1,600,000	
7	Fixed manufacturing costs[c]	480,000		720,000		864,000		1,080,000	
8	Cost of goods available for sale	2,080,000		2,320,000		2,464,000		2,680,000	
9	Deduct ending inventory[d]	(520,000)		(580,000)		(616,000)		(670,000)	
10	Cost of goods sold (at standard cost)	1,560,000		1,740,000		1,848,000		2,010,000	
11	Adjustment for production-volume variance	600,000	U	360,000	U	216,000	U	0	
12	Cost of goods sold	2,160,000		2,100,000		2,064,000		2,010,000	
13	Gross margin	3,840,000		3,900,000		3,936,000		3,990,000	
14	Marketing costs[e]	2,490,000		2,490,000		2,490,000		2,490,000	
15	Operating income	$1,350,000		$1,410,000		$1,446,000		$1,500,000	
16									
17	[a]$1,000 × 6,000 units = $6,000,000			[d]Ending inventory costs:					
18	[b]$200 × 8,000 units = $1,600,000			($200 + $60) × 2,000 units = $520,000					
19	[c]Fixed manufacturing overhead costs:			($200 + $90) × 2,000 units = $580,000					
20	$60 × 8,000 units = $ 480,000			($200 + $108) × 2,000 units = $616,000					
21	$90 × 8,000 units = $ 720,000			($200 + $135) × 2,000 units = $670,000					
22	$108 × 8,000 units = $ 864,000			[e]Marketing costs:					
23	$135 × 8,000 units = $1,080,000			$1,380,000 + ($185 × 6,000 units) = $2,490,000					

fixed manufacturing cost allocated per unit (by decreasing the denominator level used to calculate the rate).

Managers and management accountants must consider various issues when deciding whether to prorate the production-volume variance among inventories and cost of goods sold or to simply write off the variance to cost of goods sold. The objective is to write off the portion of the production-volume variance that represents the cost of capacity not used to support the production of output during the period. Determining this amount is almost always a matter of judgment.

Tax Requirements

For tax reporting purposes in the United States, the Internal Revenue Service (IRS) requires companies to assign inventoriable indirect production costs by a "method of allocation which fairly apportions such costs among the various items produced." The IRS accepts approaches that involve the use of either overhead rates (which the IRS terms the "manufacturing burden rate method") or standard costs. Under either approach, U.S. tax reporting requires end-of-period reconciliation between actual and applied indirect costs using the adjusted allocation-rate method or the proration method.[7] More interestingly, under either approach, the IRS permits the use of practical capacity to calculate budgeted fixed manufacturing cost per unit. Further, the production-volume variance generated this way can be deducted for tax purposes in the year in which the cost is incurred. The tax benefits from this policy are evident from Exhibit 7. Note that the operating income when the denominator is set to practical capacity (column D, where the production volume variance of $360,000 is written off to cost of goods sold) is lower than those under normal capacity utilization (column F) or master-budget capacity utilization (column H).

Decision Point

What are the major factors managers consider in choosing the capacity level to compute the budgeted fixed manufacturing cost rate?

Planning and Control of Capacity Costs

In addition to the issues previously discussed, managers must take a variety of other factors into account when planning capacity levels and in deciding how best to control and assign capacity costs. These other factors include the level of uncertainty about both the expected costs and the expected demand for the installed capacity; the presence of capacity-related issues in nonmanufacturing settings; and the potential use of activity-based costing techniques in allocating capacity costs.

Difficulties in Forecasting Chosen Denominator-Level Concept

Practical capacity measures the available supply of capacity. Managers can usually use engineering studies and human resource considerations (such as worker safety) to obtain a reliable estimate of this denominator level for the budget period. It is more difficult to obtain reliable estimates of demand-side denominator-level concepts, especially longer-term normal capacity utilization figures. For example, many U.S. steel companies in the 1980s believed they were in the downturn of a demand cycle that would have an upturn within two or three years. After all, steel had been a cyclical business in which upturns followed downturns, making the notion of normal capacity utilization appear reasonable. Unfortunately, the steel cycle in the 1980s did not turn up, resulting in some companies and numerous plants closing. The recent global economic slowdown demonstrated the extent to which demand projections could be inaccurate. Consider that in 2006 auto analysts forecast that annual demand in India for cars and passenger vehicles would hit 1.92 million in the year 2009–2010. In early 2009, the forecast for the same period was revised downward to 1.37 million vehicles. Inaccurate forecasts are not exclusive to the auto industry. In April

Learning Objective 7

Understand other issues that play an important role in capacity planning and control

...uncertainty regarding the expected spending on capacity costs and the demand for installed capacity, the role of capacity-related issues in nonmanufacturing areas, and the possible use of activity-based costing techniques in allocating capacity costs

---

[7] For example, Section 1.471-11 of the U.S. Internal Revenue Code states, "The proper use of the standard cost method... requires that a taxpayer must reallocate to the goods in ending inventory a pro rata portion of any net negative or net positive overhead variances." Of course, if the variances are not material in amount, they can be expensed (i.e., written off to cost of goods sold), provided the same treatment is carried out in the firm's financial reports.

2013, the world's largest miner, BHP Billiton, scrapped plans for projects worth $40 billion in Australia to reflect dropping prices for major metals in response to slowing demand from China, the largest commodities consumer. In addition to dealing with economic cycles and inaccurate forecasts, companies also face the problem of marketing managers who may overestimate their ability to regain lost sales and market share. Their estimate of "normal" demand for their product may consequently be based on an overly optimistic outlook. Master-budget capacity utilization focuses only on the expected demand for the next year. Therefore, companies can more reliably estimate master-budget capacity utilization than normal capacity utilization. However, master-budget capacity utilization is still just a forecast, and the true demand realization can be either higher or lower than this estimate.

It is important to understand that costing systems, such as normal costing or standard costing, do not recognize uncertainty the way managers recognize it. A single amount, rather than a range of possible amounts, is used as the denominator level when calculating the budgeted fixed manufacturing cost per unit in absorption costing. Consider Stassen's facility, which has an estimated practical capacity of 12,000 units. The estimated master-budget capacity utilization for 2014 is 8,000 units. However, there is still substantial doubt about the actual number of units Stassen will have to manufacture in 2014 and in future years. Managers recognize uncertainty in their capacity-planning decisions. Stassen built its current plant with a 12,000-unit practical capacity in part to provide the capability to meet possible demand surges. Even if such surges do not occur in a given period, do not conclude that capacity unused in a given period is wasted resources. The gains from meeting sudden demand surges may well require having unused capacity in some periods.

Difficulties in Forecasting Fixed Manufacturing Costs

The fixed manufacturing cost rate is based on a numerator (budgeted fixed manufacturing costs) and a denominator (some measure of capacity or capacity utilization). Our discussion so far has emphasized issues concerning the choice of the denominator. Challenging issues also arise in measuring the numerator. For example, deregulation of the U.S. electric utility industry has resulted in many electric utilities becoming unprofitable. This situation has led to write-downs in the values of the utilities' plants and equipment. The write-downs reduce the numerator because there is less depreciation expense included in the calculation of fixed capacity cost per kilowatt-hour of electricity produced. The difficulty that managers face in this situation is that the amount of write-downs is not clear-cut but, rather, a matter of judgment. In several industries, the increased emphasis on sustainability and attention to the environment has led to unexpected increases in the fixed costs of operations. On the other hand, infrastructure costs for information technology have continued to plummet and have moved from fixed to variable costs in many cases because of the capabilities offered by providers such as Amazon Web Services.

Nonmanufacturing Costs

Capacity costs also arise in nonmanufacturing parts of the value chain. Stassen may acquire a fleet of vehicles capable of distributing the practical capacity of its production facility. When actual production is below practical capacity, there will be unused-capacity cost issues with the distribution function, as well as with the manufacturing function.

Capacity cost issues are prominent in many service-sector companies, such as airlines, hospitals, and railroads—even though these companies carry no inventory and so have no inventory costing problems. For example, in calculating the fixed overhead cost per patient-day in its obstetrics and gynecology department, a hospital must decide which denominator level to use: practical capacity, normal capacity utilization, or master-budget capacity utilization. The hospital's decision may have implications for capacity management, as well as pricing and performance evaluation.

Activity-Based Costing

To maintain simplicity, the Stassen example in this chapter assumed that all costs were either variable or fixed. In particular, there were no batch-level costs and no product-sustaining costs. It is easy to see that the distinction between variable and absorption costing carries over directly into activity-based costing systems, with batch-level costs acting as variable costs and product-sustaining ones as fixed costs, as a function of the number of units produced.

In order to focus on the choice of denominator to calculate the budgeted fixed manufacturing cost rate, our Stassen example assumed that all fixed manufacturing costs had a single cost driver: telescope units produced. Activity-based costing systems have multiple overhead cost pools at the output-unit, batch, product-sustaining, and facility-sustaining levels—each with its own cost driver. In calculating activity cost rates (for fixed costs of setups and material handling, say), management must choose a capacity level for the quantity of the cost driver (setup-hours or loads moved). Should management use practical capacity, normal capacity utilization, or master-budget capacity utilization? For all the reasons described in this chapter (such as pricing and capacity management), most proponents of activity-based costing argue that managers should use practical capacity as the denominator level to calculate activity cost rates.

Decision Point

What issues must managers take into account when planning capacity levels and for assigning capacity costs?

Problem for Self-Study

Assume Stassen Company on January 1, 2014, decides to contract with another company to preassemble a large percentage of the components of its telescopes. The revised manufacturing cost structure during the 2014–2015 period is as follows:

Variable manufacturing cost per unit produced		
Direct materials	$	250
Direct manufacturing labor		20
Manufacturing overhead		5
Total variable manufacturing cost per unit produced	$	275
Fixed manufacturing costs		$480,000

Under the revised cost structure, a larger percentage of Stassen's manufacturing costs are variable for units produced. The denominator level of production used to calculate budgeted fixed manufacturing cost per unit in 2014 and 2015 is 8,000 units. Assume no other change from the data underlying Exhibits 1 and 2. Summary information pertaining to absorption-costing operating income and variable-costing operating income with this revised cost structure are as follows:

	2014	2015
Absorption-costing operating income	$1,500,000	$1,560,000
Variable-costing operating income	1,380,000	1,650,000
Difference	$ 120,000	$ (90,000)

1. Compute the budgeted fixed manufacturing cost per unit in 2014 and 2015.
2. Explain the difference between absorption-costing operating income and variable-costing operating income in 2014 and 2015, focusing on fixed manufacturing costs in beginning and ending inventory.
3. Why are these differences smaller than the differences in Exhibit 2?
4. Assume the same preceding information, except that for 2014, the master-budget capacity utilization is 10,000 units instead of 8,000. How would Stassen's absorption-costing income for 2014 differ from the $1,500,000 shown previously? Show your computations.

Required

Solution

1. $$\text{Budgeted fixed manufacturing cost per unit} = \frac{\text{Budgeted fixed manufacturing costs}}{\text{Budgeted production units}}$$

$$= \frac{\$480,000}{8,000 \text{ units}}$$

$$= \$60 \text{ per unit}$$

2. $$\begin{array}{ccc} \text{Absorption-costing} & \text{Variable-costing} & \text{Fixed manufacturing} & \text{Fixed manufacturing costs} \\ \text{operating} & - \text{ operating} & = \text{costs in ending inventory} - & \text{in beginning inventory} \\ \text{income} & \text{income} & \text{under absorption costing} & \text{under absorption costing} \end{array}$$

2014: $1,500,000 - $1,380,000 = ($60 per unit × 2,000 units) − ($60 per unit × 0 units)

$120,000 = $120,000

2015: $1,560,000 − $1,650,000 = ($60 per unit × 500 units) − ($60 per unit × 2,000 units)

−$90,000 = −$90,000

3. Subcontracting a large part of manufacturing has greatly reduced the magnitude of fixed manufacturing costs. This reduction, in turn, means differences between absorption costing and variable costing are much smaller than in Exhibit 2.

4. Given the higher master-budget capacity utilization level of 10,000 units, the budgeted fixed manufacturing cost rate for 2014 is now as follows:

$$\frac{\$480,000}{10,000 \text{ units}} = \$48 \text{ per unit}$$

The manufacturing cost per unit is $323 ($275 + $48). So, the production-volume variance for 2014 is

$$(10,000 \text{ units} - 8,000 \text{ units}) \times \$48 \text{ per unit} = \$96,000 \text{ U}$$

The absorption-costing income statement for 2014 is as follows:

Revenues: $1,000 per unit × 6,000 units	$6,000,000
Cost of goods sold:	
Beginning inventory	0
Variable manufacturing costs: $275 per unit × 8,000 units	2,200,000
Fixed manufacturing costs: $48 per unit × 8,000 units	384,000
Cost of goods available for sale	2,584,000
Deduct ending inventory: $323 per unit × 2,000 units	(646,000)
Cost of goods sold (at standard costs)	1,938,000
Adjustment for production-volume variance	96,000 U
Cost of goods sold	2,034,000
Gross margin	3,966,000
Marketing costs: $1,380,000 fixed + ($185 per unit × 6,000 units sold)	2,490,000
Operating income	$1,476,000

The higher denominator level used to calculate the budgeted fixed manufacturing cost per unit means that fewer fixed manufacturing costs are inventoried ($48 per unit × 2,000 units = $96,000) than when the master-budget capacity utilization was 8,000 units ($60 per unit × 2,000 units = $120,000). This difference of $24,000 ($120,000 − $96,000) results in operating income being lower by $24,000 relative to the prior calculated income level of $1,500,000.

▶ Decision Points

The following question-and-answer format summarizes the chapter's learning objectives.
Each decision presents a key question related to a learning objective. The guidelines are
the answer to that question.

Decision	Guidelines
1. How does variable costing differ from absorption costing?	Variable costing and absorption costing differ in only one respect: how to account for fixed manufacturing costs. Under variable costing, fixed manufacturing costs are excluded from inventoriable costs and are a cost of the period in which they are incurred. Under absorption costing, fixed manufacturing costs are inventoriable and become a part of cost of goods sold in the period when sales occur.
2. How does income differ under variable and absorption costing?	The variable-costing income statement is based on the contribution-margin format. Under it, operating income is driven by the unit level of sales. Under absorption costing, the income statement follows the gross-margin format. Operating income is driven by the unit level of production, the unit level of sales, and the denominator level used for assigning fixed costs.
3. Why might managers build up finished goods inventory if they use absorption costing?	When absorption costing is used, managers can increase current operating income by producing more units for inventory. Producing for inventory absorbs more fixed manufacturing costs into inventory and reduces costs expensed in the period. Critics of absorption costing label this manipulation of income as the major negative consequence of treating fixed manufacturing costs as inventoriable costs.
4. How does throughput costing differ from variable costing and absorption costing?	Throughput costing treats all costs except direct materials as costs of the period in which they are incurred. Throughput costing results in a lower amount of manufacturing costs being inventoried than either variable or absorption costing.
5. What are the various capacity levels a company can use to compute the budgeted fixed manufacturing cost rate?	Capacity levels can be measured in terms of capacity supplied—theoretical capacity or practical capacity. Capacity can also be measured in terms of output demanded—normal capacity utilization or master-budget capacity utilization.
6. What are the major factors managers consider in choosing the capacity level to compute the budgeted fixed manufacturing cost rate?	The major factors managers consider in choosing the capacity level to compute the budgeted fixed manufacturing cost rate are (a) effect on product costing and capacity management, (b) effect on pricing decisions, (c) effect on performance evaluation, (d) effect on financial statements, and (e) regulatory requirements.
7. What issues must managers take into account when planning capacity levels and for assigning capacity costs?	Critical factors when planning capacity levels and for assigning capacity costs include the uncertainty about the expected spending on capacity costs and the demand for the installed capacity; the role of capacity-related issues in nonmanufacturing areas; and the possible use of activity-based costing techniques in allocating capacity costs.

Appendix

Breakeven Points in Variable Costing and Absorption Costing

If variable costing is used, the breakeven point (that's where operating income is $0) is computed in the usual manner. There is only one breakeven point in this case, and it depends on (1) fixed (manufacturing and operating) costs and (2) contribution margin per unit.

The formula for computing the breakeven point under variable costing is a special case of the more general target operating income formula:

$$\text{Let } Q = \text{Number of units sold to earn the target operating income}$$

$$\text{Then } Q = \frac{\text{Total fixed costs} + \text{Target operating income}}{\text{Contribution margin per unit}}$$

Breakeven occurs when the target operating income is $0. In our Stassen illustration for 2014 (see Exhibit 1):

$$Q = \frac{(\$1,080,000 + \$1,380,000) + \$0}{(\$1,000 - (\$200 + \$185))} = \frac{\$2,460,000}{\$615}$$

$$= 4,000 \text{ units}$$

We now verify that Stassen will achieve breakeven under variable costing by selling 4,000 units:

Revenues, $1,000 × 4,000 units	$4,000,000
Variable costs, $385 × 4,000 units	1,540,000
Contribution margin, $615 × 4,000 units	2,460,000
Fixed costs	2,460,000
Operating income	$ 0

If absorption costing is used, the required number of units to be sold to earn a specific target operating income is not unique because of the number of variables involved. The following formula shows the factors that will affect the target operating income under absorption costing:

$$Q = \frac{\begin{array}{c}\text{Total} \\ \text{fixed} \\ \text{costs}\end{array} + \begin{array}{c}\text{Target} \\ \text{operating} \\ \text{income}\end{array} + \left[\begin{array}{c}\text{Fixed} \\ \text{manufacturing} \\ \text{cost rate}\end{array} \times \left(\begin{array}{c}\text{Breakeven} \\ \text{sales} \\ \text{in units}\end{array} - \begin{array}{c}\text{Units} \\ \text{produced}\end{array}\right)\right]}{\text{Contribution margin per unit}}$$

In this formula, the numerator is the sum of three terms (from the perspective of the two "+" signs), compared with two terms in the numerator of the variable-costing formula stated earlier. The additional term in the numerator under absorption costing is as follows:

$$\left[\frac{\text{Fixed manufacturing}}{\text{cost rate}} \times \left(\frac{\text{Breakeven sales}}{\text{in units}} - \frac{\text{Units}}{\text{produced}}\right)\right]$$

This term reduces the fixed costs that need to be recovered when units produced exceed the breakeven sales quantity. When production exceeds the breakeven sales quantity, some of the fixed manufacturing costs that are expensed under variable costing are not expensed under absorption costing; they are instead included in finished goods inventory. The breakeven sales quantity under absorption costing is correspondingly lower than under variable costing.[8]

---

[8] The reverse situation, where production is lower than the breakeven sales quantity, is not possible unless the firm has opening inventory. In that case, provided the variable manufacturing cost per unit and the fixed manufacturing cost rate are constant over time, the breakeven formula given is still valid. The breakeven sales quantity under absorption costing would then exceed that under variable costing.

For Stassen Company in 2014, suppose that actual production is 5,280 units. Then one breakeven point, Q, under absorption costing is as follows:

$$Q = \frac{(\$1,080,000 + \$1,380,000) + \$0 + [\$135 \times (Q - 5,280)]}{(\$1,000 - (\$200 + \$185))}$$

$$= \frac{(\$2,460,000 + \$135Q - \$712,800)}{\$615}$$

$$\$615Q = \$1,747,200 + \$135Q$$

$$\$480Q = \$1,747,200$$

$$Q = 3,640$$

We next verify that production of 5,280 units and sales of 3,640 units will lead Stassen to break even under absorption costing:

Revenues, $1,000 × 3,640 units		$3,640,000
Cost of goods sold:		
Cost of goods sold at standard cost, $335 × 3,640 units	$1,219,400	
Production-volume variance, $135 × (8,000 − 5,280) units	367,200 U	1,586,600
Gross margin		2,053,400
Marketing costs:		
Variable marketing costs, $185 × 3,640 units	673,400	
Fixed marketing costs	1,380,000	2,053,400
Operating income		$ 0

The breakeven point under absorption costing depends on (1) fixed manufacturing costs, (2) fixed operating (marketing) costs, (3) contribution margin per unit, (4) unit level of production, and (5) the capacity level chosen as the denominator to set the fixed manufacturing cost rate. For Stassen in 2014, a combination of 3,640 units sold, fixed manufacturing costs of $1,080,000, fixed marketing costs of $1,380,000, contribution margin per unit of $615, an 8,000-unit denominator level, and production of 5,280 units would result in an operating income of $0. *Note, however, that there are many combinations of these five factors that would give an operating income of $0.* For example, holding all other factors constant, a combination of 6,240 units produced and 3,370 units sold also results in an operating income of $0 under absorption costing. We provide verification of this alternative breakeven point next:

Revenues, $1,000 × 3,370 units		$3,370,000
Cost of goods sold:		
Cost of goods sold at standard cost, $335 × 3,370 units	$1,128,950	
Production-volume variance, $135 × (8,000 − 6,240) units	237,600 U	1,366,550
Gross margin		2,003,450
Marketing costs:		
Variable marketing costs, $185 × 3,370 units	623,450	
Fixed marketing costs	1,380,000	2,003,450
Operating income		$ 0

Suppose actual production in 2014 was equal to the denominator level, 8,000 units, and there were no units sold and no fixed marketing costs. All the units produced would be placed in inventory, so all the fixed manufacturing costs would be included in inventory. There would be no production-volume variance. Under these conditions, the company could break even under absorption costing with no sales whatsoever! In contrast, under variable costing, the operating loss would be equal to the fixed manufacturing costs of $1,080,000.

Terms to Learn

This chapter contains definitions of the following important terms:

absorption costing
direct costing
downward demand spiral
master-budget capacity utilization

normal capacity utilization
practical capacity
super-variable costing
theoretical capacity

throughput costing
variable costing

Assignment Material

MyAccountingLab

Questions

1 Differences in operating income between variable costing and absorption costing are due solely to accounting for fixed costs. Do you agree? Explain.

2 Why is the term *direct costing* a misnomer?

3 Do companies in either the service sector or the merchandising sector make choices about absorption costing versus variable costing?

4 Explain the main conceptual issue under variable costing and absorption costing regarding the timing for the release of fixed manufacturing overhead as expense.

5 "Companies that make no variable-cost/fixed-cost distinctions must use absorption costing, and those that do make variable-cost/fixed-cost distinctions must use variable costing." Do you agree? Explain.

6 The main trouble with variable costing is that it ignores the increasing importance of fixed costs in manufacturing companies. Do you agree? Why?

7 Give an example of how, under absorption costing, operating income could fall even though the unit sales level rises.

8 What are the factors that affect the breakeven point under (a) variable costing and (b) absorption costing?

9 Critics of absorption costing have increasingly emphasized its potential for leading to undesirable incentives for managers. Give an example.

10 What are two ways of reducing the negative aspects associated with using absorption costing to evaluate the performance of a plant manager?

11 What denominator-level capacity concepts emphasize the output a plant can supply? What denominator-level capacity concepts emphasize the output customers demand for products produced by a plant?

12 Describe the downward demand spiral and its implications for pricing decisions.

13 Will the financial statements of a company always differ when different choices at the start of the accounting period are made regarding the denominator-level capacity concept?

14 What is the IRS's requirement for tax reporting regarding the choice of a denominator-level capacity concept?

15 "The difference between practical capacity and master-budget capacity utilization is the best measure of management's ability to balance the costs of having too much capacity and having too little capacity." Do you agree? Explain.

MyAccountingLab

Exercises

16 **Variable and absorption costing, explaining operating-income differences.** Nascar Motors assembles and sells motor vehicles and uses standard costing. Actual data relating to April and May 2014 are as follows:

	A	B	C	D
1		**April**		**May**
2	Unit data			
3	Beginning inventory	0		150
4	Production	500		400
5	Sales	350		520
6	Variable costs			
7	Manufacturing cost per unit produced	$ 10,000		$ 10,000
8	Operating (marketing) cost per unit sold	3,000		3,000
9	Fixed costs			
10	Manufacturing costs	$2,000,000		$2,000,000
11	Operating (marketing) costs	600,000		600,000

The selling price per vehicle is $24,000. The budgeted level of production used to calculate the budgeted fixed manufacturing cost per unit is 500 units. There are no price, efficiency, or spending variances. Any production-volume variance is written off to cost of goods sold in the month in which it occurs.

Required

1. Prepare April and May 2014 income statements for Nascar Motors under (a) variable costing and (b) absorption costing.
2. Prepare a numerical reconciliation and explanation of the difference between operating income for each month under variable costing and absorption costing.

17 Throughput costing (continuation of 16). The variable manufacturing costs per unit of Nascar Motors are as follows:

	A	B	C
1		**April**	**May**
7	Direct material cost per unit	$6,700	$6,700
8	Direct manufacturing labor cost per unit	1,500	1,500
9	Manufacturing overhead cost per unit	1,800	1,800

Required

1. Prepare income statements for Nascar Motors in April and May 2014 under throughput costing.
2. Contrast the results in requirement 1 with those in requirement 1 of Exercise 16.
3. Give one motivation for Nascar Motors to adopt throughput costing.

18 Variable and absorption costing, explaining operating-income differences. Crystal Clear Corporation manufactures and sells 50-inch television sets and uses standard costing. Actual data relating to January, February, and March 2014 are as follows:

	January	February	March
Unit data			
Beginning inventory	0	100	100
Production	1,400	1,375	1,430
Sales	1,300	1,375	1,455
Variable costs			
Manufacturing cost per unit produced	$ 950	$ 950	$ 950
Operating (marketing) cost per unit sold	$ 725	$ 725	$ 725
Fixed costs			
Manufacturing costs	$490,000	$490,000	$490,000
Operating (marketing) costs	$120,000	$120,000	$120,000

The selling price per unit is $3,500. The budgeted level of production used to calculate the budgeted fixed manufacturing cost per unit is 1,400 units. There are no price, efficiency, or spending variances. Any production-volume variance is written off to cost of goods sold in the month in which it occurs.

1. Prepare income statements for Crystal Clear in January, February, and March 2014 under (a) variable costing and (b) absorption costing.
2. Explain the difference in operating income for January, February, and March under variable costing and absorption costing.

19 Throughput costing (continuation of 18). The variable manufacturing costs per unit of Crystal Clear Corporation are as follows:

	January	February	March
Direct material cost per unit	$550	$550	$550
Direct manufacturing labor cost per unit	175	175	175
Manufacturing overhead cost per unit	225	225	225
	$950	$950	$950

Required

1. Prepare income statements for Crystal Clear in January, February, and March 2014 under throughput costing.
2. Contrast the results in requirement 1 with those in requirement 1 of Exercise 18.
3. Give one motivation for Crystal Clear to adopt throughput costing.

20 Variable versus absorption costing. The Zwatch Company manufactures trendy, high-quality, moderately priced watches. As Zwatch's senior financial analyst, you are asked to recommend a method of inventory costing. The CFO will use your recommendation to prepare Zwatch's 2014 income statement. The following data are for the year ended December 31, 2014:

Beginning inventory, January 1, 2014	85,000 units
Ending inventory, December 31, 2014	34,500 units
2014 sales	345,400 units
Selling price (to distributor)	$22.00 per unit
Variable manufacturing cost per unit, including direct materials	$5.10 per unit
Variable operating (marketing) cost per unit sold	$1.10 per unit sold
Fixed manufacturing costs	$1,440,000
Denominator-level machine-hours	6,000
Standard production rate	50 units per machine-hour
Fixed operating (marketing) costs	$1,080,000

Required

Assume standard costs per unit are the same for units in beginning inventory and units produced during the year. Also, assume no price, spending, or efficiency variances. Any production-volume variance is written off to cost of goods sold in the month in which it occurs.

1. Prepare income statements under variable and absorption costing for the year ended December 31, 2014.
2. What is Zwatch's operating income as percentage of revenues under each costing method?
3. Explain the difference in operating income between the two methods.
4. Which costing method would you recommend to the CFO? Why?

21 Absorption and variable costing. (CMA) Osawa, Inc., planned and actually manufactured 200,000 units of its single product in 2014, its first year of operation. Variable manufacturing cost was $20 per unit produced. Variable operating (nonmanufacturing) cost was $10 per unit sold. Planned and actual fixed manufacturing costs were $600,000. Planned and actual fixed operating (nonmanufacturing) costs totaled $400,000. Osawa sold 120,000 units of product at $40 per unit.

1. Osawa's 2014 operating income using absorption costing is (a) $440,000, (b) $200,000, (c) $600,000, (d) $840,000, or (e) none of these. Show supporting calculations.
2. Osawa's 2014 operating income using variable costing is (a) $800,000, (b) $440,000, (c) $200,000, (d) $600,000, or (e) none of these. Show supporting calculations.

22 Absorption versus variable costing. Regina Company manufacturers a professional-grade vacuum cleaner and began operations in 2014. For 2014, Regina budgeted to produce and sell 20,000 units. The company had no price, spending, or efficiency variances and writes off production-volume variance to cost of goods sold. Actual data for 2014 are given as follows:

	A	B
1	Units produced	18,000
2	Units sold	17,500
3	Selling price	$ 450
4	Variable costs:	
5	Manufacturing cost per unit produced	
6	Direct materials	$ 30
7	Direct manufacturing labor	25
8	Manufacturing overhead	60
9	Marketing cost per unit sold	45
10	Fixed costs:	
11	Manufacturing costs	$1,200,000
12	Administrative costs	965,450
13	Marketing	1,366,400

1. Prepare a 2014 income statement for Regina Company using variable costing.
2. Prepare a 2014 income statement for Regina Company using absorption costing.
3. Explain the differences in operating incomes obtained in requirements 1 and 2.
4. Regina's management is considering implementing a bonus for the supervisors based on gross margin under absorption costing. What incentives will this bonus plan create for the supervisors? What modifications could Regina management make to improve such a plan? Explain briefly.

23 Variable and absorption costing, sales, and operating-income changes. Smart Safety, a three-year-old company, has been producing and selling a single type of bicycle helmet. Smart Safety uses standard costing. After reviewing the income statements for the first three years, Stuart Weil, president of Smart Safety, commented, "I was told by our accountants—and in fact, I have memorized—that our breakeven volume is 52,000 units. I was happy that we reached that sales goal in each of our first two years. But here's the strange thing: In our first year, we sold 52,000 units and indeed we broke even. Then in our second year we sold the same volume and had a positive operating income. I didn't complain, of course...but here's the bad part. In our third year, we *sold 20% more* helmets, but our *operating income fell by more than 80%* relative to the second year! We didn't change our selling price or cost structure over the past three years and have no price, efficiency, or spending variances...so what's going on?!"

	A	B	C	D
	Home	Insert	Page Layout	Formulas	Data	Review	View
	A	B	C	D
1	**Absorption Costing**			
2		**2013**	**2014**	**2015**
3	Sales (units)	52,000	52,000	62,400
4	Revenues	$2,236,000	$2,236,000	$2,683,200
5	Cost of goods sold			
6	Beginning inventory	0	0	405,600
7	Production	2,028,000	2,433,600	2,028,000
8	Available for sale	2,028,000	2,433,600	2,433,600
9	Deduct ending inventory	0	(405,600)	0
10	Adjustment for production-volume variance	0	(260,600)	0
11	Cost of goods sold	2,028,000	1,768,000	2,433,600
12	Gross margin	208,000	468,600	249,600
13	Selling and administrative expenses (all fixed)	208,000	208,000	208,000
14	Operating income	$ 0	$ 260,000	$ 41,600
15				
16	Beginning inventory	0	0	10,400
17	Production (units)	52,000	62,400	52,000
18	Sales (units)	52,000	52,000	62,400
19	Ending inventory	0	10,400	0
20	Variable manufacturing cost per unit	$ 14	$ 14	$ 14
21	Fixed manufacturing overhead costs	$1,300,000	$1,300,000	$1,300,000
22	Fixed manuf. costs allocated per unit produced	$ 25	$ 25	$ 25

Required

1. What denominator level is Smart Safety using to allocate fixed manufacturing costs to the bicycle helmets? How is Smart Safety disposing of any favorable or unfavorable production-volume variance at the end of the year? Explain your answer briefly.
2. How did Smart Safety's accountants arrive at the breakeven volume of 52,000 units?
3. Prepare a variable costing-based income statement for each year. Explain the variation in variable costing operating income for each year based on contribution margin per unit and sales volume.
4. Reconcile the operating incomes under variable costing and absorption costing for each year, and use this information to explain to Stuart Weil the positive operating income in 2014 and the drop in operating income in 2015.

24 **Capacity management, denominator-level capacity concepts.** Match each of the following numbered descriptions with one or more of the denominator-level capacity concepts by putting the appropriate letter(s) by each item:

a. Theoretical capacity
b. Practical capacity
c. Normal capacity utilization
d. Master-budget capacity utilization

1. Measures the denominator level in terms of what a plant can supply
2. Is based on producing at full efficiency all the time
3. Represents the expected level of capacity utilization for the next budget period
4. Measures the denominator level in terms of demand for the output of the plant
5. Takes into account seasonal, cyclical, and trend factors
6. Should be used for performance evaluation in the current year
7. Represents an ideal benchmark
8. Highlights the cost of capacity acquired but not used
9. Should be used for long-term pricing purposes
10. Hides the cost of capacity acquired but not used
11. If used as the denominator-level concept, would avoid the restatement of unit costs when expected demand levels change

25 Denominator-level problem. Thunder Bolt, Inc., is a manufacturer of the very popular G36 motorcycles. The management at Thunder Bolt has recently adopted absorption costing and is debating which denominator-level concept to use. The G36 motorcycles sell for an average price of $8,200. Budgeted fixed manufacturing overhead costs for 2014 are estimated at $6,480,000. Thunder Bolt, Inc., uses subassembly operators that provide component parts. The following are the denominator-level options that management has been considering:

a. Theoretical capacity—based on three shifts, completion of five motorcycles per shift, and a 360-day year—$3 \times 5 \times 360 = 5,400$.
b. Practical capacity—theoretical capacity adjusted for unavoidable interruptions, breakdowns, and so forth—$3 \times 4 \times 320 = 3,840$.
c. Normal capacity utilization—estimated at 3,240 units.
d. Master-budget capacity utilization—the strengthening stock market and the growing popularity of motorcycles have prompted the marketing department to issue an estimate for 2014 of 3,600 units.

Required

1. Calculate the budgeted fixed manufacturing overhead cost rates under the four denominator-level concepts.
2. What are the benefits to Thunder Bolt, Inc., of using either theoretical capacity or practical capacity?
3. Under a cost-based pricing system, what are the negative aspects of a master-budget denominator level? What are the positive aspects?

26 Variable and absorption costing and breakeven points. Artesa, a leading firm in the semiconductor industry, produces digital integrated circuits (ICs) for the communications and defense markets.

For the year ended December 31, 2013, Artesa sold 242,400 ICs at an average selling price of $47 per unit. The following information also relates to 2013 (assume constant unit costs and no variances of any kind):

Inventory, January 1, 2013:	32,600 ICs
Inventory, December 31, 2013:	24,800 ICs
Fixed manufacturing costs:	$1,876,800
Fixed administrative costs:	$3,284,400
Direct materials costs:	$13 per IC
Direct labor costs:	$11 per IC

Required

1. How many integrated circuits did Artesa produce in 2013?
2. Calculate the breakeven point (number of ICs sold) in 2013 under:
   a. Variable costing
   b. Absorption costing
3. Due to difficulties in obtaining high-quality silicon, Artesa expects that direct materials costs will increase to $15 per IC in 2014. Assuming all other data are the same, calculate the minimum number of ICs Artesa must sell in 2014 to break even under:
   a. Variable costing
   b. Absorption costing

27 Variable costing versus absorption costing. The Mavis Company uses an absorption-costing system based on standard costs. Total variable manufacturing cost, including direct material cost, is $3 per unit; the standard production rate is 10 units per machine-hour. Total budgeted and actual fixed manufacturing overhead costs are $420,000. Fixed manufacturing overhead is allocated at $7 per machine-hour ($420,000 ÷ 60,000 machine-hours of denominator level). Selling price is $5 per unit. Variable operating (nonmanufacturing) cost, which is driven by units sold, is $1 per unit. Fixed operating (nonmanufacturing) costs are $120,000. Beginning inventory in 2014 is 30,000 units; ending inventory is 40,000 units. Sales in 2014 are 540,000 units. The same standard unit costs persisted throughout 2013 and 2014. For simplicity, assume that there are no price, spending, or efficiency variances.

Required

1. Prepare an income statement for 2014 assuming that the production-volume variance is written off at year-end as an adjustment to cost of goods sold.
2. The president has heard about variable costing. She asks you to recast the 2014 statement as it would appear under variable costing.
3. Explain the difference in operating income as calculated in requirements 1 and 2.
4. Graph how fixed manufacturing overhead is accounted for under absorption costing. That is, there will be two lines: one for the budgeted fixed manufacturing overhead (which is equal to the actual fixed manufacturing overhead in this case) and one for the fixed manufacturing overhead allocated. Show the production-volume variance in the graph.

5. Critics have claimed that a widely used accounting system has led to undesirable buildups of inventory levels. (a) Is variable costing or absorption costing more likely to lead to such buildups? Why? (b) What can managers do to counteract undesirable inventory buildups?

MyAccountingLab

Problems

28 Variable costing and absorption costing, the All-Fixed Company. (R. Marple, adapted) It is the end of 2013. The All-Fixed Company began operations in January 2012. The company is so named because it has no variable costs. All its costs are fixed; they do not vary with output.

The All-Fixed Company is located on the bank of a river and has its own hydroelectric plant to supply power, light, and heat. The company manufactures a synthetic fertilizer from air and river water and sells its product at a price that is not expected to change. It has a small staff of employees, all paid fixed annual salaries. The output of the plant can be increased or decreased by adjusting a few dials on a control panel.

The following budgeted and actual data are for the operations of the All-Fixed Company. All-Fixed uses budgeted production as the denominator level and writes off any production-volume variance to cost of goods sold.

	2012	2013[a]
Sales	10,000 tons	10,000 tons
Production	20,000 tons	0 tons
Selling price	$ 30 per ton	$ 30 per ton
Costs (all fixed):		
Manufacturing	$280,000	$280,000
Operating (nonmanufacturing)	$ 40,000	$ 40,000

[a] Management adopted the policy, effective January 1, 2013, of producing only as much product as needed to fill sales orders. During 2013, sales were the same as for 2012 and were filled entirely from inventory at the start of 2013.

Required

1. Prepare income statements with one column for 2012, one column for 2013, and one column for the two years together using (a) variable costing and (b) absorption costing.
2. What is the breakeven point under (a) variable costing and (b) absorption costing?
3. What inventory costs would be carried in the balance sheet on December 31, 2012 and 2013, under each method?
4. Assume that the performance of the top manager of the company is evaluated and rewarded largely on the basis of reported operating income. Which costing method would the manager prefer? Why?

29 Comparison of variable costing and absorption costing. Gammaro Company uses standard costing. Tim Sweeney, the new president of Gammaro Company, is presented with the following data for 2014:

	Home	Insert	Page Layout	Formulas	Data	Review	View	
	A					B	C	
1	Gammaro Company							
2	Income Statements for the Year Ended December 31, 2014							
3						Variable	Absorption	
4						Costing	Costing	
5	Revenues					$9,350,000	$9,350,000	
6	Cost of goods sold (at standard costs)					4,695,000	5,855,000	
7	Fixed manufacturing overhead (budgeted)					1,350,000	-	
8	Fixed manufacturing overhead variances (all unfavorable):							
9	Spending					125,000	125,000	
10	Production volume					-	405,000	
11	Total marketing and administrative costs (all fixed)					1,570,000	1,570,000	
12	Total costs					7,740,000	7,955,000	
13	Operating income					$1,610,000	$1,395,000	
14								
15	Inventories (at standard costs)							
16	December 31, 2013					$1,345,000	$1,730,000	
17	December 31, 2014					45,000	215,000	

1. At what percentage of denominator level was the plant operating during 2014?
2. How much fixed manufacturing overhead was included in the 2013 and the 2014 ending inventory under absorption costing?
3. Reconcile and explain the difference in 2014 operating incomes under variable and absorption costing.
4. Tim Sweeney is concerned: He notes that despite an increase in sales over 2013, 2014 operating income has actually declined under absorption costing. Explain how this occurred.

30 Effects of differing production levels on absorption costing income: Metrics to minimize inventory buildups. Horizon Press produces textbooks for college courses. The company recently hired a new editor, Billie White, to handle production and sales of books for an introduction to accounting course. Billie's compensation depends on the gross margin associated with sales of this book. Billie needs to decide how many copies of the book to produce. The following information is available for the fall semester 2013:

Estimated sales	26,000 books
Beginning inventory	0 books
Average selling price	$ 81 per book
Variable production costs	$ 45 per book
Fixed production costs	$416,000 per semester

The fixed cost allocation rate is based on expected sales and is therefore equal to $416,000/26,000 books = $16 per book.

Billie has decided to produce either 26,000, 32,500, or 33,800 books.

1. Calculate expected gross margin if Billie produces 26,000, 32,500, or 33,800 books. (Make sure you include the production-volume variance as part of cost of goods sold.)
2. Calculate ending inventory in units and in dollars for each production level.
3. Managers who are paid a bonus that is a function of gross margin may be inspired to produce a product in excess of demand to maximize their own bonus. The chapter suggested metrics to discourage managers from producing products in excess of demand. Do you think the following metrics will accomplish this objective? Show your work.

   a. Incorporate a charge of 5% of the cost of the ending inventory as an expense for evaluating the manager.
   b. Include nonfinancial measures (such as the ones recommended earlier) when evaluating management and rewarding performance.

31 Alternative denominator-level capacity concepts, effect on operating income. Castle Lager has just purchased the Jacksonville Brewery. The brewery is two years old and uses absorption costing. It will "sell" its product to Castle Lager at $47 per barrel. Peter Bryant, Castle Lager's controller, obtains the following information about Jacksonville Brewery's capacity and budgeted fixed manufacturing costs for 2014:

	Home	Insert	Page Layout	Formulas	Data	Review	View	

	A	B	C	D	E
1		**Budgeted Fixed**	**Days of**	**Hours of**	
2	**Denominator-Level**	**Manufacturing**	**Production**	**Production**	**Barrels**
3	**Capacity Concept**	**Overhead per Period**	**per Period**	**per Day**	**per Hour**
4	Theoretical capacity	$27,900,000	358	22	545
5	Practical capacity	$27,900,000	348	20	510
6	Normal capacity utilization	$27,900,000	348	20	410
7	Master-budget capacity for each half year				
8	(a) January–June 2014	$13,950,000	174	20	315
9	(b) July–December 2014	$13,950,000	174	20	505

1. Compute the budgeted fixed manufacturing overhead rate per barrel for each of the denominator-level capacity concepts. Explain why they are different.

Inventory Costing and Capacity Analysis

2. In 2014, the Jacksonville Brewery reported these production results:

	A	B
12	Beginning inventory in barrels, 1-1-2014	0
13	Production in barrels	2,670,000
14	Ending inventory in barrels, 12-31-2014	210,000
15	Actual variable manufacturing costs	$80,634,000
16	Actual fixed manufacturing overhead costs	$26,700,000

There are no variable cost variances. Fixed manufacturing overhead cost variances are written off to cost of goods sold in the period in which they occur. Compute the Jacksonville Brewery's operating income when the denominator-level capacity is (a) theoretical capacity, (b) practical capacity, and (c) normal capacity utilization.

32 Motivational considerations in denominator-level capacity selection (continuation of 31).

Required

1. If the plant manager of the Jacksonville Brewery gets a bonus based on operating income, which denominator-level capacity concept would he prefer to use? Explain.
2. What denominator-level capacity concept would Castle Lager prefer to use for U.S. income-tax reporting? Explain.
3. How might the IRS limit the flexibility of an absorption-costing company like Castle Lager attempting to minimize its taxable income?

33 Denominator-level choices, changes in inventory levels, effect on operating income. Donaldson Corporation is a manufacturer of computer accessories. It uses absorption costing based on standard costs and reports the following data for 2014:

	A	B	C
1	Theoretical capacity	275,000	units
2	Practical capacity	265,000	units
3	Normal capacity utilization	233,200	units
4	Selling price	$ 39	per unit
5	Beginning inventory	35,000	units
6	Production	235,000	units
7	Sales volume	250,000	units
8	Variable budgeted manufacturing cost	$ 8	per unit
9	Total budgeted fixed manufacturing costs	$2,915,000	
10	Total budgeted operating (nonmanuf.) costs (all fixed)	$ 200,000	

There are no price, spending, or efficiency variances. Actual operating costs equal budgeted operating costs. The production-volume variance is written off to cost of goods sold. For each choice of denominator level, the budgeted production cost per unit is also the cost per unit of beginning inventory.

Required

1. What is the production-volume variance in 2014 when the denominator level is (a) theoretical capacity, (b) practical capacity, and (c) normal capacity utilization?
2. Prepare absorption costing–based income statements for Donaldson Corporation using theoretical capacity, practical capacity, and normal capacity utilization as the denominator levels.
3. Why is the operating income under normal capacity utilization lower than the other two scenarios?
4. Reconcile the difference in operating income based on theoretical capacity and practical capacity with the difference in fixed manufacturing overhead included in inventory.

34 Variable and absorption costing and breakeven points. Whistler, Inc., manufactures a specialized snowboard made for the advanced snowboarder. Whistler began 2014 with an inventory of 240 snowboards. During the year, it produced 900 boards and sold 995 for $750 each. Fixed production costs were $280,000, and variable production costs were $325 per unit. Fixed advertising, marketing, and other general and administrative expenses were $112,000, and variable shipping costs were $15 per board. Assume that the cost of each unit in beginning inventory is equal to 2014 inventory cost.

Required

1. Prepare an income statement assuming Whistler uses variable costing.
2. Prepare an income statement assuming Whistler uses absorption costing. Whistler uses a denominator level of 1,000 units. Production-volume variances are written off to cost of goods sold.
3. Compute the breakeven point in units sold assuming Whistler uses the following:
   a. Variable costing
   b. Absorption costing (Production = 900 boards)

4. Provide proof of your preceding breakeven calculations.
5. Assume that $20,000 of fixed administrative costs were reclassified as fixed production costs. Would this reclassification affect breakeven point using variable costing? What if absorption costing were used? Explain.
6. The company that supplies Whistler with its specialized impact-resistant material has announced a price increase of $30 for each board. What effect would this have on the breakeven points previously calculated?

35 Downward demand spiral. Gostkowski Company is about to enter the highly competitive personal electronics market with a new optical reader. In anticipation of future growth, the company has leased a large manufacturing facility and has purchased several expensive pieces of equipment. In 2013, the company's first year, Gostkowski budgets for production and sales of 24,000 units, compared with its practical capacity of 48,000. The company's cost data are as follows:

	A	B
1	Variable manufacturing costs per unit:	
2	Direct materials	$ 20
3	Direct manufacturing labor	35
4	Manufacturing overhead	9
5	Fixed manufacturing overhead	$576,000

Required

1. Assume that Gostkowski uses absorption costing and uses budgeted units produced as the denominator for calculating its fixed manufacturing overhead rate. Selling price is set at 130% of manufacturing cost. Compute Gostkowski's selling price.
2. Gostkowski enters the market with the selling price computed previously. However, despite growth in the overall market, sales are not as robust as the company had expected, and a competitor has priced its product $16 lower than Gostkowski's. Enrico Gostkowski, the company's president, insists that the competitor must be pricing its product at a loss and that the competitor will be unable to sustain that. In response, Gostkowski makes no price adjustments but budgets production and sales for 2014 at 18,000 units. Variable and fixed costs are not expected to change. Compute Gostkowski's new selling price. Comment on how Gostkowski's choice of budgeted production affected its selling price and competitive position.
3. Recompute the selling price using practical capacity as the denominator level of activity. How would this choice have affected Gostkowski's position in the marketplace? Generally, how would this choice affect the production-volume variance?

36 Absorption costing and production-volume variance—alternative capacity bases. Planet Light First (PLF), a producer of energy-efficient light bulbs, expects that demand will increase markedly over the next decade. Due to the high fixed costs involved in the business, PLF has decided to evaluate its financial performance using absorption costing income. The production-volume variance is written off to cost of goods sold. The variable cost of production is $2.40 per bulb. Fixed manufacturing costs are $1,170,000 per year. Variable and fixed selling and administrative expenses are $0.20 per bulb sold and $220,000, respectively. Because its light bulbs are currently popular with environmentally conscious customers, PLF can sell the bulbs for $9.80 each.

PLF is deciding among various concepts of capacity for calculating the cost of each unit produced. Its choices are as follows:

Theoretical capacity   900,000 bulbs
Practical capacity   520,000 bulbs
Normal capacity   260,000 bulbs (average expected output for the next three years)
Master budget capacity   225,000 bulbs expected production this year

Required

1. Calculate the inventoriable cost per unit using each level of capacity to compute fixed manufacturing cost per unit.
2. Suppose PLF actually produces 300,000 bulbs. Calculate the production-volume variance using each level of capacity to compute the fixed manufacturing overhead allocation rate.
3. Assume PLF has no beginning inventory. If this year's actual sales are 225,000 bulbs, calculate operating income for PLF using each type of capacity to compute fixed manufacturing cost per unit.

37 Operating income effects of denominator-level choice and disposal of production-volume variance (continuation of 36).

Required

1. If PLF sells all 300,000 bulbs produced, what would be the effect on operating income of using each type of capacity as a basis for calculating manufacturing cost per unit?

2. Compare the results of operating income at different capacity levels when 225,000 bulbs are sold and when 300,000 bulbs are sold. What conclusion can you draw from the comparison?

3. Using the original data (that is, 300,000 units produced and 225,000 units sold) if PLF had used the pro-ration approach to allocate the production-volume variance, what would operating income have been under each level of capacity? (Assume that there is no ending work in process.)

38 Variable and absorption costing, actual costing. The Iron City Company started business on January 1, 2014. Iron City manufactures a specialty honey beer, which it sells directly to state-owned distributors in Pennsylvania. Honey beer is produced and sold in six-packs, and in 2014, Iron City produced more six-packs than it was able to sell. In addition to variable and fixed manufacturing overhead, Iron City incurred direct materials costs of $880,000, direct manufacturing labor costs of $400,000, and fixed marketing and administrative costs of $295,000. For the year, Iron City sold a total of 180,000 six-packs for a sales revenue of $2,250,000.

Iron City's CFO is convinced that the firm should use an actual costing system but is debating whether to follow variable or absorption costing. The controller notes that Iron City's operating income for the year would be $438,000 under variable costing and $461,000 under absorption costing. Moreover, the ending finished goods inventory would be valued at $7.15 under variable costing and $8.30 under absorption costing.

Iron City incurs no variable nonmanufacturing expenses.

Required

1. What is Iron City's total contribution margin for 2014?
2. Iron City incurs fixed manufacturing costs in addition to its fixed marketing and administrative costs. How much did Iron City incur in fixed manufacturing costs in 2014?
3. How many six-packs did Iron City produce in 2014?
4. How much in variable manufacturing overhead did Iron City incur in 2014?
5. For 2014, how much in total manufacturing overhead is expensed under variable costing, either through Cost of Goods Sold or as a period expense?

39 Cost allocation, downward demand spiral. Top Catering operates a chain of 10 hospitals in the Los Angeles area. Its central food-catering facility, Topman, prepares and delivers meals to the hospitals. It has the capacity to deliver up to 1,025,000 meals a year. In 2014, based on estimates from each hospital controller, Topman budgeted for 925,000 meals a year. Budgeted fixed costs in 2014 were $1,517,000. Each hospital was charged $6.24 per meal—$4.60 variable costs plus $1.64 allocated budgeted fixed cost.

Recently, the hospitals have been complaining about the quality of Topman's meals and their rising costs. In mid-2014, Top Catering's president announces that all Top Catering hospitals and support facilities will be run as profit centers. Hospitals will be free to purchase quality-certified services from outside the system. Ron Smith, Topman's controller, is preparing the 2015 budget. He hears that three hospitals have decided to use outside suppliers for their meals, which will reduce the 2015 estimated demand to 820,000 meals. No change in variable cost per meal or total fixed costs is expected in 2015.

Required

1. How did Smith calculate the budgeted fixed cost per meal of $1.64 in 2014?
2. Using the same approach to calculating budgeted fixed cost per meal and pricing as in 2014, how much would hospitals be charged for each Topman meal in 2015? What would the reaction of the hospital controllers be to the price?
3. Suggest an alternative cost-based price per meal that Smith might propose and that might be more acceptable to the hospitals. What can Topman and Smith do to make this price profitable in the long run?

40 Cost allocation, responsibility accounting, ethics (continuation of 39). In 2015, only 740,000 Topman meals were produced and sold to the hospitals. Smith suspects that hospital controllers had systematically inflated their 2015 meal estimates.

Required

1. Recall that Topman uses the master-budget capacity utilization to allocate fixed costs and to price meals. What was the effect of production-volume variance on Topman's operating income in 2015?
2. Why might hospital controllers deliberately overestimate their future meal counts?
3. What other evidence should Top Catering's president seek to investigate Smith's concerns?
4. Suggest two specific steps that Smith might take to reduce hospital controllers' incentives to inflate their estimated meal counts.

41 Absorption, variable, and throughput costing. Tesla Motors assembles the fully electric Model S-85 automobile at its Fremont, California, plant. The standard variable manufacturing cost per vehicle in 2014 is $58,800, which consists of:

Direct materials	$36,000
Direct manufacturing labor	$10,800
Variable manufacturing overhead	$12,000

Variable manufacturing overhead is allocated to vehicles on the basis of assembly time. The standard assembly time per vehicle is 20 hours.

The Fremont plant is highly automated and has a practical capacity of 4,000 vehicles per month. The budgeted monthly fixed manufacturing overhead is $45 million. Fixed manufacturing overhead is allocated on the basis of the standard assembly time for the budgeted normal capacity utilization of the plant. For 2014, the budgeted normal capacity utilization is 3,000 vehicles per month.

Tesla started production of the Model S-85 in 2014. The actual production and sales figures for the first three months of the year are:

	January	February	March
Production	3,200	2,400	3,800
Sales	2,000	2,900	3,200

Franz Holzhausen is SVP of Tesla and director of the Fremont plant. His compensation includes a bonus that is 0.25% of quarterly operating income, calculated using absorption costing. Tesla prepares absorption-costing income statements monthly, which include an adjustment for the production-volume variance occurring in that month. There are no variable cost variances or fixed overhead spending variances in the first three months of 2014.

The Fremont plant is credited with revenue (net of marketing costs) of $96,000 for the sale of each Tesla S-85 vehicle.

Required

1. Compute (a) the fixed manufacturing cost per unit and (b) the total manufacturing cost per unit.
2. Compute the monthly operating income for January, February, and March under absorption costing. What amount of bonus is paid each month to Franz Holzhausen?
3. How much would the use of variable costing change Holzhausen's bonus each month if the same 0.25% figure were applied to variable-costing operating income?
4. Explain the differences in Holzhausen's bonuses in requirements 2 and 3.
5. How much would the use of throughput costing change Holzhausen's bonus each month if the same 0.25% figure were applied to throughput-costing operating income?
6. What are the different approaches Tesla Motors could take to reduce possible undesirable behavior associated with the use of absorption costing at its Fremont plant?

42 Costing methods and variances, comprehensive. Rob Kapito, the controller of Blackstar Paint Supply Company, has been exploring a variety of internal accounting systems. Rob hopes to get the input of Blackstar's board of directors in choosing one. To prepare for his presentation to the board, Rob applies four different cost accounting methods to the firm's operating data for 2013. The four methods are actual absorption costing, normal absorption costing, standard absorption costing, and standard variable costing.

With the help of a junior accountant, Rob prepares the following alternative income statements:

	A	B	C	D
Sales Revenue	$ 900,000	$ 900,000	$ 900,000	$ 900,000
Cost of Goods Sold	$ 375,000	$ 250,000	$ 420,000	$ 395,000
(+) Variances:				
Direct Materials	15,000	15,000	—	—
Direct Labor	5,000	5,000	—	—
Manufacturing Overhead	25,000	—	—	25,000
(+) Other Costs (All Fixed)	350,000	475,000	350,000	350,000
Total Costs	$ 770,000	$ 745,000	$ 770,000	$ 770,000
Net Income	$ 130,000	$ 155,000	$ 130,000	$ 130,000

Where applicable, Rob allocates both fixed and variable manufacturing overhead using direct labor hours as the driver. Blackstar carries no work-in-process inventory. Standard costs have been stable over time, and Rob writes off all variances to cost of goods sold. For 2013, there was no flexible budget variance for fixed overhead. In addition, the direct labor variance represents a price variance.

Required

1. Match each method below with the appropriate income statement (A, B, C, or D):

Actual Absorption costing	_____
Normal Absorption costing	_____
Standard Absorption costing	_____
Standard Variable costing	_____

2. During 2013, how did Blackstar's level of finished goods inventory change? In other words, is it possible to know whether Blackstar's finished goods inventory increased, decreased, or stayed constant during the year?
3. From the four income statements, can you determine how the actual volume of production during the year compared to the denominator (expected) volume level?
4. Did Blackstar have a favorable or unfavorable variable overhead spending variance during 2013?

Glossary

Absorption costing. Method of inventory costing in which all variable manufacturing costs and all fixed manufacturing costs are included as inventoriable costs.

Direct costing. See *variable costing*.

Downward demand spiral. Pricing context where prices are raised to spread capacity costs over a smaller number of output units. Continuing reduction in the demand for products that occurs when the prices of competitors' products are not met and, as demand drops further, higher and higher unit costs result in more and more reluctance to meet competitors' prices.

Master-budget capacity utilization. The expected level of capacity utilization for the current budget period (typically one year).

Normal capacity utilization. The level of capacity utilization that satisfies average customer demand over a period (say, two to three years) that includes seasonal, cyclical, and trend factors.

Practical capacity. The level of capacity that reduces theoretical capacity by unavoidable operating interruptions such as scheduled maintenance time, shutdowns for holidays, and so on.

Super-variable costing. See *throughput costing*.

Theoretical capacity. The level of capacity based on producing at full efficiency all the time.

Throughput costing. Method of inventory costing in which only variable direct material costs are included as inventoriable costs. Also called *super-variable costing*.

Variable costing. Method of inventory costing in which only all variable manufacturing costs are included as inventoriable costs. Also called *direct costing*.

Photo Credits

Credits are listed in order of appearance.

Photo 1: Bloomberg/Getty Images;
Photo 2: Paul Sakuma/AP Images

Cost Allocation, Customer-Profitability Analysis, and Sales-Variance Analysis

From Chapter 14 of *Cost Accounting: A Managerial Emphasis*, Fifteenth Edition. Charles T. Horngren, Srikant M. Datar, Madhav V. Rajan. Copyright © 2015 by Pearson Education, Inc. All rights reserved.

Cost Allocation, Customer-Profitability Analysis, and Sales-Variance Analysis

Companies desperately want to make their customers happy.

But how far should they go to please them, and at what price? Should a company differentiate among its customers and not treat all customers the same? The following article explains why it's so important for managers to be able to figure out the profitability of each of their customers.

Starwood Hotels: Not All Guests Are the Same[1]

In 2013, Starwood Hotels & Resorts Worldwide, Inc.—owner and operator of nine hotel brands including Westin, Sheraton, and W Hotels—announced new benefits for its most frequent customers. Starwood added features including rolling 24-hour check-in and check-out times and personal travel assistants, dubbed "ambassadors." The new perks cost the company $25 million. Why invest so much money in frequent travelers? Customer profitability-analysis shows that high-frequency guests drive a disproportionate share of Starwood's profitability.

Starwood found that just 2% of its guests drove 30% of the company's earnings before interest, taxes, depreciation, and amortization ("EBITDA"). EBITDA is a key profitability measure in the hotel industry. For 2013, Starwood expects $284 million of its projected $980 million EBITDA to come from these guests. The use of the new perks is determined by the frequency of stays in Starwood hotels, with guests who spend 100 nights a year qualifying for the highest level of service. The company estimates that the number of customers who will qualify for this level is "in the low ten thousands."

Starwood's focus on frequent travelers is part of a continuing race by hotel companies to generate more business from recurring guests. As competition grows, expect hotels to continue to match each other and ratchet up benefits for their most profitable customer segments.

To determine which product, customer, program, or department is profitable, organizations need to allocate costs. In this chapter, we build on ideas

---

[1] *Source:* Based on Alexandra Berzon, "Starwood Perks Up Loyalty Program," *Wall Street Journal* (February 1, 2012).

such as activity-based costing and provide insight into cost allocation. The emphasis in this chapter is on macro issues in cost allocation: allocation of costs to divisions and customers.

Customer-Profitability Analysis

Customer-profitability analysis is the reporting and assessment of revenues earned from customers and the costs incurred to earn those revenues. An analysis of customer differences in revenues and costs reveals why differences exist in the operating income earned from different customers. Managers use this information to ensure that customers making large contributions to the operating income of a company receive a high level of attention from the company and that loss-making customers do not use more resources than the revenues they provide. As described at the start of this chapter, at Starwood Hotels, managers use customer-profitability analysis to segment customers into profitable customers who stay frequently at the hotel and are given many perks and other customers who are much less profitable and are given less service.

Consider Astel Computers. Astel has two divisions: the Deskpoint Division manufactures and sells servers, and the Provalue Divison manufactures and sells Pentium chip-based personal computers (PCs). Exhibit 1 presents data for the Provalue Division of Astel Computers for the year ended 2013. Astel sells and distributes Provalue through two channels: (1) wholesalers who sell Provalue to retail outlets and (2) direct sales to business customers. Astel sells the same Provalue computer to wholesalers and to business customers, so the full manufacturing cost of Provalue, $680, is the same regardless of where it is sold. Provalue's listed selling price in 2013 was $1,100, but price discounts reduced the average selling price to $1,000. We focus on customer-profitability for the Provalue Division's 10 wholesale distributors.

Customer-Revenue Analysis

Consider revenues from four of Provalue's 10 wholesale customers in 2013:

	Home	Insert	Page Layout	Formulas	Data	Review	View	
	A		B		C		D	E
1					**CUSTOMER**			
2			A		B		G	J
3	Units of Provalue sold		30,000		25,000		5,000	4,000
4	List selling price		$ 1,100		$ 1,100		$ 1,100	$ 1,100
5	Price discount		$ 100		$ 50		$ 150	—
6	Invoice price		$ 1,000		$ 1,050		$ 950	$ 1,100
7	Revenues (Row 3 x Row 6)		$30,000,000		$26,250,000		$4,750,000	$4,400,000

Exhibit 1

Profitability of Provalue
Division for 2013 Using
Value-Chain Activity-
Based Costing

	Home	Insert	Page Layout	Formulas	Data	Review	View	
			A			B		C
1						**Total Amounts**		
2						**for 150,000 Units**		**Per Unit**
3						**(1)**		**(2) = (1) ÷ 150,000**
4	Revenues					$150,000,000		$1,000
5	Costs of goods sold[a] (from Exhibit 13-2)					102,000,000		680
6	Operating costs[b]							
7	R&D costs					2,400,000		16
8	Design costs of product and process					3,000,000		20
9	Marketing and administration costs					15,000,000		100
10	Distribution costs					9,000,000		60
11	Customer-service costs					3,600,000		24
12	Operating costs					33,000,000		220
13	Full cost of the product					135,000,000		900
14	Operating income					$ 15,000,000		$ 100
15								
16	[a]Cost of goods sold = Total manufacturing costs because there is no beginning or ending inventory							
17	of Provalue in 2013							
18	[b]Numbers for operating cost line-items are assumed without supporting calculations							

Two variables explain revenue differences across these four wholesale customers: (1) the number of computers they purchased and (2) the magnitude of price discounting. A **price discount** is the reduction in selling price below list selling price to encourage customers to purchase more quantities. Companies that record only the final invoice price in their information system cannot readily track the magnitude of their price discounting.[2]

Price discounts are a function of multiple factors, including the volume of product purchased (higher-volume customers receive higher discounts) and the desire to sell to a customer who might help promote sales to other customers. In some cases, discounts result from poor negotiating by a salesperson or the unwanted effect of a company's incentive plan based only on revenues. At no time, however, should price discounts stem from illegal activities such as price discrimination, predatory pricing, or collusive pricing.

Tracking price discounts by customer and by salesperson helps improve customer profitability. For example, the Provalue Division managers may decide to strictly enforce its volume-based price discounting policy. The company may also require its salespeople to obtain approval for giving large discounts to customers who do not normally qualify for them. In addition, the company could track future sales to customers who have received sizable price discounts on the basis of their "high growth potential." For example, managers should track future sales to Customer G to see if the $150-per-computer discount translates into higher future sales.

Customer revenues are one element of customer profitability. The other, equally important element is the cost of acquiring, serving, and retaining customers.

Customer-Cost Analysis

We apply to customers a **customer-cost hierarchy,** which categorizes costs related to customers into different cost pools on the basis of different types of cost drivers, or cost-allocation bases, or different degrees of difficulty

---

[2] Further analysis of customer revenues could distinguish gross revenues from net revenues. This approach highlights differences across customers in sales returns. Additional discussion of ways to analyze revenue differences across customers is in Robert S. Kaplan and Robin Cooper, *Cost and Effect: Using Integrated Cost Systems to Drive Profitability and Performance* (Boston: Harvard Business School Press, 1998), Chapter 10; and Gary Cokins, *Activity-Based Cost Management: An Executive's Guide* (New York: Wiley, 2001), Chapter 3.

in determining cause-and-effect or benefits-received relationships. The Provalue Division customer costs are composed of (1) marketing and administration costs, $15,000,000; (2) distribution costs, $9,000,000; and (3) customer-service costs, $3,600,000 (see Exhibit 1). Managers identify five categories of indirect costs in its customer-cost hierarchy:

1. **Customer output unit-level costs**—costs of activities to sell each unit (computer) to a customer. An example is product-handling costs of each computer sold.

2. **Customer batch-level costs**—costs of activities related to a group of units (computers) sold to a customer. Examples are costs incurred to process orders or to make deliveries.

3. **Customer-sustaining costs**—costs of activities to support individual customers, regardless of the number of units or batches of product delivered to the customer. Examples are costs of visits to customers or costs of displays at customer sites.

4. **Distribution-channel costs**—costs of activities related to a particular distribution channel rather than to each unit of product, each batch of product, or specific customers. An example is the salary of the manager of the Provalue Division's wholesale distribution channel.

5. **Division-sustaining costs**—costs of division activities that cannot be traced to individual customers or distribution channels. The salary of the Provalue Division manager is an example of a division-sustaining cost.

Note from these descriptions that the Provalue Division focuses on *customers*. The Provalue Division has one additional cost hierarchy category, distribution-channel costs, for the costs it incurs to support its wholesale and business-sales channels.

Customer-Level Costs

Exhibit 2 summarizes details of the costs incurred in marketing and administration, distribution, and customer service by activity. The exhibit also identifies the cost driver (where appropriate), the total costs incurred for the activity, the total quantity of the cost

Exhibit 2   Marketing, Distribution, and Customer Service Activities, Costs, and Cost Driver Information for Provalue Division in 2013

	Home	Insert	Page Layout	Formulas	Data	Review	View	
	A	B	C	D	E	F	G	H
1	Marketing, Distribution, and Customer Service Costs for 150,000 units of Provalue in 2013							
2								
3	Activity Area	Cost Driver	Total Cost of Activity	Total Quantity of Cost Driver		Rate per Unit of Cost Driver		Cost Hierarchy Category
4	(1)	(2)	(3)	(4)		(5) = (3) ÷ (4)		(6)
5	**Marketing and Administration**							
6	Sales order	Number of sales orders	$ 6,750,000	6,000	sales orders	$1,125	per sales order	Customer batch-level costs
7	Customer visits	Number of customer visits	4,200,000	750	customer visits	$5,600	per customer visit	Customer-sustaining costs
8	Wholesale channel marketing		800,000					Distribution-channel costs
9	Business-sales channel marketing		1,350,000					Distribution-channel costs
10	Provalue division administration		1,900,000					Division-sustaining costs
11	Total marketing & administration costs		$15,000,000					
12								
13	**Distribution**							
14	Product handling	Number of cubic feet moved	$ 4,500,000	300,000	cubic feet	$ 15	per cubic foot	Customer output unit-level costs
15	Regular shipments	Number of regular shipments	3,750,000	3,000	regular shipments	$1,250	per regular shipment	Customer batch-level costs
16	Rush shipments	Number of rush shipments	750,000	150	rush shipments	$5,000	per rush shipment	Customer batch-level costs
17	Total distribution costs		$ 9,000,000					
18								
19	**Customer Service**							
20	Customer service	Number of units shipped	$ 3,600,000	150,000	units shipped	$ 24	per unit shipped	Customer output unit-level costs

driver, the cost per unit of the cost driver, and the customer cost-hierarchy category for each activity.

For example, here is a breakdown of Provalue Division's $15,000,000 of marketing and administration costs:

- $6,750,000 on the sales order activity, which includes negotiating, finalizing, issuing, and collecting on 6,000 sales orders at a cost of $1,125($6,750,000 ÷ 6,000) per sales order. Sales-order costs are customer batch-level costs because these costs vary with the number of sales orders issued and not with the number of Provalue computers in a sales order.

- $4,200,000 for customer visits, which are customer-sustaining costs. The amount per customer varies with the number of visits rather than the number of units or batches of Provalue delivered to a customer.

- $800,000 on managing the wholesale channel, which are distribution-channel costs.

- $1,350,000 on managing the business-sales channel, which are distribution-channel costs.

- $1,900,000 on general administration of the Provalue Division, which are division-sustaining costs.

The Provalue Division managers are particularly interested in analyzing *customer-level indirect costs*—costs incurred in the first three categories of the customer-cost hierarchy: customer output unit–level costs, customer batch-level costs, and customer-sustaining costs. Managers want to work with customers to reduce these costs because they believe customer actions will have more impact on customer-level (indirect) costs than on distribution-channel and division-sustaining costs. Information on the quantity of cost drivers used by each of four representative wholesale customers follows:

		Home	Insert	Page Layout	Formulas	Data	Review	View	
		A		B		C	D	E	F
1							CUSTOMER		
2		Activity		Quantity of Cost Driver		A	B	G	J
3	**Marketing**								
4	Sales orders			Number of sales orders		1,200	1,000	600	300
5	Customer visits			Number of customer visits		150	100	50	25
6	**Distribution**								
7	Product handling			Number of cubic feet moved		60,000	50,000	10,000	8,000
8	Regular shipments			Number of regular shipments		600	400	300	120
9	Rush shipments			Number of rush shipments		25	5	20	3
10	**Customer Service**								
11	Customer service			Number of units shipped		30,000	25,000	5,000	4,000

Exhibit 3 shows customer-level operating income for the four wholesale customers using information on customer revenues previously presented and customer-level indirect costs, obtained by multiplying the rate per unit of cost driver (from Exhibit 2) by the quantities of the cost driver used by each customer (in the table above). Exhibit 3 shows that the Provalue Division is losing money on Customer G (the cost of resources used by Customer G exceeds revenues) while it makes money on Customer J on smaller revenues. The Provalue Division sells fewer computers to Customer B compared to Customer A but has higher operating income from Customer B than Customer A.

The Provalue Division's managers can use the information in Exhibit 3 to work with customers to reduce the quantity of activities needed to support them. Consider, for example, a comparison of Customer G and Customer J. Customer G purchases 25% more computers than Customer J purchases (5,000 versus 4,000) but the company offers Customer G significant price discounts to achieve these sales. Compared with Customer J, Customer

Exhibit 3	Customer-Profitability Analysis for Provalue Division's Four Wholesale Channel Customers for 2013

	A	B	C	D	E
		A	**B**	**G**	**J**
2	Revenues at list price	$33,000,000	$27,500,000	$5,500,000	$4,400,000
3	Price discount	3,000,000	1,250,000	750,000	-
4	Revenues	30,000,000	26,250,000	4,750,000	4,400,000
5					
6	Cost of goods sold[a]	20,400,000	17,000,000	3,400,000	2,720,000
7					
8	Gross margin	9,600,000	9,250,000	1,350,000	1,680,000
9					
10	Customer-level costs				
11	Marketing costs				
12	Sales orders[b]	1,350,000	1,125,000	675,000	337,500
13	Customer visits[c]	840,000	560,000	280,000	140,000
14	Distribution costs				
15	Product handling[d]	900,000	750,000	150,000	120,000
16	Regular shipments[e]	750,000	500,000	375,000	150,000
17	Rush shipments[f]	125,000	25,000	100,000	15,000
18	Customer service costs				
19	Customer service[g]	720,000	600,000	120,000	96,000
20					
21	Total customer-level costs	4,685,000	3,560,000	1,700,000	858,500
22					
23	Customer-level operating income	$ 4,915,000	$ 5,690,000	$ (350,000)	$ 821,500
24	[a]$680 x 30,000; 25,000; 5,000; 4,000 [b]$1,125 x 1,200; 1,000; 600; 300 [c]$5,600 x 150; 100; 50; 25 [d]$15 x 60,000; 50,000; 10,000;				
25	8,000 [e]$1,250 x 600; 400; 300; 120 [f]$5,000 x 25; 5; 20; 3 [g]$24 x 30,000; 25,000; 5,000; 4,000				

G places twice as many sales orders, requires twice as many customer visits, and generates two-and-a-half times as many regular shipments and almost seven times as many rush shipments. Selling smaller quantities of units is profitable, provided the Provalue Division's salespeople limit the amount of price discounting and customers do not use large amounts of Provalue Division's resources. For example, by implementing an additional charge for customers who use large amounts of marketing and distribution services, managers might be able to prevail upon Customer G to place fewer but larger sales orders and require fewer customer visits, regular shipments, and rush shipments while looking to increase sales in the future. The Provalue Division's managers would perform a similar analysis to understand the reasons for the lower profitability of Customer A relative to Customer B.

Owens and Minor, a distributor of medical supplies to hospitals, follows this approach. Owens and Minor strategically prices each of its services separately. For example, if a hospital wants a rush delivery or special packaging, Owens and Minor charges the hospital an additional price for each particular service. How have its customers reacted? Hospitals that value these services continue to demand and pay for them, while hospitals that do not value these services stop asking for them, saving Owens and Minor some costs. This pricing strategy influences customer behavior in a way that increases Owens and Minor's revenues or decreases its costs.

The ABC system also highlights a second opportunity for cost reduction. The Provalue Division's managers can reduce the costs of each activity by applying the value-engineering process to nonmanufacturing costs. For example, improving the efficiency of the ordering process (such as by having customers order electronically) reduces sales order costs even if customers place the same number of orders.

Decision Point

How can a company's revenues and costs differ across customers?

Simplifying the design and reducing the weight of the newly designed Provalue II for 2014 reduces the cost per cubic foot of handling Provalue and total product-handling costs. By influencing customer behavior and improving marketing, distribution, and customer service operations, Provalue Division's managers aim to reduce the nonmanufacturing cost of Provalue to $180 per computer and achieve the target cost of $720 for Provalue II.

Learning Objective 2

Identify the importance of customer-profitability profiles

...expand relationships with profitable customers and change behavior patterns of unprofitable customers and highlight that a small percentage of customers contributes a large percentage of operating income

Customer Profitability Profiles

Customer-profitability profiles are a useful tool for managers. Exhibit 4 ranks the Provalue Division's 10 wholesale customers based on customer-level operating income. (We analyzed four of these customers in Exhibit 3.)

Column 4, computed by adding the individual amounts in column 1, shows the cumulative customer-level operating income. For example, Customer C shows a cumulative income of $13,260,000 in column 4. This $13,260,000 is the sum of $5,690,000 for Customer B, $4,915,000 for Customer A, and $2,655,000 for Customer C.

Column 5 shows what percentage the $13,260,000 *cumulative* total for customers B, A, and C is of the total customer-level operating income of $15,027,500 earned in the wholesale distribution channel from all 10 customers. The three most profitable customers contribute 88% of total customer-level operating income. These customers deserve the highest service and priority. Companies try to keep their best customers happy in a number of ways, including special phone numbers and upgrade privileges for elite-level frequent flyers and free usage of luxury hotel suites and big credit limits for high rollers at casinos. In many companies, it is common for a small number of customers to contribute a high percentage of operating income. Microsoft uses the phrase "not all revenue dollars are endowed equally in profitability" to stress this point.

Exhibit 4 Cumulative Customer-Profitability Analysis for Provalue Division's Wholesale Channel Customers: Astel Computers, 2013

	Home	Insert	Page Layout	Formulas	Data	Review	View

	A	B	C	D	E	F
1	Retail Customer Code	Customer-Level Operating Income	Customer Revenue	Customer-Level Operating Income Divided by Revenue	Cumulative Customer-Level Operating Income	Cumulative Customer-Level Operating Income as a % of Total Customer-Level Operating Income
2		(1)	(2)	(3) = (1) ÷ (2)	(4)	(5) = (4) ÷ $15,027,500
3	B	$ 5,690,000	$26,250,000	21.7%	$ 5,690,000	38%
4	A	4,915,000	30,000,000	16.4%	10,605,000	71%
5	C	2,655,000	13,000,000	20.4%	13,260,000	88%
6	D	1,445,000	7,250,000	19.9%	14,705,000	98%
7	F	986,000	5,100,000	19.3%	15,691,000	104%
8	J	821,500	4,400,000	18.7%	16,512,500	110%
9	E	100,000	1,800,000	5.6%	16,612,500	111%
10	G	(350,000)	4,750,000	−7.4%	16,262,500	108%
11	H	(535,000)	2,400,000	−22.3%	15,727,500	105%
12	I	(700,000)	2,600,000	−26.9%	15,027,500	100%
13	Total	$15,027,500	$97,550,000			

Column 3 shows the profitability per dollar of revenue by customer. This measure of customer profitability indicates that, although Customer A contributes the second-highest operating income, the profitability per dollar of revenue is lowest among the top six customers because of high price discounts and higher customer-level costs. Provalue Division managers would like to increase profit margins for Customer A by decreasing price discounts or saving customer-level costs while maintaining or increasing sales. Customers D, F, and J have high profit margins but low total sales. The challenge with these customers is to maintain margins while increasing sales. With Customers E, G, H, and I, managers have the dual challenge of boosting profits and sales.

Presenting Profitability Analysis

Exhibit 5 illustrates two common ways of displaying the results of customer-profitability analysis. Managers often find the bar chart presentation in Panel A (based on Exhibit 4, Column 1) to be an intuitive way to visualize customer profitability because (1) the highly profitable customers clearly stand out and (2) the number of "unprofitable" customers and the magnitude of their losses are apparent. Panel B of Exhibit 5 is a popular alternative way to express customer profitability. It plots the contents of column 5

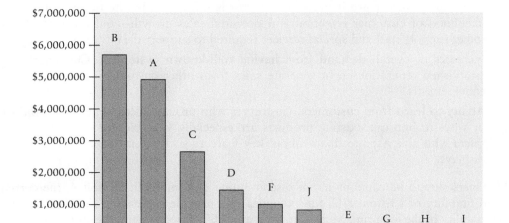

Customer-Level Operating Income

Wholesale Channel Customers

Exhibit 5

Panel A: Bar Chart of Customer-Level Operating Income for Provalue Division's Wholesale Channel Customers in 2013

Panel B: The Whale Curve of Cumulative Profitability for Provalue Division's Wholesale Channel Customers in 2013

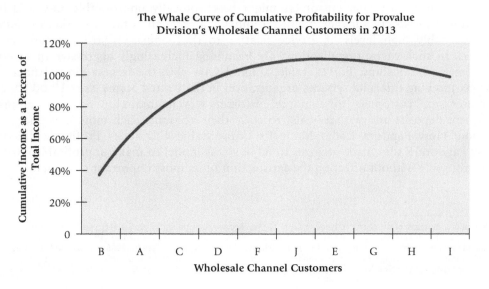

The Whale Curve of Cumulative Profitability for Provalue Division's Wholesale Channel Customers in 2013

Wholesale Channel Customers

in Exhibit 4. This chart is called the **whale curve** because it is backward-bending at the point where customers start to become unprofitable and thus resembles a humpback whale.[3]

The Provalue Division managers must explore ways to make unprofitable customers profitable. Exhibits 2 to 5 emphasize annual customer profitability. Managers should also consider other factors when allocating resources among customers, including:

- **Likelihood of customer retention.** The more likely a customer will continue to do business with a company, the more valuable the customer, for example, wholesalers who have sold Provalue each year over the last several years. Customers differ in their loyalty and their willingness to frequently "shop their business."

- **Potential for sales growth.** The higher the likely growth of the customer's sales, the more valuable the customer. Moreover, customers to whom a company can cross-sell other products profitably are more desirable, for example, wholesalers willing to distribute both Astel's Provalue and Deskpoint brands. The analysis has focused on customer profitability as it relates to Provalue. To get the full picture of Astel's relationship with a customer, managers need to do a similar customer profitability analysis for the Deskpoint Division and examine total customer profitability for those customers that sell both Provalue and Deskpoint. To simplify the exposition, we assume that the customers of the Provalue and Deskpoint divisions are distinct.

- **Long-run customer profitability.** This factor is influenced by the first two factors—likelihood of customer retention and potential sales growth—and the cost of customer-support staff and special services required to support the customer.

- **Increases in overall demand from having well-known customers.** Customers with established reputations help generate sales from other customers through product endorsements.

- **Ability to learn from customers.** Customers who provide ideas about new products or ways to improve existing products are especially valuable, for example, wholesalers who give Astel feedback about key features such as size of memory or video displays.

Managers should be cautious about discontinuing customers. In Exhibit 4, the current unprofitability of Customer G, for example, may provide misleading signals about G's profitability in the long run. Moreover, as in any ABC-based system, the costs assigned to Customer G are not all variable. In the short run, it may well be efficient for the Provalue Division managers to use spare capacity to serve G on a contribution-margin basis. Discontinuing Customer G will not eliminate all costs assigned to Customer G and may result in losing more revenues relative to costs saved.

Of course, particular customers might be chronically unprofitable and hold limited future prospects. Or they might fall outside a company's target market or require unsustainably high levels of service relative to the company's strategies and capabilities. In such cases, organizations are becoming increasingly aggressive in severing customer relationships. For example, Capital One 360, the largest direct lender and fastest-growing financial services organization in the United States, asks 10,000 "high-maintenance" customers (for example, customers who maintain low balances and make frequent deposits and withdrawals) to close their accounts each month.[4] Concepts in Action: How Pandora Radio Made Its Unprofitable Customers Profitable describes how Pandora Radio made changes to its business model to make unprofitable customers profitable without affecting the satisfaction of its most important customers.

---

[3] In practice, the curve of the chart can be quite steep. The whale curve for cumulative profitability usually reveals that the most profitable 20% of customers generate between 150% and 300% of total profits, the middle 70% of customers break even, and the least profitable 10% of customers lose from 50% to 200% of total profits (see Robert S. Kaplan and V. G. Narayanan, "Measuring and Managing Customer Profitability," *Journal of Cost Management* (September/October 2001): 1–11).

[4] See, for example, "The New Math of Customer Relationships" at http://hbswk.hbs.edu/item/5884.html.

Concepts in Action ▶ How Pandora Radio Made Its Unprofitable Customers Profitable

In 2009, Pandora Radio was growing rapidly. While the startup company was still unprofitable, widespread adoption gave founder Tim Westergren hope of turning a profit. Some venture capitalists, however, wanted Pandora to get rid of its heaviest users or at least recover the cost of supporting them. Essentially, they wanted Pandora to fire its unprofitable customers!

The venture capitalists found a troubling trend in Pandora's advertising-supported free service. The company's business model was based on selling advertising at a rate of $6 to $7 for every 1,000 customer impressions. That is, advertisers paid for reach, not duration. While Pandora streamed music at no charge to listeners, the company was contractually bound to pay a royalty on each song played. Thus, heavy users cost Pandora more. In fact, the "sweet spot" for Pandora would have been a lot of users who were in the light- to middle-usage range. Some potential investors wanted Pandora to charge the heavy users for the service or deliver more advertising to them if they listened to the radio for a longer period of time.

Westergren worried about whether such changes were really in the company's best interests, as heavy users were Pandora's greatest evangelists. Pandora ultimately decided not to fire its unprofitable customers. The company announced that free listening would be limited to 40 hours per month, but could be extended to unlimited listening for that month for $0.99. By the end of 2009, Pandora turned consistently profitable. The company grew to 43 million members, achieved $50 million in revenues, and became the second-largest volume streamer of bits on the Internet after YouTube. Today, more than 200 million users—including 140 million mobile users—enjoy music through Pandora's profitable service.

Sources: Based on Willy Shih and Halle Tesco, "Pandora Radio: Fire Unprofitable Customers?" HBS No. 9-610-077 (Boston: Harvard Business School Publishing, 2011); and "Pandora is Now 200 Million Music Fans Strong," Pandora Media, Inc. (Oakland, CA, April 9, 2013).

Using the Five-Step Decision-Making Process to Manage Customer Profitability

In this section, we apply the five-step decision-making process to help understand how managers use different types of customer analyses to allocate resources across customers.

1. *Identify the problem and uncertainties.* The problem is how to manage and allocate resources across customers.

2. *Obtain information.* Managers identify past revenues generated by each customer and customer-level costs incurred in the past to support each customer.

3. *Make predictions about the future.* Managers estimate the revenues they expect from each customer and the customer-level costs they will incur in the future. In making these predictions, managers consider the effects that future price discounts will have on revenues, the effect that pricing for different services (such as rush deliveries) will have on the demand for these services by customers, and ways to reduce the cost of providing services. For example, Deluxe Corporation, a leading check printer, initiated process modifications to rein in its cost to serve customers by opening an electronic channel to shift customers from paper to automated ordering.

4. *Make decisions by choosing among alternatives.* Managers use the customer-profitability profiles to identify the small set of customers who deserve the highest service and priority and also to identify ways to make less-profitable customers (such as Astel's Customer G) more profitable. Banks, for example, often impose minimum balance requirements on customers. Distribution firms may require minimum order quantities or levy a surcharge for smaller or customized orders. In making resource-allocation decisions, managers also consider long-term effects, such as the potential for future sales growth and the opportunity to leverage a particular customer account to make sales to other customers.

5. *Implement the decision, evaluate performance, and learn.* After the decision is implemented, managers compare actual results to predicted outcomes to evaluate the decision they made, its implementation, and ways in which they might improve profitability.

Decision Point

How do customer-profitability profiles help managers?

Learning Objective 3

Understand the cost-hierarchy-based operating income statement

…allocate only those costs that will be affected by actions at a particular hierarchical level

Cost Hierarchy-Based Operating Income Statement

Our analysis so far has focused on customer-level costs—costs of activities that the Provalue Division managers can work with customers to influence such as sales orders, customer visits, and shipments. We now consider other costs of the Provalue Division (such as R&D and design costs, costs to manage different distribution channels, and costs of division administration) and corporate costs incurred by Astel Computers (such as corporate brand advertising and general administration costs). Customer actions do not influence these costs, which raises two important questions: (1) Should these costs be allocated to customers when calculating customer profitability, and (2) if they are allocated, on what basis should they be allocated given the weak cause-and-effect relationship between these costs and customer actions? We start by considering the first question and introduce the cost-hierarchy-based operating income statement, which does not allocate the noncustomer-level costs.

Exhibit 6 shows an operating income statement for the Provalue Division for 2013. The customer-level operating income of Customers A and B in Exhibit 3 is shown in columns 3 and 4 in Exhibit 6. The format of Exhibit 6 is based on the

Exhibit 6   Income Statement of Provalue Division for 2013 Using the Cost Hierarchy

	Total	Total	Wholesale Customers A**	B**	A3		Total	Business-Sales Customers A	B	C
	(1) = (2) + (7)	(2)	(3)	(4)	(5)	(6)	(7)	(8)	(9)	(10)(11)
Revenues (at actual prices)	$150,000,000	$97,550,000	$30,000,000	$26,250,000	-	-	$52,450,000	$7,000,000	$6,250,000	- -
Cost of goods sold plus customer-level costs	125,550,000*	82,522,500	25,085,000 a	20,560,000	-	-	43,027,500	5,385,000	4,760,000	- -
Customer-level operating income	24,450,000	15,027,500	$ 4,915,000	$ 5,690,000	-	-	9,422,500	$1,615,000	$1,490,000	- -
Distribution-channel costs	2,150,000	800,000					1,350,000			
Distribution-channel-level operating income	22,300,000	$14,227,500					$ 8,072,500			
Division-sustaining costs										
Administration costs	1,900,000									
R&D Costs	2,400,000									
Design Costs	3,000,000									
Total division-sustaining costs	7,300,000									
Division operating income	$ 15,000,000									

*Cost of goods sold, $102,000,000 (Exhibit 14-1) + Sales order costs, $6,750,000 + Customer visit costs, $4,200,000 + Product handling costs, $4,500,000 + Regular shipment costs, $3,750,000 + Rush shipment costs, $750,000 + Customer service costs, $3,600,000 (all from Exhibit 14-2)

**Full details are presented in Exhibit 14-3

aCost of goods sold + total customer-level costs from Exhibit 14-3 for Customer A = $20,400,000 + $4,685,000 = $25,085,000.

Provalue Division's cost hierarchy. As described in Exhibit 2, some costs of serving customers, such as the salary of the wholesale distribution-channel manager, are not customer-level costs and are therefore not allocated to customers in Exhibit 6. Managers identify these costs as distribution-channel costs because changes in customer behavior will have no effect on these costs. Only decisions pertaining to the channel, such as a decision to discontinue wholesale distribution, will influence these costs. Managers also believe that salespeople responsible for managing individual customer accounts would lose motivation if sales bonuses were adversely affected as a result of allocating to customers distribution-channel costs over which they had minimal influence.

Next, consider division-sustaining costs such as R&D and design costs and administration costs of the Provalue Division. Managers believe there is no direct cause-and-effect relationship between these costs and customer or sales manager's actions. Under this view, allocating division-sustaining costs serves no useful purpose in decision making, performance evaluation, or motivation. Suppose, for example, that the Provalue Division allocates the $7,300,000 of division-sustaining costs to its distribution channels and that in some subsequent period this allocation results in the business-sales channel showing a loss. Should the Provalue Division shut down the business-sales distribution channel? Not if division-sustaining costs are unaffected by shutting down the business-sales distribution channel. Allocating division-sustaining costs to distribution channels gives the misleading impression that potential cost savings from discontinuing a distribution channel are greater than the likely amount.

In a cost hierarchy-based income statement, how should we treat the corporate costs for brand advertising, $1,050,000, and administration, $4,400,000, incurred by Astel Computers to support the Provalue and Deskpoint divisions? The Deskpoint Division has revenues of $200,000,000 and operating costs of $170,000,000. Exhibit 7 presents the cost hierarchy-based income statement for Astel Computers as a whole. Corporate-sustaining costs are not allocated either to divisions or to customers. That's because, as discussed earlier in the context of division-sustaining costs, there is no direct cause-and-effect relationship between these costs and the profitability of different customers. These costs are unaffected by the actions of division managers or customers, so corporate sustaining costs are subtracted as a lump-sum amount after aggregating operating incomes of the divisions.

Other managers and management accountants advocate fully allocating all costs to distribution channels and to customers because all costs are incurred to support the sales of products to customers. Allocating all corporate costs motivates division managers to examine how corporate costs are planned and controlled. Similarly allocating division costs to distribution channels motivates the managers of the distribution channels to monitor costs incurred in the division. Managers that want to calculate the full costs of serving customers must allocate all corporate, division, and distribution channel costs to customers. These managers and management accountants argue that, in the long run, customers and products must eventually be profitable on a full-cost basis. For some decisions such as pricing, allocating all costs ensures that long-run prices are set at a level to cover the cost of all resources used to produce and sell products. In this case, the sum of operating incomes of all customers equals companywide operating income.

	Home	Insert	Page Layout	Formulas	Data	Review	View	
	A				**B**	**C**	**D**	
1	Income Statement of Astel Computers for 2013 Using the Cost Hierachy							
2								
3					**Total**	**Provalue Division**	**Deskpoint Division**	
4								
5	Revenues				$350,000,000	$150,000,000	$200,000,000	
6	Division operating costs				(305,000,000)	(135,000,000)*	(170,000,000)	
7	Division operating income before corporate costs				45,000,000	$ 15,000,000	$ 30,000,000	
8	Corporate advertising				(1,050,000)			
9	Corporate administration				(4,400,000)			
10	Operating income				$ 39,550,000			
11	*135,000,000 = $125,550,000 + $2,150,000 + $7,300,000 all from Exhibit 14-6, Column 1							

Exhibit 7

Income Statement of Astel Computers for 2013 Using the Cost Hierarchy

Still other companies allocate only those corporate costs, division costs, or channel costs to customers that are widely perceived as causally related to customer actions or that provide explicit benefits to customer profitability. Corporate advertising is an example of such a cost. These companies exclude other costs such as corporate administration or donations to charitable foundations because the benefits to the customers are less evident or too remote. If a company decides not to allocate some or all corporate, division, or channel costs, it results in total company profitability being less than the sum of individual customer profitabilities.

For some decision purposes, allocating some but not all indirect costs to customers may be the preferred alternative. Consider the performance evaluation of the wholesale channel manager of the Provalue Division. The controllability notion is frequently used to justify excluding corporate costs such as salaries of the top management at corporate headquarters from responsibility accounting reports of the wholesale channel manager. Although the wholesale channel manager tends to benefit from these corporate costs, he or she has no say in ("is not responsible for") how much of these corporate resources to use or how much they cost.

Nevertheless, the value of the hierarchical format in Exhibits 6 and 7 is to distinguish among various degrees of objectivity when allocating costs so that it dovetails with the different levels at which managers make decisions and evaluate performance. The issue of when and what costs to allocate is another example of the "different costs for different purposes" theme emphasized throughout this text.

In the next section, we consider what happens if Astel's managers decided to allocate distribution channel costs (such as costs of the wholesale channel), division-sustaining costs (such as costs of R&D and design), and corporate-sustaining costs (such as corporate administration costs of Astel Computers) to individual customers.

Decision Point ▶

Why do managers prepare cost-hierarchy-based operating income statements?

Learning Objective 4 ▶

Understand criteria to guide cost-allocation decisions

...such as identifying factors that cause resources to be consumed

Criteria to Guide Cost Allocations

Exhibit 8 presents four criteria managers use to guide cost-allocation decisions. These decisions affect both the number of indirect-cost pools and the cost-allocation base for each indirect-cost pool. We emphasize the superiority of the cause-and-effect and the benefits-received criteria, especially when the purpose of cost allocation is to provide information for economic decisions or to motivate managers and employees.[5] Cause and effect is the primary criterion used in activity-based costing (ABC) applications. ABC systems use the concept of a cost hierarchy to identify the cost drivers that best demonstrate the cause-and-effect relationship between each activity and the costs in the related cost pool. The cost drivers are then chosen as cost-allocation bases. Cause and effect is often difficult to determine in the case of division-sustaining and corporate-sustaining costs. In these situations, managers and management accountants interested in allocating costs use other methods summarized in Exhibit 8.

The best way to allocate costs if cause and effect cannot be established is to use the benefits-received criterion by identifying the beneficiaries of the output of the cost object. Consider, for example, the cost of managing the wholesale channel for Provalue, such as the salary of the manager of the wholesale channel. There is no cause-and-effect relationship between these costs and sales made by wholesalers. But it is plausible to assume that the customers with higher revenues benefited more from the wholesale channel support than customers with lower revenues. The benefits-received criterion justifies allocating the costs of managing the wholesale channel of $800,000 to customers based on customer revenues.

Fairness and ability to bear are less frequently used and more problematic criteria than cause and effect or benefits received. It's difficult for two parties to agree on criteria

---

[5] The Federal Accounting Standards Advisory Board (which sets standards for management accounting for U.S. government departments and agencies) recommends the following: "Cost assignments should be performed by: (a) directly tracing costs whenever feasible and economically practicable, (b) assigning costs on a cause-and-effect basis, and (c) allocating costs on a reasonable and consistent basis" (FASAB, 1995, p. 12).

| Exhibit 8 | Criteria for Cost-Allocation Decisions |

1. Cause and Effect. Using this criterion, managers identify the variables that cause resources to be consumed. For example, managers may use number of sales orders as the variable when allocating the costs of order taking to products and customers. Cost allocations based on the cause-and-effect criterion are likely to be the most credible to operating personnel.

2. Benefits Received. Using this criterion, managers identify the beneficiaries of the outputs of the cost object. The costs of the cost object are allocated among the beneficiaries in proportion to the benefits each receives. Consider a corporatewide advertising program that promotes the general image of the corporation rather than any individual product. The costs of this program may be allocated on the basis of division revenues; the higher the revenues, the higher the division's allocated cost of the advertising program. The rationale behind this allocation is that divisions with higher revenues apparently benefited from the advertising more than divisions with lower revenues and, therefore, ought to be allocated more of the advertising costs.

3. Fairness or Equity. This criterion is often cited in government contracts when cost allocations are the basis for establishing a price satisfactory to the government and its suppliers. Cost allocation here is viewed as a "reasonable" or "fair" means of establishing a selling price in the minds of the contracting parties. For most allocation decisions, fairness is a matter of judgment rather than an operational criterion.

4. Ability to Bear. This criterion advocates allocating costs in proportion to the cost object's ability to bear costs allocated to it. An example is the allocation of corporate administration costs on the basis of division operating income. The presumption is that the more-profitable divisions have a greater ability to absorb corporate administration costs.

for fairness. What one party views as fair another party may view as unfair.[6] For example, a university may view allocating a share of general administrative costs to government contracts for scientific and medical research as fair because general administrative costs are incurred to support all activities of the university. The government may view the allocation of such costs as unfair because the general administrative costs would have been incurred by the university regardless of whether the government contract existed. Perhaps the fairest way to resolve this issue is to understand, as well as possible, the cause-and-effect relationship between the government contract activity and general administrative costs. This is difficult. In other words, fairness is more a matter of judgment than an easily implementable choice criterion.

To get a sense of the issues that arise when using the ability-to-bear criterion, consider Customer G where customer-level costs exceed revenues before any allocation of any division-sustaining or corporate-sustaining costs. This customer has no ability to bear any of the division- or corporate-sustaining costs, so under the ability-to-bear criterion none of these costs will be allocated to Customer G. Costs are not allocated because managers are expected to reduce their dependence on these more remote division- and corporate-sustaining costs (such as administration costs) to support loss-making customers in order to bring the customer relationship back to profitability. However, if the indirect costs are not reduced but simply allocated to other customers, these other customers would be subsidizing the customer that is losing money. The ability-to-bear criterion would then result in a distorted view of lower customer and service profitability for profitable customers and the potential for incorrect actions, such as increasing prices to restore profitability, which could then invite competitors to undercut artificially higher-priced services.

Most importantly, companies must weigh the costs and benefits when designing and implementing their cost allocations. Companies incur costs not only in collecting data but also in taking the time to educate managers about cost allocations. In general, the more complex the cost allocations, the higher these education costs.

---

[6] Kaplow and Shavell, in a review of the legal literature, note that "notions of fairness are many and varied. They are analyzed and rationalized by different writers in different ways, and they also typically depend upon the circumstances under consideration. Accordingly, it is not possible to identify a consensus view on these notions..." See Louis Kaplow and Steven Shavell, "Fairness Versus Welfare," *Harvard Law Review* (February 2001); and Louis Kaplow and Steven Shavell, *Fairness Versus Welfare* (Boston: Harvard University Press, 2002).

Decision Point

What criteria should managers use to guide cost-allocation decisions?

The costs of designing and implementing complex cost allocations are highly visible. Unfortunately, the benefits from using well-designed cost allocations, such as enabling managers to make better-informed sourcing decisions, pricing decisions, cost-control decisions, and so on, are difficult to measure. Nevertheless, when making cost allocations, managers should consider the benefits as well as the costs. As costs of collecting and processing information decrease, companies are building more detailed cost allocations.

Learning Objective 5

Discuss decisions faced when collecting and allocating indirect costs to customers

...determining the number of cost pools and the costs to be included in each cost pool

Fully Allocated Customer Profitability

In this section, we focus on the first purpose of cost allocation: to provide information for economic decisions, such as pricing, by measuring the full costs of delivering products to different customers based on an ABC system.

We continue with the Astel Computers example introduced earlier in this chapter and focus on the fully allocated customer profitability calculations for the 10 wholesale customers in the Provalue Division. The Provalue Division also uses a direct sales channel to sell Provalue computers directly to business customers. Recall that Astel also has another division, the Deskpoint Division, that sells servers. We will use the Astel Computers example to illustrate how costs incurred in different parts of a company can be assigned, and then reassigned, to calculate customer profitability.

We summarize the cost categories as:

- **Corporate costs**—There are two major categories of corporate costs:
  1. **Corporate advertising costs**—advertising and promotion costs to promote the Astel brand, $1,050,000.
  2. **Corporate administration costs**—executive salaries, rent, and general administration costs, $4,400,000.

- **Division costs**—The Provalue Division, which is the focus of our analysis, has three indirect-cost pools—one cost pool each corresponding to the different cost drivers for allocating division costs to distribution channels: (1) cost pool 1 that aggregates all division costs that are allocated to the wholesale and business-sales channels based on revenues of each channel; (2) cost pool 2 that accumulates R&D and design costs that are allocated to the distribution channels on some fair and equitable basis; and (3) cost pool 3 that aggregates all division costs that are allocated to the wholesale and business-sales channels based on the operating incomes of each channel before such allocations (if positive). The cost pools are *homogeneous*, that is, all costs in a cost pool have the same or similar cause-and-effect, benefits-received, or fair-and-equitable relationship with the cost-allocation base. Different cost pools need different cost allocation bases to allocate the costs in the cost pools to distribution channels.

- **Channel costs**—Each distribution channel in the Provalue Division has two indirect cost pools: (1) a cost pool that aggregates all channel costs that are allocated to customers based on customer revenues and (2) a cost pool that aggregates all channel costs that are allocated to customers based on operating incomes of customers before such allocations (if positive).

Exhibit 9 presents an overview diagram of the allocation of corporate, division, and distribution-channel indirect costs to wholesale customers of the Provalue Division. Note that the Deskpoint Division has its own indirect-cost pools used to allocate costs to its customers. These cost pools and cost-allocation bases parallel the indirect-cost pools and allocation bases for the Provalue Division.

Implementing Corporate and Division Cost Allocations

Exhibit 10 allocates all overhead costs to customers based on the overview diagram in Exhibit 9. We describe some of the allocation choices based on the criteria for allocating costs explained in Exhibit 8.

Exhibit 9 Overview Diagram for Allocating Corporate, Division, and Channel Indirect Costs to Wholesale Customers of Provalue Division

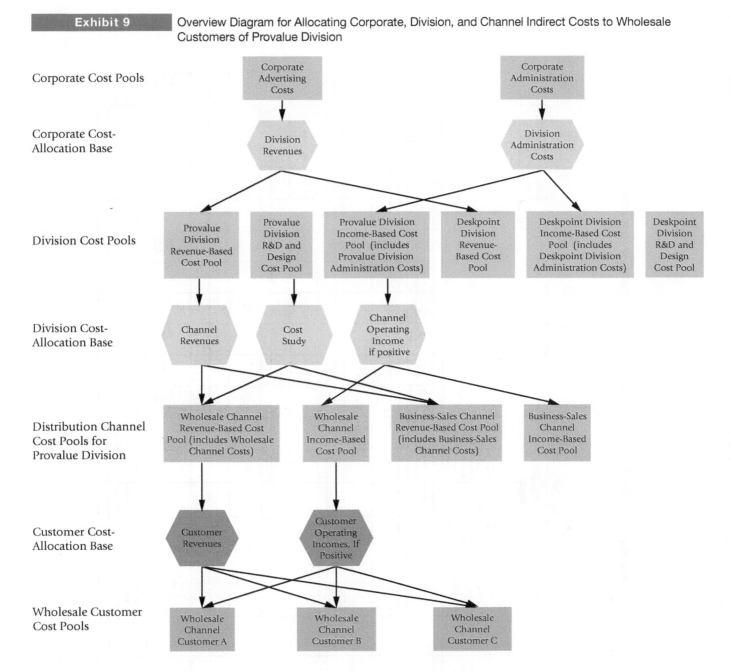

1. Start at the top of Exhibit 9 and the allocation of corporate advertising and corporate adminisitration costs based on the demands that the Provalue Division and Deskpoint Division customers place on corporate resources. The first two columns in Exhibit 10 present the allocation of corporate advertising and corporate administration costs to the Provalue and Deskpoint divisions.

   a. Astel allocates a total of $1,050,000 of corporate advertising costs to the two divisions on the basis of the revenues of each division (benefits received). It is plausible to assume that customers with higher revenues benefited more from corporate advertising costs than customers with lower revenues (see Exhibit 7):

$$\text{Provalue Division}: \$1,050,000 \times \frac{\$150,000,000}{\$150,000,000 + \$200,000,000} = \$450,000$$

$$\text{Deskpoint Division}: \$1,050,000 \times \frac{\$200,000,000}{\$150,000,000 + \$200,000,000} = \$600,000$$

Exhibit 10 Profitability of Wholesale Customers of Provalue Division After Fully Allocating Corporate, Division, and Channel Indirect Costs (in thousands, rounded)

Home | Insert | Page Layout | Formulas | Data | Review | View

Column groups: **Div Rev (B)** and **Div Admin (C)** = *Astel Corporation Cost Pools*; **Chan Rev (D)**, **R&D/Design (E)**, **Chan OI (F)** = *Provalue Division Cost Pools*; **WhRev, WhOI, BusRev, BusOI** = *Distribution Channel Cost Pools* (Provalue Division); **A–Total** = *Wholesale Channel Customers* (Provalue Division).

Row	Item	Costs Allocated Based on Division Revenues (B)	Costs Allocated Based on Division Administration Costs (C)	Costs Allocated Based on Channel Revenues (D)	R&D and Design Cost Allocation Pool (E)	Costs Allocated Based on Channel Operating Incomes (F)	Wholesale Channel Costs Allocated Based on Customer Revenues	Wholesale Channel Costs Allocated Based on Customer Operating Incomes	Business-Sales Channel Costs Allocated Based on Customer Revenues	Business-Sales Channel Costs Allocated Based on Customer Operating Incomes	A	B	C	D	E	F	G	H	I	J	Total
5	Revenues (Exhibit 14-4)										$30,000	$26,250	$13,000	$7,250	$1,800	$5,100	$4,750	$2,400	$2,600	$4,400	$97,550
6	Customer-level costs (Exh. 14-4, Col. 2–Col.1)										(25,085)	(20,560)	(10,345)	(5,605)	(1,700)	(4,114)	(5,100)	(2,935)	(3,300)	(3,578)	(82,522)
7	Customer-level operating income (Exh. 14-4)										4,915	5,690	2,655	1,445	100	986	(350)	(535)	(700)	822	15,028
8	Astel corporate advertising costs	$(1,050)																			
9	Astel corporate administration costs		$(4,400)																		
10	Allocate corporate advertising costs to divisions based on division revenues[1]	1,050		$(450)																	
11	Allocate corporate administration costs to divisions based on division administration costs[2]		4,400			$(2,090)															
12	R&D costs				$(2,400)																
13	Design costs				(3,000)																
14	Division administration costs					(1,900)															
15	Allocate corporate advertising costs from Provalue Division to wholesale channel based on channel revenues[3]			450			$(293)		$(157)												
16	Allocate R&D and Design costs to channels based on fairness[4]				5,400		(2,700)		(2,700)												
17	Distribution channel costs						(800)		(1,350)												
18	Allocate division administration costs from Provalue division to wholesale channel based on channel operating incomes[5]					3,990		$(2,725)		$(1,265)											
19	Allocate wholesale channel costs to customers based on customer revenues						3,793				(1,166)	(1,021)	(505)	(282)	(70)	(198)	(185)	(93)	(101)	(172)	(3,793)
20	Operating income before allocation of division and corporate administration										3,749	4,669	2,150	1,163	30	788	(535)	(628)	(801)	650	11,235
21	Allocate wholesale channel costs to customers based on customer operating income, if positive (ability to bear)							2,725			(774)	(964)	(444)	(240)	(6)	(163)				(134)	(2,725)
22	Fully allocated customer profitability										$ 2,975	$ 3,706	$ 1,706	$ 923	$ 24	$ 625	$ (535)	$ (628)	$ (801)	$ 516	$ 8,510

[1] $1,050 × $150,000 / ($150,000 + $200,000) = $450

[2] $4,400 × $1,900 / ($1,900 + $2,100) = $2,090

[3] $450 × $97,550 / $150,000 = $293; $450 × $52,450 / $150,000 = $157

[4] $5,400 / 2 = $2,700

[5] $3,990 × $11,235 / $16,450 = $2,725; $3,990 × $5,215 / $16,450 = $1,265

b. Using the benefits-received criterion, Astel allocates corporate administration costs of $4,400,000 to each division on the basis of division-administration costs because corporate administration's main role is to support division administration. Exhibit 6 shows division-administration costs for Provalue Division of $1,900,000. Division administration costs for Deskpoint Division are $2,100,000. The allocations are:

$$\text{Provalue Division}: \$4,400,000 \times \frac{\$1,900,000}{\$1,900,000 + \$2,100,000} = \$2,090,000$$

$$\text{Deskpoint Division}: \$4,400,000 \times \frac{\$2,100,000}{\$1,900,000 + \$2,100,000} = \$2,310,000$$

2. Next, drop down one level in Exhibit 9 and focus on the allocation of costs from the division cost pools to the distribution-channel cost pools for the Provalue Division. The three columns labeled "Provalue Division Cost Pools" in Exhibit 10 show the allocations of the Provalue Division costs to the wholesale channel and the business-sales channel.
   a. Using the benefits-received criterion, the corporate advertising cost of $450,000 that had been allocated to the Provalue Division is now reallocated to the wholesale channel and the business-sales channel on the basis of the revenues of each channel (see Exhibit 6).

$$\text{Wholesale Channel}: \$450,000 \times \frac{\$97,550,000}{\$97,550,000 + \$52,450,000} = \$292,650$$

$$\text{Business-Sales Channel}: \$450,000 \times \frac{\$52,450,000}{\$52,450,000 + \$97,550,000} = \$157,350$$

   b. The R&D costs and design costs are aggregated into one homogeneous cost pool and allocated to channels on the basis of a study analyzing the demand for R&D and design resources by the wholesale and business-sales channels. A significant amount of the R&D and design costs arise as a result of modifications to the Provalue computer demanded by the more sophisticated business customers. Using the results of the study and the fairness criterion, the Provalue Division allocates half of the R&D and design costs to the business-sales channel (and half to the wholesale channel) even though the business-sales channel accounts for only about one-third of the total sales of the Provalue Division. Exhibit 10 shows that the Provalue Division allocates $2,700,000($5,400,000 ÷ 2) each to the wholesale and business-sales channels.
   c. Each division adds the allocated corporate-administration costs to the division-administration cost pool. The costs in this cost pool are facility-sustaining costs and do not have a cause-and-effect relationship with any of the activities in the distribution channels. Astel, however, allocates all costs to products so that managers are aware of all costs when making pricing and other decisions. The Provalue Division allocates the total costs of $3,990,000 in the Provalue Division Administration cost pool to the wholesale channel and business-sales channel based on operating incomes of the wholesale and business-sales channels, representing the ability of each channel to bear division-administration costs (including allocated corporate-administration costs). The lower the operating income of a channel, the lower the division costs allocated to it. As described earlier in the chapter, the rationale for the ability-to-bear criterion is that divisions with lower incomes would work hard to reduce these overhead costs if they could manage these costs. From Exhibit 10, the operating income of the wholesale channel after subtracting all costs that have been allocated to it thus far is $11,234,850 ($15,027,500 (Cell R7) − $292,650 (Cell G15) − $2,700,000 (Cell G16) − $800,000 (Cell G17)) while the operating income of the business-sales channel is $5,215,150 (calculations not shown).

$$\text{Wholesale Channel}: \$3,990,000 \times \frac{\$11,234,850}{\$11,234,850 + \$5,215,150} = \$2,725,049$$

$$\text{Business-Sales Channel}: \$3,990,000 \times \frac{\$5,215,150}{\$11,234,850 + \$5,215,150} = \$1,264,951$$

3. Finally, focus on the bottom rows in Exhibit 9 and the allocation of costs from the distribution channel cost pools for the Provalue Division to individual wholesale channel customers. The four columns labeled "Provalue Division Distribution Channel Cost Pools" in Exhibit 10 show that the costs accumulated in the wholesale channel and the business-sales channel are allocated to customers. Exhibit 10 only presents the allocation of wholesale channel costs to wholesale customers.

   a. Some of the wholesale channel costs are allocated to individual wholesale customers on the basis of revenues because revenues are a good measure of how individual customers benefit from these costs. The costs in this cost pool total $3,792,650 and are composed of three costs: (1) $292,650 of corporate advertising costs allocated to the wholesale channel in step 2a, (2) $2,700,000 of R&D and design costs allocated to the wholesale channel in step 2b, and (3) $800,000 of costs of the wholesale-distribution channel itself (Exhibit 6). In Exhibit 10, the costs allocated to Customer A and Customer B are:

$$\text{Customer A}: \$3,792,650 \times \frac{\$30,000,000}{\$97,550,000} = \$1,166,371$$

$$\text{Customer B}: \$3,792,650 \times \frac{\$26,250,000}{\$97,550,000} = \$1,020,574$$

   b. The second wholesale channel cost pool is composed of $2,725,049 of the division-administrative costs allocated to the wholesale channel in step 2c. These costs are allocated to individual wholesale customers on the basis of operating incomes (if positive) (see Exhibit 10, row 21) because operating incomes represent the ability of customers to bear these costs. In Exhibit 10, the sum of all the positive amounts in row 20 equals $13,195, 922. The costs allocated to Customer A and Customer B are:

$$\text{Customer A}: \$2,725,049 \times \frac{\$3,748,629}{\$13,195,922} = \$774,117$$

$$\text{Customer B}: \$2,725,049 \times \frac{\$4,669,426}{\$13,195,922} = \$964,269$$

Issues in Allocating Corporate Costs to Divisions and Customers

Astel's management team makes several choices when accumulating and allocating corporate costs to divisions. We present two such issues next.

1. When allocating corporate costs to divisions, should Astel allocate only costs that vary with division activity or assign fixed costs as well? Managers allocate both variable and fixed costs to divisions and then to customers because the resulting costs are useful for making long-run strategic decisions, such as which customers to emphasize and what prices to offer. To make good long-run decisions, managers need to know the cost of all resources (whether variable or fixed in the short run) required to sell products to customers. Why? Because in the long run, firms can manage the levels of virtually all of their costs; very few costs are truly fixed. Moreover, to survive and prosper in the long run, firms must ensure that the revenues received from a customer exceed the total resources consumed to support the customer, regardless of whether these costs are variable or fixed in the short run.

   At the same time, companies that allocate corporate costs to divisions must carefully identify relevant costs for specific decisions. Suppose a division is profitable before any corporate costs are allocated but "unprofitable" after allocation of corporate costs. Should the division be closed down? The relevant corporate costs in this case are not the allocated corporate costs but those corporate costs that will be saved if the division is closed. If division profits exceed the relevant corporate costs, the division should not be closed.

2. When allocating costs to divisions, channels, and customers, how many cost pools should Astel use? One extreme is to aggregate all costs into a single cost pool. The other extreme is to have numerous individual cost pools. A major consideration is to construct **homogeneous cost pools** so that all of the costs in the cost pool have the same or a similar cause-and-effect or benefits-received relationship with the cost-allocation base.

For example, when allocating corporate costs to divisions, Astel can combine corporate advertising costs and corporate administration costs into a single cost pool if both cost categories have the same or similar cause-and-effect relationship with the same cost-allocation base. If, however, as is the case here, each cost category has a cause-and-effect or benefits-received relationship with a different cost-allocation base (for example, revenues of each division affect corporate advertising costs whereas division-administration costs of each division affect corporate administration costs), the company will prefer to maintain separate cost pools for each of these costs. Determining homogeneous cost pools requires judgment and should be revisited on a regular basis.

Managers must balance the benefit of using a multiple cost-pool system against the costs of implementing it. Advances in information-gathering technology make it more likely that multiple cost-pool systems will pass the cost–benefit test.

Decision Point

What are two key decisions managers must make when collecting costs in indirect-cost pools?

Using Fully Allocated Costs for Decision Making

How might Astel's managers use the fully allocated customer-profitability analysis in Exhibit 10? Managers frequently favor using the full cost of a product when making pricing decisions. There are similar benefits to calculating fully allocated customer costs.

Consider, for example, Customer E, who shows a profitability of $24,000 in Exhibit 10. If this customer demanded a price reduction of $50,000, how should the Provalue Division respond? Based on the analysis in Exhibit 4, Customer E shows a profitability of $100,000 and it would appear that even a $50,000 reduction in price would still leave Customer E as a profitable customer. But in the long run, Customer E must generate sufficient profits to recover all the division-support costs of the Provalue Division and the corporate costs of Astel. A $50,000 reduction in price may not be sustainable in the long run. As the Provalue Division begins making plans for Provalue II, it simultaneously must consider what it can do to better manage its customers to improve profitability.

Another advantage of allocating costs to customers is that it highlights opportunities to manage costs. For example, the manager of the wholesale channel might want to probe whether the amounts spent on corporate advertising or on R&D and design help in promoting sales to wholesale customers. These discusssions might prompt a reevalaution of the amount and type of advertising, R&D, and design activity.

Sales Variances

The customer-profitability analysis in the previous section focused on the actual profitability of individual customers within a distribution channel (wholesale, for example) and their effect on the Provalue Division's profitability for 2013. At a more strategic level, however, recall that Provalue Division sells Provalues in two different markets: wholesale and directly to businesses. The operating margins in the business-sales market are higher than the operating margins in the wholesale market. In 2013, the Provalue Division had budgeted to sell 60% of its Provalues through wholesalers and 40% directly to businesses. It sold more Provalues in total than it had budgeted, but its actual sales mix (in computers) was 66.67% to wholesalers and 33.33% directly to businesses. Regardless of the profitability of sales to individual customers within each of the wholesale and business-sales channels, the Provalue Division's actual operating income, relative to the master budget, is likely to be positively affected by the higher number of Provalues sold

Learning Objective 6

Subdivide the sales-volume variance into the sales-mix variance

…this variance arises because actual sales mix differs from budgeted sales mix

and the sales-quantity variance

…this variance arises because actual total unit sales differ from budgeted total unit sales

and the sales-quantity variance into the market-share variance

…this variance arises because actual market share differs from budgeted market share

and the market-size variance

…this variance arises because actual market size differs from budgeted market size

and negatively affected by the shift in mix toward the less profitable wholesale customers. Sales-quantity and sales-mix variances can identify the effect of each of these factors on the Provalue Division's profitability. Companies such as Cisco, GE, and Hewlett-Packard perform similar analyses because they sell their products through multiple distribution channels like the Internet, over the telephone, and retail stores.

The Provalue Division classifies all customer-level costs, other than fixed machining costs of $11,400,000, as variable costs and distribution-channel and corporate-sustaining costs as fixed costs. To simplify the sales-variance analysis and calculations, we assume that all of the variable costs are variable with respect to Provalue computers sold. (This means that average batch sizes remain the same as the total number of Provalue computers sold vary.) Without this assumption, the analysis would become more complex and would have to be done using the ABC-variance analysis approach. The basic insights, however, would not change.

Budgeted and actual operating data for 2013 are as follows:

Budget Data for 2013

	Selling Price (1)	Variable Cost per Unit (2)	Contribution Margin per Unit (3) = (1) − (2)	Sales Volume in Units (4)	Sales Mix (Based on Units) (5)	Contribution Margin (6) = (3) × (4)
Wholesale channel	$ 980	$755	$225	93,000	60%[a]	$20,925,000
Business-sales channel	1,050	775	275	62,000	40%	17,050,000
Total				155,000	100%	$37,975,000

[a]Percentage of unit sales to wholesale channel = 93,000 units ÷ 155,000 total unit = 60%.

Actual Results for 2013

	Selling Price (1)	Variable Cost per Unit (2)	Contribution Margin per Unit (3) = (1) − (2)	Sales Volume in Units (4)	Sales Mix (Based on Units) (5)	Contribution Margin (6) = (3) × (4)
Wholesale channel	$ 975.50	$749.225	$226.275	100,000	66.67%[a]	$22,627,500
Business-sales channel	1,049.00	784.55	264.45	50,000	33.33%	13,222,500
Total				150,000	100.00%	$35,850,000

[a]Percentage of unit sales to wholesale channel = 100,000 units ÷ 150,000 total unit = 66.67%.

The budgeted and actual fixed distribution-channel costs, division costs, and corporate-level costs are the same (see Exhibit 6 and Exhibit 7).

The levels of detail include the static-budget variance (level 1), the flexible-budget variance (level 2), and the sales-volume variance (level 2). The sales-quantity and sales-mix variances are level 3 variances that subdivide the sales-volume variance.[7]

Static-Budget Variance

The *static-budget variance* is the difference between an actual result and the corresponding budgeted amount in the static budget. Our analysis focuses on the difference between actual and budgeted contribution margins (column 6 in the preceding tables). The total static-budget variance is $2,125,000 U (actual contribution margin of $35,850,000 − budgeted contribution margin of $37,975,000). Exhibit 11 (columns 1 and 3) uses the columnar format to show detailed calculations of the static-budget variance. Managers can gain more insight about the static-budget variance by subdividing it into the flexible-budget variance and the sales-volume variance.

---

[7] The presentation of the variances in this chapter and the appendix draws on teaching notes prepared by J. K. Harris.

Exhibit 11   Flexible-Budget and Sales-Volume Variance Analysis of Provalue Division for 2013

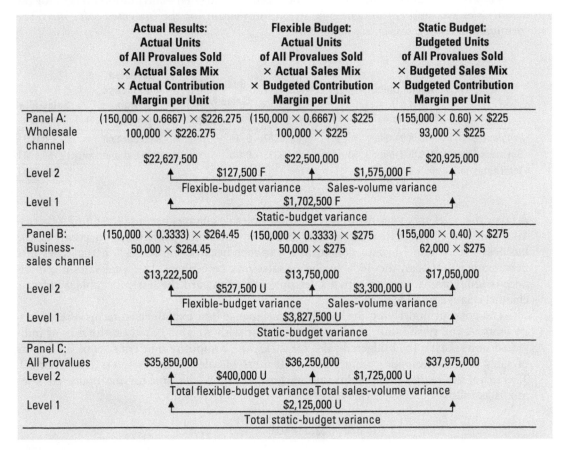

	Actual Results: Actual Units of All Provalues Sold × Actual Sales Mix × Actual Contribution Margin per Unit	Flexible Budget: Actual Units of All Provalues Sold × Actual Sales Mix × Budgeted Contribution Margin per Unit	Static Budget: Budgeted Units of All Provalues Sold × Budgeted Sales Mix × Budgeted Contribution Margin per Unit
Panel A: Wholesale channel	(150,000 × 0.6667) × $226.275 100,000 × $226.275	(150,000 × 0.6667) × $225 100,000 × $225	(155,000 × 0.60) × $225 93,000 × $225
	$22,627,500	$22,500,000	$20,925,000
Level 2	↑_____$127,500 F_____↑ Flexible-budget variance	↑_____$1,575,000 F_____↑ Sales-volume variance	
Level 1	↑_____$1,702,500 F_____↑ Static-budget variance		
Panel B: Business- sales channel	(150,000 × 0.3333) × $264.45 50,000 × $264.45	(150,000 × 0.3333) × $275 50,000 × $275	(155,000 × 0.40) × $275 62,000 × $275
	$13,222,500	$13,750,000	$17,050,000
Level 2	↑_____$527,500 U_____↑ Flexible-budget variance	↑_____$3,300,000 U_____↑ Sales-volume variance	
Level 1	↑_____$3,827,500 U_____↑ Static-budget variance		
Panel C: All Provalues	$35,850,000	$36,250,000	$37,975,000
Level 2	↑_____$400,000 U_____↑ Total flexible-budget variance	↑_____$1,725,000 U_____↑ Total sales-volume variance	
Level 1	↑_____$2,125,000 U_____↑ Total static-budget variance		

Flexible-Budget Variance and Sales-Volume Variance

The *flexible-budget variance* is the difference between an actual result and the corresponding flexible-budget amount based on actual output level in the budget period. The flexible budget contribution margin is equal to budgeted contribution margin per unit times actual units sold of each product. Exhibit 11, column 2, shows the flexible-budget calculations. The flexible budget measures the contribution margin that the Provalue Division would have budgeted for the actual quantities of cases sold. The flexible-budget variance is the difference between columns 1 and 2 in Exhibit 11. The only difference between columns 1 and 2 is that actual units sold of each product is multiplied by actual contribution margin per unit in column 1 and budgeted contribution margin per unit in column 2. The $400,000 U total flexible-budget variance arises because actual contribution margin on business sales of $264.45 per Provalue is lower than the budgeted amount of $275 per Provalue and offsets the slightly higher actual contribution margin of $226.275 versus the budgeted contribution margin of $225 on wholesale channel sales. The Provalue Division managers are aware that the lower contribution margin of $10.55 ($275 – $264.45) per computer on business sales resulted from higher variable ordering and testing costs and have put in place action plans to reduce these costs in the future.

The *sales-volume variance* is the difference between a flexible-budget amount and the corresponding static-budget amount. In Exhibit 11, the sales-volume variance shows the effect on budgeted contribution margin of the difference between actual quantity of units sold and budgeted quantity of units sold. The sales-volume variance of $1,725,000 U is the difference between columns 2 and 3 in Exhibit 11. In this case, it is unfavorable overall because while wholesale channel sales of Provalue were higher than budgeted, business sales, which are expected to be more profitable on a per computer basis, were below budget. Provalue Division managers can gain substantial insight into the sales-volume variance by subdividing it into the sales-mix variance and the sales-quantity variance.

Sales-Mix Variance

The **sales-mix variance** is the difference between (1) budgeted contribution margin for the *actual sales mix* and (2) budgeted contribution margin for the *budgeted sales mix*. The formula and computations are as follows:

	Actual Units of All Provalues Sold	×	(Actual Sales-Mix Percentage − Budgeted Sales-Mix Percentage) ×	Budgeted Contribution Margin per Unit	=	Sales-Mix Variance
Wholesale	150,000 units	×	(0.66667 − 0.60)	× $225 per unit	=	$2,250,000 F
Business-Sales	150,000 units	×	(0.33333 − 0.40)	× $275 per unit	=	2,750,000 U
Total sales-mix variance						$ 500,000 U

A favorable sales-mix variance arises for the wholesale channel because the 66.67% actual sales-mix percentage exceeds the 60% budgeted sales-mix percentage. In contrast, the business-sales channel has an unfavorable variance because the 33.33% actual sales-mix percentage is less than the 40% budgeted sales-mix percentage. The total sales-mix variance is unfavorable because actual sales mix shifted toward the less profitable wholesale channel relative to budgeted sales mix.

The concept underlying the sales-mix variance is best explained in terms of composite units. A **composite unit** is a hypothetical unit with weights based on the mix of individual units. Given the budgeted sales for 2013, the composite unit consists of 0.60 units of sales to the wholesale channel and 0.40 units of sales to the business-sales channel. Therefore, the budgeted contribution margin per composite unit for the budgeted sales mix is as follows:

$$0.60 \times \$225 + 0.40 \times \$275 = \$245^{8}$$

Similarly, for the actual sales mix, the composite unit consists of 0.66667 units of sales to the wholesale channel and 0.33333 units of sales to the business-sales channel. The budgeted contribution margin per composite unit for the actual sales mix is therefore:

$$0.66667 \times \$225 + 0.33333 \times \$275 = \$241.6667$$

The impact of the shift in sales mix is now evident. The Provalue Division obtains a lower budgeted contribution margin per composite unit of $3.3333 ($245 − $241.6667). For the 150,000 units actually sold, this decrease translates to a $500,000 U sales-mix variance ($3.3333 per unit × 150,000 units).

Managers should probe why the $500,000 U sales-mix variance occurred in 2013. Is the shift in sales mix because profitable business customers proved to be more difficult to find? Is it because of a competitor in the business-sales channel providing better service at a lower price? Or is it because the initial sales-volume estimates were made without adequate analysis of the potential market?

Exhibit 12 uses the columnar format to calculate the sales-mix variance and the sales-quantity variances.

Sales-Quantity Variance

The **sales-quantity variance** is the difference between (1) budgeted contribution margin based on *actual units sold of all products* at the budgeted mix and (2) contribution margin in the static budget (which is based on *budgeted units of all products to be sold*

---

[8] Budgeted contribution margin per composite unit can be computed in another way by dividing total budgeted contribution margin of $37,975,000 by total budgeted units of 155,000: $37,975,000 ÷ 155,000 units = $245 per unit.

| Exhibit 12 | Sales-Mix and Sales-Quantity Variance Analysis of Provalue Division for 2013 |

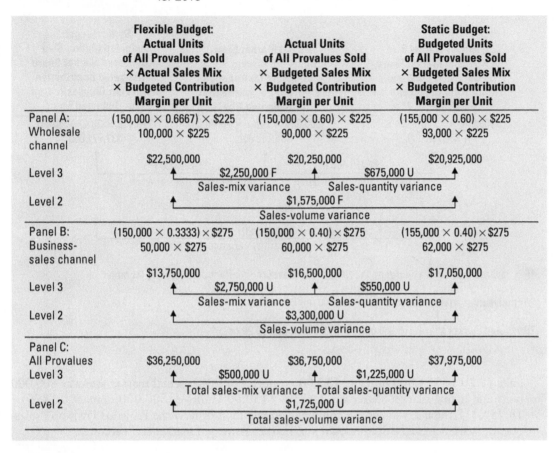

at budgeted mix). The formula and computations are as follows:

	Actual total Provalues sold − Budgeted total Provalues sold		Budgeted Sales-Mix Percentages		Budgeted Contribution Margin per Unit		Sales-Quantity Variance
Wholesale	(150,000 units − 155,000 units)	×	0.60	×	$225 per unit	=	$ 675,000 U
Business sales	(150,000 units − 155,000 units)	×	0.40	×	$275 per unit	=	550,000 U
Total sales-quantity variance							$1,225,000 U

This variance is unfavorable when actual units of all products sold are less than the budgeted units of all products sold. The Provalue Division sold 5,000 fewer Provalues than were budgeted, resulting in a $1,225,000 sales-quantity variance (also equal to budgeted contribution margin per composite unit for the budgeted sales mix times fewer units sold, $245 × 5,000). Managers would want to probe the reasons for the decrease in sales. Did lower sales come as a result of a competitor's aggressive marketing? Poorer customer service? Or decline in the overall market? Managers can gain additional insight into the causes of the sales-quantity variance by analyzing changes in Provalue Division's share of the total industry market and in the size of that market. The sales-quantity variance can be decomposed into market-share and market-size variances, as we describe in the next section.

Market-Share and Market-Size Variances

The total quantity of Provalues sold depends on overall demand for similar computers in the market, as well as Provalue Division's share of the market. Assume that the Provalue Division derived its total unit sales budget of 155,000 Provalue computers for 2013 from a management estimate of a 20% market share and a budgeted industry market size of 775,000

153

| Exhibit 13 | Market-Share and Market-Size Variance Analysis of Provalue Division of Astel Computers for 2013[a] |

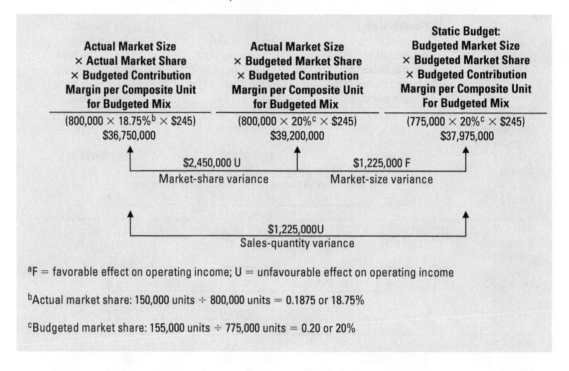

Actual Market Size × Actual Market Share × Budgeted Contribution Margin per Composite Unit for Budgeted Mix	**Actual Market Size × Budgeted Market Share × Budgeted Contribution Margin per Composite Unit for Budgeted Mix**	**Static Budget: Budgeted Market Size × Budgeted Market Share × Budgeted Contribution Margin per Composite Unit For Budgeted Mix**
(800,000 × 18.75%[b] × $245) $36,750,000	(800,000 × 20%[c] × $245) $39,200,000	(775,000 × 20%[c] × $245) $37,975,000

$2,450,000 U — Market-share variance $1,225,000 F — Market-size variance

$1,225,000 U — Sales-quantity variance

[a]F = favourable effect on operating income; U = unfavourable effect on operating income

[b]Actual market share: 150,000 units ÷ 800,000 units = 0.1875 or 18.75%

[c]Budgeted market share: 155,000 units ÷ 775,000 units = 0.20 or 20%

units $(0.20 \times 775,000 \text{ units} = 155,000 \text{ units})$. For 2013, actual market size was 800,000 units and actual market share was 18.75% $(150,000 \text{ units} \div 800,000 \text{ units} = 0.1875$ or 18.75%). Exhibit 13 shows the columnar presentation of how the Provalue Division's sales-quantity variance can be decomposed into market-share and market-size variances.

Market-Share Variance

The **market-share variance** is the difference in budgeted contribution margin for actual market size in units caused solely by *actual market share* being different from *budgeted market share*. The formula for computing the market-share variance is as follows:

$$\text{Market-share variance} = \text{Actual market size in units} \times \left(\text{Actual market share} - \text{Budgeted market share} \right) \times \text{Budgeted contribution margin per composite unit for budgeted mix}$$

$$= 800,000 \text{ units} \times (0.1875 - 0.20) \times \$245 \text{ per unit}$$

$$= \$2,450,000 \text{ U}$$

The Provalue Division lost 1.25 market-share percentage points—from the 20% budgeted share to the actual share of 18.75%. The $2,450,000 U market-share variance is the decline in contribution margin as a result of those lost sales.

Market-Size Variance

The **market-size variance** is the difference in budgeted contribution margin at budgeted market share caused solely by *actual market size in units* being different from *budgeted market size in units*. The formula for computing the market-size variance is as follows:

$$\text{Market-size variance} = \left(\text{Actual market size} - \text{Budgeted market size} \right) \times \text{Budgeted market share} \times \text{Budgeted contribution margin per composite unit for budgeted mix}$$

$$= (800,000 \text{ units} - 775,000 \text{ units}) \times 0.20 \times \$245 \text{ per unit}$$

$$= \$1,225,000 \text{ F}$$

The market-size variance is favorable because actual market size increased 3.23% [(800,000 − 775,000) ÷ 775,000 = 0.0323, or 3.23%] compared to budgeted market size.

Managers should probe the reasons for the market-size and market-share variances for 2013. Is the $1,225,000 F market-size variance because of an increase in market size that can be expected to continue in the future? If yes, the Provalue Division has much to gain by attaining or exceeding its budgeted 20% market share. Was the $2,450,000 unfavorable market-share variance because of competitors providing better offerings or greater value to customers? Did competitors aggressively cut prices to stimulate market demand? Although Provalue Divison managers reduced prices a little relative to the budget, should they have reduced prices even more, particularly for business-sales customers where Provalue sales were considerably below budget and selling prices significantly higher than the prices charged to wholesalers? Was the quality and reliability of Provalue computers as good as the quality and reliability of competitors?

Some companies place more emphasis on the market-share variance than the market-size variance when evaluating their managers. That's because they believe the market-size variance is influenced by economy-wide factors and shifts in consumer preferences that are outside the managers' control, whereas the market-share variance measures how well managers performed relative to their peers.

Be cautious when computing the market-size variance and the market-share variance. Reliable information on market size and market share is not available for all industries. The automobile, computer, and television industries are cases in which market-size and market-share statistics are widely available. In other industries, such as management consulting and personal financial planning, information about market size and market share is far less reliable.

Exhibit 14 presents an overview of the sales-mix, sales-quantity, market-share; and market-size variances for the Provalue Division. These variances can also be calculated in a multiproduct company, in which each individual product has a different contribution margin per unit. The Problem for Self-Study presents such a setting.

Decision Point

What are the two components of the sales-volume variance and two components of the sales-quantity variance?

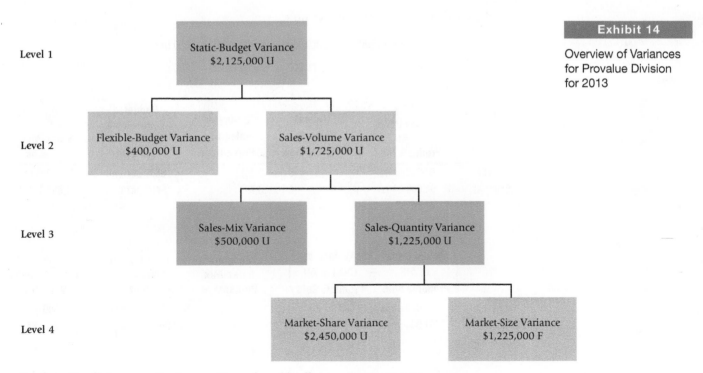

Exhibit 14

Overview of Variances for Provalue Division for 2013

Level 1 — Static-Budget Variance $2,125,000 U

Level 2 — Flexible-Budget Variance $400,000 U; Sales-Volume Variance $1,725,000 U

Level 3 — Sales-Mix Variance $500,000 U; Sales-Quantity Variance $1,225,000 U

Level 4 — Market-Share Variance $2,450,000 U; Market-Size Variance $1,225,000 F

F = favorable effect on operating income; U = unfavorable effect on operating income

Problem for Self Study

The Payne Company manufactures two types of vinyl flooring. Budgeted and actual operating data for 2013 are as follows:

	Static Budget			Actual Results		
	Commercial	Residential	Total	Commercial	Residential	Total
Unit sales in rolls	20,000	60,000	80,000	25,200	58,800	84,000
Contribution margin	$10,000,000	$24,000,000	$34,000,000	$11,970,000	$24,696,000	$36,666,000

In late 2012, a marketing research firm estimated industry volume for commercial and residential vinyl flooring for 2013 at 800,000 rolls. Actual industry volume for 2013 was 700,000 rolls.

Required

1. Compute the sales-mix variance and the sales-quantity variance by type of vinyl flooring and in total. (Compute all variances in terms of contribution margins.)
2. Compute the market-share variance and the market-size variance.
3. What insights do the variances calculated in requirements 1 and 2 provide about Payne Company's performance in 2013?

Solution

1. Actual sales-mix percentage:

$$Commercial = 25,200 \div 84,000 = 0.30, \text{ or } 30\%$$

$$Residential = 58,800 \div 84,000 = 0.70, \text{ or } 70\%$$

Budgeted sales-mix percentage:

$$Commercial = 20,000 \div 80,000 = 0.25, \text{ or } 25\%$$

$$Residential = 60,000 \div 80,000 = 0.75, \text{ or } 75\%$$

Budgeted contribution margin per unit:

$$Commercial = \$10,000,000 \div 20,000 \text{ units} = \$500 \text{ per unit}$$

$$Residential = \$24,000,000 \div 60,000 \text{ units} = \$400 \text{ per unit}$$

	Actual Units of All Products Sold	×	(Actual Sales-Mix Percentage − Budgeted Sales-Mix Percentage)	×	Budgeted Contribution Margin per Unit	=	Sales-Mix Variance
Commercial	84,000 units	×	(0.30 − 0.25)	×	$500 per unit	=	$2,100,000 F
Residential	84,000 units	×	(0.70 − 0.75)	×	$400 per unit	=	1,680,000 U
Total sales-mix variance							$ 420,000 F

	(Actual Units of All Products Sold − Budgeted Units of All Products Sold)	×	Budgeted Sales-Mix Percentage	×	Budgeted Contribution Margin per Unit	=	Sales-Quantity Variance
Commercial	(84,000 units − 80,000 units)	×	0.25	×	$500 per unit	=	$ 500,000 F
Residential	(84,000 units − 80,000 units)	×	0.75	×	$400 per unit	=	1,200,000 F
Total sales-quantity variance							$1,700,000 F

2. Actual market share = 84,000 ÷ 700,000 = 0.12, or 12%
   Budgeted market share = 80,000 ÷ 800,000 units = 0.10, or 10%

$$\begin{array}{l} \text{Budgeted contribution margin} \\ \text{per composite unit} \\ \text{of budgeted mix} \end{array} = \$34{,}000{,}000 \div 80{,}000 \text{ units} = \$425 \text{ per unit}$$

Budgeted contribution margin per composite unit of budgeted mix can also be calculated as follows:

Commercial: 500 per unit × 0.25	=	$125
Residential: 400 per unit × 0.75	=	300
Budgeted contribution margin per composite unit	=	$425

$$\begin{array}{l} \text{Market-share} \\ \text{variance} \end{array} = \begin{array}{c} \text{Actual} \\ \text{market size} \\ \text{in units} \end{array} \times \left(\begin{array}{cc} \text{Actual} & \text{Budgeted} \\ \text{market} - \text{market} \\ \text{share} & \text{share} \end{array} \right) \times \begin{array}{c} \text{Budgeted} \\ \text{contribution margin} \\ \text{per composite unit} \\ \text{for budgeted mix} \end{array}$$

$$= 700{,}000 \text{ units} \times (0.12 - 0.10) \times \$425 \text{ per unit}$$

$$= \$5{,}950{,}000 \text{ F}$$

$$\begin{array}{l} \text{Market-size} \\ \text{variance} \end{array} = \left(\begin{array}{c} \text{Actual} \\ \text{market size} - \text{market size} \\ \text{in units} \quad \text{in units} \end{array} \right) \times \begin{array}{c} \text{Budgeted} \\ \text{market} \\ \text{share} \end{array} \times \begin{array}{c} \text{Budgeted} \\ \text{contribution margin} \\ \text{per composite unit} \\ \text{for budgeted mix} \end{array}$$

$$= (700{,}000 \text{ units} - 800{,}000 \text{ units}) \times 0.10 \times \$425 \text{ per unit}$$

$$= \$4{,}250{,}000 \text{ U}$$

Note that the algebraic sum of the market-share variance and the market-size variance is equal to the sales-quantity variance: $5,950,000 F + $4,250,000 U = $1,700,000 F.

3. Both the total sales-mix variance and the total sales-quantity variance are favorable. The favorable sales-mix variance occurred because the actual mix was composed of more of the higher-margin commercial vinyl flooring. The favorable total sales-quantity variance occurred because the actual total quantity of rolls sold exceeded the budgeted amount.

   The company's large favorable market-share variance is due to a 12% actual market share compared with a 10% budgeted market share. The market-size variance is unfavorable because the actual market size was 100,000 rolls less than the budgeted market size. Payne's performance in 2013 appears to be very good. Although overall market size declined, the company sold more units than budgeted and gained market share.

▶ Decision Points

The following question-and-answer format summarizes the chapter's learning objectives. Each decision presents a key question related to a learning objective. The guidelines are the answer to that question.

Decision	Guidelines
1. How can a company's revenues and costs differ across customers?	Revenues differ because of differences in the quantity purchased and price discounts. Costs differ because different customers place different demands on a company's resources in terms of processing sales orders, making deliveries, and customer support.
2. How do customer-profitability profiles help managers?	Companies should be aware of and devote sufficient resources to maintaining and expanding relationships with customers who contribute significantly to profitability and design incentives to change behavior patterns of unprofitable customers. Customer-profitability profiles often highlight that a small percentage of customers contributes a large percentage of operating income.

Decision	Guidelines
3. Why do managers prepare cost-hierarchy-based operating incomes statements?	Cost-hierarchy-based operating income statements allocate only those costs that will be affected by actions at a particular hierarchical level. For example, costs such as sales-order costs and shipment costs are allocated to customers because customer actions can affect these costs, but costs of managing the wholesale channel are not allocated to customers because changes in customer behavior will have no effect on these costs.
4. What criteria should managers use to guide cost-allocation decisions?	Managers should use the cause-and-effect and the benefits-received criteria to guide most cost-allocation decisions. Other criteria are fairness or equity and ability to bear.
5. What are two key decisions managers must make when collecting costs in indirect-cost pools?	Two key decisions related to indirect-cost pools are the number of indirect-cost pools to form and the individual cost items to be included in each cost pool to make homogeneous cost pools. Generally, managers allocate both variable costs and costs that are fixed in the short-run.
6. What are the two components of the sales-volume variance and two components of the sales-quantity variance?	The two components of sales-volume variance are (a) the difference between actual sales mix and budgeted sales mix (the sales-mix variance) and (b) the difference between actual unit sales and budgeted unit sales (the sales-quantity variance). The two components of the the sales-quantity variance are (a) the difference between the actual market share and the budgeted market share (the market-share variance) and (b) the difference between the actual market size in units and the budgeted market size in units (the market-size variance).

Terms to Learn

The chapter contains definitions of the following important terms:

composite unit	market-share variance	sales-mix variance
customer-cost hierarchy	market-size variance	sales-quantity variance
customer-profitability analysis	price discount	whale curve
homogeneous cost pools		

Assignment Material

MyAccountingLab

Questions

1 "I'm going to focus on the customers of my business and leave cost-allocation issues to my accountant." Do you agree with this comment by a division president? Explain.

2 Why is customer-profitability analysis an important topic to managers?

3 How can a company track the extent of price discounting on a customer-by-customer basis?

4 "A customer-profitability profile highlights those customers a company should drop to improve profitability." Do you agree? Explain.

5 Give examples of three different levels of costs in a customer-cost hierarchy.

6 What information does the whale curve provide?

7 "A company should not allocate all of its corporate costs to its divisions." Do you agree? Explain.

8 What criteria might managers use to guide cost-allocation decisions? Which are the dominant criteria?

9 "Once a company allocates corporate costs to divisions, these costs should not be reallocated to the indirect-cost pools of the division." Do you agree? Explain.

10 "A company should not allocate costs that are fixed in the short run to customers." Do you agree? Explain briefly.

11 How many cost pools should a company use when allocating costs to divisions, channels, and customers?

12 Show how managers can gain insight into the causes of a sales-volume variance by subdividing the components of this variance.

13 How can the concept of a composite unit be used to explain why an unfavorable total sales-mix variance of contribution margin occurs?

14 Explain why a favorable sales-quantity variance occurs.

15 How can the sales-quantity variance be decomposed further?

Exercises

MyAccountingLab

16 Cost allocation in hospitals, alternative allocation criteria. Dave Meltzer vacationed at Lake Tahoe last winter. Unfortunately, he broke his ankle while skiing and spent two days at the Sierra University Hospital. Meltzer's insurance company received a $4,800 bill for his two-day stay. One item that caught Meltzer's attention was an $11.52 charge for a roll of cotton. Meltzer is a salesman for Johnson & Johnson and knows that the cost to the hospital of the roll of cotton is between $2.20 and $3.00. He asked for a breakdown of the $11.52 charge. The accounting office of the hospital sent him the following information:

a. Invoiced cost of cotton roll	$ 2.40
b. Cost of processing of paperwork for purchase	0.60
c. Supplies-room management fee	0.70
d. Operating-room and patient-room handling costs	1.60
e. Administrative hospital costs	1.10
f. University teaching-related costs	0.60
g. Malpractice insurance costs	1.20
h. Cost of treating uninsured patients	2.72
i. Profit component	0.60
Total	$11.52

Meltzer believes the overhead charge is outrageous. He comments, "There was nothing I could do about it. When they come in and dab your stitches, it's not as if you can say, 'Keep your cotton roll. I brought my own.'"

Required

1. Compute the overhead rate Sierra University Hospital charged on the cotton roll.
2. What criteria might Sierra use to justify allocation of the overhead items **b–i** in the preceding list? Examine each item separately and use the allocation criteria listed in Exhibit 8 in your answer.
3. What should Meltzer do about the $11.52 charge for the cotton roll?

17 Customer profitability, customer-cost hierarchy. Enviro-Tech has only two retail and two wholesale customers. Information relating to each customer for 2013 follows (in thousands):

	Wholesale Customers		**Retail Customers**	
	North America Wholesaler	**South America Wholesaler**	**Green Energy**	**Global Power**
Revenues at list prices	$375,000	$590,000	$175,000	$130,000
Discounts from list prices	25,800	47,200	8,400	590
Cost of goods sold	285,000	510,000	144,000	95,000
Delivery costs	4,550	6,710	2,230	2,145
Order processing costs	3,820	5,980	2,180	1,130
Cost of sales visit	6,300	2,620	2,620	1,575

Enviro-Tech's annual distribution-channel costs are $33 million for wholesale customers and $12 million for retail customers. The company's annual corporate-sustaining costs, such as salary for top management and general-administration costs, are $48 million. There is no cause-and-effect or benefits-received relationship between any cost-allocation base and corporate-sustaining costs. That is, Enviro-Tech could save corporate-sustaining costs only if the company completely shuts down.

Required

1. Calculate customer-level operating income using the format in Exhibit 3.
2. Prepare a customer-cost hierarchy report, using the format in Exhibit 6.
3. Enviro-Tech's management decides to allocate all corporate-sustaining costs to distribution channels: $38 million to the wholesale channel and $10 million to the retail channel. As a result,

distribution channel costs are now $71 million ($33 million + $38 million) for the wholesale channel and $22 million ($12 million + $10 million) for the retail channel. Calculate the distribution channel–level operating income. On the basis of these calculations, what actions, if any, should Enviro-Tech's managers take? Explain.

4. How might Enviro-Tech use the new cost information from its activity-based costing system to better manage its business?

18 Customer profitability, service company. Instant Service (IS) repairs printers and photocopiers for five multisite companies in a tristate area. IS's costs consist of the cost of technicians and equipment that are directly traceable to the customer site and a pool of office overhead. Until recently, IS estimated customer profitability by allocating the office overhead to each customer based on share of revenues. For 2013, IS reported the following results:

	Home	Insert	Page Layout	Formulas	Data	Review	View	

	A	B	C	D	E	F	G
1		Avery	Okie	Wizard	Grainger	Duran	Total
2	Revenues	$260,000	$200,000	$322,000	$122,000	$212,000	$1,116,000
3	Technician and equipment cost	182,000	175,000	225,000	107,000	178,000	867,000
4	Office overhead allocated	31,859	24,507	39,457	14,949	25,978	136,750
5	Operating income	$ 46,141	$ 493	$ 57,543	$ 51	$ 8,022	$ 112,250

Tina Sherman, IS's new controller, notes that office overhead is more than 10% of total costs, so she spends a couple of weeks analyzing the consumption of office overhead resources by customers. She collects the following information:

	Home	Insert	Page Layout	Formulas	Data	Review	

	I	J	K
1	Activity Area	Cost Driver Rate	
2	Service call handling	$75	per service call
3	Parts ordering	$80	per Web-based parts order
4	Billing and collection	$50	per bill (or reminder)
5	Customer database maintenance	$10	per service call

	Home	Insert	Page Layout	Formulas	Data	Review	View	

	A	B	C	D	E	F
8		Avery	Okie	Wizard	Grainger	Duran
9	Number of service calls	150	240	40	120	180
10	Number of Web-based parts orders	120	210	60	150	150
11	Number of bills (or reminders)	30	90	90	60	120

Required

1. Compute customer-level operating income using the new information that Sherman has gathered.
2. Prepare exhibits for IS similar to Exhibits 4 and 5. Comment on the results.
3. What options should IS consider, with regard to individual customers, in light of the new data and analysis of office overhead?

19 Customer profitability, distribution. Best Drugs is a distributor of pharmaceutical products. Its ABC system has five activities:

Activity Area	Cost Driver Rate in 2013
1. Order processing	$42 per order
2. Line-item ordering	$5 per line item
3. Store deliveries	$47 per store delivery
4. Carton deliveries	$4 per carton
5. Shelf-stocking	$13 per stocking-hour

Rick Flair, the controller of Best Drugs, wants to use this ABC system to examine individual customer profitability within each distribution market. He focuses first on the Ma and Pa single-store distribution market. Using only two customers helps highlight the insights available with the ABC approach. Data pertaining to these two customers in August 2013 are as follows:

	Ann Arbor Pharmacy	San Diego Pharmacy
Total orders	13	7
Average line items per order	11	19
Total store deliveries	5	7
Average cartons shipped per store delivery	21	18
Average hours of shelf-stocking per store delivery	0.5	0.75
Average revenue per delivery	$2,600	$1,900
Average cost of goods sold per delivery	$2,100	$1,700

Required

1. Use the ABC information to compute the operating income of each customer in August 2013. Comment on the results and what, if anything, Flair should do.
2. Flair ranks the individual customers in the Ma and Pa single-store distribution market on the basis of monthly operating income. The cumulative operating income of the top 20% of customers is $58,120. Best Drugs reports operating losses of $23,670 for the bottom 40% of its customers. Make four recommendations that you think Best Drugs should consider in light of this new customer-profitability information.

20 Cost allocation and decision making. Greenbold Manufacturing has four divisions named after its locations: Arizona, Colorado, Delaware, and Florida. Corporate headquarters is in Minnesota. Greenbold corporate headquarters incurs $8,400,000 per period, which is an indirect cost of the divisions. Corporate headquarters currently allocates this cost to the divisions based on the revenues of each division. The CEO has asked each division manager to suggest an allocation base for the indirect headquarters costs from among revenues, segment margin, direct costs, and number of employees. The following is relevant information about each division:

	Arizona	Colorado	Delaware	Florida
Revenues	$11,700,000	$12,750,000	$9,300,000	$8,250,000
Direct costs	7,950,000	6,150,000	6,450,000	6,900,000
Segment margin	$ 3,750,000	$ 6,600,000	$2,850,000	$1,350,000
Number of employees	3,000	6,000	2,250	750

Required

1. Allocate the indirect headquarters costs of Greenbold Manufacturing to each of the four divisions using revenues, direct costs, segment margin, and number of employees as the allocation bases. Calculate operating margins for each division after allocating headquarters costs.
2. Which allocation base do you think the manager of the Florida division would prefer? Explain.
3. What factors would you consider in deciding which allocation base Greenbold should use?
4. Suppose the Greenbold CEO decides to use direct costs as the allocation base. Should the Florida division be closed? Why or why not?

21 Cost allocation to divisions. Rembrandt Hotel & Casino is situated on beautiful Lake Tahoe in Nevada. The complex includes a 300-room hotel, a casino, and a restaurant. As Rembrandt's new controller, your manager asks you to recommend the basis the hotel should use for allocating fixed overhead costs to the three divisions in 2014. You are presented with the following income statement information for 2013:

	Hotel	Restaurant	Casino
Revenues	$16,425,000	$5,256,000	$12,340,000
Direct costs	9,819,260	3,749,172	4,248,768
Segment margin	$ 6,605,740	$1,506,828	$ 8,091,232

You are also given the following data on the three divisions:

	Hotel	Restaurant	Casino
Floor space (square feet)	80,000	16,000	64,000
Number of employees	200	50	250

You are told that you may choose to allocate indirect costs based on one of the following: direct costs, floor space, or the number of employees. Total fixed overhead costs for 2013 were $14,550,000.

1. Calculate division margins in percentage terms prior to allocating fixed overhead costs.
2. Allocate indirect costs to the three divisions using each of the three allocation bases suggested. For each allocation base, calculate division operating margins after allocations in dollars and as a percentage of revenues.
3. Discuss the results. How would you decide how to allocate indirect costs to the divisions? Why?
4. Would you recommend closing any of the three divisions (and possibly reallocating resources to other divisions) as a result of your analysis? If so, which division would you close and why?

22 **Cost allocation to divisions.** Holbrook Corporation has three divisions: pulp, paper, and fibers. Holbrook's new controller, Paul Weber, is reviewing the allocation of fixed corporate-overhead costs to the three divisions. He is presented with the following information for each division for 2013:

	Pulp	Paper	Fibers
Revenues	$ 9,800,00	$17,100,000	$25,500,000
Direct manufacturing costs	3,500,000	7,800,000	11,100,000
Division administrative costs	3,300,000	2,000,000	4,700,000
Division margin	$3,000,000	$ 7,300,000	9,700,000
Number of employees	300	150	550
Floor space (square feet)	53,200	35,340	101,460

Until now, Holbrook Corporation has allocated fixed corporate-overhead costs to the divisions on the basis of division margins. Weber asks for a list of costs that comprise fixed corporate overhead and suggests the following new allocation bases:

Fixed Corporate Overhead Costs		Suggested Allocation Bases
Human resource management	$ 2,300,000	Number of employees
Facility	3,200,000	Floor space (square feet)
Corporate administration	4,600,000	Division administrative costs
Total	$10,100,000	

1. Allocate 2013 fixed corporate-overhead costs to the three divisions using division margin as the allocation base. What is each division's operating margin percentage (division margin minus allocated fixed corporate-overhead costs as a percentage of revenues)?
2. Allocate 2013 fixed costs using the allocation bases suggested by Weber. What is each division's operating margin percentage under the new allocation scheme?
3. Compare and discuss the results of requirements 1 and 2. If division performance is linked to operating margin percentage, which division would be most receptive to the new allocation scheme? Which division would be the least receptive? Why?
4. Which allocation scheme should Holbrook Corporation use? Why? How might Weber overcome any objections that may arise from the divisions?

23 **Variance analysis, multiple products.** The Chicago Wolves play in the American Ice Hockey League. The Wolves play in the Downtown Arena, which is owned and managed by the City of Chicago. The arena has a capacity of 17,500 seats (6,500 lower-tier seats and 11,000 upper-tier seats). The arena charges the Wolves a per-ticket charge for use of its facility. All tickets are sold by the Reservation Network, which charges the Wolves a reservation fee per ticket. The Wolves' budgeted contribution margin for each type of ticket in 2013 is computed as follows:

	Lower-Tier Tickets	Upper-Tier Tickets
Selling price	$32	$14
Downtown Arena fee	9	4
Reservation Network fee	6	2
Contribution margin per ticket	$17	$ 8

The budgeted and actual average attendance figures per game in the 2013 season are as follows:

	Budgeted Seats Sold	Actual Seats Sold
Lower tier	5,500	3,600
Upper tier	7,000	6,400
Total	12,500	10,000

There was no difference between the budgeted and actual contribution margin for lower-tier or upper-tier seats.

The manager of the Wolves was unhappy that actual attendance was 20% below budgeted attendance per game, especially given the booming state of the local economy in the past six months.

Required

1. Compute the sales-volume variance for each type of ticket and in total for the Chicago Wolves in 2013. (Calculate all variances in terms of contribution margins.)
2. Compute the sales-quantity and sales-mix variances for each type of ticket and in total in 2013.
3. Present a summary of the variances in requirements 1 and 2. Comment on the results.

24   Variance analysis, working backward. The Hiro Corporation sells two brands of wine glasses: Plain and Chic. Hiro provides the following information for sales in the month of June 2014:

Static-budget total contribution margin	$15,525
Budgeted units to be sold of all glasses	2,300 units
Budgeted contribution margin per unit of Plain	$5 per unit
Budgeted contribution margin per unit of Chic	$12 per unit
Total sales-quantity variance	$2,700 U
Actual sales-mix percentage of Plain	60%

All variances are to be computed in contribution-margin terms.

Required

1. Calculate the sales-quantity variances for each product for June 2014.
2. Calculate the individual-product and total sales-mix variances for June 2014. Calculate the individual-product and total sales-volume variances for June 2014.
3. Briefly describe the conclusions you can draw from the variances.

25   Variance analysis, multiple products. Soda-King manufactures and sells two soft drinks: Kola and Limor. Budgeted and actual results for 2014 are as follows:

	Budget for 2014			Actual for 2014		
Product	Selling Price	Variable Cost per Carton	Cartons Sold	Selling Price	Variable Cost per Carton	Cartons Sold
Kola	$10.00	$5.50	500,000	$10.10	$5.75	504,300
Limor	$ 7.50	$4.00	750,000	$ 7.75	$3.70	725,700

Required

1. Compute the total sales-volume variance, the total sales-mix variance, and the total sales-quantity variance. (Calculate all variances in terms of contribution margin.) Show results for each product in your computations.
2. What inferences can you draw from the variances computed in requirement 1?

26   Market-share and market-size variances (continuation of 25). Soda-King prepared the budget for 2014 assuming a 12.5% market share based on total sales in the western region of the United States. The total soft drinks market was estimated to reach sales of 10 million cartons in the region. However, actual total sales volume in the western region was 12.3 million cartons.

Calculate the market-share and market-size variances for Soda-King in 2014. (Calculate all variances in terms of contribution margin.) Comment on the results.

Required

Problems

MyAccountingLab

27   Purposes of cost allocation. Sarah Reynolds recently started a job as an administrative assistant in the cost accounting department of Mize Manufacturing. New to the area of cost accounting, Sarah is puzzled by the fact that one of Mize's manufactured products, SR460, has a different cost depending on who asks for it. When the marketing department requested the cost of SR460 in order to determine pricing for the new catalog, Sarah was told to report one amount, but when a request came in the very next day from the financial reporting department for the cost of SR460, she was told to report a very different cost. Sarah runs a report using Mize's cost accounting system, which produces the following cost elements for one unit of SR460:

Direct materials	$57.00
Direct manufacturing labor	32.70
Variable manufacturing overhead	17.52
Allocated fixed manufacturing overhead	65.68
Research and development costs specific to SR460[a]	12.40
Marketing costs[a]	11.90
Sales commissions[a]	22.80
Allocated administrative costs of production department	10.76
Allocated administrative costs of corporate headquarters	37.20
Customer service costs[a]	6.10
Distribution costs[a]	17.60

[a]These costs are specific to SR460, but would not be eliminated if SR460 were purchased from an outside supplier. Allocated costs would be reallocated elsewhere in the company should the company cease production of SR460.

Required

1. Explain to Sarah why the cost given to the marketing and financial reporting departments would be different.
2. Calculate the cost of one unit of SR460 to determine the following:
   a. The selling price of SR460
   b. The cost of inventory for financial reporting
   c. Whether to continue manufacturing SR460 or to purchase it from an outside source (Assume that SR460 is used as a component in one of Mize's other products.)
   d. The ability of Mize's production manager to control costs

28 Customer profitability. Bracelet Delights is a new company that manufactures custom jewelry. Bracelet Delights currently has six customers referenced by customer number: 01, 02, 03, 04, 05, and 06. Besides the costs of making the jewelry, the company has the following activities:

Required

1. Customer orders. The salespeople, designers, and jewelry makers spend time with the customer. The cost driver rate is $42 per hour spent with a customer.
2. Customer fittings. Before the jewelry piece is completed, the customer may come in to make sure it looks right and fits properly. Cost driver rate is $30 per hour.
3. Rush orders. Some customers want their jewelry quickly. The cost driver rate is $90 per rush order.
4. Number of customer return visits. Customers may return jewelry up to 30 days after the pickup of the jewelry to have something refitted or repaired at no charge. The cost driver rate is $40 per return visit.

Information about the six customers follows. Some customers purchased multiple items. The cost of the jewelry is 60% of the selling price.

Customer number	01	02	03	04	05	06
Sales revenue	$850	$4,500	$280	$2,200	$5,500	$650
Cost of item(s)	$510	$2,700	$168	$1,320	$3,300	$390
Hours spent on customer order	3	10	1	8	17	5
Hours on fittings	1	6	0	0	4	0
Number of rush orders	0	2	1	2	3	0
Number of return visits	0	0	0	0	0	1

Required

1. Calculate the customer-level operating income for each customer. Rank the customers in order of most to least profitable and prepare a customer-profitability analysis, as in Exhibits 3 and 4.
2. Are any customers unprofitable? What is causing this? What should Bracelet Delights do about these customers?

29 **Customer profitability, distribution.** Green Paper Delivery has decided to analyze the profitability of five new customers. It buys recycled paper at $20 per case and sells to retail customers at a list price of $26 per case. Data pertaining to the five customers are:

	Customer				
	1	**2**	**3**	**4**	**5**
Cases sold	1,830	6,780	44,500	31,200	1,950
List selling price	$26	$26	$26	$26	$26
Actual selling price	$26	$25.20	$24.30	$25.80	$23.90
Number of purchase orders	10	18	35	16	35
Number of customer visits	3	5	12	4	12
Number of deliveries	12	28	65	25	35
Miles traveled per delivery	14	4	8	6	45
Number of expedited deliveries	0	0	0	0	3

Green Paper Delivery's five activities and their cost drivers are:

Activity	Cost Driver Rate
Order taking	$90 per purchase order
Customer visits	$75 per customer visit
Deliveries	$3 per delivery mile traveled
Product handling	$1.20 per case sold
Expedited deliveries	$250 per expedited delivery

1. Compute the customer-level operating income of each of the five retail customers now being examined (1, 2, 3, 4, and 5). Comment on the results.
2. What insights do managers gain by reporting both the list selling price and the actual selling price for each customer?
3. What factors should managers consider in deciding whether to drop one or more of the five customers?

30 **Customer profitability in a manufacturing firm.** Antelope Manufacturing makes a component called A1030. This component is manufactured only when ordered by a customer, so Antelope keeps no inventory of A1030. The list price is $115 per unit, but customers who place "large" orders receive a 12% discount on price. The customers are manufacturing firms. Currently, the salespeople decide whether an order is large enough to qualify for the discount. When the product is finished, it is packed in cases of 10. If the component needs to be exchanged or repaired, customers can come back within 10 days for free exchange or repair.

The full cost of manufacturing a unit of A1030 is $95. In addition, Antelope incurs customer-level costs. Customer-level cost-driver rates are:

Order taking	$360 per order
Product handling	$15 per case
Rush order processing	$560 per rush order
Exchange and repair costs	$50 per unit

Information about Antelope's five biggest customers follows:

	A	B	C	D	E
Number of units purchased	5,400	1,800	1,200	4,400	8,100
Discounts given	12%	12%	0	12%	12% on half the units
Number of orders	8	16	52	20	16
Number of cases	540	180	120	440	810
Number of rush orders	1	6	1	0	5
Number of units exchanged/repaired	14	72	16	40	180

All customers except E ordered units in the same order size. Customer E's order quantity varied, so E got a discount part of the time but not all the time.

1. Calculate the customer-level operating income for these five customers. Use the format in Exhibit 3. Prepare a customer-profitability analysis by ranking the customers from most to least profitable, as in Exhibit 4.
2. Discuss the results of your customer-profitability analysis. Does Antelope have unprofitable customers? Is there anything Antelope should do differently with its five customers?

31 Customer-cost hierarchy, customer profitability. Denise Nelson operates Interiors by Denise, an interior design consulting and window treatment fabrication business. Her business is made up of two different distribution channels, a consulting business in which Denise serves two architecture firms (Attractive Abodes and Better Buildings) and a commercial window treatment business in which Denise designs and constructs window treatments for three commercial clients (Cheery Curtains, Delightful Drapes, and Elegant Extras). Denise would like to evaluate the profitability of her two architecture firm clients and three commercial window treatment clients, as well as evaluate the profitability of each of the two channels and the business as a whole. Information about her most recent quarter follow:

Gross revenue from Attractive Abodes (AA)	$117,000
Gross revenue from Better Buildings (BB)	94,400
Gross revenue from Cheery Curtains (CC)	178,690
Gross revenue from Delightful Drapes (DD)	73,920
Gross revenue from Elegant Extras (EE)	36,600
Costs specific to AA	73,500
Costs specific to BB	58,600
Costs specific to CC	109,290
Costs specific to DD	57,860
Costs specific to EE	28,520
Overhead costs[a]	170,200

[a]Denise has determined that 25% of her overhead costs relate directly to her architectural business, 40% relate directly to her window treatment business, and the remainder are general in nature.

On the revenues indicated above, Denise gave a 10% discount to Attractive Abodes in order to lure it away from a competitor and gave a 5% discount to Elegant Extras for advance payment in cash.

1. Prepare a customer-cost hierarchy report for Interiors by Denise, using the format in Exhibit 6.
2. Prepare a customer-profitability analysis for the five customers, using the format in Exhibit 4.
3. Comment on the results of the preceding reports. What recommendations would you give Denise?

32 Allocation of corporate costs to divisions. Dusty Rhodes, controller of Richfield Oil Company, is preparing a presentation to senior executives about the performance of its four divisions. Summary data (dollar amounts in millions) related to the four divisions for the most recent year are as follows:

	Home	Insert	Page Layout	Formulas	Data	Review	View
	A	B	C	D	E	F	
1				DIVISIONS			
2		Oil & Gas Upstream	Oil & Gas Downstream	Chemical Products	Copper Mining	Total	
3	Revenues	$ 8,000	$16,000	$4,800	$3,200	$32,000	
4	Operating Costs	3,000	15,000	3,800	3,500	25,300	
5	Operating Income	$ 5,000	$ 1,000	$1,000	$ (300)	$ 6,700	
6							
7	Identifiable assets	$14,000	$ 6,000	$3,000	$2,000	$25,000	
8	Number of employees	9,000	12,000	6,000	3,000	30,000	

Under the existing accounting system, costs incurred at corporate headquarters are collected in a single cost pool ($3,228 million in the most recent year) and allocated to each division on the basis of its actual revenues. The top managers in each division share in a division-income bonus pool. Division income is defined as operating income less allocated corporate costs.

Rhodes has analyzed the components of corporate costs and proposes that corporate costs be collected in four cost pools. The components of corporate costs for the most recent year (dollar amounts in millions) and Rhodes' suggested cost pools and allocation bases are as follows:

	A	B	C	D	E	F
11	**Corporate Cost Category**	**Amount**	**Suggested Cost Pool**	**Suggested Allocation Base**		
12	Interest on debt	$2,000	Cost Pool 1	Identifiable assets		
13	Corporate salaries	150	Cost Pool 2			
14	Accounting and control	110	Cost Pool 2			
15	General marketing	200	Cost Pool 2	Division revenues		
16	Legal	140	Cost Pool 2			
17	Research and development	200	Cost Pool 2			
18	Public affairs	203	Cost Pool 3	Positive operating income*		
19	Personnel and payroll	225	Cost Pool 4	Number of employees		
20	Total	$3,228				
21						
22	*Because public affairs cost includes the cost of public relations staff, lobbyists, and donations to					
23	environmental charities, Rhodes proposes that this cost be allocated using operating income (if positive)					
24	of divisions, with only divisions with positive operating income included in the allocation base.					

Required

1. Discuss two reasons why Richfield Oil should allocate corporate costs to each division.
2. Calculate the operating income of each division when all corporate costs are allocated based on revenues of each division.
3. Calculate the operating income of each division when all corporate costs are allocated using the four cost pools.
4. How do you think the division managers will receive the new proposal? What are the strengths and weaknesses of Rhodes' proposal relative to the existing single-cost-pool method?

33 Cost allocation to divisions. Forber Bakery makes baked goods for grocery stores and has three divisions: bread, cake, and doughnuts. Each division is run and evaluated separately, but the main headquarters incurs costs that are indirect costs for the divisions. Costs incurred in the main headquarters are as follows:

Human resources (HR) costs	$1,900,000
Accounting department costs	1,400,000
Rent and depreciation	1,200,000
Other	600,000
Total costs	$5,100,000

The Forber upper management currently allocates this cost to the divisions equally. One of the division managers has done some research on activity-based costing and proposes the use of different allocation bases for the different indirect costs—number of employees for HR costs, total revenues for accounting department costs, square feet of space for rent and depreciation costs, and equal allocation among the divisions of "other" costs. Information about the three divisions follows:

	Bread	Cake	Doughnuts
Total revenues	$20,900,000	$4,500,000	$13,400,000
Direct costs	14,500,000	3,200,000	7,250,000
Segment margin	$ 6,400,000	$1,300,000	$ 6,150,000
Number of employees	400	100	300
Square feet of space	10,000	4,000	6,000

1. Allocate the indirect costs of Forber to each division equally. Calculate division operating income after allocation of headquarter costs.
2. Allocate headquarter costs to the individual divisions using the proposed allocation bases. Calculate the division operating income after allocation. Comment on the allocation bases used to allocate headquarter costs.
3. Which division manager do you think suggested this new allocation. Explain briefly. Which allocation do you think is "better?"

34 **Cost-hierarchy income statement and allocation of corporate, division, and channel costs to customers.** Rod Manufacturing Company produces metal rods for their customers. Its wholesale division is the focus of our analysis.

Management of the company wishes to analyze the profitability of the three key customers in the division and has gathered the following information.

	Customer A	Customer B	Customer C	Other Customers	Division
Revenue	1,054,826	1,544,680	2,210,162	480,332	5,290,000
Customer-level costs	675,378	951,669	1,517,895	266,058	3,411,000
Customer-level operating income	379,448	593,011	692,267	214,274	1,879,000
Customer-level operating income percentage	35.973%	38.391%	31.322%	44.610%	35.5%

The company allocates wholesale channel costs to customers based on one cost pool and division costs based on two cost pools as follows. Customer actions do not influence these costs.

	Total	Allocation basis
Wholesale-channel cost pool	$740,000	Customer-level operating income
Division costs		
Marketing costs	$560,000	Customer revenue
Administration costs	$240,000	Customer-level costs

1. Calculate customer profitability as a percentage of revenue after assigning customer-level costs, distribution-channel costs, and division costs. Comment on your results.
2. What are the advantages and disadvantages of Rod Manufacturing allocating wholesale-channel and division costs to customers?

35 **Cost-hierarchy income statement and allocation of corporate, division, and channel costs to customers.** Basic Boards makes keyboards that are sold to different customers in two main distribution channels. Recently, the company's profitability has decreased. Management would like to analyze the profitability of each channel based on the following information:

	Distribution Channel A	Distribution Channel B	Total
Revenue	$2,599,506	$2,690,494	$5,290,000
Customer-level costs	1,627,047	1,783,953	3,411,000
Customer-level operating income	$ 972,459	$ 906,541	$1,879,000
Customer-level operating income as a percentage of revenue	37.409%	33.694%	35.5%

The company allocates distribution costs to the two channels as follows:

	Total	Allocation basis
Distribution costs		
Marketing costs	$560,000	Channel revenue
Administration costs	$240,000	Customer-level costs

Based on a special study, the company allocates corporate costs to the two channels based on the corporate resources demanded by the channels as follows: Distribution Channel A, $440,000, and Distribution Channel B, $500,000. If the company were to close a distribution channel, none of the corporate costs would be saved.

Required

1. Calculate the operating income for each distribution channel as a percentage of revenue after assigning customer-level costs, distribution costs, and corporate costs.
2. Should Basic Boards close down any distribution channel? Explain briefly.
3. Would you allocate corporate costs to divisions? Why is allocating these costs helpful? What actions would it help you take?

36 Variance analysis, sales-mix and sales-quantity variances. Houston Infonautics, Inc., produces handheld Windows CE™-compatible organizers. Houston Infonautics markets three different handheld models: PalmPro is a souped-up version for the executive on the go, PalmCE is a consumer-oriented version, and PalmKid is a stripped-down version for the young adult market. You are Houston Infonautics' senior vice president of marketing. The CEO has discovered that the total contribution margin came in lower than budgeted, and it is your responsibility to explain to him why actual results are different from the budget. Budgeted and actual operating data for the company's third quarter of 2014 are as follows:

Budgeted Operating Data, Third Quarter 2014

	Selling Price	Variable Cost per Unit	Contribution Margin per Unit	Sales Volume in Units
PalmPro	$380	$185	$195	5,550
PalmCE	274	97	177	44,400
PalmKid	146	65	81	61,050
				111,000

Actual Operating Data, Third Quarter 2014

	Selling Price	Variable Cost per Unit	Contribution Margin per Unit	Sales Volume in Units
PalmPro	$351	$180	$ 171	4,600
PalmCE	284	92	192	49,450
PalmKid	115	73	42	60,950
				115,000

Required

1. Compute the actual and budgeted contribution margins in dollars for each product and in total for the third quarter of 2014.
2. Calculate the actual and budgeted sales mixes for the three products for the third quarter of 2014.
3. Calculate total sales-volume, sales-mix, and sales-quantity variances for the third quarter of 2014. (Calculate all variances in terms of contribution margins.)
4. Given that your CEO is known to have temper tantrums, you want to be well prepared for this meeting. In order to prepare, write a paragraph or two comparing actual results to budgeted amounts.

37 Market-share and market-size variances (continuation of 36). Houston Infonautics' senior vice president of marketing prepared his budget at the beginning of the third quarter assuming a 25% market share based on total sales. Foolinstead Research estimated that the total handheld-organizer market would reach sales of 444,000 units worldwide in the third quarter. However, actual sales in the third quarter were 500,000 units.

1. Calculate the market-share and market-size variances for Houston Infonautics in the third quarter of 2014 (calculate all variances in terms of contribution margins).
2. Explain what happened based on the market-share and market-size variances.
3. Calculate the actual market size, in units, that would have led to no market-size variance (again using budgeted contribution margin per unit). Use this market-size figure to calculate the actual market share that would have led to a zero market-share variance.

38   Variance analysis, multiple products. The Robin's Basket operates a chain of Italian gelato stores. Although the Robin's Basket charges customers the same price for all flavors, production costs vary, depending on the type of ingredients. Budgeted and actual operating data of its Washington, D.C., store for August 2014 are as follows:

Budget for August 2014

	Selling Price per Pint	Variable Cost per Pint	Contribution Margin per Pints	Sales Volume in Pints
Mint chocolate chip	$9.00	$4.80	$4.20	35,000
Vanilla	9.00	3.20	5.80	45,000
Rum raisin	9.00	5.00	4.00	20,000
				100,000

Actual for August 2014

	Selling Price per Pint	Variable Cost per Pound	Contribution Margin per Pound	Sales Volume in Pounds
Mint chocolate chip	$9.00	$4.60	$4.40	33,750
Vanilla	9.00	3.25	5.75	56,250
Rum raisin	9.00	5.15	3.85	22,500
				112,500

The Robin's Basket focuses on contribution margin in its variance analysis.

Required

1. Compute the total sales-volume variance for August 2014.
2. Compute the total sales-mix variance for August 2014.
3. Compute the total sales-quantity variance for August 2014.
4. Comment on your results in requirements 1, 2, and 3.

39   Customer profitability and ethics. KC Corporation manufactures an air-freshening device called GoodAir, which it sells to six merchandising firms. The list price of a GoodAir is $30, and the full manufacturing costs are $18. Salespeople receive a commission on sales, but the commission is based on number of orders taken, not on sales revenue generated or number of units sold. Salespeople receive a commission of $10 per order (in addition to regular salary).

KC Corporation makes products based on anticipated demand. KC carries an inventory of GoodAir, so rush orders do not result in any extra manufacturing costs over and above the $18 per unit. KC ships finished product to the customer at no additional charge for either regular or expedited delivery. KC incurs significantly higher costs for expedited deliveries than for regular deliveries. Customers occasionally return shipments to KC, and the company subtracts these returns from gross revenue. The customers are not charged a restocking fee for returns.

Budgeted (expected) customer-level cost driver rates are:

Order taking (excluding sales commission)	$15 per order
Product handling	$1 per unit
Delivery	$1.20 per mile driven
Expedited (rush) delivery	$175 per shipment
Restocking	$50 per returned shipment
Visits to customers	$125 per customer

Because salespeople are paid $10 per order, they often break up large orders into multiple smaller orders. This practice reduces the actual order-taking cost by $7 per smaller order (from $15 per order to $8 per order) because the smaller orders are all written at the same time. This lower cost rate is not included in budgeted rates because salespeople create smaller orders without telling management or the accounting department. All other actual costs are the same as budgeted costs.

Information about KC's clients follows:

	AC	DC	MC	JC	RC	BC
Total number of units purchased	225	520	295	110	390	1,050
Number of actual orders	5	20	4	6	9	18
Number of written orders	10	20*	9	12	24	36
Total number of miles driven to deliver all products	360	580	350	220	790	850
Total number of units returned	15	40	0	0	35	40
Number of returned shipments	3	2	0	0	1	5
Number of expedited deliveries	0	8	0	0	3	4

* Because DC places 20 separate orders, its order costs are $15 per order. All other orders are multiple smaller orders and so have actual order costs of $8 each.

Required

1. Classify each of the customer-level operating costs as a customer output unit–level, customer batch-level, or customer-sustaining cost.
2. Using the preceding information, calculate the expected customer-level operating income for the six customers of KC Corporation. Use the number of written orders at $15 each to calculate expected order costs.
3. Recalculate the customer-level operating income using the number of written orders but at their actual $8 cost per order instead of $15 (except for DC, whose actual cost is $15 per order). How will KC Corporation evaluate customer-level operating cost performance this period?
4. Recalculate the customer-level operating income if salespeople had not broken up actual orders into multiple smaller orders. Don't forget to also adjust sales commissions.
5. How is the behavior of the salespeople affecting the profit of KC Corporation? Is their behavior ethical? What could KC Corporation do to change the behavior of the salespeople?

Glossary

Composite unit. Hypothetical unit with weights based on the mix of individual units.

Customer-cost hierarchy. Hierarchy that categorizes costs related to customers into different cost pools on the basis of different types of cost drivers, or cost-allocation bases, or different degrees of difficulty in determining cause-and-effect or benefits-received relationships.

Customer-profitability analysis. The reporting and analysis of revenues earned from customers and the costs incurred to earn those revenues.

Homogeneous cost pool. Cost pool in which all the costs have the same or a similar cause-and-effect or benefits-received relationship with the cost-allocation base.

Market-share variance. The difference in budgeted contribution margin for actual market size in units caused solely by actual market share being different from budgeted market share.

Market-size variance. The difference in budgeted contribution margin at the budgeted market share caused solely by actual market size in units being different from budgeted market size in units.

Price discount. Reduction in selling price below list selling price to encourage increases in customer purchases.

Sales-mix variance. The difference between (1) budgeted contribution margin for the actual sales mix, and (2) budgeted contribution margin for the budgeted sales mix.

Sales-quantity variance. The difference between (1) budgeted contribution margin based on actual units sold of all products at the budgeted mix and (2) contribution margin in the static budget (which is based on the budgeted units of all products to be sold at the budgeted mix).

Whale curve. A typically backward-bending curve that represents the results from customer profitability analysis by first ranking customers from best to worst and then plotting their cumulative profitability level.

Photo Credits

Credits are listed in order of appearance.

Photo 1: Rachel Youdelman/Pearson Education, Inc.
Photo 2: Pearson Education, Inc.

Allocation of Support-Department Costs, Common Costs, and Revenues

From Chapter 15 of *Cost Accounting: A Managerial Emphasis*, Fifteenth Edition. Charles T. Horngren, Srikant M. Datar, Madhav V. Rajan. Copyright © 2015 by Pearson Education, Inc. All rights reserved.

Allocation of Support-Department Costs, Common Costs, and Revenues

Learning Objectives

1 Distinguish the single-rate method from the dual-rate method

2 Understand how the choice between allocation based on budgeted and actual rates and between budged and actual usage can affect the incentives of division managers

3 Allocate multiple support-department costs using the direct method, the step-down method, and the reciprocal method

4 Allocate common costs using the stand-alone method and the incremental method

5 Explain the importance of explicit agreement between contracting parties when the reimbursement amount is based on costs incurred

6 Understand how bundling of products causes revenue allocation issues and the methods managers use to allocate revenues

How a company allocates its overhead and internal support costs—costs related to marketing, advertising, and other internal services—among its various production departments or projects can have a big impact on how profitable those departments or projects are.

While the allocation may not affect the firm's profit as a whole, if the allocation isn't done properly, it can make some departments and projects (and their managers) look better or worse than they should profit-wise. As the following article shows, the method of allocating costs for a project affects not just the firm but also the consumer. Based on the method used, consumers may spend more, or less, for the same service.

Cost Allocation and the Future of "Smart Grid" Energy Infrastructure[1]

Across the globe, countries are adopting alternative methods of generating and distributing energy. The United States is moving toward a "Smart Grid"—that is, making transmission and power lines operate and communicate in a more effective and efficient manner using technology, computers, and software. This proposed system would also integrate with emerging clean-energy sources, such as solar farms and geothermal systems, to help create a more sustainable electricity supply that reduces carbon emissions.

Electric Power Resource Institute is an independent, nonprofit organization head-quartered in California. According to this Institute, the cost of developing the "Smart Grid" is between $338 billion and $476 billion over the next two decades. These costs include new infrastructure and technology improvements—mostly to power lines—as well as costs for upgrading the power system. Private utilities and the U.S. government will pay for the costs of "Smart Grid" development, but those costs will be recouped over time by charging energy consumers. A controversy emerged as the U.S. government debated two cost allocation methods for charging consumers. One method was

---

[1] *Sources*: Josie Garthwaite, "The $160B Question: Who Should Foot the Bill for Transmission Buildout?" *Salon.com* (March 12, 2009); Mark Jaffe, "Cost of Smart-Grid Projects Shocks Consumer Advocates," *The Denver Post* (February 14, 2010).

interconnection-wide cost allocation. Under this system, everybody in the region where a new technology was deployed would have to help pay for it. For example, if new power lines and "smart" energy meters were deployed in Denver, Colorado, everybody in Colorado would help pay for them. Supporters argued that this method would help lessen the costs of actual consumers for the significant investments in new technology.

A competing proposal would allocate costs only to utility ratepayers who actually benefited from the new "Smart Grid" system. In the previous example, only utility customers in Denver would be charged for the new power lines and energy meters. Supporters of this method believed that customers with new "Smart Grid" systems should not be subsidized by those not receiving any of the benefits.

Ultimately, the government decided to only charge the consumers who benefited. These customers would see their average monthly electricity bill increase by $9 to $12, but Smart Grid technology would provide greater grid reliability, integration of solar rooftop generation and plug-in vehicles, reductions in electricity demand, and stronger cybersecurity.

The same allocation dilemmas apply when costs of corporate support departments are allocated across multiple divisions or operating departments at manufacturing companies such as Nestle, service companies such as Comcast, merchandising companies such as Trader Joe's, and academic institutions such as Auburn University. This chapter focuses on several challenges that managers face when making decisions about cost and revenue allocations.

Allocating Support Department Costs Using the Single-Rate and Dual-Rate Methods

Learning Objective 1

Distinguish the single-rate method

...one rate for allocating costs in a cost pool

from the dual-rate method

...two rates for allocating costs in a cost pool—one for variable costs and one for fixed costs

Companies distinguish operating departments (and operating divisions) from support departments. An **operating department**, also called a **production department**, directly adds value to a product or service. Examples are manufacturing departments where products are made. A **support department**, also called a **service department**, provides the services that assist other internal departments (operating departments and other support departments) in the company. Examples of support departments are information systems, production control, materials management, and plant maintenance. Managers face two questions when allocating the costs of a support department to operating departments or divisions: (1) Should fixed costs of support departments, such as the salary of the department manager, be allocated to operating divisions? (2) If fixed costs are allocated, should variable and fixed costs of the support department be allocated in the same way? With regard to the first question, most companies believe that fixed costs of support departments should be allocated because the support department needs to incur these fixed costs to provide operating divisions with the services they require. Depending on the answer to the first question, there are two approaches to allocating support-department costs: the *single-rate cost-allocation method* and the *dual-rate cost-allocation method*.

Single-Rate and Dual-Rate Methods

The **single-rate method** does not distinguish between fixed and variable costs. It allocates costs in each cost pool (support department in this section) to cost objects (operating divisions in this section) using the same rate per unit of a single allocation base. By contrast, the **dual-rate method** partitions the cost of each support department into two pools, a variable-cost pool and a fixed-cost pool, and allocates each pool using a different cost-allocation base. When using either the single-rate method or the dual-rate method, managers can allocate support-department costs to operating divisions based on either a *budgeted* rate or the eventual *actual* cost rate. The latter approach is neither conceptually preferred nor widely used in practice (we explain why in the next section). Accordingly, we illustrate the single-rate and dual-rate methods next based on the use of *budgeted* rates.

We will use the Robinson Company example. Robinson manufactures and installs specialized machinery for the paper-making industry. In this chapter, we present a detailed accounting system to take into account the different operating and service departments within Robinson's manufacturing department.

Robinson has two operating departments—the Machining Department and the Assembly Department—where production occurs and three support departments—Plant Administration, Engineering and Production Control, and Materials Management—that provide essential services to the operating departments for manufacturing the specialized machinery.

- The Plant Adminstration Department is responsible for managing all activities in the plant. That is, its costs are incurred to support, and can be considered part of the supervision costs of, all the other departments.

- The Engineering and Production Control Department supports all the engineering activity in the other departments. In other words, its costs are incurred to support the engineering costs of the other departments and so can be considered part of the engineering costs of those departments.

- The Materials Management Department is responsible for managing and moving materials and components required for different jobs. Each job at Robinson is different and requires small quantities of unique components to be machined and assembled. Materials Management Department costs vary with the number of material-handling labor-hours incurred to support each department. The Materials Management Department invests a substantial number of material-handling labor-hours in support of the Assembly Department.

The specialized machinery that Robinson manufactures does not go through the service departments and so the costs of the service departments must be allocated to the operating departments to determine the full cost of making the specialized machinery. Once costs are accumulated in the operating departments, they can be absorbed into the different specialized machines that Robinson manufactures. Different jobs need different amounts of machining and assembly resources. Each operating department has a different overhead cost driver to absorb overhead costs to machines produced: machine-hours in the Machining Department and assembly labor-hours in the Assembly Department.

We first focus on the allocation of the Materials Management Department costs to the Machining Department and the Assembly Department. The following data relate to the 2013 budget:

Practical capacity	4,000 hours
Fixed costs of the materials management department in the 3,000 labor-hour to 4,000 labor-hour relevant range	$144,000
Budgeted usage (quantity) in labor-hours:	
Machining department	800 hours
Assembly department	2,800 hours
Total	3,600 hours

Budgeted variable cost per material-handling labor-hour in the 3,000 labor-hour to 4,000 labor-hour relevant range	$30 per hour used
Actual usage in 2013 in labor-hours:	
Machining department	1,200 hours
Assembly department	2,400 hours
Total	3,600 hours

The budgeted rates for materials management department costs can be computed based on either the demand for materials-handling services or the supply of materials-handling services. We consider the allocation of materials management department costs based first on the demand for (or usage of) materials-handling services and then on the supply of materials-handling services.

Allocation Based on the Demand for (or Usage of) Materials-handling Services

We present the single-rate method followed by the dual-rate method.

Single-Rate Method

In this method, a combined budgeted rate is used for fixed and variable costs. The rate is calculated as follows:

Budgeted usage	3,600 hours
Budgeted total cost pool: $144,000 + (3,600 hours × $30/hour)	$252,000
Budgeted total rate per hour: $252,000 ÷ 3,600 hours	$70 per hour used
Allocation rate for machining department	$70 per hour used
Allocation rate for assembly department	$70 per hour used

Note that the budgeted rate of $70 per hour is substantially higher than the $30 budgeted *variable* cost per hour. That's because the $70 rate includes an allocated amount of $40 per hour (budgeted fixed costs, $144,000 ÷ budgeted usage, $3,600 hours) for the *fixed* costs of operating the facility.

Under the single-rate method, departments are charged the budgeted rate for each hour of *actual* use of the central facility. Applying this to our example, Robinson allocates materials management department costs based on the $70 per hour budgeted rate and the actual hours the operating departments use. The support costs allocated to the two departments under this method are as follows:

Machining department: $70 per hour × 1,200 hours	$ 84,000
Assembly department: $70 per hour × 2,400 hours	$168,000

Dual-Rate Method

When a company uses the dual-rate method, managers must choose allocation bases for both the variable and fixed-cost pools of the materials management department. As in the single-rate method, variable costs are assigned based on the *budgeted* variable cost per hour of $30 for *actual* hours each department uses. However, fixed costs are assigned based on *budgeted* fixed costs per hour and the *budgeted* number of hours for each department. Given the budgeted usage of 800 hours for the machining department and 2,800 hours for the assembly department, the budgeted fixed-cost rate is $40 per hour ($144,000 ÷ 3,600 hours), as before. Because this rate is charged on the basis of the *budgeted* usage, however, the fixed costs are effectively allocated in advance as a lump sum based on the relative proportions of the materials management facilities the operating departments expect to use.

The costs allocated to the machining department in 2013 under the dual-rate method would be as follows:

Fixed costs: $40 per hour × 800 (budgeted) hours	$32,000
Variable costs: $30 per hour × 1,200 (actual) hours	36,000
Total costs	$68,000

The costs allocated to the assembly department in 2013 would be as follows:

Fixed costs: $40 per hour × 2,800 (budgeted) hours	$112,000
Variable costs: $30 per hour × 2,400 (actual) hours	72,000
Total costs	$184,000

Note that each operating department is charged the same amount for variable costs under the single-rate and dual-rate methods ($30 per hour multiplied by the actual hours of use). However, the overall assignment of costs differs under the two methods because the single-rate method allocates fixed costs of the support department based on actual usage of materials-handling resources by the operating departments, whereas the dual-rate method allocates fixed costs based on budgeted usage.

We next consider the alternative approach of allocating materials management department costs based on the capacity of materials-handling services supplied.

Allocation Based on the Supply of Capacity

We illustrate this approach using the 4,000 hours of practical capacity of the materials management department. The budgeted rate is then determined as follows:

Budgeted fixed-cost rate per hour, $144,000 ÷ 4,000 hours	$36 per hour
Budgeted variable-cost rate per hour	30 per hour
Budgeted total-cost rate per hour	$66 per hour

Using the same procedures for the single-rate and dual-rate methods as in the previous section, the Materials Management Department costs allocated to the operating departments are as follows:

Single-Rate Method

Machining department: $66 per hour × 1,200 (actual) hours	$ 79,200
Assembly department: $66 per hour × 2,400 (actual) hours	158,400
Fixed costs of unused materials-handling capacity:	
$36 per hour × 400 hours[a]	14,400

[a]400 hours = Practical capacity of 4,000 − (1,200 hours used by machining department + 2,400 hours used by assembly department).

Dual-Rate Method

Machining department

Fixed costs: $36 per hour × 800 (budgeted) hours	$28,800
Variable costs: $30 per hour × 1,200 (actual) hours	36,000
Total costs	$64,800

Assembly department

Fixed costs: $36 per hour × 2,800 (budgeted) hours	$100,800
Variable costs: $30 per hour × 2,400 (actual) hours	72,000
Total costs	$172,800
Fixed costs of unused materials-handling capacity:	
$36 per hour × 400 hours[b]	$14,400

[b]400 hours = Practical capacity of 4,000 hours − (800 hours budgeted to be used by machining department + 2,800 hours budgeted to be used by assembly department).

When a company uses practical capacity to allocate costs, the single-rate method allocates only the actual fixed-cost resources used by the machining and assembly departments, while the dual-rate method allocates the budgeted fixed-cost resources to be used by the operating departments. Unused materials management department resources are highlighted but usually not allocated to the departments.[2]

The advantage of using practical capacity to allocate costs is that it focuses management's attention on managing unused capacity. Using practical capacity also avoids burdening the user departments with the cost of unused capacity of the materials management department. In contrast, when costs are allocated on the basis of the demand for materials-handling services, all $144,000 of budgeted fixed costs, including the cost of unused capacity, are allocated to user departments. If costs are used as a basis for pricing, then charging user departments for unused capacity could result in the downward demand spiral.

Recently, the dual-rate method has been receiving more attention. Resource Consumption Accounting (RCA), an emerging management accounting system, employs an allocation procedure similar to a dual-rate system. For each cost/resource pool, cost assignment rates for fixed costs are based on practical capacity supplied, while rates for proportional costs (i.e., costs that vary with regard to the output of the resource pool) are based on planned quantities.[3]

There are advantages and disadvantages of using the single-rate and dual-rate methods. We discuss these next.

Advantages and Disadvantages of Single-Rate Method

Advantages (1) **The single-rate method is less costly to implement** because it avoids the often expensive analysis necessary to classify the individual cost items of a department into fixed and variable categories. (2) **It offers user departments some operational control over the charges they bear** by conditioning the final allocations on the actual usage of support services, rather than basing them solely on uncertain forecasts of expected demand.

Disadvantage The single-rate method may lead operating department managers to make sub-optimal decisions that are in their own best interest but that may be inefficient from the standpoint of the organization as a whole. This occurs because under the single-rate method, the allocated fixed costs of the support department appear as variable costs to the operating departments. Consider the setting where managers make allocations based on the demand for materials-handling services. In this case, each user department is charged $70 per hour under the single-rate method (recall that $40 of this charge relates to the allocated fixed costs of the materials management department). Suppose an external provider offers the machining department material-handling labor services at a rate of $55 per hour, at a time when the materials management department has unused capacity. The machining department's managers would be tempted to use this vendor because it would lower the department's costs ($55 per hour instead of the $70 per hour internal charge for materials-handling services). In the short run, however, the fixed costs of the materials management department remain unchanged in the relevant range (between 3,000 hours of usage and the practical capacity of 4,000 hours). Robinson will therefore incur an additional cost of $25 per hour if the managers were to take this offer—the difference between the $55 external purchase price and the true internal variable cost of $30 of using the materials management department.

---

[2] In our example, the costs of unused capacity under the single-rate and the dual-rate methods coincide (each equals $14,400). This occurs because the total actual usage of the facility matches the total expected usage of 3,600 hours. The budgeted cost of unused capacity (in the dual-rate method) can be either greater or lower than the actual cost (in the single-rate method), depending on whether the total actual usage is lower or higher than the budgeted usage.

[3] Other important features of Resource Consumption Accounting (RCA) include (1) the selective use of activity-based costing, (2) the nonassignment of fixed costs when causal relationships cannot be established, and (3) the depreciation of assets based on their replacement cost. RCA has its roots in the nearly 50-year-old German cost accounting system called Grenzplankostenrechnung (GPK), which is used by organizations such as Mercedes-Benz, Porsche, and Stihl. For further details, as well as illustrations of the use of RCA and GPK in organizations, see Sally Webber and Douglas B. Clinton, "Resource Consumption Accounting Applied: The Clopay Case," *Management Accounting Quarterly* (Fall 2004); and Brian Mackie, "Merging GPK and ABC on the Road to RCA," *Strategic Finance* (November 2006).

The divergence created under the single-rate method between Robinson's interests and those of its department managers is lessened when allocation is based on practical capacity. The variable cost per hour the operating department managers perceive is now $66 (rather than the $70 rate when allocation is based on budgeted usage). However, any external offer above $30 (Robinson's true variable cost) and below $66 (the single-rate charge per hour) will still result in the user manager preferring to outsource the service at the expense of Robinson's overall profits.

Advantages and Disadvantages of Dual-Rate Method

Advantages (1) **The dual-rate method guides department managers to make decisions that benefit both the organization as a whole and each department** because it signals to department managers how variable costs and fixed costs behave differently. For example, using an external provider of materials-handling services that charges more than $30 per hour would result in Robinson's being worse off than if its own materials management department were used because the latter has a variable cost of $30 per hour. Under the dual-rate method, neither department manager has an incentive to pay more than $30 per hour for an external provider because the internal charge for materials-handling services is precisely that amount. By charging the fixed costs of resources budgeted to be used by the departments as a lump sum, the dual-rate method succeeds in removing fixed costs from the department managers' consideration when making marginal decisions to outsource services. The dual-rate method therefore avoids the potential conflict of interest that can arise under the single-rate method. (2) **Allocating fixed costs based on budgeted usage helps user departments with both short-run and long-run planning because user departments know the costs allocated to them in advance.** Companies commit to infrastructure costs (such as the fixed costs of a support department) on the basis of a long-run planning horizon; budgeted usage measures the long-run demands of the user departments for support-department services.

Disadvantages (1) **The dual-rate method requires managers to distinguish variable costs from fixed costs, which is often a challenging task.** (2) **The dual-rate method does not indicate to operating managers the cost of fixed support department resources used** because fixed costs are allocated to operating departments based on budgeted rather than actual usage. Thus, the Machining Department manager is allocated fixed costs of the Materials Management Department based on the budgeted usage of 800 labor-hours even though the Machining Department actually uses 1,200 labor-hours. (3) **Allocating fixed costs on the basis of budgeted long-run usage may tempt some managers to underestimate their planned usage.** Underestimating will result in their departments bearing a lower percentage of fixed costs (assuming all other managers do not similarly underestimate their usage). If all user department managers underestimate usage, it might also lead to Robinson underestimating its total support department needs. To discourage such underestimates, some companies offer bonuses or other rewards—the "carrot" approach—to managers who make accurate forecasts of long-run usage. Other companies impose cost penalties—the "stick" approach—for underestimating long-run usage. For instance, a higher cost rate is charged after a department exceeds its budgeted usage.

Budgeted Versus Actual Costs and the Choice of Allocaton Base

The allocation methods previously outlined follow specific procedures in terms of the support department costs that are considered as well as the manner in which costs are assigned to the operating departments. In this section, we examine these choices in greater detail and consider the impact of alternative approaches. We show that the decision whether to use actual or budgeted costs, as well as the choice between actual and budgeted usage as allocation base, has a significant impact on the cost allocated to each operating department and the incentives of the operating department managers.

Budgeted Versus Actual Rates

In both the single-rate and dual-rate methods, Robinson uses budgeted rates to assign support department costs (fixed as well as variable costs). An alternative approach would involve using the actual rates based on the support costs realized during the period. This method is much less common because of the level of uncertainty it imposes on user departments. When allocations are made using budgeted rates, managers of departments to which costs are allocated know with certainty the rates to be used in that budget period. Users can then determine the amount of the service to request and—if company policy allows—whether to use the internal source or an external vendor. In contrast, when actual rates are used for cost allocation, user departments are not informed of their charges until the end of the budget period.

Budgeted rates also help motivate the manager of the support (or supplier) department (for example, the materials management department) to improve efficiency. During the budget period, the support department, not the user departments, bears the risk of any unfavorable cost variances. That's because user departments do not pay for any costs or inefficiencies of the supplier department that cause actual rates to exceed budgeted rates.

The manager of the supplier department would likely view the budgeted rates negatively if unfavorable cost variances occur due to price increases outside of his or her control. Some organizations try to identify these uncontrollable factors and relieve the support department manager of responsibility for these variances. In other organizations, the supplier department and the user department agree to share the risk (through an explicit formula) of a large, uncontrollable increase in the prices of inputs used by the supplier department. This procedure avoids imposing the risk completely on either the supplier department (as when budgeted rates are used) or the user department (as in the case of actual rates).

For the rest of this chapter, we will continue to consider only allocation methods that are based on budgeted rates.

Budgeted Versus Actual Usage

In both the single-rate and dual-rate methods, the variable costs are assigned on the basis of budgeted rates and actual usage. Because the variable costs are directly and causally linked to usage, charging them as a function of the actual usage is appropriate. Moreover, allocating variable costs on the basis of budgeted usage would provide the user departments with no incentive to control their consumption of support services.

What about the fixed costs? Consider the budget of $144,000 fixed costs at the Materials Management Department of Robinson Company. Recall that budgeted usage is 800 hours for the Machining Department and 2,800 hours for the Assembly Department. Assume that actual usage by the Machining Department is always equal to budgeted usage. We consider three cases:

Case 1: When actual usage by the Assembly Department equals budgeted usage.

Case 2: When actual usage by the Assembly Department is greater than budgeted usage.

Case 3: When actual usage by the Assembly Department is lower than budgeted usage.

Fixed-Cost Allocation Based on Budgeted Rates and Budgeted Usage

This is the dual-rate procedure outlined in the previous section. When budgeted usage is the allocation base, regardless of the actual usage of facilities (i.e., whether Case 1, 2, or 3 occurs), user departments receive a preset lump-sum fixed-cost charge. If rates are based on expected demand of $40 per hour ($144,000 ÷ 3,600 hours), the Machining Department is assigned $32,000 ($40 per hour × 800 hours) and the Assembly Department, $112,000 ($40 per hour × 2,800 hours). If rates are set using practical capacity of $36 per hour ($144,000 ÷ 4,000 hours), the Machining Department is charged $28,800 ($36 per hour × 800 hours), the Assembly Department is allocated $100,800 ($36 per hour × 2,800 hours), and the remaining $14,400 ($36 per hour × 400 hours) is the unallocated cost of excess capacity.

Fixed-Cost Allocation Based on Budgeted Rates and Actual Usage

Column 2 of Exhibit 1 shows the allocations when the budgeted rate is based on expected demand ($40 per hour), while column 3 shows the allocations when practical capacity is used to derive the rate ($36 per hour). Note that each operating department's fixed-cost allocation varies based on its actual usage of support facilities. However, variations in actual usage in one department do not affect the costs allocated to the other department. The Machining Department is allocated either $32,000 or $28,800, depending on the budgeted rate chosen, independent of the Assembly Department's actual usage.

Note, however, that this allocation procedure for fixed costs is exactly the same as that under the single-rate method. The procedure therefore shares the advantages of the single-rate method, such as advanced knowledge of budgeted rates, as well as control over the costs charged to them based on actual usage.[4] The procedure also shares the disadvantages of the single-rate method discussed in the previous section, such as charging excessively high costs, including the cost of unused capacity, when rates are based on expected usage. In Case 1, for example, actual usage equals budgeted usage of 3,600 materials-handling labor-hours and is less than the practical capacity of 4,000 labor-hours. However, all $144,000 of fixed costs of the Materials Management Department are allocated to the operating departments even though the Materials Handling Department has idle capacity. On the other hand, when actual usage (4,000 labor-hours) is more than the budgeted amount (3,600 labor-hours) as in Case 2, a total of $160,000 is allocated, which is more than the fixed costs of $144,000. This results in overallocation of fixed costs requiring end-of period adjustments.

Allocating fixed costs based on practical capacity avoids these problems by explicitly recognizing the costs of unused capacity. However, as we have discussed earlier, allocating fixed-cost rates based on actual usage induces conflicts of interest between the user departments and the firm when evaluating outsourcing possibilities.

Allocating Budgeted Fixed Costs Based on Actual Usage

Finally, consider the impact of having actual usage as the allocation base when the firm assigns total budgeted fixed costs to operating departments (rather than specifying budgeted fixed-cost rates, as we have thus far). If the budgeted fixed costs of $144,000 are

| Exhibit 1 | Effect of Variations in Actual Usage on Fixed-Cost Allocation to Operating Divisions |

	(1)		(2)		(3)		(4)	
	Actual Usage		**Budgeted Rate Based on Expected Demand**[a]		**Budgeted Rate Based on Practical Capacity**[b]		**Allocation of Budgeted Total Fixed Cost**	
Case	Mach. Dept.	Assmb. Dept.	Mach. Dept.	Assmb. Dept.	Mach. Dept.	Assmb. Dept.	Mach. Dept.	Assmb. Dept.
1	800 hours	2,800 hours	$ 32,000	$ 112,000	$ 28,800	$ 100,800	$ 32,000[c]	$ 112,000[d]
2	800 hours	3,200 hours	$ 32,000	$ 128,000	$ 28,800	$ 115,200	$ 28,800[e]	$ 115,200[f]
3	800 hours	2,400 hours	$ 32,000	$ 96,000	$ 28,800	$ 86,400	$ 36,000[g]	$ 108,000[h]

$$^a\ \frac{\$144,000}{(800+2,800)\ \text{hours}} = \$40\ \text{per hour} \qquad ^b\ \frac{\$144,000}{4,000\ \text{hours}} = \$36\ \text{per hour} \qquad ^c\ \frac{800}{(800+2,800)} \times \$144,000 \qquad ^d\ \frac{2,800}{(800+2,800)} \times \$144,000$$

$$^e\ \frac{800}{(800+3,200)} \times \$144,000 \qquad ^f\ \frac{3,200}{(800+3,200)} \times \$144,000 \qquad ^g\ \frac{800}{(800+2,400)} \times \$144,000 \qquad ^h\ \frac{2,400}{(800+2,400)} \times \$144,000$$

---

[4] The total amount of fixed costs allocated to divisions will in general not equal the actual realized costs.

allocated using budgeted usage, we are back in the familiar dual-rate setting. On the other hand, if the actual usage of the facility is the basis for allocation, the charges would equal the amounts in Exhibit 1, column 4:

- In Case 1, the fixed-cost allocation equals the amount based on budgeted usage (which is also the same as the charge under the dual-rate method based on demand for material-handling services).
- In Case 2, the fixed-cost allocation is $3,200 less to the Machining Department than the amount based on budgeted usage ($28,800 versus $32,000).
- In Case 3, the fixed-cost allocation is $4,000 more to the Machining Department than the amount based on budgeted usage ($36,000 versus $32,000).

Why does the Machining Department receive $4,000 more in costs in Case 3, even though its actual usage equals its budgeted usage? Because the total fixed costs of $144,000 are now spread over 400 fewer hours of actual total usage. In other words, the lower usage by the Assembly Department leads to an increase in the fixed costs allocated to the Machining Department. When budgeted fixed costs are allocated based on actual usage, user departments will not know their fixed-cost allocations until the end of the budget period. This method therefore shares the same flaw as those methods that rely on the use of actual cost rates rather than budgeted cost rates.

To summarize, there are excellent economic and motivational reasons to justify the precise forms of the single-rate and dual-rate methods considered in the previous section and, in particular, to recommend the dual-rate allocation procedure.

> **Decision Point**
>
> What factors should managers consider when deciding between allocation based on budgeted and actual rates, and budgeted and actual usage?

Allocating Costs of Multiple Support Departments

> **Learning Objective 3**
>
> Allocate multiple support-department costs using the direct method,
>
> …allocates support-department costs directly to operating departments
>
> the step-down method,
>
> …partially allocates support-department costs to other support departments
>
> and the reciprocal method
>
> …fully allocates support-department costs to other support departments

In the previous section, we examined general issues that arise when allocating costs from one support department to operating departments. In this section, we examine the special cost-allocation problems that arise when two or more of the support departments whose costs are being allocated provide reciprocal support to each other as well as to operating departments. An example of reciprocal support is Robinson's Materials Management Department providing material-handling labor services to all other departments, including the Engineering and Production Control Department, while also utilizing the services of the Engineering and Production Control Department for managing material-handling equipment and scheduling materials movement to the production floor. More accurate support-department cost allocations result in more accurate product, service, and customer costs.

Exhibit 2, column 6, provides details of Robinson's total budgeted manufacturing overhead costs of $1,120,000 for 2013, for example, supervision salaries, $200,000; depreciation and maintenance, $193,000; indirect labor, $195,000; and rent, utilities and insurance, $160,000. Robinson allocates the $1,120,000 of total budgeted manufacturing overhead costs to the Machining and Assembly Departments in several steps.

Step A: Trace or Allocate Each Cost to Various Support and Operating Departments. Exhibit 2, columns (1) through (5), show calculations for this step. For example, supervision salaries are traced to the departments in which the supervisors work. Supervision costs are an indirect cost of individual jobs because supervisory costs cannot be traced to individual jobs. They are a direct cost of the different departments, however, because they can be identified with each department in an economically feasible way. Rent, utilities, and insurance costs cannot be traced to each department because these costs are incurred for all of Robinson's manufacturing facility. These costs are therefore allocated to different departments on the basis of the square feet area—the cost driver for rent, utilities, and insurance costs.

Step B: Allocate Plant Administration Costs to Other Support Departments and Operating Departments. Plant adminstration supports supervisors in each department, so plant administration costs are allocated to departments on the basis of supervision costs.

| Exhibit 2 | Details of Budgeted Manufacturing Overhead at Robinson Company for 2013 and Allocation of Plant Administration Department Costs |

	A	B	C	D	E	F	G
1		**Support Departments**			**Operating Departments**		
2	**Step A**	**Plant Administration Department (1)**	**Engineering and Production Control Department (2)**	**Materials Management Department (3)**	**Machining Department (4)**	**Assembly Department (5)**	**Total (6)**
3	Plant manager's salary	$ 92,000					$ 92,000
4	Supervision salaries (traced to each department)		$ 48,000	$ 40,000	$ 52,000	$ 60,000	200,000
5	Engineering salaries (traced to each department)		110,000	36,000	60,000	24,000	230,000
6	Depreciation and maintenance (traced to each department)		39,000	55,000	79,000	20,000	193,000
7	Indirect materials (traced to each department)		20,000	12,000	11,000	7,000	50,000
8	Indirect labor (traced to each department)		43,000	77,000	37,000	38,000	195,000
9	Rent, utilities, and insurance (allocated to each department based on square feet area; $8[1] × 1,000; 2,000; 3,000; 8,000; 6,000 sq. ft.)	8,000	16,000	24,000	64,000	48,000	160,000
10	Total	$ 100,000	$276,000	$244,000	$303,000	$197,000	$1,120,000
11							
12	**Step B**						
13	Allocation of plant administration costs 0.50[2] × $48,000; $40,000; $52,000; $60,000	(100,000)	24,000	20,000	26,000	30,000	
14		$ 0	$300,000	$264,000	$329,000	$227,000	
15	[1]$160,000 ÷ 20,000 total square feet area = $8 per square foot						
16	Plant administration cost-allocation rate $= \dfrac{\text{Total plant administration costs}}{\text{Total supervision salaries}} = \dfrac{\$100,000}{\$200,000} = 0.50$						

Some companies prefer not to allocate plant adminstration costs to jobs, products, or customers because these costs are fixed and independent of the level of activity in the plant. However, most companies, like Robinson, allocate plant adminstration costs to departments and jobs, products, or customers because allocating all costs allows companies to calculate the full manufacturing costs of products. Robinson calculates the plant administration cost-allocation rate as follows:

$$\frac{\text{Plant administration}}{\text{cost-allocation rate}} = \frac{\text{Total plant administration costs}}{\text{Total supervision salaries}} = \frac{\$100,000}{\$200,000} = 0.50$$

The bottom part of Exhibit 2 shows how Robinson uses the 0.50 cost-allocation rate and supervision salaries to allocate plant adminstration costs to the other support and operating departments.

Step C: Allocate Engineering and Production Control and Materials Management Costs to the Machining and Assembly Operating Departments. Note that the two support departments whose costs are being allocated—Engineering and Production Control and Materials Management—provide reciprocal support to each other as well as support to the operating departments. That is, the Engineering and Production Control Department provides services to the Materials Management Department (for example, engineering services for material-handling equipment and scheduling material movement to the production floor), while the Materials Management Department provides services to the Engineering and Production Control Department (for example, delivering materials).

Consider again the Materials Management Department. As we saw in the previous section, this department is budgeted to provide 800 hours of materials-handling labor services to the Machining Department and 2,800 hours of materials-handling labor services to the Assembly Department. In this section, we further assume that the Materials Handling Department provides an additional 400 hours of materials-handling labor services to the Engineering and Production Control Department. Recall from the previous section that the Materials Management Department has budgeted fixed costs (for example, plant administration, depreciation, and rent) of $144,000 and budgeted variable costs (for example, indirect materials, indirect labor, and maintenance) of $30 per labor-hour. Thus, for the analysis in this section the total budgeted costs of the Materials Management Department equal $264,000 [$144,000 + $30 × (800 + 2,800 + 400) labor-hours] as shown in Exhibit 2.[5]

Exhibit 3 displays the data for budgeted overhead costs from Exhibit 2 after allocating Plant Administration Department costs but before any further interdepartment cost allocations and the services provided by each support department to the other departments. To understand the percentages in this exhibit, consider the Engineering and Production Control Department. This department supports the engineering activity in the other departments and so the costs of this department are allocated based on engineering salaries in each of the other departments. From Exhibit 2, budgeted engineering salaries are $36,000 in the Materials Management Department, $60,000 in the Machining Department, and $24,000 in the Assembly Department for a total of $120,000 ($36,000 + $60,000 + $24,000). Thus, the Engineering and Production Control Department provides support of 30% ($36,000 ÷ $120,000 = 0.30) to the Materials Management Department, 50% ($60,000 ÷ $120,000 = 0.50) to the Machining Department, and 20% ($24,000 ÷ $120,000 = 0.20) to the Assembly Department. Similarly, the Materials Management Department provides a total of 4,000 material-handling labor-hours of support work: 10% (400 ÷ 4,000 = 0.10) for the Engineering and Production Control Department, 20% (800 ÷ 4,000 = 0.20) for the Machining Department, and 70% (2,800 ÷ 4,000 = 0.70) for the Assembly Department.

We describe three methods of allocating budgeted overhead costs from the support departments to the Machining Department and the Assembly Department: *direct, step-down*, and *reciprocal*. Throughout this section, we use budgeted costs and budgeted hours. Why? Because our goal is to determine the budgeted costs of the operating departments (Machining and Assembly) after Robinson allocates the budgeted costs of the support

| Exhibit 3 | Data for Allocating Support Department Costs at Robinson Company for 2013 |

	A	B	C	D	E	F	G
		SUPPORT DEPARTMENTS			OPERATING DEPARTMENTS		
		Engineering and Production Control	Materials Management		Machining	Assembly	Total
3	Budgeted overhead costs						
4	before any interdepartment cost allocations	$300,000	$264,000		$329,000	$227,000	$1,120,000
5	Support work furnished:						
6	By Engineering and Production Control						
7	Budgeted engineering salaries	—	$36,000		$60,000	$24,000	$120,000
8	Percentage	—	30%		50%	20%	100%
9	By Materials Management						
10	Budgeted material-handling labor-hours	400	—		800	2,800	4,000
11	Percentage	10%	—		20%	70%	100%

---

[5] The previous section assumed that the Materials Management Department only provided services to the Machining and Assembly Departments and not to the Engineering and Production Control Department, resulting in total budgeted costs of $252,000 [$144,000 + $30 × (800 + 2,800) labor-hours].

departments (Materials Management and Engineering and Production Control) to the operating departments. The budgeted costs of the Machining Department will be divided by the budgeted machine-hours in the Machining Department and the budgeted costs of the Assembly Department will be divided by the budgeted direct manufacturing labor-hours in the Assembly Department to calculate the budgeted overhead allocation rates in each operating department. These overhead rates will be used to allocate overhead costs to each job as it passes through an operating department based on the actual number of machine-hours used in the Machining Department and the actual number of direct manufacturing labor-hours used in the Assembly Department. To simplify the explanation and to focus on concepts, we use the single-rate method to allocate the costs of each support department. (The Problem for Self-Study illustrates the dual-rate method for allocating reciprocal support-department costs.)

Direct Method

The **direct method** allocates each support-department's costs to operating departments only. The direct method does not allocate support department costs to other support departments. Exhibit 4 illustrates this method using the data in Exhibit 3. The base used to allocate Engineering and Production Control costs to the operating departments is the budgeted engineering salaries in the operating departments: $60,000 + $24,000 = $84,000. This amount excludes the $36,000 of budgeted engineering salaries representing services to be provided by Engineering and Production Control to Materials Management. Similarly, the base used for allocation of Materials Management costs to the operating departments is 800 + 2,800 = 3,600 budgeted material-handling labor-hours, which excludes the 400 hours of budgeted support time provided by Materials Management to Engineering and Production Control.

An equivalent approach to implementing the direct method involves calculating a budgeted rate for each support department's costs. For example, the rate for the Engineering

Exhibit 4	
Direct Method of Allocating Support-Department Costs at Robinson Company for 2013	

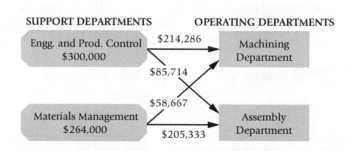

	SUPPORT DEPARTMENTS			OPERATING DEPARTMENTS		
	A	B	C	D	E	F	G
		Engineering and Production Control	Materials Management		Machining	Assembly	Total
3 Budgeted overhead costs							
4 before any interdepartment cost allocations		$300,000	$264,000		$329,000	$227,000	$1,120,000
5 Allocation of Engg. And Prod. Control (5/7, 2/7)[a]		(300,000)			214,286	85,714	
6 Allocation of Materials Management (2/9, 7/9)[b]			(264,000)		58,667	205,333	
7							
8 Total budgeted overhead of operating departments		$ 0	$ 0		$601,953	$518,047	$1,120,000
9							
10 [a] Base is ($60,000 + $24,000), or $84,000; $60,000 ÷ $84,000 = 5/7; $24,000 ÷ $84,000 = 2/7.							
11 [b] Base is (800 + 2,800), or 3,600 hours; 800 ÷ 3,600 = 2/9; 2,800 ÷ 3,600 = 7/9.							

and Production Control Department costs is ($300,000 ÷ $84,000), or 357.143%. The Machining Department is then allocated $214,286 (357.143% × $60,000), while the Assembly Department is allocated $85,714 (357.143% × $24,000). For ease of explanation throughout this section, we will use the fraction of the support department services used by other departments, rather than calculate budgeted rates, to allocate support department costs.

Most managers adopt the direct method because it is easy to use. The benefit of the direct method is simplicity. Managers do not need to predict the usage of support department services by other support departments. A disadvantage of the direct method is that it ignores information about reciprocal services provided among support departments and can therefore lead to inaccurate estimates of the cost of operating departments. We now examine a second approach, which partially recognizes the services provided among support departments.

Step-Down Method

Some organizations use the **step-down method**—also called the **sequential allocation method**—which allocates support-department costs to other support departments and to operating departments in a sequential manner that partially recognizes the mutual services provided among all support departments.

Exhibit 5 shows the step-down method. The Engineering and Production Control costs of $300,000 are allocated first. Exhibit 3 shows that Engineering and Production Control provides 30% of its services to Materials Management, 50% to Machining, and 20% to Assembly. Therefore, $90,000 is allocated to Materials Management (30% of $300,000), $150,000 to Machining (50% of $300,000), and $60,000 to Assembly (20% of $300,000). The Materials Management Department costs now total $354,000: budgeted costs of the Materials Management Department before any interdepartmental cost allocations, $264,000, plus $90,000 from the allocation of Engineering and Production Control

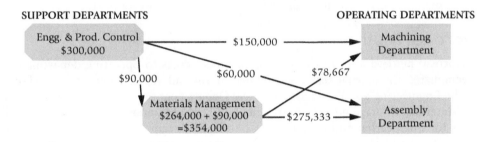

	Exhibit 5
	Step-Down Method of Allocating Support-Department Costs at Robinson Company for 2013

	A	B	C	D	E	F	G
1		SUPPORT DEPARTMENTS			OPERATING DEPARTMENTS		
2		Engineering and Production Control	Materials Management		Machining	Assembly	Total
3	Budgeted overhead costs before any						
4	interdepartment cost allocations	$300,000	$264,000		$329,000	$227,000	$1,120,000
5	Allocation of Engg. and Prod. Control (3/10, 5/10, 2/10)ᵃ	(300,000)	90,000		150,000	60,000	
6			354,000				
7	Allocation of Materials Management (2/9, 7/9)ᵇ		(354,000)		78,667	275,333	
8							
9	Total budgeted overhead of operating departments	$ 0	$ 0		$557,667	$562,333	$1,120,000
10							
11	ᵃ Base is ($36,000 + $60,000 + $24,000), or $120,000 ; $36,000 ÷ $120,000 = 3/10; $60,000 ÷ $120,000 = 5/10; $24,000 ÷ $120,000 = 2/10.						
12	ᵇ Base is (800 + 2,800), or 3,600 hours; 800 ÷ 3,600 = 2/9; 2,800 ÷ 3,600 = 7/9.						

costs to the Materials Management Department. The $354,000 is then only allocated between the two operating departments based on the proportion of the Materials Management Department services provided to Machining and Assembly. From Exhibit 3, the Materials Management Department provides 20% of its services to Machining and 70% to Assembly, so $78,667 (2/9 × $354,000) is allocated to Machining and $275,333 (7/9 × $354,000) is allocated to Assembly.

Note that this method requires managers to rank (sequence) the support departments in the order that the step-down allocation is to proceed. In our example, the costs of the Engineering and Production Control Department were allocated first to all other departments, including the Materials Management Department. The costs of the Materials Management support department were allocated second, but only to the two operating departments. Different sequences will result in different allocations of support-department costs to operating departments—for example, if the Materials Management Department costs had been allocated first and the Engineering and Production Control Department costs second. A popular step-down sequence begins with the support department that renders the highest percentage of its total services to *other support departments*. The sequence continues with the department that renders the next-highest percentage, and so on, ending with the support department that renders the lowest percentage.[6] In our example, costs of the Engineering and Production Control Department were allocated first because it provides 30% of its services to the Materials Management Department, whereas the Materials Management Department provides only 10% of its services to the Engineering and Production Control Department (see Exhibit 3).

Under the step-down method, once a support department's costs have been allocated, no subsequent support-department costs are allocated back to it. Once the Engineering and Production Control Department costs are allocated, it receives no further allocation from other (lower-ranked) support departments. The result is that the step-down method does not recognize the total services that support departments provide to each other. The reciprocal method fully recognizes all such services, as you will see next.

Reciprocal Method

The **reciprocal method** allocates support-department costs to operating departments by fully recognizing the mutual services provided among all support departments. For example, the Engineering and Production Control Department provides engineering services to the Materials Management Department. Similarly, Materials Management handles materials for Engineering and Production Control. The reciprocal method fully incorporates interdepartmental relationships into the support-department cost allocations.

Exhibit 6 presents one way to understand the reciprocal method as an extension of the step-down method. First, Engineering and Production Control costs are allocated to all other departments, including the Materials Management support department (Materials Management, 30%; Machining, 50%; Assembly, 20%). The costs in the Materials Management Department then total $354,000 ($264,000 + $90,000 from the first-round allocation), as in Exhibit 5. The $354,000 is then allocated to all other departments that the Materials Management Department supports, including the Engineering and Production Control support department—Engineering and Production Control, 10%; Machining, 20%; and Assembly, 70% (see Exhibit 3). The Engineering and Production Control costs that had been brought down to $0 now have $35,400 from the Materials Management Department allocation. These costs are again reallocated to all other departments, including Materials Management, in the same ratio that the Engineering and Production Control costs were previously assigned. Now the Materials Management Department costs that had been brought down to $0 have $10,620 from the Engineering and Production Control Department allocations. These costs are again allocated in the same ratio that the Materials Management Department costs were previously assigned.

---

[6] An alternative approach to selecting the sequence of allocations is to begin with the support department that renders the highest dollar amount of services to other support departments. The sequence ends with the allocation of the costs of the department that renders the lowest dollar amount of services to other support departments.

Exhibit 6	Reciprocal Method of Allocating Support-Department Costs Using Repeated Iterations at Robinson Company for 2013

	A	B	C	D	E	F	G
		Engineering and Production Control	Materials Management		Machining Department	Assembly Department	Total
3	Budgeted overhead costs before any						
4	interdepartment cost allocations	$300,000	$264,000		$329,000	$227,000	$1,120,000
5	1st Allocation of Engg. and Prod. Control (3/10,5/10,2/10)[a]	(300,000)	90,000		150,000	60,000	
6			354,000				
7	1st Allocation of Materials Management (1/10,2/10,7/10)[b]	35,400	(354,000)		70,800	247,800	
8	2nd Allocation of Engg. and Prod. Control (3/10,5/10,2/10)[a]	(35,400)	10,620		17,700	7,080	
9	2nd Allocation of Materials Management (1/10,2/10,7/10)[b]	1,062	(10,620)		2,124	7,434	
10	3rd Allocation of Engg. and Prod. Control (3/10,5/10,2/10)[a]	(1,062)	319		531	212	
11	3rd Allocation of Materials Management (1/10,2/10,7/10)[b]	32	(319)		63	224	
12	4th Allocation of Engg. and Prod. Control (3/10,5/10,2/10)[a]	(32)	10		16	6	
13	4th Allocation of Materials Management (1/10,2/10,7/10)[b]	1	(10)		2	7	
14	5th Allocation of Engg. and Prod. Control (3/10,5/10,2/10)[a]	(1)	0		1	0	
15							
16	Total budgeted overhead of operating departments	$ 0	$ 0		$570,237	$549,763	$1,120,000
17							
18	Total support department amounts allocated and reallocated (the numbers in parentheses in the first two columns):						
19	Engineering and Production Control: $300,000 + $35,400 + $1,062 + $32 + $1 = $336,495						
20	Materials Management: $354,000 + $10,620 + $319 + $10 = $364,949						
21							
22	[a]Base is $36,000 + $60,000 + $24,000 = $120,000; $36,000 ÷ $120,000 = 3/10; $60,000 ÷ $120,000 = 5/10; $24,000 ÷ $120,000 = 2/10						
23	[b]Base is 400 + 800 + 2,800 = 4,000 labor-hours; 400 ÷ 4,000 = 1/10; 800 ÷ 4,000 = 2/10; 2,800 ÷ 4,000 = 7/10						

Successive rounds result in smaller and smaller amounts being allocated to and reallocated from the support departments until eventually all support department costs are allocated to the Machining Department and the Assembly Department.

An alternative way to implement the reciprocal method is to formulate and solve linear equations. This implementation requires three steps.

Step 1: Express Support Department Costs and Reciprocal Relationships in the Form of Linear Equations. Let *EPC* be the *complete reciprocated costs* of Engineering and Production Control and *MM* be the *complete reciprocated costs* of Materials Management. By **complete reciprocated costs,** we mean the support department's own costs plus any interdepartmental cost allocations. We then express the data in Exhibit 3 as follows:

$$EPC = \$300,000 + 0.1\,MM \quad (1)$$

$$MM = \$264,000 + 0.3\,EPC \quad (2)$$

The $0.1MM$ term in equation (1) is the percentage of the Materials Management services *used by* Engineering and Production Control. The $0.3EPC$ term in equation (2) is the percentage of Engineering and Production Control services *used by* Materials Management. The complete reciprocated costs in equations (1) and (2) are sometimes called the **artificial costs** of the support departments.

Step 2: Solve the Set of Linear Equations to Obtain the Complete Reciprocated Costs of Each Support Department. Substituting equation (1) into (2):

$$MM = \$264,000 + [0.3\,(\$300,000 + 0.1\,MM)]$$
$$MM = \$264,000 + \$90,000 + 0.03\,MM$$
$$0.97\,MM = \$354,000$$
$$MM = \$364,949$$

Substituting this into equation (1):

$$EPC = \$300,000 + 0.1\,(\$364,949)$$
$$EPC = \$300,000 + \$36,495 = \$336,495$$

The complete reciprocated costs or artificial costs for the Materials Management Department are $364,949 and for the Engineering and Production Control Department are $336,495. The complete-reciprocated-cost figures also appear at the bottom of Exhibit 6 as the total amounts allocated and reallocated. When there are more than two support departments with reciprocal relationships, managers can use software such as Excel to calculate the complete reciprocated costs of each support department. Because the calculations involve finding the inverse of a matrix, the reciprocal method is also sometimes referred to as the **matrix method**.[7]

Step 3: Allocate the Complete Reciprocated Costs of Each Support Department to All Other Departments (Both Support Departments and Operating Departments) on the Basis of the Usage Percentages (Based on Total Units of Service Provided to All Departments). Consider the Materials Management Department. The complete reciprocated costs of $364,949 are allocated as follows:

To Engineering and Production Control $(1/10) \times \$364,949 =$	$ 36,495
To Machining $(2/10) \times \$364,949$	= $ 72,990
To Assembly $(7/10) \times \$364,949$	= $255,464
Total	$364,949

Similarly, the $336,495 in reciprocated costs of the Engineering and Production Control Department are allocated to the Materials Management Department $(3/10)$, Machining Department $(5/10)$, and Assembly Department $(2/10)$.

Exhibit 7 presents summary data based on the reciprocal method.

Robinson's $701,444 complete reciprocated costs of the support departments exceeds the budgeted amount of $564,000.

Support Department	Complete Reciprocated Costs	Budgeted Costs	Difference
Engineering and Production Control	$336,495	$300,000	$ 36,495
Materials Management	364,949	264,000	100,949
Total	$701,444	$564,000	$137,444

Each support department's complete reciprocated cost is greater than the budgeted amount because it takes into account that support costs are allocated to all departments using its services and not just to operating departments. This step ensures that the reciprocal method fully recognizes all interrelationships among support departments, as well as relationships between support and operating departments. The difference between complete reciprocated costs and budgeted costs for each support department reflects the costs allocated among support departments. The total costs allocated to the operating departments under the reciprocal method are still only $564,000 ($168,247 + $67,299 allocated from the Engineering and Production Control Department and $72,990 + $255,464 allocated from the Materials Management Department, see Exhibit 7).

---

[7] If there are n support departments, then Step 1 will yield n linear equations. Solving the equations to calculate the complete reciprocated costs then requires finding the inverse of an $n \times n$ matrix.

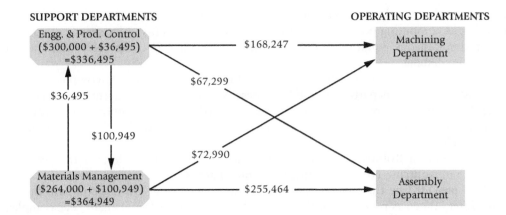

SUPPORT DEPARTMENTS

OPERATING DEPARTMENTS

Engg. & Prod. Control
($300,000 + $36,495)
=$336,495

$168,247 → Machining Department

$67,299

$36,495

$100,949

$72,990

Materials Management
($264,000 + $100,949)
=$364,949

$255,464 → Assembly Department

Exhibit 7

Reciprocal Method of Allocating Support-Department Costs Using Linear Equations at Robinson Company for 2013

	A	B	C	D	E	F	G
		SUPPORT DEPARTMENTS			**OPERATING DEPARTMENTS**		
2		**Engineering and Production Control**	**Materials Management**		**Machining**	**Assembly**	**Total**
3	Budgeted overhead costs before any						
4	interdepartment cost allocations	$300,000	$264,000		$329,000	$227,000	$1,120,000
5	Allocation of Engg. & Prod. Control (3/10, 5/10, 2/10)[a]	(336,495)	100,949		168,247	67,299	
6	Allocation of Materials Management (1/10, 2/10, 7/10)[b]	36,495	(364,949)		72,990	255,464	
7							
8	Total budgeted overhead of operating departments	$ 0	$ 0		$570,237	$549,763	$1,120,000
9							
10	[a]Base is ($36,000 + $60,000 + $24,000), or $120,000 ; $36,000 ÷ $120,000 = 3/10; $60,000 ÷ $120,000 = 5/10; $24,000 ÷ $120,000 = 2/10.						
11	[b]Base is (400 + 800 + 2,800), or 4,000 hours; 400 ÷ 4,000 = 1/10; 800 ÷ 4,000 = 2/10; 2,800 ÷ 4,000 = 7/10.						

Overview of Methods

The amount of manufacturing overhead costs allocated to the Machining and Assembly Departments will differ depending on the method used to allocate support-department costs. Differences among the three methods' allocations increase (1) as the magnitude of the reciprocal allocations increases and (2) as the differences across operating departments' usage of each support department's services increase. Note that while the final allocations under the reciprocal method are in between those under the direct and step-down methods in our example, in general, there is no relationship between the amount of costs allocated to the operating departments under the different methods. The method of allocation becomes particularly important in the case of cost-reimbursement contracts that require allocation of support-department costs. To avoid disputes, managers should always clarify the method to be used for allocation. For example, Medicare reimbursements and federal government research contracts with universities that pay for the recovery of indirect costs typically mandate use of the step-down method, with explicit requirements about the costs that can be included in the indirect cost pools.

The reciprocal method is conceptually the most precise method because it considers the mutual services provided among all support departments. The advantage of the direct and step-down methods is that they are simple for mangers to compute and understand relative to the reciprocal method. If the costs allocated to the operating departments using the direct or step-down methods closely approximate the costs allocated using the reciprocal method, managers should use the simpler direct or step-down methods. However, as computing power to perform repeated iterations (as in Exhibit 6) or to solve sets of simultaneous equations increases, more companies find the reciprocal method easier to implement.

Another advantage of the reciprocal method is that it highlights the complete reciprocated costs of support departments and how these costs differ from budgeted or actual costs of the departments. Knowing the complete reciprocated costs of a support department is a key input for decisions about whether to outsource all the services that the support department provides.

Suppose all of Robinson's support-department costs are variable over the period of a possible outsourcing contract. Consider a third party's bid to provide, say, all services currently provided by the Materials Management Department. Do not compare the bid to the $264,000 costs reported for the Materials Management Department. The complete reciprocated costs of the Materials Management Department, which include the services the Engineering and Production Control Department provides the Materials Management Department, are $364,949 to deliver 4,000 hours of material-handling labor to other departments at Robinson. The complete reciprocated costs for material-handling labor are $91.24 per hour ($364,949 ÷ 4,000 hours). Other things being equal, an external provider's bid to supply the same materials management services as Robinson's internal department at less than $364,949, or $91.24 per hour (even if much greater than $264,000) would improve Robinson's operating income.

To see this point, note that the relevant savings from shutting down the Materials Management Department are $264,000 of Materials Management Department costs *plus* $100,949 of Engineering and Production Control Department costs. By closing down the Materials Management Department, Robinson will no longer incur the 30% of reciprocated Engineering and Production Control Department costs (equal to $100,949) that were incurred to support the Materials Management Department. Therefore, the total cost savings are $364,949 ($264,000 + 100,949).[8] Neither the direct nor the step-down method can provide this relevant information for outsourcing decisions.

Calculating the Cost of Job WPP 298

Robinson uses the budgeted costs of each operating department (Machining and Assembly) to compute the rate per unit of each cost-allocation base used to allocate the indirect costs to a job (Step 5 in a job costing system). Robinson budgets 20,000 direct labor-hours for the Assembly Department (of the 28,000 total direct manufacturing labor-hours) and 10,000 machine-hours for the Machining Department.

The budgeted overhead allocation rates for each operating department by allocation method are:

Support Department Cost-Allocation Method	Total Budgeted Overhead Costs After Allocation of All Support-Department Costs		Budgeted Overhead Rate per Hour for Product-Costing Purposes	
	Machining	Assembly	Machining (10,000 machine-hours)	Assembly (20,000 labor-hours)
Direct	$601,953	$518,047	$60.20	$25.90
Step-down	557,667	562,333	55.77	28.12
Reciprocal	570,237	549,763	57.02	27.49

The next step in a job-costing system (Step 6) is to compute the indirect costs allocated to a job. For the WPP 298 job, Robinson uses 42 labor-hours in the Assembly Department (out of 88 direct manufacturing labor-hours) and 46 machine-hours in the

---

[8] Technical issues when using the reciprocal method in outsourcing decisions are discussed in Robert S. Kaplan and Anthony A. Atkinson, *Advanced Management Accounting*, 3rd ed. (Upper Saddle River, NJ: Prentice Hall, 1998, pp. 73–81).

Machining Department. The overhead costs allocated to the WPP 298 job under the three methods would be

Direct:	$3,857 (46 × $60.20 + 42 × $25.90)
Step-down:	$3,746 (46 × $55.77 + 42 × $28.12)
Reciprocal:	$3,778 (46 × $57.02 + 42 × $27.49)

The manufacturing overhead costs allocated to WPP298 differ only a little under the three methods because the WPP 298 job requires roughly equal amounts of machine-hours and assembly labor-hours. These differences would be larger if a job required many more machine-hours than assembly hours or vice versa.

Using normal costing and multiple cost-allocation bases also results in higher indirect manufacturing costs allocated to Job WPP 298, $3,778 (under the reciprocal method) compared to $3,520 allocated using direct manufacturing labor-hours as the sole allocation base. Two cost-allocation bases—machine-hours and assembly labor-hours—are better able to model the drivers of manufacturing overhead costs.

The final step (Step 7) computes the total cost of the job by adding all direct and indirect costs assigned to the job. Under the reciprocal method, the total manufacturing costs of the WPP 298 job are as follows:

Direct manufacturing costs		
Direct materials	$4,606	
Direct manufacturing labor	1,579	$6,185
Manufacturing overhead costs		
Machining Department		
($57.02 per machine-hour × 46 machine-hours)	2,623	
Assembly Department		
($27.49 per labor-hour × 42 labor-hours)	1,155	3,778
Total manufacturing costs of job WPP 298		$9,963

Note that the costs in Step 7 have four dollar amounts, each corresponding respectively to the two direct-cost and two indirect-cost categories in the costing system.

At the end of the year, actual manufacturing overhead costs of the Machining Department and the Assembly Department would be compared to the manufacturing overhead allocated for each department. To calculate the actual manufacturing overhead costs of the Machining and Assembly Departments, Robinson would need to allocate the actual costs of the Materials Management and Engineering and Production Control Departments to the Machining and Assembly Departments using the methods described in this chapter. Management accountants would then make end-of-year adjustments separately for each cost pool for under- or overallocated overhead costs.

We now consider common costs, another special class of costs for which management accountants have developed specific allocation methods.

Allocating Common Costs

A **common cost** is a cost of operating a facility, activity, or like cost object that is shared by two or more users. Common costs arise because each user obtains a lower cost by sharing than the separate cost that would result if each user operated independently.

The goal is to allocate common costs to each user in a reasonable way. Consider Jason Stevens, a graduating senior in Seattle who has been invited to a job interview with an employer in Albany. The round-trip Seattle–Albany airfare costs $1,200. A week later, Stevens is also invited to an interview with an employer in Chicago. The Seattle–Chicago round-trip airfare costs $800. Stevens decides to combine the two recruiting trips into a Seattle–Albany–Chicago–Seattle trip that will cost $1,500 in airfare. The prospective employers will reimburse Stevens for the airfare. The $1,500 is a common cost that benefits both prospective employers because it is less than the $2,000 ($1,200 + $800) that the two employers would have to pay if they operated independently.

Decision Point

What methods can managers use to allocate costs of multiple support departments to operating departments?

Learning Objective 4

Allocate common costs using the stand-alone method

...uses cost information of each user as a separate entity to allocate common costs

and the incremental method

...allocates common costs primarily to one user and the remainder to other users

What is a reasonable way to allocate the common costs of $1,500? Two methods of allocating this common cost between the two prospective employers are the stand-alone method and the incremental method.

Stand-Alone Cost-Allocation Method

The **stand-alone cost-allocation method** determines the weights for cost allocation by considering each user of the cost as a separate entity. For the common-cost airfare of $1,500, information about the separate (stand-alone) round-trip airfares ($1,200 and $800) is used to determine the allocation weights:

$$\text{Albany employer:} \frac{\$1,200}{\$1,200 + \$800} \times \$1,500 = 0.60 \times \$1,500 = \$900$$

$$\text{Chicago employer:} \frac{\$800}{\$800 + \$1,200} \times \$1,500 = 0.40 \times \$1,500 = \$600$$

Advocates of this method often emphasize the fairness or equity criterion. The method is viewed as reasonable because each employer bears a proportionate share of total costs in relation to the individual stand-alone costs.

Incremental Cost-Allocation Method

The **incremental cost-allocation method** ranks the individual users of a cost object in the order of users most responsible for the common cost and then uses this ranking to allocate cost among those users. The first-ranked user of the cost object is the *primary user* (also called the *primary party*) and is allocated costs up to the costs of the primary user as a stand-alone user. The second-ranked user is the *first-incremental user* (*first-incremental party*) and is allocated the additional cost that arises from two users instead of only the primary user. The third-ranked user is the *second-incremental user* (*second-incremental party*) and is allocated the additional cost that arises from three users instead of two users, and so on.

To see how this method works, consider again Jason Stevens and his $1,500 airfare cost. Assume the Albany employer is viewed as the primary party. Stevens' rationale is that he had already committed to go to Albany before accepting the invitation to interview in Chicago. The cost allocations would be as follows:

Party	Costs Allocated	Cumulative Costs Allocated
Albany (primary)	$1,200	$1,200
Chicago (incremental)	300 ($1,500 − $1,200)	$1,500
Total	$1,500	

The Albany employer is allocated the full Seattle–Albany airfare. The unallocated part of the total airfare is then allocated to the Chicago employer. If the Chicago employer had been chosen as the primary party, the cost allocations would have been Chicago $800 (the stand-alone round-trip Seattle–Chicago airfare) and Albany $700 ($1,500 − $800). When there are more than two parties, this method requires them to be ranked from first to last (such as by the date on which each employer invited the candidate to interview).

Under the incremental method, the primary party typically receives the highest allocation of the common costs. If the incremental users are newly formed companies or subunits, such as a new product line or a new sales territory, the incremental method may enhance their chances for short-run survival by assigning them a low allocation of the common costs. The difficulty with the method is that, particularly if a large common cost is involved, every user would prefer to be viewed as the incremental party!

One approach managers can use to avoid disputes in such situations is to use the stand-alone cost-allocation method. Another approach is to use the *Shapley value*, which considers each party as first the primary party and then the incremental party. From the calculations shown earlier, the Albany employer is allocated $1,200 as the primary party and $700 as the incremental party, for an average of $950 [($1,200 + $700) ÷ 2]. The Chicago employer is allocated $800 as the primary party and $300 as the incremental party, for an average of $550 [($800 + 300) ÷ 2]. The Shapley value method allocates, to each employer, the average of the costs allocated as the primary party and as the incremental party: $950 to the Albany employer and $550 to the Chicago employer.[9]

As our discussion suggests, allocating common costs is not clear-cut and can generate disputes. Whenever feasible, managers should specify the rules for such allocations in advance. If this is not done, then, rather than blindly follow one method or another, managers should exercise judgment when allocating common costs by thinking carefully about allocation methods that appear fair to each party. For instance, Stevens must choose an allocation method for his airfare cost that is acceptable to each prospective employer. He cannot, for example, exceed the maximum reimbursable amount of airfare for either firm. The next section discusses the role of cost data in various types of contracts, another area where disputes about cost allocation frequently arise.

Cost Allocations and Contract Disputes

Many commercial contracts include clauses based on cost accounting information. Examples include the following:

- A contract between the Department of Defense and a company designing and assembling a new fighter plane specifies that the price paid for the plane is to be based on the contractor's direct and overhead costs plus a fixed fee.

- A contract between a consulting firm and a hospital specifies that the consulting firm receive a fixed fee plus a share of the cost savings that arise from implementing the consulting firm's recommendations.

Contract disputes often arise over cost computations. Managers can reduce the areas of dispute between the contracting parties by making the "rules of the game" explicit and writing them into the contract that is signed. Such rules of the game include the definition of allowable cost items; the definitions of terms used, such as what constitutes direct labor; the permissible cost-allocation bases; and how to account for differences between budgeted and actual costs.

Contracting with the U.S. Government

The U.S. government reimburses most contractors in one of two main ways:

1. **The contractor is paid a set price without analysis of actual contract cost data.** This approach is used, for example, when there is competitive bidding, when there is adequate price competition, or when there is an established catalog with prices quoted for items sold in substantial quantities to the general public.

2. **The contractor is paid after analysis of actual contract cost data.** In some cases, when there is uncertainty about the cost to complete a job because of the nature of the task, for example, a new weapon system, the contract will explicitly state that the reimbursement amount is based on actual allocable costs plus a fixed fee.[10] This arrangement is called a *cost-plus contract*.

---

[9] For further discussion of the Shapley value, see Joel S. Demski, "Cost Allocation Games," in *Joint Cost Allocations*, ed. Shane Moriarity (University of Oklahoma Center for Economic and Management Research, 1981); Lech Kruś and Piotr Bronisz, "Cooperative Game Solution Concepts to a Cost Allocation Problem," *European Journal of Operational Research* 122:2 (April 16, 2000): 258–271.

[10] The Federal Acquisition Regulation (FAR), issued in March 2005 (see www.acquisition.gov/far/current/pdf/FAR.pdf) includes the following definition of *allocability* (in FAR 31.201-4): "A cost is allocable if it is assignable or chargeable to one or more cost objectives on the basis of relative benefits received or other equitable relationship. Subject to the foregoing, a cost is allocable to a Government contract if it:
(a) Is incurred specifically for the contract;
(b) Benefits both the contract and other work, and can be distributed to them in reasonable proportion to the benefits received; or
(c) Is necessary to the overall operation of the business, although a direct relationship to any particular cost objective cannot be shown."

All contracts with U.S. government agencies must comply with cost accounting standards issued by the **Cost Accounting Standards Board (CASB)**. For government contracts, the CASB has the exclusive authority to make, put into effect, amend, and rescind cost accounting standards and interpretations. The standards are designed to achieve *uniformity and consistency* in the measurement, assignment, and allocation of costs to government contracts within the United States.[11]

In government contracting, there is a complex interplay of political considerations and accounting principles. Terms such as *fairness* and *equity,* as well as cause and effect and benefits received, are often used in government contracts.

Fairness of Pricing

In many defense contracts, there is great uncertainty about the final cost to produce a new weapon or equipment. Such contracts are rarely subject to competitive bidding because no contractor is willing to assume all the risk of receiving a fixed price for the contract and subsequently incurring high costs to fulfill it. Therefore, setting a market-based fixed price for the contract fails to attract contractors or requires a contract price that is too high from the government's standpoint. To address this issue, the government typically assumes a major share of the risk of the potentially high costs of completing the contract. Rather than relying on selling prices as ordinarily set by suppliers in the marketplace, the government negotiates contracts on the basis of *costs plus a fixed fee.* In costs-plus-fixed-fee contracts, which often involve billions of dollars, the allocation of a specific cost, for example, general administration costs that support all contracts, may be difficult to defend on the basis of any cause-and-effect reasoning. Nonetheless, the contracting parties may still view it as a "reasonable" or "fair" means to help establish a contract amount.

Decision Point ▶

How can contract disputes over reimbursement amounts based on costs be reduced?

Some costs are "allowable"; others are "unallowable." An **allowable cost** is a cost that the contract parties agree to include in the costs to be reimbursed. Some contracts specify how allowable costs are to be determined. For example, only economy-class airfares are allowable in many U.S. government contracts. Other contracts identify cost categories that are unallowable. For example, the costs of lobbying activities and alcoholic beverages are not allowable costs in U.S. government contracts. However, the set of allowable costs is not always clear-cut. Contract disputes and allegations about overcharging the government arise from time to time (see Concepts in Action: Contract Disputes over Reimbursable Costs for the U.S. Department of Defense).

◀ **Learning Objective** 6

Understand how bundling of products

...two or more products sold for a single-price

causes revenue allocation issues

...allocating revenues to each product in the bundle to evaluate managers of individual products

and the methods managers use to allocate revenues

...using the stand-alone method or the incremental method

Bundled Products and Revenue Allocation Methods

Allocation issues can also arise when revenues from multiple products (for example, different software programs or cable and Internet packages) are bundled together and sold at a single price. The methods for revenue allocation parallel those described for common-cost allocations.

Bundling and Revenue Allocation

Revenues are inflows of assets (almost always cash or accounts receivable) companies receive for products or services provided to customers. Similar to cost allocation, **revenue allocation** occurs when revenues are related to a particular *revenue object* but cannot be traced to it in an economically feasible (cost-effective) way. A **revenue object** is anything for which a separate measurement of revenue is desired. Examples of revenue objects include products, customers, and divisions. We illustrate revenue-allocation

---

[11] Details on the Cost Accounting Standards Board are available at www.whitehouse.gov/omb/procurement/casb.html. The CASB is part of the Office of Federal Procurement Policy, U.S. Office of Management and Budget.

Concepts in Action ▷ Contract Disputes over Reimbursable Costs for the U.S. Department of Defense

For 2013, the U.S. Department of Defense budget was more than $500 billion. A portion of this money was allocated to private companies to carry out specific contracted services. In recent years, the U.S. government has pursued cases against several contractors for overcharging for services. The following examples are from cases pursued by the U.S. Department of Justice's Civil Division on behalf of the federal government.

1. Maresk Line Limited paid $31.9 million to settle allegations of overcharging the U.S Department of Defense to ship thousands of cargo containers from Middle East ports to inland destinations in Iraq and Afghanistan. The company allegedly billed in excess of the contractual rate for refrigerated-container storage, late fees, and GPS cargo tracking.

2. United Technologies Corporation was found liable for more than $473 million arising out of a contract to provide the Air Force with F-15 and F-16 aircraft engines. The company excluded discounts that it received from suppliers in its proposed prices, which led to the Department of Defense paying more than it otherwise would have paid for the engines.

3. Lockheed Martin Corporation agreed to pay $15.8 million to settle charges that it overcharged the Department of Defense for tools used on multiple contracts. Specifically, the company was accused of inflating the cost of various tools and passing along those costs to the U.S. government for eight years.

Source: Press releases from the U.S. Department of Justice, Civil Division (2011–2013).

issues for Dynamic Software Corporation, which develops, sells, and supports three software programs:

1. WordMaster, a word-processing program, released 36 months ago
2. DataMaster, a spreadsheet program, released 18 months ago
3. FinanceMaster, a budgeting and cash-management program, released six months ago with a lot of favorable media attention

Dynamic Software sells these three products individually as well as together as bundled products.

A **bundled product** is a package of two or more products (or services) that is sold for a single price but whose individual components may be sold as separate items at their own "stand-alone" prices. The price of a bundled product is typically less than the sum of the prices of the individual products sold separately. For example, banks often provide individual customers with a bundle of services from different departments (checking, safety-deposit box, and investment advisory) for a single fee. A resort hotel may offer, for a single amount per customer, a weekend package that includes services from its lodging (the room), food (the restaurant), and recreational (golf and tennis) departments. When department managers have revenue or profit responsibilities for individual products, the bundled revenue must be allocated among the individual products in the bundle.

Dynamic Software allocates revenues from its bundled product sales (called "suite sales") to individual products. Individual-product profitability is used to compensate software engineers, developers, and product managers responsible for developing and managing each product.

How should Dynamic Software allocate suite revenues to individual products? Consider information pertaining to the three "stand-alone" and "suite" products in 2013:

	Selling Price	Manufacturing Cost per Unit
Stand-alone		
WordMaster	$125	$18
DataMaster	150	20
FinanceMaster	225	25
Suite		
Word + Data	$220	
Word + Finance	280	
Finance + Data	305	
Word + Finance + Data	380	

Just as we saw in the section on common-cost allocations, the two main revenue-allocation methods are the stand-alone method and the incremental method.

Stand-Alone Revenue-Allocation Method

The **stand-alone revenue-allocation method** uses product-specific information on the products in the bundle as weights for allocating the bundled revenues to the individual products. The term *stand-alone* refers to the product as a separate (nonsuite) item. Consider the Word + Finance suite, which sells for $280. Three types of weights for the stand-alone method are as follows:

1. **Selling prices.** Using the individual selling prices of $125 for WordMaster and $225 for FinanceMaster, the weights for allocating the $280 suite revenues between the products are as follows:

$$\text{WordMaster:} \frac{\$125}{\$125 + \$225} \times \$280 = 0.357 \times \$280 = \$100$$

$$\text{FinanceMaster:} \frac{\$225}{\$125 + \$225} \times \$280 = 0.643 \times \$280 = \$180$$

2. **Unit costs.** This method uses the costs of the individual products (in this case, manufacturing cost per unit) to determine the weights for the revenue allocations.

$$\text{WordMaster:} \frac{\$18}{\$18 + \$25} \times \$280 = 0.419 \times \$280 = \$117$$

$$\text{FinanceMaster:} \frac{\$25}{\$18 + \$25} \times \$280 = 0.581 \times \$280 = \$163$$

3. **Physical units.** This method gives each product unit in the suite the same weight when allocating suite revenue to individual products. Therefore, with two products in the Word + Finance suite, each product is allocated 50% of the suite revenues.

$$\text{WordMaster:} \frac{1}{1 + 1} \times \$280 = 0.50 \times \$280 = \$140$$

$$\text{FinanceMaster:} \frac{1}{1 + 1} \times \$280 = 0.50 \times \$280 = \$140$$

These three approaches to determining weights for the stand-alone method result in very different revenue allocations to the individual products:

Revenue-Allocation Weights	WordMaster	FinanceMaster
Selling prices	$100	$180
Unit costs	117	163
Physical units	140	140

Which method do managers prefer? The selling prices method is best because the weights explicitly consider the prices customers are willing to pay for the individual products. Weighting approaches that use revenue information better capture "benefits received" by customers than unit costs or physical units.[12] The physical-units revenue-allocation method is used when managers cannot use any of the other methods (such as when selling prices are unstable or unit costs are difficult to calculate for individual products).

Incremental Revenue-Allocation Method

The **incremental revenue-allocation method** ranks individual products in a bundle according to criteria determined by management—such as the product in the bundle with the most sales—and then uses this ranking to allocate bundled revenues to individual products. The first-ranked product is the *primary product* in the bundle. The second-ranked product is the *first-incremental product*, the third-ranked product is the *second-incremental product*, and so on.

How do companies decide on product rankings under the incremental revenue-allocation method? Some organizations survey customers about the importance of each of the individual products in their purchase decision. Others rank products on the basis of the recent stand-alone sales performance of the individual products in the bundle. A third approach is for top managers to use their knowledge or intuition to decide the rankings.

Consider again the Word + Finance suite. Assume WordMaster is designated as the primary product. If the suite selling price exceeds the stand-alone price of the primary product, the primary product is allocated 100% of its *stand-alone* revenue. Because the suite price of $280 exceeds the stand-alone price of $125 for WordMaster, WordMaster is allocated revenues of $125, with the remaining revenue of $155 ($280 − $125) allocated to FinanceMaster:

Product	Revenue Allocated	Cumulative Revenue Allocated
WordMaster	$125	$125
FinanceMaster	155 ($280 − $125)	$280
Total	$280	

If the suite price is less than or equal to the stand-alone price of the primary product, the primary product is allocated 100% of the *suite* revenue. All other products in the suite receive no allocation of revenue.

Now suppose FinanceMaster is designated as the primary product and WordMaster as the first-incremental product. Then the incremental revenue-allocation method allocates revenues of the Word + Finance suite as follows:

Product	Revenue Allocated	Cumulative Revenue Allocated
FinanceMaster	$225	$225
WordMaster	55 ($280 − $225)	$280
Total	$280	

If Dynamic Software sells equal quantities of WordMaster and FinanceMaster, then the Shapley value method allocates to each product the average of the revenues allocated as the primary and first-incremental products:

WordMaster:	($125 + $55) ÷ 2 = $180 ÷ 2 =	$ 90
FinanceMaster:	($225 + $155) ÷ 2 = $380 ÷ 2 =	190
Total		$280

---

[12] Revenue-allocation issues also arise in external reporting. The AICPA's Statement of Position 97-2 (Software Revenue Recognition) states that with bundled products, revenue allocation "based on vendor-specific objective evidence (VSOE) of fair value" is required. The "price charged when the element is sold separately" is said to be "objective evidence of fair value" (see "Statement of Position 97-2," Jersey City, NJ: AICPA, 1998). In September 2009, the FASB ratified Emerging Issues Task Force (EITF) Issue 08-1, specifying that with no VSOE or third-party evidence of selling price for all units of accounting in an arrangement, the consideration received for the arrangement should be allocated to the separate units based upon their estimated relative selling prices.

What happens if the firm sells 80,000 units of WordMaster and 20,000 units of FinanceMaster in the most recent quarter? Because Dynamic Software sells four times as many units of WordMaster, its managers believe that the sales of the Word + Finance suite are four times more likely to be driven by WordMaster as the primary product. The *weighted Shapley value method* takes this fact into account. It assigns four times as much weight to the revenue allocations when WordMaster is the primary product as when FinanceMaster is the primary product, resulting in the following allocations:

WordMaster: ($125 × 4 + $55 × 1) ÷ (4 + 1) = $555 ÷ 5 = $111

FinanceMaster: ($225 × 1 + $155 × 4) ÷ (4 + 1) = $845 ÷ 5 =   169

Total $280

When there are more than two products in the suite, the incremental revenue-allocation method allocates suite revenues sequentially. Assume WordMaster is the primary product in Dynamic Software's three-product suite (Word + Finance + Data). FinanceMaster is the first-incremental product, and DataMaster is the second-incremental product. This suite sells for $380. The allocation of the $380 suite revenues proceeds as follows:

Product	Revenue Allocated	Cumulative Revenue Allocated
WordMaster	$125	$125
FinanceMaster	155 ($280 − $125)	$280 (price of Word + Finance suite)
DataMaster	100 ($380 − $280)	$380 (price of Word + Finance + Data suite)
Total	$380	

Now suppose WordMaster is the primary product, DataMaster is the first-incremental product, and FinanceMaster is the second-incremental product.

Product	Revenue Allocated	Cumulative Revenue Allocated
WordMaster	$125	$125
DataMaster	95 ($220 − $125)	$220 (price of Word + Data suite)
FinanceMaster	160 ($380 − $220)	$380 (price of Word + Data + Finance suite)
Total	$380	

The ranking of the individual products in the suite determines the revenues allocated to them. Product managers at Dynamic Software likely would have different views of how their individual products contribute to sales of the suite products. In fact, each product manager would claim to be responsible for the primary product in the Word + Finance + Data suite![13] Because the stand-alone revenue-allocation method does not require rankings of individual products in the suite, this method is less likely to cause debates among product managers.

Revenue allocations are also important for tax reasons. For example, Verizon Communications Inc., the second-largest provider of telecommunications and cable services in the United States, sells each of its services—telephone, cable television, and broadband—separately and in bundled arrangements. State and local tax laws often stipulate that if a bundle is sold and the price for each line item is not split out on the consumer's bill, then all services are taxed as telephone services, which generally carries the highest tax rate. To preclude consumers from paying higher taxes on the entire package, Verizon allocates bundled service revenue to its telephone, cable television, and broadband services

Decision Point ►

What is product bundling and how can managers allocate revenues of a bundled product to individual products in the package?

---

[13] Calculating the Shapley value mitigates this problem because each product is considered as a primary, first-incremental, and second-incremental product. Assuming equal weights on all products, the revenue allocated to each product is an average of the revenues calculated for the product under these different assumptions. In the preceding example, the interested reader can verify that this will result in the following revenue assignments: FinanceMaster, $180; WordMaster, $87.50; and DataMaster, $112.50.

based on the stand-alone selling prices of these services. Consumers then pay taxes on the amounts billed for each service. Specialized software packages, such as SureTax, help companies such as Verizon to properly recognize revenue according to the laws of each state.[14]

---

[14] SureTax, LLC, "SureTax Revenue Allocation Manager," http://www.suretax.com/solutions/suretax-revenue-allocation-manager/, accessed July 2013; Verizon Communication Inc., 2012 Annual Report (New York: Verizon Communications Inc., 2013).

Problem for Self-Study

This problem illustrates how costs of two corporate support departments are allocated to operating divisions using the dual-rate method. Fixed costs are allocated using budgeted costs and budgeted hours used by other departments. Variable costs are allocated using actual costs and actual hours used by other departments.

Computer Horizons reports the following budgeted and actual amounts for its two central corporate support departments (legal and personnel) for supporting each other and the two manufacturing divisions: the laptop division (LTD) and the work station division (WSD):

	Home	Insert	Page Layout	Formulas	Data	Review	View		
	A		B	C	D	E	F	G
1			SUPPORT			OPERATING		
2			Legal Department	Personnel Department		LTD	WSD	Total
3	**BUDGETED USAGE**							
4	Legal (hours)		—	250		1,500	750	2,500
5	(Percentages)		—	10%		60%	30%	100%
6	Personnel (hours)		2,500	—		22,500	25,000	50,000
7	(Percentages)		5%	—		45%	50%	100%
8								
9	**ACTUAL USAGE**							
10	Legal (hours)		—	400		400	1,200	2,000
11	(Percentages)		—	20%		20%	60%	100%
12	Personnel (hours)		2,000	—		26,600	11,400	40,000
13	(Percentages)		5%	—		66.5%	28.5%	100%
14	Budgeted fixed overhead costs before any							
15	interdepartment cost allocations		$360,000	$475,000		—	—	$835,000
16	Actual variable overhead costs before any							
17	interdepartment cost allocations		$200,000	$600,000		—	—	$800,000

What amount of support-department costs for legal and personnel will be allocated to LTD and WSD using (a) the direct method, (b) the step-down method (allocating the legal department costs first), and (c) the reciprocal method using linear equations?

Required

Solution

Exhibit 8 presents the computations for allocating the fixed and variable support-department costs. A summary of these costs follows:

	Laptop Division (LTD)	Work Station Division (WSD)
(a) Direct Method		
Fixed costs	$465,000	$370,000
Variable costs	470,000	330,000
	$935,000	$700,000

	Laptop Division (LTD)	Work Station Division (WSD)
(b) Step-Down Method		
Fixed costs	$458,053	$376,947
Variable costs	488,000	312,000
	$946,053	$688,947
(c) Reciprocal Method		
Fixed costs	$462,513	$372,487
Variable costs	476,364	323,636
	$938,877	$696,123

Exhibit 8	Alternative Methods of Allocating Corporate Support-Department Costs to Operating Divisions of Computer Horizons: Dual-Rate Method

| Home | Insert | Page Layout | Formulas | Data | Review | View |

	A	B	C	D	E	F	G
20		CORPORATE SUPPORT DEPARTMENTS			OPERATING DIVISIONS		
21	**Allocation Method**	Legal Department	Personnel Department		LTD	WSD	Total
22	**A. DIRECT METHOD**						
23	Fixed costs	$360,000	$475,000				
24	Legal (1,500 ÷ 2,250; 750 ÷ 2,250)	(360,000)			$240,000	$120,000	
25	Personnel (22,500 ÷ 47,500; 25,000 ÷ 47,500)		(475,000)		225,000	250,000	
26	Fixed support dept. cost allocated to operating divisions	$ 0	$ 0		$465,000	$370,000	$835,000
27	Variable costs	$200,000	$600,000				
28	Legal (400 ÷ 1,600; 1,200 ÷ 1,600)	(200,000)			$ 50,000	$150,000	
29	Personnel (26,600 ÷ 38,000; 11,400 ÷ 38,000)		(600,000)		420,000	180,000	
30	Variable support dept. cost allocated to operating divisions	$ 0	$ 0		$470,000	$330,000	$800,000
31	**B. STEP-DOWN METHOD**						
32	(Legal department first)						
33	Fixed costs	$360,000	$475,000				
34	Legal (250 ÷ 2,500; 1,500 ÷ 2,500; 750 ÷ 2,500)	(360,000)	36,000		$216,000	$108,000	
35	Personnel (22,500 ÷ 47,500; 25,000 ÷ 47,500)		(511,000)		242,053	268,947	
36	Fixed support dept. cost allocated to operating divisions	$ 0	$ 0		$458,053	$376,947	$835,000
37	Variable costs	$200,000	$600,000				
38	Legal (400 ÷ 2,000; 400 ÷ 2,000; 1,200 ÷ 2,000)	(200,000)	40,000		$ 40,000	$120,000	
39	Personnel (26,600 ÷ 38,000; 11,400 ÷ 38,000)		(640,000)		448,000	192,000	
40	Variable support dept. cost allocated to operating divisions	$ 0	$ 0		$488,000	$312,000	$800,000
41	**C. RECIPROCAL METHOD**						
42	Fixed costs	$360,000	$475,000				
43	Legal (250 ÷ 2,500; 1,500 ÷ 2,500; 750 ÷ 2,500)	(385,678)[a]	38,568		$231,407	$115,703	
44	Personnel (2,500 ÷ 50,000; 22,500 ÷ 50,000; 25,000 ÷ 50,000)	25,678	(513,568)[a]		231,106	256,784	
45	Fixed support dept. cost allocated to operating divisions	$ 0	$ 0		$462,513	$372,487	$835,000
46	Variable costs	$200,000	$600,000				
47	Legal (400 ÷ 2,000; 400 ÷ 2,000; 1,200 ÷ 2,000)	(232,323)[b]	46,465		$ 46,465	$139,393	
48	Personnel (2,000 ÷ 40,000; 26,600 ÷ 40,000; 11,400 ÷ 40,000)	32,323	(646,465)[b]		429,899	184,243	
49	Variable support dept. cost allocated to operating divisions	$ 0	$ 0		$476,364	$323,636	$800,000
50							
51	[a]FIXED COSTS	[b]VARIABLE COSTS					
52	Letting LF = Legal department fixed costs, and PF = Personnel department fixed costs, the simultaneous equations for the reciprocal method for fixed costs are	Letting LV = Legal department variable costs, and PV = Personnel department variable costs, the simultaneous equations for the reciprocal method for variable costs are					
53	$LF = \$360,000 + 0.05\,PF$	$LV = \$200,000 + 0.05\,PV$					
54	$PF = \$475,000 + 0.10\,LF$	$PV = \$600,000 + 0.20\,LV$					
55	$LF = \$360,000 + 0.05\,(\$475,000 + 0.10\,LF)$	$LV = \$200,000 + 0.05\,(\$600,000 + 0.20\,LV)$					
56	$LF = \$385,678$	$LV = \$232,323$					
57	$PF = \$475,000 + 0.10\,(\$385,678) = \$513,568$	$PV = \$600,000 + 0.20\,(\$232,323) = \$646,465$					

Decision Points

The following question-and-answer format summarizes the chapter's learning objectives. Each decision presents a key question related to a learning objective. The guidelines are the answer to that question.

Decision	Guidelines
1. When should managers use the dual-rate method over the single-rate method?	The single-rate method aggregates fixed and variable costs and allocates them to objects using a single allocation base and rate. Under the dual-rate method, costs are grouped into separate variable cost and fixed cost pools; each pool uses a different cost-allocation base and rate. If costs can be easily separated into variable and fixed costs, managers should use the dual-rate method because it provides better information for making decisions.
2. What factors should managers consider when deciding between allocation based on budgeted and actual rates and between budgeted and actual usage?	Using budgeted rates enables managers of user departments to have certainty about the costs allocated to them and insulates users from inefficiencies in the supplier department. Charging budgeted variable cost rates to users based on actual usage is causally appropriate and promotes control of resource consumption. Charging fixed cost rates on the basis of budgeted usage helps user divisions with planning and leads to goal congruence when considering outsourcing decisions.
3. What methods can managers use to allocate costs of multiple support departments to operating departments?	The three methods managers can use are the direct, the step-down, and the reciprocal methods. The direct method allocates each support department's costs to operating departments without allocating a support department's costs to other support departments. The step-down method allocates support-department costs to other support departments and to operating departments in a sequential manner that partially recognizes the mutual services provided among all support departments. The reciprocal method fully recognizes mutual services provided among all support departments.
4. What methods can managers use to allocate common costs to two or more users?	Common costs are the costs of a cost object (such as operating a facility or performing an activity) that are shared by two or more users. The stand-alone cost-allocation method uses information pertaining to each user of the cost object to determine cost-allocation weights. The incremental cost-allocation method ranks individual users of the cost object and allocates common costs first to the primary user and then to the other incremental users. The Shapley value method considers each user, in turn, as the primary and the incremental user.
5. How can contract disputes over reimbursement amounts based on costs be reduced?	Disputes can be reduced by making the cost-allocation rules as explicit as possible and including them in the contract. These rules should include details such as the allowable cost items, the acceptable cost-allocation bases, and how differences between budgeted and actual costs are to be accounted for.
6. What is product bundling, and how can managers allocate revenues of a bundled product to individual products in the package?	Bundling occurs when a package of two or more products (or services) is sold for a single price. Revenue allocation of the bundled price is required when managers of the individual products in the bundle are evaluated on product revenue or product operating income. Revenues can be allocated for a bundled product using the stand-alone method, the incremental method, or the Shapley value method.

Terms to Learn

This chapter contains definitions of the following important terms:

allowable cost	common cost	Cost Accounting Standards Board
artificial costs	complete reciprocated	(CASB)
bundled product	costs	direct method

dual-rate method	reciprocal method	stand-alone cost-allocation method
incremental cost-allocation method	revenue allocation	stand-alone revenue-allocation method
incremental revenue-allocation method	revenue object	step-down method
matrix method	service department	support department
operating department	single-rate method	
production department	sequential allocation method	

Assignment Material

Questions

1 Distinguish between the single-rate and the dual-rate methods.
2 Describe how the dual-rate method is useful to division managers in decision making.
3 How do budgeted cost rates motivate the support-department manager to improve efficiency?
4 Give examples of allocation bases used to allocate support-department cost pools to operating departments.
5 Why might a manager prefer that budgeted rather than actual cost-allocation rates be used for costs being allocated to his or her department from another department?
6 "To ensure unbiased cost allocations, fixed costs should be allocated on the basis of estimated long-run use by user-department managers." Do you agree? Why?
7 Distinguish among the three methods of allocating the costs of support departments to operating departments.
8 What is conceptually the most defensible method for allocating support-department costs? Why?
9 Distinguish between two methods of allocating common costs.
10 What role does the Cost Accounting Standards Board play when companies contract with the U.S. government?
11 What is one key way to reduce cost-allocation disputes that arise with government contracts?
12 Describe how companies are increasingly facing revenue-allocation decisions.
13 Distinguish between the stand-alone and the incremental revenue-allocation methods.
14 Identify and discuss arguments that individual product managers may put forward to support their preferred revenue-allocation method.
15 How might a dispute over the allocation of revenues of a bundled product be resolved?

Exercises

16 Single-rate versus dual-rate methods, support department. The Detroit power plant that services all manufacturing departments of MidWest Engineering has a budget for the coming year. This budget has been expressed in the following monthly terms:

Manufacturing Department	Needed at Practical Capacity Production Level (Kilowatt-Hours)	Average Expected Monthly Usage (Kilowatt-Hours)
Livonia	16,000	12,000
Warren	22,000	10,000
Dearborn	23,000	8,000
Westland	19,000	10,000
Total	80,000	40,000

The expected monthly costs for operating the power plant during the budget year are $21,600: $4,000 variable and $17,600 fixed.

Required

1. Assume that a single cost pool is used for the power plant costs. What budgeted amounts will be allocated to each manufacturing department if (a) the rate is calculated based on practical capacity and costs are allocated based on practical capacity and (b) the rate is calculated based on expected monthly usage and costs are allocated based on expected monthly usage?
2. Assume the dual-rate method is used with separate cost pools for the variable and fixed costs. Variable costs are allocated on the basis of expected monthly usage. Fixed costs are allocated on the

basis of practical capacity. What budgeted amounts will be allocated to each manufacturing department? Why might you prefer the dual-rate method?

17   Single-rate method, budgeted versus actual costs and quantities. Chocolat Inc. is a producer of premium chocolate based in Palo Alto. The company has a separate division for each of its two products: dark chocolate and milk chocolate. Chocolat purchases ingredients from Wisconsin for its dark chocolate division and from Louisiana for its milk chocolate division. Both locations are the same distance from Chocolat's Palo Alto plant.

Chocolat Inc. operates a fleet of trucks as a cost center that charges the divisions for variable costs (drivers and fuel) and fixed costs (vehicle depreciation, insurance, and registration fees) of operating the fleet. Each division is evaluated on the basis of its operating income. For 2013, the trucking fleet had a practical capacity of 50 round-trips between the Palo Alto plant and the two suppliers. It recorded the following information:

	Home	Insert	Page Layout	Formulas	Data	Review	View
			A			B	C
1						**Budgeted**	**Actual**
2	Costs of truck fleet					$115,000	$96,750
3	Number of round-trips for dark chocolate division (Palo Alto plant—Wisconsin)					30	30
4	Number of round-trips for milk chocolate division (Palo Alto plant—Louisiana)					20	15

Required

1. Using the single-rate method, allocate costs to the dark chocolate division and the milk chocolate division in these three ways.
   a. Calculate the budgeted rate per round-trip and allocate costs based on round-trips budgeted for each division.
   b. Calculate the budgeted rate per round-trip and allocate costs based on actual round-trips used by each division.
   c. Calculate the actual rate per round-trip and allocate costs based on actual round-trips used by each division.
2. Describe the advantages and disadvantages of using each of the three methods in requirement 1. Would you encourage Chocolat Inc. to use one of these methods? Explain and indicate any assumptions you made.

18   Dual-rate method, budgeted versus actual costs and quantities (continuation of 17). Chocolat Inc. decides to examine the effect of using the dual-rate method for allocating truck costs to each round-trip. At the start of 2013, the budgeted costs were as follows:

Variable cost per round-trip	$ 1,350
Fixed costs	$47,500

The actual results for the 45 round-trips made in 2013 were as follows:

Variable costs	$58,500
Fixed costs	38,250
	$96,750

Assume all other information to be the same as in Exercise 17.

Required

1. Using the dual-rate method, what are the costs allocated to the dark chocolate division and the milk chocolate division when (a) variable costs are allocated using the budgeted rate per round-trip and actual round-trips used by each division and when (b) fixed costs are allocated based on the budgeted rate per round-trip and round-trips budgeted for each division?
2. From the viewpoint of the dark chocolate division, what are the effects of using the dual-rate method rather than the single-rate method?

19   Support-department cost allocation; direct and step-down methods. Phoenix Partners provides management consulting services to government and corporate clients. Phoenix has two support departments—administrative services (AS) and information systems (IS)—and two operating departments—government consulting (GOVT) and corporate consulting (CORP). For the first quarter of 2013, Phoenix's cost records indicate the following:

	A	B	C	D	E	F	G
		SUPPORT			OPERATING		
1							
2		AS	IS		GOVT	CORP	Total
3	Budgeted overhead costs before any						
4	interdepartment cost allocations	$600,000	$2,400,000		$8,756,000	$12,452,000	$24,208,000
5	Support work supplied by AS (budgeted head count)	—	25%		40%	35%	100%
6	Support work supplied by IS (budgeted computer time)	10%	—		30%	60%	100%

Required

1. Allocate the two support departments' costs to the two operating departments using the following methods:
   a. Direct method
   b. Step-down method (allocate AS first)
   c. Step-down method (allocate IS first)

2. Compare and explain differences in the support-department costs allocated to each operating department.

3. What approaches might be used to decide the sequence in which to allocate support departments when using the step-down method?

20 Support-department cost allocation, reciprocal method (continuation of 19). Refer to the data given in Exercise 19.

Required

1. Allocate the two support departments' costs to the two operating departments using the reciprocal method. Use (a) linear equations and (b) repeated iterations.

2. Compare and explain differences in requirement 1 with those in requirement 1 of Exercise 19. Which method do you prefer? Why?

21 Direct and step-down allocation. E-books, an online book retailer, has two operating departments—corporate sales and consumer sales—and two support departments—human resources and information systems. Each sales department conducts merchandising and marketing operations independently. E-books uses number of employees to allocate human resources costs and processing time to allocate information systems costs. The following data are available for September 2013:

	A	B	C	D	E	F
1		SUPPORT DEPARTMENTS			OPERATING DEPARTMENTS	
2		Human Resources	Information Systems		Corporate Sales	Consumer Sales
3	Budgeted costs incurred before any					
4	interdepartment cost allocations	$72,700	$234,400		$998,270	$489,860
5	Support work supplied by human resources department					
6	Budgeted number of employees	—	21		42	28
7	Support work supplied by information systems department					
8	Budgeted processing time (in minutes)	320	—		1,920	1,600

Required

1. Allocate the support departments' costs to the operating departments using the direct method.

2. Rank the support departments based on the percentage of their services provided to other support departments. Use this ranking to allocate the support departments' costs to the operating departments based on the step-down method.

3. How could you have ranked the support departments differently?

22 **Reciprocal cost allocation (continuation of 21).** Consider E-books again. The controller of E-books reads a widely used textbook that states that "the reciprocal method is conceptually the most defensible." He seeks your assistance.

1. Describe the key features of the reciprocal method.
2. Allocate the support departments' costs (human resources and information systems) to the two operating departments using the reciprocal method.
3. In the case presented in this exercise, which method (direct, step-down, or reciprocal) would you recommend? Why?

Required

23 **Allocation of common costs.** Evan and Brett are students at Berkeley College. They share an apartment that is owned by Brett. Brett is considering subscribing to an Internet provider that has the following packages available:

Package	Per Month
A. Internet access	$75
B. Phone services	25
C. Internet access + phone services	90

Evan spends most of his time on the Internet ("everything can be found online now"). Brett prefers to spend his time talking on the phone rather than using the Internet ("going online is a waste of time"). They agree that the purchase of the $90 total package is a "win–win" situation.

1. Allocate the $90 between Evan and Brett using (a) the stand-alone cost-allocation method, (b) the incremental cost-allocation method, and (c) the Shapley value method.
2. Which method would you recommend they use and why?

Required

24 **Allocation of common costs.** Barbara Richardson, a self-employed consultant near Sacramento, received an invitation to visit a prospective client in Baltimore. A few days later, she received an invitation to make a presentation to a prospective client in Chicago. She decided to combine her visits, traveling from Sacramento to Baltimore, Baltimore to Chicago, and Chicago to Sacramento.

Richardson received offers for her consulting services from both companies. Upon her return, she decided to accept the engagement in Chicago. She is puzzled over how to allocate her travel costs between the two clients. She has collected the following data for regular round-trip fares with no stopovers:

Sacramento to Baltimore	$900
Sacramento to Chicago	$600

Richardson paid $1,200 for her three-leg flight (Sacramento–Baltimore, Baltimore–Chicago, Chicago–Sacramento). In addition, she paid $30 each way for limousines from her home to Sacramento Airport and back when she returned.

1. How should Richardson allocate the $1,600 airfare between the clients in Baltimore and Chicago using (a) the stand-alone cost-allocation method, (b) the incremental cost-allocation method, and (c) the Shapley value method?
2. Which method would you recommend Richardson use and why?
3. How should Richardson allocate the $60 limousine charges between the clients in Baltimore and Chicago?

Required

25 **Revenue allocation, bundled products.** Essence Company blends and sells designer fragrances. It has a Men's Fragrances Division and a Women's Fragrances Division, each with different sales strategies, distribution channels, and product offerings. Essence is now considering the sale of a bundled product called Sync consisting of one bottle of Him, a men's cologne, and one bottle of Her, a women's perfume. For the most recent year, Essence reported the following:

	A	B
1	**Product**	**Retail Price**
2	Him	$ 25.00
3	Her	$ 50.00
4	Sync (Him and Her)	$ 60.00

Allocation of Support-Department Costs, Common Costs, and Revenues

1. Allocate revenue from the sale of each unit of Sync to Him and Her using the following:
   a. The stand-alone revenue-allocation method based on selling price of each product
   b. The incremental revenue-allocation method, with Him ranked as the primary product
   c. The incremental revenue-allocation method, with Her ranked as the primary product
   d. The Shapley value method, assuming equal unit sales of Him and Her

2. Of the four methods in requirement 1, which one would you recommend for allocating Sync's revenues to Him and Her? Explain.

26 Allocation of common costs. Doug Dandy Auto Sales uses all types of media to advertise its products (television, radio, newspaper, and so on). At the end of 2013, the company president, Doug Davenport, decided that all advertising costs would be incurred by corporate headquarters and allocated to each of the company's four sales locations based on number of vehicles sold. Doug was confident that his corporate purchasing manager could negotiate better advertising contracts on a corporate-wide basis than each of the sales managers could on their own. Davenport budgeted total advertising cost for 2014 to be $1.7 million. He introduced the new plan to his sales managers just before the New Year.

The manager of the east sales location, Mike Samson, was not happy. He complained that the new allocation method was unfair and would increase his advertising costs significantly over the prior year. The east location sold high volumes of low-priced used cars and most of the corporate advertising budget was related to new car sales.

Following Mike's complaint, Doug decided to take another hard look at what each of the divisions was paying for advertising before the new allocation plan. The results were as follows:

Sales Location	Actual Number of Cars Sold in 2013	Actual Advertising Cost Incurred in 2013
East	4,620	$ 261,600
West	1,120	392,400
North	3,220	697,600
South	5,040	828,400
	14,000	$2,180,000

1. Using 2013 data as the cost bases, show the amount of the 2014 advertising cost ($1,700,000) that would be allocated to each of the divisions under the following criteria:
   a. Davenport's allocation method based on number of cars sold
   b. The stand-alone method
   c. The incremental-allocation method, with divisions ranked on the basis of dollars spent on advertising in 2013

2. Which method do you think is most equitable to the divisional sales managers? What other options might President Doug Davenport have for allocating the advertising costs?

MyAccountingLab Problems

27 Single-rate, dual-rate, and practical capacity allocation. Preston Department Store has a new promotional program that offers a free gift-wrapping service for its customers. Preston's customer-service department has practical capacity to wrap 5,000 gifts at a budgeted fixed cost of $4,950 each month. The budgeted variable cost to gift-wrap an item is $0.35. During the most recent month, the department budgeted to wrap 4,500 gifts. Although the service is free to customers, a gift-wrapping service cost allocation is made to the department where the item was purchased. The customer-service department reported the following for the most recent month:

	A	B	C
	Department	Budgeted Items Wrapped	Actual Items Wrapped
1			
2	Giftware	1,000	1,200
3	Women's Apparel	850	650
4	Fragrances	1,000	900
5	Men's Apparel	750	450
6	Domestics	900	800
7	Total	4,500	4,000

1. Using the single-rate method, allocate gift-wrapping costs to different departments in these three ways:

   a. Calculate the budgeted rate based on the budgeted number of gifts to be wrapped and allocate costs based on the budgeted use (of gift-wrapping services).

   b. Calculate the budgeted rate based on the budgeted number of gifts to be wrapped and allocate costs based on actual usage.

   c. Calculate the budgeted rate based on the practical gift-wrapping capacity available and allocate costs based on actual usage.

2. Using the dual-rate method, compute the amount allocated to each department when (a) the fixed-cost rate is calculated using budgeted costs and the practical gift-wrapping capacity, (b) fixed costs are allocated based on budgeted usage of gift-wrapping services, and (c) variable costs are allocated using the budgeted variable-cost rate and actual usage.

3. Comment on your results in requirements 1 and 2. Discuss the advantages of the dual-rate method.

28   Revenue allocation. Yang Inc. produces and sells DVDs to business people and students who are planning extended stays in China. It has been very successful with two DVDs: Beginning Mandarin and Conversational Mandarin. It is introducing a third DVD, Reading Chinese Characters. It has decided to market its new DVD in two different packages grouping the Reading Chinese Characters DVD with each of the other two language DVDs. Information about the separate DVDs and the packages follow.

DVD	Selling Price
Beginning Mandarin (BegM)	$ 72
Conversational Mandarin (ConM)	$112
Reading Chinese Characters (RCC)	$ 48
BegM + RCC	$100
ConM + RCC	$140

1. Using the selling prices, allocate revenues from the BegM + RCC package to each DVD in that package using (a) the stand-alone method; (b) the incremental method, in either order; and (c) the Shapley value method.

2. Using the selling prices, allocate revenues from the ConM + RCC package to each DVD in that package using (a) the stand-alone method; (b) the incremental method, in either order; and (c) the Shapley value method.

3. Which method is most appropriate for allocating revenues among the DVDs? Why?

29   Fixed-cost allocation. Baker University completed construction of its newest administrative building at the end of 2013. The University's first employees moved into the building on January 1, 2014. The building consists of office space, common meeting rooms (including a conference center), a cafeteria, and even a workout room for its exercise enthusiasts. The total 2014 building space of 250,000 square feet was utilized as follows:

Usage of Space	% of Total Building Space
Office space (occupied)	52%
Vacant office space	8%
Common meeting space	25%
Workout room	5%
Cafeteria	10%

The new building cost the university $60 million and was depreciated using the straight-line method over 20 years. At the end of 2014 three departments occupied the building: executive offices of the president, accounting, and human resources. Each department's usage of its assigned space was as follows:

Department	Actual Office Space Used (sq. ft.)	Planned Office Space Used (sq. ft.)	Practical Capacity Office Space (sq. ft.)
Executive	32,500	24,800	36,000
Accounting	52,000	52,080	66,000
Human resources	45,500	47,120	48,000

1. How much of the total building cost will be allocated in 2014 to each of the departments, if the total cost is allocated to each department on the basis of the following?
   a. Actual usage of the three departments
   b. Planned usage of the three departments
   c. Practical capacity of the three departments

2. Assume that Baker University allocates the total annual building cost in the following manner:
   a. All vacant office space is absorbed by the university and is not allocated to the departments.
   b. All occupied office space costs are allocated on the basis of actual square footage used.
   c. All common area costs are allocated on the basis of a department's practical capacity.
   Calculate the cost allocated to each department in 2014 under this plan. Do you think the allocation method used here is appropriate? Explain.

30   Allocating costs of support departments; step-down and direct methods. The Central Valley Company has prepared department overhead budgets for budgeted-volume levels before allocations as follows:

Support departments:		
Building and grounds	$45,000	
Personnel	300	
General plant administration	37,320	
Cafeteria: operating loss	970	
Storeroom	9,990	$ 93,580
Operating departments:		
Machining	$36,600	
Assembly	46,000	82,600
Total for support and operating departments		$176,180

Management has decided that the most appropriate inventory costs are achieved by using individual-department overhead rates. These rates are developed after support-department costs are allocated to operating departments.

Bases for allocation are to be selected from the following:

Department	Direct Manufacturing Labor-Hours	Number of Employees	Square Feet of Floor Space Occupied	Manufacturing Labor-Hours	Number of Requisitions
Building and grounds	0	0	0	0	0
Personnel[a]	0	0	2,500	0	0
General plant administration	0	40	12,000	0	0
Cafeteria: operating loss	0	10	5,000	3,000	0
Storeroom	0	5	6,000	2,000	0
Machining	8,000	55	22,000	13,000	6,000
Assembly	32,000	140	202,500	26,000	4,000
Total	40,000	250	250,000	44,000	10,000

[a]Basis used is number of employees.

1. Using the step-down method, allocate support-department costs. Develop overhead rates per direct manufacturing labor-hour for machining and assembly. Allocate the costs of the support departments in the order given in this problem. Use the allocation base for each support department you think is most appropriate.
2. Using the direct method, rework requirement 1.
3. Based on the following information about two jobs, determine the total overhead costs for each job by using rates developed in (a) requirement 1 and (b) requirement 2.

	Direct Manufacturing Labor-Hours	
	Machining	**Assembly**
Job 88	17	7
Job 89	9	20

4. The company evaluates the performance of the operating department managers on the basis of how well they managed their total costs, including allocated costs. As the manager of the Machining Department, which allocation method would you prefer from the results obtained in requirements 1 and 2? Explain.

31 **Support-department cost allocations; single-department cost pools; direct, step-down, and reciprocal methods.** The Milton Company has two products. Product 1 is manufactured entirely in department X. Product 2 is manufactured entirely in department Y. To produce these two products, the Milton Company has two support departments: A (a materials-handling department) and B (a power-generating department).

An analysis of the work done by departments A and B in a typical period follows:

| Supplied by | Used by | | | |
	A	B	X	Y
A	—	200	500	300
B	750	—	125	375

The work done in department A is measured by the direct labor-hours of materials-handling time. The work done in department B is measured by the kilowatt-hours of power. The budgeted costs of the support departments for the coming year are as follows:

	Department A (Materials Handling)	Department B (Power Generation)
Variable indirect labor and indirect materials costs	$150,000	$15,000
Supervision	45,000	25,000
Depreciation	15,000	50,000
	$210,000	$90,000
	+Power costs	+Materials-handling costs

The budgeted costs of the operating departments for the coming year are $1,250,000 for department X and $950,000 for department Y.

Supervision costs are salary costs. Depreciation in department B is the straight-line depreciation of power-generation equipment in its 19th year of an estimated 25-year useful life; it is old, but well-maintained, equipment.

1. What are the allocations of costs of support departments A and B to operating departments X and Y using (a) the direct method, (b) the step-down method (allocate department A first), (c) the step-down method (allocate department B first), and (d) the reciprocal method?

2. An outside company has offered to supply all the power needed by the Milton Company and to provide all the services of the present power department. The cost of this service will be $80 per kilowatt-hour of power. Should Milton accept? Explain.

Required

32 **Common costs.** Taylor Inc. and Victor Inc. are two small clothing companies that are considering leasing a dyeing machine together. The companies estimated that in order to meet production, Taylor needs the machine for 600 hours and Victor needs it for 400 hours. If each company rents the machine on its own, the fee will be $60 per hour of usage. If they rent the machine together, the fee will decrease to $54 per hour of usage.

1. Calculate Taylor's and Victor's respective share of fees under the stand-alone cost-allocation method.
2. Calculate Taylor's and Victor's respective share of fees using the incremental cost-allocation method. Assume Taylor to be the primary party.
3. Calculate Taylor's and Victor's respective share of fees using the Shapley value method.
4. Which method would you recommend Taylor and Victor use to share the fees?

Required

33 **Stand-alone revenue allocation.** Office Magic, Inc., sells computer hardware to end consumers. Its most popular model, the CX30 is sold as a "bundle," which includes three hardware products: a personal computer (PC) tower, a 26-inch monitor, and a color laser printer. Each of these products is made in a separate manufacturing division of Office Magic and can be purchased individually as well as in a bundle. The individual selling prices and per unit costs are as follows:

Computer Component	Individual Selling Price per Unit	Cost per Unit
PC tower	$1,140	$376
Monitor	$ 260	$200
Color laser printer	$ 600	$224
Computer bundle purchase price	$1,500	

Required

1. Allocate the revenue from the computer bundle purchase to each of the hardware products using the stand-alone method based on the individual selling price per unit.
2. Allocate the revenue from the computer bundle purchase to each of the hardware products using the stand-alone method based on cost per unit.
3. Allocate the revenue from the computer bundle purchase to each of the hardware products using the stand-alone method based on physical units (that is, the number of individual units of product sold per bundle).
4. Which basis of allocation makes the most sense in this situation? Explain your answer.

34 Support-department cost allocations; single-department cost pools; direct, step-down, and reciprocal methods. Sportz, Inc., manufactures athletic shoes and athletic clothing for both amateur and professional athletes. The company has two product lines (clothing and shoes), which are produced in separate manufacturing facilities; however, both manufacturing facilities share the same support services for information technology and human resources. The following shows total costs for each manufacturing facility and for each support department.

	Variable Costs	Fixed Costs	Total Costs by Department (in thousands)
Information technology (IT)	$ 600	$ 2,000	$ 2,600
Human resources (HR)	$ 400	$ 1,000	$ 1,400
Clothing	$2,500	$ 8,000	$10,500
Shoes	$3,000	$ 4,500	$ 7,500
Total costs	$6,500	$15,500	$22,000

The total costs of the support departments (IT and HR) are allocated to the production departments (clothing and shoes) using a single rate based on the following:

Information technology: Number of IT labor-hours worked by department
Human resources: Number of employees supported by department

Data on the bases, by department, are given as follows:

Department	IT Hours Used	Number of Employees
Clothing	5,040	220
Shoes	3,960	88
Information technology	—	92
Human resources	3,000	—

Required

1. What are the total costs of the production departments (clothing and shoes) *after* the support department costs of information technology and human resources have been allocated using (a) the direct method, (b) the step-down method (allocate information technology first), (c) the step-down method (allocate human resources first), and (d) the reciprocal method?
2. Assume that all of the work of the IT department could be outsourced to an independent company for $97.50 per hour. If Sportz no longer operated its own IT department, 30% of the fixed costs of the IT department could be eliminated. Should Sportz outsource its IT services?

35 Revenue allocation, bundled products. Premier Resorts (PR) operates a five-star hotel with a championship golf course. PR has a decentralized management structure, with three divisions:

Required

▪ Lodging (rooms, conference facilities)

▪ Food (restaurants and in-room service)

▪ Recreation (golf course, tennis courts, swimming pool, and so on)

Starting next month, PR will offer a two-day, two-person "getaway package" for $800. This deal includes the following:

	As Priced Separately
Two nights' stay for two in an ocean-view room	$ 640 ($320 per night)
Two rounds of golf (can be used by either guest)	$ 300 ($150 per round)
Candlelight dinner for two at PR's finest restaurant	$ 160 ($80 per person)
Total package value	$1,100

Jenny Lee, president of the recreation division, recently asked the CEO of PR how her division would share in the $800 revenue from the getaway package. The golf course was operating at 100% capacity. Currently, anyone booking the package was guaranteed access to the golf course. Lee noted that every "getaway" booking would displace $300 of other golf bookings not related to the package. She emphasized that the high demand reflected the devotion of her team to keeping the golf course rated one of the "Best 10 Courses in the World" by *Golf Monthly*. As an aside, she also noted that the lodging and food divisions had to turn away customers during only "peak-season events such as the New Year's period."

Required

1. Using selling prices, allocate the $800 getaway-package revenue to the three divisions using:
   a. The stand-alone revenue-allocation method
   b. The incremental revenue-allocation method (with recreation first, then lodging, and then food)

2. What are the pros and cons of the two methods in requirement 1?

3. Because the recreation division is able to book the golf course at 100% capacity, the company CEO has decided to revise the getaway package to only include the lodging and food offerings shown previously. The new package will sell for $720. Allocate the revenue to the lodging and food divisions using the following:
   a. The Shapley value method
   b. The weighted Shapley value method, assuming that lodging is three times as likely to sell as the food

36 Support-department cost allocations; direct, step-down, and reciprocal methods. Montclair Tours provides guided educational tours to college alumni associations. The company is divided into two operating divisions: domestic tours and world tours. Each of the tour divisions uses the services of the company's two support departments: Administration and Information Technology. Additionally, the Administration and Information Technology departments use the services of each other. Data concerning the past year are as follows:

	Support Departments		Operating Departments		
	Administration	Information Technology	Domestic Tours	World Tours	Total
Budgeted overhead costs before any interdepartment cost allocations	$400,000	$250,000	$1,300,000	$1,840,000	$3,790,0000
Support work furnished: by Administration					
Budgeted administration salaries	—	$ 88,000	$ 55,000	$ 77,000	$ 220,000
Percentage	—	40%	25%	35%	100%
by Information Technology					
Budgeted IT service hours	600	—	2,200	1,200	4,000
Percentage	15%	—	55%	30%	100%

Required

1. What are the total overhead costs of the operating departments (domestic and world tours) *after* the support department costs of Administration and Information Technology have been allocated using (a) the direct method, (b) the step-down method (allocate Administration first), (c) the step-down method (allocate Information Technology first), and (d) the reciprocal method?

2. Which method would you recommend that Montclair Tours use to allocate service department costs? Why?

Glossary

Allowable cost. Cost that the contract parties agree to include in the costs to be reimbursed.

Artificial costs. See *complete reciprocated costs*.

Bundled product. A package of two or more products (or services) that is sold for a single price, but whose individual components may be sold as separate items at their own "stand-alone" prices.

Common cost. Cost of operating a facility, activity, or like cost object that is shared by two or more users.

Complete reciprocated costs. The support department's own costs plus any interdepartmental cost allocations. Also called the *artificial costs* of the support department.

Cost Accounting Standards Board (CASB). Government agency that has the exclusive authority to make, put into effect, amend, and rescind cost accounting standards and interpretations thereof designed to achieve uniformity and consistency in regard to measurement, assignment, and allocation of costs to government contracts within the United States.

Direct method. Cost allocation method that allocates each support department's costs to operating departments only.

Dual-rate method. Allocation method that classifies costs in each cost pool into two pools (a variable-cost pool and a fixed-cost pool) with each pool using a different cost-allocation base.

Incremental cost-allocation method. Method that ranks the individual users of a cost object in the order of users most responsible for the common cost and then uses this ranking to allocate cost among those users.

Incremental revenue-allocation method. Method that ranks individual products in a bundle according to criteria determined by management (for example, sales), and then uses this ranking to allocate bundled revenues to the individual products.

Matrix method. See *reciprocal method*.

Operating department. Department that directly adds value to a product or service. Also called a *production department* in manufacturing companies.

Production department. See *operating department*.

Reciprocal method. Cost allocation method that fully recognizes the mutual services provided among all support departments. Also called *matrix method*.

Revenue allocation. The allocation of revenues that are related to a particular revenue object but cannot be traced to it in an economically feasible (cost-effective) way.

Revenue object. Anything for which a separate measurement of revenue is desired.

Sequential allocation method. See *step-down method*.

Service department. See *support department*.

Single-rate method. Allocation method that allocates costs in each cost pool to cost objects using the same rate per unit of a single allocation base.

Stand-alone cost-allocation method. Method that uses information pertaining to each user of a cost object as a separate entity to determine the cost-allocation weights.

Stand-alone revenue-allocation method. Method that uses product-specific information on the products in the bundle as weights for allocating the bundled revenues to the individual products.

Step-down method. Cost allocation method that partially recognizes the mutual services provided among all support departments. Also called *sequential allocation method*.

Support department. Department that provides the services that assist other internal departments (operating departments and other support departments) in the company. Also called a *service department*.

Photo Credits

Credits are listed in order of appearance.

Cost Allocation: Joint Products and Byproducts

From Chapter 16 of *Cost Accounting: A Managerial Emphasis*, Fifteenth Edition. Charles T. Horngren, Srikant M. Datar, Madhav V. Rajan. Copyright © 2015 by Pearson Education, Inc. All rights reserved.

Cost Allocation: Joint Products and Byproducts

Learning Objectives

1 Identify the splitoff point in a joint-cost situation and distinguish joint products from byproducts

2 Explain why joint costs are allocated to individual products

3 Allocate joint costs using four methods

4 Identify situations when the sales value at splitoff method is preferred when allocating joint costs

5 Explain why joint costs are irrelevant in a sell-or-process-further decision

6 Account for byproducts using two methods

Many companies, such as petroleum refiners, produce and sell two or more products simultaneously.

For example, ExxonMobil sells petroleum, natural gas, and raw liquefied petroleum gas (LPG), which are produced when the company extracts crude oil and refines it. Similarly, some companies, such as health care providers, sell or provide multiple services. The question is, "How should these companies allocate costs to 'joint' products and services?" Knowing how to allocate joint product costs isn't something that only companies need to understand. It's something that farmers have to deal with, too, especially when it comes to the lucrative production of corn to make billions of gallons of ethanol fuel.

Joint Cost Allocation and the Production of Ethanol Fuel[1]

The increased global demand for oil has driven prices higher and forced countries to look for environmentally sustainable alternatives. In the United States, the largest source of alternative fuel comes from corn-based ethanol. In 2012, the U.S. produced 13.8 billion gallons of ethanol, up from 1.7 billion gallons per year in 2001. Producing ethanol requires a significant amount of corn. Forty percent of U.S. domestic corn production is used to create ethanol fuel, but not all of that corn winds up in the ethanol that gets blended into gasoline and sold at service stations.

Most biotechnology operations, such as making ethanol, produce two or more products. While distilling corn into ethanol, cell mass from the process—such as antibiotic and yeast fermentations—separates from the liquid and becomes a distinct product, which is often sold as animal feed. This separation point, where outputs become distinctly identifiable, is called the splitoff point. Similarly, the residues from corn processing plants create secondary products including distillers' dried grains and gluten.

Accountants refer to these secondary products as byproducts. Ethanol byproducts like animal feed and gluten are accounted for by deducting the income

---

[1] *Sources:* Hacking, Andrew. 1987. Economic aspects of biotechnology. Cambridge, United Kingdom: Cambridge University Press; Leber, Jessica. 2010. Economics improve for first commercial cellulosic ethanol plants. *New York Times*, February 16; PBS. 2006. Glut of ethanol byproducts coming. *The Environmental Report*, Spring; United States Department of Energy 2013. U.S. ethanol production and the renewable fuel standard RIN bank. Press Release, June 5; Meyer, Gregory. 2013. US ethanol lobby urges brake on biofuels. *Financial Times*, April 18.

from selling these products from the cost of ethanol fuel, the major product. Because the price of ethanol is about $2 per gallon, whereas the byproducts sell for just a few cents per pound, most of the costs of production are allocated to the ethanol fuel itself, the main product. Because ethanol producers would otherwise have to pay to dispose of the byproducts, the relatively small amount of revenue earned from them just helps the firms "break even" on their production.

In the coming years, however, this may change. With ethanol production growing, corn-based animal feed byproducts are becoming more plentiful. Some ethanol manufacturers are working together to create a market for ethanol feed, which is cheaper and higher in protein than plain corn. This allows ranchers' animals to gain weight faster and at a lower cost per pound.

This chapter examines methods for allocating costs to joint products. We also examine how cost numbers appropriate for one purpose, such as external reporting, may not be appropriate for other purposes, such as decisions about the further processing of joint products.

Joint-Cost Basics

Joint costs are the costs of a production process that yields multiple products simultaneously. Consider the distillation of coal, which yields coke, natural gas, and other products. The costs of this distillation are joint costs. The **splitoff point** is the juncture in a joint production process when two or more products become separately identifiable. An example is the point at which coal becomes coke, natural gas, and other products. **Separable costs** are all costs—manufacturing, marketing, distribution, and so on—incurred beyond the splitoff point that are assignable to each of the specific products identified at the splitoff point. At or beyond the splitoff point, decisions relating to the sale or further processing of each identifiable product can be made independently of decisions about the other products.

As the examples in Exhibit 1 show, the production processes in many industries simultaneously yield two or more products, either at the splitoff point or after further processing. In each of these examples, no individual product can be produced without the accompanying products appearing, although in some cases the proportions can be varied. Joint costing allocates the joint costs to the individual products that are eventually sold.

The outputs of a joint production process can be classified into two general categories: outputs with a positive sales value and outputs with a zero sales value.[2] For example, offshore processing of hydrocarbons yields oil and natural gas, which have positive sales value; the processing also yields water, which has zero sales value and is

Learning Objective 1

Identify the splitoff point in a joint-cost situation

...the point at which two or more products become separately identifiable

and distinguish joint products

...products with high sales values

from byproducts

...products with low sales values

---

[2] Some outputs of a joint production process have "negative" revenue when their disposal costs (such as the costs of handling nonsalable toxic substances that require special disposal procedures) are considered. These disposal costs should be added to the joint production costs that are allocated to joint or main products.

| **Exhibit 1** | Examples of Joint-Cost Situations |

Industry	Separable Products at the Splitoff Point
Agriculture and Food Processing Industries	
Cocoa beans	Cocoa butter, cocoa powder, cocoa drink mix, tanning cream
Lambs	Lamb cuts, tripe, hides, bones, fat
Hogs	Bacon, ham, spare ribs, pork roast
Raw milk	Cream, liquid skim
Lumber	Lumber of varying grades and shapes
Turkeys	Breast, wings, thighs, drumsticks, digest, feather meal, poultry meal
Extractive Industries	
Coal	Coke, gas, benzol, tar, ammonia
Copper ore	Copper, silver, lead, zinc
Petroleum	Crude oil, natural gas
Salt	Hydrogen, chlorine, caustic soda
Chemical Industries	
Raw LPG (liquefied petroleum gas)	Butane, ethane, propane
Crude oil	Gasoline, kerosene, benzene, naphtha
Semiconductor Industry	
Fabrication of silicon-wafer chips	Memory chips of different quality (as to capacity), speed, life expectancy, and temperature tolerance

recycled back into the ocean. The term **product** describes any output that has a positive total sales value (or an output that enables a company to avoid incurring costs, such as an intermediate chemical product used as input in another process). The total sales value can be high or low.

When a joint production process yields one product with a high total sales value, compared with the total sales values of other products of the process, that product is called a **main product.** When a joint production process yields two or more products with high total sales values relative to the total sales values of other products, those products are called **joint products.** In contrast, products of a joint production process that have low total sales values relative to the total sales value of the main product or of joint products are called **byproducts.**

Consider some examples. If timber (logs) is processed into standard lumber and wood chips, standard lumber is a main product and wood chips are the byproduct because standard lumber has a high total sales value compared with wood chips. If, however, the logs are processed into fine-grade lumber, standard lumber, and wood chips, fine-grade lumber and standard lumber are joint products and wood chips are the byproduct. That's because both fine-grade lumber and standard lumber have high total sales values relative to wood chips.

Decision Point ▶

What do the terms joint cost and splitoff point mean, and how do joint products differ from byproducts?

Distinctions among main products, joint products, and byproducts are not so clear-cut in practice. Companies use different thresholds for determining whether the relative sales value of a product is high enough for it to be considered a joint product. Consider kerosene, obtained when refining crude oil. Based on a comparison of its sales value to the total sales values of gasoline and other products, some companies classify kerosene as a joint product whereas others classify it as a byproduct. Moreover, the classification of products—main, joint, or byproduct—can change over time, especially for products such as lower-grade semiconductor chips, whose market prices may increase or decrease by 30% or more in a year. When prices of lower-grade chips are high, they are considered joint products together with higher-grade chips; when prices of lower-grade chips fall considerably, they are considered byproducts. In practice, it is important to understand how a specific company chooses to classify its products.

Allocating Joint Costs

Before a manager is able to allocate joint costs, she must first look at the context for doing so. Joint costs must be allocated to individual products or services for several purposes, including the following:

- Computing inventoriable costs and the cost of goods sold for external and internal reporting purposes. Absorption costing is required for financial accounting and tax reporting. This necessitates the allocation of joint manufacturing or processing costs to products for calculating ending inventory values. In addition, many firms use internal accounting data based on joint cost allocations to analyze the profitability of their various divisions and evaluate the performance of division managers.

- Reimbursing companies that have some, but not all, of their products or services reimbursed under cost-plus contracts with, say, a government agency. For example, the joint costs incurred when multiple organs are removed from a single donor must be allocated to various organ centers in order to determine reimbursement rates for transplants into Medicare patients. In such cases, stringent rules typically specify the way in which joint costs are assigned to the products or services covered by the agreements. That said, fraud in defense contracting, which is often done via cost-plus contracts, remains one of the most active areas of false claim litigation under the Federal False Claims Act. A common practice is "cross-charging," where a contractor shifts joint costs from "fixed-price" defense contracts to those that are done on a cost-plus basis. Defense contractors have also attempted to secure contracts from private businesses or foreign governments by allocating an improper share of joint costs onto the cost-plus agreements they have with the U.S. government.[3]

- Regulating the rates or prices of one or more of the jointly produced products or services. This issue is critical in the extractive and energy industries, in which output prices are regulated to yield a fixed return on a cost basis that includes joint cost allocations. In telecommunications, a firm with significant market power has some products subject to price regulation (e.g., interconnection) and other activities that are unregulated (such as equipment rentals to end-users). In this case, joint costs must be allocated to ensure that costs are not transferred from unregulated services to regulated ones.

- For any commercial litigation or insurance settlement situation in which the costs of joint products or services are key inputs.

Concepts in Action: Are Charitable Organizations Allocating Joint Costs in a Misleading Way? outlines another scenario in which joint cost allocations are important and have also been the subject of some controversy.

Approaches to Allocating Joint Costs

Two approaches are used to allocate joint costs.

- **Approach 1.** Allocate joint costs using *market-based* data such as revenues. This chapter illustrates three methods that use this approach:
  1. Sales value at splitoff method
  2. Net realizable value (NRV) method
  3. Constant gross-margin percentage NRV method
- **Approach 2.** Allocate joint costs using *physical measures*, such as the weight, quantity (physical units), or volume of the joint products.

We can use the cause-and-effect and benefits-received criteria for guiding cost-allocation decisions. Joint costs do not have a cause-and-effect relationship with individual products because the production process simultaneously yields multiple products. Using the benefits-received criterion leads to a preference for

---

[3] See, for example, www.dodig.mil/iginformation/IGInformationReleases/3eSettlementPR.pdf.

Concepts in Action

Are Charitable Organizations Allocating Joint Costs in a Misleading Way?

Whether seeking to help children or eradicate disease, charities raise money from philanthropic donors to fulfill their public-interest missions. In the United States, charities that use direct mailings or other activities that combine a public education effort with fundraising appeals must allocate the joint costs related to these activities to programs, fundraising, and administration. Some critics say that joint-cost allocation can be used to mislead donors by disguising high fundraising costs and over-reporting funds used for an organization's mission.

According to the Financial Accounting Standards Board, charities are supposed to allocate joint costs only in certain circumstances. They must design the activity to get people to take a specific action to support their mission—for example, contact a public official, recycle waste, or reduce health risks. Additionally, they must select recipients because they are able to take that action or would benefit from it—not because they are likely donors. The main accounting issue is the following: for mailings, which are common for charities, to which category should the joint costs of the envelope and postage (usually the largest component of the total cost of the activity) be charged?

The American Heart Association, for example, allocated $227.5 million out of total spending of almost $596 million to joint costs and spent 78% on programs according to its 2012 tax form. If joint costs were discounted, program spending falls to 51%.

Many charities believe that joint costs, if used appropriately, reward efficiency because a charity can combine multiple goals in a single campaign and reflect that in its breakdown of costs. Others argue that joint costs allow charities to overstate the program portion of its work, thus misleading donors into believing that more is being done for the public than is really the case. With nonprofit watchdogs, including Charity Navigator and the Better Business Bureau, looking closely at the practices of U.S. charities, joint costs will likely remain in the nonprofit spotlight.

Source: Christopher Jones and Andrea Roberts, "Management of Financial Information in Charitable Organizations: The Case of Joint-Cost Allocations," *The Accounting Review* 81(1) (January 2006); Suzanne Perry, "Watchdog Cracks Down on Misleading Statements on Fundraising Costs," *The Chronicle of Philanthropy* (February 10, 2013); "Watchdog Barks Louder on Cost Allocation Issues," *The NonProfit Times* (October 1, 2012).

methods under approach 1 because revenues are, in general, a better indicator of benefits received than physical measures. Mining companies, for example, receive more benefit from 1 ton of gold than they do from 10 tons of coal.

In the simplest joint production process, the joint products are sold at the splitoff point without further processing. Example 1 illustrates the two methods that apply in this case: the sales value at splitoff method and the physical-measure method. Then we introduce joint production processes that yield products that require further processing beyond the splitoff point. Example 2 illustrates the NRV method and the constant-gross margin percentage NRV method. To help you focus on key concepts, we use numbers and amounts that are smaller than the numbers that are typically found in practice.

The exhibits in this chapter use the following symbols to distinguish a joint or main product from a byproduct:

Joint Product or Main Product   Byproduct

To compare the methods, we report gross-margin percentages for individual products under each method.

> Example 1: Farmland Dairy purchases raw milk from individual farms and processes it until the splitoff point, when two products—cream and liquid skim—emerge. These two products are sold to an independent company, which markets and distributes them to supermarkets and other retail outlets.
>
> In May 2014, Farmland Dairy processes 110,000 gallons of raw milk. During processing, 10,000 gallons are lost due to evaporation and spillage, yielding 25,000 gallons of cream and 75,000 gallons of liquid skim. The data are summarized as follows:

	A	B	C
1		**Joint Costs**	
2	Joint costs (costs of 110,000 gallons raw milk and processing to splitoff point)	$400,000	
3			
4		**Cream**	**Liquid Skim**
5	Beginning inventory (gallons)	0	0
6	Production (gallons)	25,000	75,000
7	Sales (gallons)	20,000	30,000
8	Ending inventory (gallons)	5,000	45,000
9	Selling price per gallon	$ 8	$ 4

Exhibit 2 depicts the basic relationships in this example.

How much of the $400,000 joint costs should be allocated to the cost of goods sold of 20,000 gallons of cream and 30,000 gallons of liquid skim, and how much should be allocated to the ending inventory of 5,000 gallons of cream and 45,000 gallons of liquid skim? We begin by illustrating the two methods that use the properties of the products at the splitoff point: the sales value at splitoff method and the physical-measure method.

Sales Value at Splitoff Method

The **sales value at splitoff method** allocates joint costs to joint products produced during the accounting period on the basis of the relative total sales value at the splitoff point.

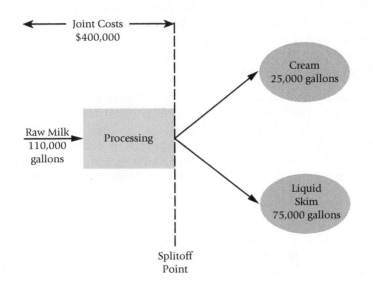

Exhibit 2

Example 1: Overview of Farmland Dairy

Exhibit 3	Joint-Cost Allocation and Product-Line Income Statement Using Sales Value at Splitoff Method: Farmland Dairy for May 2014

	A	B	C	D
		Cream	Liquid Skim	Total
1	PANEL A: Allocation of Joint Costs Using Sales Value at Splitoff Method	Cream	Liquid Skim	Total
2	Sales value of total production at splitoff point			
3	(25,000 gallons × $8 per gallon; 75,000 gallons × $4 per gallon)	$200,000	$300,000	$500,000
4	Weighting ($200,000 ÷ $500,000; $300,000 ÷ 500,000)	0.40	0.60	
5	Joint costs allocated (0.40 × $400,000; 0.60 × $400,000)	$160,000	$240,000	$400,000
6	Joint production cost per gallon			
7	($160,000 ÷ 25,000 gallons; $240,000 ÷ 75,000 gallons)	$ 6.40	$ 3.20	
8				
9	PANEL B: Product-Line Income Statement Using Sales Value at Splitoff Method for May 2014	Cream	Liquid Skim	Total
10	Revenues (20,000 gallons × $8 per gallon; 30,000 gallons × $4 per gallon)	$160,000	$120,000	$280,000
11	Cost of goods sold (joint costs)			
12	Production costs (0.40 × $400,000; 0.60 × $400,000)	160,000	240,000	400,000
13	Deduct ending inventory (5,000 gallons × $6.40 per gallon; 45,000 gallons × $3.20 per gallon)	32,000	144,000	176,000
14	Cost of goods sold (joint costs)	128,000	96,000	224,000
15	Gross margin	$ 32,000	$ 24,000	$ 56,000
16	Gross margin percentage ($32,000 ÷ $160,000; $24,000 ÷ $120,000; $56,000 ÷ $280,000)	20%	20%	20%

Using this method for Example 1, Exhibit 3, Panel A, shows how joint costs are allocated to individual products to calculate the cost per gallon of cream and liquid skim for valuing ending inventory. This method uses the sales value of the *entire production of the accounting period* (25,000 gallons of cream and 75,000 gallons of liquid skim), not just the quantity sold (20,000 gallons of cream and 30,000 gallons of liquid skim). The reason this method does not rely solely on the quantity sold is that the joint costs were incurred on all units produced, not just the portion sold during the current period. Exhibit 3, Panel B, presents the product-line income statement using the sales value at splitoff method. Note that the gross-margin percentage for each product is 20% because the sales value at splitoff method allocates joint costs to each product in proportion to the sales value of total production (cream: $160,000 ÷ $200,000 = 80%; liquid skim: $240,000 ÷ $300,000 = 80%). Therefore, the gross-margin percentage for each product manufactured in May 2014 is the same: 20%.[4]

Note how the sales value at splitoff method follows the benefits-received criterion of cost allocation: Costs are allocated to products in proportion to their revenue-generating power (their expected revenues). The cost-allocation base (total sales value at splitoff) is expressed in terms of a common denominator (the amount of revenues) that is systematically recorded in the accounting system. To use this method, selling prices must exist for all products at the splitoff point.

Physical-Measure Method

The **physical-measure method** allocates joint costs to joint products produced during the accounting period on the basis of a *comparable* physical measure, such as the relative weight, quantity, or volume at the splitoff point. In Example 1, the $400,000 joint costs produced 25,000 gallons of cream and 75,000 gallons of liquid skim. Using the number of gallons produced as the physical measure, Exhibit 4, Panel A, shows how joint costs are allocated to individual products to calculate the cost per gallon of cream and liquid skim.

---

[4] Suppose Farmland Dairy has beginning inventory of cream and liquid milk in May 2014 and when this inventory is sold, Farmland earns a gross margin different from 20%. Then the gross-margin percentage for cream and liquid skim will not be the same. The relative gross-margin percentages will depend on how much of the sales of each product came from beginning inventory and how much came from current-period production.

Exhibit 4	Joint-Cost Allocation and Product-Line Income Statement Using Physical-Measure Method: Farmland Dairy for May 2014

	Home Insert Page Layout Formulas Data Review View			
	A	B	C	D
1	PANEL A: Allocation of Joint Costs Using Physical-Measure Method	Cream	Liquid Skim	Total
2	Physical measure of total production (gallons)	25,000	75,000	100,000
3	Weighting (25,000 gallons ÷ 100,000 gallons; 75,000 gallons ÷ 100,000 gallons)	0.25	0.75	
4	Joint costs allocated (0.25 × $400,000; 0.75 × $400,000)	$100,000	$300,000	$400,000
5	Joint production cost per gallon ($100,000 ÷ 25,000 gallons; $300,000 ÷ 75,000 gallons)	$ 4.00	$ 4.00	
6				
7	PANEL B: Product-Line Income Statement Using Physical-Measure Method for May 2014	Cream	Liquid Skim	Total
8	Revenues (20,000 gallons × $8 per gallon; 30,000 gallons × $4 per gallon)	$160,000	$120,000	$280,000
9	Cost of goods sold (joint costs)			
10	Production costs (0.25 × $400,000; 0.75 × $400,000)	100,000	300,000	400,000
11	Deduct ending inventory (5,000 gallons × $4 per gallon; 45,000 gallons × $4 per gallon)	20,000	180,000	200,000
12	Cost of goods sold (joint costs)	80,000	120,000	200,000
13	Gross margin	$ 80,000	$ 0	$ 80,000
14	Gross margin percentage ($80,000 ÷ $160,000; $0 ÷ $120,000; $80,000 ÷ $280,000)	50%	0%	28.6%

Because the physical-measure method allocates joint costs on the basis of the number of gallons, the cost per gallon is the same for both products. Exhibit 4, Panel B, presents the product-line income statement using the physical-measure method. The gross-margin percentages are 50% for cream and 0% for liquid skim.

Under the benefits-received criterion, the physical-measure method is much less desirable than the sales value at splitoff method. Why? Because the physical measure of the individual products may have no relationship to their respective revenue-generating abilities. Consider a gold mine that extracts ore containing gold, silver, and lead. Using a common physical measure (tons) would result in almost all costs being allocated to lead, the product that weighs the most but has the lowest revenue-generating power. This method of cost allocation is inconsistent with the main reason the mining company is incurring mining costs—to earn revenues from gold and silver, not lead. When a company uses the physical-measure method in a product-line income statement, products that have a high sales value per ton, like gold and silver, would show a large "profit," and products that have a low sales value per ton, like lead, would show sizable losses.

Obtaining comparable physical measures for all products is not always straightforward. Consider the joint costs of producing oil and natural gas; oil is a liquid and gas is a vapor. To use a physical measure, the oil and gas need to be converted to the energy equivalent for oil and gas, British thermal units (BTUs). Using some physical measures to allocate joint costs may require assistance from technical personnel outside of accounting.

Determining which products of a joint process to include in a physical-measure computation can greatly affect the allocations to those products. Outputs with no sales value (such as dirt in gold mining) are always excluded. Although many more tons of dirt than gold are produced, costs are not incurred to produce outputs that have zero sales value. Byproducts are also often excluded from the denominator used in the physical-measure method because of their low sales values relative to the joint products or the main product. The general guideline for the physical-measure method is to include only the joint-product outputs in the weighting computations.

Net Realizable Value Method

In many cases, products are processed beyond the splitoff point to bring them to a marketable form or to increase their value above their selling price at the splitoff point. For example, when crude oil is refined, the gasoline, kerosene, benzene, and naphtha must be processed further before they can be sold. To illustrate, let's extend the Farmland Dairy example.

Example 2: Assume the same data as in Example 1 except that both cream and liquid skim can be processed further:

- Cream → Buttercream: 25,000 gallons of cream are further processed to yield 20,000 gallons of buttercream at additional processing costs of $280,000. Buttercream, which sells for $25 per gallon, is used in the manufacture of butter-based products.

- Liquid Skim → Condensed Milk: 75,000 gallons of liquid skim are further processed to yield 50,000 gallons of condensed milk at additional processing costs of $520,000. Condensed milk sells for $22 per gallon.

- Sales during May 2014 are 12,000 gallons of buttercream and 45,000 gallons of condensed milk.

Exhibit 5, Panel A, depicts how (a) raw milk is converted into cream and liquid skim in the joint production process and (b) how cream is separately processed into buttercream and liquid skim is separately processed into condensed milk. Panel B shows the data for Example 2.

| Exhibit 5 | Example 2: Overview of Farmland Dairy |

PANEL A: Graphical Presentation of Process for Example 2

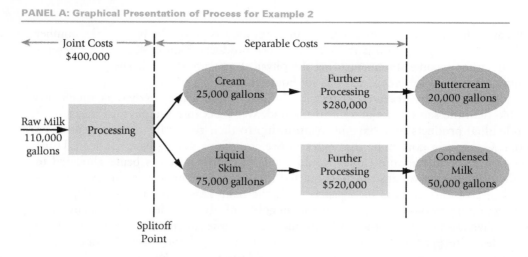

PANEL B: Data for Example 2

	A	B	C	D	E
1		**Joint Costs**		**Buttercream**	**Condensed Milk**
2	Joint costs (costs of 110,000 gallons raw milk and processing to splitoff point)	$400,000			
3	Separable cost of processing 25,000 gallons cream into 20,000 gallons buttercream			$280,000	
4	Separable cost of processing 75,000 gallons liquid skim into 50,000 gallons condensed milk				$520,000
5					
6		**Cream**	**Liquid Skim**	**Buttercream**	**Condensed Milk**
7	Beginning inventory (gallons)	0	0	0	0
8	Production (gallons)	25,000	75,000	20,000	50,000
9	Transfer for further processing (gallons)	25,000	75,000		
10	Sales (gallons)			12,000	45,000
11	Ending inventory (gallons)	0	0	8,000	5,000
12	Selling price per gallon	$ 8	$ 4	$ 25	$ 22

Exhibit 6	Joint-Cost Allocation and Product-Line Income Statement Using NRV Method: Farmland Dairy for May 2014

	A	B	C	D
		Buttercream	Condensed Milk	Total
1	**PANEL A: Allocation of Joint Costs Using Net Realizable Value Method**			
2	Final sales value of total production during accounting period			
3	(20,000 gallons × $25 per gallon; 50,000 gallons × $22 per gallon)	$500,000	$1,100,000	$1,600,000
4	Deduct separable costs	280,000	520,000	800,000
5	Net realizable value at splitoff point	$220,000	$ 580,000	$ 800,000
6	Weighting ($220,000 ÷ $800,000; $580,000 ÷ $800,000)	0.275	0.725	
7	Joint costs allocated (0.275 × $400,000; 0.725 × $400,000)	$110,000	$ 290,000	$ 400,000
8	Production cost per gallon			
9	([$110,000 + $280,000] ÷ 20,000 gallons; [$290,000 + $520,000] ÷ 50,000 gallons)	$ 19.50	$ 16.20	
10				
11	**PANEL B: Product-Line Income Statement Using Net Realizable Value Method for May 2014**	Buttercream	Condensed Milk	Total
12	Revenues (12,000 gallons × $25 per gallon; 45,000 gallons × $22 per gallon)	$300,000	$ 990,000	$1,290,000
13	Cost of goods sold			
14	Joint costs (0.275 × $400,000; 0.725 × $400,000)	110,000	290,000	400,000
15	Separable costs	280,000	520,000	800,000
16	Production costs	390,000	810,000	1,200,000
17	Deduct ending inventory (8,000 gallons × $19.50 per gallon; 5,000 gallons × $16.20 per gallon)	156,000	81,000	237,000
18	Cost of goods sold	234,000	729,000	963,000
19	Gross margin	$ 66,000	$ 261,000	$ 327,000
20	Gross margin percentage ($66,000 ÷ $300,000; $261,000 ÷ $990,000; $327,000 ÷ $1,290,000)	22.0%	26.4%	25.3%

The **net realizable value (NRV) method** allocates joint costs to joint products produced during the accounting period on the basis of their relative NRV—final sales value minus separable costs. The NRV method is typically used in preference to the sales value at splitoff method only when selling prices for one or more products at splitoff do not exist. Using this method for Example 2, Exhibit 6, Panel A, shows how joint costs are allocated to individual products to calculate cost per gallon of buttercream and condensed milk. Panel B presents the product-line income statement using the NRV method. The gross-margin percentages are 22.0% for buttercream and 26.4% for condensed milk.

The NRV method is often implemented using simplifying assumptions. For example, even when the selling prices of joint products vary frequently, companies implement the NRV method using a given set of selling prices throughout the accounting period. Similarly, even though companies may occasionally change the number or sequence of processing steps beyond the splitoff point in order to adjust to variations in input quality or local conditions, they assume a specific constant set of such steps when implementing the NRV method.

Constant Gross-Margin Percentage NRV Method

The **constant gross-margin percentage NRV method** allocates joint costs to joint products produced during the accounting period in such a way that each individual product achieves an identical gross-margin percentage. The method works backward in that the overall gross margin is computed first. Then, for each product, this gross-margin percentage and any separable costs are deducted from the final sales value of production in order to back into the joint cost allocation for that product. The method can be broken down into three discrete steps. Exhibit 7, Panel A, shows these steps for allocating the $400,000 joint costs between buttercream and condensed milk in the Farmland Dairy example. Refer to the panel for an illustration of each step as we describe it.

Step 1: **Compute the Overall Gross Margin Percentage.** The overall gross-margin percentage for all joint products together is calculated first. This is based on the final sales value of *total production* during the accounting period, not the *total revenues* of the period. Accordingly, Exhibit 7, Panel A, uses $1,600,000, the final expected sales value of the entire output of buttercream and condensed milk, not the $1,290,000 in actual sales revenue for the month of May.

Exhibit 7	Joint-Cost Allocation and Product-Line Income Statement Using Constant Gross-Margin Percentage NRV Method: Farmland Dairy for May 2014

	A	B	C	D
	Home Insert Page Layout Formulas Data Review View			
1	**PANEL A: Allocation of Joint Costs Using Constant Gross-Margin Percentage NRV Method**			
2	**Step 1**			
3	Final sales value of total production during accounting period: (20,000 gallons × $25 per gallon) + (50,000 gallons × $22 per gallon)	$1,600,000		
4	Deduct joint and separable costs ($400,000 + $280,000 + $520,000)	1,200,000		
5	Gross margin	$ 400,000		
6	Gross margin percentage ($400,000 ÷ $1,600,000)	25%		
7		**Buttercream**	**Condensed Milk**	**Total**
8	**Step 2**			
9	Final sales value of total production during accounting period: (20,000 gallons × $25 per gallon; 50,000 gallons × $22 per gallon)	$ 500,000	$1,100,000	$1,600,000
10	Deduct gross margin, using overall gross-margin percentage (25% × $500,000; 25% × $1,100,000)	125,000	275,000	400,000
11	Total production costs	375,000	825,000	1,200,000
12	**Step 3**			
13	Deduct separable costs	280,000	520,000	800,000
14	Joint costs allocated	$ 95,000	$ 305,000	$ 400,000
15				
16	**PANEL B: Product-Line Income Statement Using Constant Gross-Margin Percentage NRV Method for May 2014**	**Buttercream**	**Condensed Milk**	**Total**
17	Revenues (12,000 gallons × $25 per gallon; 45,000 gallons × $22 per gallon)	$ 300,000	$ 990,000	$1,290,000
18	Cost of goods sold			
19	Joint costs (from Panel A)	95,000	305,000	400,000
20	Separable costs	280,000	520,000	800,000
21	Production costs	375,000	825,000	1,200,000
22	Deduct ending inventory			
23	(8,000 gallons × $18.75 per gallon[a]; 5,000 gallons × $16.50 per gallon[b])	150,000	82,500	232,500
24	Cost of goods sold	225,000	742,500	967,500
25	Gross margin	$ 75,000	$ 247,500	$ 322,500
26	Gross margin percentage ($75,000 ÷ $300,000; $247,500 ÷ $990,000; $322,500 ÷ $1,290,000)	25%	25%	25%
27				
28	[a]Total production costs of buttercream ÷ Total production of buttercream = $375,000 ÷ 20,000 gallons = $18.75 per gallon.			
29	[b]Total production costs of condensed milk ÷ Total production of condensed milk = $825,000 ÷ 50,000 gallons = $16.50 per gallon.			

Step 2: Compute the Total Production Costs for Each Product. The gross margin (in dollars) for each product is computed by multiplying the overall gross-margin percentage by the product's final sales value of total production. The difference between the final sales value of total production and the gross margin then yields the total production costs that the product must bear.

Step 3: Compute the Allocated Joint Costs. As the final step, the separable costs for each product are deducted from the total production costs that the product must bear to obtain the joint-cost allocation for that product.

Exhibit 7, Panel B, presents the product-line income statement for the constant gross-margin percentage NRV method.

The constant gross-margin percentage NRV method is the only method whereby products can receive negative allocations. This may be required in order to bring the gross-margin percentages of relatively unprofitable products up to the overall average. The constant gross-margin percentage NRV method also differs from the other two market-based joint-cost-allocation methods described earlier in another fundamental way. Neither the sales value at splitoff method nor the NRV method takes account of profits earned either before or after the splitoff point when allocating the joint costs. In contrast, the constant gross-margin percentage NRV method allocates both joint costs and profits: The gross margin is allocated to the joint products in order to determine the joint-cost allocations so that the resulting gross-margin percentage for each product is the same.

Decision Point ▶

What methods can be used to allocate joint costs to individual products?

Choosing an Allocation Method

Which method of allocating joint costs should be used? When selling-price data exist at the splitoff, the sales value at splitoff method is preferred, even if further processing is done. The following are reasons why:

1. **Measure of benefits received.** The sales value at splitoff is the best measure of the benefits received by joint products relative to all other methods of allocating joint costs. It is a meaningful basis for allocating joint costs because generating revenues is the reason why a company incurs joint costs in the first place. It is also sometimes possible to vary the physical mix of final output and thereby produce more or less market value by incurring more or less joint costs. In such cases, there is a clear causal link between total cost and total output value, thereby further validating the use of the sales value at splitoff method.[5]

2. **Independent of further processing decisions.** The sales value at splitoff method does not require information on the processing steps after the splitoff, if there are any. In contrast, the NRV and constant gross-margin percentage NRV methods require information on (a) the specific sequence of further processing decisions, (b) the separable costs of further processing, and (c) the point at which individual products will be sold.

3. **Common allocation basis.** As with other market-based approaches, the sales value at splitoff method provides a common basis for allocating joint costs to products, namely revenue. In contrast, the physical-measure at splitoff method may lack an easily identifiable common basis for cost allocation.

4. **Simplicity.** The sales value at splitoff method is simple. In contrast, the NRV and constant gross-margin percentage NRV methods can be complex for operations with multiple products and multiple splitoff points. This complexity increases when managers make frequent changes to the sequence of post-splitoff processing decisions or to the point at which individual products are sold.

When the selling prices of all products at the splitoff point are unavailable, the NRV method is the best alternative. It attempts to approximate the sales values at splitoff by subtracting from final selling prices the separable costs incurred after the splitoff point. The NRV method assumes that all the markup (the profit margin) is attributable to the joint process and none of the markup is attributable to the separable costs. This is unrealistic if, for example, a firm uses a special patented technology in its separable process or innovative marketing that enables it to generate significant profits. Despite this limitation, the NRV method is commonly used when selling prices at splitoff are not available as it provides a better measure of the benefits received than either the constant gross-margin percentage NRV method or the physical-measure method.

The constant gross-margin percentage NRV method treats the joint products as though they comprise a single product. This method calculates the aggregate gross-margin percentage, applies this percentage to each product, and views the residual after separable costs are accounted for as the amount of joint costs assigned to each product. Consequently, unlike the NRV method, the benefits received by each of the joint products at the splitoff point don't have to be measured. Also, the constant gross-margin percentage method recognizes that the profit margin is not just attributable to the joint process but is also derived from the costs incurred after splitoff. The drawback of the method is that it assumes that the profit margin is identical across products; that is, all products are assumed to have the same ratio of cost to sales value. Such a situation is uncommon when companies offer a diverse set of products.

Although there are difficulties in using the physical-measure method—such as lack of congruence with the benefits-received criterion—there are instances when it may be

---

[5] In the semiconductor industry, for example, the use of cleaner facilities, higher-quality silicon wafers, and more sophisticated equipment (all of which require higher joint costs) shifts the distribution of output to higher-quality memory devices with more market value. For details, see James F. Gatti and D. Jacque Grinnell, "Joint Cost Allocations: Measuring and Promoting Productivity and Quality Improvements," *Journal of Cost Management* (2000). The authors also demonstrate that joint cost allocations based on market value are preferable for promoting quality and productivity improvements.

preferred. In settings where end prices are volatile or the process after splitoff is long or uncertain, the presence of a comparable physical measure at splitoff would favor use of the method. This is true, for instance, in the chemical and oil refining industries. The physical-measure method is also useful when joint cost allocations are used as the basis for setting market prices, as in rate regulation. It avoids the circular reasoning of using selling prices to allocate the costs on which prices (rates) are based.

Not Allocating Joint Costs

Some companies choose to not allocate joint costs to products due to the complexity of their production or extraction processes and the difficulty of gathering a sufficient amount of data to allocate the costs correctly. For example, a survey of nine sawmills in Norway revealed that none of them allocated joint costs. The study's authors noted that the "interviewed sawmills considered the joint cost problem very interesting, but pointed out that the problem is not easily solved."[6]

Rather than allocating joint costs, some firms simply subtract them directly from total revenues in the management accounts. If substantial inventories exist, the firms carry their product inventories at NRV. Companies in the meatpacking, canning, and mining industries often use variations of this approach. Accountants do not ordinarily record inventories at NRV because this practice recognizes the income on each product at the time it is completed but *before* it is sold. To deal with this problem, some of these companies carry their inventories at NRV minus an estimated operating income margin. When any end-of-period inventories are sold in the next period, the cost of goods sold then equals this carrying value. This approach is akin to the "production method" of accounting for byproducts, which we describe later in this chapter.

Decision Point

When is the sales value at splitoff method considered preferable for allocating joint costs to individual products and why?

Learning Objective 5

Explain why joint costs are irrelevant in a sell-or-process-further decision

...because joint costs are the same whether or not further processing occurs

Why Joint Costs Are Irrelevant for Decision Making

Relevant revenues are expected future revenues that differ among alternative courses of action, and *relevant costs* are expected future costs that differ among alternative courses of action. These concepts can be applied to decisions on whether a joint product or main product should be sold at the splitoff point or processed further.

Sell-or-Process-Further Decisions

Consider Farmland Dairy's decision to either sell the joint products, cream and liquid skim, at the splitoff point or to further process them into buttercream and condensed milk. The decision to incur additional costs for further processing should be based on the incremental operating income attainable beyond the splitoff point. Example 2 assumed it was profitable for both cream and liquid skim to be further processed into buttercream and condensed milk, respectively. The incremental analysis for the decision to process further is as follows:

Further Processing Cream into Buttercream	
Incremental revenues	
($25/gallon × 20,000 gallons) − ($8/gallon × 25,000 gallons)	$300,000
Deduct incremental processing costs	280,000
Increase in operating income from buttercream	$ 20,000
Further Processing Liquid Skim into Condensed Milk	
Incremental revenues	
($22/gallon × 50,000 gallons) − ($4/gallon × 75,000 gallons)	$800,000
Deduct incremental processing costs	520,000
Increase in operating income from condensed milk	$280,000

---

[6] For further details, see Torgrim Tunes, Anders Q. Nyrud, and Birger Eikenes, "Cost and Performance Management in the Sawmill Industry," *Scandinavian Forest Economics* (2006).

In this example, the operating income increases for both products, so the manager decides to process cream into buttercream and liquid skim into condensed milk. *Note that the $400,000 joint costs incurred before the splitoff point are irrelevant in deciding whether to process further.* Why? Because the joint costs of $400,000 are the same whether the products are sold at the splitoff point or processed further. What matters is the incremental income from additional processing.

Incremental costs are the additional costs incurred for an activity, such as further processing. *Do not assume all separable costs in joint-cost allocations are incremental costs.* Some separable costs may be fixed costs, such as the lease cost on buildings where the further processing is done; some separable costs may be sunk costs, such as depreciation on the equipment that converts cream into buttercream; and some separable costs may be allocated costs, such as corporate costs allocated to the condensed milk operations. None of these costs will differ between the alternatives of selling products at the splitoff point or processing further; therefore, they are irrelevant.

Decision Making and Performance Evaluation

The potential conflict between cost concepts used for decision making and cost concepts used for evaluating the performance of managers often arises when sell-or-process-further decisions are being made. To see how, let us continue with Example 2. Suppose the *allocated* fixed corporate and administrative costs of further processing cream into buttercream equal $30,000 and that these costs will be allocated only to buttercream and to the manager's product-line income statement if buttercream is produced. How might this policy affect the decision to process further?

As we have seen, on the basis of incremental revenues and incremental costs, Farmland's operating income will increase by $20,000 if it processes cream into buttercream. However, producing the buttercream also results in an additional charge for allocated fixed costs of $30,000. If the manager is evaluated on a full-cost basis (that is, after allocating all costs), processing cream into buttercream will lower the manager's performance-evaluation measure by $10,000 (incremental operating income, $20,000 – allocated fixed costs, $30,000). Therefore, the manager may be tempted to sell the cream at the splitoff point and not process it into buttercream.

A similar conflict can also arise with joint products. Returning to Example 1, suppose Farmland Dairy has the option of selling raw milk at a profit of $20,000. From a decision-making standpoint, the company would maximize its operating income by processing raw milk into cream and liquid skim because the total revenues from selling both joint products ($500,000, see Exhibit 3) exceed the joint costs ($400,000) by $100,000, which is greater than the $20,000 profit from selling the raw milk. Suppose, however, the cream and liquid-skim product lines are managed by different managers, each of whom is evaluated based on a product-line income statement. If the physical-measure method of joint-cost allocation is used and the selling price per gallon of liquid skim falls below $4.00 per gallon, the liquid-skim product line will show a loss (from Exhibit 4, revenues will be less than $120,000, but cost of goods sold will be unchanged at $120,000). The manager of the liquid-skim line will therefore prefer, from a performance-evaluation standpoint, to not produce liquid skim but rather to sell the raw milk.

Farmland Dairy's performance-evaluation conflicts will be less severe if it uses any of the market-based methods of joint-cost allocations—sales value at splitoff, NRV, or constant gross-margin percentage NRV—because each of these methods allocates costs using revenues, which generally leads to a positive income for each joint product.

Pricing Decisions

Firms should be wary of using the full cost of a joint product (that is, the cost after joint costs are allocated) as the basis for making pricing decisions. Why? Because in many situations, there is no direct cause-and-effect relationship that identifies the resources demanded by each joint product that can then be used as a basis for pricing. In fact, the use of the sales value at splitoff or the net realizable value method to allocate joint costs

Decision Point

Are joint costs relevant in a sell-or-process-further decision?

results in a reverse effect: The selling prices of joint products drive joint-cost allocations, rather than cost allocations serving as the basis for the pricing of joint products! Of course, the principles of pricing apply to the joint process as a whole. Even if the firm cannot alter the mix of products generated by the joint process, it must ensure that the joint products generate a sufficient amount of combined revenue in the long run to cover the joint costs of processing.

Learning Objective 6

Account for byproducts using two methods

...recognize in financial statements at time of production or at time of sale

Accounting for Byproducts

Joint production processes can yield not only joint products and main products but also byproducts. Although their total sales values are relatively low, the byproducts in a joint production process can affect the allocation of joint costs. Moreover, byproducts can be quite profitable for a firm. Wendy's, the fast food chain, uses surplus hamburger patties in its "rich and meaty" chili and, because it cooks meat specifically for the chili only 10% of the time, makes great margins even at a price of $0.99 for an eight-ounce serving of chili.

Let's consider a two-product example consisting of a main product and a byproduct.

Example 3: The Westlake Corporation processes timber into fine-grade lumber and wood chips, which are used as mulch in gardens and lawns.

- Fine-grade lumber (the main product)—sells for $6 per board foot (b.f.)
- Wood chips (the byproduct)—sells for $1 per cubic foot (c.f.)

The data for July 2014 are as follows:

	Beginning Inventory	Production	Sales	Ending Inventory
Fine-grade lumber (b.f.)	0	50,000	40,000	10,000
Wood chips (c.f.)	0	4,000	1,200	2,800

The joint manufacturing costs for these products in July 2014 are $250,000. They consist of $150,000 for direct materials and $100,000 for conversion costs. Both products are sold at the splitoff point without further processing, as Exhibit 8 shows.

We present two byproduct accounting methods: the production method and the sales method. The production method recognizes byproducts in the financial statements when their production is completed. The sales method delays recognizing byproducts until they are sold.[7] Exhibit 9 presents the income statement of Westlake Corporation under both methods.

Exhibit 8

Example 3: Overview of Westlake Corporation

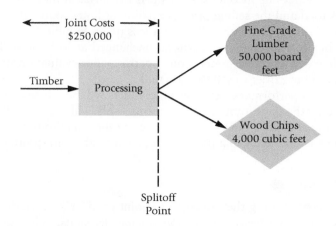

[7] For a discussion of joint cost allocation and byproduct accounting methods, see P. Douglas Marshall and Robert F. Dombrowski, "A Small Business Review of Accounting for Primary Products, Byproducts and Scrap," *The National Public Accountant* (February/March 2003): 10–13.

Exhibit 9	Income Statements of Westlake Corporation for July 2014 Using the Production and Sales Methods for Byproduct Accounting

	Production Method	Sales Method
Revenues		
Main product: Fine-grade lumber (40,000 b.f. × $6 per b.f.)	$240,000	$240,000
Byproduct: Wood chips (1,200 c.f. × $1 per c.f.)	—	1,200
Total revenues	240,000	241,200
Cost of goods sold		
Total manufacturing costs	250,000	250,000
Deduct byproduct revenue and inventory (4,000 c.f. × $1 per c.f.)	(4,000)	—
Net manufacturing costs	246,000	250,000
Deduct main-product inventory	(49,200)[a]	(50,000)[b]
Cost of goods sold	196,800	200,000
Gross margin	$ 43,200	$ 41,200
Gross-margin percentage ($43,200 ÷ $240,000; $41,200 ÷ $241,200)	18.00%	17.08%
Inventoriable costs (end of period):		
Main product: Fine-grade lumber	$ 49,200	$ 50,000
Byproduct: Wood chips (2,800 c.f. × $1 per c.f.)[c]	2,800	0

[a](10,000 ÷ 50,000) × net manufacturing cost = (10,000 ÷ 50,000) × $246,000 = $49,200
[b](10,000 ÷ 50,000) × total manufacturing cost = (10,000 ÷ 50,000) × $250,000 = $50,000
[c]Recorded at selling prices.

Production Method: Byproducts Recognized at Time Production Is Completed

This method recognizes the byproduct in the financial statements—the 4,000 cubic feet of wood chips—in the month it is produced, July 2014. The NRV from the byproduct produced is offset against the costs of the main product. The following journal entries illustrate the production method:

1.	Work in Process	150,000	
	Accounts Payable		150,000
	To record the direct materials purchased and used in production during July.		
2.	Work in Process	100,000	
	Various accounts such as Wages Payable and Accumulated Depreciation		100,000
	To record the conversion costs in the production process during July; examples include energy, manufacturing supplies, all manufacturing labor, and plant depreciation.		
3.	Byproduct Inventory—Wood Chips (4,000 c.f. × $1 per c.f.)	4,000	
	Finished Goods—Fine-Grade Lumber ($250,000 − $4,000)	246,000	
	Work in Process ($150,000 + $100,000)		250,000
	To record the cost of goods completed during July.		
4a.	Cost of Goods Sold [(40,000 b.f. ÷ 50,000 b.f.) × $246,000]	196,800	
	Finished Goods—Fine-Grade Lumber		196,800
	To record the cost of the main product sold during July.		
4b.	Cash or Accounts Receivable (40,000 b.f. × $6 per b.f.)	240,000	
	Revenues—Fine-Grade Lumber		240,000
	To record the sales of the main product during July.		
5.	Cash or Accounts Receivable (1,200 c.f. × $1 per c.f.)	1,200	
	Byproduct Inventory—Wood Chips		1,200
	To record the sales of the byproduct during July.		

The production method reports the byproduct inventory of wood chips in the balance sheet at its $1 per cubic foot selling price [(4,000 cubic feet − 1,200 cubic feet) × $1 per cubic foot = $2,800].

One variation of this method would be to report the byproduct inventory at its NRV reduced by a normal profit margin, say 20%: $2,800 − 20% × $2,800 = $2,240.[8] When the byproduct inventory is sold in a subsequent period, the income statement will match the selling price, $2,800, with the "cost" reported for the byproduct inventory, $2,240, resulting in a byproduct operating income of $560 ($2,800 − $2,240).

Sales Method: Byproducts Recognized at Time of Sale

With this method, no journal entries are made for byproducts until they are sold. At that time, the byproduct revenues are reported in the income statement. The revenues are either grouped with other sales, included as other income, or deducted from the cost of goods sold. In the Westlake Corporation example, byproduct revenues in July 2014 are $1,200 (1,200 cubic feet × $1 per cubic foot) because only 1,200 cubic feet of wood chips are sold in July (of the 4,000 cubic feet produced). The journal entries are as follows:

1. and 2.	*Same as for the production method.*		
	Work in Process	150,000	
	Accounts Payable		150,000
	Work in Process	100,000	
	Various accounts such as Wages Payable and Accumulated Depreciation		100,000
3.	Finished Goods—Fine-Grade Lumber	250,000	
	Work in Process		250,000
	To record the cost of the main product completed during July.		
4a.	Cost of Goods Sold [(40,000 b.f. ÷ 50,000 b.f.) × $250,000]	200,000	
	Finished Goods—Fine-Grade Lumber		200,000
	To record the cost of the main product sold during July.		
4b.	Same as for the production method.		
	Cash or Accounts Receivable (40,000 b.f. × $6 per b.f.)	240,000	
	Revenues—Fine-Grade Lumber		240,000
5.	Cash or Accounts Receivable	1,200	
	Revenues—Wood Chips		1,200
	To record the sales of the byproduct during July.		

Decision Point

What methods can be used to account for byproducts and which of them is preferable?

Which method should a company use? The production method for accounting for byproducts is consistent with the matching principle and is the preferred method. This method recognizes the byproduct inventory in the accounting period in which it is produced and simultaneously reduces the cost of manufacturing the main or joint products, thereby better matching the revenues and expenses from selling the main product. However, the sales method is simpler and is often used in practice, primarily because the dollar amounts of byproducts are immaterial. The drawback of the sales method is that it allows a firm to "manage" its reported earnings by timing the sale of byproducts. For example, to boost its revenues and income slightly, a firm might store the byproducts for several periods and then sell them when the revenues and profits from the main product or joint products are low.

---

[8] One way to make this calculation is to assume all products have the same "normal" profit margin, as in the constant gross-margin percentage NRV method. Alternatively, the company might allow products to have different profit margins based on an analysis of the margins earned by other companies that sell these products individually.

Problem for Self-Study

Inorganic Chemicals (IC) processes salt into various industrial products. In July 2014, IC incurred joint costs of $100,000 to purchase salt and convert it into two products: caustic soda and chlorine. Although there is an active outside market for chlorine, IC processes all 800 tons of chlorine it produces into 500 tons of PVC (polyvinyl chloride), which is then sold. There were no beginning or ending inventories of salt, caustic soda, chlorine, or PVC in July. Information for July 2014 production and sales follows:

	A	B	C	D
		Home Insert Page Layout Formulas Data Review View		
1		**Joint Costs**		**PVC**
2	Joint costs (costs of salt and processing to splitoff point)	$100,000		
3	Separable cost of processing 800 tons chlorine into 500 tons PVC			$20,000
4				
5		**Caustic Soda**	**Chlorine**	**PVC**
6	Beginning inventory (tons)	0	0	0
7	Production (tons)	1,200	800	500
8	Transfer for further processing (tons)		800	
9	Sales (tons)	1,200		500
10	Ending inventory (tons)	0	0	0
11	Selling price per ton in active outside market (for products not actually sold)		$ 75	
12	Selling price per ton for products sold	$ 50		$ 200

Required

1. Allocate the joint costs of $100,000 between caustic soda and PVC under (a) the sales value at splitoff method and (b) the physical-measure method.
2. Allocate the joint costs of $100,000 between caustic soda and PVC under the NRV method.
3. Under the three allocation methods in requirements 1 and 2, what is the gross-margin percentage of (a) caustic soda and (b) PVC?
4. Lifetime Swimming Pool Products offers to purchase 800 tons of chlorine in August 2014 at $75 per ton. Assume all other production and sales data are the same for August as they were for July. This sale of chlorine to Lifetime would mean that no PVC would be produced by IC in August. How would accepting this offer affect IC's August 2014 operating income?

Solution

The following picture provides a visual illustration of the main facts in this problem.

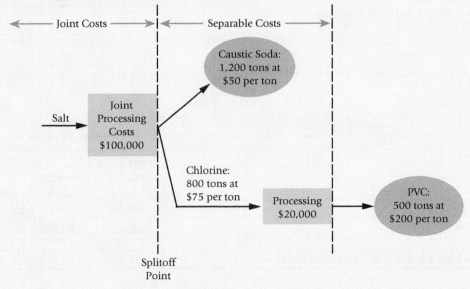

Note that caustic soda is sold as is while chlorine, despite having a market value at splitoff, is sold only in processed form as PVC. The goal is to allocate the joint costs of $100,000 to the final products—caustic soda and PVC. However, because PVC exists only in the form of chlorine at the splitoff point, we use chlorine's sales value and physical measure as the basis for allocating joint costs to PVC under the sales value at splitoff and physical measure at splitoff methods. Detailed calculations are shown next.

1a. Sales value at splitoff method

	A	B	C	D
	Home Insert Page Layout Formulas Data Review View			
1	Allocation of Joint Costs Using Sales Value at Splitoff Method	Caustic Soda	PVC/Chlorine	Total
2	Sales value of total production at splitoff point			
3	(1,200 tons × $50 per ton; 800 × $75 per ton)	$60,000	$60,000	$120,000
4	Weighting ($60,000 ÷ $120,000; $60,000 ÷ $120,000)	0.50	0.50	
5	Joint costs allocated (0.50 × $100,000; 0.50 × $100,000)	$50,000	$50,000	$100,000

1b. Physical-measure method

	A	B	C	D
	Home Insert Page Layout Formulas Data Review View			
8	Allocation of Joint Costs Using Physical-Measure Method	Caustic Soda	PVC/Chlorine	Total
9	Physical measure of total production (tons)	1,200	800	2,000
10	Weighting (1,200 tons ÷ 2,000 tons; 800 tons ÷ 2,000 tons)	0.60	0.40	
11	Joint cost allocated (0.60 × $100,000; 0.40 × $100,000)	$60,000	$40,000	$100,000

2. Net realizable value (NRV) method

	A	B	C	D
	Home Insert Page Layout Formulas Data Review View			
14	Allocation of Joint Costs Using Net Realizable Value Method	Caustic Soda	PVC	Total
15	Final sales value of total production during accounting period			
16	(1,200 tons × $50 per ton; 500 tons × $200 per ton)	$60,000	$100,000	$160,000
17	Deduct separable costs to complete and sell	0	20,000	20,000
18	Net realizable value at splitoff point	$60,000	$ 80,000	$140,000
19	Weighting ($60,000 ÷ $140,000; $80,000 ÷ $140,000)	3/7	4/7	
20	Joint costs allocated (3/7 × $100,000; 4/7 × $100,000)	$42,857	$ 57,143	$100,000

3a. Gross-margin percentage of caustic soda

	A	B	C	D
	Home Insert Page Layout Formulas Data Review View			
23	Caustic Soda	Sales Value at Splitoff Point	Physical Measure	NRV
24	Revenues (1,200 tons × $50 per ton)	$60,000	$60,000	$60,000
25	Cost of goods sold (joint costs)	50,000	60,000	42,857
26	Gross margin	$10,000	$ 0	$17,143
27	Gross margin percentage ($10,000 ÷ $60,000; $0 ÷ $60,000; $17,143 ÷ $60,000)	16.67%	0.00%	28.57%

3b. Gross-margin percentage of PVC

	A	B	C	D
30	PVC	Sales Value at Splitoff Point	Physical Measure	NRV
31	Revenues (500 tons × $200 per ton)	$100,000	$100,000	$100,000
32	Cost of goods sold			
33	Joint costs	50,000	40,000	57,143
34	Separable costs	20,000	20,000	20,000
35	Cost of goods sold	70,000	60,000	77,143
36	Gross margin	$ 30,000	$ 40,000	$ 22,857
37	Gross margin percentage ($30,000 ÷ $100,000; $40,000 ÷ $100,000; $22,857 ÷ $100,000)	30.00%	40.00%	22.86%

4. Sale of chlorine versus processing into PVC

	A	B
40	Incremental revenue from processing 800 tons of chlorine into 500 tons of PVC	
41	(500 tons × $200 per ton) – (800 tons × $75 per ton)	$40,000
42	Incremental cost of processing 800 tons of chlorine into 500 tons of PVC	20,000
43	Incremental operating income from further processing	$20,000

If IC sells 800 tons of chlorine to Lifetime Swimming Pool Products instead of further processing it into PVC, its August 2014 operating income will be reduced by $20,000.

▶ Decision Points

The following question-and-answer format summarizes the chapter's learning objectives. Each decision presents a key question related to a learning objective. The guidelines are the answer to that question.

Decision	Guidelines
1. What do the terms joint cost and splitoff point mean, and how do joint products differ from byproducts?	A joint cost is the cost of a single production process that yields multiple products simultaneously. The splitoff point is the juncture in a joint production process when the products become separately identifiable. Joint products have high total sales values at the splitoff point. A byproduct has a low total sales value at the splitoff point relative to the total sales value of a joint or main product.
2. Why are joint costs allocated to individual products?	The purposes for allocating joint costs to products include inventory costing for financial accounting and internal reporting, cost reimbursement, insurance settlements, rate regulation, and product-cost litigation.
3. What methods can be used to allocate joint costs to individual products?	The methods to allocate joint costs to products are the sales value at splitoff, physical-measure, NRV, and constant gross-margin percentage NRV methods.

Decision	Guidelines
4. When is the sales value at splitoff method considered preferable for allocating joint costs to individual products and why?	The sales value at splitoff method is preferred when market prices exist at splitoff because using revenues is consistent with the benefits-received criterion; further, the method does not depend on subsequent decisions made about further processing and is simple.
5. Are joint costs relevant in a sell-or-process-further decision?	No, joint costs and how they are allocated are irrelevant because they are the same regardless of whether further processing occurs.
6. What methods can be used to account for byproducts, and which of them is preferable?	The production method recognizes byproducts in financial statements at the time of their production, whereas the sales method recognizes byproducts in financial statements at the time of their sale. The production method is conceptually superior, but the sales method is often used in practice because the dollar amounts of byproducts are immaterial.

Terms to Learn

This chapter contains definitions of the following important terms:

byproducts	main product	separable costs
constant gross-margin percentage NRV method	net realizable value (NRV) method	splitoff point
joint costs	physical-measure method	
joint products	product	
	sales value at splitoff method	

Assignment Material

MyAccountingLab

Questions

1 Give two examples of industries in which joint costs are found. For each example, what are the individual products at the splitoff point?

2 What is a joint cost? What is a separable cost?

3 Distinguish between a joint product and a byproduct.

4 Why might the number of products in a joint-cost situation differ from the number of outputs? Give an example.

5 Provide three reasons for allocating joint costs to individual products or services.

6 Why does the sales value at splitoff method use the sales value of the total production in the accounting period and not just the revenues from the products sold?

7 Describe a situation in which the sales value at splitoff method cannot be used but the NRV method can be used for joint-cost allocation.

8 Distinguish between the sales value at splitoff method and the NRV method.

9 Give two limitations of the physical-measure method of joint-cost allocation.

10 How might a company simplify its use of the NRV method when final selling prices can vary sizably in an accounting period and management frequently changes the point at which it sells individual products?

11 Why is the constant gross-margin percentage NRV method sometimes called a "joint-cost-allocation and a profit-allocation" method?

12 "Managers must decide whether a product should be sold at splitoff or processed further. The sales value at splitoff method of joint-cost allocation is the best method for generating the information managers need for this decision." Do you agree? Explain.

13 "Managers should consider only additional revenues and separable costs when making decisions about selling at splitoff or processing further." Do you agree? Explain.

14 Describe two major methods to account for byproducts.

15 Why might managers seeking a monthly bonus based on attaining a target operating income prefer the sales method of accounting for byproducts rather than the production method?

Exercises

16 **Joint-cost allocation, insurance settlement.** Quality Chicken grows and processes chickens. Each chicken is disassembled into five main parts. Information pertaining to production in July 2014 is as follows:

Parts	Pounds of Product	Wholesale Selling Price per Pound When Production Is Complete
Breasts	100	$0.55
Wings	20	0.20
Thighs	40	0.35
Bones	80	0.10
Feathers	10	0.05

Joint cost of production in July 2014 was $50.

A special shipment of 40 pounds of breasts and 15 pounds of wings has been destroyed in a fire. Quality Chicken's insurance policy provides reimbursement for the cost of the items destroyed. The insurance company permits Quality Chicken to use a joint-cost-allocation method. The splitoff point is assumed to be at the end of the production process.

1. Compute the cost of the special shipment destroyed using the following:
   a. Sales value at splitoff method
   b. Physical-measure method (pounds of finished product)
2. What joint-cost-allocation method would you recommend Quality Chicken use? Explain.

Required

17 **Joint products and byproducts (continuation of 16).** Quality Chicken is computing the ending inventory values for its July 31, 2014, balance sheet. Ending inventory amounts on July 31 are 15 pounds of breasts, 4 pounds of wings, 6 pounds of thighs, 5 pounds of bones, and 2 pounds of feathers.

Quality Chicken's management wants to use the sales value at splitoff method. However, management wants you to explore the effect on ending inventory values of classifying one or more products as a byproduct rather than a joint product.

1. Assume Quality Chicken classifies all five products as joint products. What are the ending inventory values of each product on July 31, 2014?
2. Assume Quality Chicken uses the production method of accounting for byproducts. What are the ending inventory values for each joint product on July 31, 2014, assuming breasts and thighs are the joint products and wings, bones, and feathers are byproducts?
3. Comment on differences in the results in requirements 1 and 2.

Required

18 **Net realizable value method.** Stenback Company is one of the world's leading corn refiners. It produces two joint products—corn syrup and corn starch—using a common production process. In July 2014, Stenback reported the following production and selling-price information:

	A	B	C	D
1		**Corn Syrup**	**Corn Starch**	**Joint Costs**
2	Joint costs (costs of processing corn to splitoff point)			$329,000
3	Separable cost of processing beyond splitoff point	$406,340	$97,060	
4	Beginning inventory (cases)	0	0	
5	Production and Sales (cases)	13,000	5,900	
6	Ending inventory (cases)	0	0	
7	Selling price per case	$51	$26	

Allocate the $329,000 joint costs using the NRV method.

Required

19 **Alternative joint-cost-allocation methods, further-process decision.** The Wood Spirits Company produces two products—turpentine and methanol (wood alcohol)—by a joint process. Joint costs amount to $120,000 per batch of output. Each batch totals 10,000 gallons: 25% methanol and 75% turpentine. Both products are processed further without gain or loss in volume. Separable processing costs are methanol, $3 per gallon, and turpentine, $2 per gallon. Methanol sells for $21 per gallon. Turpentine sells for $14 per gallon.

1. How much of the joint costs per batch will be allocated to turpentine and to methanol, assuming that joint costs are allocated based on the number of gallons at splitoff point?

Required

2. If joint costs are allocated on an NRV basis, how much of the joint costs will be allocated to turpentine and to methanol?

3. Prepare product-line income statements per batch for requirements 1 and 2. Assume no beginning or ending inventories.

4. The company has discovered an additional process by which the methanol (wood alcohol) can be made into a pleasant-tasting alcoholic beverage. The selling price of this beverage would be $60 a gallon. Additional processing would increase separable costs $9 per gallon (in addition to the $3 per gallon separable cost required to yield methanol). The company would have to pay excise taxes of 20% on the selling price of the beverage. Assuming no other changes in cost, what is the joint cost applicable to the wood alcohol (using the NRV method)? Should the company produce the alcoholic beverage? Show your computations.

20 Alternative methods of joint-cost allocation, ending inventories. The Cook Company operates a simple chemical process to convert a single material into three separate items, referred to here as X, Y, and Z. All three end products are separated simultaneously at a single splitoff point.

Products X and Y are ready for sale immediately upon splitoff without further processing or any other additional costs. Product Z, however, is processed further before being sold. There is no available market price for Z at the splitoff point.

The selling prices quoted here are expected to remain the same in the coming year. During 2014, the selling prices of the items and the total amounts sold were as follows:

- X—68 tons sold for $1,200 per ton
- Y—480 tons sold for $900 per ton
- Z—672 tons sold for $600 per ton

The total joint manufacturing costs for the year were $580,000. Cook spent an additional $200,000 to finish product Z.

There were no beginning inventories of X, Y, or Z. At the end of the year, the following inventories of completed units were on hand: X, 132 tons; Y, 120 tons; Z, 28 tons. There was no beginning or ending work in process.

1. Compute the cost of inventories of X, Y, and Z for balance sheet purposes and the cost of goods sold for income statement purposes as of December 31, 2014, using the following joint cost allocation methods:
   a. NRV method
   b. Constant gross-margin percentage NRV method

2. Compare the gross-margin percentages for X, Y, and Z using the two methods given in requirement 1.

21 Joint-cost allocation, process further. Sinclair Oil & Gas, a large energy conglomerate, jointly processes purchased hydrocarbons to generate three nonsalable intermediate products: ICR8, ING4, and XGE3. These intermediate products are further processed separately to produce crude oil, natural gas liquids (NGL), and natural gas (measured in liquid equivalents). An overview of the process and results for August 2014 are shown here. (Note: The numbers are small to keep the focus on key concepts.)

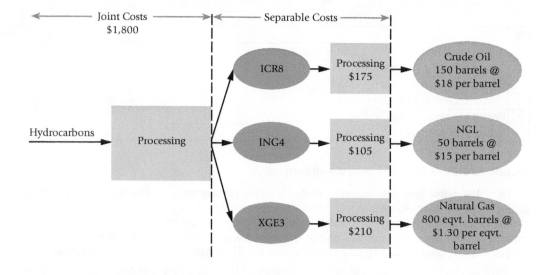

A new federal law has recently been passed that taxes crude oil at 30% of operating income. No new tax is to be paid on natural gas liquid or natural gas. Starting August 2014, Sinclair Oil & Gas must report a separate product-line income statement for crude oil. One challenge facing Sinclair Oil & Gas is how to allocate the joint cost of producing the three separate salable outputs. Assume no beginning or ending inventory.

1. Allocate the August 2014 joint cost among the three products using the following:
   a. Physical-measure method
   b. NRV method

Required

2. Show the operating income for each product using the methods in requirement 1.
3. Discuss the pros and cons of the two methods to Sinclair Oil & Gas for making decisions about product emphasis (pricing, sell-or-process-further decisions, and so on).
4. Draft a letter to the taxation authorities on behalf of Sinclair Oil & Gas that justifies the joint-cost-allocation method you recommend Sinclair use.

22 Joint-cost allocation, sales value, physical measure, NRV methods. Fancy Foods produces two types of microwavable products: beef-flavored ramen and shrimp-flavored ramen. The two products share common inputs such as noodle and spices. The production of ramen results in a waste product referred to as stock, which Fancy dumps at negligible costs in a local drainage area. In June 2014, the following data were reported for the production and sales of beef-flavored and shrimp-flavored ramen:

	Home Insert Page Layout Formulas Data Review		
	A	B	C
1		**Joint Costs**	
2	Joint costs (costs of noodles, spices, and other inputs and processing to splitoff point)	$400,000	
3			
4		**Beef Ramen**	**Shrimp Ramen**
5	Beginning inventory (tons)	0	0
6	Production (tons)	20,000	28,000
7	Sales (tons)	20,000	28,000
8	Selling price per ton	$ 5	$ 20

Due to the popularity of its microwavable products, Fancy decides to add a new line of products that targets dieters. These new products are produced by adding a special ingredient to dilute the original ramen and are to be sold under the names Special B and Special S, respectively. Following are the monthly data for all the products:

	Home Insert Page Layout Formulas Data Review View				
	A	B	C	D	E
11		**Joint Costs**		**Special B**	**Special S**
12	Joint costs (costs of noodles, spices, and other inputs and processing to splitoff point)	$400,000			
13	Separable costs of processing 20,000 tons of Beef Ramen into 25,000 tons of Special B			$100,000	
14	Separable cost of processing 28,000 tons of Shrimp Ramen into 34,000 tons of Special S				$238,000
15					
16		**Beef Ramen**	**Shrimp Ramen**	**Special B**	**Special S**
17	Beginning inventory (tons)	0	0	0	0
18	Production (tons)	20,000	28,000	25,000	34,000
19	Transfer for further processing (tons)	20,000	28,000		
20	Sales (tons)			25,000	34,000
21	Selling price per ton	$ 5	$ 20	$ 17	$ 33

1. Calculate Fancy's gross-margin percentage for Special B and Special S when joint costs are allocated using the following:
   a. Sales value at splitoff method
   b. Physical-measure method
   c. Net realizable value method

2. Recently, Fancy discovered that the stock it is dumping can be sold to cattle ranchers at $4 per ton. In a typical month with the production levels shown, 6,000 tons of stock are produced and can be sold by incurring marketing costs of $12,400. Sandra Dashel, a management accountant, points out that treating the stock as a joint product and using the sales value at splitoff method, the stock product would lose about $2,435 each month, so it should not be sold. How did Dashel arrive at that final number, and what do you think of her analysis? Should Fancy sell the stock?

23 Joint cost allocation: Sell immediately or process further. Illinois Soy Products (ISP) buys soybeans and processes them into other soy products. Each ton of soybeans that ISP purchases for $340 can be converted for an additional $190 into 575 pounds of soy meal and 160 gallons of soy oil. A pound of soy meal can be sold at splitoff for $1.24 and soy oil can be sold in bulk for $4.25 per gallon.

ISP can process the 575 pounds of soy meal into 725 pounds of soy cookies at an additional cost of $380. Each pound of soy cookies can be sold for $2.24 per pound. The 160 gallons of soy oil can be packaged at a cost of $240 and made into 640 quarts of Soyola. Each quart of Soyola can be sold for $1.35.

1. Allocate the joint cost to the cookies and the Soyola using the following:
   a. Sales value at splitoff method
   b. NRV method

2. Should ISP have processed each of the products further? What effect does the allocation method have on this decision?

24 Accounting for a main product and a byproduct. (Cheatham and Green, adapted) Tasty, Inc., is a producer of potato chips. A single production process at Tasty, Inc., yields potato chips as the main product and a byproduct that can also be sold as a snack. Both products are fully processed by the splitoff point, and there are no separable costs.

For September 2014, the cost of operations is $500,000. Production and sales data are as follows:

	Production (in pounds)	Sales (in pounds)	Selling Price per Pound
Main Product:			
Potato Chips	52,000	42,640	$16
Byproduct	8,500	6,500	$10

There were no beginning inventories on September 1, 2014.

1. What is the gross margin for Tasty, Inc., under the production method and the sales method of byproduct accounting?
2. What are the inventory costs reported in the balance sheet on September 30, 2014, for the main product and byproduct under the two methods of byproduct accounting in requirement 1?

25 Joint costs and decision making. Jack Bibby is a prospector in the Texas Panhandle. He has also been running a side business for the past couple of years. Based on the popularity of shows such as "Rattlesnake Nation," there has been a surge of interest from professionals and amateurs to visit the northern counties of Texas to capture snakes in the wild. Jack has set himself up as a purchaser of these captured snakes.

Jack purchases rattlesnakes in good condition from "snake hunters" for an average of $11 per snake. Jack produces canned snake meat, cured skins, and souvenir rattles, although he views snake meat as his primary product. At the end of the recent season, Jack Bibby evaluated his financial results:

	Meat	Skins	Rattles	Total
Sales revenues	$33,000	$8,800	$2,200	$44,000
Share of snake cost	19,800	5,280	1,320	26,400
Processing expenses	6,600	990	660	8,250
Allocated overhead	4,400	660	440	5,500
Income (loss)	$ 2,200	$1,870	($ 220)	$ 3,850

The cost of snakes is assigned to each product line using the *relative* sales value of meat, skins, and rattles (i.e., the percentage of total sales generated by each product). Processing expenses are directly traced to each product line. Overhead costs represent Jack's basic living expenses. These are allocated to each product line on the basis of processing expenses.

Jack has a philosophy of every product line paying for itself and is determined to cut his losses on rattles.

Required

1. Should Jack Bibby drop rattles from his product offerings? Support your answer with computations.
2. An old miner has offered to buy every rattle "as is" for $0.60 per rattle (note: "as is" refers to the situation where Jack only removes the rattle from the snake and no processing costs are incurred). Assume that Jack expects to process the same number of snakes each season. Should he sell rattles to the miner? Support your answer with computations.

26   Joint costs and byproducts. (W. Crum adapted) Royston, Inc., is a large food-processing company. It processes 150,000 pounds of peanuts in the peanuts department at a cost of $180,000 to yield 12,000 pounds of product A, 65,000 pounds of product B, and 16,000 pounds of product C.

- Product A is processed further in the salting department to yield 12,000 pounds of salted peanuts at a cost of $27,000 and sold for $12 per pound.

- Product B (raw peanuts) is sold without further processing at $3 per pound.

- Product C is considered a byproduct and is processed further in the paste department to yield 16,000 pounds of peanut butter at a cost of $12,000 and sold for $6 per pound.

The company wants to make a gross margin of 10% of revenues on product C and needs to allow 20% of revenues for marketing costs on product C. An overview of operations follows:

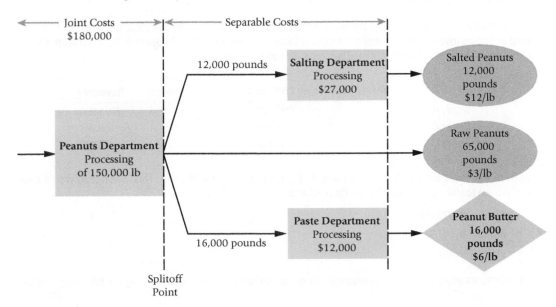

Required

1. Compute unit costs per pound for products A, B, and C, treating C as a byproduct. Use the NRV method for allocating joint costs. Deduct the NRV of the byproduct produced from the joint cost of products A and B.
2. Compute unit costs per pound for products A, B, and C, treating all three as joint products and allocating joint costs by the NRV method.

Problems

MyAccountingLab

27   Methods of joint-cost allocation, ending inventory. Tivoli Labs produces a drug used for the treatment of hypertension. The drug is produced in batches. Chemicals costing $60,000 are mixed and heated, creating a reaction; a unique separation process then extracts the drug from the mixture. A batch yields a total of 2,500 gallons of the chemicals. The first 2,000 gallons are sold for human use while the last 500 gallons, which contain impurities, are sold to veterinarians.

The costs of mixing, heating, and extracting the drug amount to $90,000 per batch. The output sold for human use is pasteurized at a total cost of $120,000 and is sold for $585 per gallon. The product sold to veterinarians is irradiated at a cost of $10 per gallon and is sold for $410 per gallon.

In March, Tivoli, which had no opening inventory, processed one batch of chemicals. It sold 1,700 gallons of product for human use and 300 gallons of the veterinarian product. Tivoli uses the net realizable value method for allocating joint production costs.

1. How much in joint costs does Tivoli allocate to each product?
2. Compute the cost of ending inventory for each of Tivoli's products.
3. If Tivoli were to use the constant gross-margin percentage NRV method instead, how would it allocate its joint costs?
4. Calculate the gross margin on the sale of the product for human use in March under the constant gross-margin percentage NRV method.
5. Suppose that the separation process also yields 300 pints of a toxic byproduct. Tivoli currently pays a hauling company $5,000 to dispose of this byproduct. Tivoli is contacted by a firm interested in purchasing a modified form of this byproduct for a total price of $6,000. Tivoli estimates that it will cost about $30 per pint to do the required modification. Should Tivoli accept the offer?

28   Alternative methods of joint-cost allocation, product-mix decisions. The Eastern Oil Company buys crude vegetable oil. Refining this oil results in four products at the splitoff point: A, B, C, and D. Product C is fully processed by the splitoff point. Products A, B, and D can individually be further refined into Super A, Super B, and Super D. In the most recent month (December), the output at the splitoff point was as follows:

- Product A, 275,000 gallons
- Product B, 100,000 gallons
- Product C, 75,000 gallons
- Product D, 50,000 gallons

The joint costs of purchasing and processing the crude vegetable oil were $105,000. Eastern had no beginning or ending inventories. Sales of product C in December were $45,000. Products A, B, and D were further refined and then sold. Data related to December are as follows:

	Separable Processing Costs to Make Super Products	Revenues
Super A	$240,000	$375,000
Super B	60,000	150,000
Super D	45,000	75,000

Eastern had the option of selling products A, B, and D at the splitoff point. This alternative would have yielded the following revenues for the December production:

- Product A, $75,000
- Product B, $62,500
- Product D, $67,500

1. Compute the gross-margin percentage for each product sold in December, using the following methods for allocating the $105,000 joint costs:
   a. Sales value at splitoff
   b. Physical-measure
   c. NRV
2. Could Eastern have increased its December operating income by making different decisions about the further processing of products A, B, or D? Show the effect on operating income of any changes you recommend.

29   Comparison of alternative joint-cost-allocation methods, further-processing decision, chocolate products. The Cocoa Factory manufactures and distributes chocolate products. It purchases cocoa beans and processes them into two intermediate products: chocolate-powder liquor base and milk-chocolate liquor base. These two intermediate products become separately identifiable at a single splitoff point. Every 2,000 pounds of cocoa beans yields 50 gallons of chocolate-powder liquor base and 50 gallons of milk-chocolate liquor base.

The chocolate-powder liquor base is further processed into chocolate powder. Every 50 gallons of chocolate-powder liquor base yield 650 pounds of chocolate powder. The milk-chocolate liquor base is further processed into milk chocolate. Every 50 gallons of milk-chocolate liquor base yield 1,070 pounds of milk chocolate.

Production and sales data for August 2014 are as follows (assume no beginning inventory):

▪ Cocoa beans processed, 28,000 pounds

▪ Costs of processing cocoa beans to splitoff point (including purchase of beans), $62,000

	Production	Sales	Selling Price	Separable Processing Costs
Chocolate powder	9,100 pounds	6,500 pounds	$ 9 per pound	$50,100
Milk chocolate	14,980 pounds	13,500 pounds	$10 per pound	$60,115

Cocoa Factory fully processes both of its intermediate products into chocolate powder or milk chocolate. There is an active market for these intermediate products. In August 2014, Cocoa Factory could have sold the chocolate-powder liquor base for $20 a gallon and the milk-chocolate liquor base for $60 a gallon.

Required

1. Calculate how the joint costs of $62,000 would be allocated between chocolate powder and milk chocolate under the following methods:
   a. Sales value at splitoff
   b. Physical-measure (gallons)
   c. NRV
   d. Constant gross-margin percentage NRV
2. What are the gross-margin percentages of chocolate powder and milk chocolate under each of the methods in requirement 1?
3. Could Cocoa Factory have increased its operating income by a change in its decision to fully process both of its intermediate products? Show your computations.

30 Joint-cost allocation, process further or sell. (CMA, adapted) Doughty Sawmill, Inc., (DSI) purchases logs from independent timber contractors and processes the logs into three types of lumber products:

▪ Studs for residential buildings (walls, ceilings)

▪ Decorative pieces (fireplace mantels, beams for cathedral ceilings)

▪ Posts used as support braces (mine support braces, braces for exterior fences on ranch properties)

These products are the result of a joint sawmill process that involves removal of bark from the logs, cutting the logs into a workable size (ranging from 8 to 16 feet in length), and then cutting the individual products from the logs.
The joint process results in the following costs of products for a typical month:

Direct materials (rough timber logs)	$ 485,000
Debarking (labor and overhead)	65,000
Sizing (labor and overhead)	215,000
Product cutting (labor and overhead)	255,000
Total joint costs	$1,020,000

Product yields and average sales values on a per-unit basis from the joint process are as follows:

Product	Monthly Output of Materials at Splitoff Point	Fully Processed Selling Price
Studs	82,000 units	$ 6
Decorative pieces	2,000 units	110
Posts	18,000 units	16

The studs are sold as rough-cut lumber after emerging from the sawmill operation without further processing by DSI. Also, the posts require no further processing beyond the splitoff point. The decorative pieces must be planed and further sized after emerging from the sawmill. This additional processing costs $110,000 per month and normally results in a loss of 10% of the units entering the process. Without this planing and sizing process, there is still an active intermediate market for the unfinished decorative pieces in which the selling price averages $70 per unit.

Required

1. Based on the information given for Doughty Sawmill, allocate the joint processing costs of $1,020,000 to the three products using:
   a. Sales value at splitoff method
   b. Physical-measure method (volume in units)
   c. NRV method

2. Prepare an analysis for Doughty Sawmill that compares processing the decorative pieces further, as it currently does, with selling them as a rough-cut product immediately at splitoff.

3. Assume Doughty Sawmill announced that in six months it will sell the unfinished decorative pieces at splitoff due to increasing competitive pressure. Identify at least three types of likely behavior that will be demonstrated by the skilled labor in the planing-and-sizing process as a result of this announcement. Include in your discussion how this behavior could be influenced by management.

31   Joint-cost allocation. Clover Dairy Products Corp. buys one input, full-cream milk, and refines it in a churning process. From each gallon of milk Clover produces three cups of butter and nine cups of buttermilk. During May 2014, Clover bought 12,000 gallons of milk for $44,500. Clover spent another $18,860 on the churning process to separate the milk into butter and buttermilk. Butter could be sold immediately for $4.40 per pound and buttermilk could be sold immediately for $2.40 per quart (note: two cups = one pound; four cups = one quart).

Clover chooses to process the butter further into spreadable butter by mixing it with canola oil, incurring an additional cost of $3.20 per pound. This process results in two tubs of spreadable butter for each pound of butter processed. Each tub of spreadable butter sells for $4.60.

Required

1. Allocate the $63,360 joint cost to the spreadable butter and the buttermilk using the following:
   a. Physical-measure method (using cups) of joint cost allocation
   b. Sales value at splitoff method of joint cost allocation
   c. NRV method of joint cost allocation
   d. Constant gross margin percentage NRV method of joint cost allocation

2. Each of these measures has advantages and disadvantages; what are they?

3. Some claim that the sales value at splitoff method is the best method to use. Discuss the logic behind this claim.

32   Further processing decision (continuation of 31). Clover has decided that buttermilk may sell better if it was marketed for baking and sold in pints. This would involve additional packaging at an incremental cost of $0.70 per pint. Each pint could be sold for $1.50 (note: one quart = two pints).

Required

1. If Clover uses the sales value at splitoff method, what combination of products should Clover sell to maximize profits?

2. If Clover uses the physical-measure method, what combination of products should Clover sell to maximize profits?

3. Explain the effect that the different cost allocation methods have on the decision to sell the products at splitoff or to process them further.

33   Joint-cost allocation with a byproduct. Mat Place purchases old tires and recycles them to produce rubber floor mats and car mats. The company washes, shreds, and molds the recycled tires into sheets. The floor and car mats are cut from these sheets. A small amount of rubber shred remains after the mats are cut. The rubber shreds can be sold to use as cover for paths and playgrounds. The company can produce 25 floor mats, 75 car mats, and 40 pounds of rubber shreds from 100 old tires.

In May, Mat Place, which had no beginning inventory, processed 125,000 tires and had joint production costs of $600,000. Mat Place sold 25,000 floor mats, 85,000 car mats, and 43,000 pounds of rubber shreds. The company sells each floor mat for $12 and each car mat for $6. The company treats the rubber shreds as a byproduct that can be sold for $0.70 per pound.

Required

1. Assume that Mat Place allocates the joint costs to floor mats and car mats using the sales value at splitoff method and accounts for the byproduct using the production method. What is the ending inventory cost for each product and gross margin for Mat Place?

2. Assume that Mat Place allocates the joint costs to floor mats and car mats using the sales value at splitoff method and accounts for the byproduct using the sales method. What is the ending inventory cost for each product and gross margin for Mat Place?

3. Discuss the difference between the two methods of accounting for byproducts, focusing on what conditions are necessary to use each method.

34 Byproduct-costing journal entries (continuation of 33). The Mat Place's accountant needs to record the information about the joint and byproducts in the general journal, but is not sure what the entries should be. The company has hired you as a consultant to help its accountant.

Required

1. Show journal entries at the time of production and at the time of sale assuming the Mat Place accounts for the byproduct using the production method.
2. Show journal entries at the time of production and at the time of sale assuming the Mat Place accounts for the byproduct using the sales method.

35 Process further or sell, byproduct. (CMA, adapted) Newcastle Mining Company (NMC) mines coal, puts it through a one-step crushing process, and loads the bulk raw coal onto river barges for shipment to customers.

NMC's management is currently evaluating the possibility of further processing the raw coal by sizing and cleaning it and selling it to an expanded set of customers at higher prices. The option of building a new sizing and cleaning plant is ruled out as being financially infeasible. Instead, Amy Kimbell, a mining engineer, is asked to explore outside-contracting arrangements for the cleaning and sizing process. Kimbell puts together the following summary:

	A	B	C
	Home Insert Page Layout Formulas Data Review View		
1	Selling price of raw coal	$30 per ton	
2	Cost of producing raw coal	$21 per ton	
3	Selling price of sized and cleaned coal	$34 per ton	
4	Annual raw coal output	9,000,000 tons	
5	Percentage of material weight loss in sizing/cleaning coal	6%	
6			
7		**Incremental Costs of Sizing & Cleaning Processes**	
8	Direct labor	$790,000 per year	
9	Supervisory personnel	$190,000 per year	
10	Heavy equipment: rental, operating, maintenance costs	$35,000 per month	
11	Contract sizing and cleaning	$3.30 per ton of raw coal	
12	Outbound rail freight	$250 per 600-ton rail car	
13			
14	Percentage of sizing/cleaning waste that can be salvaged for coal fines	75%	
15	Range of costs per ton for preparing coal fine for sale	$3	$5
16	Range of coal fine selling prices (per ton)	$14	$25

Kimbell also learns that 75% of the material loss that occurs in the cleaning and sizing process can be salvaged as coal fines, which can be sold to steel manufacturers for their furnaces. The sale of coal fines is erratic and NMC may need to stockpile them in a protected area for up to one year. The selling price of coal fines ranges from $14 to $25 per ton and costs of preparing coal fines for sale range from $3 to $5 per ton.

Required

1. Prepare an analysis to show whether it is more profitable for NMC to continue selling raw bulk coal or to process it further through sizing and cleaning. (Ignore coal fines in your analysis.)
2. How would your analysis be affected if the cost of producing raw coal could be held down to $20 per ton?
3. Now consider the potential value of the coal fines and prepare an addendum that shows how their value affects the results of your analysis prepared in requirement 1.

36 **Joint-cost allocation, process further or sell.** Iridium Technologies manufactures a variety of flash memory chips at its main foundry in Anam, Korea. Some chips are sold by Iridium to makers of electronic equipment while others are embedded into consumer products for sale under Iridium's house label, Celeron. At Anam, Iridium produces three chips that arise from a common production process. The first chip, Apple, is sold to a maker of smartphones and personal computers. The second chip, Broadcom, is intended for a wireless and broadband communication firm. Iridium uses the third chip to manufacture and market a solid-state device under the Celeron name.

Data regarding these three products for the fiscal year ended June 30, 2014, are given below.

	Apple	Broadcom	Celeron
Units produced	510,000	990,000	1,500,000
Selling price per unit at splitoff	$ 7.00	$ 4.00	—
Separable costs	—	—	$8,400,000
Final selling price per unit	—	—	$ 10.00

Iridium incurred joint product costs up to the splitoff point of $10,800,000 during the fiscal year.

The head of Iridium, Amala Peterman, is considering a variety of alternatives that would potentially change the way the three products are processed and sold. Proposed changes for each product are as follows:

- Apple chips can be incorporated into Iridium's own memory stick. However, this additional processing causes a loss of 55,000 units of Apple. The separable costs to further process Apple chips are estimated to be $1,500,000 annually. The memory stick would sell for $11 per unit.

- Iridium's R&D unit has recommended that the company process Broadcom further into a 3D vertical chip and sell it to a high-end vendor of datacenter products. The additional processing would cost $2,000,000 annually and would result in 25% more units of product. The 3D vertical chip sells for $5.00 per unit.

- The third chip is currently incorporated into a solid-state device under the Celeron name. Galaxy Electronics has approached Iridium with an offer to purchase this chip at the splitoff point for $4.75 per unit.

1. Allocate the $10,800,000 joint production cost to Apple, Broadcom, and Celeron using the NRV method.
2. Identify which of the three joint products Iridium should sell at the splitoff point in the future and which of the three the company should process further to maximize operating income. Support your decisions with appropriate computations.

37 **Methods of joint-cost allocation, comprehensive.** Kardash Cosmetics purchases flowers in bulk and processes them into perfume. From a certain mix of petals, the firm uses Process A to generate Seduction, its high-grade perfume, as well as a certain residue. The residue is then further treated, using Process B, to yield Romance, a medium-grade perfume. An ounce of residue typically yields an ounce of Romance.

In July, the company used 25,000 pounds of petals. Costs involved in Process A, i.e., reducing the petals to Seduction and the residue, were:

Direct Materials - $440,000; Direct Labor - $220,000; Overhead Costs - $110,000.
The additional costs of producing Romance in Process B were:

Direct Materials - $22,000; Direct Labor - $50,000; Overhead Costs - $40,000.
During July, Process A yielded 7,000 ounces of Seduction and 49,000 ounces of residue. From this, 5,000 ounces of Seduction were packaged and sold for $109.50 an ounce. Also, 28,000 ounces of Romance were processed in Process B and then packaged and sold for $31.50 an ounce. The other 21,000 ounces remained as residue. Packaging costs incurred were $137,500 for Seduction and $196,000 for Romance. The firm has no beginning inventory on July 1.

If it so desired, the firm could have sold unpackaged Seduction for $56 an ounce and the residue from Process A for $24 an ounce.

1. What is the joint cost of the firm to be allocated to Seduction and Romance?
2. Under the physical measure method, how would the joint costs be allocated to Seduction and Romance?
3. Under the sales value at splitoff method, what portion of the joint costs would be allocated to Seduction and Romance, respectively?

4. What is the estimated net realizable value per ounce of Seduction and Romance?
5. Under the net realizable value method, what portion of the joint costs would be allocated to Seduction and Romance, respectively?
6. What is the gross margin percentage for the firm as a whole?
7. Allocate the joint costs to Seduction and Romance under the constant gross-margin percentage NRV method.
8. If you were the manager of Kardash Cosmetics, would you continue to process the petal residue into Romance perfume? Explain your answer.

Glossary

Byproducts. Products from a joint production process that have low total sales values compared with the total sales value of the main product or of joint products.

Constant gross-margin percentage NRV method. Method that allocates joint costs to joint products in such a way that the overall gross-margin percentage is identical for the individual products.

Joint costs. Costs of a production process that yields multiple products simultaneously.

Joint products. Two or more products that have high total sales values compared with the total sales values of other products yielded by a joint production process.

Main product. Product from a joint production process that has a high total sales value compared with the total sales values of all other products of the joint production process.

Net realizable value (NRV) method. Method that allocates joint costs to joint products on the basis of final sales value minus separable costs of total production of the joint products during the accounting period.

Physical-measure method. Method that allocates joint costs to joint products on the basis of the relative weight, volume, or other physical measure at the splitoff point of total production of these products during the accounting period.

Product. Any output that has a positive total sales value (or an output that enables an organization to avoid incurring costs).

Sales value at splitoff method. Method that allocates joint costs to joint products on the basis of the relative total sales value at the splitoff point of the total production of these products during the accounting period.

Separable costs. All costs (manufacturing, marketing, distribution, and so on) incurred beyond the splitoff point that are assignable to each of the specific products identified at the splitoff point.

Splitoff point. The juncture in a joint-production process when two or more products become separately identifiable.

Photo Credits

Process Costing

From Chapter 17 of *Cost Accounting: A Managerial Emphasis,* Fifteenth Edition. Charles T. Horngren, Srikant M. Datar,
Madhav V. Rajan. Copyright © 2015 by Pearson Education, Inc. All rights reserved.

Process Costing

Learning Objectives

1 Identify the situations in which process-costing systems are appropriate

2 Understand the basic concepts of process costing and compute average unit costs

3 Describe the five steps in process costing and calculate equivalent units

4 Use the weighted-average method and first-in, first-out (FIFO) method of process costing

5 Apply process-costing methods to situations with transferred-in costs

6 Understand the need for hybrid-costing systems such as operation costing

Many companies use mass-production techniques to produce identical or similar units of a product or service:

Apple (smartphones), Coca-Cola (soft drinks), ExxonMobil (gasoline), JP MorganChase (processing of checks), and Novartis (pharmaceuticals). Managerial accountants at companies like these use process costing because it helps them (1) determine how many units of the product the firm has on hand at the end of an accounting reporting period, (2) evaluate the units' stages of completion, and (3) assign costs to units produced and in inventory. There are different methods for process costing (for example, the FIFO or weighted-average methods) that are based on different assumptions about the flow of product costs. As you learned in your financial accounting class, the choice of method results in different operating income and affects the taxes a company pays and the performance evaluation of managers. At times, variations in international rules and customs also determine the method chosen. In the case of ExxonMobil, differences in inventory accounting rules for the United States versus Europe have a large impact on the company's profits and tax liability.

ExxonMobil and Accounting Differences in the Oil Patch[1]

In 2013, ExxonMobil was ranked second in the *Fortune* 500 annual ranking of the largest U.S. companies, with revenue of $453 billion and more than $44 billion in profits. Believe it or not, however, by one measure ExxonMobil's profits are *understated*.

ExxonMobil, like most U.S. energy companies, uses last-in, first-out (LIFO) accounting for financial reporting. Under LIFO, ExxonMobil records its cost of inventory at the latest price paid for crude oil in the open market, even though it is often selling oil produced at a much lower cost. This increases the company's cost of goods sold, which in turn reduces profit and tax payments.

Assigning costs to inventory is a critical part of process costing, and a company's choice of method can result in substantially different profits. For instance, ExxonMobil's 2012 net income would have been $4.3 billion lower under FIFO. However, if ExxonMobil had used FIFO accounting in prior years, its operating income over the years would have been higher by $21.3 billion. Assuming a marginal tax rate of 35%, this would have resulted in an incremental tax burden of almost $7.5 billion.

It is interesting to note that International Financial Reporting Standards (IFRS) do not permit the use of LIFO accounting. European oil companies such as Royal Dutch Shell and British Petroleum must use the first-in, first-out (FIFO) methodology instead

---

[1] *Source:* Exxon Mobil Corporation, 2012 Annual Report (Irving, TX: Exxon Mobil Corporation, 2013); Izabella Kaminska, "Shell, BP, and the Increasing Cost of Inventory," *Financial Times*. "FT Alphaville" blog (April 29, 2010); David Reilly, "Big Oil's Accounting Methods Fuel Criticism," *Wall Street Journal* (August 8, 2006).

when accounting for inventory, thereby preventing them from receiving the favorable inventory accounting treatment enjoyed by ExxonMobil.

Companies such as ExxonMobil, Kellogg (cereals), and AB InBev (beer) produce many identical or similar units of a product using mass-production techniques. The focus of these companies on individual production processes gives rise to process costing. This chapter describes how companies use process-costing methods to determine the costs of products or services and to value inventory and the cost of goods sold.

Illustrating Process Costing

Learning Objective 1

Identify the situations in which process-costing systems are appropriate

...when masses of identical or similar units are produced

Before examining process costing in more detail, let's briefly discuss the distinction between job costing and process costing. Job-costing and process-costing systems are best viewed as ends of a continuum:

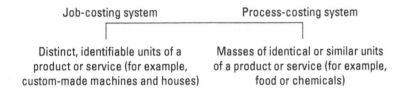

Job-costing system — Process-costing system

Distinct, identifiable units of a product or service (for example, custom-made machines and houses)

Masses of identical or similar units of a product or service (for example, food or chemicals)

In a *process-costing system*, the unit cost of a product or service is obtained by assigning total costs to many identical or similar units of output. In other words, unit costs are calculated by dividing total costs incurred by the number of units of output from the production process. In a manufacturing process-costing setting, each unit receives the same or similar amounts of direct material costs, direct manufacturing labor costs, and indirect manufacturing costs (manufacturing overhead).

The main difference between process costing and job costing is the *extent of averaging* used to compute the unit costs of products or services. In a job-costing system, individual jobs use different quantities of resources, so it would be incorrect to cost each job at the same average production cost. In contrast, when identical or similar units of products or services are mass-produced rather than processed as individual jobs, process costing is used to calculate an average production cost for all units produced. Some processes such as clothes manufacturing have aspects of both process costing (the cost per unit of each operation, such as cutting or sewing, is identical) and job costing (different materials are used in different batches of clothing, say, wool versus cotton). The final section in this chapter describes "hybrid" costing systems that combine elements of both job and process costing.

Consider the following example: Suppose that Pacific Electronics manufactures a variety of cell phone models. These models are assembled in the assembly department. Upon completion, units are transferred to the testing department. We focus on the assembly department process for one model, SG-40. All units of SG-40 are identical and must meet a set of demanding performance specifications. The process-costing system for SG-40 in the assembly department has a single direct-cost category—direct materials—and a single indirect-cost category—conversion costs. Conversion costs are all manufacturing costs other than direct material costs, including manufacturing labor, energy, plant depreciation, and so on. As the following figure shows, direct materials, such as a phone's circuit board, antenna, and microphone, are added at the beginning of the assembly process. Conversion costs are added evenly during assembly.

The following graphic represents these facts:

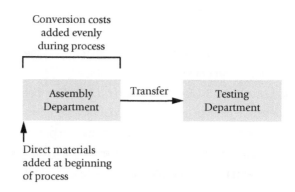

Process-costing systems separate costs into cost categories according to *when costs are introduced into the process.* Often, as in our Pacific Electronics example, only two cost classifications—direct materials and conversion costs—are necessary to assign costs to products. Why only two? Because *all* direct materials are added to the process at one time and all conversion costs generally are added to the process evenly through time. Sometimes the situation is different.

1. If two different direct materials—such as the circuit board and microphone—are added to the process at different times, two different direct-materials categories would be needed to assign these costs to products.

2. If manufacturing labor costs are added to the process at a different time compared to other conversion costs, an additional cost category—direct manufacturing labor costs— would be needed to assign these costs to products.

We illustrate process costing using three cases of increasing complexity:

▪ **Case 1**—Process costing with zero beginning and zero ending work-in-process inventory of SG-40. (That is, all units are started and fully completed within the accounting period.) *This case presents the most basic concepts of process costing and illustrates the averaging of costs.*

▪ **Case 2**—Process costing with zero beginning work-in-process inventory and some ending work-in-process inventory of SG-40. (That is, some units of SG-40 started during the accounting period are incomplete at the end of the period.) *This case introduces the five steps of process costing and the concept of equivalent units.*

▪ **Case 3**—Process costing with both some beginning and some ending work-in-process inventory of SG-40. *This case adds more complexity and illustrates the effects the weighted-average and first-in, first-out (FIFO) methods have on the cost of units completed and the cost of work-in-process inventory.*

Case 1: Process Costing with No Beginning or Ending Work-in-Process Inventory

On January 1, 2014, there was no beginning inventory of SG-40 units in the assembly department. During the month of January, Pacific Electronics started, completely assembled, and transferred 400 units to the testing department.

Data for the assembly department for January 2014 are as follows:

Physical Units for January 2014

Work in process, beginning inventory (January 1)	0 units
Started during January	400 units
Completed and transferred out during January	400 units
Work in process, ending inventory (January 31)	0 units

Physical units refer to the number of output units, whether complete or incomplete. In January 2014, all 400 physical units started were completed.

Total Costs for January 2014

Direct materials costs added during January	$32,000
Conversion costs added during January	24,000
Total assembly department costs added during January	$56,000

Pacific Electronics records direct materials costs and conversion costs in the assembly department as these costs are incurred. The cost per unit is then calculated by dividing the total costs incurred in a given accounting period by the total units produced in that period. So, the assembly department cost of an SG-40 is $56,000 ÷ 400 units = $140 per unit:

Direct material cost per unit ($32,000 ÷ 400 units)	$ 80
Conversion cost per unit ($24,000 ÷ 400 units)	60
Assembly department cost per unit	$140

Decision Point

How are average unit costs computed when no inventories are present?

Case 1 applies whenever a company produces a homogeneous product or service but has no incomplete units when each accounting period ends, which is a common situation in service-sector organizations. For example, a bank can adopt this process-costing approach to compute the unit cost of processing 100,000 customer deposits made in a month because each deposit is processed in the same way regardless of the amount of the deposit.

Learning Objective 3

Describe the five steps in process costing

...to assign total costs to units completed and to units in work in process

and calculate equivalent units

...output units adjusted for incomplete units

Case 2: Process Costing with Zero Beginning and Some Ending Work-in-Process Inventory

In February 2014, Pacific Electronics places another 400 units of SG-40 into production. Because all units placed into production in January were completely assembled, there is no beginning inventory of partially completed units in the assembly department on February 1. Some customers order late, so not all units started in February are completed by the end of the month. Only 175 units are completed and transferred to the testing department.

Data for the assembly department for February 2014 are as follows:

	A	B	C	D	E
		Physical Units (SG-40s) (1)	**Direct Materials** (2)	**Conversion Costs** (3)	**Total Costs** (4) = (2) + (3)
2	Work in process, beginning inventory (February 1)	0			
3	Started during February	400			
4	Completed and transferred out during February	175			
5	Work in process, ending inventory (February 28)	225			
6	Degree of completion of ending work in process		100%	60%	
7	Total costs added during February		$32,000	$18,600	$50,600

The 225 partially assembled units as of February 28, 2014, are fully processed for direct materials because all direct materials in the assembly department are added at the beginning of the assembly process. Conversion costs, however, are added evenly during assembly.

An assembly department supervisor estimates that the partially assembled units are, on average, 60% complete with respect to conversion costs.

The accuracy of the completion estimate of conversion costs depends on the care, skill, and experience of the estimator and the nature of the conversion process. Estimating the degree of completion is usually easier for direct material costs than for conversion costs because the quantity of direct materials needed for a completed unit and the quantity of direct materials in a partially completed unit can be measured more accurately. In contrast, the conversion sequence usually consists of a number of operations, each for a specified period of time, at various steps in the production process.[2] The degree of completion for conversion costs depends on the proportion of the total conversion costs needed to complete one unit (or a batch of production) that has already been incurred on the units still in process.

Department supervisors and line managers are most familiar with the conversion process, so they most often estimate completion rates for conversion costs. However, in some industries, such as semiconductor manufacturing, no exact estimate is possible because manufacturing occurs inside sealed environments that can be opened only when the process is complete. In other settings, such as the textile industry, vast quantities of unfinished products such as shirts and pants make the task of estimation too costly. In these cases, to calculate the conversion costs, managers assume that all work in process in a department is complete to some preset degree (for example, one-third, one-half, or two-thirds).

Because some units are fully assembled and some are only partially assembled, a common metric is needed to compare the work that's been done on them and, more importantly, obtain a total measure of the work done. The concept we will use in this regard is that of *equivalent units*. We will explain this concept in greater detail next as part of the set of five steps required to calculate (1) the cost of fully assembled units in February 2014 and (2) the cost of partially assembled units still in process at the end of that month, for Pacific Electronics. The five steps of process costing are as follows:

Step 1:   Summarize the flow of physical units of output.

Step 2:   Compute output in terms of equivalent units.

Step 3:   Summarize the total costs to account for.

Step 4:   Compute the cost per equivalent unit.

Step 5:   Assign the total costs to the units completed and to the units in ending work-in-process inventory.

Summarizing the Physical Units and Equivalent Units (Steps 1 and 2)

In **Step 1,** managers track the physical units of output. Recall that physical units are the number of output units, whether complete or incomplete. The physical-units column of Exhibit 1 tracks where the physical units came from (400 units started) and where they went (175 units completed and transferred out and 225 units in ending inventory). Remember that when there is no beginning inventory, the number of units started must equal the sum of units transferred out and ending inventory.

Because not all 400 physical units are fully completed, in **Step 2,** managers compute the output in *equivalent units*, not in *physical units*. **Equivalent units** are a derived measure of output calculated by (1) taking the quantity of each input (factor of production) in units completed and in incomplete units of work in process and (2) converting the quantity of input into the amount of completed output units that could be produced with that quantity of input. To see what is meant by equivalent units, suppose that during a month, 50 physical units were started but not completed. Managers estimate that the 50 units in ending inventory are 70% complete for conversion costs. Now, suppose all the conversion costs represented in these units were used to make fully completed units instead. How many completed units would that have resulted in? The answer is 35 units.

---

[2] For example, consider the conventional tanning process for converting hide to leather. Obtaining 250–300 kg of leather requires putting one metric ton of raw hide through as many as 15 steps: from soaking, liming, and pickling to tanning, dyeing, and fatliquoring, the step in which oils are introduced into the skin before the leather is dried.

Exhibit 1

Summarize the Flow
of Physical Units and
Compute Output in
Equivalent Units for the
Assembly Department
for February 2014

	Home	Insert	Page Layout	Formulas	Data	Review	View		
	A					B	C		D
1						(Step 1)	(Step 2)		
2							Equivalent Units		
3	Flow of Production					Physical Units	Direct Materials		Conversion Costs
4	Work in process, beginning					0			
5	Started during current period					400			
6	To account for					400			
7	Completed and transferred out during current period					175	175		175
8	Work in process, ending[a]					225			
9	(225 × 100%; 225 × 60%)						225		135
10	Accounted for					400			
11	Equivalent units of work done in current period						400		310
12									
13	[a]Degree of completion in this department; direct materials, 100%; conversion costs, 60%.								

Why? Because the conversion costs incurred to produce 50 units that are each 70% complete could have instead generated 35 (0.70 × 50) units that are 100% complete. The 35 units are referred to as *equivalent units* of output. That is, in terms of the work done on them, the 50 partially completed units are considered equivalent to 35 completed units.

Note that equivalent units are calculated separately for each input (such as direct materials and conversion costs). Moreover, every completed unit, by definition, is composed of one equivalent unit of each input required to make it. This chapter focuses on equivalent-unit calculations in manufacturing settings, but the calculations can be used in nonmanufacturing settings as well. For example, universities convert their part-time student enrollments into "full-time student equivalents" to get a better measure of faculty–student ratios over time. Without this adjustment, an increase in part-time students would lead to a lower faculty–student ratio. This would erroneously suggest a decline in the quality of instruction when, in fact, part-time students take fewer academic courses and do not need the same number of instructors as full-time students do.

When calculating the equivalent units in Step 2, focus on quantities. Disregard dollar amounts until after the equivalent units are computed. In the Pacific Electronics example, all 400 physical units—the 175 fully assembled units and the 225 partially assembled units—are 100% complete with respect to direct materials because all direct materials are added in the assembly department at the start of the process. Therefore, Exhibit 1 shows that the output is 400 *equivalent units* for direct materials: 175 equivalent units for the 175 physical units assembled and transferred out and 225 equivalent units for the 225 physical units in ending work-in-process inventory.

The 175 fully assembled units have also incurred all of their conversion costs. The 225 partially assembled units in ending work in process are 60% complete (on average). Therefore, their conversion costs are *equivalent* to the conversion costs incurred by 135 fully assembled units (225 × 60% = 135). Hence, Exhibit 1 shows that the output is a total of 310 *equivalent units* for the conversion costs: 175 equivalent units for the 175 physical units assembled and transferred out and 135 equivalent units for the 225 physical units in ending work-in-process inventory.

Calculating Product Costs (Steps 3, 4, and 5)

Exhibit 2 shows Steps 3, 4, and 5. Together, they are called the *production cost worksheet.*

In **Step 3**, managers summarize the total costs to account for. Because the beginning balance of work-in-process inventory is zero on February 1, the total costs to account for (that is, the total charges or debits to the Work in Process—Assembly account) consist only of costs added during February: $32,000 in direct materials and $18,600 in conversion costs, for a total of $50,600.

| | Exhibit 2 | | Summarize the Total Costs to Account For, Compute the Cost per Equivalent Unit, and Assign Costs to the Units Completed and Units in Ending Work-in-Process Inventory for the Assembly Department for February 2014 |

	Home	Insert	Page Layout	Formulas	Data	Review	View			

	A	B	C	D	E
1			Total Production Costs	Direct Materials	Conversion Costs
2	(Step 3)	Costs added during February	$50,600	$32,000	$18,600
3		Total costs to account for	$50,600	$32,000	$18,600
4					
5	(Step 4)	Costs added in current period	$50,600	$32,000	$18,600
6		Divide by equivalent units of work done in current period (Exhibit 17-1)		÷ 400	÷ 310
7		Cost per equivalent unit		$ 80	$ 60
8					
9	(Step 5)	Assignment of costs:			
10		Completed and transferred out (175 units)	$24,500	$(175^a \times \$80)$ +	$(175^a \times \$60)$
11		Work in process, ending (225 units):	26,100	$(225^b \times \$80)$ +	$(135^b \times \$60)$
12		Total costs accounted for	$50,600	$32,000 +	$18,600
13					
14	[a] Equivalent units completed and transferred out from Exhibit 17-1, step 2.				
15	[b] Equivalent units in ending work in process from Exhibit 17-1, step 2.				

In **Step 4,** managers calculate the cost per equivalent unit separately for the direct materials costs and conversion costs. This is done by dividing the direct material costs and conversion costs added during February by their related quantities of equivalent units of work done in February (as calculated in Exhibit 1).

To see why it is important to understand equivalent units in unit-cost calculations, compare the conversion costs for January and February 2014. The $18,600 in total conversion costs for the 400 units worked on during February are lower than the $24,000 in total conversion costs for the 400 units worked on in January. However, the conversion costs to fully assemble a unit are the same: $60 per unit in both January and February. Total conversion costs are lower in February because fewer equivalent units of conversion-costs work were completed in that month than in January (310 in February versus 400 in January). Note that using physical units instead of equivalent units would have resulted in a conversion cost per unit of just $46.50 ($18,600 ÷ 400 units) for February, which is down from $60 in January. This incorrect costing might lead the firm's managers to believe that the assembly department achieved efficiencies that lowered the conversion costs of the SG-40 when in fact the costs had not declined.

Once the cost per equivalent unit is calculated for both the direct materials and conversion costs, managers can move to **Step 5:** assigning the total direct materials and conversion costs to the units completed and transferred out and to the units still in process at the end of February 2014. As Exhibit 2 shows, this is done by multiplying the equivalent output units for each input by the cost per equivalent unit. For example, the total costs (direct materials and conversion costs assigned to the 225 physical units in ending work-in-process inventory are as follows:

Direct material costs of 225 equivalent units (calculated in Step 2) × $80 cost per equivalent unit of direct materials (calculated in Step 4)	$18,000
Conversion costs of 135 equivalent units (calculated in Step 2) × $60 cost per equivalent unit of conversion costs (calculated in Step 4)	8,100
Total cost of ending work-in-process inventory	$26,100

Note that the total costs to account for in Step 3 ($50,600) equal the total costs accounted for in Step 5.

Journal Entries

Journal entries in process-costing systems are similar to the entries made in job-costing systems with respect to direct materials and conversion costs. The main difference is that, when process costing is used, there is one Work in Process account for each process. In our example, there are accounts for (1) Work in Process—Assembly and (2) Work in Process—Testing. Pacific Electronics purchases direct materials as needed. These materials are delivered directly to the assembly department. Using the amounts from Exhibit 2, the summary journal entries for February are as follows:

1. Work in Process—Assembly   32,000
      Accounts Payable Control   32,000
   To record the direct materials purchased and used in production
   during February.

2. Work in Process—Assembly   18,600
      Various accounts such as Wages Payable Control and Accumulated
      Depreciation   18,600
   To record the conversion costs for February; examples include energy,
   manufacturing supplies, all manufacturing labor, and plant depreciation.

3. Work in Process—Testing   24,500
      Work in Process—Assembly   24,500
   To record the cost of goods completed and transferred from assembly
   to testing during February.

Exhibit 3 shows a general framework for the flow of costs through T-accounts. Notice how entry 3 for $24,500 follows the physical transfer of goods from the assembly to the testing department. The T-account Work in Process—Assembly shows February 2014's ending balance of $26,100, which is the beginning balance of Work in Process—Assembly in March 2014. It is important to ensure that all costs have been accounted for and that the ending inventory of the current month is the beginning inventory of the following month.

Earlier, we discussed the importance of accurately estimating the completion percentages for conversion costs. We can now calculate the effect of incorrect estimates of the degree of completion of units in ending work in process. Suppose, for example, that Pacific

Decision Point

What are the five steps in a process-costing system and how are equivalent units calculated?

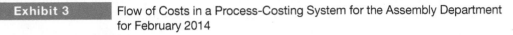

| Exhibit 3 | Flow of Costs in a Process-Costing System for the Assembly Department for February 2014 |

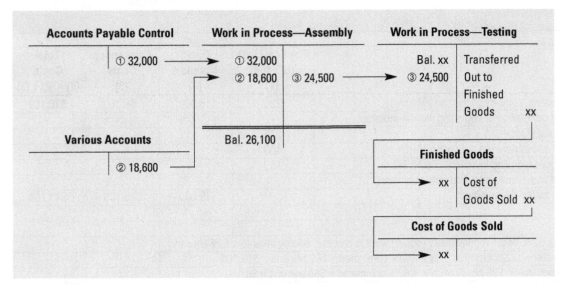

Electronics' managers overestimate the degree of completion for conversion costs at 80% instead of 60%. The computations would change as follows:

- Exhibit 1, Step 2

    Equivalent units of conversion costs in ending Work in Process—Assembly = 80% × 225 = 180

    Equivalent units of conversion costs for work done in the current period = 175 + 180 = 355

- Exhibit 2, Step 4

    Cost per equivalent unit of conversion costs = $18,600 ÷ 355 = $52.39

    Cost per equivalent unit of direct materials is the same, $80

- Exhibit 2, Step 5

    Cost of 175 units of goods completed and transferred out = 175 × $80 + 175 × $52.39 = $23,168.25

This amount is lower than the $24,500 of costs assigned to goods completed and transferred out calculated in Exhibit 2. Overestimating the degree of completion decreases the costs assigned to goods transferred out and eventually to cost of goods sold and increases operating income.

Managers must ensure that department supervisors avoid introducing personal biases into estimates of degrees of completion. To show better performance, for example, a department supervisor might report a higher degree of completion resulting in overstated operating income. If performance for the period is very good, the department supervisor may be tempted to report a lower degree of completion, reducing income in the current period. This has the effect of reducing the costs carried in ending inventory and the costs carried to the following year in beginning inventory. In other words, estimates of degree of completion can help to smooth earnings from one period to the next.

To guard against the possibility of bias, managers should ask supervisors specific questions about the process they followed to prepare estimates. Top management should always emphasize obtaining the correct answer, regardless of how it affects reported performance. This emphasis drives ethical actions throughout the organization.

Learning Objective 4

Use the weighted-average method of process costing

...assigns costs based on total costs and equivalent units completed to date

and the first-in, first-out (FIFO) method of process costing

...to assign costs based on costs and equivalent units of work done in the current period

Case 3: Process Costing with Some Beginning and Some Ending Work-in-Process Inventory

At the beginning of March 2014, Pacific Electronics had 225 partially assembled SG-40 units in the assembly department. It started production of another 275 units in March. The data for the assembly department for March are as follows:

	Home	Insert	Page Layout	Formulas	Data	Review	View			
	A					B	C	D	E
1						Physical Units (SG-40s) (1)	Direct Materials (2)	Conversion Costs (3)	Total Costs (4) = (2) + (3)
2	Work in process, beginning inventory (March 1)					225	$18,000[a]	$8,100[a]	$26,100
3	Degree of completion of beginning work in process						100%	60%	
4	Started during March					275.			
5	Completed and transferred out during March					400			
6	Work in process, ending inventory (March 31)					100			
7	Degree of completion of ending work in process						100%	50%	
8	Total costs added during March						$19,800	$16,380	$36,180
9									
10									
11	[a]Work in process, beginning inventory (equals work in process, ending inventory for February)								
12	Direct materials: 225 physical units × 100% completed × $80 per unit = $18,000								
13	Conversion costs: 225 physical units × 60% completed × $60 per unit = $8,100								

Pacific Electronics now has incomplete units in both beginning work-in-process inventory and ending work-in-process inventory for March 2014. We can still use the five steps described earlier to calculate (1) the cost of units completed and transferred out and (2) the cost of ending work-in-process inventory. To assign costs to each of these categories, however, we first need to choose an inventory-valuation method. We next describe the five-step approach for two key methods—the *weighted-average method* and the *first-in, first-out method*. These different valuation methods produce different costs for the units completed and for the ending work-in-process inventory when the unit cost of inputs changes from one period to the next.

Weighted-Average Method

The **weighted-average process-costing method** calculates the cost per equivalent unit of all *work done to date* (regardless of the accounting period in which it was done) and assigns this cost to equivalent units completed and transferred out of the process and to equivalent units in ending work-in-process inventory. The weighted-average cost is the total of all costs entering the Work in Process account (whether the costs are from beginning work in process or from work started during the current period) divided by total equivalent units of work done to date. We now describe the weighted-average method using the five-step procedure.

Step 1: **Summarize the Flow of Physical Units of Output.** The physical-units column in Exhibit 4 shows where the units came from—225 units from beginning inventory and 275 units started during the current period—and where the units went—400 units completed and transferred out and 100 units in ending inventory.

Step 2: **Compute the Output in Terms of Equivalent Units.** We use the relationship shown in the following equation:

$$\begin{array}{c} \text{Equivalent units} \\ \text{in beginning work} \\ \text{in process} \end{array} + \begin{array}{c} \text{Equivalent units} \\ \text{of work done in} \\ \text{current period} \end{array} = \begin{array}{c} \text{Equivalent units} \\ \text{completed and transferred} \\ \text{out in current period} \end{array} + \begin{array}{c} \text{Equivalent units} \\ \text{in ending work} \\ \text{in process} \end{array}$$

Although we are interested in calculating the left side of the preceding equation, it is easier to calculate this sum using the equation's right side: (1) the equivalent units completed and transferred out in the current period plus (2) the equivalent units in ending work in process. *Note that the stage of completion of the current-period beginning work in process is not used in this computation.*

The equivalent-units columns in Exhibit 4 show the equivalent units of work done to date: 500 equivalent units of direct materials and 450 equivalent units of conversion

Exhibit 4

	Home	Insert	Page Layout	Formulas	Data	Review	View		
	A					B	C	D	
1						(Step 1)	(Step 2)		
2							Equivalent Units		
3	Flow of Production					Physical Units	Direct Materials	Conversion Costs	
4	Work in process, beginning (given)					225			
5	Started during current period (given)					275			
6	To account for					500			
7	Completed and transferred out during current period					400	400	400	
8	Work in process, ending[a] (given)					100			
9	(100 × 100%; 100 × 50%)						100	50	
10	Accounted for					500			
11	Equivalent units of work done to date						500	450	
12									
13	[a]Degree of completion in this department; direct materials, 100%; conversion costs, 50%.								

Summarize the Flow of Physical Units and Compute Output in Equivalent Units Using the Weighted-Average Method for the Assembly Department for March 2014

| Exhibit 5 | | Summarize the Total Costs to Account For, Compute the Cost per Equivalent Unit, and Assign Costs to the Units Completed and Units in Ending Work-in-Process Inventory Using the Weighted-Average Method for the Assembly Department for March 2014 |

			Home Insert Page Layout Formulas Data Review View		
	A	B	C	D	E
1			Total Production Costs	Direct Materials	Conversion Costs
2	(Step 3)	Work in process, beginning (given, p. 672)	$26,100	$18,000	$ 8,100
3		Costs added in current period (given, p. 672)	36,180	19,800	16,380
4		Total costs to account for	$62,280	$37,800	$24,480
5					
6	(Step 4)	Costs incurred to date		$37,800	$24,480
7		Divide by equivalent units of work done to date (Exhibit 17-4)		÷ 500	÷ 450
8		Cost per equivalent unit of work done to date		$ 75.60	$ 54.40
9					
10	(Step 5)	Assignment of costs:			
11		Completed and transferred out (400 units)	$52,000	$(400^a \times \$75.60)$	$+(400^a \times \$54.40)$
12		Work in process, ending (100 units):	10,280	$(100^b \times \$75.60)$	$+ (50^b \times \$54.40)$
13		Total costs accounted for	$62,280	$37,800	$ + $24,480
14					
15	^{a}Equivalent units completed and transferred out from Exhibit 17-4, Step 2.				
16	^{b}Equivalent units in ending work in process from Exhibit 17-4, Step 2.				

costs. All completed and transferred-out units are 100% complete with regard to both their direct materials and conversion costs. Partially completed units in ending work in process are 100% complete with regard to their direct materials costs (because the direct materials are introduced at the beginning of the process) and 50% complete with regard to their conversion costs, based on estimates from the assembly department manager.

Step 3: **Summarize the Total Costs to Account For.** Exhibit 5 presents Step 3. The total costs to account for in March 2014 are described in the example data:

Beginning work in process	
(direct materials, $18,000 + conversion costs, $8,100)	$26,100
Costs added during March	
(direct materials, $19,800 + conversion costs, $16,380)	36,180
Total costs to account for in March	$62,280

Step 4: **Compute the Cost per Equivalent Unit.** Exhibit 5, Step 4, shows how the weighted-average cost per equivalent unit for direct materials and conversion costs is computed. The weighted-average cost per equivalent unit is obtained by dividing the sum of the costs for beginning work in process plus the costs for work done in the current period by the total equivalent units of work done to date. For example, we calculate the weighted-average conversion cost per equivalent unit in Exhibit 5 as follows:

Total conversion costs (beginning work in process,	
$8,100 + work done in current period, $16,380)	$24,480
Divided by the total equivalent units of work done to date (equivalent units	
of conversion costs in beginning work in process and in work done in current period)	÷ 450
Weighted-average cost per equivalent unit	$ 54.40

Step 5: Assign Costs to the Units Completed and to Units in Ending Work-in-Process Inventory. Step 5 in Exhibit 5 takes the equivalent units completed and transferred out and the equivalent units in ending work in process (calculated in Exhibit 4, Step 2) and assigns dollar amounts to them using the weighted-average cost per equivalent unit for the direct materials and conversion costs calculated in Step 4. For example, the total costs of the 100 physical units in ending work in process are as follows:

Direct materials:
100 equivalent units × weighted-average cost per equivalent unit of $75.60	$ 7,560
Conversion costs:	
50 equivalent units × weighted-average cost per equivalent unit of $54.40	2,720
Total costs of ending work in process	$10,280

The following table summarizes total costs to account for ($62,280) and how they are accounted for in Exhibit 5. The arrows indicate that the costs of units completed and transferred out and units in ending work in process are calculated using weighted-average total costs obtained after merging costs of beginning work in process and costs added in the current period.

Costs to Account For			Costs Accounted for Calculated on a Weighted-Average Basis	
Beginning work in process	$26,100		Completed and transferred out	$52,000
Costs added in current period	36,180		Ending work in process	10,280
Total costs to account for	$62,280		Total costs accounted for	$62,280

Before proceeding, review Exhibits 4 and 5 to check your understanding of the weighted-average method. Note: Exhibit 4 deals with only physical and equivalent units, not costs. Exhibit 5 shows the cost amounts.

Using amounts from Exhibit 5, the summary journal entries under the weighted-average method for March 2014 are as follows:

1. Work in Process—Assembly	19,800	
Accounts Payable Control		19,800

To record the direct materials purchased and used in production during March.

2. Work in Process—Assembly	16,380	
Various accounts such as Wages Payable Control and Accumulated Depreciation		16,380

To record the conversion costs for March; examples include energy, manufacturing supplies, all manufacturing labor, and plant depreciation.

3. Work in Process—Testing	52,000	
Work in Process—Assembly		52,000

To record the cost of goods completed and transferred from assembly to testing during March.

The T-account Work in Process—Assembly, under the weighted-average method, is as follows:

Work in Process—Assembly

Beginning inventory, March 1	26,100	③ Completed and transferred	52,000
① Direct materials	19,800	out to Work in Process—	
② Conversion costs	16,380	Testing	
Ending inventory, March 31	10,280		

First-In, First-Out Method

The **first-in, first-out (FIFO) process-costing method** (1) assigns the cost of the previous accounting period's equivalent units in beginning work-in-process inventory to the first units completed and transferred out of the process and (2) assigns the cost of equivalent units worked on during the *current* period first to complete the beginning inventory, next to start and complete new units, and finally to units in ending work-in-process inventory. The FIFO method assumes that the earliest equivalent units in work in process are completed first.

A *distinctive feature of the FIFO process-costing method is that work done on the beginning inventory before the current period is kept separate from work done in the current period.* The costs incurred and units produced in the current period are used to calculate the cost per equivalent unit of work done in the current period. In contrast, the equivalent-unit and cost-per-equivalent-unit calculations under the weighted-average method *merge* the units and costs in beginning inventory with the units and costs of work done in the current period.

We now describe the FIFO method using the five-step procedure.

Step 1: Summarize the Flow of Physical Units of Output. Exhibit 6, Step 1, traces the flow of the physical units of production and explains how they are calculated under the FIFO method.

- The first physical units assumed to be completed and transferred out during the period are 225 units from beginning work-in-process inventory.

- The March data indicate that 400 physical units were completed during March. The FIFO method assumes that of these 400 units, 175 units (400 units − 225 units from beginning work-in-process inventory) must have been started and completed during March.

- The ending work-in-process inventory consists of 100 physical units—the 275 physical units started minus the 175 units that were started and completed.

- The physical units "to account for" equal the physical units "accounted for" (500 units).

Step 2: Compute the Output in Terms of Equivalent Units. Exhibit 6 also presents the computations for Step 2 under the FIFO method. *The equivalent-unit calculations for each cost category focus on equivalent units of work done in the current period (March) only.*

Flow of Production	Physical Units (Step 1)	Direct Materials (Step 2) Equivalent Units	Conversion Costs
Work in process, beginning (given, p. 673)	225	(work done before current period)	
Started during current period (given, p. 673)	275		
To account for	500		
Completed and transferred out during current period:			
From beginning work in process[a]	225		
[225 × (100% − 100%); 225 × (100% − 60%)]		0	90
Started and completed	175[b]		
(175 × 100%; 175 × 100%)		175	175
Work in process, ending[c] (given, p. 673)	100		
(100 × 100%; 100 × 50%)		100	50
Accounted for	500		
Equivalent units of work done in current period		275	315

[a]Degree of completion in this department; direct materials, 100%; conversion costs, 60%.
[b]400 physical units completed and transferred out minus 225 physical units completed and transferred out from beginning work-in-process inventory.
[c]Degree of completion in this department: direct materials, 100%; conversion costs, 50%.

Under the FIFO method, the equivalent units of work done in March on the beginning work-in-process inventory equal 225 physical units times *the percentage of work remaining to be done in March to complete these units*: 0% for direct materials, because the beginning work in process is 100% complete for direct materials, and 40% for conversion costs, because the beginning work in process is 60% complete for conversion costs. The results are 0 (0% × 225) equivalent units of work for direct materials and 90 (40% × 225) equivalent units of work for conversion costs.

The equivalent units of work done on the 175 physical units started and completed equals 175 units times 100% for both direct materials and conversion costs because all work on these units is done in the current period.

The equivalent units of work done on the 100 units of ending work in process equal 100 physical units times 100% for direct materials (because all direct materials for these units are added in the current period) and 50% for conversion costs (because 50% of the conversion-costs work on these units is done in the current period).

Step 3: **Summarize the Total Costs to Account For.** Exhibit 7 presents Step 3 and summarizes the $62,280 in total costs to account for in March 2014 (the costs of the beginning work in process, $26,100, and the costs added in the current period, $36,180).

Step 4: **Compute the Cost per Equivalent Unit.** Exhibit 7 shows the Step 4 computation of the cost per equivalent unit of *work done in the current period only* for the direct materials and conversion costs. For example, the conversion cost per equivalent

	Exhibit 7	Summarize the Total Costs to Account For, Compute the Cost per Equivalent Unit, and Assign Costs to the Units Completed and Units in Ending Work-in-Process Inventory Using the FIFO Method for the Assembly Department for March 2014

	A	B	C	D	E
1			Total Production Costs	Direct Material	Conversion Costs
2	(Step 3)	Work in process, beginning (given, p. 672)	$26,100	$18,000	$ 8,100
3		Costs added in current period (given, p. 672)	36,180	19,800	16,380
4		Total costs to account for	$62,280	$37,800	$24,480
5					
6	(Step 4)	Costs added in current period		$19,800	$16,380
7		Divide by equivalent units of work done in current period (Exhibit 17-6)		÷ 275	÷ 315
8		Cost per equivalent unit of work done in current period		$ 72	$ 52
9					
10	(Step 5)	Assignment of costs:			
11		Completed and transferred out (400 units):			
12		Work in process, beginning (225 units)	$26,100	$18,000 + $8,100	
13		Costs added to beginning work in process in current period	4,680	(0[a] × $72) + (90[a] × $52)	
14		Total from beginning inventory	30,780		
15		Started and completed (175 units)	21,700	(175[b] × $72) + (175[b] × $52)	
16		Total costs of units completed and transferred out	52,480		
17		Work in process, ending (100 units):	9,800	(100[c] × $72) + (50[c] × $52)	
18		Total costs accounted for	$62,280	$37,800 + $24,480	
19					
20		[a]Equivalent units used to complete beginning work in process from Exhibit 17-6, Step 2.			
21		[b]Equivalent units started and completed from Exhibit 17-6, Step 2.			
22		[c]Equivalent units in ending work in process from Exhibit 17-6, Step 2.			

unit of $52 is obtained by dividing the current-period conversion costs of $16,380 by the current-period conversion-costs equivalent units of 315.

Step 5: Assign Costs to the Units Completed and Units in Ending Work-in-Process Inventory. Exhibit 7 shows the assignment of costs under the FIFO method. The costs of work done in the current period are assigned (1) first to the additional work done to complete the beginning work-in-process inventory, then (2) to work done on units started and completed during the current period, and finally (3) to ending work-in-process inventory. *Step 5 takes each quantity of equivalent units calculated in Exhibit 6, Step 2, and assigns dollar amounts to them (using the cost-per-equivalent-unit calculations in Step 4).* The goal is to use the cost of work done in the current period to determine the total costs of all units completed from beginning inventory and from work started and completed in the current period and the costs of ending work-in-process inventory.

Of the 400 completed units, 225 units are from beginning inventory and 175 units are started and completed during March. The FIFO method starts by assigning the costs of the beginning work-in-process inventory of $26,100 to the first units completed and transferred out. As we saw in Step 2, an additional 90 equivalent units of conversion costs are needed to complete these units in the current period. The current-period conversion cost per equivalent unit is $52, so $4,680 (90 equivalent units × $52 per equivalent unit) of additional costs are incurred to complete the beginning inventory. The total production costs for units in beginning inventory are $26,100 + $4,680 = $30,780. The 175 units started and completed in the current period consist of 175 equivalent units of direct materials and 175 equivalent units of conversion costs. These units are costed at the cost per equivalent unit in the current period (direct materials, $72, and conversion costs, $52) for a total production cost of $21,700 [175 × ($72 + $52)].

Under FIFO, the ending work-in-process inventory comes from units that were started but not fully completed during the current period. The total costs of the 100 partially assembled physical units in ending work in process are as follows:

Direct materials:	
100 equivalent units × $72 cost per equivalent unit in March	$7,200
Conversion costs:	
50 equivalent units × $52 cost per equivalent unit in March	2,600
Total cost of work in process on March 31	$9,800

The following table summarizes the total costs to account for and the costs accounted for under FIFO, which are $62,280 in Exhibit 7. Notice how the FIFO method keeps separate the layers of the beginning work-in-process costs and the costs added in the current period. The arrows indicate where the costs in each layer go—that is, to units completed and transferred out or to ending work in process. Be sure to include the costs of the beginning work-in-process inventory ($26,100) when calculating the costs of units completed.

Costs to Account for		Costs Accounted for Calculated on a FIFO Basis	
		Completed and transferred out	
Beginning work in process	$26,100	Beginning work in process	$26,100
Costs added in current period	36,180	Used to complete beginning work in process	4,680
		Started and completed	21,700
		Completed and transferred out	52,480
		Ending work in process	9,800
Total costs to account for	$62,280	Total costs accounted for	$62,280

Before proceeding, review Exhibits 6 and 7 to check your understanding of the FIFO method. Note: Exhibit 6 deals with only physical and equivalent units, not costs. Exhibit 7 shows the cost amounts.

The journal entries under the FIFO method are identical to the journal entries under the weighted-average method except for one difference. The entry to record the cost of goods completed and transferred out would be $52,480 under the FIFO method instead of $52,000 under the weighted-average method.

Keep in mind that FIFO is applied within each department to compile the cost of units *transferred out*. As a practical matter, however, units *transferred in* during a given period usually are carried at a single average unit cost. For example, in the preceding example, the assembly department uses FIFO to distinguish between monthly batches of production. The resulting average cost of each SG-40 unit transferred out of the assembly department is $52,480 ÷ 400 units = $131.20. The testing department, however, costs these units (which consist of costs incurred in both February and March) at one average unit cost ($131.20 in this example). If this averaging were not done, the attempt to track costs on a pure FIFO basis throughout a series of processes would be cumbersome. As a result, the FIFO method should really be called a *modified* or *department* FIFO method.

Comparing the Weighted-Average and FIFO Methods

Consider the summary of the costs assigned to units completed and to units still in process under the weighted-average and FIFO process-costing methods in our example for March 2014:

	Weighted Average (from Exhibit 5)	FIFO (from Exhibit 7)	Difference
Cost of units completed and transferred out	$52,000	$52,480	+ $480
Work in process, ending	10,280	9,800	− $480
Total costs accounted for	$62,280	$62,280	

The weighted-average ending inventory is higher than the FIFO ending inventory by $480, or 4.9% ($480 ÷ $9,800 = 0.049, or 4.9%). This would be a significant difference when aggregated over the many thousands of products Pacific Electronics makes. When completed units are sold, the weighted-average method in our example leads to a lower cost of goods sold and, therefore, higher operating income than the FIFO method does. To see why, recall the data. For the beginning work-in-process inventory, the direct materials cost per equivalent unit is $80 and the conversion cost per equivalent unit is $60. These costs are greater, respectively, than the $72 direct materials cost and the $52 conversion cost per equivalent unit of work done during the current period. The current-period costs could be lower due to a decline in the prices of direct materials and conversion-cost inputs or as a result of Pacific Electronics becoming more efficient in its processes by using smaller quantities of inputs per unit of output or both.

FIFO assumes that (1) all the higher-cost units from the previous period in beginning work in process are the first to be completed and transferred out of the process and (2) the ending work in process consists of only the lower-cost current-period units. The weighted-average method, however, smooths out the cost per equivalent unit by assuming that (1) more of the lower-cost units are completed and transferred out and (2) some of the higher-cost units are placed in ending work in process. The decline in the current-period cost per equivalent unit results in a lower cost of units completed and transferred out and a higher ending work-in-process inventory under the weighted-average method relative to FIFO.

Managers use information from process-costing systems to make pricing and product-mix decisions and understand how well a firm's processes are performing. FIFO provides managers with information about changes in the costs per unit from one period to the next. Managers can use this data to adjust selling prices based on current conditions (for example, based on the $72 direct material cost and $52 conversion cost in March). The managers can also more easily evaluate the firm's cost performance relative to either a budget or the previous period (for example, both unit direct materials and conversion costs have declined relative to the prior period). By focusing on the work done and the costs of work done during the current period, the FIFO method provides valuable information for these planning and control purposes.

The weighted-average method merges unit costs from different accounting periods, obscuring period-to-period comparisons. For example, the weighted-average method would lead managers at Pacific Electronics to make decisions based on the $75.60 direct materials and $54.40 conversion costs, rather than the costs of $72 and $52 prevailing in the current period. However, costs are relatively easy to compute using the weighted-average method, and it results in a more-representative average unit cost when input prices fluctuate markedly from month to month.

The cost of units completed and, hence, a firm's operating income differ materially between the weighted-average and FIFO methods when (1) the direct materials or conversion cost per equivalent unit varies significantly from period to period and (2) the physical-inventory levels of the work in process are large relative to the total number of units transferred out of the process. As changes in unit costs and inventory levels across periods decrease, the difference in the costs of units completed under the weighted-average and FIFO methods also decreases.[3]

When the cost of units completed under the weighted-average and FIFO methods differs substantially, which method should a manager choose? In a period of falling prices, as in the Pacific Electronics case, the higher cost of goods sold under the FIFO method will lead to lower operating income and lower tax payments, saving the company cash and increasing the company's value. FIFO is the preferred choice, but managers may not make this choice. If the manager's compensation, for instance, is based on operating income, the manager may prefer the weighted-average method, which increases operating income even though it results in higher tax payments. Top managers must carefully design compensation plans to encourage managers to take actions that increase a company's value. For example, the compensation plan might reward after-tax cash flow metrics, in addition to operating income metrics, to align decision making and performance evaluation.

Occasionally, choosing a process-costing method can be more difficult. Suppose, for example, that by using FIFO a company would violate its debt covenants (agreements between a company and its creditors that the company will maintain certain financial ratios) resulting in its loans coming due. In this case, a manager may prefer the weighted-average method even though it results in higher taxes because the company does not have the liquidity to repay its loans.

In a period of rising prices, the weighted-average method will decrease taxes because cost of goods sold will be higher and operating income lower. Recall the vignette at the start of this chapter that describes how ExxonMobil uses the last-in, first-out (LIFO) method (not presented in this chapter) to save taxes.[4]

Finally, how is activity-based costing related to process costing? Like activity-based processing, each process—assembly, testing, and so on—can be considered a different (production) activity. However, no additional activities need to be identified within each process to use process costing. That's because products are homogeneous and use the resources of each process in a uniform way. The bottom line is that activity-based costing has less applicability in process-costing environments, especially when compared to the significant role it plays in job costing. *The appendix illustrates the use of the standard costing method for the assembly department.*

Decision Point

What are the weighted-average and first-in, first-out (FIFO) methods of process costing? Under what conditions will they yield different levels of operating income?

---

[3] For example, suppose the beginning work-in-process inventory for March was 125 physical units (instead of 225), and suppose the costs per equivalent unit of work done in the current period (March) were direct materials, $75, and conversion costs, $55. Assume that all other data for March are the same as in our example. In this case, the cost of units completed and transferred out would be $52,833 under the weighted-average method and $53,000 under the FIFO method. The work-in-process ending inventory would be $10,417 under the weighted-average method and $10,250 under the FIFO method (calculations not shown). These differences are much smaller than in the chapter example. The weighted-average ending inventory is higher than the FIFO ending inventory by only $167 ($10,417 − $10,250), or 1.6% ($167 ÷ $10,250 = 0.016), compared with 4.9% higher in the chapter example.

[4] Students not familiar with the LIFO method need only note that in a period of rising prices, the LIFO method reduces operating income and taxes even more than the weighted-average method.

Transferred-In Costs in Process Costing

Learning Objective **5**

Apply process-costing methods to situations with transferred-in costs

...using weighted-average and FIFO methods

Many process-costing systems have two or more departments or processes in the production cycle. As units move from department to department, the related costs are also transferred by monthly journal entries. **Transferred-in costs** (also called **previous-department costs**) are costs incurred in previous departments that are carried forward as the product's cost when it moves to a subsequent process in the production cycle.

We now extend our Pacific Electronics example to the testing department. As the assembly process is completed, the assembly department of Pacific Electronics immediately transfers SG-40 units to the testing department. Conversion costs are added evenly during the testing department's process. At the *end of the testing process*, the units receive additional direct materials, including crating and other packing materials to prepare them for shipment. As units are completed in testing, they are immediately transferred to Finished Goods. The testing department costs consist of transferred-in costs, as well as direct materials and conversion costs added during testing.

The following diagram represents these facts:

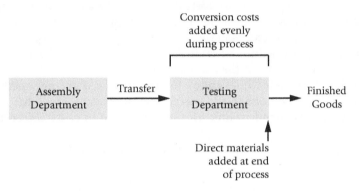

The data for the testing department for March 2014 are as follows:

	A	B	C	D	E
1		**Physical Units (SG-40s)**	**Transferred-In Costs**	**Direct Materials**	**Conversion Costs**
2	Work in process, beginning inventory (March 1)	240	$33,600	$ 0	$18,000
3	Degree of completion, beginning work in process		100%	0%	62.5%
4	Transferred in during March	400			
5	Completed and transferred out during March	440			
6	Work in process, ending inventory (March 31)	200			
7	Degree of completion, ending work in process		100%	0%	80%
8	Total costs added during March				
9	Direct materials and conversion costs			$13,200	$48,600
10	Transferred in (Weighted-average from Exhibit 17-5)[a]		$52,000		
11	Transferred in (FIFO from Exhibit 17-7)[a]		$52,480		
12					
13	[a]The transferred-in costs during March are different under the weighted-average method (Exhibit 17-5) and the FIFO method (Exhibit 17-7). In our example, beginning work-in-process inventory, $51,600 ($33,600 + $0 + $18,000), is the same under both the weighted-average and FIFO inventory methods because we assume costs per equivalent unit to be the same in both January and February. If costs per equivalent unit had been different in the two months, work-in-process inventory at the end of February (beginning of March) would be costed differently under the weighted-average and FIFO methods. The basic approach to process costing with transferred-in costs, however, would still be the same as what we describe in this section.				

Transferred-in costs are treated as if they are a separate type of direct material added at the beginning of the process. That is, the transferred-in costs are always 100% complete at the beginning of the process in the new department. When successive departments are involved, the transferred units from one department become all or a part of the direct materials of the next department; however, they are called transferred-in costs, not direct material costs.

Transferred-In Costs and the Weighted-Average Method

To examine the weighted-average process-costing method with transferred-in costs, we use the five-step procedure described earlier to assign the costs of the testing department to units completed and transferred out and to the units in ending work in process.

Exhibit 8 shows Steps 1 and 2. The computations are similar to the calculations of equivalent units under the weighted-average method for the assembly department in Exhibit 4. The one difference here is that we have transferred-in costs as an additional input. All units, whether completed and transferred out during the period or in ending work in process, are always fully complete with respect to transferred-in costs. The reason is that the transferred-in costs are the costs incurred in the assembly department, and any units received in the testing department must have first been completed in the assembly department. However, the direct material costs have a zero degree of completion in both beginning and ending work-in-process inventories because, in the testing department, direct materials are introduced at the *end* of the process.

Exhibit 9 describes Steps 3, 4, and 5 for the weighted-average method. Beginning work in process and work done in the current period are combined for the purposes of computing the cost per equivalent unit for the transferred-in costs, direct materials costs, and conversion costs.

The journal entry for the transfer from testing to Finished Goods (see Exhibit 9) is as follows:

Finished Goods Control	120,890	
Work in Process—Testing		120,890
To record cost of goods completed and transferred from testing to Finished Goods.		

Exhibit 8   Summarize the Flow of Physical Units and Compute Output in Equivalent Units Using the Weighted-Average Method for the Testing Department for March 2014

	A	B	C	D	E
1		(Step 1)		(Step 2)	
2				Equivalent Units	
3	**Flow of Production**	**Physical Units**	**Transferred-In Costs**	**Direct Materials**	**Conversion Costs**
4	Work in process, beginning (given, p. 681)	240			
5	Transferred in during current period (given, p. 681)	400			
6	To account for	640			
7	Completed and transferred out during current period	440	440	440	440
8	Work in process, ending[a] (given, p. 681)	200			
9	(200 × 100%; 200 × 0%; 200 × 80%)		200	0	160
10	Accounted for	640			
11	Equivalent units of work done to date		640	440	600
12					
13	[a]Degree of completion in this department; transferred-in costs, 100%; direct materials, 0%; conversion costs, 80%.				

Exhibit 9	Summarize the Total Costs to Account For, Compute the Cost per Equivalent Unit, and Assign Costs to the Units Completed and Units in Ending Work-in-Process Inventory Using the Weighted-Average Method for the Testing Department for March 2014

	Home	Insert	Page Layout	Formulas	Data	Review	View		
	A	B		C	D	E	F		
1				Total Production Costs	Transferred-In Costs	Direct Materials	Conversion Costs		
2	(Step 3)	Work in process, beginning (given, p. 681)		$ 51,600	$33,600	$ 0	$18,000		
3		Costs added in current period (given, p. 681)		113,800	52,000	13,200	48,600		
4		Total costs to account for		$165,400	$85,600	$13,200	$66,600		
5									
6	(Step 4)	Costs incurred to date			$85,600	$13,200	$66,600		
7		Divide by equivalent units of work done to date (Exhibit 17-8)			÷ 640	÷ 440	÷ 600		
8		Cost per equivalent unit of work done to date			$133.75	$ 30.00	$111.00		
9									
10	(Step 5)	Assignment of costs:							
11		Completed and transferred out (440 units)		$120,890	(440[a] × $133.75) +	(440[a] × $30) +	(440[a] × $111)		
12		Work in process, ending (200 units):		44,510	(200[b] × $133.75) +	(0[b] × $30) +	(160[b] × $111)		
13		Total costs accounted for		$165,400	$85,600 +	$13,200 +	$66,600		
14									
15	[a]Equivalent units completed and transferred out from Exhibit 17-8, Step 2.								
16	[b]Equivalent units in ending work in process from Exhibit 17-8, Step 2.								

Entries in the Work in Process—Testing account (see Exhibit 9) are as follows:

Work in Process—Testing

Beginning inventory, March 1	51,600	Transferred out	120,890
Transferred-in costs	52,000		
Direct materials	13,200		
Conversion costs	48,600		
Ending inventory, March 31	44,510		

Transferred-In Costs and the FIFO Method

To examine the FIFO process-costing method with transferred-in costs, we again use the five-step procedure. Exhibit 10 shows Steps 1 and 2. Other than accounting for transferred-in costs, computing the equivalent units is the same as under the FIFO method for the assembly department (see Exhibit 6).

Exhibit 11 describes Steps 3, 4, and 5. In Step 3, the $165,880 in total costs to account for under the FIFO method differ from the total costs under the weighted-average method, which are $165,400. This is because of the difference in the costs of completed units transferred in from the assembly department under the two methods—$52,480 under FIFO and $52,000 under the weighted-average method. The cost per equivalent unit for the current period in Step 4 is calculated on the basis of costs transferred in and work done in the current period only. Step 5 then accounts for the total costs of $165,880 by assigning them to the units transferred out and those in ending work-in-process inventory. Again, other than considering transferred-in costs, the calculations mirror those under the FIFO method for the assembly department (in Exhibit 7).

Exhibit 10	Summarize the Flow of Physical Units and Compute Output in Equivalent Units Using the FIFO Method for the Testing Department for March 2014

	Home	Insert	Page Layout	Formulas	Data	Review	View				
	A							B	C	D	E
1								(Step 1)		(Step 2)	
2										Equivalent Units	
3	Flow of Production							Physical Units	Transferred-In Costs	Direct Materials	Conversion Costs
4	Work in process, beginning (given, p. 681)							240	(work done before current period)		
5	Transferred in during current period (given, p. 681)							400			
6	To account for							640			
7	Completed and transferred out during current period:										
8	From beginning work in process[a]							240			
9	[240 × (100% − 100%); 240 × (100% − 0%); 240 × (100% − 62.5%)]								0	240	90
10	Started and completed							200[b]			
11	(200 × 100%; 200 × 100%; 200 × 100%)								200	200	200
12	Work in process, ending[c] (given, p. 681)							200			
13	(200 × 100%; 200 × 0%; 200 × 80%)								200	0	160
14	Accounted for							640			
15	Equivalent units of work done in current period								400	440	450
16											
17	[a]Degree of completion in this department: transferred-in costs, 100%; direct materials, 0%; conversion costs, 62.5%.										
18	[b]440 physical units completed and transferred out minus 240 physical units completed and transferred out from beginning										
19	work-in-process inventory.										
20	[c]Degree of completion in this department: transferred-in costs, 100%; direct materials, 0%; conversion costs, 80%.										

Remember that in a series of interdepartmental transfers, each department is regarded as separate and distinct for accounting purposes. The journal entry for the transfer from testing to Finished Goods (see Exhibit 11) is as follows:

Finished Goods Control	122,360	
Work in Process—Testing		122,360
To record the cost of goods completed and transferred from testing to Finished Goods.		

The entries in the Work in Process—Testing account (see Exhibit 11) are as follows:

Work in Process—Testing

Beginning inventory, March 1	51,600	Transferred out	122,360
Transferred-in costs	52,480		
Direct materials	13,200		
Conversion costs	48,600		
Ending inventory, March 31	43,520		

Points to Remember About Transferred-In Costs

Some points to remember when accounting for transferred-in costs are as follows:

1. Be sure to include the transferred-in costs from previous departments in your calculations.

2. When calculating the costs to be transferred using the FIFO method, do not overlook costs assigned in the previous period to units that were in process at the beginning of the current period but are now included in the units transferred. For example, do not overlook the $51,600 in Exhibit 11.

| Exhibit 11 | Summarize the Total Costs to Account For, Compute the Cost per Equivalent Unit, and Assign Costs to the Units Completed and Units in Ending Work-in-Process Inventory Using the FIFO Method for the Testing Department for March 2014 |

	A	B	C	D	E	F
			Total Production Costs	**Transferred-In Cost**	**Direct Material**	**Conversion Costs**
1						
2	(Step 3)	Work in process, beginning (given, p. 681)	$ 51,600	$33,600	$ 0	$18,000
3		Costs added in current period (given, p. 681)	114,280	52,480	13,200	48,600
4		Total costs to account for	$165,880	$86,080	$13,200	$66,600
5						
6	(Step 4)	Costs added in current period		$52,480	$13,200	$48,600
7		Divide by equivalent units of work done in current period (Exhibit 17-10)		÷ 400	÷ 440	÷ 450
8		Cost per equivalent unit of work done in current period		$131.20	$ 30	$ 108
9						
10	(Step 5)	Assignment of costs:				
11		Completed and transferred out (440 units)				
12		Work in process, beginning (240 units)	$ 51,600	$33,600 +	$0 +	$18,000
13		Costs added to beginning work in process in current period	16,920	(0ᵃ × $131.20) +	(240ᵃ × $30) +	(90ᵃ × $108)
14		Total from beginning inventory	68,520			
15		Started and completed (200 units)	53,840	(200ᵇ × $131.20) +	(200ᵇ × $30) +	(200ᵇ × $108)
16		Total costs of units completed and transferred out	122,360			
17		Work in process, ending (200 units):	43,520	(200ᶜ × $131.20) +	(0ᶜ × $30) +	(160ᶜ × $108)
18		Total costs accounted for	$165,880	$86,080 +	$13,200 +	$66,600
19						
20	ᵃEquivalent units used to complete beginning work in process from Exhibit 17-10, Step 2.					
21	ᵇEquivalent units started and completed from Exhibit 17-10, Step 2.					
22	ᶜEquivalent units in ending work in process from Exhibit 17-10, Step 2.					

3. Unit costs may fluctuate between periods. Therefore, transferred units may contain batches accumulated at different unit costs. For example, the 400 units transferred in at $52,480 in Exhibit 11 using the FIFO method consist of units that have different unit costs of direct materials and conversion costs when these units were worked on in the assembly department (see Exhibit 7). Remember, however, that when these units are transferred to the testing department, they are costed at *one average unit cost* of $131.20 ($52,480 ÷ 400 units), as in Exhibit 11.

4. Units may be measured in different denominations in different departments. Consider each department separately. For example, unit costs could be based on kilograms in the first department and liters in the second department. Accordingly, as units are received in the second department, their measurements must be converted to liters.

Decision Point

How are the weighted-average and FIFO process-costing methods applied to transferred-in costs?

Hybrid Costing Systems

Product-costing systems do not always fall neatly into either job-costing or process-costing categories. Many production systems are hybrid systems in which both mass production and customization occur. Consider Ford Motor Company. Automobiles are manufactured in a continuous flow (suited to process costing), but individual units may be customized with different engine sizes, transmissions, music systems, and so on (which requires job costing). A **hybrid-costing system** blends characteristics from both job-costing and process-costing systems. Managers must design product-costing systems to fit the particular characteristics of different production systems.

Firms that manufacture closely related standardized products (for example, various types of televisions, dishwashers, washing machines, and shoes) tend to use hybrid-costing

Learning Objective 6

Understand the need for hybrid-costing systems such as operation costing

...when product-costing does not fall into job-costing or process-costing categories

Concepts in Action

Hybrid Costing for Customized Shoes at Adidas

Adidas has been designing and manufacturing athletic footwear for nearly 90 years. Although shoemakers have long individually crafted shoes for professional athletes, Adidas took this concept a step further when it initiated the *mi adidas* program.

The mi adidas customization offering is available online and in retail stores around the world. Consumers can choose from more than 200 styles across seven sports and lifestyle categories. Along with competitors Nike and New Balance, mi adidas offers the opportunity to create individual, custom shoes for performance, fit, and design. Once the designs are created and purchased, the design and product data are transferred to manufacturing plants where the product is then built to order and shipped directly to the consumer.

Adidas uses a hybrid-costing system. Accounting for individual customization requires job costing, but the similar process used to make sneakers lends itself to process costing. The cost of making each pair of shoes is calculated by accumulating all production costs and dividing by the number of shoes made. In other words, even though each pair of shoes is different, the conversion cost is roughly the same.

The combination of customization with certain features of mass production is called mass customization. It is the consequence of being able to digitize information that individual customers indicate is important to them. Various products that companies can customize within a mass-production setting (including personal computers, jeans, and bicycles) still require job costing of materials and considerable human intervention. However, as manufacturing systems become flexible, companies are also using process costing to account for the standardized conversion costs.

Sources: Tien, Ellen. 2011. These (custom) colors do run. *New York Times*, April 7; Kamenev, Marina. 2006. Adidas' high tech footwear. *Bloomberg Businessweek*, November 3; Seifert, Ralf. 2003. The "mi adidas" mass customization initiative. IMD No. 159. Lausanne, Switzerland: International Institute for Management Development.

systems. They use process costing to account for the conversion costs and job costing for the material and customizable components. Consider Nike, which has a message for shoppers looking for the hottest new shoe design: Just do it … yourself! Athletic apparel manufacturers have long individually crafted shoes for professional athletes. Now, Nike is making it possible for other customers to design their own shoes and clothing. Using the Internet and mobile applications, Nike's customers can personalize with their own colors and patterns for Jordan-brand sneakers and other apparel. Concepts in Action: Hybrid Costing for Customized Shoes at Adidas describes customization and the use of a hybrid-costing system at Nike's main rival, Adidas. The next section explains *operation costing*, a common type of hybrid-costing system.

Overview of Operation-Costing Systems

An **operation** is a standardized method or technique performed repetitively, often on different materials, resulting in different finished goods. Multiple operations are usually conducted within a department. For instance, a suit maker may have a cutting operation and a hemming operation within a single department. The term *operation*, however, is often used loosely. It may be a synonym for a department or process. For example, some companies may call their finishing department a finishing process or a finishing operation.

An **operation-costing system** is a hybrid-costing system applied to batches of similar, but not identical, products. Each batch of products is often a variation of a single design, and it proceeds through a sequence of operations. Within each operation, all product units are treated exactly alike, using identical amounts of the operation's resources. A key point in the operation system is that each batch does not necessarily move through the same operations as other batches. Batches are also called production runs.

In a company that makes suits, managers may select a single basic design for every suit to be made, but depending on specifications, each batch of suits varies somewhat from other batches. Batches may vary with respect to the material used or the type of stitching. Semiconductors, textiles, and shoes are also manufactured in batches and may have similar variations from batch to batch.

An operation-costing system uses work orders that specify the needed direct materials and step-by-step operations. Product costs are compiled for each work order. Direct materials that are unique to different work orders are specifically identified with the appropriate work order, as in job costing. However, each unit is assumed to use an identical amount of conversion costs for a given operation, as in process costing. A single average conversion cost per unit is calculated for each operation. This is done by dividing the total conversion costs for that operation by the number of units that pass through it. This average cost is then assigned to each unit passing through the operation. Units that do not pass through an operation are not allocated any costs for that operation. There were only two cost categories—direct materials and conversion costs—in the examples we have discussed. However, operation costing can have more than two cost categories. The costs in each category are identified with specific work orders using job-costing or process-costing methods as appropriate.

Managers find operation costing useful in cost management because operation costing focuses on control of physical processes, or operations, of a given production system. For example, in clothing manufacturing, managers are concerned with fabric waste, how many fabric layers can be cut at one time, and so on. Operation costing measures, in financial terms, how well managers have controlled physical processes.

Illustrating an Operation-Costing System

The Baltimore Clothing Company, a clothing manufacturer, produces two lines of blazers for department stores: those made of wool and those made of polyester. Wool blazers use better-quality materials and undergo more operations than polyester blazers do. The operations information on work order 423 for 50 wool blazers and work order 424 for 100 polyester blazers is as follows:

	Work Order 423	Work Order 424
Direct materials	Wool	Polyester
	Satin full lining	Rayon partial lining
	Bone buttons	Plastic buttons
Operations		
1. Cutting cloth	Use	Use
2. Checking edges	Use	Do not use
3. Sewing body	Use	Use
4. Checking seams	Use	Do not use
5. Machine sewing of collars and lapels	Do not use	Use
6. Hand sewing of collars and lapels	Use	Do not use

The cost data for these work orders, started and completed in March 2014, are as follows:

	Work Order 423	Work Order 424
Number of blazers	50	100
Direct materials costs	$ 6,000	$3,000
Conversion costs allocated:		
Operation 1	580	1,160
Operation 2	400	—
Operation 3	1,900	3,800
Operation 4	500	—
Operation 5	—	875
Operation 6	700	—
Total manufacturing costs	$10,080	$8,835

As in process costing, all product units in any work order are assumed to consume identical amounts of conversion costs of a particular operation. Baltimore's operation-costing system uses a budgeted rate to calculate the conversion costs of each operation. The budgeted rate for Operation 1 (amounts assumed) is as follows:

$$
\begin{aligned}
\text{Operation 1 budgeted conversion-cost rate for 2014} &= \frac{\text{Operation 1 budgeted conversion costs for 2014}}{\text{Operation 1 budgeted product units for 2014}} \\
&= \frac{\$232{,}000}{20{,}000 \text{ units}} \\
&= \$11.60 \text{ per unit}
\end{aligned}
$$

The budgeted conversion costs of Operation 1 include labor, power, repairs, supplies, depreciation, and other overhead of this operation. If some units have not been completed (so all units in Operation 1 have not received the same amounts of conversion costs), the conversion-cost rate is computed by dividing the budgeted conversion costs by the *equivalent units* of the conversion costs, as in process costing.

As the company manufactures blazers, managers allocate the conversion costs to the work orders processed in Operation 1 by multiplying the $11.60 conversion cost per unit by the number of units processed. Conversion costs of Operation 1 for 50 wool blazers (Work Order 423) are $11.60 per blazer × 50 blazers = $580 and for 100 polyester blazers (Work Order 424) are $11.60 per blazer × 100 blazers = $1,160. When equivalent units are used to calculate the conversion-cost rate, costs are allocated to work orders by multiplying the conversion cost per equivalent unit by the number of equivalent units in the work order. The direct material costs of $6,000 for the 50 wool blazers (Work Order 423) and $3,000 for the 100 polyester blazers (Work Order 424) are specifically identified with each order, as in job costing. The basic point of operation costing is this: Operation unit costs are assumed to be the same regardless of the work order, but direct material costs vary across orders when the materials for each work order vary.

Journal Entries

The actual conversion costs for Operation 1 in March 2014—assumed to be $24,400, including the actual costs incurred for work order 423 and work order 424—are entered into a Conversion Costs Control account:

1. Conversion Costs Control	24,400	
Various accounts (such as Wages Payable		
Control and Accumulated Depreciation)		24,400

The summary journal entries for assigning the costs to polyester blazers (work order 424) follow. Entries for wool blazers would be similar. Of the $3,000 of direct materials for work order 424, $2,975 are used in Operation 1, and the remaining $25 of materials are used in another operation. The journal entry to record direct materials used for the 100 polyester blazers in March 2014 is as follows:

2. Work in Process, Operation 1	2,975	
Materials Inventory Control		2,975

The journal entry to record the allocation of conversion costs to products uses the budgeted rate of $11.60 per blazer times the 100 polyester blazers processed, or $1,160:

3. Work in Process, Operation 1	1,160	
Conversion Costs Allocated		1,160

The journal entry to record the transfer of the 100 polyester blazers (at a cost of $2,975 + $1,160) from Operation 1 to Operation 3 (polyester blazers do not go through Operation 2) is as follows:

4. Work in Process, Operation 3	4,135	
Work in Process, Operation 1		4,135

After posting these entries, the Work in Process, Operation 1, account appears as follows:

Work in Process, Operation 1

② Direct materials	2,975	④ Transferred to Operation 3	4,135
③ Conversion costs allocated	1,160		
Ending inventory, March 31	0		

The costs of the blazers are transferred through the operations in which blazers are worked on and then to finished goods in the usual manner. Costs are added throughout the fiscal year in the Conversion Costs Control account and the Conversion Costs Allocated account. Any overallocation or underallocation of conversion costs is disposed of in the same way as overallocated or underallocated manufacturing overhead in a job-costing system.

> **Decision Point**
>
> What is an operation-costing system and when is it a better approach to product costing?

Problem for Self-Study

Allied Chemicals operates a thermo-assembly process as the second of three processes at its plastics plant. Direct materials in thermo-assembly are added at the end of the process. Conversion costs are added evenly during the process. The following data pertain to the thermo-assembly department for June 2014:

	Home	Insert	Page Layout	Formulas	Data	Review	View		
	A					B	C	D	E
1						Physical Units	Transferred-In Costs	Direct Materials	Conversion Costs
2	Work in process, beginning inventory					50,000			
3	Degree of completion, beginning work in process						100%	0%	80%
4	Transferred in during current period					200,000			
5	Completed and transferred out during current period					210,000			
6	Work in process, ending inventory					?			
7	Degree of completion, ending work in process						100%	0%	40%

Compute equivalent units under (1) the weighted-average method and (2) the FIFO method.

Required

Solution

1. The weighted-average method uses equivalent units of work done to date to compute cost per equivalent unit. The calculations of equivalent units follow:

	Home	Insert	Page Layout	Formulas	Data	Review	View			

	A	B	C	D	E
1		(Step 1)		(Step 2)	
2				Equivalent Units	
3	**Flow of Production**	**Physical Units**	**Transferred-In Costs**	**Direct Materials**	**Conversion Costs**
4	Work in process, beginning (given)	50,000			
5	Transferred in during current period (given)	200,000			
6	To account for	250,000			
7	Completed and transferred out during current period	210,000	210,000	210,000	210,000
8	Work in process, ending[a]	40,000[b]			
9	(40,000 × 100%; 40,000 × 0%; 40,000 × 40%)		40,000	0	16,000
10	Accounted for	250,000			
11	Equivalent units of work done to date		250,000	210,000	226,000
12					
13	[a]Degree of completion in this department: transferred-in costs, 100%; direct materials, 0%; conversion costs, 40%.				
14	[b]250,000 physical units to account for minus 210,000 physical units completed and transferred out.				

2. The FIFO method uses equivalent units of work done in the current period only to compute cost per equivalent unit. The calculations of equivalent units follow:

	Home	Insert	Page Layout	Formulas	Data	Review	View			

	A	B	C	D	E
1		(Step 1)		(Step 2)	
2				Equivalent Units	
3	**Flow of Production**	**Physical Units**	**Transferred-In Costs**	**Direct Materials**	**Conversion Costs**
4	Work in process, beginning (given)	50,000			
5	Transferred in during current period (given)	200,000			
6	To account for	250,000			
7	Completed and transferred out during current period:				
8	From beginning work in process[a]	50,000			
9	[50,000 × (100% – 100%); 50,000 × (100% – 0%); 50,000 × (100% – 80%)]		0	50,000	10,000
10	Started and completed	160,000[b]			
11	(160,000 × 100%; 160,000 × 100%; 160,000 × 100%)		160,000	160,000	160,000
12	Work in process, ending[c]	40,000[d]			
13	(40,000 × 100%; 40,000 × 0%; 40,000 × 40%)		40,000	0	16,000
14	Accounted for	250,000			
15	Equivalent units of work done in current period		200,000	210,000	186,000
16					
17	[a]Degree of completion in this department: transferred-in costs, 100%; direct materials, 0%; conversion costs, 80%.				
18	[b]210,000 physical units completed and transferred out minus 50,000 physical units completed and transferred out from beginning work-in-process inventory.				
19	[c]Degree of completion in this department: transferred-in costs, 100%; direct materials, 0%; conversion costs, 40%.				
20	[d]250,000 physical units to account for minus 210,000 physical units completed and transferred out.				

▶ Decision Points

The following question-and-answer format summarizes the chapter's learning objectives. Each decision presents a key question related to a learning objective. The guidelines are the answer to that question.

Decision	Guidelines
1. Under what conditions is a process-costing system used?	A process-costing system is used to determine cost of a product or service when masses of identical or similar units are produced. Industries using process-costing systems include the food, textiles, and oil-refining industries.
2. How are average unit costs computed when no inventories are present?	Average unit costs are computed by dividing the total costs in a given accounting period by the total units produced in that period.
3. What are the five steps in a process-costing system, and how are equivalent units calculated?	The five steps in a process-costing system are (1) summarize the flow of physical units of output, (2) compute the output in terms of equivalent units, (3) summarize the total costs to account for, (4) compute the cost per equivalent unit, and (5) assign the total costs to units completed and to units in ending work-in-process inventory. An equivalent unit is a derived measure of output that (a) takes the quantity of each input (factor of production) in units completed or in incomplete units in work in process and (b) converts the quantity of input into the amount of completed output units that could be made with that quantity of input.
4. What are the weighted-average and first-in, first-out (FIFO) methods of process costing? Under what conditions will they yield different levels of operating income?	The weighted-average method computes unit costs by dividing total costs in the Work in Process account by total equivalent units completed to date and assigns this average cost to units completed and to units in ending work-in-process inventory. The first-in, first-out (FIFO) method computes unit costs based on costs incurred during the current period and equivalent units of work done in the current period. Operating income can differ materially between the two methods when (1) direct material or conversion cost per equivalent unit varies significantly from period to period and (2) physical-inventory levels of work in process are large in relation to the total number of units transferred out of the process.
5. How are the weighted-average and FIFO process-costing methods applied to transferred-in costs?	The weighted-average method computes transferred-in costs per unit by dividing the total transferred-in costs to date by the total equivalent transferred-in units completed to date and assigns this average cost to units completed and to units in ending work-in-process inventory. The FIFO method computes the transferred-in costs per unit based on the costs transferred in during the current period and equivalent units of transferred-in costs of work done in the current period. The FIFO method assigns transferred-in costs in the beginning work-in-process inventory to units completed and costs transferred in during the current period first to complete the beginning inventory, next to start and complete new units, and finally to units in ending work-in-process inventory.
6. What is an operation-costing system, and when is it a better approach to product costing?	Operation costing is a hybrid-costing system that blends characteristics from both job-costing (for direct materials) and process-costing systems (for conversion costs). It is a better approach to product costing when production systems share some features of custom-order manufacturing and other features of mass-production manufacturing.

Appendix

Standard-Costing Method of Process Costing

Accounting in a standard-costing system involves making entries using standard costs and then isolating variances from these standards in order to support management control. This appendix describes how the principles of standard costing can be employed in process-costing systems.

Benefits of Standard Costing

Companies that use process-costing systems produce masses of identical or similar units of output. In such companies, it is fairly easy to budget for the quantities of inputs needed to produce a unit of output. Standard cost per input unit can then be multiplied by input quantity standards to develop a standard cost per output unit.

The weighted-average and FIFO methods become very complicated when used in process industries, such as textiles, ceramics, paints, and packaged food, that produce a wide variety of similar products. For example, a steel-rolling mill uses various steel alloys and produces sheets of varying sizes and finishes. The different types of direct materials used and the operations performed are few, but used in various combinations, they yield a wide variety of products. In these cases, if the broad averaging procedure of *actual* process costing were used, the result would be inaccurate costs for each product. Therefore, managers in these industries typically use the standard-costing method of process costing.

Under the standard-costing method, teams of design and process engineers, operations personnel, and management accountants work together to determine *separate* standard costs per equivalent unit on the basis of different technical processing specifications for each product. Identifying standard costs for each product overcomes the disadvantage of costing all products at a single average amount, as under actual costing.

Computations Under Standard Costing

We return to the assembly department of Pacific Electronics, but this time we use standard costs. Assume the same standard costs apply in February and March 2014. Data for the assembly department are as follows:

	Physical Units (SG-40s) (1)	Direct Materials (2)	Conversion Costs (3)	Total Costs (4) = (2) + (3)
Standard cost per unit		$ 74	$ 54	
Work in process, beginning inventory (March 1)	225			
Degree of completion of beginning work in process		100%	60%	
Beginning work in process inventory at standard costs		$16,650[a]	$ 7,290[a]	$23,940
Started during March	275			
Completed and transferred out during March	400			
Work in process, ending inventory (March 31)	100			
Degree of completion of ending work in process		100%	50%	
Actual total costs added during March		$19,800	$16,380	$36,180
[a]Work in process, beginning inventory at standard costs				
Direct materials: 225 physical units × 100% completed × $74 per unit = $16,650				
Conversion costs: 225 physical units × 60% completed × $54 per unit = $7,290				

We illustrate the standard-costing method of process costing using the five-step procedure.

Exhibit 12

Summarize the Flow
of Physical Units and
Compute Output
in Equivalent Units
Using the Standard-
Costing Method for the
Assembly Department
for March 2014

	Home	Insert	Page Layout	Formulas	Data	Review	View		
			A		B	C	D	
1					(Step 1)	(Step 2)		
2						Equivalent Units		
3			Flow of Production		Physical Units	Direct Materials	Conversion Costs	
4	Work in process, beginning (given, p. 692)				225			
5	Started during current period (given, p. 692)				275			
6	To account for				500			
7	Completed and transferred out during current period:							
8	From beginning work in process[a]				225			
9	[225 × (100% − 100%); 225 × (100% − 60%)]					0	90	
10	Started and completed				175[b]			
11	(175 × 100%; 175 × 100%)					175	175	
12	Work in process, ending[c] (given, p. 692)				100			
13	(100 × 100%; 100 × 50%)					100	50	
14	Accounted for				500			
15	Equivalent units of work done in current period					275	315	
16								
17	[a]Degree of completion in this department: direct materials, 100%; conversion costs, 60%.							
18	[b]400 physical units completed and transferred out minus 225 physical units completed and transferred out from beginning work-in-process inventory.							
19	[c]Degree of completion in this department: direct materials, 100%; conversion costs, 50%.							

Exhibit 12 presents Steps 1 and 2. These steps are identical to the steps described for the FIFO method in Exhibit 6 because, as in FIFO, the standard-costing method also assumes that the earliest equivalent units in beginning work in process are completed first. Work done in the current period for direct materials is 275 equivalent units. Work done in the current period for conversion costs is 315 equivalent units.

Exhibit 13 describes Steps 3, 4, and 5. In Step 3, total costs to account for (that is, the total debits to Work in Process—Assembly) differ from total debits to Work in Process—Assembly under the actual-cost-based weighted-average and FIFO methods. That's because, as in all standard-costing systems, the debits to the Work in Process account are at standard costs, rather than actual costs. These standard costs total $61,300 in Exhibit 13. In Step 4, costs per equivalent unit are standard costs: direct materials, $74, and conversion costs, $54. *Therefore, costs per equivalent unit do not have to be computed as they were for the weighted-average and FIFO methods.*

Exhibit 13, Step 5, assigns total costs to units completed and transferred out and to units in ending work-in-process inventory, as in the FIFO method. Step 5 assigns amounts of standard costs to equivalent units calculated in Exhibit 12. These costs are assigned (1) first to complete beginning work-in-process inventory, (2) next to start and complete new units, and (3) finally to start new units that are in ending work-in-process inventory. Note how the $61,300 total costs accounted for in Step 5 of Exhibit 13 equal total costs to account for.

Accounting for Variances

Process-costing systems using standard costs record actual direct material costs in Direct Materials Control and actual conversion costs in Conversion Costs Control (similar to Variable and Fixed Overhead Control). In the journal entries that follow, the first two record these *actual costs*. In entries 3 and 4a, the Work-in-Process—Assembly account accumulates direct material costs and conversion costs at *standard*

| | Exhibit 13 | | Summarize the Total Costs to Account For, Compute the Cost per Equivalent Unit, and Assign Costs to the Units Completed and Units in Ending Work-in-Process Inventory Using the Standard-Costing Method for the Assembly Department for March 2014 |

	A	B	C	D	E	F	G
1			Total Production Costs	Direct Materials		Conversion Costs	
2	(Step 3)	Work in process, beginning (given, p. 692)					
3		Direct materials, 225 × $74; Conversion costs, 135 × $54	$23,940	$16,650		$ 7,290	
4		Costs added in current period at standard costs					
5		Direct materials, 275 × $74; Conversion costs, 315 × $54	37,360	20,350		17,010	
6		Total costs to account for	$61,300	$37,000		$24,300	
7							
8	(Step 4)	Standard cost per equivalent unit (given, p. 692)		$ 74		$ 54	
9							
10	(Step 5)	Assignment of costs at standard costs:					
11		Completed and transferred out (400 units):					
12		Work in process, beginning (225 units)	$23,940	$16,650	+	$ 7,290	
13		Costs added to beginning work in process in current period	4,860	(0[a] × $74)	+	(90[a] × $54)	
14		Total from beginning inventory	28,800				
15		Started and completed (175 units)	22,400	(175[b] × $74)	+	(175[b] × $54)	
16		Total costs of units completed and transferred out	51,200				
17		Work in process, ending (100 units):	10,100	(100[c] × $74)	+	(50[c] × $54)	
18		Total costs accounted for	$61,300	$37,000	+	$24,300	
19							
20	Summary of variances for current performance:						
21	Costs added in current period at standard costs (see Step 3 above)			$20,350		$17,010	
22	Actual costs incurred (given, p. 692)			$19,800		$16,380	
23	Variance			$ 550	F	$ 630	F
24							
25	[a]Equivalent units used to complete beginning work in process from Exhibit 17-12, Step 2.						
26	[b]Equivalent units started and completed from Exhibit 17-12, Step 2.						
27	[c]Equivalent units in ending work in process from Exhibit 17-12, Step 2.						

costs. Entries 3 and 4b isolate total variances. The final entry transfers out completed goods at standard costs.

1. Assembly Department Direct Materials Control (at actual costs)   19,800
   Accounts Payable Control   19,800

   To record the direct materials purchased and used in production during March. This cost control account is debited with actual costs.

2. Assembly Department Conversion Costs Control (at actual costs)   16,380
   Various accounts such as Wages Payable Control and Accumulated Depreciation   16,380

   To record the assembly department conversion costs for March. This cost control account is debited with actual costs.

   Entries 3, 4, and 5 use standard cost amounts from Exhibit 13.

3. Work in Process—Assembly (at standard costs)   20,350
   Direct Materials Variances   550
   Assembly Department Direct Materials Control   19,800

   To record the standard costs of direct materials assigned to units worked on and total direct materials variances.

4a. Work in Process—Assembly (at standard costs)	17,010	
Assembly Department Conversion Costs Allocated		17,010
To record the conversion costs allocated at standard rates to the units worked on during March.		
4b. Assembly Department Conversion Costs Allocated	17,010	
Conversion Costs Variances		630
Assembly Department Conversion Costs Control		16,380
To record the total conversion costs variances.		
5. Work in Process—Testing (at standard costs)	51,200	
Work in Process—Assembly (at standard costs)		51,200
To record the standard costs of units completed and transferred out from assembly to testing.		

Variances arise under standard costing, as in entries 3 and 4b. That's because the standard costs assigned to products on the basis of work done in the current period do not equal actual costs incurred in the current period. Recall that variances that result in higher income than expected are termed favorable, while those that reduce income are unfavorable. From an accounting standpoint, favorable cost variances are credit entries, while unfavorable ones are debits. In the preceding example, both direct materials and conversion cost variances are favorable. This is also reflected in the "F" designations for both variances in Exhibit 13.

Variances can be analyzed in little or great detail for planning and control purposes. Sometimes direct materials price variances are isolated at the time direct materials are purchased and only efficiency variances are computed in entry 3. Exhibit 14 shows how the costs flow through the general-ledger accounts under standard costing.

Exhibit 14 Flow of Standard Costs in a Process-Costing System for the Assembly Department for March 2014

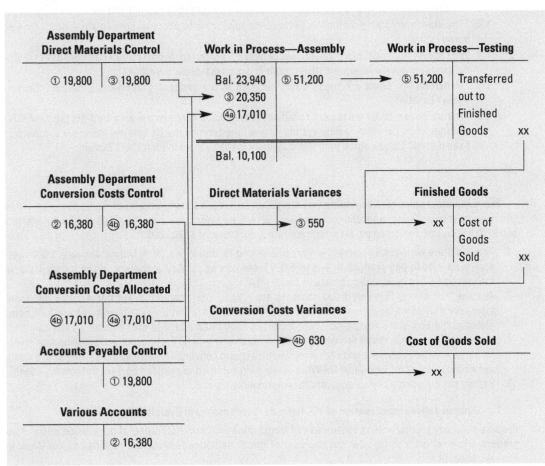

Terms to Learn

This chapter contains definitions of the following important terms:

equivalent units

first-in, first-out (FIFO) process-costing
  method

hybrid-costing system

operation

operation-costing system

previous-department costs

transferred-in costs

weighted-average process-costing
  method

Assignment Material

MyAccountingLab

Questions

1 Give three examples of industries that use process-costing systems.

2 In process costing, why are costs often divided into two main classifications?

3 Explain equivalent units. Why are equivalent-unit calculations necessary in process costing?

4 What problems might arise in estimating the degree of completion of semiconductor chips in a semiconductor plant?

5 Name the five steps in process costing when equivalent units are computed.

6 Name the three inventory methods commonly associated with process costing.

7 Describe the distinctive characteristic of weighted-average computations in assigning costs to units completed and to units in ending work in process.

8 Describe the distinctive characteristic of FIFO computations in assigning costs to units completed and to units in ending work in process.

9 Why should the FIFO method be called a modified or department FIFO method?

10 Identify a major advantage of the FIFO method for purposes of planning and control.

11 Identify the main difference between journal entries in process costing and job costing.

12 "The standard-costing method is particularly applicable to process-costing situations." Do you agree? Why?

13 Why should the accountant distinguish between transferred-in costs and additional direct material costs for each subsequent department in a process-costing system?

14 "Transferred-in costs are those costs incurred in the preceding accounting period." Do you agree? Explain.

15 "There's no reason for me to get excited about the choice between the weighted-average and FIFO methods in my process-costing system. I have long-term contracts with my materials suppliers at fixed prices." Do you agree with this statement made by a plant controller? Explain.

MyAccountingLab

Exercises

16 Equivalent units, zero beginning inventory. Candid, Inc., is a manufacturer of digital cameras. It has two departments: assembly and testing. In January 2014, the company incurred $800,000 on direct materials and $805,000 on conversion costs, for a total manufacturing cost of $1,605,000.

Required

1. Assume there was no beginning inventory of any kind on January 1, 2014. During January, 5,000 cameras were placed into production and all 5,000 were fully completed at the end of the month. What is the unit cost of an assembled camera in January?

2. Assume that during February 5,000 cameras are placed into production. Further assume the same total assembly costs for January are also incurred in February, but only 4,000 cameras are fully completed at the end of the month. All direct materials have been added to the remaining 1,000 cameras. However, on average, these remaining 1,000 cameras are only 60% complete as to conversion costs. (a) What are the equivalent units for direct materials and conversion costs and their respective costs per equivalent unit for February? (b) What is the unit cost of an assembled camera in February 2014?

3. Explain the difference in your answers to requirements 1 and 2.

17 Journal entries (continuation of 16). Refer to requirement 2 of Exercise 16.

Required

Prepare summary journal entries for the use of direct materials and incurrence of conversion costs. Also prepare a journal entry to transfer out the cost of goods completed. Show the postings to the Work in Process account.

18 Zero beginning inventory, materials introduced in middle of process. Pilar Chemicals has a mixing department and a refining department. Its process-costing system in the mixing department has two direct materials cost categories (chemical P and chemical Q) and one conversion costs pool. The following data pertain to the mixing department for July 2014:

Units	
Work in process, July 1	0
Units started	100,000
Completed and transferred to refining department	70,000
Costs	
Chemical P	$600,000
Chemical Q	140,000
Conversion costs	360,000

Chemical P is introduced at the start of operations in the mixing department, and chemical Q is added when the product is three-fourths completed in the mixing department. Conversion costs are added evenly during the process. The ending work in process in the mixing department is two-thirds complete.

Required

1. Compute the equivalent units in the mixing department for July 2014 for each cost category.
2. Compute (a) the cost of goods completed and transferred to the refining department during July and (b) the cost of work in process as of July 31, 2014.

19 Weighted-average method, equivalent units. The assembly division of Fenton Watches, Inc., uses the weighted-average method of process costing. Consider the following data for the month of May 2014:

	Physical Units (Watches)	Direct Materials	Conversion Costs
Beginning work in process (May 1)[a]	80	$ 493,360	$ 91,040
Started in May 2014	500		
Completed during May 2014	460		
Ending work in process (May 31)[b]	120		
Total costs added during May 2014		$3,220,000	$1,392,000

[a]Degree of completion: direct materials, 90%; conversion costs, 40%.
[b]Degree of completion: direct materials, 60%; conversion costs, 30%.

Required

Compute equivalent units for direct materials and conversion costs. Show physical units in the first column of your schedule.

20 Weighted-average method, assigning costs (continuation of 19).

Required

For the data in Exercise 19, summarize the total costs to account for, calculate the cost per equivalent unit for direct materials and conversion costs, and assign costs to the units completed (and transferred out) and units in ending work in process.

21 FIFO method, equivalent units. Refer to the information in Exercise 19. Suppose the assembly division at Fenton Watches, Inc., uses the FIFO method of process costing instead of the weighted-average method.

Required

Compute equivalent units for direct materials and conversion costs. Show physical units in the first column of your schedule.

22 FIFO method, assigning costs (continuation of 21).

Required

For the data in Exercise 19, use the FIFO method to summarize the total costs to account for, calculate the cost per equivalent unit for direct materials and conversion costs, and assign costs to units completed (and transferred out) and to units in ending work in process.

23 Operation costing. Whole Goodness Bakery needs to determine the cost of two work orders for the month of June. Work order 215 is for 2,400 packages of dinner rolls, and work order 216 is for 2,800 loaves of multigrain bread. Dinner rolls are mixed and cut into individual rolls before being baked and then packaged. Multigrain loaves are mixed and shaped before being baked, sliced, and packaged. The following information applies to work order 215 and work order 216:

	Work Order 215	Work Order 216
Quantity (packages)	2,400	2,800
Operations		
1. Mix	Use	Use
2. Shape loaves	Do not use	Use
3. Cut rolls	Use	Do not use
4. Bake	Use	Use
5. Slice loaves	Do not use	Use
6. Package	Use	Use

Selected budget information for June follows:

	Dinner Rolls	Multigrain Loaves	Total
Packages	9,600	13,000	22,600
Direct material costs	$5,280	$11,700	$ 16,980

Budgeted conversion costs for each operation for June follow:

Mixing	$18,080
Shaping	3,250
Cutting	1,440
Baking	14,690
Slicing	1,300
Packaging	16,950

Required

1. Using budgeted number of packages as the denominator, calculate the budgeted conversion-cost rates for each operation.
2. Using the information in requirement 1, calculate the budgeted cost of goods manufactured for the two June work orders.
3. Calculate the cost per package of dinner rolls and multigrain loaves for work order 215 and 216.

24 Weighted-average method, assigning costs. Tomlinson Corporation is a biotech company based in Milpitas. It makes a cancer-treatment drug in a single processing department. Direct materials are added at the start of the process. Conversion costs are added evenly during the process. Tomlinson uses the weighted-average method of process costing. The following information for July 2014 is available.

		Equivalent Units	
	Physical Units	Direct Materials	Conversion Costs
Work in process, July 1	8,700[a]	8,700	2,175
Started during July	34,500		
Completed and transferred out during July	32,000	32,000	32,000
Work in process, July 31	11,200[b]	11,200	7,840

[a]Degree of completion: direct materials, 100%; conversion costs, 25%.
[b]Degree of completion: direct materials, 100%; conversion costs, 70%.

Total Costs for July 2014

Work in process, beginning		
Direct materials	$61,500	
Conversion costs	43,200	$104,700
Direct materials added during July		301,380
Conversion costs added during July		498,624
Total costs to account for		$904,704

1. Calculate the cost per equivalent unit for direct materials and conversion costs.
2. Summarize the total costs to account for, and assign them to units completed (and transferred out) and to units in ending work in process.

25 FIFO method, assigning costs.

1. Do Exercise 24 using the FIFO method.
2. Tomlinson's management seeks to have a more consistent cost per equivalent unit. Which method of process costing should the company choose and why?

26 Transferred-in costs, weighted-average method.
Trendy Clothing, Inc., is a manufacturer of winter clothes. It has a knitting department and a finishing department. This exercise focuses on the finishing department. Direct materials are added at the end of the process. Conversion costs are added evenly during the process. Trendy uses the weighted-average method of process costing. The following information for June 2014 is available.

	Home	Insert	Page Layout	Formulas	Data	Review	View	

	A	B	C	D	E
1		Physical Units (tons)	Transferred-In Costs	Direct Materials	Conversion Costs
2	Work in process, beginning inventory (June 1)	60	$ 60,000	$ 0	$24,000
3	Degree of completion, beginning work in process		100%	0%	50%
4	Transferred in during June	100			
5	Completed and transferred out during June	120			
6	Work in process, ending inventory (June 30)	40			
7	Degree of completion, ending work in process		100%	0%	75%
8	Total costs added during June		$117,000	$27,000	$62,400

1. Calculate equivalent units of transferred-in costs, direct materials, and conversion costs.
2. Summarize the total costs to account for, and calculate the cost per equivalent unit for transferred-in costs, direct materials, and conversion costs.
3. Assign costs to units completed (and transferred out) and to units in ending work in process.

27 Transferred-in costs, FIFO method.
Refer to the information in Exercise 26. Suppose that Trendy uses the FIFO method instead of the weighted-average method in all of its departments. The only changes to Exercise 26 under the FIFO method are that total transferred-in costs of beginning work in process on June 1 are $45,000 (instead of $60,000) and total transferred-in costs added during June are $114,000 (instead of $117,000).

Do Exercise 26 using the FIFO method. Note that you first need to calculate equivalent units of work done in the current period (for transferred-in costs, direct materials, and conversion costs) to complete beginning work in process, to start and complete new units, and to produce ending work in process.

28 Operation costing.
Purex produces three different types of detergents: Breeze, Fresh, and Joy. The company uses four operations to manufacture the detergents: spray drying, mixing, blending, and packaging. Breeze and Fresh are produced in powder form in the mixing department, while Joy is produced in liquid form in the blending department. The powder detergents are packed in 50-ounce paperboard cartons, and the liquid detergent is packed in 50-ounce bottles made of recycled plastic.

Purex applies conversion costs based on labor-hours in the spray drying department. It takes 1½ minutes to mix the ingredients for a 50-ounce container for each product. Conversion costs are applied based on the number of containers in the mixing and blending departments and on the basis of machine-hours in the packaging department. It takes 0.3 minutes of machine time to fill a 50-ounce container, regardless of the product.

The budgeted number of containers and expected direct materials cost for each type of detergent are as follows:

	Breeze	Fresh	Joy
Number of 50-ounce containers	11,000	8,000	21,000
Direct materials cost	$21,450	$20,000	$52,500

The budgeted conversion costs for each department for July are as follows:

Department	Budgeted Conversion Cost
Spray Drying	$ 8,000
Mixing	22,800
Blending	30,450
Packaging	1,000

1. Calculate the conversion cost rates for each department.
2. Calculate the budgeted cost of goods manufactured for Breeze, Fresh, and Joy for the month of July.
3. Calculate the cost per 50-ounce container for each type of detergent for the month of July.

29 Standard-costing with beginning and ending work in process. Priscilla's Pearls Company (PPC) is a manufacturer of knock-off jewelry. Priscilla attends Fashion Week in New York City every September and February to gauge the latest fashion trends in jewelry. She then makes jewelry at a fraction of the cost of those designers who participate in Fashion Week. This fall's biggest item is triple-stranded pearl necklaces. Because of her large volume, Priscilla uses process costing to account for her production. In October, she had started some of the triple strands. She continued to work on those in November. Costs and output figures are as follows:

Priscilla's Pearls Company Process Costing
For the Month Ended November 30, 2014

	Units	Direct Materials	Conversion Costs
Standard cost per unit		$ 2.40	$ 9.00
Work in process, beginning inventory (Nov. 1)	29,000	$ 69,600	$ 156,600
Degree of completion of beginning work in process		100%	60%
Started during November	124,200		
Completed and transferred out	127,000		
Work in process, ending inventory (Nov. 30)	26,200		
Degree of completion of ending work in process		100%	40%
Total costs added during November		$327,500	$1,222,000

1. Compute equivalent units for direct materials and conversion costs. Show physical units in the first column of your schedule.
2. Compute the total standard costs of pearls transferred out in November and the total standard costs of the November 30 inventory of work in process.
3. Compute the total November variances for direct materials and conversion costs.

MyAccountingLab Problems

30 Equivalent units, comprehensive. Louisville Sports manufactures baseball bats for use by players in the major leagues. A critical requirement for elite players is that each bat they use have an identical look and feel. As a result, Louisville uses a dedicated process to produce bats to each player's specifications.

One of Louisville's key clients is Ryan Brown of the Green Bay Brewers. Producing his bat involves the use of three materials—ash, cork, and ink—and a sequence of 20 standardized steps. Materials are added as follows:

Ash: This is the basic wood used in bats. Eighty percent of the ash content is added at the start of the process; the rest is added at the start of the 16th step of the process.

Cork: This is inserted into the bat in order to increase Ryan's bat speed. Half of the cork is introduced at the beginning of the seventh step of the process; the rest is added at the beginning of the 14th step.

Ink: This is used to stamp Ryan's name on the finished bat and is added at the end of the process.

Of the total conversion costs, 6% are added during each of the first 10 steps of the process, and 4% are added at each of the remaining 10 steps.

On May 1, 2014, Louisville had 100 bats in inventory. These bats had completed the ninth step of the process as of April 30, 2014. During May, Louisville put another 60 bats into production. At the end of May, Louisville was left with 40 bats that had completed the 12th step of the production process.

1. Under the weighted-average method of process costing, compute equivalent units of work done for each relevant input for the month of May.

2. Under the FIFO method of process costing, compute equivalent units of work done for each relevant input for the month of May.

31 Weighted-average method. Larsen Company manufactures car seats in its San Antonio plant. Each car seat passes through the assembly department and the testing department. This problem focuses on the assembly department. The process-costing system at Larsen Company has a single direct-cost category (direct materials) and a single indirect-cost category (conversion costs). Direct materials are added at the beginning of the process. Conversion costs are added evenly during the process. When the assembly department finishes work on each car seat, it is immediately transferred to testing.

Larsen Company uses the weighted-average method of process costing. Data for the assembly department for October 2014 are as follows:

	Physical Units (Car Seats)	Direct Materials	Conversion Costs
Work in process, October 1[a]	5,000	$1,250,000	$ 402,750
Started during October 2014	20,000		
Completed during October 2014	22,500		
Work in process, October 31[b]	2,500		
Total costs added during October 2014		$4,500,000	$2,337,500

[a]Degree of completion: direct materials,?%; conversion costs, 60%.
[b]Degree of completion: direct materials,?%; conversion costs, 70%.

Required

1. For each cost category, compute equivalent units in the assembly department. Show physical units in the first column of your schedule.
2. What issues should the manager focus on when reviewing the equivalent units calculation?
3. For each cost category, summarize total assembly department costs for October 2014 and calculate the cost per equivalent unit.
4. Assign costs to units completed and transferred out and to units in ending work in process.

32 Journal entries (continuation of 31).

Prepare a set of summarized journal entries for all October 2014 transactions affecting Work in Process—Assembly. Set up a T-account for Work in Process—Assembly and post your entries to it.

Required

33 FIFO method (continuation of 31).

1. Do Problem 31 using the FIFO method of process costing. Explain any difference between the cost per equivalent unit in the assembly department under the weighted-average method and the FIFO method.
2. Should Larsen's managers choose the weighted-average method or the FIFO method? Explain briefly.

Required

34 Transferred-in costs, weighted-average method (related to 31 to 33). Larsen Company, as you know, is a manufacturer of car seats. Each car seat passes through the assembly department and testing department. This problem focuses on the testing department. Direct materials are added when the testing department process is 90% complete. Conversion costs are added evenly during the testing department's process. As work in assembly is completed, each unit is immediately transferred to testing. As each unit is completed in testing, it is immediately transferred to Finished Goods.

Larsen Company uses the weighted-average method of process costing. Data for the testing department for October 2014 are as follows:

	Physical Units (Car Seats)	Transferred-In Costs	Direct Materials	Conversion Costs
Work in process, October 1[a]	7,500	$2,932,500	$ 0	$ 835,460
Transferred in during October 2014	?			
Completed during October 2014	26,300			
Work in process, October 31[b]	3,700			
Total costs added during October 2014		$7,717,500	$9,704,700	$3,955,900

[a]Degree of completion: transferred-in costs,?%; direct materials,?%; conversion costs, 70%.
[b]Degree of completion: transferred-in costs,?%; direct materials,?%; conversion costs, 60%.

Required

1. What is the percentage of completion for (a) transferred-in costs and direct materials in beginning work-in-process inventory and (b) transferred-in costs and direct materials in ending work-in-process inventory?
2. For each cost category, compute equivalent units in the testing department. Show physical units in the first column of your schedule.
3. For each cost category, summarize total testing department costs for October 2014, calculate the cost per equivalent unit, and assign costs to units completed (and transferred out) and to units in ending work in process.
4. Prepare journal entries for October transfers from the assembly department to the testing department and from the testing department to Finished Goods.

35 Transferred-in costs, FIFO method (continuation of 34). Refer to the information in Problem 34. Suppose that Larsen Company uses the FIFO method instead of the weighted-average method in all of its departments. The only changes to Problem 34 under the FIFO method are that total transferred-in costs of beginning work in process on October 1 are $2,800,000 (instead of $2,932,500) and that total transferred-in costs added during October are $7,735,250 (instead of $7,717,500).

Required

Using the FIFO process-costing method, complete Problem 34.

36 Weighted-average method. McKnight Handcraft is a manufacturer of picture frames for large retailers. Every picture frame passes through two departments: the assembly department and the finishing department. This problem focuses on the assembly department. The process-costing system at McKnight has a single direct-cost category (direct materials) and a single indirect-cost category (conversion costs). Direct materials are added when the assembly department process is 10% complete. Conversion costs are added evenly during the assembly department's process.

McKnight uses the weighted-average method of process costing. Consider the following data for the assembly department in April 2014:

	Physical Unit (Frames)	Direct Materials	Conversion Costs
Work in process, April 1[a]	60	$ 1,530	$ 156
Started during April 2014	510		
Completed during April 2014	450		
Work in process, April 30[b]	120		
Total costs added during April 2014		$17,850	$11,544

[a]Degree of completion: direct materials, 100%; conversion costs, 40%.
[b]Degree of completion: direct materials, 100%; conversion costs, 15%.

Required

1. Summarize the total assembly department costs for April 2014, and assign them to units completed (and transferred out) and to units in ending work in process.
2. What issues should a manager focus on when reviewing the equivalent units calculation?

37 FIFO method (continuation of 36).

Required

1. Complete Problem 36 using the FIFO method of process costing.
2. If you did Problem 36, explain any difference between the cost of work completed and transferred out and the cost of ending work in process in the assembly department under the weighted-average method and the FIFO method. Should McKnight's managers choose the weighted-average method or the FIFO method? Explain briefly.

38 Transferred-in costs, weighted-average method. Publishers, Inc., has two departments: printing and binding. Each department has one direct-cost category (direct materials) and one indirect-cost category (conversion costs). This problem focuses on the binding department. Books that have undergone the printing process are immediately transferred to the binding department. Direct material is added when the binding process is 70% complete. Conversion costs are added evenly during binding operations. When those operations are done, the books are immediately transferred to Finished Goods. Publishers, Inc., uses the weighted-average method of process costing. The following is a summary of the April 2014 operations of the binding department.

	Physical Units (books)	Transferred-In Costs	Direct Materials	Conversion Costs
1				
2 Beginning work in process	1,260	$ 39,060	$ 0	$16,380
3 Degree of completion, beginning work in process		100%	0%	50%
4 Transferred in during April 2014	2,880			
5 Completed and transferred out during April	3,240			
6 Ending work in process (April 30)	900			
7 Degree of completion, ending work in process		100%	0%	70%
8 Total costs added during April		$155,520	$28,188	$84,240

1. Summarize total binding department costs for April 2014, and assign these costs to units completed (and transferred out) and to units in ending work in process.
2. Prepare journal entries for April transfers from the printing department to the binding department and from the binding department to Finished Goods.

39 Transferred-in costs, FIFO method. Refer to the information in Problem 38. Suppose that Publishers, Inc., uses the FIFO method instead of the weighted-average method in all of its departments. The only changes to Problem 38 under the FIFO method are that total transferred-in costs of beginning work in process on April 1 are $44,100 (instead of $39,060) and that total transferred-in costs added during April are $149,760 (instead of $155,520).

1. Using the FIFO process-costing method, complete Problem 38.
2. If you did Problem 38, explain any difference between the cost of work completed and transferred out and the cost of ending work in process in the binding department under the weighted-average method and the FIFO method.

40 Transferred-in costs, weighted-average and FIFO methods. Portland Pale Ale, Inc., makes a variety of specialty beers at its main brewery in Oregon. Production of beer occurs in three main stages: mashing, boiling, and fermenting. Consider the fermenting department, where direct materials (bottles and other packaging) are added at the end of the process. Conversion costs are added evenly during the process.

Portland Pale Ale provides the following information related to its top-selling Gypsum Ale for the fermenting department for the month of July:

	Physical Units (Cases)	Transferred-In Costs	Direct Materials	Conversion Costs
Beginning work in process	2,500	$116,000	$ 0	$ 37,500
Transferred in during July from boiling department	10,000			
Completed during July	10,500			
Ending work in process, July 31	2,000			
Total costs added during July		$384,000	$110,775	$152,250

The units in beginning work in process are 25% complete for conversion costs, while the units in ending inventory are 50% complete for conversion costs.

1. Using the weighted-average method, summarize the total fermenting department costs for July, and assign costs to units completed (and transferred out) and to units in ending work in process.
2. Assume that the FIFO method is used for the fermenting department. Under FIFO, the transferred-in costs for work-in-process beginning inventory in July are $115,680 (instead of $116,000 under the weighted-average method), and the transferred-in costs during July from the boiling department are $376,000 (instead of $384,000 under the weighted-average method). All other data are unchanged. Summarize the total fermenting department costs for July, and assign costs to units completed and transferred out and to units in ending work in process using the FIFO method.

41 Multiple processes or operations, costing. The Sedona Company is dedicated to making products that meet the needs of customers in a sustainable manner. Sedona is best known for its KLN water bottle, which is a BPA-free, dishwasher-safe, bubbly glass bottle in a soft silicone sleeve.

The production process consists of three basic operations. In the first operation, the glass is formed by remelting cullets (broken or refuse glass). In the second operation, the glass is assembled with the silicone gasket and sleeve. The resulting product is finished in the final operation with the addition of the polypropylene cap.

Consulting studies have indicated that of the total conversion costs required to complete a finished unit, the forming operation requires 60%, the assembly 30%, and the finishing 10%.

The following data are available for March 2014 (there is no opening inventory of any kind):

Cullets purchased	$67,500
Silicone purchased	$24,000
Polypropylene used	$ 6,000
Total conversion costs incurred	$68,850
Ending inventory, cullets	$ 4,500
Ending inventory, silicone	$ 3,000
Number of bottles completed and transferred	12,000
Inventory in process at the end of the month:	
Units formed but not assembled	4,000
Units assembled but not finished	2,000

Required

1. What is the cost per equivalent unit for conversion costs for KLN bottles in March 2014?
2. Compute the cost per equivalent unit with respect to each of the three materials: cullets, silicone, and polypropylene.
3. What is the cost of goods completed and transferred out?
4. What is the cost of goods formed but not assembled?
5. What is the cost of goods assembled but not finished?

42 Benchmarking, ethics. Amanda McNall is the corporate controller of Scott Quarry. Scott Quarry operates 12 rock-crushing plants in Scott County, Kentucky, that process huge chunks of limestone rock extracted from underground mines.

Given the competitive landscape for pricing, Scott's managers pay close attention to costs. Each plant uses a process-costing system, and at the end of every quarter, each plant manager submits a production report and a production-cost report. The production report includes the plant manager's estimate of the percentage of completion of the ending work in process as to direct materials and conversion costs, as well as the level of processed limestone inventory. McNall uses these estimates to compute the cost per equivalent unit of work done for each input for the quarter. Plants are ranked from 1 to 12, and the three plants with the lowest cost per equivalent unit for direct materials and conversion costs are each given a bonus and recognized in the company newsletter.

McNall has been pleased with the success of her benchmarking program. However, she has recently received anonymous emails that two plant managers have been manipulating their monthly estimates of percentage of completion in an attempt to obtain the bonus.

Required

1. Why and how might managers manipulate their monthly estimates of percentage of completion and level of inventory?
2. McNall's first reaction is to contact each plant controller and discuss the problem raised by the anonymous communications. Is that a good idea?
3. Assume that each plant controller's primary reporting responsibility is to the plant manager and that each plant controller receives the phone call from McNall mentioned in requirement 2. What is the ethical responsibility of each plant controller (a) to Amanda McNall and (b) to Scott Quarry in relation to the equivalent-unit and inventory information each plant provides?
4. How might McNall learn whether the data provided by particular plants are being manipulated?

43 Standard-costing method. Hi-sense Technologies produces stripped-down phones for sale to customers in frontier economies. The firm purchases used or obsolete models of specific smartphone models. It removes nonstandard applications, installs open source Android software, and unlocks the phone so it can operate on GSM networks. Hi-sense's most popular offering is the iZoom phone.

Given the importance of scaling and cost control for the success of its business model, Hi-sense uses a standard-costing system. The following information is available for the second quarter of 2014 (April 1–June 30):

Physical and Equivalent Units for iZoom
For the Second Quarter of 2014

	Physical Units	Equivalent Units	
		Direct Materials	Conversion Costs
Completion of beginning work in process	1,158,000	—	521,100
Started and completed	1,014,000	1,014,000	1,014,000
Work on ending work in process	2,180,400	2,180,400	1,308,240
Units to account for	4,352,400	3,194,400	2,843,340

	Costs
Cost of units completed from beginning work in process	$ 9,206,100
Cost of new units started and completed	8,061,300
Cost of units completed in the second quarter	17,267,400
Cost of ending work in process	14,630,484
Total costs accounted for	$31,897,884

1. What are the completion percentages of iZoom phones in beginning work-in-process inventory with respect to the two inputs?
2. What are the completion percentages of iZoom phones in ending work-in-process inventory with respect to the two inputs?
3. What are the standard costs per unit for direct materials and conversion costs?
4. What is the total cost of work-in-process inventory as of April 1, 2014 (the start of the second quarter)?

Glossary

Equivalent units. Derived amount of output units that (a) takes the quantity of each input (factor of production) in units completed and in incomplete units of work in process and (b) converts the quantity of input into the amount of completed output units that could be produced with that quantity of input.

First-in, first-out (FIFO) process-costing method. Method of process costing that assigns the cost of the previous accounting period's equivalent units in beginning work-in-process inventory to the first units completed and transferred out of the process, and assigns the cost of equivalent units worked on during the current period first to complete beginning inventory, next to start and complete new units, and finally to units in ending work-in-process inventory.

Hybrid-costing system. Costing system that blends characteristics from both job-costing systems and process-costing systems.

Operation. A standardized method or technique that is performed repetitively, often on different materials, resulting in different finished goods.

Operation-costing system. Hybrid-costing system applied to batches of similar, but not identical, products. Each batch of products is often a variation of a single design, and it proceeds through a sequence of operations, but each batch does not necessarily move through the same operations as other batches. Within each operation, all product units use identical amounts of the operation's resources.

Previous-department costs. See transferred-in costs.

Transferred-in costs. Costs incurred in previous departments that are carried forward as the product's costs when it moves to a subsequent process in the production cycle. Also called previous department costs.

Weighted-average process-costing method. Method of process costing that assigns the equivalent-unit cost of the work done to date (regardless of the accounting period in which it was done) to equivalent units completed and transferred out of the process and to equivalent units in ending work-in-process inventory.

Photo Credits

Credits are listed in order of appearance.

Inventory Management, Just-in-Time, and Simplified Costing Methods

From Chapter 20 of *Cost Accounting: A Managerial Emphasis,* Fifteenth Edition. Charles T. Horngren, Srikant M. Datar, Madhav V. Rajan. Copyright © 2015 by Pearson Education, Inc. All rights reserved.

Inventory Management, Just-in-Time, and Simplified Costing Methods

Learning Objectives

1 Identify six categories of costs associated with goods for sale

2 Balance ordering costs with carrying costs using the economic-order-quantity (EOQ) decision model

3 Identify the effect of errors that can arise when using the EOQ decision model and ways to reduce conflicts between the EOQ model and models used for performance evaluation

4 Describe why companies are using just-in-time (JIT) purchasing

5 Distinguish materials requirements planning (MRP) systems from just-in-time (JIT) systems for manufacturing

6 Identify the features and benefits of a just-in-time production system

7 Describe different ways backflush costing can simplify traditional inventory-costing systems

8 Understand the principles of lean accounting

Suppose you could receive a large quantity discount for a product that you regularly use, but the discount requires you to buy a year's supply of it and make a large up-front expenditure.

Would you take the quantity discount? Companies face similar decisions because firms pay a price for tying up money in inventory sitting on their shelves or elsewhere. Money tied up in inventory is a particularly serious problem when times are tough. Companies such as Costco work very hard to keep their inventories low.

Costco Aggressively Manages Its Inventory to Thrive in Tough Times[1]

Costco is widely known for its $55-a-year membership fee and its massive, austere warehouses stocked floor to ceiling with large portions of everything from soap to soda. With 627 Costco warehouses around the world, Costco stocks *fewer* items than its competitors and employs innovative inventory management practices that successfully reduce costs throughout its global operations.

The average grocery store carries around 40,000 items, but Costco limits its offerings to about 4,000 products or 90% less, reducing the costs of carrying inventory. Costco also employs a just-in-time inventory management system, which includes sharing data directly with many of its largest suppliers. Companies like PepsiCo and Kraft Foods can track sales performance of items on a warehouse-by-warehouse basis and ship products to replenish Costco's shelves only as needed. These inventory management techniques have allowed Costco to outperform its competitors. Costco turns its inventory more than 12 times a year, far more often than other retailers.

Occasionally, the company leverages its 87 million square feet of warehouse space to reduce its purchasing costs. For example, when Procter & Gamble recently announced a 6% price increase for its paper goods, Costco bought 258 truckloads of paper towels at the old rate and stored them in its distribution centers and warehouses.

Inventory management is important because materials costs often account for more than 40% of total costs of manufacturing companies and more than 70% of total

---

[1] *Source:* McGregor, Jena. 2008. Costco's artful discounts. *BusinessWeek*, October 20; Brad Stone, "Costco CEO Craig Jelinek Leads the Cheapest, Happiest Company in the World," *Bloomberg Businessweek* (June 6, 2013); Liz Parks, "Sharing the View," NRF Stores (February 2006); and Costco Wholesale Company, 2012 Annual Report (Issaquah, Washington: Costco Wholesale Company, 2012).

costs in merchandising companies. In this chapter, we describe the components of inventory costs, relevant costs for different inventory-related decisions, and how planning and control systems, such as just-in-time systems, can reduce inventory.

Inventory Management in Retail Organizations

Learning Objective 1

Identify six categories of costs associated with goods for sale

...purchasing, ordering, carrying, stockout, quality, and shrinkage

Inventory management includes planning, coordinating, and controlling activities related to the flow of inventory into, through, and out of an organization. Consider this breakdown of operations for three major retailers for which cost of goods sold constitutes their largest cost item.

	Kroger	Costco	Walmart
Revenues	100.0%	100.0%	100.0%
Deduct costs:			
Cost of goods sold	79.4%	87.6%	75.1%
Selling and administration costs	15.4%	9.6%	18.9%
Other costs, interest, and taxes	3.7%	1.1%	2.2%
Total costs	98.5%	98.3%	96.2%
Net income	1.5%	1.7%	3.8%

The low percentages of net income to revenues mean that improving the purchase and management of goods for sale can cause dramatic percentage increases in net income.

Costs Associated with Goods for Sale

There are a number of different types of costs associated with inventory other than the cost of the actual goods purchased. The costs associated with inventory fall into the following six categories:

1. **Purchasing costs** are the cost of goods acquired from suppliers, including incoming freight costs. These costs usually make up the largest cost category of goods in inventory. Discounts for various purchase-order sizes and supplier payment terms affect purchasing costs.

2. **Ordering costs** are the costs of preparing and issuing purchase orders, receiving and inspecting the items included in the orders, and matching invoices received, purchase orders, and delivery records to make payments. Ordering costs include the cost of obtaining purchase approvals, as well as other special processing costs.

3. **Carrying costs** are costs that arise while goods are being held in inventory. Carrying costs include the opportunity cost of the investment tied up in inventory and the costs associated with storage, such as space rental, insurance, and obsolescence.

4. **Stockout costs** are costs that arise when a company runs out of a particular item for which there is customer demand, a *stockout*. The company must act quickly to

replenish inventory to meet that demand or suffer the costs of not meeting it. A company may respond to a stockout by expediting an order from a supplier, which can be expensive because of additional ordering and manufacturing costs plus any associated transportation costs. Or the company may lose sales due to the stockout. In this case, the opportunity cost of the stockout includes the lost contribution margin on the sale not made plus any contribution margin lost on future sales due to customer ill will.

5. **Costs of quality** are the costs incurred to prevent and appraise, or the costs arising as a result of, quality issues. Quality problems arise, for example, because products get spoiled or broken or are mishandled while products are moved in and out of the warehouse. There are four categories of quality costs: prevention costs, appraisal costs, internal failure costs, and external failure costs.

6. **Shrinkage costs** result from theft by outsiders, embezzlement by employees, misclassifications, and clerical errors. Shrinkage is measured by the difference between (a) the cost of inventory recorded on the books (after correcting errors) and (b) the cost of inventory when physically counted. Shrinkage can often be an important measure of management performance. Consider, for example, the grocery business, where operating income percentages hover around 2%. With such small margins, it is easy to see why one of a store manager's prime responsibilities is controlling inventory shrinkage. A $1,000 increase in shrinkage will erase the operating income from sales of $50,000 (2% × $50,000 = $1,000). Because shrinkage costs generally increase when a firm's inventory increases, most firms try not to hold more inventory than necessary.

Note that not all inventory costs are available in financial accounting systems. For example, opportunity costs are not recorded in these systems but are a significant component in several of these cost categories.

Information-gathering technology increases the reliability and timeliness of inventory information and reduces the costs related to inventory. For example, barcoding technology allows a scanner to record individual units purchased and sold. As soon as a unit is scanned, a record of its movement is created, which helps a firm better manage its purchasing, carrying, and stockout costs. In the next several sections, we consider how relevant costs are computed for different inventory-related decisions in merchandising companies.

Decision Point

What are the six categories of costs associated with goods for sale?

Learning Objective 2

Balance ordering costs with carrying costs using the economic-order-quantity (EOQ) decision model

...choose the inventory quantity per order to minimize these costs

The Economic-Order-Quantity Decision Model

How much should a firm order of a given product? The **economic order quantity (EOQ)** is a decision model that, under a given set of assumptions, calculates the optimal quantity of inventory to order.

- The simplest version of the EOQ model assumes there are only ordering and carrying costs because these are the most common costs of inventory.
- The same quantity is ordered at each reorder point.
- Demand, ordering costs, and carrying costs are known with certainty. The **purchase-order lead time**, the time between placing an order and its delivery, is also known with certainty.
- The purchasing cost per unit is unaffected by the order quantity. This assumption makes purchasing costs irrelevant to determining the EOQ because the purchase price is the same, whatever the order size.
- No stockouts occur. The basis for this assumption is that the costs of stockouts are so high that managers maintain adequate inventory to prevent them.
- When deciding on the size of a purchase order, managers consider the costs of quality and shrinkage costs only to the extent that these costs affect ordering or carrying costs.

Note that EOQ analysis ignores purchasing costs, stockout costs, costs of quality, and shrinkage costs. Also note that managers only consider relevant costs when making decisions. In a later section we will discuss how to identify the relevant ordering and carrying costs. At this point, we simply note that EOQ is the order quantity that minimizes the sum of a company's relevant ordering and carrying costs. The sum of the costs is the firm's *relevant total ordering and carrying costs* of inventory. The relevant total costs are calculated as follows:

Relevant total costs = Relevant ordering costs + Relevant carrying costs

We use the following notations:

D = Demand in units for a specified period (one year in this example)

Q = Size of each order (order quantity)

$$\text{Number of purchase orders per period (one year)} = \frac{\text{Demand in units for a period (one year)}}{\text{Size of each order (order quantity)}} = \frac{D}{Q}$$

Average inventory in units = $\dfrac{Q}{2}$, because each time the inventory goes down to 0, an order for Q units is received. The inventory varies from Q to 0, so the average inventory is $\dfrac{0 + Q}{2}$.

P = Relevant ordering cost per purchase order

C = Relevant carrying cost of one unit in stock for the time period used for D (one year)

For any order quantity, Q,

$$\text{Annual relevant ordering costs} = \begin{pmatrix} \text{Number of} & \text{Relevant ordering} \\ \text{purchase orders} \times & \text{cost per} \\ \text{per year} & \text{purchase order} \end{pmatrix} = \left(\frac{D}{Q} \times P \right)$$

$$\text{Annual relevant carrying costs} = \begin{pmatrix} & \text{Annual} \\ \text{Average inventory} \times & \text{relevant carrying} \\ \text{in units} & \text{cost per unit} \end{pmatrix} = \left(\frac{Q}{2} \times C \right)$$

$$\text{Annual relevant total costs} = \begin{matrix} \text{Annual} \\ \text{relevant ordering} \\ \text{costs} \end{matrix} + \begin{matrix} \text{Annual} \\ \text{relevant carrying} \\ \text{costs} \end{matrix} = \left(\frac{D}{Q} \times P \right) + \left(\frac{Q}{2} \times C \right)$$

The order quantity that minimizes annual relevant total costs is

$$EOQ = \sqrt{\frac{2DP}{C}}$$

The EOQ model is solved using calculus, but the key intuition is that relevant total costs are minimized when relevant ordering costs equal relevant carrying costs. If carrying costs are less (greater) than ordering costs, the total costs can be reduced by increasing (decreasing) the order quantity. To solve for EOQ, we set

$$\left(\frac{Q}{2} \times C \right) = \left(\frac{D}{Q} \times P \right)$$

Multiplying both sides by $\dfrac{2Q}{C}$, we get $Q^2 = \dfrac{2DP}{C}$

$$Q = \sqrt{\frac{2DP}{C}}$$

The formula indicates that EOQ increases with higher demand and/or higher ordering costs and decreases with higher carrying costs.

Let's see how EOQ analysis works. Glare Shade sells sunglasses. This problem focuses on Glare Shade's basic sunglasses, UX1. Glare Shade purchases the UX1s from

Rytek at $14 a unit. Rytek pays for all incoming freight. No inspection is necessary at Glare Shade because Rytek supplies quality merchandise. Glare Shade's annual demand is 13,000 units of UX1s, at a rate of 250 units per week. Glare Shade requires a 15% annual rate of return on its investment. Relevant ordering cost per purchase order is $200.

The relevant carrying cost per unit per year is as follows:

Required annual return on investment, 0.15 × $14	$2.10
Relevant costs of insurance, materials handling, breakage, shrinkage, and so on, per year	3.10
Total	$5.20

What is the EOQ for ordering UX1 sunglasses?

Substituting $D = 13,000$ units per year, $P = \$200$ per order, and $C = \$5.20$ per unit per year, in the EOQ formula, we get

$$EOQ = \sqrt{\frac{2 \times 13,000 \times \$200}{\$5.20}} = \sqrt{1,000,000} = 1,000 \text{ units}$$

Purchasing 1,000 units per order minimizes total relevant ordering and carrying costs. Therefore, the number of deliveries each period (1 year in this example) is as follows:

$$\frac{D}{EOQ} = \frac{13,000}{1,000} = 13 \text{ deliveries}$$

Recall the annual relevant total costs $(RTC) = \left(\frac{D}{Q} \times P\right) + \left(\frac{Q}{2} \times C\right)$

For $Q = 1,000$ units,

$$RTC = \frac{13,000 \times \$200}{1,000} + \frac{1,000 \times \$5.20}{2}$$
$$= \$2,600 + \$2,600 = \$5,200$$

Exhibit 1 graphs the annual relevant total costs of ordering (DP/Q) and carrying inventory $(QC/2)$ under various order sizes (Q), and it illustrates the tradeoff between these two types of costs. The larger the order quantity, the lower the annual relevant ordering

---

Exhibit 1   Graphic Analysis of Ordering Costs and Carrying Costs for UX1 Sunglasses at Glare Shade

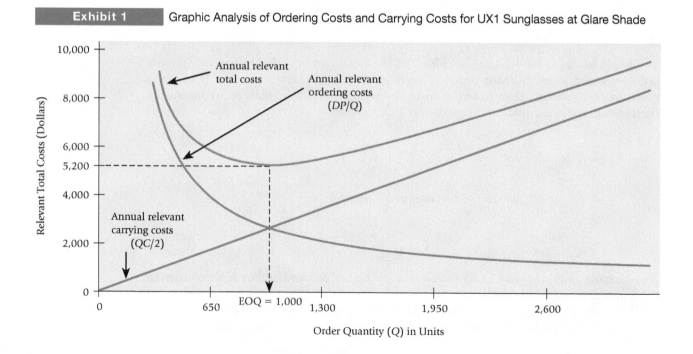

costs, but the higher the annual relevant carrying costs. *The annual relevant total costs are at a minimum at the EOQ at which the relevant ordering and carrying costs are equal.*

When to Order, Assuming Certainty

The second decision Glare Shade's managers face is *when to order* the units. The **reorder point** is the quantity level of inventory on hand that triggers a new purchase order. The reorder point is simplest to compute when both demand and the purchase-order lead time are known with certainty:

$$\text{Reorder point} = \frac{\text{Number of units sold}}{\text{per time period}} \times \frac{\text{Purchase-order}}{\text{lead time}}$$

Suppose the purchase-order lead time for UX1s is 2 weeks:

Economic order quantity	1,000 units
Number of units sold per week	250 units per week (13,000 units ÷ 52 weeks)
Purchase-order lead time	2 weeks

Reorder point = 250 units per week × 2 weeks = 500 units

Glare Shade will order 1,000 units of UX1s each time its inventory falls to 500 units.[2] Exhibit 2 shows the behavior of the inventory level of UX1 units, assuming demand occurs uniformly during each week. If the purchase-order lead time is 2 weeks, a new order will be placed when the inventory level falls to 500 units, so the 1,000 units ordered will be received at the precise time that inventory reaches zero.

Safety Stock

If Glare Shade's managers are uncertain about demand or the purchase-order lead time or if they are uncertain about the quantities of UX1s Rytek can provide, they will hold safety stock. **Safety stock** is inventory held at all times regardless of the quantity of inventory ordered using the EOQ model. Companies use safety stock as a buffer against unexpected increases in demand, uncertainty about lead time, and unavailability of stock from

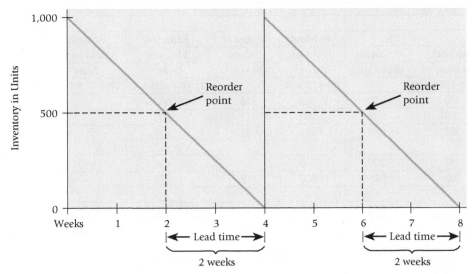

Exhibit 2

Inventory Level of UX1 Sunglasses at Glare Shade[a]

[a] This exhibit assumes that demand and purchase-order lead time are certain:
Demand = 250 UX1 sunglasses per week
Purchase-order lead time = 2 weeks

---

[2] This handy but special formula does not apply when receipt of the order fails to increase inventory to the reorder-point quantity (for example, when lead time is 3 weeks and the order is a 1-week supply). In these cases, orders will overlap.

suppliers. Suppose Glare Shade's managers are uncertain about demand. They expect the demand for UX1s to be 250 units per week, but it could be as high as 400 units per week or as low as 100 units per week. If stockout costs are very high, the managers will want to hold a safety stock of 300 units and incur higher carrying costs. The 300 units equal the maximum excess demand of $150(400 - 250)$ units per week times the 2 weeks of purchase-order lead time. If stockout costs are minimal, no safety stock will be held to avoid incurring the additional carrying costs.

Managers use a frequency distribution based on prior daily or weekly levels of demand to compute safety-stock levels. Assume that one of the following levels of demand for UX1s will occur over the 2-week purchase-order lead time.

Total Demand for 2 Weeks	200 Units	300 Units	400 Units	500 Units	600 Units	700 Units	800 Units
Probability (sums to 1.00)	0.06	0.09	0.20	0.30	0.20	0.09	0.06

We see that 500 units is the most likely level of demand for 2 weeks because it has the highest probability of occurrence. We see also a 0.35 probability that demand will be 600, 700, or 800 units $(0.20 + 0.09 + 0.06 = 0.35)$.

If a customer wants to buy UX1s and the store has none in stock, Glare Shade can "rush" them to the customer at an additional cost to Glare Shade of $4 per unit. The relevant stockout costs in this case are $4 per unit. The optimal safety-stock level is the quantity of safety stock that minimizes the sum of annual relevant stockout and carrying costs. Note that Glare Shade will place 13 orders per year for UX1s and will incur the same ordering costs whatever level of safety stock it chooses. Therefore, ordering costs are irrelevant for the safety-stock decision. Recall that the relevant carrying cost for UX1s is $5.20 per unit per year.

Exhibit 3 tabulates the annual relevant total stockout and carrying costs when the reorder point is 500 units. Over the 2-week purchase-order lead time, stockouts can occur if demand is 600, 700, or 800 units because these levels exceed the 500 units in

Exhibit 3	Computation of Safety Stock for Glare Shade When Reorder Point Is 500 Units

	Home	Insert	Page Layout	Formulas	Data	Review	View		
	A	B	C	D	E	F	G	H	I
1	Safety	Demand							
2	Stock	Levels			Relevant	Number of	Expected	Relevant	Relevant
3	Level	Resulting	Stockout	Probability	Stockout	Orders	Stockout	Carrying	Total
4	in Units	in Stockouts	in Units[a]	of Stockout	Costs[b]	per Year[c]	Costs[d]	Costs[e]	Costs
5	(1)	(2)	(3) = (2) – 500 – (1)	(4)	(5) = (3) × $4	(6)	(7) = (4) × (5) × (6)	(8) = (1) × $5.20	(9) = (7) + (8)
6	0	600	100	0.20	$ 400	13	$1,040		
7		700	200	0.09	800	13	936		
8		800	300	0.06	1,200	13	936		
9							$2,912	$ 0	$2,912
10	100	700	100	0.09	400	13	$ 468		
11		800	200	0.06	800	13	624		
12							$1,092	$ 520	$1,612
13	200	800	100	0.06	400	13	$ 312	$1,040	$1,352
14	300	-	-	-	-	-	$ 0[f]	$1,560	$1,560
15									
16	[a]Demand level resulting in stockouts – Inventory available during lead time (excluding safety stock), 500 units – Safety stock.								
17	[b]Stockout in units × Relevant stockout costs of $4.00 per unit.								
18	[c]Annual demand, 13,000 ÷ 1,000 EOQ = 13 orders per year.								
19	[d]Probability of stockout × Relevant stockout costs × Number of orders per year.								
20	[e]Safety stock × Annual relevant carrying costs of $5.20 per unit (assumes that safety stock is on hand at all times and that there is no overstocking								
21	caused by decreases in expected usage).								
22	[f]At a safety stock level of 300 units, no stockout will occur and, hence, expected stockout costs = $0.								

stock at the time Glare Shade places the purchase orders. Consequently, Glare Shade only evaluates safety stock levels of 0, 100, 200, and 300 units of UX1s. If the safety stock is 0 units, Glare Shade will incur stockout costs if demand is 600, 700, or 800 units but will have no additional carrying costs. At the other extreme, if the safety stock is 300 units, Glare Shade will never incur stockout costs but will have higher carrying costs. As Exhibit 3 shows, the firm's annual relevant total stockout and carrying costs are lowest ($1,352) when a safety stock of 200 units of UX1s is maintained. Therefore, 200 units is the optimal safety-stock level. The 200 units of safety stock is the extra stock that Glare Shade always maintains. For example, Glare Shade's total inventory of UX1s at the time of reordering its EOQ of 1,000 units would be 700 units (the reorder point of 500 units plus safety stock of 200 units).

Estimating Inventory-Related Relevant Costs and Their Effects

How do Glare Shade's managers calculate the annual relevant inventory-related costs, such as the relevant carrying, stockout, and ordering costs?

We start by discussing the relevant inventory carrying costs of $5.20 per unit per year, which consist of the *relevant incremental costs* plus the *relevant opportunity cost of capital*. What are the *relevant incremental costs* of carrying inventory? Only those costs, such as warehouse rent, warehouse workers' salaries, costs of obsolescence, costs of shrinkage, costs of breakage, and costs of insurance, that change with the quantity of inventory held. The salaries paid to clerks, stock keepers, and materials handlers are irrelevant if they are unaffected by changes in inventory levels. Suppose, however, that as inventories increase (decrease), total salary costs increase (decrease) as clerks, stock keepers, and materials handlers are added (transferred to other activities or laid off). In this case, the salaries paid are relevant costs of carrying inventory. Similarly, costs of storage space owned that cannot be used for other profitable purposes when inventories decrease are irrelevant. But if the space has other profitable uses or if total rental cost is tied to the amount of space occupied, storage costs are relevant costs of carrying inventory.

What is the *relevant opportunity cost of capital*? It is the return forgone by investing capital in inventory rather than elsewhere. It is calculated as the required rate of return multiplied by the per-unit costs of acquiring inventory, such as the purchase price of units, incoming freight, and incoming inspection. Opportunity costs are also computed on investments (say, in equipment) if these investments are affected by changes in inventory levels.

In the case of stockouts, the relevant incremental cost is the cost of expediting an order from a supplier. The relevant opportunity cost is (1) the lost contribution margin on sales forgone because of the stockout and (2) the lost contribution margin on future sales forgone as a result of customer ill will.

The relevant ordering costs are only those ordering costs that change with the number of orders placed (for example, the costs of preparing and issuing purchase orders and receiving and inspecting materials).

Cost of a Prediction Error

Predicting relevant costs is difficult and seldom flawless, which raises the question, "What is the cost when actual relevant costs differ from the estimated relevant costs used for decision making?"

Suppose Glare Shade's relevant ordering costs per purchase order for UX1s are $100, but the manager predicts them to be $200 when calculating the order quantity. We can calculate the cost of this "prediction" error using a three-step approach.

Step 1: Compute the Monetary Outcome from the Best Action That Could Be Taken, Given the *Actual* Amount of the Cost Input (Cost per Purchase Order). This is the benchmark—that is, the decision the manager would have made if the manager had

Decision Point

What does the EOQ decision model help managers do, and how do managers decide on the safety-stock levels?

Learning Objective 3

Identify the effect of errors that can arise when using the EOQ decision model

...errors in predicting parameters have a small effect on costs

and ways to reduce conflicts between the EOQ model and models used for performance evaluation

...by making the two models congruent

known the correct ordering cost against which actual performance can be measured. Using $D = 13{,}000$ units of UX1 per year, $P = \$100$, and $C = \$5.20$ per unit per year,

$$EOQ = \sqrt{\frac{2DP}{C}}$$

$$= \sqrt{\frac{2 \times 13{,}000 \times \$100}{\$5.20}} = \sqrt{500{,}000}$$

$$= 707 \text{ units (rounded)}$$

Glare Shade's annual relevant total costs when the $EOQ = 707$ units are as follows:

$$RTC = \frac{DP}{Q} + \frac{QC}{2}$$

$$= \frac{13{,}000 \times \$100}{707} + \frac{707 \times \$5.20}{2}$$

$$= \$1{,}839 + \$1{,}838 = \$3{,}677$$

Step 2: Compute the Monetary Outcome from the Best Action Based on the Incorrect *Predicted* Amount of the Cost Input (Cost per Purchase Order). In this step, the manager calculates the order quantity based on the prediction (that later proves to be wrong) that the ordering cost is $200. When this is the case, the best action is to purchase 1,000 units in each order. However, the actual cost of the purchase order is only $100. Consequently, the actual annual relevant total costs when $D = 13{,}000$ units per year, $Q = 1{,}000$ units, $P = \$100$, and $C = \$5.20$ per unit per year are as follows:

$$RTC = \frac{13{,}000 \times \$100}{1{,}000} + \frac{1{,}000 \times \$5.20}{2}$$

$$= \$1{,}300 + \$2{,}600 = \$3{,}900$$

Step 3: Compute the Difference Between the Monetary Outcomes from Step 1 and Step 2.

	Monetary Outcome
Step 1	$3,677
Step 2	3,900
Difference	$ (223)

The cost of the prediction error, $223, is less than 7% of the relevant total costs of $3,677. Note that the annual relevant-total-costs curve in Exhibit 1 is somewhat flat over the range of order quantities from 700 to 1,300 units. That is, the annual relevant cost is roughly the same even if misestimating the relevant carrying and ordering costs results in an EOQ quantity of 1,000 plus 30% (1,300) or 1,000 minus 30% (700). *The square root in the EOQ model diminishes the effect of estimation errors because it results in the effects of the incorrect numbers becoming smaller.*

In the next section, we consider a planning-and-control and performance-evaluation issue that frequently arises when managing inventory.

Conflicts Between the EOQ Decision Model and Managers' Performance Evaluation

What happens if the order quantity based on the EOQ decision model differs from the order quantity managers would choose to make their own performance look best? Consider, for example, opportunity costs. As we have seen, the EOQ model takes into account opportunity costs because these costs are relevant costs when calculating inventory carrying costs. However, managers evaluated on financial accounting numbers, which is often the case, will ignore opportunity costs. Why? Because financial accounting only records actual transactions, not the costs of opportunities forgone. Managers interested in making their own performance look better will only focus on measures used to evaluate their performance. Conflicts will then arise between the EOQ model's optimal order quantity and the order quantity that managers regard as optimal.

As a result of ignoring some of the carrying costs (the opportunity costs), managers will be inclined to purchase larger lot sizes of materials than the lot sizes calculated according to the EOQ model, particularly if larger lot sizes result in lower purchase prices. As we discussed in the previous section, the cost of these suboptimal choices is small if the quantities purchased are close to the EOQ. However, if the lot sizes become much greater, the cost to the company can be quite large. Moreover, if we consider other costs, such as costs of quality and shrinkage of holding large inventories, the cost to the company of purchasing in large lot sizes is even greater. To achieve congruence between the EOQ decision model and managers' performance evaluations, companies such as Walmart design performance-evaluation systems that charge managers responsible for managing inventory levels with carrying costs that include a required return on investment.

Decision Point

How do errors in predicting the parameters of the EOQ model affect costs? How can companies reduce the conflict between the EOQ decision model and models used for performance evaluation?

Just-in-Time Purchasing

Just-in-time (JIT) purchasing is the purchase of materials (or goods) so that they are delivered just as needed for production (or sales). Consider Hewlett-Packard's (HP's) JIT purchasing: HP has long-term agreements with suppliers of the major components of its printers. Each supplier is required to make frequent deliveries of small orders directly to the production floor, based on the production schedules HP provides them. The suppliers work hard to keep their commitments because any failure on their part will result in HP's assembly plant not meeting its scheduled deliveries of printers.

Learning Objective 4

Describe why companies are using just-in-time (JIT) purchasing

...high carrying costs, costs of quality, and shrinkage costs, low ordering costs, high-quality suppliers, and reliable supply chains

JIT Purchasing and EOQ Model Parameters

Suppose Glare Shade's managers believe that the current purchasing policies might result in the carrying costs of the firm's inventories (parameter C in the EOQ model) being much greater than what they had estimated because of higher warehousing, handling, insurance, and equipment costs. Suppose they also believe that the cost of placing a purchase order (parameter P in the EOQ model) is likely to decrease because of the following:

- Glare Shade is establishing long-term purchasing agreements that define the price and quality terms it has with its suppliers over an extended period. No additional negotiations need to take place before supplies can be ordered.

- New electronic systems allow Glare Shade to place purchase orders, tally delivery records, and make payments to suppliers more cost effectively.

- Glare Shade is using purchase-order cards (similar to consumer credit cards such as VISA and MasterCard). As long as purchasing personnel stay within preset total and individual-transaction dollar limits, traditional labor-intensive procurement-approval procedures are not required.

Exhibit 4 tabulates the sensitivity of the EOQ to changes in carrying and ordering costs of UX1s. Exhibit 4 supports moving toward JIT purchasing because, as the company's relevant carrying costs increase and relevant ordering costs per purchase order decrease, the EOQ decreases and ordering frequency increases.

Relevant Costs of JIT Purchasing

JIT purchasing is not guided solely by the EOQ model because that model only emphasizes the tradeoff between relevant carrying and ordering costs. Inventory management, however, also includes accounting for a company's purchasing costs, stockout costs, costs of quality, and shrinkage costs. Glare Shade's managers are concerned that ordering and storing large quantities of UX1 units have contributed to defective and broken units and shrinkage. So, the company begins implementing JIT purchasing by asking the

Exhibit 4

Sensitivity of EOQ to
Variations in Relevant
Ordering and Carrying
Costs for UX1
Sunglasses

	A	B	C	D	E	F	G
	Home	Insert	Page Layout	Formulas	Data	Review	View
1				Economic Order Quantity in Units			
2				at Different Ordering and Carrying Costs			
3	Annual Demand (D) =	13,000	units				
4							
5	Relevant Carrying Costs			Relevant Ordering Costs per Purchase Order (P)			
6	Per unit per Year (C)			$ 200	$150	$100	$ 30
7	$ 5.20			1,000	866	707	387
8	7.00			862	746	609	334
9	10.00			721	624	510	279
10	15.00			589	510	416	228

supplier of UX1 units to make more frequent deliveries of smaller sizes. Glare Shade has recently established an Internet business-to-business purchase-order link with its supplier, Rytek. Glare Shade triggers a purchase order for UX1s by a single computer entry. Payments are made electronically for batches of deliveries, rather than for each individual delivery. These changes reduce the company's ordering costs from $200 to only $2 per purchase order! Glare Shade will use the Internet purchase-order link whether or not it shifts to JIT purchasing. We next evaluate the effect JIT purchasing has on quality and costs.

Description of Item	Current Purchasing Practice	JIT Purchasing Practice
Deliveries	1,000 units purchased 13 times per year	100 units purchased 130 times per year (5 times every 2 weeks)
Purchasing costs	$14 per unit	$14.02 per unit (Note: Many companies do not pay a higher price for more frequent deliveries.)
Inspection of units	Units inspected at the time of receipt at a cost of $0.05 per unit to identify units that need to be returned	Units not inspected because Rytek ensures that quality UX1 sunglasses are delivered to support Glare Shade's JIT purchasing.
Required rate of return on investment	15%	15%
Relevant carrying cost of insurance, materials handling, storage, etc.	$3.10 per unit of average inventory per year	$3.00 per unit of average inventory per year (lower insurance, materials handling, and storage rates)
Customer return costs	$10 for shipping and processing a defective unit returned by a customer. The high quality of units supplied by Rytek and Glare Shade's inspection procedures will result in no units being returned by customers.	$10 for shipping and processing a defective unit returned by a customer. The high quality of units supplied by Rytek will result in no units being returned by customers.
Stockout costs	No stockout costs because demand and purchase-order lead times during each 4-week period (52 weeks ÷ 13 deliveries) are known with certainty.	More stockouts because demand variations and delays in supplying units are more likely in the short time intervals between orders under JIT purchasing. Glare Shade expects to incur stockout costs on 150 units of UX1 per year under the JIT purchasing policy. When a stockout occurs, Glare Shade must rush-order units at an additional cost of $4 per unit.

| Exhibit 5 | Annual Relevant Costs of Current Purchasing Policy and JIT Purchasing Policy for UX1 Sunglasses |

	A	B	C	D	E	F	G	H	I	J
1					Relevant Costs Under					
2			Current Purchasing Policy					JIT Purchasing Policy		
3	Relevant Items	Relevant Cost per Unit		Quantity per Year	Total Costs		Relevant Cost per Unit		Quantity per Year	Total Costs
4	(1)	(2)		(3)	(4) = (2) × (3)		(5)		(6)	(7) = (5) × (6)
5	Purchasing costs	$14.00	per unit	13,000	$182,000		$14.02	per unit	13,000	$182,260
6	Ordering costs	$ 2.00	per order	13	26		$ 2.00	per order	130	260
7	Inspection costs	$ 0.05	per unit	13,000	650		$ -	per unit	-	-
8	Opportunity carrying costs	$ 2.10[a]	per unit of average inventory per year	500[b]	1,050		$ 2.10[a]	per unit of average inventory per year	50[c]	105
9	Other carrying costs (insurance, materials handling, etc.)	$ 3.10	per unit of average inventory per year	500[b]	1,550		$ 3.00	per unit of average inventory per year	50[c]	150
10	Customer return costs	$10.00	per unit returned	0	0		$10.00	per unit returned	0	0
11	Stockout costs	$ 4.00	per unit	0	0		$ 4.00	per unit	150	600
12	Total annual relevant costs				$185,276					$183,375
13	Annual difference in favor of JIT Purchasing					$1,901				
14										
15	[a]Purchasing cost per unit × 0.15 per year									
16	[b]Order quantity/2 = 1,000/2 = 500 units									
17	[c]Order quantity/2 = 100/2 = 50 units									

Should Glare Shade implement the JIT purchasing option of 130 deliveries of UX1 per year? Exhibit 5 compares Glare Shade's relevant total costs under the current purchasing policy and the JIT policy. It shows net cost savings of $1,901 per year by shifting to a JIT purchasing policy. The benefits of JIT purchasing arise from lower carrying and inspection costs as a result of better quality. JIT purchasing gives Glare Shade's managers immediate feedback about quality problems by reducing the "safety net" large quantities of inventory afford.

Supplier Evaluation and Relevant Costs of Quality and Timely Deliveries

Companies that implement JIT purchasing choose their suppliers carefully and develop long-term supplier relationships. Some suppliers are better positioned than others to support JIT purchasing. For example, the corporate strategy of Frito-Lay, a supplier of potato chips and other snack foods, emphasizes service, consistency, freshness, and the quality of the products the company delivers. As a result, Frito-Lay makes deliveries to retail outlets more frequently than many of its competitors.

What are the relevant total costs when choosing suppliers? Consider again the UX1 units purchased by Glare Shade. Denton Corporation, another supplier of UX1 sunglasses, offers to supply all the units that Glare Shade needs. Glare Shade requires the supplier to deliver 100 units 130 times per year (5 times every 2 weeks). Glare Shade will establish an Internet-based purchase-order link with whichever supplier it chooses, trigger a purchase order for UX1 units by a single computer entry, and make payments electronically for batches of deliveries, rather than for each individual delivery. As discussed earlier, the company's ordering costs will be only $2 per purchase order. The following table provides information about Denton versus Rytek. Rytek charges a higher price than Denton but also supplies higher-quality UX1s. The information about Rytek is the same as that presented earlier under JIT purchasing in Exhibit 5.

Description of Item	Purchasing Terms from Rytek	Purchasing Terms from Denton
Purchasing costs	$14.02 per unit	$13.80 per unit
Inspection of UX1s	Glare Shade has bought UX1s from Rytek in the past and knows that it will deliver quality UX1s on time. UX1s supplied by Rytek require no inspection.	Denton does not enjoy a sterling reputation for quality, so Glare Shade plans to inspect UX1s at a cost of $0.05 per UX1.
Required rate of return on investment	15%	15%
Relevant carrying cost of insurance, materials handling, storage, etc.	$3.00 per unit per year	$2.90 per unit per year because of lower purchasing costs
Customer return costs	Glare Shade estimates $10 for shipping and processing a defective UX1 unit returned by a customer. Fortunately, the high quality of units supplied by Rytek will result in no units being returned by customers.	Glare Shade estimates $10 for shipping and processing a defective UX1 unit returned by a customer and product returns of 2.5% of all units sold.
Stockout costs	Glare Shade expects to incur stockout costs on 150 UX1 units each time resulting in a rush-order at a cost of $4 per unit.	Denton has less control over its processes, so Glare Shade expects to incur stockout costs on 360 UX1 units each time initiating rush orders at a cost of $4 per unit

Exhibit 6 shows the relevant total costs of purchasing from Rytek and Denton. Even though Denton is offering a lower price per unit, there is a net cost savings of $1,873 per year by purchasing UX1s from Rytek because of lower inspection, customer returns, and stockout costs. The benefit of purchasing from Rytek could be even greater if purchasing high-quality UX1s from Rytek enhances Glare Shade's reputation and increases customer goodwill, leading to higher sales and profitability in the future.

Exhibit 6   Annual Relevant Costs of JIT Purchasing for UX1 Sunglasses from Rytek and Denton

	A	B	C	D	E	F	G	H	I	J
1					Relevant Cost of JIT Purchasing From					
2			Rytek					Denton		
3	Relevant Items	Relevant Cost per Unit		Quantity per Year	Total Costs		Relevant Cost per Unit		Quantity per Year	Total Costs
4	(1)	(2)		(3)	(4) = (2) × (3)		(5)		(6)	(7) = (5) × (6)
5	Purchasing costs	$14.02	per unit	13,000	$182,260		$13.80	per unit	13,000	$179,400
6		$ 2.00	per order	130	260		2.00	per order	130	260
7	Inspection costs	-	per unit	-	-		0.05	per unit	13,000	650
8	Opportunity carrying costs	$ 2.10[a]	per unit of average inventory per year	50[b]	105		2.07[a]	per unit of average inventory per year	50[b]	103
9	Other carrying costs (insurance, materials handling, etc.)	$ 3.00	per unit of average inventory per year	50[b]	150		2.90	per unit of average inventory per year	50[b]	145
10	Customer return costs	$10.00	per unit returned	0	0		10.00	per unit returned	325[c]	3,250
11	Stockout costs	$ 4.00	per unit	150	600		4.00	per unit	360	1,440
12	Total annual relevant costs				$183,375					$185,248
13	Annual difference in favor of Rytek					$1,873				
14										
15	[a]Purchasing cost per unit × 0.15 per year									
16	[b]Order quantity ÷ 2 = 100 ÷ 2 = 50 units									
17	[c]2.5% of units returned × 13,000 units									

JIT Purchasing, Planning and Control, and Supply-Chain Analysis

Retailers' inventory levels depend on the demand patterns of their customers and supply relationships with their distributors and manufacturers, the suppliers to their manufacturers, and so on. The *supply chain* describes the flow of goods, services, and information from the initial sources of materials and services to the delivery of products to consumers, regardless of whether those activities occur in the same company or in other companies. Retailers can purchase inventories on a JIT basis only if activities throughout the supply chain are properly planned, coordinated, and controlled.

Procter and Gamble's (P&G's) experience with its Pampers product illustrates the gains from supply-chain coordination. Retailers selling Pampers found that the weekly demand for the product varied because families purchased disposable diapers randomly. Anticipating even more demand variability and lacking information about available inventory with P&G, retailers' orders to P&G became more variable. This, in turn, increased variability of orders at P&G's suppliers, resulting in high levels of inventory at all stages in the supply chain.

How did P&G respond to these problems? By sharing information and planning and coordinating activities throughout the supply chain among retailers, P&G, and P&G's suppliers. Sharing sales information reduced the level of uncertainty that P&G and its suppliers had about retail demand for the product and led to (1) fewer stockouts at the retail level, (2) reduced manufacturing of Pampers not immediately needed by retailers, (3) fewer manufacturing orders that had to be "rushed" or "expedited," and (4) lower inventories held by each company in the supply chain. The benefits of supply chain coordination at P&G have been so great that retailers such as Walmart have contracted with P&G to manage their inventories on a just-in-time basis. This practice is called *supplier- or vendor-managed inventory*. Coordinating supply chains, however, can be difficult because supply-chain partners don't always share accurate and timely information about their sales, inventory levels, and sales forecasts with one another. Some of the reasons for these challenges are communication problems, trust issues between the companies, incompatible information systems, and limited people and financial resources.

Decision Point

Why are companies using just-in-time (JIT) purchasing?

Inventory Management, MRP, and JIT Production

We now turn our attention from purchasing to managing the production inventories of manufacturing companies. Two of the most widely used systems to plan and implement inventory activities within plants are materials requirements planning (MRP) and just-in-time (JIT) production.

Materials Requirements Planning

A **materials requirements planning (MRP) system** is a "push-through" system that manufactures finished goods for inventory on the basis of demand forecasts. Companies such as Guidant, which manufactures medical devices, and Philips, which makes consumer electronic products, use MRP systems. To determine outputs at each stage of production, MRP uses (1) the demand forecasts for final products; (2) a bill of materials detailing the materials, components, and subassemblies for each final product; and (3) information about a company's inventories of materials, components, and products. Taking into account the lead time required to purchase materials and to manufacture components and finished products, a master production schedule specifies the quantity and timing of each item to be produced. Once production starts as scheduled, the output of each department is pushed through the production line.

Maintaining accurate inventory records and costs is critical in an MRP system. For example, after becoming aware of the full costs of carrying finished goods inventory in its MRP system, National Semiconductor contracted with FedEx to airfreight its microchips

Learning Objective 5

Distinguish materials requirements planning (MRP) systems

...manufacturing products based on demand forecasts

from just-in-time (JIT) systems for manufacturing

...manufacturing products only upon receiving customer orders

from a central location in Singapore to customer sites worldwide instead of storing the chips at geographically dispersed warehouses.

Just-in-Time (JIT) Production

Decision Point

How do materials requirements planning (MRP) systems differ from just-in-time (JIT) production systems?

In contrast, JIT production is a "demand-pull" approach, which is used by companies such as Toyota in the automobile industry, Dell in the computer industry, and Braun in the appliance industry. **Just-in-time (JIT) production,** which is also called **lean production,** is a "demand-pull" manufacturing system that manufactures each component in a production line as soon as, and only when, needed by the next step in the production line. Demand triggers each step of the production process, starting with customer demand for a finished product at the end of the process and working all the way back to the demand for direct materials at the beginning of the process. In this way, demand pulls an order through the production line. The demand-pull feature of JIT production systems results in close coordination among workstations and smooths the flow of goods, despite low quantities of inventory. JIT production systems help companies meet the demand for high-quality products on time and at the lowest possible cost.

Features of JIT Production Systems

Learning Objective 6

Identify the features and benefits of a just-in-time production system

...for example, organizing work in manufacturing cells, improving quality, and reducing manufacturing lead time to reduce costs and earn higher margins

A JIT production system has these features:

- Production is organized in **manufacturing cells,** which are work areas with different types of equipment grouped together to make related products. Materials move from one machine to another, and various operations are performed in sequence, minimizing materials-handling costs.

- Workers are hired and trained to be multiskilled and capable of performing a variety of operations and tasks, including minor repairs and routine equipment maintenance.

- Defects are aggressively eliminated. Because of the tight links between workstations and the minimal inventories at each workstation, defects arising at one workstation quickly affect other workstations in the line. JIT creates an urgency for solving problems immediately and eliminating the root causes of defects as quickly as possible. Low levels of inventories allow workers to trace problems to and solve problems at earlier workstations in the production process, where the problems likely originated.

- The *setup time,* the time required to get equipment, tools, and materials ready to start the production of a component or product, and the *manufacturing cycle time,* the time from when an order is received by manufacturing until it becomes a finished good, are reduced. Setup costs correspond to the ordering costs P in the EOQ model. Reducing the setup time and its costs makes production in smaller batches economical, which in turn reduces inventory levels. Reducing the manufacturing cycle time enables a company to respond faster to changes in customer demand (see also Concepts in Action: After the Encore: Just-in-Time Live Concert Recordings).

- Suppliers are selected on the basis of their ability to deliver quality materials in a timely manner. Most companies implementing *JIT production* also implement *JIT purchasing.* JIT plants expect JIT suppliers to make timely deliveries of high-quality goods directly to the production floor.

We next present a relevant-cost analysis for deciding whether to implement a JIT production system.

Costs and Benefits of JIT Production

As we have seen, JIT production clearly lowers a company's carrying costs of inventory. But there are other benefits of lower inventories: heightened emphasis on improving quality by eliminating the specific causes of rework, scrap, and waste, and lower manufacturing cycle times. It is important, therefore, when computing the relevant benefits and costs of reducing inventories in JIT production systems for managers to take into account all benefits and all costs.

Consider Hudson Corporation, a manufacturer of brass fittings. Hudson is considering implementing a JIT production system. To implement JIT production, Hudson must incur $100,000 in annual tooling costs to reduce setup times. Hudson expects that JIT production will reduce its average inventory by $500,000 and that the relevant costs of insurance, storage, materials handling, and setups will decline by $30,000 per year. The company's required rate of return on its inventory investments is 10% per year. Should Hudson implement a JIT production system? On the basis of the information provided, we would be tempted to say "no" because the annual relevant total cost savings amount to $80,000 [(10% of $500,000) + $30,000)], which is less than the additional annual tooling costs of $100,000.

Our analysis, however, is incomplete. We have not considered the other benefits of lower inventories associated with JIT production. Hudson estimates that implementing JIT will improve quality and reduce rework on 500 units each year, resulting in savings of $50 per unit. Also, better quality and faster delivery will allow Hudson to charge $2 more per unit on the 20,000 units that it sells each year.

The annual relevant benefits and costs from implementing JIT equal the following:

Incremental savings in insurance, storage, materials handling, and set up	$ 30,000
Incremental savings in inventory carrying costs (10% × $500,000)	50,000
Incremental savings from reduced rework ($50 per unit × 500 units)	25,000
Additional contribution margin from better quality and faster delivery ($2 per unit × 20,000 units)	40,000
Incremental annual tooling costs	(100,000)
Net incremental benefit	$ 45,000

Therefore, Hudson *should* implement a JIT production system.

JIT in Service Industries

JIT purchasing and production methods can be used in service industries as well. For example, inventories and supplies, and the associated labor costs to manage them, represent more than a third of the costs in most hospitals. By implementing a JIT purchasing and distribution system, Eisenhower Memorial Hospital in Palm Springs, California, reduced its inventories and supplies by 90% in 18 months. McDonald's has adapted JIT production practices to making hamburgers.[3] Before, McDonald's precooked a batch of hamburgers that were placed under heat lamps to stay warm until ordered. If the hamburgers didn't sell within a specified period of time, they were discarded, resulting in high inventory holding costs and spoilage costs. Moreover, the quality of hamburgers deteriorated the longer they sat under the heat lamps. A customer placing a special order for a hamburger (such as a hamburger with no cheese) had to wait for it to be cooked. Now McDonald's cooks hamburgers only when they are ordered. By increasing the quality of hamburgers and reducing the time needed for special orders, JIT has led to greater customer satisfaction.

We next turn our attention to planning and control of production systems.

Enterprise Resource Planning (ERP) Systems[4]

Enterprise resource planning systems are frequently used in conjunction with JIT production. An **enterprise resource planning (ERP) system** is an integrated set of software modules covering a company's accounting, distribution, manufacturing, purchasing, human resources, and other functions. Real-time information is collected in a single database and simultaneously fed into all of the software applications, giving personnel greater visibility into the company's end-to-end business processes. For example, using an ERP system,

---

[3] Charles Atkinson, "McDonald's, A Guide to the Benefits of JIT," *Inventory Management Review* (November 8, 2005). http://www.inventorymanagementreview.org/2005/11/mcdonalds_a_gui.html.

[4] For an excellent discussion, see Thomas H. Davenport, "Putting the Enterprise into the Enterprise System," *Harvard Business Review* (July–August 1998); also see A. Cagilo, "Enterprise Resource Planning Systems and Accountants: Towards Hybridization?" *European Accounting Review* (May 2003).

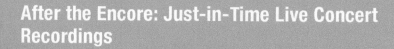

Concepts in Action ▶ After the Encore: Just-in-Time Live Concert Recordings

Each year, millions of music fans flock to concerts to see artists ranging from Pearl Jam to the Dave Matthews Band. When fans stop by the merchandise stand to pick up a T-shirt or poster after the show ends, they often have another option: buying a professional recording of the concert they just saw! Just-in-time production, enabled by advances in technology, now allows fans to relive the live concert experience just a few minutes after the final chord is played.

Live concert recordings have long been hampered by production and distribution difficulties. Live albums typically sold few copies, and retail outlets that profit from volume-driven merchandise turnover, like Best Buy, were somewhat reluctant to carry them.

Several companies, including Live Nation and Nugs.net, now employ microphones, recording and audio mixing hardware and software, and an army of high-speed computers to produce concert recordings during the show. As soon as each song is complete, engineers burn that track onto hundreds of CDs or USB drives. At the end of the show, they have to burn only one last song. Once completed, the recordings are packaged and rushed to merchandise stands throughout the venue for instant sale.

Sources: Sabra Chartrand, "How to Take the Concert Home." *New York Times* (May 3, 2004); Stephen Humphries, "Get Your Official 'Bootleg' Here," *Christian Science Monitor* (November 21, 2003); Eliot Van Buskirk, "Apple Unveils 'Live Music' in iTunes," *Wired Business* (blog), November 24, 2009, http://www.wired.com/business/, accessed July 2013; and Clyde Smith, "Nugs.net Appetizer Puts Direct-to-Fan Download Sales In Facebook Newsfeed," Hypebot.com (blog), August 12, 2011, http://www.hypebot.com/, accessed July 2013.

a salesperson can generate a contract for a customer in Germany, verify the customer's credit limits, and place a production order. The system will then use this same information to schedule manufacturing in, say, Brazil, requisition materials from inventory, order components from suppliers, and schedule shipments. Simultaneously the system credits the salesperson with his or her commission and records all the costing and financial accounting information. An ERP system also allows a company to shift its manufacturing and distribution plans rapidly in response to changes in supply and demand.

Companies believe that an ERP system is essential to support JIT initiatives because of the effect it has on lead times. For example, using an ERP system, Autodesk, a maker of computer-aided design software, reduced order lead time from 2 weeks to 1 day. Fujitsu, an information technology company, reduced its lead time from 18 days to 1.5 days.

ERP systems are large and unwieldy. Because of their complexity, the suppliers of ERP systems such as SAP and Oracle provide software units that are standard but that can be customized at significant cost. Without some customization, unique and distinctive features that confer strategic advantage will not be available. The challenge when implementing ERP systems is to strike the proper balance between the lower cost and reliability of standardized systems and the strategic benefits that accrue from customization. Companies such as Netsuite are developing ERP systems for small and medium-sized enterprises that are easier to customize using cloud-based computing and providing the software as a service.

Performance Measures and Control in JIT Production

In addition to their personal observations, managers use financial and nonfinancial measures to evaluate and control JIT production. We now describe these measures and indicate the effect JIT systems are expected to have on these measures.

1. Financial performance measures, such as the inventory turnover ratio (cost of goods sold ÷ average inventory), which is expected to increase

2. Nonfinancial performance measures of inventory, quality, and time such as the following:

- Number of days of inventory on hand, expected to decrease
- Units produced per hour, expected to increase

- $\dfrac{\text{Number of units scrapped or requiring rework}}{\text{Total number of units started and completed}}$, expected to decrease

- Manufacturing cycle time, expected to decrease

- $\dfrac{\text{Total setup time for machines}}{\text{Total manufacturing time}}$, expected to decrease

Personal observation and nonfinancial performance measures provide the most timely, intuitive, and easy-to-understand measures of manufacturing performance. Rapid, meaningful feedback is critical because the lack of inventories in a demand-pull system makes it urgent for managers to detect and solve problems quickly.

Effect of JIT Systems on Product Costing

By reducing materials handling, warehousing, and inspection, JIT systems reduce overhead costs. JIT systems also aid in the direct tracing of some costs usually classified as indirect. For example, the use of manufacturing cells makes it cost-effective to trace materials handling, machine operating, and inspection costs to specific products or product families made in these cells. These costs then become direct costs of those products. Also, the use of multiskilled workers in these cells allows the costs of setup, maintenance, and quality inspection to be traced as direct costs. These changes have prompted some companies using JIT to adopt simplified product-costing methods that dovetail with JIT production and that are less costly to operate than traditional costing systems. We examine two of these methods next: backflush costing and lean accounting.

Decision Point

What are the features and benefits of a just-in-time (JIT) production system?

Backflush Costing

Organizing manufacturing in cells, reducing defects and manufacturing cycle times, and ensuring the timely delivery of materials enable a company's purchasing, production, and sales to occur in quick succession with minimal inventories. The absence of inventories makes choices about cost-flow assumptions (such as weighted average or first-in, first-out) or inventory-costing methods (such as absorption or variable costing) unimportant: All manufacturing costs of the accounting period flow directly into cost of goods sold. The rapid conversion of direct materials into finished goods that are immediately sold greatly simplifies the costing system.

Learning Objective 7

Describe different ways backflush costing can simplify traditional inventory-costing systems

...for example, by not recording journal entries for work in process, purchase of materials, or production of finished goods

Simplified Normal or Standard Costing Systems

Traditional normal or standard-costing systems use **sequential tracking**, which is a costing system in which the recording of the journal entries occurs in the same order as actual purchases and progress in production. Costs are tracked sequentially as products pass through each of the following four stages:

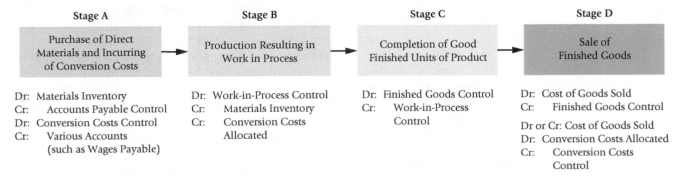

Stage A	Stage B	Stage C	Stage D
Purchase of Direct Materials and Incurring of Conversion Costs	Production Resulting in Work in Process	Completion of Good Finished Units of Product	Sale of Finished Goods

Dr: Materials Inventory
Cr: Accounts Payable Control
Dr: Conversion Costs Control
Cr: Various Accounts
    (such as Wages Payable)
	Dr: Work-in-Process Control
	Cr: Materials Inventory
	Cr: Conversion Costs
	    Allocated
		Dr: Finished Goods Control
		Cr: Work-in-Process
		    Control
			Dr: Cost of Goods Sold
			Cr: Finished Goods Control
			
			Dr or Cr: Cost of Goods Sold
			Dr: Conversion Costs Allocated
			Cr: Conversion Costs
			    Control

A sequential-tracking costing system has four *trigger points*, corresponding to Stages A, B, C, and D. A **trigger point** is a stage in the cycle, from the purchase of direct materials and incurring of conversion costs (Stage A) to the sale of finished goods (Stage D), at which journal entries are made in the accounting system. The journal entries (with Dr. representing debits and Cr. representing credits) for each stage are displayed below the box for that stage.

An alternative approach to sequential tracking is backflush costing. **Backflush costing** is a costing system that omits recording some of the journal entries relating to the stages from the purchase of direct materials to the sale of finished goods. When journal entries for one or more stages are omitted, the journal entries for a subsequent stage use normal or standard costs to work backward to "flush out" the costs in the cycle for which journal entries were *not* made. When inventories are minimal, as in JIT production systems, backflush costing simplifies costing systems without losing much information.

Consider the following data for the month of April for Silicon Valley Computer (SVC), which produces keyboards for personal computers.

- There are no beginning inventories of direct materials and no beginning or ending work-in-process inventories.

- SVC has only one direct manufacturing cost category (direct materials) and one indirect manufacturing cost category (conversion costs). All manufacturing labor costs are included in conversion costs.

- From its bill of materials and an operations list (description of operations to be undergone), SVC determines that the standard direct materials cost per keyboard unit is $19 and the standard conversion cost is $12.

- SVC purchases $1,950,000 of direct materials. To focus on the basic concepts, we assume SVC has no direct materials variances. Actual conversion costs equal $1,260,000. SVC produces 100,000 good keyboard units and sells 99,000 units.

- Any underallocated or overallocated conversion costs are written off to cost of goods sold at the end of April.

We use three examples to illustrate backflush costing. *They differ in the number and placement of trigger points.*

Example 1: The three trigger points for journal entries are Purchase of direct materials and incurring of conversion costs (Stage A), Completion of good finished units of product (Stage C), and Sale of finished goods (Stage D).

Note that there is no journal entry for Production resulting in work in process (Stage B) because this method is used when work-in-process inventory is minimal (units started are quickly converted to finished goods).

SVC records two inventory accounts:

Type	Account Title
Combined materials inventory and materials in work in process	Materials and In-Process Inventory Control
Finished goods	Finished Goods Control

Exhibit 7, Panel A, summarizes the journal entries for Example 1 with three trigger points: Purchase of direct materials and incurring of conversion costs, Completion of good finished units of product, and Sale of finished goods (and recognizing under- or overallocated costs). For each stage, the backflush costing entries for SVC are shown on the left. The comparable entries under sequential tracking (costing) are shown on the right.

Consider first the entries for the purchase of direct materials and incurring of conversion costs (Stage A). As described earlier, the inventory account under backflush costing combines direct materials and work in process. When materials are purchased, these costs increase (are debited to) the Materials and In-Process Inventory Control account. Under the sequential tracking approach, the direct materials and work-in-process accounts are separate, so the purchase of direct materials is debited to Materials Inventory Control. Actual conversion costs are recorded as incurred under backflush costing, just as in sequential tracking, and they increase (are debited to) Conversion Costs Control.

Exhibit 7	Journal Entries and General Ledger Overview for Backflush Costing and Journal Entries for Sequential Tracking with Three Trigger Points: Purchase of Direct Materials and Incurring of Conversion Costs, Completion of Good Finished Units of Product, and Sale of Finished Goods

PANEL A: Journal Entries

Backflush Costing				Sequential Tracking		

Stage A: Record Purchase of Direct Materials and Incurring of Conversion Costs

1. Record Direct Materials Purchased.

	Backflush			Sequential	
Entry (A1)	Materials and In-Process Inventory Control	1,950,000		Materials Inventory Control	1,950,000	
	Accounts Payable Control		1,950,000	Accounts Payable Control		1,950,000

2. Record Conversion Costs Incurred.

Entry (A2)	Conversion Costs Control	1,260,000		Conversion Costs Control	1,260,000	
	Various accounts (such as Wages			Various accounts (such as Wages		1,260,000
	Payable Control)		1,260,000	Payable Control)		

Stage B: Record Production Resulting in Work in Process.

Entry (B1)	No Entry Recorded			Work-in-Process Control	3,100,000	
				Materials Inventory Control		1,900,000
				Conversion Costs Allocated		1,200,000

Stage C: Record Cost of Good Finished Units Completed.

Entry (C1)	Finished Goods Control	3,100,000		Finished Goods Control	3,100,000	
	Materials and In-Process Inventory Control		1,900,000	Work-in-Process Control		3,100,000
	Conversion Costs Allocated		1,200,000			

Stage D: Record Cost of Finished Goods Sold (and Under- or Overallocated Conversion Costs).

1. Record Cost of Finished Goods Sold.

Entry (D1)	Cost of Goods Sold	3,069,000		Cost of Goods Sold	3,069,000	
	Finished Goods Control		3,069,000	Finished Goods Control		3,069,000

2. Record Underallocated or Overallocated Conversion Costs.

Entry (D2)	Conversion Costs Allocated	1,200,000		Conversion Costs Allocated	1,200,000	
	Cost of Goods Sold	60,000		Cost of Goods Sold	60,000	
	Conversion Costs Control		1,260,000	Conversion Costs Control		1,260,000

PANEL B: General Ledger Overview for Backflush Costing

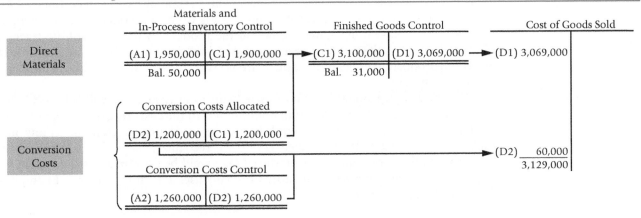

The coding that appears in parentheses for each entry indicates the stage in the production process that the entry relates to as presented in the text.

Next consider the entries for production resulting in work in process (Stage B). Recall that 100,000 units were started into production in April and that the standard cost for the units produced is $31 ($19 direct materials + $12 conversion costs) per unit. Under backflush costing, no entry is recorded in Stage B because work-in-process inventory is minimal and all units are quickly converted to finished goods. Under sequential tracking, work-in-process inventory is increased as manufacturing occurs and later decreased as manufacturing is completed and the product becomes a finished good.

The entries to record the completion of good finished units (Stage C) give backflush costing its name. The costs have not been recorded sequentially with the flow of the product along its production route through work in process and finished goods. Instead, the output trigger point reaches *back* and pulls ("*flushes*") the standard direct material costs from Materials and In-Process Inventory Control and the standard conversion costs for manufacturing the finished goods. Under the sequential tracking approach, Finished Goods Control is debited (increased) and Work-in-Process Control is credited (decreased) as manufacturing is completed and finished goods are produced. The net effect of Stages B and C under sequential tracking is the same as the effect under backflush costing (except for the name of the inventory account).

Finally consider the entries to record the sale of finished goods (and under- or over-allocated conversion costs) (Stage D). The standard cost of 99,000 units sold in April equals $3,069,000 (99,000 units × $31 per unit). The entries to record the cost of finished goods sold are exactly the same under backflush costing and sequential tracking.

Actual conversion costs may be underallocated or overallocated in an accounting period. There are various ways to dispose of underallocated or overallocated manufacturing overhead costs. Companies that use backflush costing typically have low inventories, so prorating underallocated or overallocated conversion costs between work in process, finished goods, and cost of goods sold is seldom necessary. Generally, companies write off underallocated or overallocated conversion costs to cost of goods sold only at the end of the fiscal year. Other companies, like SVC, record the write-off monthly. The journal entry to dispose of the difference between actual conversion costs incurred and standard conversion costs allocated is exactly the same under backflush costing and sequential tracking.

The April 30 ending inventory balances under backflush costing are as follows:

Materials and In-Process Inventory Control ($1,950,000 − $1,900,000)	$50,000
Finished Goods Control, 1,000 units × $31/unit (or $3,100,000 − $3,069,000)	31,000
Total	$81,000

The April 30 ending inventory balances under sequential tracking would be exactly the same except that the inventory account would be Materials Inventory Control. Exhibit 7, Panel B, provides a general-ledger overview of this version of backflush costing.

The elimination of the typical Work-in-Process Control account reduces the amount of detail in the accounting system. Units on the production line may still be tracked in physical terms, but there is "no assignment of costs" to specific work orders while they are in the production cycle. In fact, there are no work orders or labor-time records in the accounting system.

The three trigger points to make journal entries in Example 1 will lead SVC's backflush costing system to report costs that are similar to the costs reported under sequential tracking when SVC has minimal work-in-process inventory. In Example 1, any inventories of direct materials or finished goods are recognized in SVC's backflush costing system when they are acquired or produced (as would be done in a costing system using sequential tracking). International Paper Company uses a method similar to Example 1 in its specialty papers plant.

Accounting for Variances

Accounting for variances between actual and standard costs is basically the same under all standard-costing systems. Suppose that in Example 1, SVC had an unfavorable direct materials price variance of $42,000. Then the journal entry would be as follows:

Materials and In-Process Inventory Control	1,950,000	
Direct Materials Price Variance	42,000	
Accounts Payable Control		1,992,000

Direct materials costs are often a large proportion of total manufacturing costs, sometimes as much as 60%. Consequently, many companies measure the direct materials efficiency variance in total by physically comparing what remains in direct materials inventory against what should remain based on the output of finished goods for the accounting period. In our example, suppose that such a comparison showed an unfavorable materials efficiency variance of $30,000. The journal entry would be as follows:

Direct Materials Efficiency Variance	30,000	
Materials and In-Process Inventory Control		30,000

The underallocated or overallocated conversion costs are split into various overhead variances (spending variance, efficiency variance, and production-volume variance). Each variance is closed to the Cost of Goods Sold account, if it is immaterial in amount.

Example 2: The two trigger points are Purchase of direct materials and incurring of conversion costs (Stage A) and Sale of finished goods (Stage D).

This example uses the SVC data to illustrate a backflush costing that differs more from sequential tracking than the backflush costing in Example 1. This example and Example 1 have the same first trigger point, purchase of direct materials and incurring of conversion costs. But the second trigger point in Example 2 is the sale, not the completion, of finished goods. *Note that there is no journal entry for Production resulting in work in process (Stage B) and Completion of good finished units of product (Stage C) because this method is used when there are minimal work-in-process and finished goods inventories (units started are quickly converted into finished goods that are immediately sold).*
In this example, there is only one inventory account: direct materials, whether the materials are in storerooms, in process, or in finished goods.

Type	Account Title
Combines direct materials inventory and any direct materials in work-in-process and finished goods inventories	Inventory Control

Exhibit 8, Panel A, summarizes the journal entries for Example 2 with two trigger points: Purchase of direct materials and incurring of conversion costs and Sale of finished goods (and recognizing under- or overallocated costs). As in Example 1, for each stage, the backflush costing entries for SVC are shown on the left. The comparable entries under sequential tracking are shown on the right.

The entries for direct materials purchased and conversion costs incurred (Stage A) are the same as in Example 1, except that the inventory account is called Inventory Control. As in Example 1, no entry is made to record the production of work-in-process inventory (Stage B) because the work-in-process inventory is minimal. When finished goods are completed (Stage C), no entry is recorded because the completed units are expected to be sold quickly and the finished goods inventory is expected to be minimal. As finished goods are sold (Stage D), the cost of goods sold is calculated as 99,000 units sold × $31 per unit = $3,069,000, which is composed of direct materials costs (99,000 units × $19 per unit = $1,881,000) and conversion costs allocated (99,000 units × $12 per unit = $1,188,000). This is the same Cost of Goods Sold calculated under sequential tracking as described in Example 1.

Under this method of backflush costing, conversion costs are not inventoried because no entries are recorded when finished goods are produced in Stage C. That is, compared with sequential tracking, Example 2 does not assign $12,000 ($12 per unit × 1,000 units) of conversion costs to finished goods inventory produced but not sold. Of the $1,260,000 in conversion

| **Exhibit 8** | Journal Entries and General Ledger Overview for Backflush Costing and Journal Entries for Sequential Tracking with Two Trigger Points: Purchase of Direct Materials and Incurring of Conversion Costs and Sale of Finished Goods |

PANEL A: Journal Entries

Backflush Costing			**Sequential Tracking**		

Stage A: Record Purchase of Direct Materials and Incurring of Conversion Costs

1. Record Direct Materials Purchased.

| Entry (A1) | Inventory: Control | 1,950,000 | | Materials Inventory Control | 1,950,000 | |
| | Accounts Payable Control | | 1,950,000 | Accounts Payable Control | | 1,950,000 |

2. Record Conversion Costs Incurred.

| Entry (A2) | Conversion Costs Control | 1,260,000 | | Conversion Costs Control | 1,260,000 | |
| | Various accounts (such as Wages Payable Control) | | 1,260,000 | Various accounts (such as Wages Payable Control) | | 1,260,000 |

Stage B: Record Production Resulting in Work in Process.

Entry (B1)	No Entry Recorded			Work-in-Process Control	3,100,000	
				Materials Inventory Control		1,900,000
				Conversion Costs Allocated		1,200,000

Stage C: Record Cost of Good Finished Units Completed.

| Entry (C1) | No Entry Recorded | | | Finished Goods Control | 3,100,000 | |
| | | | | Work-in-Process Control | | 3,100,000 |

Stage D: Record Cost of Finished Goods Sold (and Under- or Overallocated Conversion Costs).

1. Record Cost of Finished Goods Sold.

Entry (D1)	Cost of Goods Sold	3,069,000		Cost of Goods Sold	3,069,000	
	Inventory Control		1,881,000	Finished Goods Control		3,069,000
	Conversion Costs Allocated		1,188,000			

2. Record Underallocated or Overallocated Conversion Costs.

Entry (D2)	Conversion Costs Allocated	1,188,000		Conversion Costs Allocated	1,200,000	
	Cost of Goods Sold	72,000		Cost of Goods Sold	60,000	
	Conversion Costs Control		1,260,000	Conversion Costs Control		1,260,000

PANEL B: General Ledger Overview for Backflush Costing

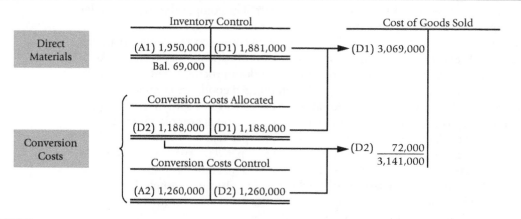

The coding that appears in parentheses for each entry indicates the stage in the production process that the entry relates to as presented in the text.

costs, $1,188,000 is allocated at standard cost to the units sold. The remaining $72,000 ($1,260,000 − $1,188,000) of conversion costs is underallocated compared to $60,000 under sequential tracking. Entry (D2) presents the journal entry if SVC, like many companies, writes off these underallocated costs monthly as additions to the Cost of Goods Sold account.

The April 30 ending balance of the Inventory Control account is $69,000 ($1,950,000 − $1,881,000). This balance represents the $50,000 direct materials still on hand + $19,000 direct materials embodied in the 1,000 finished units manufactured but not sold during the period. Finished goods inventory under sequential tracking is: direct materials, $19,000 + conversion costs, $12,000 for a total of $31,000. Exhibit 8, Panel B, provides a general-ledger overview of Example 2. The approach described in Example 2 closely approximates the costs computed using sequential tracking when a company holds minimal work-in-process and finished goods inventories.

Toyota's cost accounting system at its Kentucky plant is similar to this example. Two advantages of this system are (1) it removes the incentive for managers to produce for inventory because conversion costs are recorded as period costs instead of inventoriable costs and (2) it focuses managers on sales.

Example 3: The two trigger points are Completion of good finished units of product (Stage C) and Sale of finished goods (Stage D).

This example has two trigger points. In contrast to Example 2, the first trigger point in Example 3 is delayed until Stage C, SVC's completion of good finished units of product. *Note that there are no journal entries for Purchase of direct materials and incurring of conversion costs (Stage A) and Production resulting in work in process (Stage B) because this method is used when there are minimal direct materials and work-in-process inventories (direct materials purchased are quickly placed into production and then quickly converted into finished goods).* Exhibit 9, Panel A, summarizes the journal entries for Example 3 with two trigger points: Completion of good finished units of product and Sale of finished goods (and recognizing under- or overallocated costs). As in Examples 1 and 2, for each stage, the backflush costing entries for SVC are shown on the left. The comparable entries under sequential tracking are shown on the right.

No entry is made for direct materials purchases of $1,950,000 (Stage A) because the acquisition of direct materials is not a trigger point in this form of backflush costing. As in Examples 1 and 2, actual conversion costs are recorded as incurred and no entry is made to record production resulting in work-in-process inventory (Stage B). The cost of 100,000 good finished units completed (Stage C) is recorded at standard cost of $31 ($19 direct materials + $12 conversion costs) per unit as in Example 1 except that Accounts Payable Control is credited (instead of Materials and In-Process Inventory Control) because no entry had been made when direct materials were purchased in Stage A. Note that at the end of April, $50,000 of direct materials purchased have not yet been placed into production ($1,950,000 − $1,900,000 = $50,000), nor have the cost of those direct materials been entered into the inventory-costing system. The Example 3 version of backflush costing is suitable for a JIT production system in which both direct materials inventory and work-in-process inventory are minimal. As finished goods are sold (Stage D), the cost of goods sold is calculated as 99,000 units sold × $31 per unit = $3,069,000. This is the same Cost of Goods sold calculated under sequential tracking. The Finished Goods Control account has a balance of $31,000 under both this form of backflush costing and sequential tracking. The journal entry to dispose of the difference between the actual conversion costs incurred and standard conversion costs allocated is the same under backflush costing and sequential tracking. The only difference between this form of backflush costing and sequential tracking is that direct materials inventory of $50,000 (and the corresponding Accounts Payable Control) is not recorded, which is no problem if direct materials inventories are minimal. Exhibit 9, Panel B, provides a general-ledger overview of Example 3.

Extending Example 3, backflush costing systems could use the sale of finished goods as the only trigger point. This version of backflush costing is most suitable for a JIT production system with minimal direct materials, work-in-process, and finished goods inventories. That's because this backflush costing system maintains no inventory accounts.

Exhibit 9   Journal Entries and General Ledger Overview for Backflush Costing and Journal Entries for Sequential Tracking with Two Trigger Points: Completion of Good Finished Units of Product and Sale of Finished Goods

PANEL A: Journal Entries

	Backflush Costing			Sequential Tracking	

Stage A: Record Purchase of Direct Materials and Incurring of Conversion Costs.

1. Record Direct Materials Purchased.

	Backflush Costing			Sequential Tracking	
Entry (A1)	No Entry Recorded			Materials Inventory Control	1,950,000	
				Accounts Payable Control		1,950,000

2. Record Conversion Costs Incurred.

Entry (A2)	Conversion Costs Control	1,260,000		Conversion Costs Control	1,260,000	
	Various accounts (such as Wages Payable Control)		1,260,000	Various accounts (such as Wages Payable Control)		1,260,000

Stage B: Record Production Resulting in Work in Process.

Entry (B1)	No Entry Recorded			Work-in-Process Control	3,100,000	
				Materials Inventory Control		1,900,000
				Conversion Costs Allocated		1,200,000

Stage C: Record Cost of Good Finished Units Completed.

Entry (C1)	Finished Goods Control	3,100,000		Finished Goods Control	3,100,000	
	Accounts Payable Control		1,900,000	Work-in-Process Control		3,100,000
	Conversion Costs Allocated		1,200,000			

Stage D: Record Cost of Finished Goods Sold (and Under- or Overallocated Conversion Costs).

1. Record Cost of Finished Goods Sold.

Entry (D1)	Cost of Goods Sold	3,069,000		Cost of Goods Sold	3,069,000	
	Finished Goods Control		3,069,000	Finished Goods Control		3,069,000

2. Record Underallocated or Overallocated Conversion Costs.

Entry (D2)	Conversion Costs Allocated	1,200,000		Conversion Costs Allocated	1,200,000	
	Cost of Goods Sold	60,000		Cost of Goods Sold	60,000	
	Conversion Costs Control		1,260,000	Conversion Costs Control		1,260,000

PANEL B: General Ledger Overview for Backflush Costing

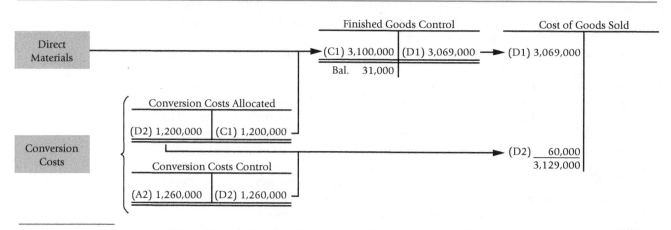

The coding that appears in parentheses for each entry indicates the stage in the production process that the entry relates to as presented in the text.

Special Considerations in Backflush Costing

The accounting procedures illustrated in Examples 1, 2, and 3 do not strictly adhere to Generally Accepted Accounting Principles (GAAP). For example, work-in-process inventory, which is an asset, exists but is not recognized in the financial accounting system. Advocates of backflush costing, however, cite the generally accepted accounting principle of materiality in support of the various versions of backflush costing. As the three examples illustrate, backflush costing can approximate the costs that would be reported under sequential tracking by varying the number of trigger points and where they are located. If significant amounts of direct materials inventory or finished goods inventory exist, adjusting entries can be incorporated (as explained next).

Suppose there are material differences in a company's operating income and inventories based on a backflush costing system and a conventional standard-costing system. A journal entry can be recorded to adjust the backflush number to comply with GAAP. For example, the backflush entries in Example 2 would result in expensing all conversion costs to the Cost of Goods Sold account ($1,188,000 at standard costs + $72,000 write-off of underallocated conversion costs = $1,260,000). But suppose conversion costs were regarded as sufficiently material in amount to be included in the Inventory Control account. Then entry (D2) in Example 2, closing the Conversion Costs accounts, would change as follows:

Original entry (D2)	Conversion Costs Allocated	1,188,000	
	Cost of Goods Sold	72,000	
	Conversion Costs Control		1,260,000
Revised entry (D2)	Conversion Costs Allocated	1,188,000	
	Inventory Control (1,000 units × $12)	12,000	
	Cost of Goods Sold	60,000	
	Conversion Costs Control		1,260,000

Critics say backflush costing leaves no audit trails—the ability of the accounting system to pinpoint the uses of resources at each step in the production process. However, the absence of sizable amounts of materials inventory, work-in-process inventory, and finished goods inventory means managers can keep track of operations by personal observations, computer monitoring, and nonfinancial measures.

What are the implications of JIT and backflush costing systems for activity-based costing (ABC) systems? Simplifying the production process, as a JIT system does, makes more of the costs direct and reduces the extent of overhead cost allocations. Simple ABC systems are often adequate for companies implementing JIT. These simple ABC systems work well with backflush costing. Costs from ABC systems yield a more accurate budgeted conversion cost per unit for different products in the backflush costing system. The activity-based cost information is also useful for product costing, decision making, and cost management.

Lean Accounting

Another simplified product costing system that can be used with JIT (or lean production) systems is *lean accounting*. When a company utilizes JIT production, it has to focus on the entire value chain of business functions (from suppliers to manufacturing to customers) in order to reduce inventories, lead times, and waste. The improvements throughout the value chain that result have led some companies with JIT systems to develop organizational structures and costing systems that focus on value streams, which are all the value-added activities needed to design, manufacture, and deliver a given product or product line to customers. For example, a value stream can include the activities needed to develop and engineer products, advertise and market those products, process orders, purchase and receive materials, manufacture and ship orders, bill customers, and collect

Decision Point

How does backflush costing simplify traditional inventory costing?

Learning Objective 8

Understand the principles of lean accounting

...focus on costing value streams rather than products and limit arbitrary allocations

payments. The use of manufacturing cells in JIT systems helps keep a company focused on its value streams.

Lean accounting is a costing method that focuses on value streams, as distinguished from individual products or departments, thereby eliminating waste in the accounting process.[5] If a company makes multiple, related products in a single value stream, it does not compute product costs for the individual products. Instead, it traces many actual costs directly to the value stream. Tracing more costs as direct costs to value streams is possible because companies using lean accounting often dedicate resources to individual value streams. We now illustrate lean accounting for Manuela Corporation.

Manuela Corporation manufactures toner cartridges and ink cartridges for use with its printers. It makes two models of toner cartridges in one manufacturing cell and two models of ink cartridges in another manufacturing cell. The following table lists revenues, operating costs, operating income, and other information for the different products.

	Toner Cartridges		Ink Cartridges	
	Model A	Model B	Model C	Model D
Revenues	$600,000	$700,000	$800,000	$550,000
Direct materials	340,000	400,000	410,000	270,000
Direct manufacturing labor	70,000	78,000	105,000	82,000
Manufacturing overhead costs (e.g., equipment lease, supervision, and unused facility costs)	112,000	130,000	128,000	103,000
Rework costs	15,000	17,000	14,000	10,000
Design costs	20,000	21,000	24,000	18,000
Marketing and sales costs	30,000	33,000	40,000	28,000
Total costs	587,000	679,000	721,000	511,000
Operating income	$ 13,000	$ 21,000	$ 79,000	$ 39,000
Direct materials purchased	$350,000	$420,000	$430,000	$285,000
Unused facility costs	$ 22,000	$ 38,000	$ 18,000	$ 15,000

Using lean accounting principles, Manuela's managers calculate the value-stream operating costs and operating income for toner cartridges and ink cartridges, not individual models, as follows:

	Toner Cartridges	Ink Cartridges
Revenues ($600,000 + $700,000; $800,000 + $550,000)	$1,300,000	$1,350,000
Direct materials used ($340,000 + $400,000; $410,000 + $270,000)	740,000	680,000
Direct manufacturing labor ($70,000 + $78,000; $105,000 + $82,000)	148,000	187,000
Manufacturing overhead (after deducting unused facility costs) ($112,000 − $22,000) + ($130,000 − $38,000); ($128,000 − $18,000) + ($103,000 − $15,000)	182,000	198,000
Design costs ($20,000 + $21,000; $24,000 + $18,000)	41,000	42,000
Marketing and sales costs ($30,000 + $33,000; $40,000 + $28,000)	63,000	68,000
Total value stream operating costs	1,174,000	1,175,000
Value-stream operating income	$ 126,000	$ 175,000

---

[5] See Bruce L. Baggaley, "Costing by Value Stream," *Journal of Cost Management* (May–June 2003).

To gain insights, Manuela's lean accounting system, like many lean accounting systems, compares value-stream costs against costs that include costs of all purchased materials. Doing so keeps the company focused on reducing its direct materials and work-in-process inventory. In our example, the cost of direct material purchases exceeds the cost of direct materials used.

Manuela allocates its facility costs (such as depreciation, property taxes, and leases) to value streams based on the square footage each value stream uses. This encourages managers to use less space for production and for holding and moving inventory. Note that Manuela does not consider unused facility costs when calculating its manufacturing overhead costs of value streams. Instead, it treats these costs as plant or business unit expenses. Manuela excludes unused facility costs because it only includes in its value-stream costs those costs that add value. Increasing the visibility of unused capacity costs creates incentives to reduce these costs or to find alternative uses for the company's capacity. Manuela also excludes rework costs when calculating its value-stream costs and operating income because these costs are non-value-added costs. Companies also exclude from value-stream costs common costs such as corporate or support-department costs that cannot reasonably be assigned to value streams.

The analysis shows that although the total cost of the toner cartridges based on direct materials purchases rather than direct materials used is $1,296,000 [$587,000 + $679,000 + ($350,000 − $340,000) + ($420,000 − $400,000)], the value-stream cost using lean accounting is $1,174,000 (90.6% × $1,296,000). The difference between the two indicates that there are opportunities for improving the company's profitability by reducing unused facility and rework costs and by purchasing direct materials only as needed for production. Making improvements is particularly important because Manuela's value-stream operating income is only 9.7% ($126,000 ÷ $1,300,000) of its revenues. Manuela's ink cartridges portray a different picture. The total cost for ink cartridges based on direct materials purchases rather than direct materials used is $1,267,000 [$721,000 + $511,000 + ($430,000 − $410,000) + ($285,000 − $270,000)], whereas the value-stream cost using lean accounting is $1,175,000 (92.7% × $1,267,000). The ink cartridges value stream has low unused facility and rework costs and is more efficient. Moreover, the ink cartridges also have higher value-stream operating income profitability of 13% ($175,000 ÷ $1,350,000).

Lean accounting is much simpler than traditional product costing. Why? Because calculating actual product costs by value streams requires less overhead allocation. Consistent with JIT and lean production, lean accounting emphasizes improvements in the value chain from suppliers to customers. Lean accounting encourages practices—such as reducing direct materials and work-in-process inventories, improving quality, using less space, and eliminating unused capacity—that reflect the goals of JIT production.

Critics of lean accounting charge that it does not compute the costs of individual products, which makes it less useful for making decisions. Proponents of lean accounting argue that the lack of individual product costs is not a problem because most decisions are made at the product line level rather than the individual product level and that pricing decisions are based on the value created for the customer (market prices) and not product costs.

Another criticism of lean accounting is that it excludes certain support costs and unused capacity costs. As a result, the decisions based on only value-stream costs will look profitable because they do not consider all costs. Proponents of lean accounting argue that the method overcomes this problem by adding a larger markup on value-stream costs to compensate for some of these excluded costs. Moreover, in a competitive market, prices will eventually settle at a level that represents a reasonable markup above a product's value-stream costs because customers will be unwilling to pay for non-value-added costs. The goal must therefore be to eliminate non-value-added costs.

A final criticism of lean accounting is that, like backflush costing, it does not correctly account for inventories under Generally Accepted Accounting Principles (GAAP). However, the method's proponents are quick to point out that in lean accounting environments, work-in-process and finished goods inventories are immaterial from an accounting perspective.

◄ Decision Point

How is lean accounting different from traditional costing systems?

Problems for Self-Study

Problem 1

Lee Company has a Singapore plant that manufactures MP3 players. One component is an XT chip. Expected demand is for 5,200 of these chips in March 2013. Lee estimates the ordering cost per purchase order to be $250. The monthly carrying cost for one unit of XT in stock is $5.

Required

1. Compute the EOQ for the XT chip.
2. Compute the number of deliveries of XT in March 2013.

Solution

$$EOQ = \sqrt{\frac{2 \times 5{,}200 \times \$250}{\$5}}$$

$$= 721 \text{ chips (rounded)}$$

$$\text{Number of deliveries} = \frac{5{,}200}{721}$$

$$= 8 \text{(rounded)}$$

Problem 2

Littlefield Company uses a backflush costing system with three trigger points:

- Purchase of direct materials
- Completion of good finished units of product
- Sale of finished goods

There are no beginning inventories. Information for April 2013 is as follows:

Direct materials purchased	$880,000	Conversion costs allocated	$ 400,000
Direct materials used	$850,000	Costs transferred to finished goods	$1,250,000
Conversion costs incurred	$422,000	Cost of goods sold	$1,190,000

Required

1. Prepare journal entries for April (without disposing of underallocated or overallocated conversion costs). Assume there are no direct materials variances.
2. Under an ideal JIT production system, how would the amounts in your journal entries differ from the journal entries in requirement 1?

Solution

1. Journal entries for April are as follows:

Entry (A1)	Materials and In-Process Inventory Control	880,000	
	Accounts Payable Control		880,000
	(direct materials purchased)		
Entry (A2)	Conversion Costs Control	422,000	
	Various accounts (such as Wages Payable Control)		422,000
	(conversion costs incurred)		
Entry (C1)	Finished Goods Control	1,250,000	
	Materials and In-Process Inventory Control		850,000
	Conversion Costs Allocated		400,000
	(standard cost of finished goods completed)		
Entry (D1)	Cost of Goods Sold	1,190,000	
	Finished Goods Control		1,190,000
	(standard costs of finished goods sold)		

2. Under an ideal JIT production system, if the manufacturing lead time per unit is very short, there would be zero inventories at the end of each day. Entry (C1) would be $1,190,000 finished goods production [to match finished goods sold in entry (D1)], not $1,250,000. If the marketing department could only sell goods costing $1,190,000, the JIT production system would call for direct materials purchases and conversion costs of lower than $880,000 and $422,000, respectively, in entries (A1) and (A2).

▶ Decision Points

The following question-and-answer format summarizes the chapter's learning objectives. Each decision presents a key question related to a learning objective. The guidelines are the answer to that question.

Decision	Guidelines
1. What are the six categories of costs associated with goods for sale?	The six categories are purchasing costs (costs of goods acquired from suppliers), ordering costs (costs of preparing a purchase order and receiving goods), carrying costs (costs of holding inventory of goods for sale), stockout costs (costs arising when a customer demands a unit of product and that unit is not on hand), costs of quality (prevention, appraisal, internal failure, and external failure costs), and shrinkage costs (the costs resulting from theft by outsiders, embezzlement by employees, misclassifications, and clerical errors).
2. What does the EOQ decision model help managers do, and how do managers decide on the safety-stock levels?	The economic-order-quantity (EOQ) decision model helps managers to calculate the optimal quantity of inventory to order by balancing ordering costs and carrying costs. The larger the order quantity, the higher are the annual carrying costs and the lower the annual ordering costs. The EOQ model includes costs recorded in the financial accounting system as well as opportunity costs of carrying inventory that are not recorded in the financial accounting system. Managers choose a level of safety stock to minimize the stockout costs and the carrying costs of holding more inventory.
3. How do errors in predicting the parameters of the EOQ model affect costs? How can companies reduce the conflict between the EOQ decision model and models used for performance evaluation?	The cost of prediction errors when using the EOQ model is small. To reduce the conflict between the EOQ decision model and the performance evaluation model, companies should include the opportunity cost of investment in inventory when evaluating managers. The opportunity cost of investment tied up in inventory is a key input in the EOQ decision model that is often ignored in the performance-evaluation model.
4. Why are companies using just-in-time (JIT) purchasing?	Just-in-time (JIT) purchasing is making purchases in small order quantities just as needed for production (or sales). JIT purchasing is a response to high carrying costs and low ordering costs. JIT purchasing increases the focus of companies and suppliers on quality and timely deliveries. Companies coordinate their activities and reduce inventories throughout the supply chain, from the initial sources of materials and services to the delivery of products to consumers.
5. How do materials requirements planning (MRP) systems differ from just-in-time (JIT) production systems?	Materials requirements planning (MRP) systems use a "push-through" approach whereby finished goods are manufactured on the basis of demand forecasts. Just-in-time (JIT) production systems use a "demand-pull" approach in which goods are manufactured only after receiving customer orders.

Decision	Guidelines
6. What are the features and benefits of a just-in-time (JIT) production system?	JIT production systems (a) organize production in manufacturing cells, (b) hire and train multiskilled workers, (c) emphasize total quality management, (d) reduce manufacturing lead time and setup time, and (e) build strong supplier relationships. The benefits of JIT production include lower costs and higher margins from better flow of information, higher quality, and faster delivery as well as simpler accounting systems.
7. How does backflush costing simplify traditional inventory costing?	Traditional inventory-costing systems use sequential tracking, in which recording of the journal entries occurs in the same order as actual purchases and progress in production. Most backflush costing systems do not record journal entries for the work-in-process stage of production. Some backflush costing systems also do not record entries for either the purchase of direct materials or the completion of finished goods.
8. How is lean accounting different from traditional costing systems?	Lean accounting assigns costs to value streams rather than to products. Non-value-added costs, unused capacity costs, and costs that cannot be easily traced to value streams are not allocated but instead expensed.

Terms to Learn

This chapter contains definitions of the following important terms:

backflush costing

carrying costs

economic order quantity (EOQ)

enterprise resource planning (ERP)
  system

inventory management

just-in-time (JIT) production

just-in-time (JIT) purchasing

lean accounting

lean production

manufacturing cells

materials requirements planning
  (MRP) system

ordering costs

purchase-order lead time

purchasing costs

reorder point

safety stock

sequential tracking

shrinkage costs

stockout costs

trigger point

value streams

Assignment Material

Questions

1 Why do better decisions regarding the purchasing and managing of goods for sale frequently cause dramatic percentage increases in net income?

2 Name six cost categories that are important in managing goods for sale in a retail company.

3 What assumptions are made when using the simplest version of the economic-order-quantity (EOQ) decision model?

4 Give examples of costs included in annual carrying costs of inventory when using the EOQ decision model.

5 Give three examples of opportunity costs that typically are not recorded in accounting systems, although they are relevant when using the EOQ model in the presence of demand uncertainty.

6 What are the steps in computing the cost of a prediction error when using the EOQ decision model?

7 Why might goal-congruence issues arise when managers use an EOQ model to guide decisions on how much to order?

8 "JIT purchasing has many benefits but also some risks." Do you agree? Explain briefly.

9 What are three factors causing reductions in the cost to place purchase orders for materials?

10 "You should always choose the supplier who offers the lowest price per unit." Do you agree? Explain.

11 What is supply-chain analysis, and how can it benefit manufacturers and retailers?

12 What are the main features of JIT production, and what are its benefits and costs?

13 Distinguish inventory-costing systems using sequential tracking from those using backflush costing.

14 Describe three different versions of backflush costing.

15 Discuss the differences between lean accounting and traditional cost accounting.

Exercises

16 **Economic order quantity for retailer.** Fan Base (FB) operates a megastore featuring sports merchandise. It uses an EOQ decision model to make inventory decisions. It is now considering inventory decisions for its Los Angeles Galaxy soccer jerseys product line. This is a highly popular item. Data for 2013 are as follows:

Expected annual demand for Galaxy jerseys	10,000
Ordering cost per purchase order	$200
Carrying cost per year	$7 per jersey

Each jersey costs FB $40 and sells for $80. The $7 carrying cost per jersey per year consists of the required return on investment of $4.80 ($12\% \times \$40$ purchase price) plus $2.20 in relevant insurance, handling, and storage costs. The purchasing lead time is 7 days. FB is open 365 days a year.

1. Calculate the EOQ.
2. Calculate the number of orders that will be placed each year.
3. Calculate the reorder point.

Required

17 **Economic order quantity, effect of parameter changes (continuation of 16).** Athletic Textiles (AT) manufactures the Galaxy jerseys that Fan Base (FB) sells to its customers. AT has recently installed computer software that enables its customers to conduct "one-stop" purchasing using state-of-the-art Web site technology. FB's ordering cost per purchase order will be $30 using this new technology.

1. Calculate the EOQ for the Galaxy jerseys using the revised ordering cost of $30 per purchase order. Assume all other data from Exercise 16 are the same. Comment on the result.
2. Suppose AT proposes to "assist" FB. AT will allow FB customers to order directly from the AT Web site. AT would ship directly to these customers. AT would pay $10 to FB for every Galaxy jersey purchased by one of FB's customers. Comment qualitatively on how this offer would affect inventory management at FB. What factors should FB consider in deciding whether to accept AT's proposal?

Required

18 **EOQ for a retailer.** The Denim World sells fabrics to a wide range of industrial and consumer users. One of the products it carries is denim cloth, used in the manufacture of jeans and carrying bags. The supplier for the denim cloth pays all incoming freight. No incoming inspection of the denim is necessary because the supplier has a track record of delivering high-quality merchandise. The purchasing officer of the Denim World has collected the following information:

Annual demand for denim cloth	26,400 yards
Ordering cost per purchase order	$165
Carrying cost per year	20% of purchase costs
Safety-stock requirements	None
Cost of denim cloth	$9 per yard

The purchasing lead time is 2 weeks. The Denim World is open 250 days a year (50 weeks for 5 days a week).

1. Calculate the EOQ for denim cloth.
2. Calculate the number of orders that will be placed each year.
3. Calculate the reorder point for denim cloth.

Required

19 **EOQ for manufacturer.** Turfpro Company produces lawn mowers and purchases 4,500 units of a rotor blade part each year at a cost of $30 per unit. Turfpro requires a 15% annual rate of return on investment. In addition, the relevant carrying cost (for insurance, materials handling, breakage, etc.) is $3 per unit per year. The relevant ordering cost per purchase order is $75.

1. Calculate Turfpro's EOQ for the rotor blade part.
2. Calculate Turfpro's annual relevant ordering costs for the EOQ calculated in requirement 1.
3. Calculate Turfpro's annual relevant carrying costs for the EOQ calculated in requirement 1.
4. Assume that demand is uniform throughout the year and known with certainty so there is no need for safety stocks. The purchase-order lead time is half a month. Calculate Turfpro's reorder point for the rotor blade part.

Required

20 Sensitivity of EOQ to changes in relevant ordering and carrying costs, cost of prediction error. Alpha Company's annual demand for its only product, XT-590, is 10,000 units. Alpha is currently analyzing possible combinations of relevant carrying cost per unit per year and relevant ordering cost per purchase order, depending on the company's choice of supplier and average levels of inventory. This table presents three possible combinations of carrying and ordering costs.

Relevant Carrying Cost per Unit per Year	Relevant Ordering Cost per Purchase Order
$10	$400
$20	$200
$40	$100

Required

1. For each of the relevant ordering and carrying-cost alternatives, determine (a) EOQ and (b) annual relevant total costs.
2. How does your answer to requirement 1 give insight into the impact of changes in relevant ordering and carrying costs on EOQ and annual relevant total costs? Explain briefly.
3. Suppose the relevant carrying cost per unit per year was $20 and the relevant ordering cost per purchase order was $200. Suppose further that Alpha calculates EOQ after incorrectly estimating relevant carrying cost per unit per year to be $10 and relevant ordering cost per purchase order to be $400. Calculate the actual annual relevant total costs of Alpha's EOQ decision. Compare this cost to the annual relevant total costs that Alpha would have incurred if it had correctly estimated the relevant carrying cost per unit per year of $20 and the relevant ordering cost per purchase order of $200 that you have already calculated in requirement 1. Calculate and comment on the cost of the prediction error.

21 JIT production, relevant benefits, relevant costs. The Colonial Hardware Company manufactures specialty brass door handles at its Lynchburg plant. Colonial is considering implementing a JIT production system. The following are the estimated costs and benefits of JIT production:

a. Annual additional tooling costs would be $200,000.
b. Average inventory would decline by 80% from the current level of $2,000,000.
c. Insurance, space, materials-handling, and setup costs, which currently total $600,000 annually, would decline by 25%.
d. The emphasis on quality inherent in JIT production would reduce rework costs by 30%. Colonial currently incurs $400,000 in annual rework costs.
e. Improved product quality under JIT production would enable Colonial to raise the price of its product by $8 per unit. Colonial sells 40,000 units each year.

Colonial's required rate of return on inventory investment is 15% per year.

Required

1. Calculate the net benefit or cost to Colonial if it adopts JIT production at the Lynchburg plant.
2. What nonfinancial and qualitative factors should Colonial consider when making the decision to adopt JIT production?
3. Suppose Colonial implements JIT production at its Lynchburg plant. Give examples of performance measures Colonial could use to evaluate and control JIT production. What would be the benefit of Colonial implementing an enterprise resource planning (ERP) system?

22 Backflush costing and JIT production. Grand Devices Corporation assembles handheld computers that have scaled-down capabilities of laptop computers. Each handheld computer takes 6 hours to assemble. Grand Devices uses a JIT production system and a backflush costing system with three trigger points:

- Purchase of direct materials and incurring of conversion costs
- Completion of good finished units of product
- Sale of finished goods

There are no beginning inventories of materials or finished goods and no beginning or ending work-in-process inventories. The following data are for August 2013:

Direct materials purchased	$2,958,000	Conversion costs incurred	$777,600
Direct materials used	$2,937,600	Conversion costs allocated	$806,400

Grand Devices records direct materials purchased and conversion costs incurred at actual costs. It has no direct materials variances. When finished goods are sold, the backflush costing system "pulls through" standard direct material cost ($102 per unit) and standard conversion cost ($28 per unit). Grand Devices produced 28,800 finished units in August 2013 and sold 28,400 units. The actual direct material cost per unit in August 2013 was $102, and the actual conversion cost per unit was $27.

1. Prepare summary journal entries for August 2013 (without disposing of under- or overallocated conversion costs).
2. Post the entries in requirement 1 to T-accounts for applicable Materials and In-Process Inventory Control, Finished Goods Control, Conversion Costs Control, Conversion Costs Allocated, and Cost of Goods Sold.
3. Under an ideal JIT production system, how would the amounts in your journal entries differ from those in requirement 1?

Required

23 Backflush costing, two trigger points, materials purchase and sale (continuation of 22). Assume the same facts as in Exercise 22, except that Grand Devices now uses a backflush costing system with the following two trigger points:

■ Purchase of direct materials and incurring of conversion costs

■ Sale of finished goods

The Inventory Control account will include direct materials purchased but not yet in production, materials in work in process, and materials in finished goods but not sold. No conversion costs are inventoried. Any under- or overallocated conversion costs are written off monthly to Cost of Goods Sold.

1. Prepare summary journal entries for August, including the disposition of under- or overallocated conversion costs.
2. Post the entries in requirement 1 to T-accounts for Inventory Control, Conversion Costs Control, Conversion Costs Allocated, and Cost of Goods Sold.

Required

24 Backflush costing, two trigger points, completion of production and sale (continuation of 22). Assume the same facts as in Exercise 22, except now Grand Devices uses only two trigger points, Completion of good finished units of product and Sale of finished goods. Any under- or overallocated conversion costs are written off monthly to Cost of Goods Sold.

1. Prepare summary journal entries for August, including the disposition of under- or overallocated conversion costs.
2. Post the entries in requirement 1 to T-accounts for Finished Goods Control, Conversion Costs Control, Conversion Costs Allocated, and Cost of Goods Sold.

Required

Problems

MyAccountingLab

25 EOQ, uncertainty, safety stock, reorder point. Chadwick Shoe Co. produces and sells an excellent-quality walking shoe. After production, the shoes are distributed to 20 warehouses around the country. Each warehouse services approximately 100 stores in its region. Chadwick uses an EOQ model to determine the number of pairs of shoes to order for each warehouse from the factory. Annual demand for Warehouse OR2 is approximately 120,000 pairs of shoes. The ordering cost is $250 per order. The annual carrying cost of a pair of shoes is $2.40 per pair.

1. Use the EOQ model to determine the optimal number of pairs of shoes per order.
2. Assume each month consists of approximately 4 weeks. If it takes 1 week to receive an order, at what point should warehouse OR2 reorder shoes?
3. Although OR2's average weekly demand is 2,500 pairs of shoes ($120,000 \div 12 \text{ months} \div 4 \text{ weeks}$), demand each week may vary with the following probability distribution:

Required

Total demand for 1 week	2,000 pairs	2,250 pairs	2,500 pairs	2,750 pairs	3,000 pairs
Probability (sums to 1.00)	0.04	0.20	0.52	0.20	0.04

If a store wants shoes and OR2 has none in stock, OR2 can "rush" them to the store at an additional cost of $2 per pair. How much safety stock should Warehouse OR2 hold? How will this affect the reorder point and reorder quantity?

26 EOQ, uncertainty, safety stock, reorder point. Stewart Corporation is a major automobile manufacturer. It purchases steering wheels from Coase Corporation. Annual demand is 10,400 steering wheels per year or 200 steering wheels per week. The ordering cost is $100 per order. The annual carrying cost is $13 per steering wheel. It currently takes 1.5 weeks to supply an order to the assembly plant.

1. What is the optimal number of steering wheels that Stewart's managers should order according to the EOQ model?
2. At what point should managers reorder the steering wheels, assuming that both demand and purchase-order lead time are known with certainty?

Required

3. Now assume that demand can vary during the 1.5-week purchase-order lead time. The following table shows the probability distribution of various demand levels:

Total Demand for Steering Wheels for 1.5 Weeks	Probability of Demand (sums to 1)
100	0.15
200	0.20
300	0.40
400	0.20
500	0.05

If Stewart runs out of stock, it would have to rush order the steering wheels at an additional cost of $9 per steering wheel. How much safety stock should the assembly plant hold? How will this affect the reorder point and reorder quantity.

27 MRP, EOQ, and JIT. Tech Works Corp. produces J-Pods, music players that can download thousands of songs. Tech Works forecasts that demand in 2014 will be 48,000 J-Pods. The variable production cost of each J-Pod is $54. In its MRP system, due to the large $10,000 cost per setup, Tech Works plans to produce J-Pods once a month in batches of 4,000 each. The carrying cost of a unit in inventory is $17 per year.

1. Using the MRP system, what is the annual cost of producing and carrying J-Pods in inventory? (Assume that, on average, half of the units produced in a month are in inventory.)
2. A new manager at Tech Works has suggested that the company use the EOQ model to determine the optimal batch size to produce. (To use the EOQ model, Tech Works needs to treat the setup cost in the same way it would treat ordering cost in a traditional EOQ model.) Determine the optimal batch size and number of batches. Round up the number of batches to the nearest whole number. What would be the annual cost of producing and carrying J-Pods in inventory if it uses the optimal batch size? Compare this cost to the cost calculated in requirement 1. Comment briefly.
3. Tech Works is also considering switching from its MRP system to a JIT system. This will result in producing J-Pods in batch sizes of 600 J-Pods and will reduce obsolescence, improve quality, and result in a higher selling price. The frequency of production batches will force Tech Works to reduce setup time and will result in a reduction in setup cost. The new setup cost will be $500 per setup. What is the annual cost of producing and carrying J-Pods in inventory under the JIT system?
4. Compare the models analyzed in the previous parts of the problem. What are the advantages and disadvantages of each?

28 Effect of management evaluation criteria on EOQ model. Computer Depot purchases one model of computer at a wholesale cost of $300 per unit and resells it to end consumers. The annual demand for the company's product is 600,000 units. Ordering costs are $1,200 per order and carrying costs are $75 per computer, including $30 in the opportunity cost of holding inventory.

1. Compute the optimal order quantity using the EOQ model.
2. Compute (a) the number of orders per year and (b) the annual relevant total cost of ordering and carrying inventory.
3. Assume that when evaluating the manager, the company excludes the opportunity cost of carrying inventory. If the manager makes the EOQ decision excluding the opportunity cost of carrying inventory, the relevant carrying cost would be $45, not $75. How would this affect the EOQ amount and the actual annual relevant cost of ordering and carrying inventory?
4. What is the cost impact on the company of excluding the opportunity cost of carrying inventory when making EOQ decisions? Why do you think the company currently excludes the opportunity costs of carrying inventory when evaluating the manager's performance? What could the company do to encourage the manager to make decisions more congruent with the goal of reducing total inventory costs?

29 JIT purchasing, relevant benefits, relevant costs. (CMA, adapted) The Greene Corporation is an automotive supplier that uses automatic turning machines to manufacture precision parts from steel bars. Greene's inventory of raw steel averages $300,000. John Oates, president of Greene, and Helen Gorman, Greene's controller, are concerned about the costs of carrying inventory. The steel supplier is willing to supply steel in smaller lots at no additional charge. Gorman identifies the following effects of adopting a JIT inventory program to virtually eliminate steel inventory:

- Without scheduling any overtime, lost sales due to stockouts would increase by 35,000 units per year. However, by incurring overtime premiums of $20,000 per year, the increase in lost sales could be reduced to 20,000 units per year. This would be the maximum amount of overtime that would be feasible for Greene.

- Two warehouses currently used for steel bar storage would no longer be needed. Greene rents one warehouse from another company under a cancelable leasing arrangement at an annual cost of

$45,000. The other warehouse is owned by Greene and contains 12,000 square feet. Three-fourths of the space in the owned warehouse could be rented for $1.25 per square foot per year. Insurance and property tax costs totaling $7,000 per year would be eliminated.

Greene's required rate of return on investment is 20% per year. Greene's budgeted income statement for the year ending December 31, 2014, (in thousands) is:

Revenues (900,000 units)		$ 5,400
Cost of goods sold		
Variable costs	$2,025	
Fixed costs	725	
Total costs of goods sold		2,750
Gross margin		2,650
Marketing and distribution costs		
Variable costs	$ 450	
Fixed costs	750	
Total marketing and distribution costs		1,200
Operating income		$ 1,450

Required

1. Calculate the estimated dollar savings (loss) for the Greene Corporation that would result in 2014 from the adoption of JIT purchasing.
2. Identify and explain other factors that Greene should consider before deciding whether to adopt JIT purchasing.

30 Supply chain effects on total relevant inventory cost. Peach Computer Co. outsources the production of motherboards for its computers. It is currently deciding which of two suppliers to use: Alpha or Beta. Due to differences in the product failure rates in the two companies, 5% of motherboards purchased from Alpha will be inspected and 25% of motherboards purchased from Beta will be inspected. The following data refer to costs associated with Alpha and Beta:

	Alpha	Beta
Number of orders per year	50	50
Annual motherboards demanded	10,000	10,000
Price per motherboard	$108	$105
Ordering cost per order	$13	$10
Inspection cost per unit	$6	$6
Average inventory level	100 units	100 units
Expected number of stockouts	100	300
Stockout cost (cost of rush order) per stockout	$4	$6
Units returned by customers for replacing motherboards	50	500
Cost of replacing each motherboard	$30	$30
Required annual return on investment	10%	10%
Other carrying cost per unit per year	$3.50	$3.50

Required

1. What is the relevant cost of purchasing from Alpha and Beta?
2. What factors other than cost should Peach consider?

31 Supply chain effects on total relevant inventory cost. Joe's Deli orders specially-made sandwich buns from two different suppliers: Gold Star Breads and Grandma's Bakery. Joe's Deli would like to use only one of the suppliers in the future. Due to variations in quality, Joe's would need to inspect 30% of Gold Star's buns and 60% of Grandma's. The following data refer to costs associated with the two suppliers.

	Gold Star	Grandma's
Number of orders per year	100	100
Annual buns demanded	2,400	2,400
Price per bun	$ 2.50	$ 2.00
Ordering cost per order	$ 10.00	$ 12.00
Inspection cost per bun	$ 0.50	$ 0.50
Average inventory level	200	200

	Gold Star	Grandma's
Expected number of stockouts	10	10
Stockout cost of rush order	$ 10.00	$ 3.00
Estimated sandwiches returned by customers because of defective buns	60	100
Cost of fixing sandwiches returned by customers because of defective buns	$ 1.50	$ 1.50
Opportunity cost of investment	12%	12%
Other carrying costs per bun per year	$ 0.50	$ 0.50

Required

1. What is the relevant cost of purchasing from Gold Star and Grandma's?
2. What factors other than cost should Joe's Deli consider?

32 Backflush costing and JIT production. The Grand Meter Corporation manufactures electrical meters. For August, there were no beginning inventories of direct materials and no beginning or ending work in process. Grand Meter uses a JIT production system and backflush costing with three trigger points for making entries in the accounting system:

- Purchase of direct materials and incurring of conversion costs
- Completion of good finished units of product
- Sale of finished goods

Grand Meter's August standard cost per meter is direct materials, $25, and conversion cost, $20. Grand Meter has no direct materials variances. The following data apply to August manufacturing:

Direct materials purchased	$550,000	Number of finished units manufactured	21,000
Conversion costs incurred	$440,000	Number of finished units sold	20,000

Required

1. Prepare summary journal entries for August (without disposing of under- or overallocated conversion costs). Assume no direct materials variances.
2. Post the entries in requirement 1 to T-accounts for Materials and In-Process Inventory Control, Finished Goods Control, Conversion Costs Control, Conversion Costs Allocated, and Cost of Goods Sold.

33 Backflush, two trigger points, materials purchase and sale (continuation of 32). Assume that the second trigger point for Grand Meter Corporation is the sale—rather than the completion—of finished goods. Also, the inventory account is confined solely to direct materials, whether these materials are in a storeroom, in work in process, or in finished goods. No conversion costs are inventoried. They are allocated to the units sold at standard costs. Any under- or overallocated conversion costs are written off monthly to Cost of Goods Sold.

Required

1. Prepare summary journal entries for August, including the disposition of under- or overallocated conversion costs. Assume no direct materials variances.
2. Post the entries in requirement 1 to T-accounts for Inventory Control, Conversion Costs Control, Conversion Costs Allocated, and Cost of Goods Sold.

34 Backflush, two trigger points, completion of production and sale (continuation of 32). Assume the same facts as in Problem 33 except now there are only two trigger points: Completion of good finished units of product and Sale of finished goods.

Required

1. Prepare summary journal entries for August, including the disposition of under- or overallocated conversion costs. Assume no direct materials variances.
2. Post the entries in requirement 1 to T-accounts for Finished Goods Control, Conversion Costs Control, Conversion Costs Allocated, and Cost of Goods Sold.

35 Lean accounting. Reliable Security Devices (RSD) has introduced a just-in-time production process and is considering the adoption of lean accounting principles to support its new production philosophy. The company has two product lines: Mechanical Devices and Electronic Devices. Two individual products are made in each line. Product-line manufacturing overhead costs are traced directly to product lines and then allocated to the two individual products in each line. The company's traditional cost-accounting system allocates all plant-level facility costs and some corporate overhead costs to individual products. The latest accounting report using traditional cost accounting methods included the following information (in thousands of dollars):

	Mechanical Devices		Electronic Devices	
	Product A	Product B	Product C	Product D
Sales	$1,400	$1,000	$1,800	$900
Direct material (based on quantity used)	400	200	500	150
Direct manufacturing labor	300	150	400	120
Manufacturing overhead (equipment lease, supervision, production control)	180	240	400	190
Allocated plant-level facility costs	100	80	160	60
Design and marketing costs	190	100	210	84
Allocated corporate overhead costs	30	20	40	16
Operating income	$200	$210	$90	$280

RSD has determined that each of the two product lines represents a distinct value stream. It has also determined that out of the $400,000 ($100,000 + $80,000 + $160,000 + $60,000) plant-level facility costs, product A occupies 22% of the plant's square footage, product B occupies 18%, product C occupies 36%, and product D occupies 14%. The remaining 10% of square footage is not being used. Finally, RSD has decided that in order to identify inefficiencies, direct material should be expensed in the period it is purchased, rather than when the material is used. According to purchasing records, direct material purchase costs during the period were as follows:

	Mechanical Devices		Electronic Devices	
	Product A	Product B	Product C	Product D
Direct material (purchases)	$420	$240	$500	$180

Required

1. What are the cost objects in RSD's lean accounting system?
2. Compute operating income for the cost objects identified in requirement 1 using lean accounting principles. What would you compare this operating income against? Comment on your results.

36 JIT production, relevant benefits, relevant costs, ethics. Perez Container Corporation is considering implementing a JIT production system. The new system would reduce current average inventory levels of $4,000,000 by 75%, but it would require a much greater dependency on the company's core suppliers for on-time deliveries and high-quality inputs. The company's operations manager, Jim Ingram, is opposed to the idea of a new JIT system because he is concerned that the new system (a) will be too costly to manage; (b) will result in too many stockouts; and (c) will lead to the layoff of his employees, several of whom are currently managing inventory. He believes that these layoffs will affect the morale of his entire production department. The management accountant, Sue Winston, is in favor of the new system because of its likely cost savings. Jim wants Sue to rework the numbers because he is concerned that top management will give more weight to financial factors and not give due consideration to nonfinancial factors such as employee morale. In addition to the reduction in inventory described previously, Sue has gathered the following information for the upcoming year regarding the JIT system:

- Annual insurance and warehousing costs for inventory would be reduced by 60% of current budgeted level of $700,000.
- Payroll expenses for current inventory management staff would be reduced by 15% of the budgeted total of $1,200,000.
- Additional annual costs for JIT system implementation and management, including personnel costs, would equal $440,000.
- The additional number of stockouts under the new JIT system is estimated to be 5% of the total number of shipments annually. Ten thousand shipments are budgeted for the upcoming year. Each stockout would result in an average additional cost of $500.
- Perez's required rate of return on inventory investment is 10% per year.

Required

1. From a financial perspective, should Perez adopt the new JIT system?
2. Should Sue Winston rework the numbers?
3. How should she manage Jim Ingram's concerns?

Glossary

Backflush costing. Costing system that omits recording some of the journal entries relating to the stages from purchase of direct materials to the sale of finished goods.

Carrying costs. Costs that arise while holding inventory of goods for sale.

Economic order quantity (EOQ). Decision model that calculates the optimal quantity of inventory to order under a set of assumptions.

Enterprise resource planning (ERP) system. An integrated set of software modules covering a company's accounting, distribution, manufacturing, purchasing, human resources, and other functions.

Inventory management. Planning, coordinating, and controlling activities related to the flow of inventory into, through, and out of an organization.

Just-in-time (JIT) production. Demand-pull manufacturing system in which each component in a production line is produced as soon as, and only when, needed by the next step in the production line. Also called *lean production*.

Just-in-time (JIT) purchasing. The purchase of materials (or goods) so that they are delivered just as needed for production (or sales).

Lean accounting. Costing method that supports creating value for the customer by costing the entire value stream, not individual products or departments, thereby eliminating waste in the accounting process.

Lean production. See *just-in-time (JIT) production*.

Manufacturing cells. Grouping of all the different types of equipment used to make a given product.

Materials requirements planning (MRP). Push-through system that manufactures finished goods for inventory on the basis of demand forecasts.

Ordering costs. Costs of preparing, issuing, and paying purchase orders, plus receiving and inspecting the items included in the orders.

Purchase-order lead time. The time between placing an order and its delivery.

Purchasing costs. Cost of goods acquired from suppliers including incoming freight or transportation costs.

Reorder point. The quantity level of inventory on hand that triggers a new purchase order.

Safety stock. Inventory held at all times regardless of the quantity of inventory ordered using the EOQ model.

Sequential tracking. Approach in a product-costing system in which recording of the journal entries occurs in the same order as actual purchases and progress in production.

Shrinkage costs. Costs that result from theft by outsiders, embezzlement by employees, misclassifications, and clerical errors.

Stockout costs. Costs that result when a company runs out of a particular item for which there is customer demand. The company must act to meet that demand or suffer the costs of not meeting it.

Trigger point. Refers to a stage in the cycle from purchase of direct materials to sale of finished goods at which journal entries are made in the accounting system.

Value streams. All valued-added activities needed to design, manufacture, and deliver a given product or product line to customers.

Photo Credits

Capital Budgeting
and Cost Analysis

From Chapter 21 of *Cost Accounting: A Managerial Emphasis,* Fifteenth Edition. Charles T. Horngren, Srikant M. Datar, Madhav V. Rajan. Copyright © 2015 by Pearson Education, Inc. All rights reserved.

Capital Budgeting and Cost Analysis

Learning Objectives

1 Understand the five stages of capital budgeting for a project

2 Use and evaluate the two main discounted cash flow (DCF) methods: the net present value (NPV) method and the internal rate-of-return (IRR) method

3 Use and evaluate the payback and discounted payback methods

4 Use and evaluate the accrual accounting rate-of-return (AARR) method

5 Identify relevant cash inflows and outflows for capital budgeting decisions

6 Understand issues involved in implementing capital budgeting decisions and evaluating managerial performance

7 Explain how managers can use capital budgeting to achieve their firms' strategic goals

Should Honda open a new plant in China or India?

Should Sony invest in developing the next generation of PlayStation consoles? Should the Gap discontinue its children's clothing line and expand its women's athletic clothing line? Working closely with accountants, top executives have to figure out how and when to best allocate the firm's financial resources among alternative opportunities to create future value for the company. Because it's hard to know what the future holds and how much projects will ultimately cost, this can be a challenging task, but it's one that managers must constantly confront. To meet this challenge, companies such as Target and Chevron have developed special groups to make project-related capital budgeting decisions. This chapter explains the different methods managers use to get the "biggest bang" for the firm's "buck" in terms of the projects they undertake.

Capital Budgeting Powers Decisions at the TVA[1]

The Tennessee Valley Authority (TVA) is the United States' largest public power provider and is wholly owned by the U.S. government. Although owned by the federal government, TVA is not financed with tax dollars; rather, the utility's funding comes from the sale of power to its customers. Recently, TVA faced a difficult strategic decision: ensuring sufficient power generation while at the same time continuing to provide affordable power to a growing number of customers in its service area.

At the same time, TVA was replacing a significant part of its existing power generation capability. TVA previously announced plans to retire multiple coal power plants by 2018 to reach its goal of becoming a clean energy leader. Potential sources of new power generation included the construction of nuclear, natural gas, coal, wind, and solar plants. The power generation options had differing costs, expected cash flows, and useful lives. Moreover, TVA's construction decisions were constrained by a limited capital budget. TVA turned to net present value (NPV) and internal rate-of-return (IRR) calculations to guide its decision making.

After extensive calculations, TVA discovered that the NPV and IRR of natural gas, nuclear, and wind plants were positive. The NPV of solar and coal plants was negative, and their IRR was below TVA's cost of capital (calculated as the current yield to maturity on 30-year government debt plus an added 1% premium). In 2012, four renewable wind-power sources located in Kansas, Illinois, and Iowa began delivery to the TVA power grid and construction began on a new gas-fired combustion turbine/combined

[1] *Sources:* Bob Wood, Steven Isbell, and Cass Larson, "The Tennessee Valley Authority: The Cost of Power." *IMA Educational Case Journal*, Volume 5, Number 4 (Montvale, NJ: Institute of Management Accountants, Inc., December 2012); and "TVA Releases Cost, Schedule Estimates for Watts Bar Nuclear Unit 2," Tennessee Valley Authority press release (Knoxville, TN, April 5, 2012).

cycle generating power plant. Additionally, the Watts Bar Unit 2 nuclear power generator is scheduled to begin operation in 2015. Construction on the unit, originally started in the mid-'80s, was resumed with updated technologies. TVA is also developing a smart grid deployment plan that will help customers better understand the costs and benefits of these new power sources.

Just as at the TVA, managers at companies such as Target, Honda, Sony, and the Gap face challenging investment decisions. In this chapter, we introduce several capital budgeting methods used to evaluate long-term investment projects. These methods help managers choose the projects that will contribute the most value to their organizations.

Stages of Capital Budgeting

Capital budgeting is the process of making long-run planning decisions for investments in projects. In much of accounting, income is calculated on a period-by-period basis. In choosing investments, however, managers make a selection from among multiple projects, each of which may span several periods. Exhibit 1 illustrates these two different yet intersecting dimensions of cost analysis: (1) horizontally across, as the *project dimension*, and (2) vertically upward, as the *accounting-period dimension*. Each project is represented as a horizontal rectangle starting and ending at different times and stretching over time spans longer than one year. The vertical rectangle for the 2015 accounting period, for example, represents the dimensions of income determination and routine annual planning and control that cut across all projects that are ongoing that year.

To make capital budgeting decisions, managers analyze each project by considering all the life-span cash flows from its initial investment through its termination. This process is analogous to life-cycle budgeting and costing. For example, when Honda considers producing a new model of automobile, it begins by estimating all potential revenues from the project as well as any costs that will be incurred during its life cycle, which may be as long as 10 years. Only after examining the potential costs and benefits across all of the business functions in the value chain, from research and development (R&D) to customer service, across the entire life span of the new-car project does Honda decide whether the new model is a wise investment.

Learning Objective 1

Understand the five stages of capital budgeting for a project

...identify projects; obtain information; make predictions; make decisions; and implement the decision, evaluate performance, and learn

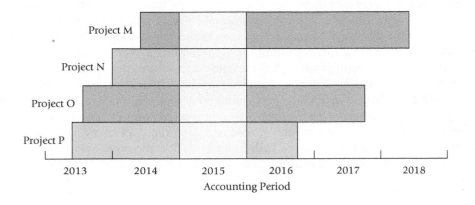

Exhibit 1

The Project and Time Dimensions of Capital Budgeting

Managers use capital budgeting as a decision-making and a control tool. Like the five-step decision process, there are five stages to the capital budgeting process:

Stage 1: Identify Projects. *Identify potential capital investments that agree with the organization's strategy.* For example, Nike, an industry leader in product differentiation, makes significant investments in product innovation, engineering, and design, hoping to develop the next generation of high-quality sportswear. Alternatively, managers could promote products that improve productivity and efficiency as a cost-leadership strategy. For example, Dell's strategy of cost leadership includes outsourcing certain components to lower-cost contract manufacturing facilities located overseas. Identifying which types of capital projects to invest in is largely the responsibility of a firm's top managers.

Stage 2: Obtain Information. *Gather information from all parts of the value chain to evaluate alternative projects.* Returning to the new car example at Honda, in this stage, the firm's top managers ask the company's marketing managers for potential revenue numbers, plant managers for assembly times, and suppliers for prices and the availability of key components. Lower-level managers are asked to validate the data provided and to explain the assumptions underlying them. The goal is to encourage open and honest communication that results in accurate estimates so that the best investment decisions are made. Some projects will be rejected at this stage. For example, suppose Honda learns that the car cannot be built using existing plants. It may then opt to cancel the project altogether. At Akzo-Nobel, a global paints and coating company, the chief sustainability officer reviews projects against a set of environmental criteria and has the power to reject projects that do not meet the criteria or lack an acceptable explanation for why the company's sustainability factors were not considered.

Stage 3: Make Predictions. *Forecast all potential cash flows attributable to the alternative projects.* A new project generally requires a firm to make a substantial initial outlay of capital, which is recouped over time through annual cash inflows and the disposal value of the project's assets after it is terminated. Consequently, investing in a new project requires the firm to forecast its cash flows several years into the future. BMW, for example, estimates yearly cash flows and sets its investment budgets accordingly using a 12-year planning horizon. Because of the significant uncertainty associated with these predictions, firms typically analyze a wide range of alternate circumstances. In the case of BMW, the marketing group is asked to estimate a band of possible sales figures within a 90% confidence interval. Firms also attempt to ensure that estimates, especially for the later years of a project, are grounded in realistic scenarios. It is tempting for managers to introduce biases into these projections in order to drive the outcome of the capital budgeting process to their preferred choice. This effect is exacerbated by the fact that managers may not expect to be employed at the firm during those years and therefore cannot be held accountable for their estimates.

Stage 4: Make Decisions by Choosing Among Alternatives. *Determine which investment yields the greatest benefit and the least cost to the organization.* Using the quantitative information obtained in stage 3, the firm uses any one of several capital budgeting methodologies to determine which project best meets organizational goals. While capital budgeting calculations are typically limited to financial information, managers use their judgment and intuition to factor in qualitative information and strategic considerations as well. For example, even if a proposed new line of cars meets its financial targets on a standalone basis, Honda might decide not to pursue the line if it is not aligned with the strategic imperatives of the company on matters such as brand positioning, industry leadership in safety and technology, and fuel consumption. Considerations of environmental sustainability might also favor certain projects that currently appear unprofitable. For example, UPS relaxes the company's minimum rate of return on vehicles that have the potential to reduce fuel use and costs. Similarly, Sealed Air is willing to accept projects with a lower projected return if they look promising with regard to reducing greenhouse gas emissions. Finally, managers spend a significant amount of time assessing the risks of a project, in terms of both the uncertainty of the estimated cash flows as well as the potential downside risks of the project (as well as to the firm as a whole) if the worst-case scenario were to occur.

Stage 5: Implement the Decision, Evaluate Performance, and Learn. Given the complexities of capital investment decisions and their long-time horizons, this stage can be separated into two phases:

- *Obtain funding and make the investments selected in stage 4.* The sources of funding include internally generated cash as well as equity and debt securities sold in capital markets. Making capital investments is often an arduous task, laden with the purchase of many different goods and services. If Honda opts to build a new car, it must order steel, aluminum, paint, and so on. If some of the materials are unavailable, managers must determine the economic feasibility of using alternative inputs.

- *Track realized cash flows, compare against estimated numbers, and revise plans if necessary.* As the cash outflows and inflows begin to accumulate, managers can verify whether the predictions made in stage 3 agree with the actual flows of cash from the project. When the BMW group initially released the Mini Cooper in 2001, its sales were substantially higher than the original demand estimates. BMW responded by manufacturing more cars. It also expanded the Mini line to include convertibles and the larger Clubman model.

  It is equally important for a company to abandon projects that are performing poorly relative to expectations. A natural bias for managers is to escalate their commitment to a project they chose to implement for fear of revealing they made an incorrect capital budgeting decision. It is in the firm's and the managers' long-term interest, however, to acknowledge the mistake when it is clear that the project is not financially sustainable. For example, in April 2012, TransAlta, a Canadian electricity generator, halted a CA$1.4 billion project to capture carbon in the province of Alberta. After spending CA$30 million on engineering and design studies, the firm realized that the revenue from carbon sales and the costs of reducing emissions were insufficient to make the project economically viable.

To illustrate capital budgeting, consider Vector Transport. Vector operates bus lines throughout the United States, often providing transportation services on behalf of local transit authorities. Several of Vector's buses are nearing the end of their useful lives and are requiring increased operating and maintenance costs. Customers have also complained that the buses lack adequate storage, flexible seating configurations, and newer amenities such as wireless Internet access. The firm has made a commitment to act in an environmentally responsible manner and will only pursue projects that do minimal harm to the ecosystem. Accordingly, in stage 1, Vector's managers decide to look for replacement buses that generate low emissions. In the information-gathering stage (stage 2), the company learns that as early as 2014, it could feasibly begin purchasing and using diesel electric hybrid buses that have Wi-Fi and also offer greater comfort and storage. After collecting additional data, Vector begins to forecast its future cash flows if it invests in the new buses (stage 3). Vector estimates that it can purchase a hybrid bus with a useful life of 5 years for a net after-tax initial investment of $648,900, which is calculated as follows:[2]

Cost of new hybrid bus	$660,000
Investment in working capital	30,000
Cash flow from disposing of existing bus (after-tax)	(41,100)
Net initial investment for new bus	$648,900

Working capital refers to the difference between current assets and current liabilities. New projects often require additional investments in current assets such as inventories and receivables. In the case of Vector, the purchase of the new bus is accompanied by an incremental outlay of $30,000 for supplies, replacement batteries, and spare parts inventory. At the end of the project, the $30,000 in current assets is liquidated, resulting in a cash inflow. However, because of the rapid nature of improvements in hybrid technology, the bus itself is believed to have no terminal disposal value after 5 years.

---

[2] For the purposes of exposition, we study the capital budgeting problem for replacing one bus, rather than a fleet of buses.

Managers estimate that by introducing the new hybrid buses, operating cash inflows (cash revenues minus cash operating costs) will increase by $180,000 (after tax) in the first 4 years and by $150,000 in year 5. This arises from higher ticket prices and increases in ridership because of new customers who are drawn to the amenities of the hybrid bus, as well as savings in fuel, maintenance, and operating costs. To simplify the analysis, suppose that all cash flows occur at the end of each year. Note that cash flow at the end of the fifth year also increases by $180,000—$150,000 in operating cash inflows and $30,000 in working capital. Management next calculates the costs and benefits of the proposed project (stage 4). This chapter discusses four capital budgeting methods to analyze financial information: (1) net present value (NPV), (2) internal rate-of-return (IRR), (3) payback, and (4) accrual accounting rate-of-return (AARR). Both the net present value (NPV) and internal rate-of-return (IRR) methods use *discounted cash flows,* which we discuss in the next section.

Decision Point ▶

What are the five stages of capital budgeting?

Learning Objective **2** ▶

Use and evaluate the two main discounted cash flow (DCF) methods: the net present value (NPV) method and the internal rate-of-return (IRR) method

...to explicitly consider all project cash flows and the time value of money

Discounted Cash Flow

Discounted cash flow (DCF) methods measure all expected future cash inflows and outflows of a project discounted back to the present point in time. The key feature of DCF methods is the **time value of money,** which means that a dollar (or any other monetary unit) received today is worth more than a dollar received at any future time. The reason is that $1 received today can be invested at, say, 10% per year so that it grows to $1.10 at the end of one year. The time value of money is the opportunity cost (the return of $0.10 forgone per year) from not having the money today. In this example, $1 received 1 year from now is worth $1 ÷ 1.10 = $0.9091 today. Similarly, $100 received 1 year from now will be weighted by 0.9091 to yield a discounted cash flow of $90.91, which is today's value of that $100 next year. In this way, discounted cash flow methods explicitly measure cash flows in terms of the time value of money. Note that DCF focuses exclusively on cash inflows and outflows rather than on operating income as calculated under accrual accounting.

The compound interest tables and formulas used in DCF analysis are in Appendix: Notes on Compound Interest and Interest Tables. If you are unfamiliar with compound interest, do not proceed until you have studied Appendix: Notes on Compound Interest and Interest Tables, as the tables in the appendix will be used frequently in this chapter.

The two DCF methods we describe are the net present value (NPV) method and the internal rate-of-return (IRR) method. Both DCF methods use the **required rate of return (RRR),** the minimum acceptable annual rate of return on an investment. The RRR is internally set, usually by upper management, and typically represents the return that an organization could expect to receive elsewhere for an investment of comparable risk. The RRR is also called the **discount rate, hurdle rate, cost of capital,** or **opportunity cost of capital.** Let's suppose the CFO at Vector has set the required rate of return for the firm's investments at 8% per year.

Net Present Value Method

The **net present value (NPV) method** calculates the expected monetary gain or loss from a project by discounting all expected future cash inflows and outflows back to the present point in time using the required rate of return. To use the NPV method, apply the following three steps:

Step 1: Draw a Sketch of Relevant Cash Inflows and Outflows. The right side of Exhibit 2 shows arrows that depict the cash flows of the new hybrid bus. The sketch helps the decision maker visualize and organize the data in a systematic way. *Note that parentheses denote relevant cash outflows throughout all of the exhibits in this chapter.* Exhibit 2 includes the outflow for the acquisition of the new bus at the start of year 1 (also referred to as end of year 0) and the inflows over the subsequent 5 years. The NPV method specifies cash flows regardless of their source, such as operations, the purchase or sale of equipment, or an investment in or recovery of working capital. However, accrual-accounting

Exhibit 2 Net Present Value Method: Vector's Hybrid Bus

	A	B	C	D	E	F	G	H	I
1			Net initial investment	$648,900					
2			Useful life	5 years					
3			Annual cash flow	$180,000					
4			Required rate of return	8%					
5									
6		Present Value	Present Value of	Sketch of Relevant Cash Flows at End of Each Year					
7		of Cash Flow	$1 Discounted at 8%	0	1	2	3	4	5
8	Approach 1: Discounting Each Year's Cash Flow Separately[a]								
9	Net initial investment	$(648,900) ←	1.000 ←	$(648,900)					
10		166,680 ←	0.926 ←		$180,000				
11		154,260 ←	0.857 ←			$180,000			
12	Annual cash inflow	142,920 ←	0.794 ←				$180,000		
13		132,300 ←	0.735 ←					$180,000	
14		122,580 ←	0.681 ←						$180,000
15	NPV if new bus purchased	$ 69,840							
16									
17	Approach 2: Using Annuity Table[b]								
18	Net initial investment	$(648,900) ←	1.000 ←	$(648,900)					
19					$180,000	$180,000	$180,000	$180,000	$180,000
20									
21	Annual cash inflow	718,740 ←	3.993 ←						
22	NPV if new bus purchased	$ 69,840							
23									
24	*Note:* Parentheses denote relevant cash outflows throughout all exhibits in Chapter 21.								
25	[a] Present values from Table 2, Appendix A, at the end of the book. For example, $0.857 = 1 \div (1.08)^2$.								
26	[b] Annuity present value from Table 4, Appendix A. The annuity value of 3.993 is the sum of the individual discount rates $0.926 + 0.857 + 0.794 + 0.735 + 0.681$.								

concepts such as sales made on credit or noncash expenses are not included because the focus is on *cash* inflows and outflows.

Step 2: Discount the Cash Flows Using the Correct Compound Interest Table from Appendix: Notes on Compound Interest and Interest Tables and Sum Them. In the Vector example, we can discount each year's cash flow separately using Table 2, or we can compute the present value of an annuity, a series of equal cash flows at equal time intervals, using Table 4. (Both tables are in Appendix: Notes on Compound Interest and Interest Tables.) If we use Table 2, we find the discount factors for periods 1–5 under the 8% column. Approach 1 in Exhibit 2 uses the five discount factors. To obtain the present value amount, multiply each discount factor by the corresponding amount represented by the arrow on the right in Exhibit 2 (−$648,900 × 1.000; $180,000 × 0.926; and so on to $180,000 × 0.681). Because the investment in the new bus produces an annuity, we may also use Table 4. Under Approach 2, we find that the annuity factor for five periods under the 8% column is 3.993, which is the sum of the five discount factors used in Approach 1. We multiply the uniform annual cash inflow by this factor to obtain the present value of the inflows ($718,740 = $180,000 × 3.993). Subtracting the initial investment then reveals the NPV of the project as $69,840 ($69,840 = $718,740 − $648,900).

Step 3: Make the Project Decision on the Basis of the Calculated NPV. An NPV that is zero or positive suggest that from a financial standpoint, the company should accept the project because its expected rate of return equals or exceeds the required rate of return. If the NPV is negative, the company should reject the project because its expected rate of return is below the required rate of return.

Exhibit 2 calculates an NPV of $69,840 at the required rate of return of 8% per year. The project is acceptable based on financial information. The cash flows from the project are adequate (1) to recover the net initial investment in the project and (2) to earn a return greater than 8% per year on the investment tied up in the project over its useful life.

Managers must also weigh nonfinancial factors such as the effect that purchasing the bus will have on Vector's brand. This is a nonfinancial factor because the financial benefits that accrue from Vector's brand are very difficult to estimate. Nevertheless, managers must consider brand effects before reaching a final decision. Suppose, for example, that the NPV of the hybrid bus is negative. Vector's managers might still decide to buy the bus if it maintains Vector's technological image and reputation for environmental responsibility. These are factors that could increase Vector's financial outcomes in the future, such as by attracting more riders or generating additional contracts from government transit agencies. For example, Alcoa, an aluminum producer, has found that its sustainability track record gives it better access to large markets such as Brazil, where a positive environmental record is becoming an important component in selecting products.

Pause here. Do not proceed until you understand what you see in Exhibit 2. Compare Approach 1 with Approach 2 in Exhibit 2 to see how Table 4 in Appendix: Notes on Compound Interest and Interest Tables merely aggregates the present value factors of Table 2. That is, the fundamental table is Table 2. Table 4 simply reduces calculations when there is an annuity.

Internal Rate-of-Return Method

The **internal rate-of-return (IRR) method** calculates the discount rate at which an investment's present value of all expected cash inflows equals the present value of its expected cash outflows. That is, the IRR is the discount rate that makes NPV = $0. Exhibit 3 shows the cash flows and the NPV of Vector's hybrid project using a 12% annual

Exhibit 3   Internal Rate-of-Return Method: Vector's Hybrid Bus[a]

	A	B	C	D	E	F	G	H	I
1			Net initial investment	$648,900					
2			Useful life	5 years					
3			Annual cash flow	$180,000					
4			Annual discount rate	12%					
5									
6		Present Value	Present Value of	Sketch of Relevant Cash Flows at End of Each Year					
7		of Cash Flow	$1 Discounted at 12%	0	1	2	3	4	5
8	Approach 1: Discounting Each Year's Cash Flow Separately[b]								
9	Net initial investment	$(648,900) ←	1.000 ←	$(648,900)					
10		160,740 ←	0.893 ←		$180,000				
11		143,460 ←	0.797 ←			$180,000			
12	Annual cash inflow	128,160 ←	0.712 ←				$180,000		
13		114,480 ←	0.636 ←					$180,000	
14		102,060 ←	0.567 ←						$180,000
15	NPV if new bus purchased	$ 0							
16	(the zero difference proves that								
17	the internal rate of return is 12%)								
18									
19	Approach 2: Using Annuity Table[c]								
20	Net initial investment	$(648,900) ←	1.000 ←	$(648,900)					
21					$180,000	$180,000	$180,000	$180,000	$180,000
22									
23	Annual cash inflow	648,900 ←	3.605 ←						
24	NPV if new bus purchased	$ 0							
25									
26	Note: Parentheses denote relevant cash outflows throughout all exhibits in Chapter 21.								
27	[a]The internal rate of return is computed by methods explained on pp. 808–809.								
28	[b]Present values from Table 2, Appendix A, at the end of the book.								
29	[c]Annuity present value from Table 4, Appendix A. The annuity table value of 3.605 is the sum of the individual discount rates 0.893 + 0.797 + 0.712 + 0.636 + 0.567.								

discount rate. At a 12% discount rate, the NPV of the project is $0. Therefore, the IRR is 12% per year.

Managers or analysts solving capital budgeting problems typically use a calculator or computer program to provide the internal rate of return. The following trial-and-error approach can also provide the answer.

Step 1: Use a discount rate and calculate the project's NPV.

Step 2: If the calculated NPV is less than zero, use a lower discount rate. (A *lower* discount rate will *increase* the NPV. Remember that we are trying to find a discount rate for which the NPV = $0.) If the NPV exceeds zero, use a higher discount rate to lower the NPV. Keep adjusting the discount rate until the NPV does equal $0. In the Vector example, a discount rate of 8% yields an NPV of +$69,840 (see Exhibit 2). A discount rate of 14% yields an NPV of −$30,960 (3.433, the present value annuity factor from Table 4, × $180,000 minus $648,900). Therefore, the discount rate that makes the NPV equal $0 must lie between 8% and 14%. We use 12% and get NPV = $0. Hence, the IRR is 12% per year.

Computing the IRR is easier when the cash inflows are constant, as in our Vector example. Information from Exhibit 3 can be expressed as follows:

$$\$648,900 = \text{Present value of annuity of } \$180,000 \text{ at } X\% \text{ per year for 5 years}$$

Or what factor F in Table 4 (in Appendix: Notes on Compound Interest and Interest Tables) will satisfy this equation?

$$\$648,900 = \$180,000F$$

$$F = \$648,900 \div \$180,000 = 3.605$$

On the five-period line of Table 4, find the percentage column that is closest to 3.605. It is exactly 12%. If the factor (F) falls between the factors in two columns, straight-line interpolation is used to approximate the IRR. This interpolation is illustrated in the Problem for Self-Study.

Managers accept a project only if its IRR equals or exceeds the firm's RRR (required rate of return). In the Vector example, the hybrid bus has an IRR of 12%, which is greater than the RRR of 8%. On the basis of financial factors, Vector should invest in the new bus. In general, the NPV and IRR decision rules result in consistent project acceptance or rejection decisions. If the IRR exceeds the RRR, then the project has a positive NPV (favoring acceptance). If the IRR equals the RRR, then NPV equals $0, so the company is indifferent between accepting and rejecting the project. If the IRR is less than the RRR, the NPV is negative (favoring rejection). Obviously, managers prefer projects with higher IRRs to projects with lower IRRs, if all other things are equal. The IRR of 12% means the cash inflows from the project are adequate to (1) recover the net initial investment in the project and (2) earn a return of exactly 12% on the investment tied up in the project over its useful life.

Comparing the Net Present Value and Internal Rate-of-Return Methods

The NPV method is the preferred method for selecting projects because its use leads to shareholder value maximization. At an intuitive level, this occurs because the NPV measure captures the value, in today's dollars, of the surplus the project generates for the firm's shareholders over and above the required rate of return.[3] Next, we highlight some of the limitations of the IRR method relative to the NPV technique.

One advantage of the NPV method is that it's expressed in dollars, not in percentages. Therefore, we can sum NPVs of individual projects to calculate an NPV of a combination or portfolio of projects. In contrast, the IRRs of individual projects cannot be added or averaged to represent the IRR of a combination of projects.

---

[3] More detailed explanations of the preeminence of the NPV criterion can be found in corporate finance texts.

A second advantage of NPV is that it can be expressed as a unique number. From the sign and magnitude of this number, the firm can then make an accurate assessment of the financial consequences of accepting or rejecting the project. Under the IRR method, it is possible that more than one IRR may exist for a given project. In other words, there may be multiple discount rates that equate the NPV of a set of cash flows to zero. This is especially true when the signs of the cash flows switch over time; that is, when there are outflows, followed by inflows, followed by additional outflows, and so forth. In such cases, it is difficult to know which of the IRR estimates should be compared to the firm's required rate of return.

A third advantage of the NPV method is that it can be used when the RRR varies over the life of a project. Suppose Vector's management sets an RRR of 10% per year in years 1 and 2 and 14% per year in years 3, 4, and 5. Total present value of the cash inflows can be calculated as $633,780 (computations not shown). It is not possible to use the IRR method in this case. That's because different RRRs in different years mean there is no single RRR that the IRR (a single figure) can be compared against to decide if the project should be accepted or rejected.

Finally, in some situations, the IRR method is prone to indicating erroneous decisions. This can occur when mutually exclusive projects with unequal lives or unequal levels of initial investment are being compared to one another. The reason is that the IRR method implicitly assumes that project cash flows can be reinvested at the *project's* rate of return. The NPV method, in contrast, accurately assumes that project cash flows can only be reinvested at the *company's* required rate of return.

Despite its limitations, the IRR method is widely used.[4] Why? Probably because managers find the percentage return computed under the IRR method easy to understand and compare. Moreover, in most instances where a single project is being evaluated, their decisions would likely be unaffected by using IRR or NPV.

Sensitivity Analysis

To present the basics of the NPV and IRR methods, we have assumed that the expected values of cash flows will occur *for certain*. In reality, there is much uncertainty associated with predicting future cash flows. To examine how a result will change if the predicted financial outcomes are not achieved or if an underlying assumption changes, managers use *sensitivity analysis*, or "what-if" technique.

A common way to apply sensitivity analysis for capital budgeting decisions is to vary each of the inputs to the NPV calculation by a certain percentage and assess the effect on the project's NPV. Sensitivity analysis can take on other forms as well. Suppose a manager at Vector believes the firm's forecasted cash flows are difficult to predict. She asks, "What are the minimum annual cash inflows that make the investment in a new hybrid bus acceptable—that is, what inflows lead to an $NPV = \$0$?" For the data in Exhibit 2, let A = annual cash flow and let the NPV = $0. The net initial investment is $648,900, and the present value factor at the 8% required annual rate of return for a 5-year annuity of $1 is 3.993. Then

$$NPV = \$0$$
$$3.993A - \$648{,}900 = \$0$$
$$3.993A = \$648{,}900$$
$$A = \$162{,}509$$

At the discount rate of 8% per year, the annual (after tax) cash inflows can decrease to $162,509 (a decline of $180,000 − $162,509 = $17,491) before the NPV falls to $0. If the manager believes she can attain annual cash inflows of at least $162,509, she can justify investing in the hybrid bus on financial grounds.

---

[4] In a survey, John Graham and Campbell Harvey found that 75.7% of CFOs always or almost always used IRR for capital budgeting decisions, while a slightly smaller number, 74.9%, always or almost always used the NPV criterion.

Exhibit 4

Net Present Value Calculations for Vector's Hybrid Bus Under Different Assumptions of Annual Cash Flows and Required Rates of Return[a]

	A	B	C	D	E	F
1	Required	Annual Cash Flows				
2	Rate of Return	$ 140,000	$160,000	$180,000	$200,000	$220,000
3	8%	$ (89,880)	$ (10,020)	$ 69,840	$149,700	$229,560
4	10%	$(118,160)	$ (42,340)	$ 33,480	$109,300	$185,120
5	12%	$(144,200)	$ (72,100)	$ 0	$ 72,100	$144,200
6						
7	[a]All calculated amounts assume the project's useful life is 5 years.					

Exhibit 4 shows that variations in the annual cash inflows or the RRR significantly affect the NPV of the hybrid bus project. NPVs can also vary with different useful lives of a project. Sensitivity analysis helps managers to focus on decisions that are most sensitive to different assumptions and to worry less about decisions that are not so sensitive. It is also an important risk-management tool because it provides information to managers about the downside risks of projects as well as their potential impact on the health of the overall firm.

Decision Point

What are the two primary discounted cash flow (DCF) methods for project evaluation?

Payback Method

Learning Objective 3

Use and evaluate the payback and discounted payback methods

...to calculate the time it takes to recoup the investment

We now consider the third method for analyzing the financial aspects of projects. The **payback method** measures the time it will take to recoup, in the form of expected future cash flows, the net initial investment in a project. Like the NPV and IRR methods, the payback method does not distinguish among the sources of cash flows, such as those from operations, purchase or sale of equipment, or investment or recovery of working capital. As you will see, the payback method is simpler to calculate when a project has uniform cash flows than when cash flows are uneven over time.

Uniform Cash Flows

The hybrid bus Vector is considering buying costs $648,900 and generates a *uniform* $180,000 in cash flow every year of its 5-year expected useful life. The payback period is calculated as follows:

$$\text{Payback period} = \frac{\text{Net initial investment}}{\text{Uniform increase in annual future cash flows}}$$

$$= \frac{\$648,900}{\$180,000} = 3.6 \text{ years}[5]$$

The payback method highlights liquidity, a factor that often plays a role in capital budgeting decisions, particularly when the investments are large. Managers prefer projects with shorter payback periods (projects that are more liquid) to projects with longer payback periods, if all other things are equal. Projects with shorter payback periods give an organization more flexibility because funds for other projects become available sooner. Also, managers are less confident about cash flow predictions that stretch far into the future, again favoring shorter payback periods.

Unlike the NPV and IRR methods where managers select the RRR, under the payback method, managers choose a cutoff period for the project. Projects with payback

---

[5] Cash inflows from the new hybrid bus occur uniformly *throughout* the year, but for simplicity in calculating NPV and IRR, we assume they occur at the *end* of each year. A literal interpretation of this assumption would imply a payback of 4 years because Vector will only recover its investment when cash inflows occur at the end of year 4. The calculations shown in the chapter, however, better approximate Vector's payback on the basis of uniform cash flows throughout the year.

periods that are shorter than the cutoff period are considered acceptable, and those with payback periods that are longer than the cutoff period are rejected. Japanese companies favor the payback method over other methods and use cutoff periods ranging from 3 to 5 years depending on the risks involved with the project.[6] In general, modern risk management calls for using shorter cutoff periods for riskier projects. If Vector's cutoff period under the payback method is 3 years, it will reject the new bus.

The payback method is easy to understand. As in DCF methods, the payback method is not affected by accrual accounting conventions such as depreciation. Payback is a useful measure when (1) preliminary screening of many proposals is necessary, (2) interest rates are high, and (3) the expected cash flows in later years of a project are highly uncertain. Under these conditions, companies give much more weight to cash flows in early periods of a capital budgeting project and to recovering the investments they have made, thereby making the payback criterion especially relevant.

Two weaknesses of the payback method are that (1) it fails to explicitly incorporate the time value of money and (2) it does not consider a project's cash flows after the payback period. Consider an alternative to the $648,900 hybrid bus. Another hybrid bus, one with a 3-year useful life and no terminal disposal value, requires only a $540,000 net initial investment and will also result in cash inflows of $180,000 per year. First, compare the payback periods:

$$\text{Bus 1} = \frac{\$648,900}{\$180,000} = 3.6 \text{ years}$$

$$\text{Bus 2} = \frac{\$540,000}{\$180,000} = 3.0 \text{ years}$$

The payback criterion favors bus 2, which has a shorter payback. If the cutoff period were 3 years, bus 1 would fail to meet the payback criterion.

Consider next the NPV of the two investment options using Vector's 8% required rate of return for the hybrid bus investment. At a discount rate of 8%, the NPV of bus 2 is −$76,140 (2.577, the present value annuity factor for 3 years at 8% per year from Table 4, times $180,000 = $463,860 minus net initial investment of $540,000). Bus 1, as we know, has a positive NPV of $69,840 (from Exhibit 2). The NPV criterion suggests Vector should acquire bus 1. Bus 2, which has a negative NPV, would fail to meet the NPV criterion.

The payback method gives a different answer from the NPV method in this example because the payback method ignores cash flows after the payback period and ignores the time value of money. Another problem with the payback method is that choosing too short a cutoff period can lead to projects with high short-run cash flows being selected. Projects with long-run, positive NPVs will tend to be rejected. Despite these differences, companies find it useful to look at both NPV and payback when making capital investment decisions.

Nonuniform Cash Flows

When cash flows are not uniform, the payback computation takes a cumulative form: The cash flows over successive years are accumulated until the amount of net initial investment is recovered. Suppose Venture Law Group is considering purchasing video-conferencing equipment for $150,000. The equipment is expected to provide a total cash savings of $340,000 over the next 5 years, due to reduced travel costs and more effective use of associates' time. The cash savings occur uniformly throughout each year but are not uniform across years.

---

[6] A 2010 survey of Japanese firms found that 50.2% of them often or always used the payback method to make capital budgeting decisions. The NPV method came in a distant second at 30.5% (see Tomonari Shinoda, "Capital Budgeting Management Practices in Japan," *Economic Journal of Hokkaido University* 39 (2010): 39–50).

Year	Cash Savings	Cumulative Cash Savings	Net Initial Investment Unrecovered at End of Year
0	—	—	$150,000
1	$50,000	$ 50,000	100,000
2	55,000	105,000	45,000
3	60,000	165,000	—
4	85,000	250,000	—
5	90,000	340,000	—

The chart shows that payback occurs during the third year. Straight-line interpolation within the third year reveals that the final $45,000 needed to recover the $150,000 investment (that is, $150,000 − $105,000 recovered by the end of year 2) will be achieved three-quarters of the way through year 3 (in which $60,000 of cash savings occur):

$$\text{Payback period} = 2 \text{ years} + \left(\frac{\$45,000}{\$60,000} \times 1 \text{ year} \right) = 2.75 \text{ years}$$

It is relatively simple to adjust the payback method to incorporate the time value of money by using a similar cumulative approach. The **discounted payback method** calculates the amount of time required for the discounted expected future cash flows to recoup the net initial investment in a project. For the videoconferencing example, we can modify the preceding chart by discounting the cash flows at the 8% required rate of return.

Year (1)	Cash Savings (2)	Present Value of $1 Discounted at 8% (3)	Discounted Cash Savings (4) = (2) × (3)	Cumulative Discounted Cash Savings (5)	Net Initial Investment Unrecovered at End of Year (6)
0	—	1.000	—	—	$150,000
1	$50,000	0.926	$46,300	$ 46,300	103,700
2	55,000	0.857	47,135	93,435	56,565
3	60,000	0.794	47,640	141,075	8,925
4	85,000	0.735	62,475	203,550	—
5	90,000	0.681	61,290	264,840	—

The fourth column shows the present values of the future cash savings. It is evident from the chart that discounted payback occurs between years 3 and 4. At the end of the third year, $8,925 of the initial investment is still unrecovered. Comparing this to the $62,475 in present value of savings achieved in the fourth year, straight-line interpolation then reveals that the discounted payback period is exactly one-seventh of the way into the fourth year:

$$\text{Discounted payback period} = 3 \text{ years} + \left(\frac{\$8,925}{\$62,475} \times 1 \text{ year} \right) = 3.14 \text{ years}$$

The discounted payback does incorporate the time value of money, but is still subject to the other criticism of the payback method—that cash flows beyond the discounted payback period are ignored, resulting in a bias toward projects with high short-run cash flows. Companies such as Hewlett-Packard value the discounted payback method (HP refers to it as "breakeven time") because they view longer-term cash flows as inherently unpredictable in high-growth industries, such as technology.

Finally, the videoconferencing example has a single cash outflow of $150,000 in year 0. When a project has multiple cash outflows occurring at different points in time, these outflows are first aggregated to obtain a total cash-outflow figure for the project. For computing the payback period, the cash flows are simply added, with no adjustment for the time value of money. For calculating the discounted payback period, the present values of the outflows are added instead.

Decision Point

What are the payback and discounted payback methods? What are their main weaknesses?

**Learning
Objective** 4

Use and evaluate the
accrual accounting
rate-of-return (AARR)
method

...after-tax operating
income divided by
investment

Accrual Accounting Rate-of-Return Method

We now consider a fourth method for analyzing the financial aspects of capital budgeting projects. The **accrual accounting rate-of-return (AARR) method** divides the average annual (accrual accounting) income of a project by a measure of the investment in it. We illustrate this method for Vector using the project's net initial investment as the amount in the denominator:

$$\frac{\text{Accrual accounting}}{\text{rate of return}} = \frac{\begin{array}{c}\text{Increase in expected average}\\\text{annual after-tax operating income}\end{array}}{\text{Net initial investment}}$$

If Vector purchases the new hybrid bus, its net initial investment is $648,900. The increase in the expected average annual after-tax operating cash inflows is $174,000. This amount is the expected after-tax total operating cash inflows of $870,000 ($180,000 for 4 years and $150,000 in year 5), divided by the time horizon of 5 years. Suppose that the new bus results in additional depreciation deductions of $120,000 per year ($132,000 in annual depreciation for the new bus, relative to $12,000 per year on the existing bus).[7] The increase in the expected average annual after-tax income is therefore $54,000 (the difference between the cash flow increase of $174,000 and the depreciation increase of $120,000). The AARR on net initial investment is computed as:

$$AARR = \frac{\$174,000 - \$120,000}{\$648,900} = \frac{\$54,000 \text{ per year}}{\$648,900} = 0.083, \text{ or } 8.3\% \text{ per year}$$

The 8.3% figure for AARR indicates the average rate at which a dollar of investment generates after-tax operating income. The new hybrid bus has a low AARR for two reasons: (1) the use of the net initial investment as the denominator and (2) the use of income as the numerator, which necessitates deducting depreciation charges from the annual operating cash flows. To mitigate the first issue, many companies calculate AARR using an average level of investment. This alternative procedure recognizes that the book value of the investment declines over time. In its simplest form, average investment for Vector is calculated as the arithmetic mean of the net initial investment of $648,900 and the net terminal cash flow of $30,000 (terminal disposal value of hybrid bus of $0, plus the terminal recovery of working capital of $30,000):

$$\frac{\text{Average investment}}{\text{over 5 years}} = \frac{\text{Net initial investment} + \text{Net terminal cash flow}}{2}$$

$$= \frac{\$648,900 + \$30,000}{2} = \$339,450$$

The AARR on average investment is then calculated as follows:

$$AARR = \frac{\$54,000}{\$339,450} = 0.159, \text{ or } 15.9\% \text{ per year}$$

Our point here is that companies vary in how they calculate the AARR. There is no uniformly preferred approach. Be sure you understand how the AARR is defined in each individual situation. Projects with AARRs that exceed a specific required rate of return are regarded as acceptable (the higher the AARR, the better the project is considered to be).

The AARR method is similar to the IRR method in that both calculate a rate-of-return percentage. The AARR method calculates the return using operating-income numbers after considering accruals and taxes, whereas the IRR method calculates the return using after-tax cash flows and the time value of money. Because cash flows and time value of money are central to capital budgeting decisions, the IRR method is regarded as better than the AARR method.

---

[7] We provide further details on these numbers in the next section.

AARR computations are easy to understand, and they use numbers reported in the financial statements. The AARR gives managers an idea of how the accounting numbers they will report in the future will be affected if a project is accepted. Unlike the payback method, which ignores cash flows after the payback period, the AARR method considers income earned *throughout* a project's expected useful life. Unlike the NPV method, the AARR method uses accrual accounting income numbers, it does not track cash flows, and it ignores the time value of money. Critics of the AARR method argue that these are its drawbacks.

Overall, keep in mind that companies frequently use multiple methods for evaluating capital investment decisions. When different methods lead to different rankings of projects, more weight should be given to the NPV method because the assumptions made by the NPV method are most consistent with making decisions that maximize a company's value.

Decision Point

What are the strengths and weaknesses of the accrual accounting rate-of-return (AARR) method for evaluating long-term projects?

Relevant Cash Flows in Discounted Cash Flow Analysis

Learning Objective 5

Identify relevant cash inflows and outflows for capital budgeting decisions

...the differences in expected future cash flows resulting from the investment

So far, we have examined methods for evaluating long-term projects in settings where the expected future cash flows of interest were assumed to be known. One of the biggest challenges in capital budgeting, particularly DCF analysis, however, is determining which cash flows are relevant in making an investment selection. Relevant cash flows are the differences in expected future cash flows as a result of making the investment. In the Vector example, the relevant cash flows are the differences in expected future cash flows that will result from continuing to use one of the firm's old buses versus purchasing a new hybrid bus. *When reading this section, focus on identifying expected future cash flows and the differences in expected future cash flows.*

To illustrate relevant cash flow analysis, consider a more complex version of the Vector example with these additional assumptions:

- Vector is a profitable company. The income tax rate is 40% of operating income each year.
- The before-tax additional operating cash inflows from the hybrid bus are $220,000 in years 1–4 and $170,000 in year 5.
- For tax purposes, Vector uses the straight-line depreciation method and assumes there is no terminal disposal value of the bus.
- Gains or losses on the sale of depreciable assets are taxed at the same rate as ordinary income.
- The tax effects of cash inflows and outflows occur at the same time that the cash inflows and outflows occur.
- Vector uses an 8% required rate of return for discounting after-tax cash flows.

The data for the buses follow:

	Old Bus	New Hybrid Bus
Purchase price	—	$660,000
Current book value	$60,000	—
Current disposal value	28,500	Not applicable
Terminal disposal value five years from now	0	0
Annual depreciation	12,000[a]	132,000[b]
Working capital required	6,000	36,000

[a]$60,000 ÷ 5 years = $12,000 annual depreciation.
[b]$660,000 ÷ 5 years = $132,000 annual depreciation.

Relevant After-Tax Flows

We use the concepts of differential cost and differential revenue. We compare (1) the after-tax cash outflows as a result of replacing the old bus with (2) the additional after-tax cash inflows generated from using the new bus rather than the old bus.

Exhibit 5	

Effect on Cash Flow from Operations, Net of Income Taxes, in Year 1 for Vector's Investment in the New Hybrid Bus

PANEL A: Two Methods Based on the Income Statement

C	Operating cash inflows from investment in bus	$220,000
D	Additional depreciation deduction	120,000
OI	Increase in operating income	100,000
T	Income taxes (Income tax rate $t \times OI$) =	
	40% × $100,000	40,000
NI	Increase in net income	$ 60,000
	Increase in cash flow from operations, net of income taxes	
	Method 1: $C - T$ = $220,000 − $40,000 = $180,000; or	
	Method 2: $NI + D$ = $60,000 + $120,000 = $180,000	

PANEL B: Item-by-Item Method

	Effect of cash operating flows	
C	Operating cash inflows from investment in bus	$220,000
$t \times C$	Deduct income tax cash outflow at 40%	88,000
$C \times (1 - t)$	After-tax cash flow from operations	$132,000
	(excluding the depreciation effect)	
	Effect of depreciation	
D	Additional depreciation deduction, $120,000	
$t \times D$	Income tax cash savings from additional depreciation	
	deduction at 40% × $120,000	48,000
$C \times (1 - t) + t \times D$	Cash flow from operations, net of income taxes	$180,000

As Benjamin Franklin said, "Two things in life are certain: death and taxes." Income taxes are a fact of life for most corporations and individuals. It is important first to understand how income taxes affect cash flows in each year. Exhibit 5 shows how investing in the new bus will affect Vector's cash flow from operations and its income taxes in year 1. Recall that Vector will generate $220,000 in before-tax additional operating cash inflows by investing in the new bus, but it will record additional depreciation of $120,000 ($132,000 − $12,000) for tax purposes.

Panel A shows, using two methods based on the income statement, that the year 1 cash flow from operations, net of income taxes, equals $180,000. The first method focuses on cash items only, the $220,000 operating cash inflows minus income taxes of $40,000. The second method starts with the $60,000 increase in net income (calculated after subtracting the $120,000 additional depreciation deductions for income tax purposes) and adds back the $120,000 because depreciation is an operating cost that reduces net income but is a noncash item itself.

Panel B of Exhibit 5 describes a third method frequently used to compute the cash flow from operations, net of income taxes. The easiest way to interpret the third method is to think of the government as a 40% (equal to the tax rate) partner in Vector. Each time Vector obtains operating cash inflows, C, its income is higher by C, so it will pay 40% of the operating cash inflows (0.40C) in taxes. This results in additional after-tax cash operating flows of $C - 0.40C$, which in this example is $220,000 − (0.40 × $220,000) = $132,000, or $220,000 × (1 − 0.40) = $132,000.

To achieve the higher operating cash inflows, C, Vector incurs higher depreciation charges, D, from investing in the new bus. Depreciation costs do not directly affect cash flows because depreciation is a noncash cost, but higher depreciation cost *lowers* Vector's taxable income by D, saving income tax cash outflows of 0.40D, which in this example is 0.40 × $120,000 = $48,000.

Letting t = tax rate, cash flow from operations, net of income taxes, in this example equals the operating cash inflows, C, minus the tax payments on these inflows, $t \times C$, plus the tax savings on depreciation deductions, $t \times D$: $220,000 − (0.40 × $220,000) + (0.40 × $120,000) = $220,000 − $88,000 + $48,000 = $180,000.

By the same logic, each time Vector has a gain on the sale of assets, G, it will show tax outflows, $t \times G$; and each time Vector has a loss on the sale of assets, L, it will show tax benefits or savings of $t \times L$.

Categories of Cash Flows

A capital investment project typically has three categories of cash flows: (1) the net initial investment in the project, which includes the acquisition of assets and any associated additions to working capital, minus the after-tax cash flow from the disposal of existing assets; (2) the after-tax cash flow from operations (including income tax cash savings from annual depreciation deductions) each year; and (3) the after-tax cash flow from disposing of an asset and recovering any working capital invested at the termination of the project. We use the Vector example to discuss these three categories.

As you work through the cash flows in each category, refer to Exhibit 6. This exhibit sketches the relevant cash flows for Vector's decision to purchase the new bus as described in items 1–3 here. Note that the total relevant cash flows for each year equal the relevant cash flows used in Exhibits 2 and 3 to illustrate the NPV and IRR methods.

1. **Net Initial Investment.** Three components of net-initial-investment cash flows are (a) the cash outflow to purchase the hybrid bus, (b) the cash outflow for working capital, and (c) the after-tax cash inflow from the current disposal of the old bus.

   1a. *Initial bus investment.* These outflows, made for purchasing plant and equipment, occur at the beginning of the project's life and include cash outflows for transporting and installing the equipment. In the Vector example, the $660,000 cost (including transportation and initial preparation) of the hybrid bus is an outflow in year 0. These cash flows are relevant to the capital budgeting decision because they will be incurred only if Vector decides to purchase the new bus.

   1b. *Initial working-capital investment.* Initial investments in plant and equipment are usually accompanied by additional investments in working capital. These additional investments take the form of current assets, such as accounts receivable and inventories, minus current liabilities, such as accounts payable. Working-capital investments are similar to plant and equipment investments in that they require

	Exhibit 6	Relevant Cash Inflows and Outflows for Vector's Hybrid Bus

	A	B	C	D	E	F	G	H
1			Sketch of Relevant Cash Flows at End of Each Year					
2			0	1	2	3	4	5
3	1a.	Initial hybrid bus investment	$(660,000)					
4	1b.	Initial working-capital investment	(30,000)					
5	1c.	After-tax cash inflow from current disposal						
6		of old bus	41,100					
7	Net initial investment		(648,900)					
8	2a.	Annual after-tax cash flow from operations						
9		(excluding the depreciation effect)		$ 132,000	$ 132,000	$ 132,000	$ 132,000	$ 102,000
10	2b.	Income tax savings from annual						
11		depreciation deductions		48,000	48,000	48,000	48,000	48,000
12	3a.	After-tax cash flow from terminal disposal						
13		of bus						0
14	3b.	After-tax cash flow from recovery of						
15		working capital						30,000
16	Total relevant cash flows,							
17		as shown in Exhibits 21-2 and 21-3	$(648,900)	$ 180,000	$180,000	$180,000	$180,000	$180,000
18								

cash. The magnitude of the investment generally increases as a function of the level of additional sales generated by the project. However, the exact relationship varies based on the nature of the project and the operating cycle of the industry. For a given dollar of sales, a maker of heavy equipment, for example, would require more working capital support than Vector, which in turn has to invest more in working capital than a retail grocery store.

The Vector example assumes a $30,000 additional investment in working capital if the hybrid bus is acquired. The additional working-capital investment is the difference between the working capital required to operate the new bus ($36,000) and that required to operate the old bus ($6,000). The $30,000 additional investment, a consequence of the higher cost of replacement batteries and spare parts for the technologically advanced new bus, is a cash outflow in year 0 and is returned, that is, becomes a cash inflow, at the end of year 5.

1c. *After-tax cash flow from current disposal of old bus.* Any cash received from disposal of the old bus is a relevant cash inflow (in year 0) because it is a cash flow that differs between the alternatives of investing and not investing in the new bus. Vector will dispose of the old bus for $28,500 only if it invests in the new hybrid bus. The book value (which is original cost minus accumulated depreciation) of the old equipment is generally irrelevant to the decision because it is a past, or sunk, cost. However, when tax considerations are included, the book value does play a role because it determines the gain or loss on the sale of the bus and, therefore, the taxes paid (or saved) on the transaction.

Consider the tax consequences of disposing of the old bus. We first have to compute the gain or loss on disposal:

Current disposal value of old bus	$ 28,500
Deduct current book value of old bus	60,000
Loss on disposal of bus	$(31,500)

Any loss on the sale of assets lowers taxable income and results in tax savings. The after-tax cash flow from disposal of the old bus is as follows:

Current disposal value of old bus	$28,500
Tax savings on loss (0.40 × $31,500)	12,600
After-tax cash inflow from current disposal of old bus	$41,100

The sum of items **1a**, **1b**, and **1c** appears in Exhibit 6 as the year 0 net initial investment for the new hybrid bus. It equals $648,900 (initial bus investment, $660,000, plus additional working-capital investment, $30,000, minus the after-tax cash inflow from current disposal of the old bus, $41,100).[8]

2. **Cash Flow from Operations.** This category includes the difference between each year's cash flow from operations under the two alternatives. Organizations make capital investments to generate future cash inflows. These inflows may result from producing and selling additional goods or, as for Vector, from savings in fuel, maintenance, and operating costs and the additional revenue from higher ticket prices as well as new customers who wish to take advantage of the greater comfort and accessibility of the hybrid bus. The annual cash flow from operations can be net outflows in some years. For example, Chevron periodically upgrades its oil extraction equipment, and when it does, the cash flow from operations tends to be negative for the site being upgraded. However, in the long run, the upgrades are NPV positive. Always focus on the cash flow from operations, not on revenues and expenses under accrual accounting.

Vector's additional operating cash inflows—$220,000 in each of the first 4 years and $170,000 in the fifth year—are relevant because they are expected future cash flows that will differ depending on whether the firm purchases the new bus. The after-tax effects of these cash flows follow.

---

[8] To illustrate the case when there is a gain on disposal, suppose that the old bus could be sold now for $70,000 instead. Then the firm would record a gain on disposal of $10,000 ($70,000 less the book value of $60,000), resulting in additional tax payments of $4,000 (0.40 tax rate × $10,000 gain). The after-tax cash inflow from current disposal would therefore equal $66,000 (the disposal value of $70,000, less the tax payment of $4,000).

2a. *Annual after-tax cash flow from operations (excluding the depreciation effect).* The 40% tax rate reduces the benefit of the $220,000 additional operating cash inflows for years 1–4 with the new hybrid bus. The after-tax cash flow (excluding the depreciation effect) is:

Annual cash flow from operations with new bus	$220,000
Deduct income tax payments (0.40 × $220,000)	88,000
Annual after-tax cash flow from operations	$132,000

For year 5, the after-tax cash flow (excluding the depreciation effect) is as follows:

Annual cash flow from operations with new bus	$170,000
Deduct income tax payments (0.40 × $170,000)	68,000
Annual after-tax cash flow from operations	$102,000

Exhibit 6, item **2a**, shows that the after-tax cash flows are $132,000 in each of years 1 through 4 and $102,000 for year 5.

To reinforce the idea about focusing on cash flows, consider the following additional fact about Vector. Suppose its total administrative costs will not change whether the company purchases a new bus or keeps the old one. The administrative costs are allocated to individual buses—Vector has several—on the basis of the costs for operating each bus. Because the new hybrid bus would have lower operating costs, the administrative costs allocated to it would be $30,000 less than the amount allocated to the bus it would replace. How should Vector incorporate the $30,000 decrease in allocated administrative costs in the relevant cash flow analysis?

To answer that question, we need to ask, "Do *total* administrative costs decrease at Vector Transport as a result of acquiring the new bus?" In our example, they do not. They remain the same whether or not the new bus is acquired. *Only the administrative costs allocated to individual buses change.* The administrative costs allocated to the new bus are $30,000 less than the amount allocated to the bus it would replace. This $30,000 difference in costs would be allocated to *other* buses in the company. That is, no cash flow savings in total costs would occur. Therefore, the $30,000 should not be included as part of the annual cash savings from operations.

Next consider the effects of depreciation. *The depreciation line item is itself irrelevant in a DCF analysis.* That's because depreciation is a noncash allocation of costs, whereas DCF is based on inflows and outflows of *cash*. If a DCF method is used, the initial cost of equipment is regarded as a *lump-sum* outflow of cash in year 0. Deducting depreciation expenses from operating cash inflows would result in counting the lump-sum amount twice. *However, depreciation results in income tax cash savings. These tax savings are a relevant cash flow.*

2b. *Income tax cash savings from annual depreciation deductions.* Tax deductions for depreciation, in effect, partially offset the cost of acquiring the new hybrid bus. By purchasing the new bus, Vector is able to deduct $132,000 in depreciation each year, relative to the $12,000 depreciation on the old bus. The additional annual depreciation deduction of $120,000 results in incremental income tax cash savings of $120,000 × 0.4, or $48,000 annually. Exhibit 6, item **2b**, shows these $48,000 amounts for years 1 through 5.[9]

For economic-policy reasons, usually to encourage (or in some cases, discourage) investments, tax laws specify which depreciation methods and which depreciable lives are permitted. Suppose the government permitted accelerated depreciation to be used, allowing for higher depreciation deductions in earlier years. Should Vector then use accelerated depreciation? Yes, because there is a general rule in tax planning for profitable companies such as Vector: When there

---

[9] If Vector were a nonprofit foundation not subject to income taxes, cash flow from operations would equal $220,000 in years 1 through 4 and $170,000 in year 5. The revenues would not be reduced by 40% nor would there be income tax cash savings from the depreciation deduction.

is a legal choice, take the depreciation (or any other deduction) sooner rather than later. Doing so causes the (cash) income tax savings to occur earlier, which increases a project's NPV.

3. **Terminal Disposal of Investment.** The disposal of an investment generally increases cash inflow of a project at its termination. An error in forecasting the disposal value is seldom critical for a long-duration project because the present value of the amounts to be received in the distant future is usually small. For Vector, the two components of the terminal disposal value of an investment are (a) the after-tax cash flow from the terminal disposal of buses and (b) the after-tax cash flow from recovery of working capital.

3a. *After-tax cash flow from terminal disposal of buses.* At the end of the useful life of the project, the bus's terminal disposal value is usually considerably less than the net initial investment (and sometimes zero). The relevant cash inflow is the difference in the expected after-tax cash inflow from terminal disposal at the end of 5 years under the two alternatives. Disposing of both the existing and the new bus will result in a zero after-tax cash inflow in year 5. Hence, there is no difference in the disposal-related after-tax cash inflows of the two alternatives.

Because both the existing and new bus have disposal values that equal their book values at the time of their disposal (in each case, this value is $0), there are no tax effects for either alternative. What if either the existing or the new bus had a terminal value that differed from its book value at the time of disposal? In that case, the approach for computing the terminal inflow is identical to that for calculating the after-tax cash flow from current disposal illustrated earlier in part 1c.

3b. *After-tax cash flow from terminal recovery of working-capital investment.* The initial investment in working capital is usually fully recouped when the project is terminated. At that time, inventories and accounts receivable necessary to support the project are no longer needed. Vector receives cash equal to the book value of its working capital. Thus, there is no gain or loss on working capital and, hence, no tax consequences. The relevant cash inflow is the difference in the expected working capital recovered under the two alternatives. At the end of year 5, Vector recovers $36,000 cash from working capital if it invests in the new hybrid bus versus $6,000 if it continues to use the old bus. The relevant cash inflow at the end of year 5 if Vector invests in the new bus is thus $30,000 ($36,000 − $6,000).

Some capital investment projects *reduce* working capital. Assume that a computer-integrated manufacturing (CIM) project with a 7-year life will reduce inventories and, hence, working capital by $20 million from, say, $50 million to $30 million. This reduction will be represented as a $20 million cash *inflow* for the project in year 0. At the end of 7 years, the recovery of working capital will show a relevant incremental cash *outflow* of $20 million. That's because, at the end of year 7, the company recovers only $30 million of working capital under CIM, rather than the $50 million of working capital it would have recovered had it not implemented CIM.

Exhibit 6 shows items **3a** and **3b** in the "year 5" column. The relevant cash flows in Exhibit 6 serve as inputs for the four capital budgeting methods described earlier in the chapter.

Decision Point ▶

What are the relevant cash inflows and outflows for capital budgeting decisions? How should accrual accounting concepts be considered?

Learning Objective 6 ▶

Understand issues involved in implementing capital budgeting decisions and evaluating managerial performance

...the importance of post-investment audits and the correct choice of performance measures

Project Management and Performance Evaluation

We have so far looked at ways to identify relevant cash flows and techniques for analyzing them. The final stage (stage 5) of capital budgeting begins with implementing the decision and managing the project.[10] This includes management control of the investment activity itself, as well as the project as a whole.

---

[10] In this section, we do not consider the different options for financing a project (refer to a text on corporate finance for details).

Capital budgeting projects, such as purchasing a hybrid bus or videoconferencing equipment, are easier to implement than projects involving building shopping malls or manufacturing plants. The building projects are more complex, so monitoring and controlling the investment schedules and budgets are critical to successfully completing the investment activity. This leads to the second dimension of stage 5 in the capital budgeting process: evaluate performance and learn.

Post-Investment Audits

A post-investment audit provides managers with feedback about the performance of a project so they can compare the actual results to the costs and benefits expected at the time the project was selected. Suppose the actual outcomes (such as the additional operating cash flows from Vector's purchase of a new hybrid bus) are much lower than expected. Managers must then determine if this result occurred because the original estimates were overly optimistic or because of implementation problems. Either of these explanations is a concern.

Optimistic estimates can result in managers accepting a project they should reject. To discourage unrealistic forecasts, companies such as DuPont maintain records comparing the actual results of the firm's projects to the estimates individual managers either made or signed off on when seeking approval for capital investments. Post-investment audits prevent managers from overstating the expected cash inflows from projects and accepting projects they should reject. Implementation problems, such as weak project management, poor quality control, or inadequate marketing, are also a concern. Post-investment audits help to alert senior management to these problems so they can be quickly corrected.

Companies should perform post-investment audits with thought and care, and only after the outcomes of projects are fully known. Performing audits too early can be misleading. In addition, obtaining actual results to compare against estimates is often difficult. For example, in any particular period, macroeconomic factors, such as the weather and changes in fuel prices, can greatly affect the ridership on buses and the costs of running them. Consequently, the overall additional net revenues from Vector's new hybrid bus may not be immediately comparable to the estimated revenues. A better evaluation would look at the average revenues across a couple of seasons.

Performance Evaluation

As the preceding discussion suggests, ideally one should evaluate managers on a project-by-project basis and look at how well managers achieve the amounts and timing of forecasted cash flows. In practice, however, companies often evaluate managers based on aggregate information, especially when multiple projects are under way at any point in time. It is important then for companies to ensure that the method of evaluation does not conflict with the use of the NPV method for making capital budgeting decisions. For example, suppose Vector uses the accrual accounting rate of return generated in each period to assess its managers. We know the managers should purchase the hybrid bus because it has a positive NPV of $69,840. However, they may reject the project if the AARR of 8.3% on the net initial investment is lower than the minimum accounting rate of return Vector requires them to achieve.

There is an inconsistency between promoting the NPV method as best for capital budgeting decisions and then using a different method to evaluate performance. Even though the NPV method is best for capital budgeting decisions, managers will be tempted to make those decisions based on the method on which they are being evaluated. The temptation becomes more pronounced if managers are frequently transferred (or promoted) or if their bonuses are affected by the level of year-to-year income earned under accrual accounting.

Other conflicts between decision making and performance evaluation persist even if a company uses similar measures for both purposes. If the AARR on the hybrid bus exceeds the minimum required AARR but is below Vector's current AARR in the region, the manager may still be tempted to reject purchase of the hybrid bus because the lower AARR of the hybrid bus will reduce the AARR of the entire region and hurt the manager's reported performance. Or consider an example where the cash inflows from the hybrid bus occur mostly in the later years of the project. Then, even if the project's AARR exceeds the current AARR of the projects overseen by the manager (as well as the minimum

◄ **Decision Point**
What conflicts can arise between using DCF methods for capital budgeting decisions and accrual accounting for performance evaluation? How can these conflicts be reduced?

required return), the manager may still reject the purchase because for the first few years it will have a negative effect on the rate of return earned under accrual accounting.

Learning Objective 7

Explain how managers can use capital budgeting to achieve their firms' strategic goals

...make critical investments aligned with the firm's objectives but whose benefits are uncertain or difficult to estimate

Strategic Considerations in Capital Budgeting

Managers consider a company's strategic goals when making capital budgeting decisions. Strategic decisions by United Airlines, Westin Hotels, FedEx, and Pizza Hut to expand in Europe and Asia required capital investments in several countries (also see Concepts in Action: International Capital Budgeting at Disney). The strategic decision by Barnes & Noble to support book sales over the Internet required capital investments creating barnesandnoble.com and an Internet infrastructure. AOL's desire to create an enhanced digital destination with greater appeal for consumers and advertisers led to its purchase of *The Huffington Post*, as well as increased investment in editorial staff and sales representatives and higher marketing expenses. AstraZeneca's decision to develop Nexium as a patented replacement drug for its blockbuster Prilosec to prevent the formation of gastric acid led to major investments in R&D and marketing. Toyota's decision to offer a line of hybrids across both its Toyota and Lexus platforms required start-up investments to form a hybrid division and ongoing investments to fund the division's continuing research efforts.

Concepts in Action ▶ International Capital Budgeting at Disney

The Walt Disney Company, one of the world's leading entertainment producers with $42 billion in 2012 revenue, spends about $1 billion annually in capital investments on its theme park business. These funds are invested in new theme parks, rides and attractions, and other park construction and improvements.

Years ago, Disney developed a robust capital budgeting approval process. Project approval relied heavily on projected returns on capital investment as measured by net present value (NPV) and internal rate-of-return (IRR) calculations. This worked well for Disney's investments in its domestic theme park business, but the company experienced challenges when it considered building the DisneySea theme park near Tokyo, Japan.

While capital budgeting in the United States relies on discounted cash flow analysis, Japanese firms frequently use the average accounting return (AAR) method instead. AAR is analogous to an accrual accounting rate-of-return (AARR) measure based on average investment. However, it focuses on the first few years of a project (5 years, in the case of DisneySea) and ignores terminal values.

Disney discovered that the difference in capital budgeting techniques between U.S. and Japanese firms reflected the difference in corporate governance in the two countries. The use of NPV and IRR in the United States underlined a focus on shareholder-value maximization. On the other hand, the preference for AAR in Japan reflected the importance of achieving complete consensus among all parties affected by the investment decision.

When the DisneySea project was evaluated, it was found to have a positive NPV but a negative AAR. To account for the differences in philosophies and capital budgeting techniques, managers at Disney introduced a third calculation method called average cash flow return (ACFR). This hybrid method measured the average cash flow over the first 5 years, with the asset assumed to be sold for book value at the end of that period as a fraction of the initial investment in the project. The resulting ratio was found to exceed the return on Japanese government bonds and hence to yield a positive return for DisneySea. As a result, the park was constructed next to Tokyo Disneyland and has since become a profitable addition to Disney's Japanese operations.

Sources: Misawa, Mitsuru. 2006. Tokyo Disneyland and the DisneySea Park: Corporate governance and differences in capital budgeting concepts and methods between American and Japanese companies. University of Hong Kong No. HKU568, Hong Kong: University of Hong Kong Asia Case Research Center; and The Walt Disney Company. 2013. 2012 annual report. Burbank, CA: The Walt Disney Company.

Capital investment decisions that are strategic in nature require managers to consider a broad range of factors that may be difficult to estimate. Consider some of the difficulties of justifying investments made by companies such as Mitsubishi, Sony, and Audi in computer-integrated manufacturing (CIM) technology. In CIM, computers give instructions that quickly and automatically set up and run equipment to manufacture many different products. Quantifying these benefits requires some notion of how quickly consumer demand will change in the future. CIM technology also increases worker knowledge of and experience with automation; however, the benefit of this knowledge and experience is difficult to measure. Managers must develop judgment and intuition to make these decisions.

Investment in Research and Development

Companies such as GlaxoSmithKline, in the pharmaceutical industry, and Intel, in the semiconductor industry, regard R&D projects as important strategic investments. The distant payoffs from R&D investments, however, are more uncertain than other investments such as new equipment purchases. On the positive side, R&D investments are often staged: As time unfolds, companies can increase or decrease the resources committed to a project based on how successful it has been up to that point. This option feature of R&D investments, called real options, is an important aspect of R&D investments and increases the NPV of these investments because a company can limit its losses when things are going badly and take advantage of new opportunities when things are going well. As an example, a pharmaceutical company can increase or decrease its investment in an R&D joint venture based on the progress of the clinical trials of new drugs being developed by the venture.

Customer Value and Capital Budgeting

Finally, note that managers can use the framework described in this chapter to both evaluate investment projects and to make strategic decisions regarding which customers to invest in. Consider Potato Supreme, which makes potato products for sale to retail outlets. It is currently analyzing two of its customers: Shine Stores and Always Open. Potato Supreme predicts the following cash flow from operations, net of income taxes (in thousands), from each customer account for the next 5 years:

	2014	2015	2016	2017	2018
Shine Stores	$1,450	$1,305	$1,175	$1,058	$ 950
Always Open	690	1,160	1,900	2,950	4,160

Which customer is more valuable to Potato Supreme? Looking at only the current period, 2014, Shine Stores provides more than double the cash flow compared to Always Open ($1,450 versus $690). A different picture emerges, however, if you look at the entire 5-year horizon. Potato Supreme anticipates Always Open's orders to increase; meanwhile, it expects Shine Stores' orders to decline. Using Potato Supreme's 10% RRR, the NPV of the Always Open customer is $7,610, compared with $4,591 for Shine Stores (computations not shown). Note how NPV captures in its estimate of customer value the future growth of Always Open. Potato Supreme uses this information to allocate more resources and salespeople to service the Always Open account. Potato Supreme can also use NPV calculations to examine the effects of alternative ways of increasing customer loyalty and retention, such as introducing frequent-purchaser cards.

A comparison of year-to-year changes in customer NPV estimates highlights whether managers have been successful in maintaining long-run profitable relationships with their customers. Suppose the NPV of Potato Supreme's customer accounts declines by 15% in a year. The firm's managers can then examine the reasons for the decline, such as aggressive pricing by competitors, and devise new-product development and marketing strategies for the future.

Capital One, a financial-services company, uses NPV to estimate the value of different credit-card customers. Cellular telephone companies such as Sprint and Verizon Wireless attempt to sign up customers for multiple years of service. The objective is to prevent "customer churn"—that is, customers switching frequently from one company to another. The higher the probability is of a customer switching, the lower the customer's NPV.

◀ **Decision Point**

How can managers use capital budgeting to achieve strategic goals?

Problem for Self-Study

Part A

Returning to the Vector hybrid bus project, assume that Vector is a *nonprofit organization* and that the expected additional operating cash inflows are $240,000 in years 1 through 4 and $210,000 in year 5. Using data given earlier, the net initial investment is $661,500 (new bus, $660,000, plus additional working capital, $30,000, minus terminal disposal value of old bus, $28,500). All other facts are unchanged: a 5-year useful life, no terminal disposal value, and an 8% RRR. Year 5 cash inflows are $240,000, which includes a $30,000 recovery of working capital.

Calculate the following:
1. Net present value
2. Internal rate of return
3. Payback
4. Accrual accounting rate of return on net initial investment

Solution

1. $NPV = (\$240,000 \times 3.993) - \$661,500$

   $= \$958,320 - \$661,500 = \$296,820$

2. There are several approaches to computing IRR. One is to use a calculator with an IRR function. This approach gives an IRR of 23.8%. Another approach is to use Table 4 in Appendix: Notes on Compound Interest and Interest Tables:

$$\$661,500 = \$240,000F$$

$$F = \frac{\$661,500}{\$240,000} = 2.756$$

On the five-period line of Table 4, the column closest to 2.756 is 24%. To obtain a more-accurate number, use straight-line interpolation:

	Present Value Factors	
22%	2.864	2.864
IRR	—	2.756
24%	2.745	—
Difference	0.119	0.108

$$IRR = 22\% + \frac{0.108}{0.119}(2\%) = 23.8\% \text{ per year}$$

3. $\text{Payback period} = \dfrac{\text{Net initial investment}}{\text{Uniform increase in annual future cash flows}}$

   $= \$661,500 \div \$240,000 = 2.76 \text{ years}$

4. $AARR = \dfrac{\text{Increase in expected average annual operating income}}{\text{Net initial investment}}$

   $\text{Increase in expected average annual operating cash inflows} = [(\$240,000 \times 4) + \$210,000] \div 5 \text{ years}$

   $= \$1,170,000 \div 5 = \$234,000$

   $\text{Increase in annual depreciation} = \$120,000(\$132,000 - \$12,000)$

   $\text{Increase in expected average annual operating income} = \$234,000 - \$120,000 = \$114,000$

   $AARR = \dfrac{\$114,000}{\$661,500} = 17.2\% \text{ per year}$

Part B

Assume that Vector is subject to income tax at a 40% rate. All other information from Part A is unchanged. Compute the NPV of the new hybrid bus project.

Solution

To save space, Exhibit 7 shows the calculations using a format slightly different from the format used in this chapter. Item **2a** is where the new cash flow assumptions affect the NPV analysis (compared with Exhibit 6). All other amounts in Exhibit 7 are identical to the corresponding amounts in Exhibit 6. For years 1 through 4, after-tax cash flow (excluding the depreciation effect) is as follows:

Annual cash flow from operations with new bus	$240,000
Deduct income tax payments (0.40 × $240,000)	96,000
Annual after-tax cash flow from operations	$144,000

For year 5, after-tax cash flow (excluding the depreciation effect) is as follows:

Annual cash flow from operations with new bus	$210,000
Deduct income tax payments (0.40 × $210,000)	84,000
Annual after-tax cash flow from operations	$126,000

NPV in Exhibit 7 is $125,928. As computed in Part A, NPV when there are no income taxes is $296,820. The difference in these two NPVs illustrates the impact of income taxes in capital budgeting analysis.

Exhibit 7   Net Present Value Method Incorporating Income Taxes: Vector's Hybrid Bus with Revised Annual Cash Flow from Operations

		Home Insert Page Layout Formulas Data Review View								
	A	B	C	D	E	F	G	H	I	J
1			Present Value	Present Value of		Sketch of Relevant Cash Flows at End of Year				
2			of Cash Flow	$1 Discounted at 8%	0	1	2	3	4	5
3	1a.	Initial hybrid bus investment	$(660,000) ← 1.000 ←		$(660,000)					
4										
5	1b.	Initial working-capital investment	(30,000) ← 1.000 ←		$ (30,000)					
6	1c.	After-tax cash inflow from current disposal								
7		of old bus	41,100 ← 1.000 ←		$ 41,100					
8		Net initial investment	(648,900)							
9	2a.	Annual after-tax cash flow from operations								
10		(excluding the depreciation effect)								
11		Year 1	133,344 ← 0.926 ←			$144,000				
12		Year 2	123,408 ← 0.857 ←				$144,000			
13		Year 3	114,336 ← 0.794 ←					$144,000		
14		Year 4	105,840 ← 0.735 ←						$144,000	
15		Year 5	85,806 ← 0.681 ←							$126,000
16	2b.	Income tax cash savings from annual								
17		depreciation deductions								
18		Year 1	44,448 ← 0.926 ←			$ 48,000				
19		Year 2	41,136 ← 0.857 ←				$ 48,000			
20		Year 3	38,112 ← 0.794 ←					$ 48,000		
21		Year 4	35,280 ← 0.735 ←						$ 48,000	
22		Year 5	32,688 ← 0.681 ←							$ 48,000
23	3.	After-tax cash flow from recovery of								
24		a. Terminal disposal of bus	0 ← 0.681 ←							$ 0
25		b. Recovery of working capital	20,430 ← 0.681 ←							$ 30,000
26		NPV if new hybrid bus purchased	$ 125,928							
27										

▶ Decision Points

The following question-and-answer format summarizes the chapter's learning objectives. Each decision presents a key question related to a learning objective. The guidelines are the answer to that question.

Decision	Guidelines
1. What are the five stages of capital budgeting?	Capital budgeting is long-run planning for proposed investment projects. The five stages of capital budgeting are as follows: (1) Identify projects: Identify potential capital investments aligned with the organization's strategy; (2) Obtain information: Gather information from all parts of the value chain to evaluate alternative projects; (3) Make predictions: Forecast all potential cash flows attributable to the alternative projects; (4) Choose among alternatives: Determine which investment yields the greatest benefit and the least cost to the organization; and (5) Implement the decision, evaluate performance, and learn: Obtain funding and make the investments selected in stage 4; track the realized cash flows, compare them against estimated numbers, and revise plans if necessary.
2. What are the two primary discounted cash flow (DCF) methods for project evaluation?	The two main DCF methods are the net present value (NPV) method and the internal rate-of-return (IRR) method. The NPV method calculates the expected net monetary gain or loss from a project by discounting to the present all expected future cash inflows and outflows, using the required rate of return. A project is acceptable in financial terms if it has a positive NPV. The IRR method computes the rate of return (also called the discount rate) at which a project's present value of expected cash inflows equals the present value of its expected cash outflows. A project is acceptable in financial terms if its IRR exceeds the required rate of return. DCF is the best approach to capital budgeting. It explicitly includes all project cash flows and recognizes the time value of money. The NPV method is the preferred DCF method.
3. What are the payback and discounted payback methods? What are their main weaknesses?	The payback method measures the time it will take to recoup, in the form of cash inflows, the total cash amount invested in a project. The payback method neglects the time value of money and ignores cash flows beyond the payback period. The discounted payback method measures the time taken for the present value of cash inflows to equal the present value of cash outflows. It adjusts for the time value of money but overlooks cash flows after the discounted payback period.
4. What are the strengths and weaknesses of the accrual accounting rate-of-return (AARR) method for evaluating long-term projects?	The accrual accounting rate of return (AARR) divides an accrual accounting measure of average annual income from a project by an accrual accounting measure of its investment. AARR gives managers an idea of how accepting a project will affect a firm's future reported accounting profitability. However, AARR uses accrual accounting income numbers, does not track cash flows, and ignores the time value of money.
5. What are the relevant cash inflows and outflows for capital budgeting decisions? How should accrual accounting concepts be considered?	Relevant cash inflows and outflows in a DCF analysis are the differences in expected future cash flows as a result of making the investment. Only cash inflows and outflows matter; accrual accounting concepts are irrelevant for DCF methods. For example, the income taxes saved as a result of depreciation deductions are relevant because they decrease cash outflows, but the depreciation itself is a noncash item.

Decision	Guidelines
6. What conflicts can arise between using DCF methods for capital budgeting decisions and accrual accounting for performance evaluation? How can these conflicts be reduced?	Using accrual accounting to evaluate the performance of a manager may create conflicts with the use of DCF methods for capital budgeting. Frequently, the decision made using a DCF method will not report good "operating income" results in the project's early years under accrual accounting. For this reason, managers are tempted to not use DCF methods even though the decisions based on them would be in the best interests of the company as a whole over the long run. This conflict can be reduced by evaluating managers on a project-by-project basis and by looking at their ability to achieve the amounts and timing of forecasted cash flows.
7. How can managers use capital budgeting to achieve strategic goals?	A company's strategy is the source of its strategic capital budgeting decisions. Such decisions require managers to consider a broad range of factors that may be difficult to estimate. Managers must develop judgment and intuition to make these decisions. R&D projects, for example, are important strategic investments, with distant and usually highly uncertain payoffs.

Appendix

Capital Budgeting and Inflation

The Vector example (Exhibits 2 to 6) does not include adjustments for inflation in the relevant revenues and costs. **Inflation** is the decline in the general purchasing power of the monetary unit, such as dollars. An inflation rate of 10% per year means that an item bought for $100 at the beginning of the year will cost $110 at the end of the year.

Why is it important to account for inflation in capital budgeting? Because declines in the general purchasing power of the monetary unit will inflate future cash flows above what they would have been in the absence of inflation. These inflated cash flows will cause the project to look better than it really is unless the analyst recognizes that the inflated cash flows are measured in dollars that have less purchasing power than the dollars that were initially invested. When analyzing inflation, distinguish real rate of return from nominal rate of return:

Real rate of return is the rate of return demanded to cover investment risk if there is no inflation. The real rate is made up of two elements: (1) a risk-free element (the pure rate of return on risk-free long-term government bonds when there is no expected inflation) and (2) a business-risk element (that's the risk premium demanded for bearing risk).

Nominal rate of return is the rate of return demanded to cover investment risk and the decline in general purchasing power of the monetary unit as a result of expected inflation. The nominal rate is made up of three elements: (a) a risk-free element when there is no expected inflation, (b) a business-risk element, and (c) an inflation element. Items (a) and (b) make up the real rate of return to cover investment risk. The inflation element is the premium above the real rate. The rates of return earned in the financial markets are nominal rates because investors want to be compensated both for the investment risks they take and for the expected decline in the general purchasing power, as a result of inflation, of the money they get back.

Assume that the real rate of return for investments in high-risk cellular data-transmission equipment at Network Communications is 20% per year and that the expected inflation rate is 10% per year. Nominal rate of return is as follows:

$$\text{Nominal rate} = (1 + \text{Real rate})(1 + \text{Inflation rate}) - 1$$
$$= (1 + 0.20)(1 + 0.10) - 1$$
$$= (1.20 \times 1.10) - 1 = 1.32 - 1 = 0.32, \text{ or } 32\%$$

Nominal rate of return is related to the real rate of return and the inflation rate:

Real rate of return	0.20
Inflation rate	0.10
Combination (0.20 × 0.10)	0.02
Nominal rate of return	0.32

Note the nominal rate, 0.32, is slightly higher than 0.30, the real rate (0.20) plus the inflation rate (0.10). That's because the nominal rate recognizes that inflation of 10% also decreases the purchasing power of the real rate of return of 20% earned during the year. The combination component represents the additional compensation investors seek for the decrease in the purchasing power of the real return earned during the year because of inflation.[11]

Net Present Value Method and Inflation

When incorporating inflation into the NPV method, the key is *internal consistency*. There are two internally consistent approaches:

1. **Nominal approach**—predicts cash inflows and outflows in nominal monetary units *and* uses a nominal rate as the required rate of return
2. **Real approach**—predicts cash inflows and outflows in real monetary units *and* uses a real rate as the required rate of return

We will limit our discussion to the simpler nominal approach. Consider an investment that is expected to generate sales of 100 units and a net cash inflow of $1,000 ($10 per unit) each year for 2 years *absent inflation*. Assume cash flows occur at the end of each year. If inflation of 10% is expected each year, net cash inflows from the sale of each unit would be $11 ($10 × 1.10) in year 1 and $12.10 ($11 × 1.10, or $10 × (1.10)^2) in year 2, resulting in net cash inflows of $1,100 in year 1 and $1,210 in year 2. The net cash inflows of $1,100 and $1,210 are nominal cash inflows because they include the effects of inflation. *Nominal cash flows are the cash flows that are recorded in the accounting system.* The cash inflows of $1,000 each year are real cash flows. The accounting system does not record these cash flows. The nominal approach is easier to understand and apply because it uses nominal cash flows from accounting systems and nominal rates of return from financial markets.

Assume that Network Communications can purchase equipment to make and sell a cellular data-transmission product at a net initial investment of $750,000. It is expected to have a 4-year useful life and no terminal disposal value. An annual inflation rate of 10% is expected over this 4-year period. Network Communications requires an after-tax nominal rate of return of 32%. The following table presents the predicted amounts of real (that's assuming no inflation) and nominal (that's after considering cumulative inflation) net cash inflows from the equipment over the next 4 years (excluding the $750,000 investment in the equipment and before any income tax payments):

Year (1)	Before-Tax Cash Inflows in Real Dollars (2)	Cumulative Inflation Rate Factor[a] (3)	Before-Tax Cash Inflows in Nominal Dollars (4) = (2) × (3)
1	$500,000	$(1.10)^1 = 1.1000$	$550,000
2	600,000	$(1.10)^2 = 1.2100$	726,000
3	600,000	$(1.10)^3 = 1.3310$	798,600
4	300,000	$(1.10)^4 = 1.4641$	439,230

[a]1.10 = 1.00 + 0.10 inflation rate.

---

[11] The real rate of return can be expressed in terms of the nominal rate of return as follows:

$$\text{Real rate} = \frac{1 + \text{Nominal rate}}{1 + \text{Inflation rate}} - 1 = \frac{1 + 0.32}{1 + 0.10} - 1 = 0.20, \text{ or } 20\%$$

Exhibit 8   Net Present Value Method Using Nominal Approach to Inflation for Network Communication's New Equipment

	A	B	C	D	E	F	G	H	I	J	K	L
						Present	Present Value					
1						Value of	Discount Factor[a] at		Sketch of Relevant Cash Flows at End of Each Year			
2						Cash Flow	32%	0	1	2	3	4
3												
4	1.	Net initial investment										
5		Year	Investment Outflows									
6		0	$(750,000)			$(750,000)	←— 1.000 ←—	$(750,000)				
7	2a.	Annual after-tax cash flow from										
8		operations (excluding the depreciation effect)										
9			Annual		Annual							
10			Before-Tax	Income	After-Tax							
11			Cash Flow	Tax	Cash Flow							
12		Year	from Operations	Outflows	from Operations							
13		(1)	(2)	(3) = 0.40 x (2)	(4) = (2) - (3)							
14		1	$550,000	$220,000	$330,000	250,140	←— 0.758 ←—		$330,000			
15		2	726,000	290,400	435,600	250,034	←— 0.574 ←—			$435,600		
16		3	798,600	319,440	479,160	208,435	←— 0.435 ←—				$479,160	
17		4	439,230	175,692	263,538	86,704	←— 0.329 ←—					$263,538
18						795,313						
19	2b.	Income tax cash savings from annual										
20		depreciation deductions										
21		Year	Depreciation	Tax Cash Savings								
22		(1)	(2)	(3) = 0.40 x (2)								
23		1	$187,500[b]	$75,000		56,850	←— 0.758 ←—		$ 75,000			
24		2	187,500	75,000		43,050	←— 0.574 ←—			$ 75,000		
25		3	187,500	75,000		32,625	←— 0.435 ←—				$ 75,000	
26		4	187,500	75,000		24,675	←— 0.329 ←—					$ 75,000
27						157,200						
28	NPV if new equipment purchased					$ 202,513						
29												
30												
31	[a]The nominal discount rate of 32% is made up of the real rate of return of 20% and the inflation rate of 10% [(1 + 0.20) (1 + 1.10)] − 1 = 0.32.											
32	[b]$750,000 ÷ 4 = $187,500											

We continue to make the simplifying assumption that cash flows occur at the end of each year. The income tax rate is 40%. For tax purposes, the cost of the equipment will be depreciated using the straight-line method.

Exhibit 8 shows the calculation of NPV using cash flows in nominal dollars and using a nominal discount rate. The calculations in Exhibit 8 include the net initial bus investment, annual after-tax cash flows from operations (excluding the depreciation effect), and income tax cash savings from annual depreciation deductions. The NPV is $202,513, and, based on financial considerations alone, Network Communications should purchase the equipment.

Terms to Learn

This chapter contains definitions of the following important terms:

accrual accounting rate-of-return
  (AARR) method
capital budgeting
cost of capital
discount rate
discounted cash flow (DCF)
  methods

discounted payback method
hurdle rate
inflation
internal rate-of-return (IRR)
  method
net present value (NPV)
  method

nominal rate of return
opportunity cost of capital
payback method
real rate of return
required rate of return
  (RRR)
time value of money

Assignment Material

Questions

1 "Capital budgeting has the same focus as accrual accounting." Do you agree? Explain.

2 List and briefly describe each of the five stages in capital budgeting.

3 What is the essence of the discounted cash flow methods?

4 "Only quantitative outcomes are relevant in capital budgeting analyses." Do you agree? Explain.

5 How can sensitivity analysis be incorporated in DCF analysis?

6 What is the payback method? What are its main strengths and weaknesses?

7 Describe the accrual accounting rate-of-return method. What are its main strengths and weaknesses?

8 "The trouble with discounted cash flow methods is that they ignore depreciation." Do you agree? Explain.

9 "Let's be more practical. DCF is not the gospel. Managers should not become so enchanted with DCF that strategic considerations are overlooked." Do you agree? Explain.

10 "All overhead costs are relevant in NPV analysis." Do you agree? Explain.

11 Bill Watts, president of Western Publications, accepts a capital budgeting project proposed by division X. This is the division in which the president spent his first 10 years with the company. On the same day, the president rejects a capital budgeting project proposal from division Y. The manager of division Y is incensed. She believes that the division Y project has an internal rate of return at least 10 percentage points higher than the division X project. She comments, "What is the point of all our detailed DCF analysis? If Watts is panting over a project, he can arrange to have the proponents of that project massage the numbers so that it looks like a winner." What advice would you give the manager of division Y?

12 Distinguish different categories of cash flows to be considered in an equipment-replacement decision by a taxpaying company.

13 Describe three ways income taxes can affect the cash inflows or outflows in a motor-vehicle-replacement decision by a taxpaying company.

14 How can capital budgeting tools assist in evaluating a manager who is responsible for retaining customers of a cellular telephone company?

15 Distinguish the nominal rate of return from the real rate of return.

Exercises

16 **Exercises in compound interest, no income taxes.** To be sure that you understand how to use the tables in Appendix: Notes on Compound Interest and Interest Tables, solve the following exercises. Ignore income tax considerations. The correct answers, rounded to the nearest dollar, appear later in the chapter.

1. You have just won $10,000. How much money will you accumulate at the end of 10 years if you invest it at 8% compounded annually? At 10%?

2. Ten years from now, the unpaid principal of the mortgage on your house will be $154,900. How much do you need to invest today at 4% interest compounded annually to accumulate the $154,900 in 10 years?

3. If the unpaid mortgage on your house in 10 years will be $154,900, how much money do you need to invest at the end of each year at 10% to accumulate exactly this amount at the end of the 10th year?

4. You plan to save $7,500 of your earnings at the end of each year for the next 10 years. How much money will you accumulate at the end of the 10th year if you invest your savings compounded at 8% per year?

5. You have just turned 65 and an endowment insurance policy has paid you a lump sum of $250,000. If you invest the sum at 8%, how much money can you withdraw from your account in equal amounts at the end of each year so that at the end of 10 years (age 75) there will be nothing left?

6. You have estimated that for the first 10 years after you retire you will need a cash inflow of $65,000 at the end of each year. How much money do you need to invest at 8% at your retirement age to obtain this annual cash inflow? At 12%?

7. The following table shows two schedules of prospective operating cash inflows, each of which requires the same net initial investment of $10,000 now:

Annual Cash Inflows

Year	Plan A	Plan B
1	$ 3,000	$ 1,000
2	5,000	2,000
3	2,000	3,000
4	3,000	4,000
5	2,000	5,000
Total	$15,000	$15,000

The required rate of return is 8% compounded annually. All cash inflows occur at the end of each year. In terms of net present value, which plan is more desirable? Show your computations.

17 **Capital budgeting methods, no income taxes.** Riverbend Company runs hardware stores in a tristate area. Riverbend's management estimates that if it invests $250,000 in a new computer system, it can save $65,000 in annual cash operating costs. The system has an expected useful life of 8 years and no terminal disposal value. The required rate of return is 8%. Ignore income tax issues in your answers. Assume all cash flows occur at year-end except for initial investment amounts.

1. Calculate the following for the new computer system:
   a. Net present value
   b. Payback period
   c. Discounted payback period
   d. Internal rate of return (using the interpolation method)
   e. Accrual accounting rate of return based on the net initial investment (assume straight-line depreciation)

2. What other factors should Riverbend consider in deciding whether to purchase the new computer system?

Required

18 **Capital budgeting methods, no income taxes.** City Hospital, a nonprofit organization, estimates that it can save $28,000 a year in cash operating costs for the next 10 years if it buys a special-purpose eye-testing machine at a cost of $110,000. No terminal disposal value is expected. City Hospital's required rate of return is 14%. Assume all cash flows occur at year-end except for initial investment amounts. City Hospital uses straight-line depreciation.

1. Calculate the following for the special-purpose eye-testing machine:
   a. Net present value
   b. Payback period
   c. Internal rate of return
   d. Accrual accounting rate of return based on net initial investment
   e. Accrual accounting rate of return based on average investment

2. What other factors should City Hospital consider in deciding whether to purchase the special-purpose eye-testing machine?

Required

19 **Capital budgeting, income taxes.** Assume the same facts as in Exercise 18 except that City Hospital is a taxpaying entity. The income tax rate is 30% for all transactions that affect income taxes.

1. Do requirement 1 of Exercise 18.
2. How would your computations in requirement 1 be affected if the special-purpose machine had a $10,000 terminal disposal value at the end of 10 years? Assume depreciation deductions are based on the $110,000 purchase cost and zero terminal disposal value using the straight-line method. Answer briefly in words without further calculations.

Required

20 **Capital budgeting with uneven cash flows, no income taxes.** America Cola is considering the purchase of a special-purpose bottling machine for $65,000. It is expected to have a useful life of 4 years with no terminal disposal value. The plant manager estimates the following savings in cash operating costs:

Year	Amount
1	$25,000
2	22,000
3	21,000
4	20,000
Total	$88,000

Southern Cola uses a required rate of return of 18% in its capital budgeting decisions. Ignore income taxes in your analysis. Assume all cash flows occur at year-end except for initial investment amounts.

Calculate the following for the special-purpose bottling machine:

Required

1. Net present value
2. Payback period
3. Discounted payback period
4. Internal rate of return (using the interpolation method)
5. Accrual accounting rate of return based on net initial investment (Assume straight-line depreciation. Use the average annual savings in cash operating costs when computing the numerator of the accrual accounting rate of return.)

21 **Comparison of projects, no income taxes.** (CMA, adapted) New Tech Corporation is a rapidly growing biotech company that has a required rate of return of 8%. It plans to build a new facility in Santa Clara County. The building will take 2 years to complete. The building contractor offered New Bio a choice of three payment plans, as follows:

- **Plan I:** Payment of $325,000 at the time of signing the contract and $4,825,000 upon completion of the building. The end of the second year is the completion date.
- **Plan II:** Payment of $1,675,000 at the time of signing the contract and $1,675,000 at the end of each of the 2 succeeding years.
- **Plan III:** Payment of $425,000 at the time of signing the contract and $1,650,000 at the end of each of the 3 succeeding years.

Required

1. Using the net present value method, calculate the comparative cost of each of the three payment plans being considered by New Tech.
2. Which payment plan should New Tech choose? Explain.
3. Discuss the financial factors, other than the cost of the plan, and the nonfinancial factors that should be considered in selecting an appropriate payment plan.

22 **Payback and NPV methods, no income taxes.** (CMA, adapted) Andrews Construction is analyzing its capital expenditure proposals for the purchase of equipment in the coming year. The capital budget is limited to $5,000,000 for the year. Lori Bart, staff analyst at Andrews, is preparing an analysis of the three projects under consideration by Corey Andrews, the company's owner.

	Home	Insert	Page Layout	Formulas	Data	Review	View
		A		B	C	D	
1				Project A	Project B	Project C	
2	Projected cash outflow						
3	Net initial investment			$3,000,000	$1,500,000	$4,000,000	
4							
5	Projected cash inflows						
6	Year 1			$1,000,000	$ 400,000	$2,000,000	
7	Year 2			1,000,000	900,000	2,000,000	
8	Year 3			1,000,000	800,000	200,000	
9	Year 4			1,000,000		100,000	
10							
11	Required rate of return			10%	10%	10%	

1. Because the company's cash is limited, Andrews thinks the payback method should be used to choose between the capital budgeting projects.
   a. What are the benefits and limitations of using the payback method to choose between projects?
   b. Calculate the payback period for each of the three projects. Ignore income taxes. Using the payback method, which projects should Andrews choose?

2. Bart thinks that projects should be selected based on their NPVs. Assume all cash flows occur at the end of the year except for initial investment amounts. Calculate the NPV for each project. Ignore income taxes.

3. Which projects, if any, would you recommend funding? Briefly explain why.

23   DCF, accrual accounting rate of return, working capital, evaluation of performance, no income taxes. Century Lab plans to purchase a new centrifuge machine for its New Hampshire facility. The machine costs $137,500 and is expected to have a useful life of 8 years, with a terminal disposal value of $37,500. Savings in cash operating costs are expected to be $31,250 per year. However, additional working capital is needed to keep the machine running efficiently. The working capital must continually be replaced, so an investment of $10,000 needs to be maintained at all times, but this investment is fully recoverable (will be "cashed in") at the end of the useful life. Century Lab's required rate of return is 14%. Ignore income taxes in your analysis. Assume all cash flows occur at year-end except for initial investment amounts. Century Lab uses straight-line depreciation for its machines.

1. Calculate net present value.
2. Calculate internal rate of return.
3. Calculate accrual accounting rate of return based on net initial investment.
4. Calculate accrual accounting rate of return based on average investment.
5. You have the authority to make the purchase decision. Why might you be reluctant to base your decision on the DCF methods?

24   New equipment purchase, income taxes. Ella's Bakery plans to purchase a new oven for its store. The oven has an estimated useful life of 4 years. The estimated pretax cash flows for the oven are as shown in the table that follows, with no anticipated change in working capital. Ella's Bakery has a 14% after-tax required rate of return and a 35% income tax rate. Assume depreciation is calculated on a straight-line basis for tax purposes using the initial oven investment and estimated terminal disposal value of the oven. Assume all cash flows occur at year-end except for initial investment amounts.

Home Insert Page Layout Formulas Data Review View					
A	B	C	D	E	F
1		Relevant Cash Flows at End of Each Year			
2	0	1	2	3	4
3 Initial machine investment	$(186,000)				
4 Annual cash flow from operations (excluding the depreciation effect)		$77,000	$77,000	$77,000	$77,000
5 Cash flow from terminal disposal of over					$ 6,000

1. Calculate (a) net present value, (b) payback period, and (c) internal rate of return.
2. Calculate accrual accounting rate of return based on net initial investment.

25   New equipment purchase, income taxes. Nikola Inc. is considering the purchase of a new industrial electric motor to improve efficiency at its Rochester plant. The motor has an estimated useful life of 5 years. The estimated pretax cash flows for the motor are shown in the table that follows, with no anticipated change in working capital. Nikola has a 10% after-tax required rate of return and a 30% income tax rate. Assume depreciation is calculated on a straight-line basis for tax purposes. Assume all cash flows occur at year-end except for initial investment amounts.

Home Insert Page Layout Formulas Data Review View						
A	B	C	D	E	F	G
1		Relevant Cash Flows at End of Each Year				
2	0	1	2	3	4	5
3 Initial motor investment	$(75,000)					
4 Annual cash flow from operations (excluding the depreciation effect)		$25,000	$25,000	$25,000	$25,000	$25,000
5 Cash flow from terminal disposal of motor						$ 0

Required

1. Calculate (a) net present value, (b) payback period, (c) discounted payback period, and (d) internal rate of return.
2. Compare and contrast the capital budgeting methods in requirement 1.

26   Project choice, taxes. Harrison Ventures has invested in a variety of retail outlets in key mall locations. Harrison is contemplating an investment in upgrading the furnishings and fittings of these properties. The upgrades will require an up-front investment of $100,000. Harrison estimates that they will yield incremental margins of $43,000 annually due to higher foot traffic and sales and require incremental cash maintenance costs of $15,000 annually. Harrison expects the life span of these improvements at 5 years and estimates a terminal disposal value of $20,000.

Harrison faces a 30% income tax rate. It depreciates assets on a straight-line basis (to terminal value) for tax purposes. The required rate of return on investments is 12%.

Required

1. What is the expected increase in annual net income from investing in the improvements?
2. Calculate the accrual accounting rate of return based on average investment.
3. Is the project worth investing in from an NPV standpoint?
4. Suppose the tax authorities are willing to let Harrison depreciate the project down to zero over its useful life. If Harrison plans to liquidate the project in 5 years, should it take this option? Quantify the impact of this choice on the NPV of the project.

27   Customer value. Ortel Telecom sells telecommunication products and services to a variety of small businesses. Two of Ortel's key clients are Square and Cloudburst, both fast-growing technology start-ups located in New York City. Ortel has compiled information regarding its transactions with Square and Cloudburst for 2014, as well as its expectations regarding their interactions for the next 3 years:

	Home	Insert	Page Layout	Formulas	Data	Review
	A	B	C	D	E
1		Expected Annual percentage increase		2014		
2		Square	Cloudburst	Square	Cloudburst
3	Sales revenues	6%	5.5%	$567,000	$3,510,000
4	Cost of sales	5%	4.5%	$364,800	$3,060,000
5	Net cash flow			$202,200	$450,000

Ortel's transactions with Square and Cloudburst are in cash. Assume that they occur at year-end. Ortel is headquartered in the Cayman Islands and pays no income taxes. The owners of Ortel insist on a required rate of return of 12%.

Required

1. What is the expected net cash flow from Square and Cloudburst for the next 3 years?
2. Based on the net present value from cash flows over the next 3 years, is Cloudburst or Square a more valuable customer for Ortel?
3. Cloudburst threatens to switch to another supplier unless Ortel gives a 10% price reduction on all sales starting in 2015. Calculate the 3-year NPV of Cloudburst after incorporating the 10% discount. Should Ortel continue to transact with Cloudburst? What other factors should it consider before making its final decision?

28   Selling a plant, income taxes. (CMA, adapted) The Lucky Seven Company is an international clothing manufacturer. Its Redmond plant will become idle on December 31, 2014. Peter Laney, the corporate controller, has been asked to look at three options regarding the plant:

- **Option 1:** The plant, which has been fully depreciated for tax purposes, can be sold immediately for $900,000.
- **Option 2:** The plant can be leased to the Preston Corporation, one of Lucky Seven's suppliers, for 4 years. Under the lease terms, Preston would pay Lucky Seven $220,000 rent per year (payable at year-end) and would grant Lucky Seven a $40,000 annual discount off the normal price of fabric purchased by Lucky Seven. (Assume that the discount is received at year-end for each of the 4 years.) Preston would bear all of the plant's ownership costs. Lucky Seven expects to sell this plant for $150,000 at the end of the 4-year lease.

- **Option 3:** The plant could be used for 4 years to make souvenir jackets for the Olympics. Fixed overhead costs (a cash outflow) before any equipment upgrades are estimated to be $20,000 annually for the 4-year period. The jackets are expected to sell for $55 each. Variable cost per unit is expected to be $43. The following production and sales of jackets are expected: 2015, 18,000 units; 2016, 26,000 units; 2017, 30,000 units; 2018, 10,000 units. In order to manufacture the jackets, some of the plant equipment would need to be upgraded at an immediate cost of $160,000. The equipment would be depreciated using the straight-line depreciation method and zero terminal disposal value over the 4 years it would be in use. Because of the equipment upgrades, Lucky Seven could sell the plant for $270,000 at the end of 4 years. No change in working capital would be required.

Lucky Seven treats all cash flows as if they occur at the end of the year, and it uses an after-tax required rate of return of 10%. Lucky Seven is subject to a 35% tax rate on all income, including capital gains.

1. Calculate net present value of each of the options and determine which option Lucky Seven should select using the NPV criterion.
2. What nonfinancial factors should Lucky Seven consider before making its choice?

Problems

29 Equipment replacement, no income taxes. Clean Chips is a manufacturer of prototype chips based in Dublin, Ireland. Next year, in 2015, Clean Chips expects to deliver 535 prototype chips at an average price of $55,000. Clean Chips' marketing vice president forecasts growth of 65 prototype chips per year through 2021. That is, demand will be 535 in 2015, 600 in 2016, 665 in 2017, and so on.

The plant cannot produce more than 525 prototype chips annually. To meet future demand, Clean Chips must either modernize the plant or replace it. The old equipment is fully depreciated and can be sold for $4,300,000 if the plant is replaced. If the plant is modernized, the costs to modernize it are to be capitalized and depreciated over the useful life of the updated plant. The old equipment is retained as part of the modernize alternative. The following data on the two options are available:

	Modernize	Replace
Initial investment in 2015	$36,800,000	$61,700,000
Terminal disposal value in 2021	$7,000,000	$17,000,000
Useful life	7 years	7 years
Total annual cash operating costs per prototype chip	$35,500	$26,000

Clean Chips uses straight-line depreciation, assuming zero terminal disposal value. For simplicity, we assume no change in prices or costs in future years. The investment will be made at the beginning of 2015, and all transactions thereafter occur on the last day of the year. Clean Chips' required rate of return is 10%.

There is no difference between the modernize and replace alternatives in terms of required working capital. Clean Chips has a special waiver on income taxes until 2021.

1. Sketch the cash inflows and outflows of the modernize and replace alternatives over the 2015–2021 period.
2. Calculate payback period for the modernize and replace alternatives.
3. Calculate net present value of the modernize and replace alternatives.
4. What factors should Clean Chips consider in choosing between the alternatives?

30 Equipment replacement, income taxes (continuation of 29). Assume the same facts as in Problem 29, except that the plant is located in Austin, Texas. Clean Chips has no special waiver on income taxes. It pays a 30% tax rate on all income. Proceeds from sales of equipment above book value are taxed at the same 30% rate.

1. Sketch the after-tax cash inflows and outflows of the modernize and replace alternatives over the 2015–2021 period.
2. Calculate the net present value of the modernize and replace alternatives.
3. Suppose Clean Chips is planning to build several more plants. It wants to have the most advantageous tax position possible. Clean Chips has been approached by Spain, Malaysia, and Australia to construct plants in their countries. Use the data in Problem 29 and this problem to briefly describe in qualitative terms the income tax features that would be advantageous to Clean Chips.

31 DCF, sensitivity analysis, no income taxes. (CMA, adapted) Invigor Corporation is an international manufacturer of fragrances for women. Management at Invigor is considering expanding the product line to men's fragrances. From the best estimates of the marketing and production managers, annual sales (all for cash) for this new line are 1,200,000 units at $50 per unit; cash variable cost is $20 per unit; and cash fixed costs are $8,000,000 per year. The investment project requires $70,000,000 of cash outflow and has a project life of 8 years.

At the end of the 8-year useful life, there will be no terminal disposal value. Assume all cash flows occur at year-end except for initial investment amounts.

Men's fragrance is a new market for Invigor, and management is concerned about the reliability of the estimates. The controller has proposed applying sensitivity analysis to selected factors. Ignore income taxes in your computations. Invigor's required rate of return on this project is 12%.

Required

1. Calculate the net present value of this investment proposal.
2. Calculate the effect on the net present value of the following two changes in assumptions. (Treat each item independently of the other.)
   a. 10% reduction in the selling price
   b. 10% increase in the variable cost per unit
3. Discuss how management would use the data developed in requirements 1 and 2 in its consideration of the proposed capital investment.

32 NPV and AARR, goal-congruence issues. Eric Ishton, a manager of the Plate Division for the Stone Ware Manufacturing company, has the opportunity to expand the division by investing in additional machinery costing $430,000. He would depreciate the equipment using the straight-line method and expects it to have no residual value. It has a useful life of 8 years. The firm mandates a required after-tax rate of return of 12% on investments. Eric estimates annual net cash inflows for this investment of $110,000 before taxes and an investment in working capital of $7,500. The tax rate is 30%.

Required

1. Calculate the net present value of this investment.
2. Calculate the accrual accounting rate of return based on net initial investment for this project.
3. Should Eric accept the project? Will Eric accept the project if his bonus depends on achieving an accrual accounting rate of return of 12%? How can this conflict be resolved?

33 Payback methods, even and uneven cash flows. Cardinal Laundromat is trying to enhance the services it provides to customers, mostly college students. It is looking into the purchase of new high-efficiency washing machines that will allow for the laundry's status to be checked via smartphone.

Cardinal estimates the cost of the new equipment at $186,000. The equipment has a useful life of 9 years. Cardinal expects cash fixed costs of $82,000 per year to operate the new machines, as well as cash variable costs in the amount of 5% of revenues. Cardinal evaluates investments using a cost of capital of 6%.

Required

1. Calculate the payback period and the discounted payback period for this investment, assuming Cardinal expects to generate $180,000 in revenues every year from the new machines.
2. Assume instead that Cardinal expects the following uneven stream of cash revenues from installing the new washing machines:

	Home	Insert	Page Layout		Formulas	Data	Review	View	
	A	B	C	D	E	F	G	H	I	J
1	Year	1	2	3	4	5	6	7	8	9
2	Projected revenue	$110,000	$100,000	$150,000	$95,000	$165,000	$205,000	$150,000	$165,000	$170,000

Based on this estimated revenue stream, what are the payback and discounted payback periods for the investment?

34 Replacement of a machine, income taxes, sensitivity. (CMA, adapted) The Frooty Company is a family-owned business that produces fruit jam. The company has a grinding machine that has been in use for 3 years. On January 1, 2014, Frooty is considering the purchase of a new grinding machine. Frooty has two options: (1) continue using the old machine or (2) sell the old machine and purchase a new machine. The seller of the new machine isn't offering a trade-in. The following information has been obtained:

			Home	Insert	Page Layout	Formulas	Data	Review	View
	A						B		C
1							**Old Machine**		**New Machine**
2	Initial purchase cost of machines						$150,000		$190,000
3	Useful life from acquisition date (years)						8		5
4	Terminal disposal value at the end of useful life on Dec. 31, 2018, assumed for depreciation purposes						$ 20,000		$ 25,000
5	Expected annual cash operating costs:								
6	Variable cost per can of jam						$ 0.25		$ 0.19
7	Total fixed costs						$ 25,000		$ 24,000
8	Depreciation method for tax purposes						Straight line		Straight line
9	Estimated disposal value of machines:								
10	January 1, 2014						$ 68,000		$190,000
11	December 31, 2018						$ 12,000		$ 22,000
12	Expected cans of jam made and sold each year						475,000		475,000

Frooty is subject to a 34% income tax rate. Assume that any gain or loss on the sale of machines is treated as an ordinary tax item and will affect the taxes paid by Frooty in the year in which it occurs. Frooty's after-tax required rate of return is 12%. Assume all cash flows occur at year-end except for initial investment amounts.

Required

1. A manager at Frooty asks you whether it should buy the new machine. To help in your analysis, calculate the following:
   a. One-time after-tax cash effect of disposing of the old machine on January 1, 2014
   b. Annual recurring after-tax cash operating savings from using the new machine (variable and fixed)
   c. Cash tax savings due to differences in annual depreciation of the old machine and the new machine
   d. Difference in after-tax cash flow from terminal disposal of new machine and old machine
2. Use your calculations in requirement 1 and the net present value method to determine whether Frooty should use the old machine or acquire the new machine.
3. How much more or less would the recurring after-tax cash operating savings of the new machine need to be for Frooty to earn exactly the 12% after-tax required rate of return? Assume that all other data about the investment do not change.

35 **Recognizing cash flows for capital investment projects.** Johnny Buster owns Entertainment World, a place that combines fast food, innovative beverages, and arcade games. Worried about the shifting tastes of younger audiences, Johnny contemplates bringing in new simulators and virtual reality games to maintain customer interest.

As part of this overhaul, Johnny is also looking at replacing his old Guitar Hero equipment with a Rock Band Pro machine. The Guitar Hero setup was purchased for $25,200 and has accumulated depreciation of $23,000, with a current trade-in value of $2,700. It currently costs Johnny $600 per month in utilities and another $5,000 a year in maintenance to run the Guitar Hero equipment. Johnny feels that the equipment could be kept in service for another 11 years, after which it would have no salvage value.

The Rock Band Pro machine is more energy-efficient and durable. It would reduce the utilities costs by 30% and cut the maintenance cost in half. The Rock Band Pro costs $49,000 and has an expected disposal value of $5,000 at the end of its useful life of 11 years.

Johnny charges an entrance fee of $5 per hour for customers to play an unlimited number of games. He does not believe that replacing Guitar Hero with Rock Band Pro will have an impact on this charge or materially change the number of customers who will visit Entertainment World.

Required

1. Johnny wants to evaluate the Rock Band Pro project using capital budgeting techniques. To help him, read through the problem and separate the cash flows into four groups: (1) net initial investment cash flows, (2) cash flow savings from operations, (3) cash flows from terminal disposal of investment, and (4) cash flows not relevant to the capital budgeting problem.
2. Assuming a tax rate of 40%, a required rate of return of 8%, and straight-line depreciation over the remaining useful life of equipment, should Johnny purchase Rock Band Pro?

36 NPV, inflation and taxes. Cheap-O Foods is considering replacing all 10 of its old cash registers with new ones. The old registers are fully depreciated and have no disposal value. The new registers cost $899,640 (in total). Because the new registers are more efficient than the old registers, Cheap-O will have annual incremental cash savings from using the new registers in the amount of $192,000 per year. The registers have a 7-year useful life and no terminal disposal value and are depreciated using the straight-line method. Cheap-O requires an 8% real rate of return.

Required

1. Given the preceding information, what is the net present value of the project? Ignore taxes.
2. Assume the $192,000 cost savings are in current real dollars and the inflation rate is 5.5%. Recalculate the NPV of the project.
3. Based on your answers to requirements 1 and 2, should Cheap-O buy the new cash registers?
4. Now assume that the company's tax rate is 30%. Calculate the NPV of the project assuming no inflation.
5. Again assuming that the company faces a 30% tax rate, calculate the NPV of the project under an inflation rate of 5.5%.
6. Based on your answers to requirements 4 and 5, should Cheap-O buy the new cash registers?

37 NPV of information system, income taxes. Saina Supplies leases and sells materials, tools, and equipment and also provides add-on services such as ground maintenance and waterproofing to construction and mining sites. The company has grown rapidly over the past few years. The owner, Saina Torrance, feels that for the company to continue to scale, it needs to install a professional information system rather than relying on intuition and Excel analyses. After some research, Saina's CFO reports back with the following data about a data warehousing and analytics system that she views as promising:

- The system will cost $750,000. For tax purposes, it can be depreciated straight-line to a zero terminal value over a 5-year useful life. However, the CFO expects that the system will still be worth $50,000 at that time.

- There is an additional $75,000 annual fee for software upgrades and technical support from the vendor.

- The ability to provide better services and to target and reach more clients as a result of the new system will directly result in a $500,000 increase in revenues for Saina in the first year after installation. Revenues will grow by 5% each year thereafter. Saina's contribution margin is 60%.

- Due to greater efficiency in ordering and dispatching supplies, as well as in collecting receivables, the firm's working-capital requirements will decrease by $100,000.

- Saina will also be able to reduce the amount of warehouse space it currently leases, saving $40,000 annually in the process.

- Saina Supplies pays an income tax of 30% and requires an after-tax rate of return of 12%.

Assume that all cash flows occur at year-end except for initial investment amounts.

Required

1. If Saina decides to purchase and install the new information system, what is the expected incremental after-tax cash flow from operations during each of the 5 years?
2. Compute the net present value of installing the information system at Saina Supplies.
3. In addition to the analysis in requirement 2, what nonfinancial factors you would consider in making the decision about the information system?

Answers to Exercises in Compound Interest (Exercise 16)

The general approach to these exercises centers on a key question: Which of the four basic tables in Appendix: Notes on Compound Interest and Interest Tables should be used? No computations should be made until this basic question has been answered with confidence.

1. **From Table 1.** The $10,000 is the present value P of your winnings. Their future value S in 10 years will be as follows:

$$S = P(1 + r)^n$$

The conversion factor, $(1 + r)^n$, is on line 10 of Table 1.

Substituting at 8%: $S = \$10,000(2.159) = \$21,590$

Substituting at 10%: $S = \$10,000(2.594) = \$25,940$

2. **From Table 2.** The $154,900 is a future value. You want the present value of that amount. $P = S \div (1 + r)^n$. The conversion factor, $1 \div (1 + r)^n$, is on line 10 of Table 2. Substituting,

$$P = \$154,900(.676) = \$104,712.40$$

3. **From Table 3.** The $154,900 is a future value. You are seeking the uniform amount (annuity) to set aside annually. Note that $1 invested each year for 10 years at 10% has a future value of $15.937 after 10 years, from line 10 of Table 3.

$$\$154,900/15.937 = \$9,719.52$$

4. **From Table 3.** You need to find the future value of an annuity of $7,500 per year. Note that $1 invested each year for 10 years at 8% has a future value of $14.487 after 10 years.

$$\$7,500(14.487) = \$108,652.50$$

5. **From Table 4.** When you reach age 65, you will get $250,000, a present value at that time. You need to find the annuity that will exactly exhaust the invested principal in 10 years. To pay yourself $1 each year for 10 years when the interest rate is 8% requires you to have $6.710 today, from line 10 of Table 4.

$$\$250,000/6.710 = \$37,257.82$$

6. **From Table 4.** You need to find the present value of an annuity for 10 years at 8% and at 12%:

$$8\%: \$65,000(6.710) = \$436,150.00$$

$$12\%: \$65,000(5.650) = \$367,250.00$$

7. Plan A is preferable. The NPV of plan A exceeds that of plan B by $851.

		Plan A		Plan B	
Year	PV Factor at 8%	Cash Inflows	PV of Cash Inflows	Cash Inflows	PV of Cash Inflows
0	1.000	$(10,000)	$ (10,000)	$(10,000)	$ (10,000)
1	0.926	3,000	2,778	1,000	926
2	0.857	5,000	4,285	2,000	1,714
3	0.794	2,000	1,588	3,000	2,382
4	0.735	3,000	2,205	4,000	2,940
5	0.681	2,000	1,362	5,000	3,405
			$ 2,218		$ 1,367

Even though plans A and B have the same total cash inflows over the 5 years, plan A is preferred because it has greater cash inflows occurring earlier.

Glossary

Accrual accounting rate-of-return (AARR) method. Capital budgeting method that divides an accrual accounting measure of average annual income of a project by an accrual accounting measure of its investment. See also *return on investment (ROI)*.

Capital budgeting. The making of long-run planning decisions for investments in projects.

Cost of capital. See *required rate of return (RRR)*.

Discount rate. See *required rate of return (RRR)*.

Discounted cash flow (DCF) methods. Capital budgeting methods that measure all expected future cash inflows and outflows of a project as if they occurred at the present point in time.

Discounted payback method. Capital budgeting method that calculates the amount of time required for the discounted expected future cash flows to recoup the net initial investment in a project.

Hurdle rate. See *required rate of return (RRR)*.

Inflation. The decline in the general purchasing power of the monetary unit, such as dollars.

Internal rate-of-return (IRR) method. Capital budgeting discounted cash flow (DCF) method that calculates the discount rate at which the present value of expected cash inflows from a project equals the present value of its expected cash outflows.

Net present value (NPV) method. Capital budgeting discounted cash flow (DCF) method that calculates the expected monetary gain or loss from a project by discounting all expected future cash inflows and outflows to the present point in time, using the required rate of return.

Nominal rate of return. Made up of three elements: (a) a risk-free element when there is no expected inflation, (b) a business-risk element, and (c) an inflation element.

Opportunity cost of capital. See *required rate of return (RRR)*.

Payback method. Capital budgeting method that measures the time it will take to recoup, in the form of expected future cash flows, the net initial investment in a project.

Real rate of return. The rate of return demanded to cover investment risk (with no inflation). It has a risk-free element and a business-risk element.

Required rate of return (RRR). The minimum acceptable annual rate of return on an investment. Also called the *discount rate*, *hurdle rate*, *cost of capital*, or *opportunity cost of capital*.

Time value of money. Takes into account that a dollar (or any other monetary unit) received today is worth more than a dollar received at any future time.

Photo Credits

Credits are listed in order of appearance.

Photo 1: Wade Payne/AP Images
Photo 2: Yoshikazu Tsuno/AFP/Getty Images/Newscom

Index